Networking

ALL-IN-ONE

for
dummies®
A Wiley Brand

Networking

ALL-IN-ONE

for
dummies®
A Wiley Brand

Networking

ALL-IN-ONE

7th Edition

by Doug Lowe

for
dummies®
A Wiley Brand

Networking All-in-One For Dummies®, 7th Edition

Published by: **John Wiley & Sons, Inc.**, 111 River Street, Hoboken, NJ 07030-5774, www.wiley.com

Copyright © 2018 by John Wiley & Sons, Inc., Hoboken, New Jersey

Published simultaneously in Canada

For general information on our other products and services, please contact our Customer Care Department within the U.S. at 877-762-2974, outside the U.S. at 317-572-3993, or fax 317-572-4002. For technical support, please visit https://hub.wiley.com/community/support/dummies.

Wiley publishes in a variety of print and electronic formats and by print-on-demand. Some material included with standard print versions of this book may not be included in e-books or in print-on-demand. If this book refers to media such as a CD or DVD that is not included in the version you purchased, you may download this material at http://booksupport.wiley.com. For more information about Wiley products, visit www.wiley.com.

Library of Congress Control Number: 2018934082

ISBN 978-1-119-47160-8 (pbk); ISBN 978-1-119-47162-2 (ebk); ISBN 978-1-119-47159-2 (ebk)

Manufactured in the United States of America

10 9 8 7 6 5 4 3 2 1

Contents at a Glance

Table of Contents

Introduction

Welcome to the seventh edition of *Networking All-in-One For Dummies,* the one networking book that's designed to replace an entire shelf full of the dull and tedious networking books you'd otherwise have to buy. This book contains all the basic and not-so-basic information you need to know to get a network up and running and to stay on top of the network as it grows, develops problems, and encounters trouble.

If you're just getting started as a network administrator, this book is ideal. As a network administrator, you have to know about a lot of different topics: installing and configuring network hardware and software, planning a network, working with TCP/IP, securing your network, working with mobile devices, virtualizing your servers, backing up your data, managing cloud services, and many others.

You can, and probably eventually will, buy separate books on each of these topics. It won't take long before your bookshelf is bulging with 10,000 or more pages of detailed information about every imaginable nuance of networking. But before you're ready to tackle each of those topics in depth, you need to get a bird's-eye picture. This book is the ideal way to do that.

And if you already own 10,000 pages or more of network information, you may be overwhelmed by the amount of detail and wonder, "Do I really need to read 1,000 pages about BIND to set up a simple DNS server?" or "Do I really need a 6-pound book to show me how to install Linux?" Truth is, most 1,000-page networking books have about 100 or so pages of really useful information — the kind you use every day — and about 900 pages of excruciating details that apply mostly to networks at places like NASA and the CIA.

The basic idea of this book is that I've tried to wring out the 100 or so most useful pages of information on nine different networking topics: network basics, building a network, network administration and security, troubleshooting and disaster planning, working with TCP/IP, home networking, wireless networking, Windows server operating systems, and Linux.

So whether you've just been put in charge of your first network or you're a seasoned pro, you've found the right book.

About This Book

Networking All-in-One For Dummies, 7th Edition, is intended to be a reference for all the great things (and maybe a few not-so-great things) that you may need to know when you're setting up and managing a network. You can, of course, buy a huge 1,000-page book on each of the networking topics covered in this book. But then, who would you get to carry them home from the bookstore for you? And where would you find the shelf space to store them? In this book, you get the information you need all conveniently packaged for you in between one set of covers.

This book doesn't pretend to be a comprehensive reference for every detail of these topics. Instead, this book shows you how to get up and running fast so that you have more time to do the things you really want to do. Designed using the easy-to-follow *For Dummies* format, this book helps you get the information you need without laboring to find it.

Networking All-in-One For Dummies, 7th Edition, is a big book made up of several smaller books — minibooks, if you will. Each of these minibooks covers the basics of one key element of network management, such as setting up network hardware, installing a network operating system, or troubleshooting network problems. Whenever one big thing is made up of several smaller things, confusion is always a possibility. That's why *Networking All-in-One For Dummies,* 7th Edition, is designed to have multiple access points (I hear an acronym coming on — MAP!) to help you find what you want. At the beginning of the book is a detailed table of contents that covers the entire book. Then each minibook begins with a minitable of contents that shows you at a glance what chapters are included in that minibook. Useful running heads appear at the top of each page to point out the topic discussed on that page. And handy thumb tabs run down the side of the pages to help you find each minibook quickly. Finally, a comprehensive index lets you find information anywhere in the entire book.

This isn't the kind of book you pick up and read from start to finish, as though it were a cheap novel. (If I ever see you reading it at the beach, I'll kick sand in your face.) This book is more like a reference — the kind of book you can pick up, turn to just about any page, and start reading. You don't have to memorize anything in this book. It's a need-to-know book: You pick it up when you need to know something. Need to know how to set up a DHCP server in Windows? Pick up the book. Need to know how to create a user account in Linux? Pick up the book. Otherwise, put it down, and get on with your life.

Within this book, you may note that some web addresses break across two lines of text. If you're reading this book in print and want to visit one of these web pages, simply key in the web address exactly as it's noted in the text, pretending as though the line break doesn't exist. If you're reading this as an e-book, you've got it easy — just click the web address to be taken directly to the web page.

Foolish Assumptions

As I was writing this book, I made a few assumptions about you, the reader:

>> **You are responsible for or would like to be responsible for a computer network.** The network we speak of may be small – just a few computers, or large – consisting of dozens or even hundreds of computers. The network may already exist, or it may be a network you would like to build. But one way or another, I assume that managing the network is, at least in part, your responsibility.

>> **You are an experienced computer user.** You don't need to be an expert, but this book assumes a modest level of experience with computers.

>> **You are familiar with Windows.** This book touches on Mac and Linux networks, but the primary focus is on creating and managing networks of Windows computers.

Icons Used in This Book

Like any *For Dummies* book, this book is chock-full of helpful icons that draw your attention to items of particular importance. You find the following icons throughout this book:

TECHNICAL STUFF

Hold it — technical stuff is just around the corner. Read on only if you have your pocket protector.

TIP

Pay special attention to this icon; it lets you know that some particularly useful tidbit is at hand.

REMEMBER

Did I tell you about the memory course I took?

WARNING

Danger, Will Robinson! This icon highlights information that may help you avert disaster.

Beyond the Book

In addition to what you're reading right now, this product also comes with a free access-anywhere Cheat Sheet that includes tables where you can record key network and Internet connection information, the RJ-45 pin connections, private IP address ranges, and useful websites for networking information. To get this Cheat Sheet, simply go to www.dummies.com and type **Networking All-in-One For Dummies Cheat Sheet** in the Search box.

Where to Go from Here

Yes, you can get there from here. With this book in hand, you're ready to plow right through the rugged networking terrain. Browse the table of contents, and decide where you want to start. Be bold! Be courageous! Be adventurous! And above all, have fun!

1
Networking Basics

Contents at a Glance

IN THIS CHAPTER

» Considering why networking is useful (and is everywhere)

» Telling the difference between servers and clients

» Assessing how networks change computing life

» Examining network topology

» Identifying (and offering sympathy to) the network administrator

Chapter **1**

Welcome to Networking

omputer networks get a bad rap in the movies. In the 1980s, the *Terminator* movies featured Skynet, a computer network that becomes self-aware (a computer network of the future), takes over the planet, builds deadly terminator robots, and sends them back through time to kill everyone unfortunate enough to have the name Sarah Connor. In the *Matrix* movies, a vast and powerful computer network enslaves humans and keeps them trapped in a simulation of the real world. And in the 2015 blockbuster *Spectre*, James Bond goes rogue (again) to prevent the Evil Genius Ernst Blofeld from taking over the world (again) by linking the computer systems of all the world's intelligence agencies together to form a single all-powerful evil network that spies on everybody.

Fear not. These bad networks exist only in the dreams of science-fiction writers. Real-world networks are much more calm and predictable. Although sophisticated networks do seem to know a lot about you, they don't think for themselves and they don't evolve into self-awareness. And although they can gather a sometimes disturbing amount of information about you, they aren't trying to kill you, even if your name is Sarah Connor.

Now that you're over your fear of networks, you're ready to breeze through this chapter. It's a gentle, even superficial, introduction to computer networks, with a slant toward the concepts that can help you use a computer that's attached to a network. This chapter goes easy on the details; the detailed and boring stuff comes later.

Defining a Network

A *network* is nothing more than two or more computers connected by a cable or by a wireless radio connection so that they can exchange information.

Of course, computers can exchange information in ways other than networks. Most of us have used what computer nerds call the *sneakernet*. That's where you copy a file to a flash drive or other portable storage device and then walk the data over to someone else's computer. (The term *sneakernet* is typical of computer nerds' feeble attempts at humor.)

The whole problem with the sneakernet is that it's slow, and it wears a trail in your carpet. One day, some penny-pinching computer geeks discovered that connecting computers with cables was cheaper than replacing the carpet every six months. Thus, the modern computer network was born.

You can create a simple computer network by hooking together all the computers in your office with cables and using the computer's *network interface* (an electronic circuit that resides inside your computer and has a special jack on the computer's backside). Then you tweak a few simple settings in the computer's operating system (OS) software, and — *voilà!* — you have a working network. That's all there is to it.

If you don't want to mess with cables, you can create a wireless network instead. In a wireless network, the computers use wireless network adapters that communicate via radio signals. All modern laptop computers have built-in wireless network adapters, as do most desktop computers. (If yours doesn't, you can purchase a separate wireless network adapter that plugs into one of the computer's USB ports.)

Figure 1-1 shows a typical network with four computers. You can see that all four computers are connected by a network cable to a central network device: the *switch*. You can also see that Ward's computer has a fancy laser printer attached to it. Because of the network, June, Wally, and the Beaver can also use this laser printer.

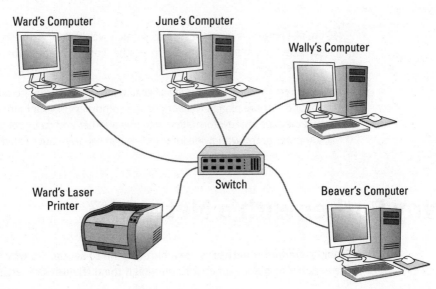

Ward's Computer

June's Computer

Wally's Computer

Switch

Ward's Laser
Printer

Beaver's Computer

FIGURE 1-1:
A typical network.

Computer networking has its own strange vocabulary. Although you don't have to know every esoteric networking term, it helps to be acquainted with a few of the basic buzzwords:

**TECHNICAL
STUFF**

>> **LAN:** Networks are often called LANs, short for *local area network.*

LAN is the first *three-letter acronym* (TLA) of this book. You don't really need to remember it or any of the many TLAs that follow. You may guess that the acronym for *four-letter acronym* is *FLA.* Wrong! A four-letter acronym is an *ETLA,* which stands for *extended three-letter acronym.* After all, it just wouldn't be right if the acronym for *four-letter acronym* had only three letters.

>> **On the network:** Every computer connected to the network is said to be "on the network." The technical term (which you can forget) for a computer that's on the network is a *node.*

>> **Online, offline:** When a computer is turned on and can access the network, the computer is *online.* When a computer can't access the network, it's *offline.* A computer can be offline for several reasons. The computer can be turned off, the user may have disabled the network connection, the computer may be broken, the cable that connects it to the network can be unplugged, or a wad of gum can be jammed into the disk drive.

>> **Up, down:** When a computer is turned on and working properly, it's *up.* When a computer is turned off, broken, or being serviced, it's *down.* Turning off a computer is sometimes called *taking it down.* Turning it back on is sometimes called *bringing it up.*

>> **Local, remote:** A resource such as a disk drive is *local* if it resides in your computer. It's *remote* if it resides in another computer somewhere else on your network.

>> **Internet:** The *Internet* is a huge amalgamation of computer networks strewn about the entire planet. Networking the computers in your home or office so that they can share information with one another and connecting your computer to the worldwide Internet are two separate but related tasks.

Why Bother with a Network?

Frankly, computer networks are a bit of a pain to set up. So, why bother? Because the benefits of having a network outweigh the difficulties of setting one up.

You don't have to be a PhD to understand the benefits of networking. In fact, you learned everything you need to know in kindergarten: Networks are all about sharing. Specifically, networks are about sharing three things: files, resources, and programs.

Sharing files

Networks enable you to share information with other computers on the network. Depending on how you set up your network, you can share files with your network friends in several different ways. You can send a file from your computer directly to a friend's computer by attaching the file to an email message and then mailing it. Or you can let your friend access your computer over the network so that your friend can retrieve the file directly from your hard drive. Yet another method is to copy the file to a disk on another computer and then tell your friend where you put the file so that your friend can retrieve it later. One way or the other, the data travels to your friend's computer over the network cable and not on a CD or DVD or flash drive, as it would in a sneakernet.

Sharing resources

You can set up certain computer resources — such as hard drives or printers — so that all computers on the network can access them. For example, the laser printer attached to Ward's computer in Figure 1-1 is a *shared resource*, which means that anyone on the network can use it. Without the network, June, Wally, and the Beaver would have to buy their own laser printers.

Hard drives can be shared resources, too. In fact, you must set up a hard drive as a shared resource to share files with other users. Suppose that Wally wants to share a file with the Beaver, and a shared hard drive has been set up on June's computer. All Wally has to do is copy his file to the shared hard drive in June's computer and tell the Beaver where he put it. Then, when the Beaver gets around to it, he can copy the file from June's computer to his own (unless, of course, that hooligan Eddie Haskell deletes the file first).

TIP

You can share other resources, too, such as an Internet connection. In fact, sharing an Internet connection is one of the main reasons why many networks are created.

Sharing programs

Instead of keeping separate copies of programs on each person's computer, put programs on a drive that everyone shares. For example, if ten computer users all use a particular program, you can purchase and install ten copies of the program, one for each computer. Or you can purchase a ten-user license for the program and then install just one copy of the program on a shared drive. Each of the ten users can then access the program from the shared hard drive.

In most cases, however, running a shared copy of a program over the network is unacceptably slow. A more common way of using a network to share programs is to copy the program's installation disks or CDs to a shared network drive. Then you can use that copy to install a separate copy of the program on each user's local hard drive. For example, Microsoft Office enables you to do this if you purchase a license from Microsoft for each computer on which you install Office.

The advantage of installing Office from a shared network drive is that you don't have to lug around the installation disks or CDs to each user's computer. And the system administrator can customize the network installation so that the software is installed the same way on each user's computer. (However, these benefits are significant only for larger networks. If your network has fewer than about ten computers, you're probably better off installing the program separately on each computer directly from the installation disks or CDs.)

WARNING

Remember that purchasing a single-user copy of a program and then putting it on a shared network drive — so that everyone on the network can access it — is illegal. If five people use the program, you need to either purchase five copies of the program or purchase a network license that specifically allows five or more users.

That being said, many software manufacturers sell their software with a concurrent usage license, which means that you can install the software on as many computers as you want, but only a certain number of people can use the software at any given time. Usually, special licensing software that runs on one of the network's server computers keeps track of how many people are currently using the software. This type of license is frequently used with more specialized (and expensive) software, such as accounting systems or computer drafting systems.

Another benefit of networking is that networks enable computer users to communicate with one another over the network. The most obvious way networks allow computer users to communicate is by passing messages back and forth, using email or instant-messaging programs. Networks also offer other ways to communicate: For example, you can hold online meetings over the network. Network users who have inexpensive video cameras (webcams) attached to their computers can have videoconferences. You can even play a friendly game of Hearts over a network — during your lunch break, of course.

Servers and Clients

The network computer that contains the hard drives, printers, and other resources that are shared with other network computers is a *server*. This term comes up repeatedly, so you have to remember it. Write it on the back of your left hand.

Any computer that's not a server is a *client*. You have to remember this term, too. Write it on the back of your right hand.

Only two kinds of computers are on a network: servers and clients. Look at your left hand and then look at your right hand. Don't wash your hands until you memorize these terms.

The distinction between servers and clients in a network has parallels in sociology — in effect, a sort of class distinction between the "haves" and "have-nots" of computer resources:

>> Usually, the most powerful and expensive computers in a network are the servers. There's a good technical reason: All users on the network share the server's resources.

>> The cheaper and less-powerful computers in a network are the clients. *Clients* are the computers used by individual users for everyday work. Because clients' resources don't have to be shared, they don't have to be as fancy.

» Most networks have more clients than servers. For example, a network with ten clients can probably get by with one server.

» In many networks, a clean line of demarcation exists between servers and clients. In other words, a computer functions as either a server or a client, not both. For the sake of an efficient network, a server can't become a client, nor can a client become a server.

» Other (usually smaller) networks can be more evenhanded by allowing any computer in the network to be a server and allowing any computer to be both a server and a client at the same time.

Dedicated Servers and Peers

In some networks, a server computer is a server computer and nothing else. It's dedicated to the sole task of providing shared resources, such as hard drives and printers, to be accessed by the network client computers. This type of server is a *dedicated server* because it can perform no other task than network services.

Some smaller networks take an alternative approach by enabling any computer on the network to function as both a client and a server. Thus, any computer can share its printers and hard drives with other computers on the network. And while a computer is working as a server, you can still use that same computer for other functions, such as word processing. This type of network is a *peer-to-peer network* because all the computers are thought of as *peers*, or equals.

Here are some points to ponder concerning the differences between dedicated server networks and peer-to-peer networks while you're walking the dog tomorrow morning:

» Peer-to-peer networking features are built into Windows. Thus, if your computer runs Windows, you don't have to buy any additional software to turn your computer into a server. All you have to do is enable the Windows server features.

» The network server features that are built into desktop versions of Windows (such as Windows 7 and 8) aren't particularly efficient because these versions of Windows weren't designed primarily to be network servers.

REMEMBER

If you dedicate a computer to the task of being a full-time server, use a special server operating system rather than the standard Windows desktop operating system. A *server operating system* is specially designed to handle networking functions efficiently.

- The most commonly used server operating systems are the server versions of Windows. As of this writing, the current server version of Windows is Windows Server 2016. However, many companies still use the previous version (Windows Server 2012), and a few even use its predecessor, Windows Server 2008.

- Another popular server operating system is *Linux*. Linux is popular because it's free. However, it requires more expertise to set up than Windows Server.

» Many networks are both peer-to-peer *and* dedicated-server networks at the same time. These networks have

- At least one server computer that runs a server operating system such as Windows Server 2016

- Client computers that use the server features of Windows to share their resources with the network

TIP

» Besides being dedicated, your servers should also be sincere.

What Makes a Network Tick?

To use a network, you don't really have to know much about how it works. Still, you may feel a little bit better about using the network if you realize that it doesn't work by voodoo. A network may seem like magic, but it isn't. The following list describes the inner workings of a typical network:

» **Network interface:** Inside any computer attached to a network is a special electronic circuit called the *network interface.* The network interface has either an external jack into which you can plug a network cable — or, in the case of a wireless network interface, an antenna.

» **Network cable:** The network cable physically connects the computers. It plugs into the network interface card (NIC) on the back of your computer.

The type of network cable most commonly used is twisted-pair cable, so named because it consists of several pairs of wires twisted together in a certain way. Twisted-pair cable superficially resembles telephone cable. However, appearances can be deceiving. Most phone systems are wired using a lower grade of cable that doesn't work for networks.

For the complete lowdown on networking cables, see Chapter 2 of this minibook.

TIP

Network cable isn't necessary when wireless networking is used. For more information about wireless networking, see Chapter 2 of this minibook.

» **Network switch:** Networks built with twisted-pair cabling require one or more switches. A *switch* is a box with a bunch of cable connectors. Each computer on the network is connected by cable to the switch. The switch, in turn, connects all the computers to each other.

TECHNICAL STUFF

In the early days of twisted-pair networking, devices known as *hubs* were used rather than switches. The term *hub* is sometimes used to refer to switches, but true hubs went out of style sometime around the turn of the century.

I explain much more about switches and hubs in Chapter 2 of this minibook.

» **Network router:** A router is used to connect two networks. Typically, a router is used to connect your network to the Internet. Figure 1-2 shows what the Cleaver family network would look like if they added a router to connect to the Internet. As you can see, the router is connected to the switch and also to the Internet. As a result, any computer that's connected to the switch can also reach the Internet via the router.

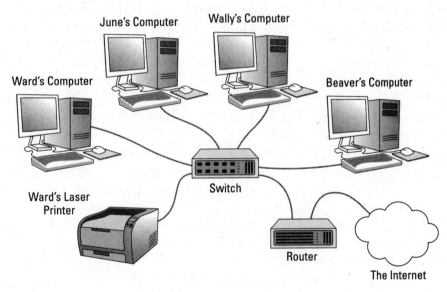

FIGURE 1-2: Connecting to the Internet via a router.

TECHNICAL STUFF

In networks with just a few computers, the network switch and router are often combined into a single device. By combining a router and a switch in a single box, you can easily connect several computers to the Internet and to each other.

» **Wireless networks:** In a wireless network, most cables and switches are moot. Radio transmitters and receivers take the place of cables.

The main advantage of wireless networking is its flexibility: No cables to run through walls or ceilings, and client computers can be located anywhere within range of the network broadcast.

There are trade-offs, though. For example, wireless networks are inherently less secure than a cabled network because anyone within range can intercept the radio signals. In addition, cabled networks are inherently faster and more stable than wireless networks.

Figure 1-3 shows how the Cleaver's network might look if they used a single device that combines a wireless router, which also includes a built-in switch. In this example, Ward's printer and computer are connected by wires because they're in the same room as the router. June's, Wally's, and the Beave's computers are connected wirelessly, so no cables are required.

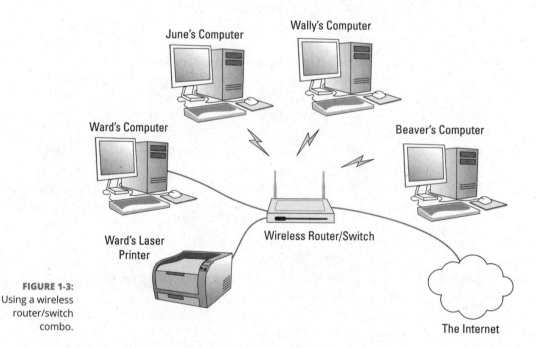

FIGURE 1-3:
Using a wireless router/switch combo.

» **Network software:** Of course, the software makes the network work. To make any network work, a whole bunch of software has to be set up just right. For peer-to-peer networking with Windows, you have to play with the Control Panel to get networking to work. And a server operating system such as Windows Server 2016 requires a substantial amount of tweaking to get it to work just right.

Networks Big and Small

Networks come in all sizes and shapes. In fact, networks are commonly based on the geographical size they cover, as described in the following list:

>> **Local area networks (LANs):** In this type of network, computers are relatively close together, such as within the same office or building.

Don't let the descriptor "local" fool you. A LAN doesn't imply that a network is small. A LAN can contain hundreds or even thousands of computers. What makes a network a LAN is that all its connected computers are located within close proximity. Usually a LAN is contained within a single building, but a LAN can extend to several buildings on a campus, provided that the buildings are close to each other (typically within 300 feet of each other, although greater distances are possible with special equipment).

>> **Wide area networks (WANs):** These networks span a large geographic territory, such as an entire city or a region or even a country. WANs are typically used to connect two or more LANs that are relatively far apart. For example, a WAN may connect an office in San Francisco with an office in New York.

REMEMBER

The geographic distance, not the number of computers involved, makes a network a WAN. If an office in San Francisco and an office in New York each has only one computer, the WAN will have a grand sum of two computers — but will span more than 3,000 miles.

>> **Metropolitan area networks (MANs):** This kind of network is smaller than a typical WAN but larger than a LAN. Typically, a MAN connects two or more LANs within the same city that are far enough apart that the networks can't be connected via a simple cable or wireless connection.

It's Not a Personal Computer Anymore!

If I had to choose one point that I want you to remember from this chapter more than anything else, it's this: After you hook up your personal computer (PC) to a network, it's not a "personal" computer anymore. You're now part of a network of computers, and in a way, you've given up one of the key concepts that made PCs so successful in the first place: independence.

I got my start in computers back in the days when mainframe computers ruled the roost. *Mainframe computers* are big, complex machines that used to fill entire rooms and had to be cooled with chilled water. My first computer was a water-cooled

Binford Hex Core Model 2000. Argh, argh, argh. (I'm not making up the part about the water. A plumber was often required to install a mainframe computer. In fact, the really big ones were cooled by liquid nitrogen. I *am* making up the part about the Binford Hex Core 2000.)

Mainframe computers required staffs of programmers and operators in white lab coats just to keep them going. The mainframes had to be carefully managed. A whole bureaucracy grew up around managing them.

Mainframe computers used to be the dominant computers in the workplace. Personal computers changed all that: They took the computing power out of the big computer room and put it on the user's desktop, where it belongs. PCs severed the tie to the centralized control of the mainframe computer. With a PC, a user could look at the computer and say, "This is mine — all mine!" Mainframes still exist, but they're not nearly as popular as they once were.

But networks have changed everything all over again. In a way, it's a change back to the mainframe-computer way of thinking: central location, distributed resources. True, the network isn't housed in the basement and doesn't have to be installed by a plumber. But you can no longer think of "your" PC as your own. You're part of a network — and like the mainframe, the network has to be carefully managed.

Here are several ways in which a network robs you of your independence:

>> **You can't just indiscriminately delete files from the network.** They may not be yours.

>> **You're forced to be concerned about network security.** For example, a server computer has to know who you are before it allows you to access its files. So you have to know your user ID and password to access the network. This precaution prevents some 15-year-old kid from hacking his way into your office network by using its Internet connection and stealing all your computer games.

>> **You may have to wait for shared resources.** Just because Wally sends something to Ward's printer doesn't mean that it immediately starts to print. The Beav may have sent a two-hour print job before that. Wally just has to wait.

>> **You may have to wait for access to documents.** You may try to retrieve an Excel spreadsheet file from a network drive, only to discover that someone else is using it. Like Wally, you just have to wait.

>> **You don't have unlimited storage space.** If you copy a 100GB video file to a server's drive, you may get calls later from angry co-workers complaining that no room is left on the server's drive for their important files.

>> **Your files can become infected from viruses given to you by someone over the network.** You may then accidentally infect other network users.

>> **You have to be careful about saving sensitive files on the server.** If you write an angry note about your boss and save it on the server's hard drive, your boss may find the memo and read it.

>> **The server computer must be up and running at all times.** For example, if you turn Ward's computer into a server computer, Ward can't turn his computer off when he's out of the office. If he does, you can't access the files stored on his computer.

>> **If your computer is a server, you can't just turn it off when you're finished using it.** Someone else may be accessing a file on your hard drive or printing on your printer.

Understanding Network Topology

The term *network topology* refers to the shape of how the computers and other network components are connected to each other. There are several different types of network topologies, each with advantages and disadvantages.

In the following discussion of network topologies, I use two important terms:

>> **Node:** A *node* is a device that's connected to the network. For your purposes here, a node is the same as a computer. Network topology deals with how the nodes of a network are connected to each other.

>> **Packet:** A *packet* is a message that's sent over the network from one node to another node. The packet includes the address of the node that sent the packet, the address of the node the packet is being sent to, and data.

Bus topology

The first type of network topology is called a *bus*, in which nodes are strung together in a line, as shown in Figure 1-4. The key to understanding how a bus topology works is to think of the entire network as a single cable, with each node "tapping" into the cable so it can listen in on the packets being sent over that cable. If you're old enough to remember party lines, you get the idea.

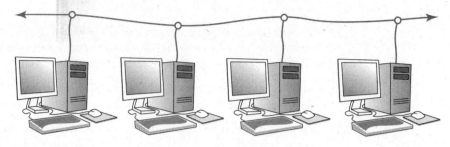

FIGURE 1-4:
Bus topology.

In a bus topology, every node on the network can see every packet that's sent on the cable. Each node looks at each packet to determine whether the packet is intended for it. If so, the node claims the packet. If not, the node ignores the packet. This way, each computer can respond to data sent to it and ignore data sent to other computers on the network.

If the cable in a bus network breaks, the entire network is effectively disabled. Obviously, the nodes on opposite sides of the break can continue to communicate with each other, because data can't span the gap created by the break. But even those nodes that are on the same side of the break may not be able to communicate with each other, because the open end of the cable left by the break disrupts the proper transmission of electrical signals.

In the early days of Ethernet networking, bus topology was commonplace. Although bus topology has given way to star topology (see the next section) for most networks today, many networks today still have elements that rely on bus topology.

Star topology

In a star topology, each network node is connected to a central device called a *hub* or a *switch*, as shown in Figure 1-5. Star topologies are commonly used with LANs.

If a cable in a star network breaks, only the node connected to that cable is isolated from the network. The other nodes can continue to operate without interruption — unless, of course, the node that's isolated because of the break happens to be the file server.

TECHNICAL
STUFF

You should be aware of the somewhat technical distinction between a hub and a switch. Simply put, a *hub* doesn't know anything about the computers that are connected to each of its ports. So when a computer connected to the hub sends a packet to a computer that's connected to another port, the hub sends a duplicate copy of the packet to all its ports. In contrast, a switch knows which computer is connected to each of its ports. As a result, when a switch receives a packet intended for a particular computer, it sends the packet only to the port that the recipient is connected to.

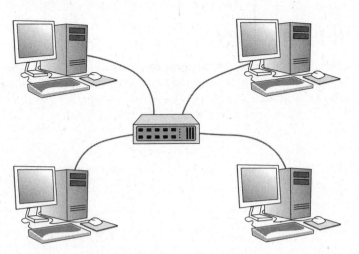

FIGURE 1-5:
Star topology.

Strictly speaking, only networks that use switches have a true star topology. If the network uses a hub, the network topology has the physical appearance of a star, but it's actually a bus. That's because when a hub is used, each computer on the network sees all the packets sent over the network, just like in a bus topology. In a true star topology, as when a switch is used, each computer sees only those packets that were sent specifically to it, as well as packets that were specifically sent to all computers on the network (those types of packets are called *broadcast packets*).

Expanding stars

Physicists say that the universe is expanding, and network administrators know they're right. A simple bus or star topology is suitable only for small networks, with a dozen or so computers. But small networks inevitably become large networks as more computers are added. For larger networks, it's common to create more complicated topologies that combine stars and buses.

For example, a bus can be used to connect several stars. In this case, two or more hubs or switches are connected to each other using a bus. Each of these hubs or switches is then the center of a star that connects two or more computers to the network. This type of arrangement is commonly used in buildings that have two or more distinct workgroups. The bus that connects the switches is sometimes called a *backbone.*

Another way to expand a star topology is to use a technique called *daisy-chaining.* When you use daisy-chaining, a switch is connected to another switch as if it were one of the nodes on the star. Then this second switch serves as the center of a second star.

Ring topology

A third type of network topology is called a *ring* (see Figure 1-6). In a ring topology, packets are sent around the circle from computer to computer. Each computer looks at each packet to decide whether the packet was intended for it. If not, the packet is passed on to the next computer in the ring.

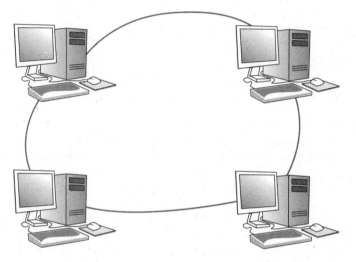

FIGURE 1-6:
Ring topology.

Years ago, ring topologies were common in LANs, as two popular networking technologies used rings: ARCNET and token ring. ARCNET is still used for certain applications such as factory automation, but it's rarely used in business networks. token ring is still a popular network technology for IBM midrange computers. Although plenty of token ring networks are still in existence, not many new networks use token ring any more.

Ring topology was also used by FDDI, one of the first types of fiber-optic network connections. FDDI has given way to more efficient fiber-optic techniques, however. So ring networks have all but vanished from business networks.

Mesh topology

A fourth type of network topology, known as *mesh*, has multiple connections between each of the nodes on the network, as shown in Figure 1-7. The advantage of a mesh topology is that if one cable breaks, the network can use an alternative route to deliver its packets.

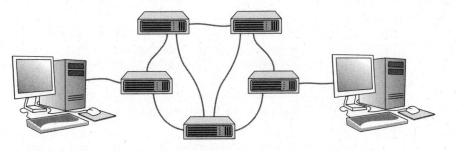

FIGURE 1-7:
Mesh topology.

Mesh networks aren't very practical in a LAN setting. For example, to network eight computers in a mesh topology, each computer would have to have seven network interface cards, and 28 cables would be required to connect each computer to the seven other computers in the network. Obviously, this scheme isn't very scalable.

However, mesh networks are common for metropolitan or wide area networks. These networks use routers to route packets from network to network. For reliability and performance reasons, routers are usually arranged in a way that provides multiple paths between any two nodes on the network in a mesh-like arrangement.

The Network Administrator

Because so much can go wrong — even with a simple network — designating one person as network administrator is important. This way, someone is responsible for making sure that the network doesn't fall apart or get out of control.

The network administrator doesn't have to be a technical genius. In fact, some of the best network administrators are complete idiots when it comes to technical stuff. What's important is that the administrator is organized. That person's job is to make sure that plenty of space is available on the file server, that the file server is backed up regularly, and that new employees can access the network, among other tasks.

The network administrator's job also includes solving basic problems that the users themselves can't solve — and knowing when to call in an expert when something really bad happens. It's a tough job, but somebody's got to do it. Here are a few tips that might help:

>> In small companies, picking the network administrator by drawing straws is common. The person who draws the shortest straw loses and becomes administrator.

>> Of course, the network administrator can't be a *complete* technical idiot. I was lying about that. (For those of you in Congress, the word is *testifying*.) I exaggerated to make the point that organizational skills are more important than technical skills. The network administrator needs to know how to do various maintenance tasks. Although this knowledge requires at least a little technical know-how, the organizational skills are more important.

Because network administration is such an important job, all the chapters in Books 8 and 9 are devoted to it.

IN THIS CHAPTER

» Looking at the various elements that make up a typical network infrastructure

» Considering how standards and protocols are used in networking

» Examining the elements of a network's cable infrastructure

» Learning how network data is transmitted via packets

» Looking at the issues of collisions in wired and wireless networks

Chapter **2**

Network Infrastructure

I n this chapter, I cover the key concepts of local area networks — that is, networks that are contained within a single location. Although this chapter may seem a little abstract, you'll be much better prepared to design and implement a solid local area network if you have a good understanding of these concepts from the very beginning.

I go into more depth on many of the concepts presented in this chapter in Book 2, which dives deeper into the various networking standards and protocols.

Introducing Infrastructure

As I mention in the preceding chapter, a *local area network* (LAN) is a network that connects computers and other devices that are located in relatively close proximity to one another. Most LANs are contained to a single building, although it's possible to create LANs that span several buildings at a single site, provided the buildings are close to one another. For the purposes of this chapter, I stick to LANs that operate within a single building and support anywhere from a few dozen to a few hundred users.

LANs exist to connect computing devices such as workstation computers, servers, printers, scanners, cameras, and so on, together. The essence of a network is the *physical infrastructure* that enables the connections. The infrastructure is similar to the infrastructure of a city. A city's infrastructure has many physical elements, including roads, stop signs and stop lights, water supply lines, storm water drains, sewage lines and treatment plants, electrical distribution cables, transformers, and much more.

Similarly, the infrastructure of a network consists of physical elements:

>> **Cables:** These run through walls and ceiling spaces, through conduits, between floors, and wherever else they need to go to reach their destinations.

>> **Patch panels:** These allow cables to be organized at a central location.

>> **Network switches:** A *switch* is an intermediate device that sits between the networked devices that allows those devices to communicate with each other. In a real way, switches are the core of the network; without switches, computers wouldn't be able to talk.

>> **At least one router:** A *router* enables the network to the outside world. The most common use of a router is to connect the LAN to the Internet. However, routers can also be used to connect one LAN to another. I tell you more about routers in Chapter 3 of this minibook.

Introducing Network Protocols and Standards

To operate efficiently, the infrastructure of a network consists of devices that conform to well-known standards and protocols. A *protocol* provides a precise sequence of steps that each element of a network must follow to enable communications. Protocols also define the precise format of all data that is exchanged in a network. For example, the Internet Protocol (IP) defines the format of IP addresses: four eight-bit numbers called *octets* whose decimal values range from 0 to 255, as in 10.0.101.155.

A *standard* is a detailed definition of a protocol that has been established by a standards organization and that vendors follow when they create products. Without standards, it would be impossible for one vendor's products to work with another vendor's. Because of standards, you can instead purchase equipment from different vendors with the assurance that they'll work together.

Network standards are organized into a framework called the Open Systems Interconnection (OSI) Reference Model. The OSI Reference Model establishes a hierarchy for protocols so that each protocol can deal with just one part of the overall task of data communications. The OSI Reference Model identifies seven distinct layers at which a protocol may operate:

>> **Physical (layer 1):** Describes the mechanical and electrical details of network components such as cables, connectors, and network interfaces.

>> **Data link (layer 2):** Describes the basic techniques that networks use to uniquely identify devices on the network (typically via a MAC address) and the means for one device to send information over the physical layer to another device, in the form of data packets. Switches operate at the data link layer, which means that they manage the efficient transmission of data packets from one device to another.

>> **Network (layer 3):** Handles the routing of data across networks. Routers operate at the network layer.

>> **Transport (layer 4):** Provides for reliable delivery of packets.

>> **Session (layer 5):** Establishes sessions between network applications.

>> **Presentation (layer 6):** Converts data so that systems that use different data formats can exchange information.

>> **Application (layer 7):** Allows applications to request network services.

Although the upper layers of the OSI model (layers 4 through 7) are equally important, in this chapter and the next, I focus on the first three layers of the OSI model — physical, data link, and network. These layers are the ones where the most common types of networking hardware such as cables, interfaces, switches, and routers operate.

Although many different network protocols and standards can be used in various layers of the OSI model, the most common standard found at layers 1 and 2 is Ethernet. Similarly, the most common standard at layer 3 is IP. I cover more about Ethernet and IP in Chapters 2 and 3 of Book 2, but keep in mind that most of what follows in this chapter is related to Ethernet and IP.

Understanding Cable Infrastructure

You can find much more about the details of working with network cable in Book 3, Chapter 1, as well as Book 4, Chapter 1. But before we get too far, I want to give you an overview of what's involved with cabling together a network.

For starters, network cable and all the bits and pieces that go along with it are the most important components of layer 1 of the OSI Reference Model. The following sections describe the most important layer 1 and cabling details you need to know.

Twisted-pair cable

There are several varieties of cable you can choose from, but the most common is called *twisted-pair*. It's called that because inside the outer sheath of the cable are four pairs of small insulated wire. The wires are 24 gauge, which means they're about half a millimeter in diameter. These pairs are color coded: blue, green, orange, and brown. For each pair, there is one solid color wire and one striped wire — so, the blue pair consists of a solid blue wire and a blue-and-white striped wire.

The two wires that make up each pair are twisted together in a way that prevents the electrical signals within each pair from interfering with the other pairs. To accomplish this, each pair is twisted at a different rate.

The maximum length of a single run of Cat-5e cable is 100 meters.

Cat-5e cable is able to carry network data at speeds of up to 1 gigabit per second (Gbps). The newer and somewhat more expensive Cat-6 cable can carry data at up to 10 Gbps but can sustain that speed for only 55 meters.

RJ45 connectors

Twisted-pair cable is attached to network devices using a special type of connector called an RJ45, which is a small block of plastic with eight metal contacts. RJ45 connectors resemble a telephone connector but are larger (telephone connectors have just four electrical contacts). For the cable to meet Cat-5e standards, the twists of the individual pairs must be maintained all the way up to the RJ45 connector.

RJ45 connectors come in both male (plug) and female (receptacle) varieties. Typically, the male connector is installed on the cables and the female connectors are installed in equipment. Thus, to connect a cable to a computer, you plug the male RJ45 plug on the cable into the female RJ45 receptacle on the computer.

Patch panels and patch cables

A *patch panel* is a group of RJ45 receptacles on a single metal plate, usually attached to a 19-inch equipment rack. Patch panels are used to bring cables run from individual computer locations to a single location where they can then be patched to other equipment using patch cables. A *patch cable* is simply a short length of twisted-pair cable with an RJ45 plug on both ends. Patch cables are usually 3 to 10 feet in length, but longer lengths are occasionally used.

Patch panels typically have either 24 or 48 ports. Depending on the size of your network, you may have more than one patch panel at a single location. For example, a large network may have four 48-port patch panels to support a total of 192 computers.

A patch panel by itself doesn't actually *do* anything. Its job is simply to provide a central collecting point for all your network cables so that you can easily use patch cables to connect the cables to other devices, such as switches or servers.

Repeaters and hubs

A *repeater* is a layer-1 device that is designed to circumvent the maximum length limitation of twisted-pair network cables. A repeater contains two RJ45 ports, which are connected internally by an amplifier. Electrical signals received on either of the two ports are boosted by the amplifier and sent through the other port. Thus, the cables on both ends of the repeater can be up to 100 meters. The repeater effectively doubles the reach of the cable.

A *hub* is a repeater with more than two ports. For example, a hub may have four or eight ports. These ports can each connect to another device on the network such as a client computer, a server, or a printer. A port on a hub can also connect to another hub, so that (for example) an eight-port hub can connect to seven computers and another eight-port hub, which can connect to seven more computers. In this way, two eight-port hubs can connect 14 computers to each other.

There are two very important things to know about hubs.

The *second* most important thing to know about hubs is that an electrical signal received on any of the hub's ports is amplified and repeated on all the other ports in the hub. So, in an eight-port hub, any electrical signals received on port 1 are amplified and then sent out on ports 2 through 8. Any devices that are connected to ports 2 through 8 see the signals that were received on port 1. The same is true for signals received on any of the other ports; for example, any signals received on port 4 will be amplified and repeated on ports 1 through 3 as well as ports 5 through 8.

That's the second most important thing to know. The *first* most important thing to know about hubs is that they're almost never used anymore. That's because simply repeating all incoming signals on all ports is an incredibly bad idea, for reasons that will become apparent later in this chapter and in Chapter 3 of this minibook. If your network still has hubs, you should seriously consider replacing them with switches, which are described in the next section and further explained in the next chapter.

Switches

A *switch* is a layer-2 device that is similar to a hub in that it allows you to connect more than one device, and packets received on one port are relayed to other ports. The difference, however, is that a switch is able to examine the actual contents of the data that it receives. As I explain in the "Understanding Packets" section, later in this chapter, data is sent in units called *packets* that contain a destination address. A switch looks at this destination address and repeats the incoming packet only on the port that can deliver the packet to the intended destination.

For example, suppose Computer A is connected to switch port 1, and Computer D is connected to switch port 4. If Computer A sends a packet to Computer D, that packet is received on switch port 1. The switch knows that Computer D is connected to switch port 4, so the switch sends the packet out on switch port 4. In this way, Computer D receives the packet. The computers or devices that are connected to the other ports on the switch are not bothered with the packet intended for Computer D.

If that doesn't make a lot of sense, don't worry: It will. The next two sections in this chapter explain the concept of MAC addresses, which are how networks identify the intended recipients of data packets, as well as how data packets work. Then, in Chapter 3 of this minibook, I dive deeper into how switches do their magic.

Understanding Ports, Interfaces, and MAC Addresses

A *network interface* is the electronic circuitry that allows a device to connect to a network. Each network interface provides a *port*, which is the plug-in point for the interface. Generally speaking, the terms *port* and *interface* are synonymous.

A network interface might be a separate add-on card for a computer, in which case the interface is called a *network interface card* (NIC). On some devices, such as printers, separate network interface cards are still common. But nearly all desktop and laptop computers have a network interface built into the computer's motherboard, so separate NICs are rarely used on desktop computers or laptops. NICs are still widely used on servers, however, as servers are often configured with two or more interfaces; using a separate card for the interface allows for more flexibility.

TIP

The term *adapter* is often used as a synonym for *interface.* Port, interface, adapter — three words that mean the same thing.

Every network interface must have a unique identifier called a *MAC address.* (*MAC* stands for *media access control,* but that won't be on the test.) Each MAC address is unique throughout the entire world. I have no idea whether MAC addresses are unique throughout the galaxy; it's entirely possible that the computer system on some invading alien spacecraft would have a MAC address that is the same as your laptop, but if that were to happen, I doubt you'd be too concerned about fixing your network.

MAC addresses are important because they provide the means for a network to keep track of the devices that make up the network. Without MAC addresses, it would be impossible to know what devices are on the network. And it would be impossible to send information to a particular device or to know which particular device sent information.

TIP

The term *physical address* is sometimes used as a synonym for *MAC address.* The two terms are interchangeable.

TECHNICAL STUFF

MAC addresses are a part of layer 2 of the OSI Reference Model, called the link layer. This layer is responsible for the exchange of basic information on a network. The ability to uniquely identify every device on a network is a key component of enabling that to happen.

MAC addresses are 48 bits in length, which means that more than 280 trillion devices can be assigned unique MAC addresses before we run out. When written, MAC addresses are written in six *octets* separated by hyphens. An octet is a group of eight binary bits, written as a two-digit number in hexadecimal notation, which uses the letters A through F in addition to the digits 0 through 9 to represent the value of each octet. A typical MAC address looks like this:

```
48-2C-6A-1E-59-3D
```

If you want to see the MAC address of your computer's network adapter, open a command prompt and type **ipconfig /all**. Scroll through the output from this command to see the MAC address (ipconfig calls is a physical address) for each interface on your computer. For example, here's the ipconfig output for the built-in adapter on my SurfaceBook:

```
Ethernet adapter Ethernet 2:

    Media State ... ... ... ... .... : Media disconnected
    Connection-specific DNS Suffix . : bcf-engr.pri
    Description ... ... ... ... ... : Surface Ethernet Adapter
    Physical Address... ... ... ... .: 58-82-A8-9C-A7-28
    DHCP Enabled... ... ... ... ... .: Yes
    Autoconfiguration Enabled ... .. : Yes
```

Here, you can see the MAC address is 58-82-A8-9C-A7-28.

TIP

A MAC address is technically associated with a network interface, not with the device that uses that interface. For example, if your computer's motherboard has a network interface built in, the MAC address of the network interface is pretty much married to the motherboard. However, if your computer has a separate NIC, the MAC address is a part of the card, not the computer that the card is plugged into. If you remove the interface card from one computer and install it in another, the MAC address travels with the card.

REMEMBER

The key points to remember here are that in order for a computer, printer, or any other device to connect to a network, that device must contain a network interface. That interface has a unique MAC address, which is the primary way that the network can distinguish one device from another.

Understanding Packets

When two or more devices are connected to a network via cables plugged into their network interfaces, those devices can exchange information with one another. This bit of magic is accomplished through the use of *packets*, which are relatively small units of data that are sent and received through the network interface and cables. A network packet always originates at a single network interface, called the *sender*, and it's usually (but not always) sent to a single network interface, called the *destination*.

A packet is very similar to an envelope that you would send through standard mail delivery. It includes the MAC address of both the sender and the destination, as well as some other interesting header information, along with a *payload* that contains the actual data being sent by the packet. You can think of the payload as what you would put in an envelope you want to send through the mail. You wouldn't dream of dropping an envelope in the mail without writing the recipient's address, as well as your own address, on the envelope. So it is with packets.

The payload of an Ethernet packet may be a packet created by some higher-level protocol, such as IP. This is analogous to putting a letter in an envelope, putting that envelope in a larger envelope, and sending it through the mail. When the recipient receives your mail, she opens the envelope only to find another envelope that must be opened. That envelope may itself contain another envelope and so on, like Russian nesting dolls.

**TECHNICAL
STUFF**

The term *frame* is often used instead of *packet*, but technically they're not quite the same. Every packet begins with a *preamble*, which consists of 56 bits of alternating zeros and ones. This preamble is used by the electronic circuitry of the interfaces to get their clocks synchronized properly so they can accurately read the rest of the packet. It's the rest of the packet that is technically called the *frame*. In other words, a *packet* consists of a *preamble* followed by a *frame*. Because the preamble is of concern only to the electronic engineers that design network interfaces, most non-engineers use the terms *packet* and *frame* interchangeably.

Ethernet has a standard packet format that all packets sent on an Ethernet network must follow. An Ethernet packet contains the following information:

>> **Preamble:** The preamble consists of 56 bits of alternating ones and zeros and is used to synchronize the precise timing required to read packet data.

>> **Start-of-frame marker:** A start-of-frame marker is a single byte that indicates that the frame is about to begin.

>> **Destination MAC address (six bytes).**

>> **Sender MAC address (six bytes).**

>> **Tag:** The tag, which is used to support virtual local area networks (VLANs), is optional. A VLAN lets you divide two or more distinct LANs on a shared physical infrastructure (for example, cables and switches). (For more information about VLANs, see Chapter 3 of this minibook, as well as Book 3, Chapter 1.)

>> **Ethertype (two bytes):** This field indicates the specific protocol that is contained in the payload.

>> **Payload:** The payload contains the actual data being sent by the packet. The payload can be anywhere from 46 to 1,500 bytes. If the information that needs to be sent is longer than 1,500 bytes, the information must be broken into two or more packets, sent separately, and then reassembled when the packets reach their destination. (The tasks of breaking up and reassembling the data are handled by protocols at higher layers in the OSI framework; Ethernet itself has no understanding of what is in the packets it sends.)

>> **Frame check sequence (four bytes):** The frame check sequence (FCS) is used to ensure that the frame data was sent correctly. Basically, the interface that sends the packet uses an algorithm to calculate a four-byte number based on the contents of the frame and saves this number in the FCS field. When the packet is received, the receiving interface repeats the calculation, and then makes sure that the number recorded in the FCS portion of the packet matches the number it calculated. If the numbers disagree, the packet got garbled in transmission and is discarded.

Note that the details of an Ethernet packet are not really of much concern when you design and implement a network. Here are the main points to remember:

>> Ethernet packets contain the MAC addresses of the sender and the receiver.

>> The payload of an Ethernet packet is almost always a packet created by another higher-level protocol such as IP.

>> Ethernet packets can contain a tag field used to implement VLANs, which provide an important means of organizing a large network into smaller parts that can be more easily managed.

Understanding Collisions

One of the basic principles of Ethernet is that multiple devices can be connected to media (that is, cables), and that all devices connected to this media can and should examine every packet that is sent on the media. In other words, Ethernet uses shared media.

Every packet contains the MAC address of the intended recipient. So, when an interface detects an incoming packet, it inspects the recipient MAC address and compares it with its own MAC address. If the addresses match, the interface passes the packet up to the next higher protocol on the protocol stack (typically, the IP protocol). If the addresses don't match, the interface assumes that the packet doesn't belong to the interface, so the interface simply ignores the packet.

The use of hubs on an Ethernet propagates the shared cable through the network. That's because a hub simply amplifies any packet that arrives on any of its ports and then forwards the amplified packet to all the other ports in the hub. So, if you use a 12–port hub to connect 12 computers together, all 12 of the computers will see all the packets generated by any of the other computers. And if two or more of the computers try to transmit a packet at the same time, the packets will collide.

Ethernet has been very successful — in fact, it has become one of the most widely used networking protocols of all time. However, Ethernet's shared media approach has a basic problem: It doesn't scale well. When two or more interfaces are shared on a single cable, there is always the possibility that two or more interfaces will try to send information at the same time. This is called a *collision*. The result of a collision between two packets is that both packets will be destroyed in the process and will need to be sent again.

In a small network with just a few computers, collisions happen now and again but aren't a big deal. However, in a large network with dozens or hundreds of devices, collisions can become a constant annoyance. In fact, collisions can become such a problem that the network slows to a halt and no one is able to get anything done at all.

TIP

As a result, it's important to design a network in a way that reduces the possibility of collisions becoming a problem. Fortunately, that's easy to do with modern network equipment: All you have to do is use switches instead of hubs. Switches all but eliminate the problem of collisions by forwarding network packets only to the cable segments that the destination devices are connected to rather than forwarding them throughout the entire network.

You learn more about how this works and why it's so important in Chapter 3 of this minibook.

Understanding Broadcast Packets

Not all packets on an Ethernet network are intended for a single destination. Instead, some packets, called *broadcast packets,* are intended to be received by every device on the network. To send a broadcast packet, the sending interface sets the destination MAC address to FF-FF-FF-FF-FF-FF — that is, all ones. Then, all interfaces that receive the packet inspect the destination, see that the packet is a broadcast, and pass the packet up to the next higher protocol.

One of the most common users of broadcast packets is Dynamic Host Configuration Protocol (DHCP), which allows computers that join a network to be assigned an IP address. When a network interface is first connected to a network, it sends out a broadcast message requesting the address of the network's DHCP server. Every device on the network sees this packet. But only the DHCP service will respond.

As you see in the next chapter, broadcast packets can sometimes cause a serious problem on your network. All networks should be planned in a way that minimizes problems caused by broadcast packets.

Understanding Wireless Networks

As I mention in Chapter 1 of this minibook, a *wireless network* is a network in which radio signals are used to connect devices to the network rather than physical cables. You learn much more about wireless networks in Book 2, Chapter 1, as well as Book 4, Chapter 2. But for now, I want you to keep the following points in mind:

>> **Just like a wired network, a device connecting to a wireless network does so via a network interface.** A wireless interface, also known as a wireless adapter, includes a radio transmitter and receiver rather than a physical cable connection.

>> **Every wireless network adapter has a MAC address.**

>> **Rather than a switch or a hub, wireless devices connect to a wireless access point (WAP).**

>> **Collisions are possible (likely, actually) on a WAP, just as they are on a hub.** Unfortunately, there is no equivalent to a wireless switch that reduces the collision problem. WAPs are essentially hubs in that every device that connects to the access point is competing for the same bandwidth. Whenever the WAP sends a packet, all devices connected to the access point must inspect the packet to determine the MAC address destination. And if two devices try to send packets at the same time, a collision will occur. This is one of the inherent reasons that wireless networking is slower than wired networking.

Chapter **3**

Switches, Routers, and VLANs

I n this chapter, I dig deeper into two of the most basic and ubiquitous network-ing devices: switches and routers. Every network has at least one switch and one router, and all but the smallest networks have more than one switch. These components are the basic building blocks of networks, so understanding what they do and how they work is essential to properly designing, implementing, and maintaining a network that functions well.

Besides switches and routers, this chapter also introduces the concept of virtual local area networks (VLANs). A VLAN is a fancy technique that lets you split a single physical network into two or more logical networks. VLANs are one of the key techniques for organizing a network in a way that will allow the network to scale up as your organization grows. Small networks don't need to worry about VLANs, but even in a relatively small network, it pays to know what VLANs are. Introducing VLANs into your network before you actually need them will simplify your life as your network grows.

Understanding Switches

In the previous chapter, I explain that a *hub* is a layer-1 device that simply repeats all incoming network data to all its output ports. In other words, if a hub has eight ports, any input data that arrives on port 1 will be amplified and repeated on ports 2 through 8. A hub is an unintelligent device — the hub doesn't know or care what the intended destination of the incoming data is. It simply sends the data to all its ports, hoping that the intended recipient is on one of those ports. (Actually, using the term *hope* here is misleading, because as I said, the hub not only doesn't know who the intended recipient is but doesn't even care. Hubs have no capacity for hope.)

Figure 3-1 shows a simple network with four computers connected via a hub. In this example, Computer 1 is sending data to Computer 4. As the figure shows, the hub doesn't know that the intended recipient is Computer 4, so it sends the data not just to Computer 4, but also to Computer 2 and Computer 3 as well.

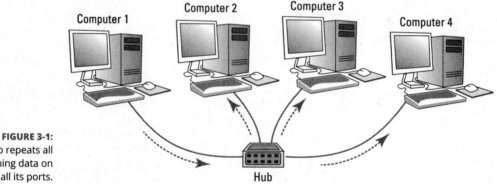

FIGURE 3-1:
A hub repeats all incoming data on all its ports.

To understand why hubs even exist, or at least did exist in the distant past, we need a little history lesson. Ethernet was invented in the late 1970s and first became commercially available in 1980. From the very beginning, Ethernet used what is called *shared media* to connect devices in a network. The basic idea of Ethernet is that data is sent over network cables in the form of *packets*, which follow a well-defined structure. The key elements of the original Ethernet were (and still are) as follows:

>> **All devices on the network can access all data sent over the network.** That's why the network cable itself is considered to be *shared media*.

>> **Every device on the network has a unique identifier called a MAC address.** I cover MAC addresses in the preceding chapter. As a quick reminder, MAC addresses are 48 bits long and are written as six octets

separated by hyphens. For example, 21–76–3D–7A–F6–1E is a valid MAC address.

>> **A data packet includes the MAC address of the packet's intended recipient, as well as the MAC address of the sender.**

>> **Every device on the network receives every packet that is sent on the network and examines the destination MAC address to determine whether the packet is intended for it.** If so, the device says, "Mine!" and stores the packet to be processed by other protocols higher up the food chain (that is, at higher levels in the OSI Reference Model). If the destination MAC address doesn't match the device's, the device says "Hmph!" and simply ignores the packet.

All the devices on the network do this examination, keeping only the packets that belong to them and ignoring all the others.

>> **If the destination MAC address is all ones (represented as** FF–FF–FF–FF–FF–FF**), the packet is called a *broadcast packet*.** When a broadcast packet is sent, every device on the network looks at the destination MAC address, sees that the packet is a broadcast packet, and says, "Mine!" Broadcast packets are received by every device on the network.

>> **Every once in a while, two devices try to send a packet at the exact same time.** When that happens, both packets are garbled. The result is called a *collision*. When collisions happen, both senders wait for a brief amount of randomly generated time and then try again. The collision probably won't happen again. But if it does, the senders wait and try again later.

So, that's a recap of the basic operation of the Ethernet networking system. Because it was a great system when it was invented, it quickly replaced the two dominant network technologies that were popular at the time, ARCNET and token ring. But unfortunately, Ethernet had a few serious problems lurking under the surface that proved to be a problem for larger networks:

>> **The frequency of collisions rises exponentially with the number of devices added to the network.** When you get too many devices, collisions happen all the time, and devices spend way too much time resending packets, sometimes having to resend them over and over again until a collision doesn't happen. This results in the network becoming much slower as it grows larger.

>> **The frequency of broadcast packets can quickly increase as more devices are added to the network, further adding to the performance problem and the likelihood of collisions.**

>> **Security is difficult to enforce, because every device on the network *must* examine every packet that comes its way.** Even though devices are supposed to ignore packets that aren't meant for them, there is no way to ensure that they do so.

Switches to the rescue!

A switch is essentially an intelligent hub that has the ability to actually look at the contents of the packets it processes and make intelligent decisions about what to do with them. A hub is a layer-1 device, which means that it can do nothing but receive and amplify electrical signals. In contrast, switches are layer-2 devices, which means they can actually inspect the layer-2 packets and act intelligently based on the content of each packet.

A switch examines the destination MAC address of every packet it receives and forwards the packet only to the port that leads to the packet's intended destination. Thus, packets aren't repeated on ports that don't contain the packets' destination.

Figure 3-2 shows the same simple network that was shown in Figure 3-1, but this time with a switch instead of a hub. As you can see, the switch is smart enough to know that the data sent by Computer 1 is intended for Computer 4. So it sends the data only to Computer 4; the switch leaves Computer 2 and Computer 3 alone so they can concentrate on other work.

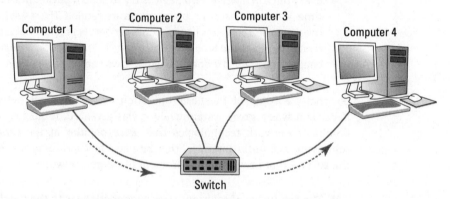

FIGURE 3-2:
Unlike a hub, a switch knows where to send its data.

In order to accomplish intelligent forwarding, a switch must know what devices are connected to each of its ports. In the next section, you see how a switch learns what devices are connected to each of its ports.

Learning

For a switch to do its job, it needs to know what devices are connected to each of its ports. More specifically, the switch needs to know what MAC addresses are reachable via each of its ports. It does this in an ingeniously simple way: It simply learns. Whenever a packet is received on any of the switch's ports, the switch examines the sending MAC address in the packet. The switch rightly assumes that if it received a packet from a given MAC address on a given port, the switch can reach that MAC address via that port. For example, if a switch receives a packet from Computer C on port 3, the switch has learned that Computer C is reachable on port 3. The switch adds this information to the MAC address table. This table is sometimes referred to as a *forwarding database,* because it keeps track of which port packets intended for a given destination should be forwarded to. The MAC address table simply keeps a tally of which MAC addresses are reachable on each port of the switch. Suppose the MAC address for Computer C is 21–76–3D–7A–F6–1E. If the switch receives a packet from port 3 with that MAC address, it would add the following entry to the MAC address table:

Port	MAC Address
3	21–76–3D–7A–F6–1E

In this way, the switch has learned that Computer C is reachable via port 3.

After a short time, the switch will likely receive packets from all its ports and will associate the sender's MAC address with each port:

Port	MAC Address
1	40–20–08–78–84–52
2	21–76–3D–7A–F6–1E
3	21–76–3D–7A–F6–1E
4	21–76–3D–7A–F6–1E
5	76–2F–F9–C8–B6–08
6	FC–78–B6–07–52–EA
7	CD–34–E4–B3–2C–76
8	1C–FD–E0–63–21–C0

It's important to keep in mind that a switch port might actually connect to more than one device. For example, suppose port 5 isn't connected to a computer but to another switch, which in turn has three other computers connected to it. In that case, the first switch can receive packets from three different computers on port 5. Then, the switch records each distinct MAC address in its MAC address table, something like this:

Port	MAC Address
1	40–20–08–78–84–52
2	21–76–3D–7A–F6–1E
3	21–76–3D–7A–F6–1E
4	21–76–3D–7A–F6–1E
5	76–2F–F9–C8–B6–08
5	D6–4E–69–86–E9–F7
5	06–C1–15–A2–BA–60
6	FC–78–B6–07–52–EA
7	CD–34–E4–B3–2C–76
8	1C–FD–E0–63–21–C0

The process of building the MAC address table is called *learning,* and is one of the three basic functions of a switch. The other two are *forwarding* and *flooding,* as described in the next two sections.

Forwarding

Now that you know about the MAC address table, you should have a good idea of how a switch knows which ports to forward incoming packets to: The switch simply looks up the destination MAC address in the table and sends the packet out through the corresponding port.

For example, if the switch receives a packet on port 1 intended for MAC address CD–34–E4–B3–2C–76, the switch looks up that MAC address in the table, finds that the MAC address can be reached on port 7, and forwards the packet out to port 7. This process, called *forwarding,* is the second basic function of a switch.

Switches have memory buffers associated with each port that allow the switch to store a complete packet before forwarding it to the destination port. This allows the switch to hold onto the packet for a bit if necessary before forwarding it. For example, the destination port may be busy sending out a packet received from a different port. Or, the destination port may be busy receiving a packet. In either case, when the port becomes free, the switch can transmit the packet to its destination.

It's important to understand that the switch does not modify the packet in any way prior to sending it. What gets sent out to the destination port is an exact replica of what was received on the incoming port. When the destination device receives the packet, the device has no idea that the packet passed through the switch. In other words, no tracing information is added to the packet by the switch.

It's also important to know that, at least at this level of operation of the switch, the switch has no idea or concern for the contents of the Ethernet frame's payload. In particular, the switch is not concerned with the possibility that the payload may be an IP packet, which in turn contains an IP address. Switching does not rely on or even know about IP addresses. Switching is a layer-2 function, and layer 2 is concerned with MAC addresses. IP addresses are a layer-3 concern and, thus, are hidden from switches.

TECHNICAL STUFF

Here's where I have to tell you that I lied. It isn't exactly true that switches don't care about IP addresses. Many advanced switches have layer-3 features that *do* look at the IP address. But when they do, they're acting more like routers than switches. *Routers* work at layer 3 and, therefore, deal with IP addresses. I have more to say about that later in this chapter, in the "Understanding Routers" section.

So, to recap, when a switch receives a packet on one of its ports, the switch looks in the Ethernet frame to determine the destination MAC address. The switch then looks that address up in its MAC address table, determines which port is associated with the destination address, and forwards the packet on to that port.

Which begs the question: What happens if the switch doesn't recognize the destination MAC address in the forwarding database? The answer is found in the next section.

Flooding

When a switch receives a packet that is intended for a MAC address that isn't in the switch's internal MAC address table, the switch has no way to know what port to forward the packet to. In that case, the switch has no option but to revert to acting like a hub: The switch simply forwards the packet on all available ports other than the one the packet arrived on, of course. This is called *flooding*, which is the third function of a switch (the first two being *learning* and *forwarding*).

The packet will be forwarded even to ports for which the switch has already learned a MAC address. This is necessary because a single port can be a pathway to more than one MAC address, as is the case when the port is connected to another switch.

Flooding is similar to broadcasting, but it isn't quite the same. A broadcast packet is a packet that is intended for every recipient on the network. Thus, a switch must forward broadcast packets to every port. In contrast, flooding results when the packet has a single destination, but the switch doesn't know how to reach it. Thus, the switch sends the packet to every port in the hopes that one of them will lead to the destination.

Hopefully, flooding doesn't happen too often. There's a very good chance that the destination device will receive the packet and send a reply back to the sender. In that case, the switch will record the MAC address of the recipient in its table. Then, the next time a packet intended for that destination is reached, the switch will be able to forward it to the correct port rather than flood the network again.

Looking Deeper into Switches

In the previous sections, you learned about the three basic functions of a switch:

>> **Learning:** The switch learns what devices are reachable on each of its ports.

>> **Forwarding:** The switch forwards incoming packets just to the correct port based on the intended destination.

>> **Flooding:** The switch forwards incoming packets to all ports when it hasn't yet learned how to reach the intended destination.

In the following sections, I dig deeper into the operation of switches to explain more about how they operate.

Collision domains

One of the main benefits of switches over hubs is that switches minimize the frequency of collisions on the network. Consider a four-port switch in which Computers 1, 2, 3, and 4 are connected to ports 1, 2, 3, and 4. If port 1 receives a packet from Computer 1 that is intended for Computer 2, the switch will forward the packet to port 2. If, at the same time, port 3 receives a packet intended for Computer 4, the switch will forward that packet to port 4. Both of these packets can travel on the network at the same time because at no time will they exist on the same set of network interfaces or cables. Thus, the packets will never collide.

In contrast, if these four computers were connected with a hub, the packets would collide because the two packets would be forwarded to all the ports, not just the ports connected to the destination computers.

This reduction of collisions is so fundamental to what a switch does that a common definition of what a switch is reads like this: *A switch is a device that divides collision domains.* A *collision domain* is a segment of a network on which collisions are possible. In an old-style Ethernet network built with hubs, the entire network is a single collision domain because all the network interfaces that connect to the network will see all packets that travel on the network. But when a switch is used, the network is divided into separate collision domains.

In a switched network, each collision domain consists of just two network interfaces: the port on the switch and the port on the destination device (typically a computer, but possibly another switch). An eight-port switch divides a single collision domain with eight devices into eight separate collision domains, each with only two devices.

Switches don't completely eliminate collisions. For example, suppose a switch has received a packet intended for a computer, and that computer attempts to send a packet at the same moment that the switch attempts to forward the received packet to the computer. In that case, the two packets collide, and both the switch and the computer must wait and try again a bit later.

Bridging

A *bridge* is a device that is very similar to a switch, but it typically has fewer ports — perhaps as few as two. The primary purpose of a bridge is to provide a link between two networks, so some bridges have just two ports. Like a switch, a bridge examines the destination MAC address of every packet it receives and forwards the packet to the other side of the bridge only if the bridge knows that the destination is on the other side.

Technically speaking, a switch is simply a multi-port bridge. The distinction is mostly a historical one, because bridges were invented and widely used before switches. Before switches became inexpensive, large Ethernet networks used multiple hubs to connect computers and other devices, and a few bridges would be introduced into the network to break up large collision domains. Now that switches are common, you don't see separate bridging devices much anymore.

However, one function that a bridge can perform can come in handy: A bridge can be used to connect two different types of networks. For example, suppose your main network uses Cat-5e cable, but you also have a smaller network that uses fiber-optic cable. You can use a bridge to link these two types of networks. The bridge would have two ports: One Cat-5e port and one fiber-optic port. When the bridge receives a packet on the Cat-5e port, it forwards it to the fiber-optic port, and vice versa.

All switches can perform this type of bridging to connect Cat-5e devices that operate at different speeds. For example, most computers have network interfaces that operate at 1 gigabit per second (Gbps). But many printers have slower, 100 megabits per second (Mbps) connections. The ports on a switch can automatically detect the speed of the device on the other end of the cable, so you can plug a 1 Gbps computer or a 100 Mbps printer into a switch port. The switch will automatically take care of buffering and forwarding packets received from the 1 Gbps devices to the slower 100 Mbps devices.

Some switches also include ports that allow you to connect the switch to even faster networks that use 10 Gbps copper or fiber-optic cable, as described in the next section.

SFP ports and uplinks

Some switches have special ports called *small form-factor pluggable* (SFP) *ports*. You can use an SFP port to connect a variety of different types of high-speed networks, including 10 Gb Ethernet (which uses copper cable) or 8 Gb Fibre Channel, which uses fiber-optic cables. In this way, the SFP ports allow the switch to bridge 100 Mbps or 1 Gbps Cat-5e networks with faster copper or fiber-optic networks.

One of the most common uses of SFP ports is to connect switches to each port at speeds faster than 1 Gbps. The interconnection between two switches is often called an *uplink*. It makes sense to use high-speed uplinks because the uplink ports are likely to be the busiest ports on the switch. For example, suppose you have a network with 80 computers in which 40 of the computers are connected to one switch (call it Switch A) and the other 40 computers are connected to a second switch (Switch B). If a computer on switch A sends a packet to a computer on Switch B, that packet must travel through the uplink ports to get from Switch A to Switch B. So, you can expect that the uplink ports will carry as much as 40 times the amount of traffic that the other ports carry.

Another common use of SFP is to connect switches to server computers. This also makes sense, because the ports that connect to your servers will carry much more traffic than the ports that connect to workstations. In order to connect a switch to a server using an SFP port, both the switch and the server must have SFP ports. So you'll need to make sure both your servers and your switches have SFP ports.

Broadcast domains

Earlier in this chapter (in the "Understanding Switches" section), I mention that packets whose destination MAC addresses are all ones (FF-FF-FF-FF-FF-FF) are intended to be received by all devices that see the packet. Such packets are called *broadcast packets*.

The scope of the devices that broadcast packets are intended for is called the *broadcast domain.* Ordinarily, a switch forwards broadcast packets to all the ports on the switch except the port on which the broadcast packet was received. Thus, the broadcast domain consists of all the devices connected to the switch, either directly or indirectly through another switch.

In many cases, allowing broadcast packets to travel throughout a large network is not a good idea. If the network is large, broadcast packets may consume a significant amount of the total bandwidth available on the network, slowing down other more important traffic.

You may be surprised to discover just how much broadcast traffic actually happens on a large network. The most common type of broadcast packet is an Address Resolution Protocol (ARP) request. ARP is the protocol used to determine the MAC address of a given IP address. If one IP device wants to send a packet to another IP device, the sender needs to know the MAC address of the recipient. So, the sender broadcasts an ARP request, which is essentially the question "Does anyone know the MAC address of this particular IP address? If so, please let me know."

Reducing the amount of broadcast traffic on a network is a key way to improve the network's overall performance. One of the best ways to do that is to segment the network in a way that splits up the broadcast domains. There are two ways to do this: by using routers, which are described in the next section, or by using VLANs, which are described later in this chapter, in the "Understanding VLANs" section.

Managed and unmanaged switches

Most advanced switches have management features built in to them, which means that you can monitor and configure the switch remotely, usually by logging in to a web console. To accomplish this, the switch has a small web server built into it to provide the management console. In addition, the switch itself must have an IP address.

In contrast, inexpensive consumer-grade switches that you would purchase at a retail store are usually unmanaged switches. Unmanaged switches are often appropriate for small networks, but if you have more than a few dozen computers on your network, I suggest you invest in managed switches to give you more control over your network.

With a managed switch, you can monitor traffic over the switch, which can be useful when troubleshooting network issues. In addition, you can often configure certain functions for each port of the switch. Among the most important features you can configure are VLANs, which allow you to actually create separate layer-2 networks on a single switch. I cover VLANs in greater detail later in this chapter, in the "Understanding VLANs" section.

Understanding Routers

A *router* is a layer-3 device, which means it works at the network layer of the OSI Reference Model. In practical terms, that means that routers know about IP addresses. At least one router is a vital component of any modern network.

A router differs from a switch in the following ways:

» **Switches work with MAC addresses and know nothing about IP addresses.** In contrast, routers work with IP addresses.

» **Routers can facilitate communication between IP networks with different subnets.** For example, if your organization has a 10.0.100.x network and a 192.168.0.x network, a router can enable packets to get from the 10.0.100.x network to the 192.168.0.x network, and vice versa. A switch can't do that. (For more about subnets, refer to Book 2, Chapter 3.)

» **Routers also enable a private network to communicate with the Internet.** For example, suppose you want to connect your network to the Internet via a broadband cable provider such as Comcast. The cable provider will give you a network interface that has a public IP address. You must then use a router to exchange packets from your private network to the Internet via the public IP address. A switch can't do that for you.

» **Switches split up collision domains.** The segments created by switches are still part of the same broadcast domain. In contrast, routers split up broadcast domains. So, broadcast packets do not cross the boundaries created by routers. (Actually, as I explain in the "Understanding VLANs" section, later in this chapter, switches can also break up broadcast domains.)

» **Switches typically have a large number of ports — often as many as 48 in a single switch.** Routers usually have fewer ports, typically between two and eight. (However, routers for very large networks may have many more ports. For example, Cisco makes a router that can accommodate as many as 256 ports in a single chassis.)

The basic operation of a router is fairly simple. Consider the simple network depicted in Figure 3-3. Here, an organization has two separate IP networks, one using a 10.0.100.x subnet and the other using 192.168.0.x. (In both cases, the subnet mask is 255.255.255.0. Again, for more information about subnetting, refer to Book 2, Chapter 3.) A router is used to connect these two networks. On either side of the router is a switch, and each switch has just one computer connected. On the 10.0.100.x side, the computer's IP address is 10.0.100.50. On the 192.168.0.x side, the computer's IP address is 192.168.0.50. (For simplicity, I only show one

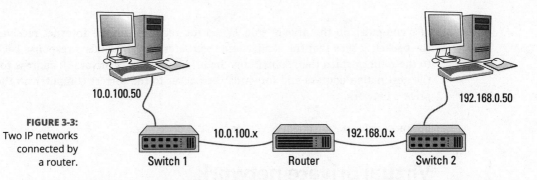

FIGURE 3-3:
Two IP networks
connected by
a router.

10.0.100.50

192.168.0.50

10.0.100.x

192.168.0.x

Switch 1

Router

Switch 2

computer connected to the switches on either side of the router, but in the real world there would probably be many more.)

Now suppose that the computer on the left side of the figure (10.0.100.50) needs to send a packet over to the computer on the right side of the figure (192.168.0.50). The sending computer forms the packet and sends it to Switch 1. Switch 1, in turn, sends the packet to the router. The router examines the destination IP address and determines that the destination computer is on the 192.168.0.50 network, so it forwards the packet over to Switch 2. Switch 2, in turn, forwards the packet to the destination computer.

Note that this exchange is actually considerably more complicated than the previous description lets on. For one thing, the switches — which don't know about IP addresses — must determine the MAC addresses not only of the sending and receiving computers, but also of the router. And the router must also know the MAC addresses of the two switches. You'll learn more about how this type of routing actually happens in Book 2, Chapter 4. But for now, I think you get the general idea.

The following sections describe a few of the other features commonly provided by routers.

Network address translation

When a router is used to connect a private network to the Internet, one of the router's most important functions is routing traffic from all the computers on the private side of the router to the public side, which usually has just a single public IP address. To accomplish this magic, the router uses network address translation (NAT).

In short, when a computer on the private side of the network sends a packet through the router to the Internet, the router substitutes its own public IP address as the sender address, and keeps track of the fact that it sent a packet on behalf of a computer on the private side. When the recipient on the Internet receives the packet, it sees that the sender was the router. It then sends a response back to the router, which then substitutes the original sender's private IP address for the destination address and forwards the packet to the correct computer on the private network.

For more information about NAT, see Book 2, Chapter 4.

Virtual private network

A *virtual private network* (VPN) is a secure connection between two private networks over a public network (in other words, over the Internet). All the data that flows over the VPN is encrypted, so anyone who steals packets from the VPN will find them unintelligible; only the parties on either end of the VPN are able to decrypt the packets.

VPN connections are often called *tunnels*, because they provide an isolated pathway from one point to another through the Internet. The only way to gain meaningful access to a VPN tunnel is at either end.

There are two common uses for VPNs:

>> **To provide remote workers with secure access to your company network:** To do that, you set up a VPN on the router, and then provide your remote workers with the credentials necessary to access the VPN. The remote workers can run a software VPN client on their home computers or laptops to connect to your company network.

>> **To establish a tunnel directly between routers on two networks that are separated geographically:** For example, suppose you have offices in Los Angeles and Las Vegas. You can use routers on both networks to establish a VPN tunnel between them. This effectively joins the networks together, so that devices on the Los Angeles network can freely exchange packets with devices on the Las Vegas network, and vice versa.

Figure 3-4 shows this arrangement. As you can see, the routers in both Los Angeles and Las Vegas are connected through the Internet via a VPN tunnel. This tunnel enables computers in Los Angeles and Las Vegas to communicate freely and securely with each other.

For more information about working with VPN tunnels, refer to Book 4, Chapter 6.

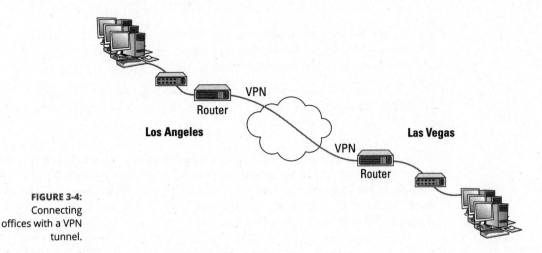

FIGURE 3-4:
Connecting offices with a VPN tunnel.

Understanding VLANs

The final topic for this whirlwind introduction to switches and routers is the concept of VLANs. Most advanced switches allow you to create VLANs.

As its name suggests, a VLAN is a virtual network that runs on top of your actual physical network. VLANs work at layer 2 of the OSI model, which means that they're related MAC addresses, not IP addresses. That said, there is usually a direct correlation between VLANs and IP subnets. If (or when) your network grows large enough that you want to set up two or more subnets to better manage it, you'll probably also want to set up two or more VLANs, one for each of your subnets.

A VLAN can divide a single switch into two virtual switches that behave exactly as if they were separate switches. This means the following:

>> If a port on one VLAN receives a packet intended for a destination on the same VLAN, the switch forwards the packet to the destination port, the same as if VLANs were not in use.

>> When a port on one VLAN receives a packet intended for a destination on the same VLAN that the switch has not yet learned, the switch will flood only those ports that are on the destination VLAN — not all the ports on the switch. Thus, VLANs can reduce traffic caused by flooding.

>> When a broadcast packet is received, the switch will forward the packet only to those ports that are on the same VLAN. In other words, VLANs can break up broadcast domains in the same way that a router can.

>> If a port on one VLAN receives a packet intended for a different VLAN, a router is required to link the networks. That's because separate VLANs are, for all intents and purposes, separate networks.

That being said, most switches that support VLANs also support *trunk ports,* which can switch traffic between VLANs. A trunk port is a port that can handle traffic for two or more VLANs.

To use VLANs, you must manually configure each port of your switches to operate on the appropriate VLAN. By default, all switches regardless of manufacturer are configured out of the box so that all ports operate on a VLAN named VLAN1. To create a new VLAN, you simply create a name for the new VLAN, then configure the ports that will talk on the new VLAN.

In VLAN terminology, a port that is configured to operate on a single VLAN is called an *access port.* Ports that are configured to work on more than one VLAN are called *trunk ports.* By default, all switch ports are configured as access ports on VLAN1.

Note that if you have more than one switch in your network, you can configure VLANs to work across the switches. For example, you can create a VLAN for your company's accounting department — let's call it VLAN-Acct. Then you can configure ports on any of your switches as access ports on VLAN-Acct. In this way, your entire accounting staff can operate on the accounting VLAN.

Chapter **4**

Servers and Virtualization

S ervers are the lifeblood of any network. They provide the shared resources that network users crave, such as file storage, databases, email, web services, and so on. Choosing which servers your network needs and selecting the type of equipment you use to implement your servers are among the key decisions you'll make when you set up a network.

In this chapter, I take a quick look at what is important in a server. First, I cover the basic functions of a server operating system. Then I survey the various types of servers most networks need. Then I turn my attention to important matters to consider when selecting the kind of hardware a server should run on. And finally, I look quickly at the idea of virtualizing your entire server environment.

Understanding Network Operating Systems

The server operating system is what enables your server computers to function as servers rather than as ordinary Windows clients. Server operating systems provide essential functions such as providing basic security services, sharing disk storage and printers, and so on. Here are some of these core server operating system features:

Network services

Obviously, a server operating system must provide networking capabilities in order for it to function on a network. If your client computers can't connect to your servers, your network will be useless. For this reason, it's a good idea to make sure your server computers are equipped with more than one network interface. That way, if one of the interfaces fails, the other can pick up the slack and keep your server connected to your network.

In addition to basic network connectivity, one of your servers will typically be responsible for providing some essential software services that are required to keep a network operating in an efficient manner. One of these is called Dynamic Host Configuration Protocol (DHCP); it's the service that recognizes computers and other devices that want to join the network, providing each with a unique address so that all the devices on the network can identify one another. For more information about this vital service, refer to Book 2, Chapter 5.

A second basic service that is provided by one of the servers on your network is called Domain Name System (DNS). This service is what enables people to use network names instead of the actual addresses that are handed out by DHCP. It's also the service that enables people to browse the World Wide Web using addresses such as www.dummies.com rather than cryptic addresses. For more information about this important service, please refer to Book 2, Chapter 6.

File-sharing services

One of the most important functions of a server operating system is to share resources with other network users. The most common resource that's shared is the server's *file system* — organized disk space that a server must be able to share (in whole or in part) with other users. In effect, those users can treat the server's disk space as an extension of their own computers' disk space.

The server operating system allows the system administrator to determine which portions of the server's file system to share.

 Although an entire hard drive can be shared, it isn't commonly done. Instead, individual folders are shared. The administrator can control which users are allowed to access each shared folder.

TIP

Because file sharing is the reason why many network servers exist, server operating systems have more sophisticated disk management features than are found in desktop operating systems. For example, most server operating systems can manage two or more hard drives as though they were a single drive. In addition, most can create a *mirror* — an automatic backup copy of a drive — on a second drive.

Multitasking

Only one user at a time uses a desktop computer; however, multiple users simultaneously use server computers. As a result, a server operating system must provide support for multiple users who access the server remotely via the network.

At the heart of multiuser support is *multitasking*, which is the capability of an operating system to execute more than one program (a task or a process) at a time. Multitasking operating systems are like the guy who used to spin plates balanced on sticks on the old *Ed Sullivan Show* back in the 1950s. He'd run from plate to plate, trying to keep them all spinning so they wouldn't fall off the sticks — and just for grins, he was blindfolded or rode on a unicycle.

Although multitasking creates the appearance that two or more programs are executing on the computer at one time, in reality, a computer with a single processor can execute only one program at a time. The operating system switches the CPU from one program to another to create the appearance that several programs are executing simultaneously, but at any given moment, only one of the programs is actually executing. The others are patiently waiting for their turns. (However, if the computer has more than one CPU, the CPUs *can* execute programs simultaneously, which is multiprocessing.)

For multitasking to work reliably, the server operating system must completely isolate the executing programs from each other. Otherwise, one program may perform an operation that adversely affects another program. Multitasking operating systems do this by providing each task with its own unique address space that makes it almost impossible for one task to affect memory that belongs to another task.

Directory services

Directories are everywhere — and were, even in the days when they were all hard copy. When you needed to make a phone call, you looked up the number in a phone directory. When you needed to find the address of a client, you looked her up in your Rolodex. And then there were the nonbook versions: When you needed to find the Sam Goody store at a shopping mall (for example), you looked for the mall directory — usually, a lighted sign showing what was where.

Networks have directories, too, providing information about the resources that are available on the network: users, computers, printers, shared folders, and files. Directories are essential parts of any server operating system.

The most popular modern directory service is called *Active Directory*. Active Directory is a standard component of all Windows operating systems, and because it's so popular, most other operating systems support it as well. Active Directory is a database that organizes information about a network and all its computers and users. It's simple enough to use for networks with just a few computers and users, but powerful enough to work with large networks containing tens of thousands of computers and users. Figure 4-1 shows the Active Directory Users and Computers tool, which manages Active Directory user and computer accounts on Windows Server 2016.

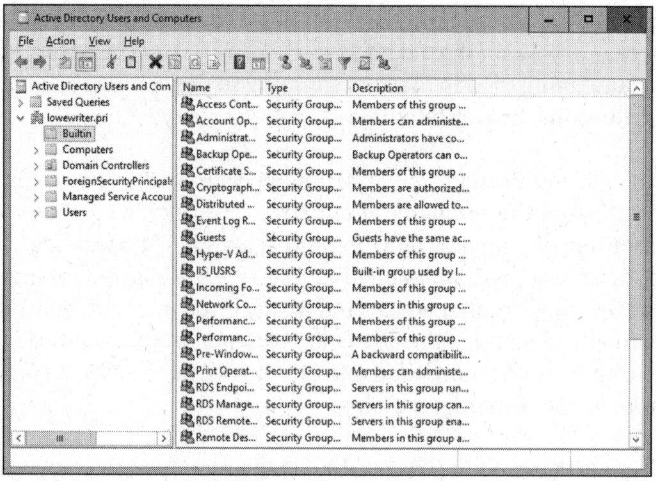

FIGURE 4-1:
Managing Active Directory Users and Computers.

Security services

All server operating systems must provide some measure of security to protect the network from unauthorized access. Hacking seems to be the national pastime these days. With most computer networks connected to the Internet, anyone anywhere in the world can — and probably will — try to break into your network.

The most basic type of security is handled through *user accounts,* which grant individual users the right to access the network resources and govern which resources the user can access. User accounts are secured by passwords; therefore, good password policy is a cornerstone of any security system. Most server operating systems give you some standard tools for maintaining network security:

» **Establish password policies.** For example, you can mandate that passwords have a minimum length and include a mix of letters and numerals.

» **Set passwords to expire after a certain number of days.** Network users must change their passwords frequently.

» **Encrypt network data.** A data-encryption capability scrambles data before it's sent over the network or saved on disk, making unauthorized use a lot more difficult.

Good encryption is the key to setting up a virtual private network (VPN), which enables network users to securely access a network from a remote location by using an Internet connection.

TIP

» **Manage digital certificates.** Digital certificates are used to ensure that users are who they say they are and files are what they claim to be.

The overwhelming majority of business networks rely on server versions of Windows, known as Windows Server. Microsoft periodically releases updated versions of Windows Server, so Windows Server is frequently improved, and older versions are occasionally rendered obsolete. Currently, the most commonly used versions are Windows Server 2008, Windows Server 2012, Windows Server 2012 Release 2, and the latest-and-greatest version, known as Windows Server 2016.

But Windows Server is not the only server operating system at your disposal. Many servers — especially those whose primary responsibility is to host websites — use Linux instead of Windows Server. Apple also makes an excellent server operating system, known as OS X Server.

What's Important in a Server

The following sections point out some general things to keep in mind when selecting the equipment that a server should run on.

Scalability

The ability to increase the size and capacity of the server computer without unreasonable hassle. Purchasing a server computer that just meets your current needs is a major mistake because (rest assured) your needs will double within a year. If at all possible, equip your servers with far more disk space, RAM, and processor power than you currently need.

Reliability

The old adage "you get what you pay for" applies especially well to server computers. Why spend $5,000 on a server computer when you can buy one with seemingly similar specifications at a discount electronics store for a mere $1,000? The main reason: reliability. When a client computer fails, only the person who uses that computer is affected. When a server fails, however, everyone on the network is affected. The less-expensive computer is probably made of inferior components that are more likely to fail, and does not have redundant components built in. (For example, many server computers have two power supplies, two CPUs, two or more network interfaces, and other redundant components.)

Availability

This concept is closely related to reliability. When a server computer fails, how long does it take to correct the problem and get the server up and running again? Server computers are designed so their components can be easily diagnosed and replaced, which minimizes the downtime that results when a component fails. In some servers, components are *hot swappable* (certain components can be replaced without shutting down the server). Some servers are fault-tolerant so that they can continue to operate even if a major component fails.

Service and support

Service and support are often overlooked factors when picking computers. If a component in a server computer fails, do you have someone on site qualified to repair the broken computer? If not, you should get an on-site maintenance contract for the computer.

WARNING

Don't settle for a maintenance contract that requires you to take the computer in to a repair shop or, worse, mail it to a repair facility. You can't afford to be without your server that long. Get a maintenance contract that provides for on-site service and repair of your server, 24 hours a day, 7 days a week.

Components of a Server Computer

The hardware components that make up a typical server computer are similar to the components used in less-expensive client computers. However, server computers are usually built from higher-grade components than client computers for the reasons given in the preceding section. The following paragraphs describe the typical components of a server computer:

Motherboard

A motherboard is the computer's main electronic circuit board to which all the other components of your computer are connected. More than any other component, the motherboard *is* the computer. All other components attach to the motherboard.

The major components on the motherboard include the processor (CPU); supporting circuitry (the chipset); memory (RAM); expansion slots; a hard drive controller; USB ports for devices such as keyboards and mice; a graphics adapter; and one or more network interfaces.

Processor

The CPU is the brain of the computer. Although the processor isn't the only component that affects overall system performance, it's the one that most people think of first when deciding what type of server to purchase. At the time of this writing, most servers used one of several variations of Intel's Xeon processor. These processors are designed specifically for server computers rather than client computers, and offer from 4 to 22 independent processor cores, depending on the model.

Each motherboard is designed to support a particular type of processor. CPUs come in two basic mounting styles: slot or socket. However, you can choose from several types of slots and sockets, so you have to make sure that the motherboard supports the specific slot or socket style used by the CPU. Some server motherboards have two or more slots or sockets to hold two or more CPUs.

TECHNICAL STUFF

Clock speed refers to how fast the basic clock that drives the processor's operation ticks. In theory, the faster the clock speed, the faster the processor. However, clock speed alone is reliable only for comparing processors within the same family. What matters more in a server is the number of processor cores. The more cores the server has, the more tasks the server can perform simultaneously. Since servers are in the business of supporting many clients, being able to do many tasks simultaneously is a huge benefit for server performance.

What's more, processor cores utilize a technology called *hyperthreading*, which effectively lets each processor core juggle two threads at once. (In general terms, a *thread* is a sequence of instructions that performs a single task.) Because each core can handle two simultaneous threads, a processor with four cores can handle eight concurrent threads.

Many server motherboards can support two separate processors, which doubles the potential workload of the server. For example, if the server has two 8-core

Servers and Virtualization

processors, the server has a total of 16 cores available for its workload. Because of hyperthreading, each of these 16 cores can handle 2 threads, so the server can handle 32 concurrent threads.

Memory

Don't scrimp on memory. People rarely complain about servers having too much memory. The total memory capacity of the server depends on the motherboard. It isn't unusual to see servers configured with anywhere from 32GB to 512GB of RAM.

Hard drives

Most desktop computers use inexpensive consumer-grade SATA hard drives, which are adequate for individual users. Because of their low cost, SATA drives are sometimes also used in inexpensive servers. But because performance and reliability are important in servers, many servers rely on faster and more reliable SCSI or Serial Attached SCSI (SAS) disk drives instead. For the best performance, solid state drives (SSDs) can be used. These drives have no mechanical parts, so they are considerably faster than traditional spinning disks.

Network interfaces

The network connection is one of the most important parts of any server. Ideally, your server should have at least two network interfaces. Additional network interfaces not only improve the performance of your server, but also make it more reliable: If one of the network interfaces should fail, the others can pick up the ball.

Video

Fancy graphics aren't that important for a server computer. You don't need to equip your server with an expensive video card; the video interface that's built in to the motherboard will suffice. (This is one of the few areas where it's acceptable to cut costs on a server.)

Power supply

Because a server usually has more devices than a typical desktop computer, it requires a larger power supply (typically 600 watts). If the server houses a large number of hard drives, it may require an even larger power supply.

Because the power supply is one of the most likely components to fail, many server computers have two built-in power supplies for redundancy. That way, if one of the power supplies should fail, the other can pick up the load and keep the server running.

Considering Server Form Factors

Form factor refers to the size, shape, and packaging of a hardware device. Server computers typically come in one of three form factors:

Tower case

Most servers are housed in a traditional tower case, similar to the tower cases used for desktop computers. A typical server tower case is 18 inches high, 20 inches deep, and 9 inches wide with room inside for a motherboard, five or more hard drives, and other components.

Some server cases include advanced features specially designed for servers, such as redundant power supplies (so both servers can continue operating if one of the power supplies fails), hot-swappable fans, and hot-swappable disk drive bays. (*Hot-swappable* components can be replaced without powering down the server.)

Rack mount

If you need only a few servers, tower cases are fine. You can just place the servers next to each other on a table or in a cabinet that's specially designed to hold servers. If you need more than a few servers, though, space can quickly become an issue. For example, what if your departmental network requires a bank of ten file servers? You'd need a pretty long table.

Rack-mount servers are designed to save space when you need more than a few servers in a confined area. A rack-mount server is housed in a small chassis that's designed to fit into a standard 19-inch equipment rack. The rack allows you to vertically stack servers to save space.

Blade servers

Blade servers are designed to save even more space than rack-mount servers. A *blade server* is a server on a single card that can be mounted alongside other blade servers in a blade chassis, which itself fits into a standard 19-inch equipment rack. A typical blade chassis holds six or more servers, depending on the manufacturer.

One of the key benefits of using blade servers is that you don't need a separate power supply for each server. Instead, the blade enclosure provides power for all its blade servers. Some blade server systems provide rack-mounted power supplies that can serve several blade enclosures mounted in a single rack.

In addition, the blade enclosure provides keyboard, video, and mouse (KVM) switching so that you don't have to use a separate KVM switch. You can control any of the servers in a blade server network from a single keyboard, monitor, and mouse. (For more information, see the sidebar, "Saving space with a KVM switch.")

Another big benefit of using blade servers is that they drastically cut down the amount of cable clutter. With rack-mount servers, each server requires its own power, keyboard, video, mouse, and network cables. With blade servers, a single set of cables can service all the servers in a blade enclosure.

SAVING SPACE WITH A KVM SWITCH

If you have more than two or three servers in one location, consider getting a KVM switch to save space by connecting several server computers to a single keyboard, monitor, and mouse. Then, you can control any of the servers from a single keyboard, monitor, and mouse by turning a dial or by pressing a button on the KVM switch.

Simple KVM switches are mechanical affairs that let you choose from 2–16 (or more) computers. More elaborate KVM switches can control more computers, using a pop-up menu or a special keyboard combination to switch among computers. Some advanced KVMs can even control a mix of PCs and Macintosh computers from a single keyboard, monitor, and mouse.

To find more information about KVM switches, search online for *KVM*.

Considering Virtualization

One final consideration for this chapter is the concept of virtualization. Throughout this chapter, I use the term *server* to refer both to an operating system that provides services such as file sharing or directory services, as well as to the hardware on which that operating system runs. However, in many (if not most) modern network environments, a single physical computer system is used to run more than *virtual machines* (VMs). A VM is a simulation of an actual computer system. This concept is called *virtualization*. When virtualization is used, a single physical server computer actually runs more than one virtual server.

Virtualization is the reason that server computer hardware often has such high performance specifications, such as dual processors with multiple cores each and a large amount of RAM (256GB or more). In most environments, no single server really needs that much capacity. But when a single physical computer is responsible for running multiple virtual servers, the physical server must have sufficient capacity to run all its virtual servers.

If this concept seems confusing at first, don't sweat it. You'll learn more about virtualization in Book 3, Chapter 4, and in the five chapters of Book 5.

Chapter **5**

Cloud Computing

The world's two most popular science-fiction franchises — *Star Wars* and *Star Trek* — both feature cities that are suspended in the clouds. In *Star Wars Episode V: The Empire Strikes Back,* Han takes the *Millennium Falcon* to Cloud City, hoping that his friend Lando Calrissian can help repair their damaged hyperdrive. And in the original *Star Trek* series episode "The Cloud Minders," the crew of the *Enterprise* visits a city named Stratos, which is suspended in the clouds.

Coincidence? Perhaps. Or maybe Gene Roddenberry and George Lucas both knew that the future would be in the clouds. At any rate, the future of computer networking is rapidly heading for the clouds. Cloud computing, to be specific. This chapter is a brief introduction to cloud computing. You discover what it is, the pros and cons of adopting it, and what services are provided by the major cloud computer providers.

Introducing Cloud Computing

The basic idea behind cloud computing is to outsource one or more of your networked computing resources to the Internet. "The cloud" represents a new way of handling common computer tasks. Following are just a few examples of how the cloud way differs from the traditional way:

- >> **Email services**

  - *Traditional:* Provide email services by installing Microsoft Exchange on a local server computer. Then your clients can connect using Microsoft Outlook to connect to the Exchange server to send and receive email.

  - *Cloud:* Contract with an Internet-based email provider, such as Google Mail (Gmail) or Microsoft's Exchange Online. Cloud-based email services typically charge a low monthly per-user fee, so the amount you pay for your email service depends solely on the number of email users you have.

- >> **Disk storage**

  - *Traditional:* Set up a local file server computer with a large amount of shared disk space.

  - *Cloud:* Sign up for an Internet file storage service and then store your data on the Internet. Cloud-based file storage typically charges a small monthly per-gigabyte fee, so you pay only for the storage you use. The disk capacity of cloud-based storage is essentially unlimited.

- >> **Accounting services**

  - *Traditional:* Purchase expensive accounting software and install it on a local server computer.

  - *Cloud:* Sign up for a web-based accounting service. Then all your accounting data is saved and managed on the provider's servers, not on yours.

Looking at the Benefits of Cloud Computing

Cloud computing is a different — and, in many ways, better — approach to networking. Here are a few of the main benefits of moving to cloud-based networking:

- >> **Cost-effective:** Cloud-based computing typically is less expensive than traditional computing. Consider a typical file server application: To implement a file server, first you must purchase a file server computer with enough disk space to accommodate your users' needs, which amounts to 1TB of disk storage. You want the most reliable data storage possible, so you purchase a server-quality computer and fully redundant disk drives. For the sake of this discussion, figure that the total price of the server — including its disk drive, the operating system license, and the labor cost of setting it up — is about $10,000. Assuming that the server will last for four years, that totals about $2,500 per year.

If you instead acquire your disk storage from a cloud-based file-sharing service, you can expect to pay about one fourth of that amount for an equivalent amount of storage.

The same economies apply to most other cloud-based solutions. Cloud-based email solutions, for example, typically cost around $5 per month per user — well less than the cost of setting up and maintaining an on-premises Microsoft Exchange Server.

» **Scalable:** So what happens if you guess wrong about the storage requirements of your file server, and your users end up needing 2TB instead of just 1TB? With a traditional file server, you must purchase additional disk drives to accommodate the extra space. Sooner than you want, you'll run out of capacity in the server's cabinet. Then you'll have to purchase an external storage cabinet. Eventually, you'll fill that up, too.

Now suppose that after you expand your server capacity to 2TB, your users' needs contract to just 1TB. Unfortunately, you can't return disk drives for a refund.

REMEMBER

With cloud computing, you pay only for the capacity you're actually using, and you can add capacity whenever you need it. In the file server example, you can write as much data as you need to the cloud storage. Each month, you're billed according to your actual usage. Thus, you don't have to purchase and install additional disk drives to add storage capacity.

» **Reliable:** Especially for smaller businesses, cloud services are much more reliable than in-house services. Just a week before I wrote this chapter, the tape drive that a friend uses to back up his company's data failed. As a result, he was unable to back up data for three days while the tape drive was repaired. Had he been using cloud-based backup, he could have restored his data immediately and wouldn't have been without backups for those four days.

The reason for the increased reliability of cloud services is simply a matter of scale. Most small businesses can't afford the redundancies needed to make their computer operations as reliable as possible. My friend's company can't afford to buy two tape drives so that an extra is available in case the main one fails.

By contrast, cloud services are usually provided by large companies such as Amazon, Google, Microsoft, and IBM. These companies have state-of-the-art data centers with multiple redundancies for their cloud services. Cloud storage may be kept on multiple servers so that if one server fails, others can take over the load. In some cases, these servers are in different data centers in different parts of the country. Thus, your data will still be available even in the event of a disaster that shuts down an entire data system.

>> **Hassle-free:** Face it, IT can be a hassle. With cloud-based services, you basically outsource the job of complex system maintenance chores, such as software upgrade, patches, hardware maintenance, backup, and so on. You get to consume the services while someone else takes care of making sure that the services run properly.

>> **Globally accessible:** One of the best things about cloud services is that they're available anywhere you have an Internet connection. Suppose that you have offices in five cities. Using traditional computing, each office would require its own servers, and you'd have to carefully design systems that allowed users in each of the offices to access shared data.

With cloud computing, each office simply connects to the Internet to access the cloud applications. Cloud-based applications are also great if your users are mobile because they can access the applications anywhere they can find an Internet connection.

Detailing the Drawbacks of Cloud Computing

Although cloud computing has many advantages over traditional techniques, it isn't without its drawbacks. The following sections outline some of the most significant roadblocks to adopting cloud computing.

>> **Entrenched applications:** Your organization may depend on entrenched applications that don't lend themselves especially well to cloud computing — or that at least require significant conversion efforts to migrate to the cloud. For example, you might use an accounting system that relies on local file storage.

Fortunately, many cloud providers offer assistance with this migration. And in many cases, the same application that you run locally can be run in the cloud, so no conversion is necessary.

>> **Internet connection speed:** Cloud computing shifts much of the burden of your network to your Internet connection. Your users used to access their data on local file servers over gigabit-speed connections; now they must access data over slower bandwidth Internet connections.

REMEMBER

Although you can upgrade your connection to higher speeds, doing so will cost money — money that may well offset the money you otherwise save from migrating to the cloud.

» **Internet connection reliability:** The cloud resources you access may feature all the redundancy in the world, but if your users access the cloud through a single Internet connection, that connection becomes a key point of vulnerability. Should it fail, any applications that depend on the cloud will be unavailable. If those applications are mission-critical, business will come to a halt until the connection is restored.

Here are two ways to mitigate this risk:

● *Make sure that you're using an enterprise-class Internet connection.* Enterprise-class connections are more expensive but provide much better fault tolerance and repair service than consumer-class connections do.

● *Provide redundant connections if you can.* That way, if one connection fails, traffic can be rerouted through alternative connections.

» **Security threats:** You can bet your life that hackers throughout the world are continually probing for ways to break through the security perimeter of all the major cloud providers. When they do, your data may be exposed.

The best way to mitigate this threat is to ensure that strong password policies are enforced.

Examining Three Basic Kinds of Cloud Services

Three distinct kinds of services can be provided via the cloud: applications, platforms, and services (infrastructure). The following paragraphs describe these three types of cloud services in greater detail.

Applications

Most often referred to as *Software as a Service (SaaS)*, fully functional applications can be delivered via the cloud. One of the best-known examples is *G Suite* (formerly known as *Google Apps*), which is a suite of cloud-based office applications designed to compete directly with Microsoft's traditional office applications, including Word, Excel, PowerPoint, Access, and Outlook. G Suite can also replace the back-end software often used to support Microsoft Office, including Exchange and SharePoint.

When you use a cloud-based application, you don't have to worry about any of the details that are commonly associated with running an application on your network, such as deploying the application and applying product upgrades and software patches. Cloud-based applications usually charge a small monthly fee based on the number of users running the software, so costs are low.

Also, as a cloud-based application user, you don't have to worry about providing the hardware or operating system platform on which the application will run. The application provider takes care of that detail for you, so you can focus simply on developing the application to best serve your users' needs.

Platforms

Also referred to as *Platform as a Service (PaaS)*, this class of service refers to providers that give you access to a remote virtual operating platform on which you can build your own applications.

At the simplest level, a PaaS provider gives you a complete, functional remote virtual machine that's fully configured and ready for you to deploy your applications to. If you use a web provider to host your company's website, you're already using PaaS: Most web host providers give you a functioning Linux system, fully configured with all the necessary servers, such as Apache or MySQL. All you have to do is build and deploy your web application on the provider's server.

More-complex PaaS solutions include specialized software that your custom applications can tap to provide services such as data storage, online order processing, and credit card payments. One of the best-known examples of this type of PaaS provider is Amazon.

REMEMBER

When you use PaaS, you take on the responsibility of developing your own custom applications to run on the remote platform. The PaaS provider takes care of the details of maintaining the platform itself, including the base operating system and the hardware on which the platform runs.

Infrastructure

If you don't want to delegate the responsibility of maintaining operating systems and other elements of the platform, you can use *Infrastructure as a Service (IaaS)*. When you use IaaS, you're purchasing raw computing power that's accessible via the cloud. Typically, IaaS provides you access to a remote virtual machine. It's up to you to manage and configure the remote machine however you want.

Public Clouds versus Private Clouds

The most common form of cloud computing uses what is known as a *public cloud* — that is, cloud services that are available to anyone in the world via the Internet. G Suite is an excellent example of a public cloud service. Anyone with access to the Internet can access the public cloud services of G Suite: Just point your browser to http://gsuite.google.com.

A public cloud is like a public utility, in that anyone can subscribe to it on a pay-as-you-go basis. One of the drawbacks of public cloud services is that they're inherently insecure. When you use a public cloud service, you're entrusting your valuable data to a third party that you cannot control. Sure, you can protect your access to your public cloud services by using strong passwords, but if your account names and passwords are compromised, your public cloud services can be hacked into, and your data can be stolen. Every so often, we all hear news stories about how this company's or that company's back-door security has been compromised.

Besides security, another drawback of public cloud computing is that it's dependent on high-speed, reliable Internet connections. Your cloud service provider may have all the redundancy in the world, but if your connection to the Internet goes down, you won't be able to access your cloud services. And if your connection is slow, your cloud services will be slow.

A *private cloud* mimics many of the features of cloud computing but is implemented on private hardware within a local network, so it isn't accessible to the general public. Private clouds are inherently more secure because the general public can't access them. Also, they're dependent only on private network connections, so they aren't subject to the limits of a public Internet connection.

TIP

As a rule, private clouds are implemented by large organizations that have the resources available to create and maintain their own cloud servers.

A relative newcomer to the cloud computing scene is the *hybrid cloud,* which combines the features of public and private clouds. Typically, a hybrid cloud system uses a small private cloud that provides local access to some of the applications and the public cloud for others. You might maintain your most frequently used data on a private cloud for fast access via the local network and use the public cloud to store archives and other less frequently used data, for which performance isn't as much of an issue.

Introducing Some of the Major Cloud Providers

Hundreds, if not thousands, of companies provide cloud services. Most of the cloud computing done today, however, is provided by just a few providers, which are described in the following sections.

Amazon

By far the largest provider of cloud services in the world is Amazon. Amazon launched its cloud platform — Amazon Web Services (AWS) — in 2006. Since then, hundreds of thousands of customers have signed up. Some of the most notable users of AWS include Netflix, Pinterest, and Instagram.

AWS includes the following features:

>> **Amazon CloudFront:** A PaaS content-delivery system designed to deliver web content to large numbers of users.

>> **Amazon Elastic Compute Cloud:** Also called Amazon EC2. An IaaS system that provides access to raw computing power.

>> **Amazon Simple Storage Service:** Also called Amazon S3. Provides web-based data storage for unlimited amounts of data.

>> **Amazon Simple Queue Service:** Also called Amazon SQS. Provides a data transfer system that lets applications send messages to other applications. SQS enables you to build applications that work together.

>> **Amazon Virtual Private Cloud:** Also called Amazon VPC. Uses virtual private network (VPN) connections to connect your local network to Amazon's cloud services.

For more information about Amazon Web Services, refer to Book 5, Chapter 4.

Google

Google is also one of the largest providers of cloud services. Its offerings include the following:

>> **G Suite:** A replacement for Microsoft Office that provides basic email, word processing, spreadsheet, and database functions via the cloud. G Suite is free to the general public and can even be used free by small business (up to

50 users). For larger businesses, Google offers an advanced version, G Suite for Business. For $5 per month per user, you get extra features, such as 25GB of email data per user, archiving, and advanced options for customizing your account policies.

>> **Google Drive:** A cloud-based solution that lets you work with Google cloud data directly from within Microsoft Office applications.

>> **Google App Engine:** A PaaS interface that lets you develop your own applications that work with Google's cloud services.

>> **Google Cloud Print:** Allows you to connect your printers to the cloud so that they can be accessed from anywhere.

>> **Google Maps:** A Global Information System (GIS).

Microsoft

Microsoft has its own cloud strategy, designed in part to protect its core business of operating systems and Office applications against competition from other cloud providers, such as Google Apps.

The following paragraphs summarize several of Microsoft's cloud offerings:

>> **Microsoft Office 365:** A cloud-based version of Microsoft Office. According to Microsoft's website, Office 365 provides "anywhere access to cloud-based email, web conferencing, file sharing, and Office Web Apps at a low predictable monthly cost." For more information, check out www.office365.com.

>> **Windows Azure:** A PaaS offering that lets you build websites, deploy virtual machines that run Windows Server or Linux, or access cloud versions of server applications such as SQL Server.

For more information about Azure, refer to Book 5, Chapter 3.

Getting Into the Cloud

After you wrap your head around just how cool cloud computing can be, what should you do to take your network toward the cloud? Allow me to make a few recommendations:

>> **Don't depend on a poor Internet connection.** First and foremost, before you take any of your network operations to the cloud, make sure that you're

not dependent on a consumer-grade Internet connection if you decide to adopt cloud computing. Consumer-grade Internet connections can be fast, but when an outage occurs, there's no telling how long you'll wait for the connection to be repaired. You definitely don't want to wait for hours or days while the cable company thinks about sending someone out to your site. Instead, spend the money for a high-speed enterprise-class connection that can scale as your dependence on it increases.

>> **Assess what applications you may already have running on the cloud.** If you use Gmail rather than Exchange for your email, congratulations! You've already embraced the cloud. Other examples of cloud services that you may already be using include a remote web or FTP host, Dropbox or another file-sharing service, Carbonite or another online backup service, a payroll service, and so on.

>> **Don't move to the cloud all at once.** Start by identifying a single application that lends itself to the cloud. If your engineering firm archives projects when they close and wants to get them off your primary file server but keep them readily available, look to the cloud for a file storage service.

>> **Go with a reputable company.** Google, Amazon, and Microsoft are all huge companies with proven track records in cloud computing. Many other large and established companies also offer cloud services. Don't stake your company's future on a company that didn't exist six months ago.

>> **Research, research, research.** Pour yourself into the web, and buy a few books. *Hybrid Cloud For Dummies,* by Judith Hurwitz, Marcia Kaufman, Dr. Fern Halper, and Daniel Kirsch (Wiley), is a good place to start.

2

Understanding Network Protocols

Contents at a Glance

Chapter **1**

Network Protocols and Standards

P rotocols and standards make networks work together. Protocols make it possible for the various components of a network to communicate with each other, and standards make it possible for different manufacturers' network components to work together. This chapter introduces you to the protocols and standards that you're most likely to encounter when building and maintaining a network.

Understanding Protocols

A *protocol* is simply a set of rules that enable effective communications to occur. You encounter protocols every day and probably don't even realize it. When you pay for groceries with a debit card, the clerk tells you how much the groceries cost, and then you swipe your debit card in the card reader, punch in your security code, indicate whether you want cash back, enter the amount of the cash back if you so indicated, and verify the total amount. You then cross your fingers behind your back and say a quiet prayer while the machine authorizes the purchase. Assuming the amount is authorized, the machine prints out your receipt.

Here's another example of an everyday protocol: making a phone call. You probably take most of the details of the phone-calling protocol for granted, but it's pretty complicated if you think about it:

>> When you pick up a phone, you listen for a dial tone before dialing the number (unless you're using a cellphone). If you don't hear a dial tone, you know that someone else in your family is talking on the phone, or something is wrong with your phone.

>> When you hear the dial tone, you dial the number of the party you want to reach. If the person you want to call is in the same area code, you simply dial that person's seven-digit phone number. If the person is in a different area code, you dial 1, the three-digit area code, and the person's seven-digit phone number.

>> If you hear a series of long ringing tones, you wait until the other person answers the phone. If the phone rings a certain number of times with no answer, you hang up and try again later. If you hear a voice say, "Hello," you begin a conversation with the other party. If the person on the other end of the phone has never heard of you, you say, "Sorry, wrong number," hang up, and try again.

>> If you hear a voice that rambles on about how they're not home but they want to return your call, you wait for a beep and leave a message.

>> If you hear a series of short tones, you know the other person is talking to someone else on the phone. So you hang up and try again later.

>> If you hear a sequence of three tones that increase in pitch, followed by a recorded voice that says "We're sorry . . ." you know that the number you dialed is invalid. Either you dialed the number incorrectly, or the number has been disconnected.

You get the point. Exchanges — using a debit card or making a phone call — follow the same rules every time they happen.

REMEMBER

Computer networks depend upon many different types of protocols. These protocols are very rigidly defined, and for good reason. Network cards must know how to talk to other network cards to exchange information, operating systems must know how to talk to network cards to send and receive data on the network, and application programs must know how to talk to operating systems to know how to retrieve a file from a network server.

Protocols come in many different types. At the lowest level, protocols define exactly what type of electrical signal represents a 1 and what type of signal represents a 0. At the highest level, protocols allow (say) a computer user in the United States to send an email to another computer user in New Zealand — and in between are many other levels of protocols. You find out more about these levels of protocols (often called "layers") in the upcoming section, "Seeing the Seven Layers of the OSI Reference Model."

TIP

Protocols tend to be used together in matched sets called *protocol suites.* The two most popular protocol suites for networking are TCP/IP and Ethernet. TCP/IP, originally developed for Unix networks, is the protocol of the Internet and most local area networks (LANs). Ethernet is a low-level protocol that spells out the electrical characteristics of the network hardware used by most LANs. A third important protocol is IPX/SPX, which is an alternative to TCP/IP, and originally developed for NetWare networks. In the early days of networking, IPX/SPX was widely used in LANs, but TCP/IP is now the preferred protocol.

Understanding Standards

As I mention earlier, a *standard* is an agreed-upon definition of a protocol. In the early days of computer networking, each computer manufacturer developed its own networking protocols. As a result, you couldn't easily mix equipment from different manufacturers on a single network.

Then along came standards to save the day. Hurrah! Because standards are industry-wide protocol definitions not tied to a particular manufacturer, you can mix and match equipment from different vendors. As long as the equipment implements the standard protocols, it should be able to coexist on the same network.

Many organizations are involved in setting standards for networking. The five most important organizations are

>> **American National Standards Institute (ANSI):** The official standards organization in the United States. ANSI is pronounced *AN-see.* www.ansi.org

>> **Institute of Electrical and Electronics Engineers (IEEE):** An international organization that publishes several key networking standards — in particular, the official standard for the Ethernet networking system (known officially as IEEE 802.3). IEEE is pronounced *eye-triple-E.* www.ieee.org

» **International Organization for Standardization (ISO):** A federation of more than 100 standards organizations throughout the world. If I had studied French in high school, I'd probably understand why the acronym for International Organization for Standardization is ISO, and not IOS. www.iso.org

» **Internet Engineering Task Force (IETF):** The organization responsible for the protocols that drive the Internet. www.ietf.org

» **World Wide Web Consortium (W3C):** An international organization that handles the development of standards for the World Wide Web. www.w3.org

Seeing the Seven Layers of the OSI Reference Model

"OSI" sounds like the name of a top-secret government agency you hear about only in Tom Clancy novels. What it really stands for in the networking world is Open Systems Interconnection, as in the Open Systems Interconnection Reference Model, affectionately known as the *OSI model.*

The OSI model breaks the various aspects of a computer network into seven distinct layers. These layers are kind of like the layers of an onion: Each successive layer envelops the layer beneath it, hiding its details from the levels above. The OSI model is also like an onion in that if you start to peel it apart to have a look inside, you're bound to shed a few tears.

The OSI model is not a networking standard in the same sense that Ethernet and TCP/IP are networking standards. Rather, the OSI model is a framework into which the various networking standards can fit. The OSI model specifies what aspects of a network's operation can be addressed by various network standards. So, in a sense, the OSI model is sort of a standard of standards.

Table 1-1 summarizes the seven layers of the OSI model.

The first three layers are sometimes called the *lower layers.* They deal with the mechanics of how information is sent from one computer to another over a network. Layers 4–7 are sometimes called the *upper layers.* They deal with how application software can relate to the network through application programming interfaces.

The following sections describe each of these layers in greater detail.

TABLE 1-1

The Seven Layers of the OSI Model

Layer	Name	Description
1	Physical	Governs the layout of cables and devices, such as repeaters and hubs.
2	Data Link	Provides MAC* addresses to uniquely identify network nodes and a means for data to be sent over the physical layer in the form of packets. Bridges and switches are layer 2 devices.
3	Network	Handles routing of data across network segments.
4	Transport	Provides for reliable delivery of packets.
5	Session	Establishes sessions between network applications.
6	Presentation	Converts data so that systems that use different data formats can exchange information.
7	Application	Allows applications to request network services.

*MAC = Media Access Control. Read more about MAC and bridges and switches in "The data link layer."

REMEMBER

The seven layers of the OSI model are a somewhat idealized view of how networking protocols should work. In the real world, actual networking protocols don't follow the OSI model to the letter. The real world is always messier. Still, the OSI model provides a convenient — if not completely accurate — conceptual picture of how networking works.

The physical layer

The bottom layer of the OSI model is the *physical layer.* It addresses the physical characteristics of the network, such as the types of cables used to connect devices, the types of connectors used, how long the cables can be, and so on. For example, the Ethernet standard for 10BaseT cable specifies the electrical characteristics of the twisted-pair cables, the size and shape of the connectors, the maximum length of the cables, and so on. The star, bus, ring, and mesh network topologies described in Chapter 1 of this minibook apply to the physical layer.

Another aspect of the physical layer is the electrical characteristics of the signals used to transmit data over the cables from one network node to another. The physical layer doesn't define any meaning to those signals other than the basic binary values of 1 and 0. The higher levels of the OSI model must assign meanings to the bits that are transmitted at the physical layer.

One type of physical layer device commonly used in networks is a *repeater,* which is used to regenerate the signal whenever you need to exceed the cable length allowed by the physical layer standard. 10BaseT hubs are also physical layer devices. Technically, they're known as *multiport repeaters* because the purpose of a hub is to regenerate every packet received on any port on all the hub's other ports. Repeaters and hubs don't examine the contents of the packets that they regenerate, though. If they did, they would be working at the data link layer, and not at the physical layer.

The *network adapter* (also called a network interface card; NIC) installed in each computer on the network is a physical layer device. You can display information about the network adapter (or adapters) installed in a Windows computer by displaying the adapter's Properties dialog box, as shown in Figure 1-1. To access this dialog box in Windows, open the Control Panel, choose Network and Sharing Center, and then choose Change Adapter Settings. Then right-click the Local Area Connection icon and choose Properties from the menu that appears.

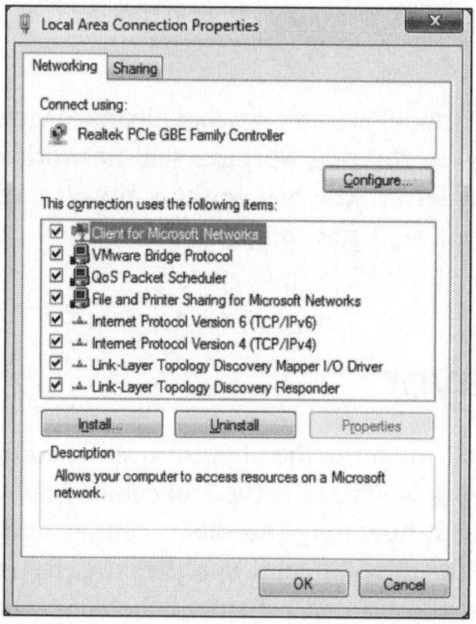

FIGURE 1-1:
The Properties dialog box for a network adapter.

The data link layer

The *data link layer* is the lowest layer at which meaning is assigned to the bits that are transmitted over the network. Data link protocols address things, such as the size of each packet of data to be sent, a means of addressing each packet so that it's delivered to the intended recipient, and a way to ensure that two or more nodes don't try to transmit data on the network at the same time.

The data link layer also provides basic error detection and correction to ensure that the data sent is the same as the data received. If an uncorrectable error occurs, the data link standard must specify how the node is to be informed of the error so that it can retransmit the data.

At the data link layer, each device on the network has an address: the Media Access Control (MAC). This address is hard-wired into every network device by the manufacturer. MAC addresses are unique; no two network devices made by any manufacturer anywhere in the world can have the same MAC address.

You can see the MAC address for a computer's network adapter by opening a command window and running the `ipconfig /all` command, as shown in Figure 1-2. In this example, the MAC address of the network card is 00-40-F4-CD-A9-50. (The `ipconfig` command refers to the MAC address as the *physical address*.)

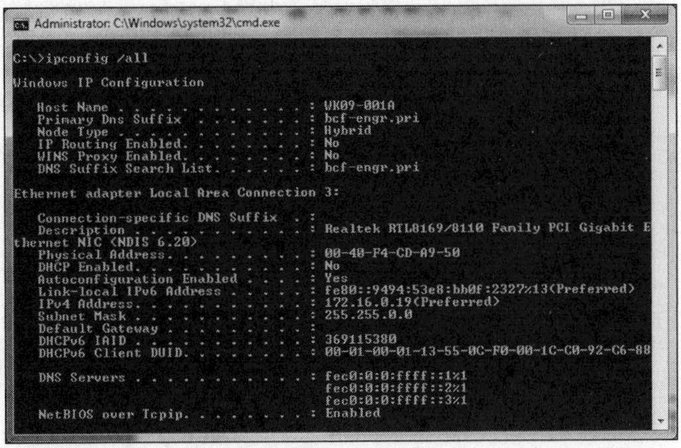

FIGURE 1-2:
Display the MAC address of a network adapter.

One of the most import functions of the data link layer is to provide a way for packets to be sent safely over the physical media without interference from other nodes attempting to send packets at the same time. The two most popular ways to do this are CSMA/CD and token passing. (Take a deep breath. CSMA/CD stands for Carrier Sense Multiple Access/Collision Detection.) Ethernet networks use CSMA/CD, and token ring networks use token passing.

TECHNICAL STUFF

Two types of data link layer devices are commonly used on networks:

>> **Bridge:** An intelligent repeater that's aware of the MAC addresses of the nodes on either side of the bridge and can forward packets accordingly.

>> **Switch:** An intelligent hub that examines the MAC address of arriving packets to determine which port to forward the packet to.

CSMA/CD IS A MOUTHFUL!

An important function of the data link layer is to make sure that two computers don't try to send packets over the network at the same time. If they do, the signals will collide with each other, and the transmission will be garbled. Ethernet accomplishes this feat by using CSMA/CD. This phrase is a mouthful, but if you take it apart piece by piece, you'll get an idea of how it works.

- *Carrier Sense* means that whenever a device wants to send a packet over the network media, it first listens to the network media to see whether anyone else is already sending a packet. If it doesn't hear any other signals on the media, the computer assumes that the network is free, so it sends the packet.

- *Multiple Access* means that nothing prevents two or more devices from trying to send a message at the same time. Sure, each device listens before sending. However, suppose that two devices listen, hear nothing, and then proceed to send their packets at the same time? Picture what happens when you and someone else arrive at a four-way stop sign at the same time. You wave the other driver on, he or she waves you on, you wave, he or she waves, you both wave, and then you both go at the same time.

- *Collision Detection* means that after a device sends a packet, it listens carefully to see whether the packet crashes into another packet. This is kind of like listening for the screeching of brakes at the four-way stop. If the device hears the screeching of brakes, it waits a random period of time and then tries to send the packet again. Because the delay is random, two packets that collide are sent again after different delay periods, so a second collision is unlikely.

CSMA/CD works pretty well for smaller networks. After a network hits about 30 computers, however, packets start to collide like crazy, and the network slows to a crawl. When that happens, the network should be divided into two or more separate sections that are sometimes called *collision domains*.

The network layer

The *network layer* handles the task of routing network messages from one computer to another. The two most popular layer 3 protocols are IP (which is usually paired with TCP) and IPX (typically paired with SPX for use with Novell and Windows networks).

Network layer protocols provide two important functions: logical addressing and routing. The following sections describe these functions.

Logical addressing

As I mention earlier, every network device has a physical address — a MAC address — assigned to the device at the factory. When you buy a network interface card to install into a computer, the MAC address of that card is fixed and can't be changed. So what happens if you want to use some other addressing scheme to refer to the computers and other devices on your network? This is where the concept of logical addressing comes in; with a logical address, you can access a network device by using an address that you assign.

Logical addresses are created and used by network layer protocols, such as IP or IPX. The network layer protocol translates logical addresses to MAC addresses. For example, if you use IP as the network layer protocol, devices on the network are assigned IP addresses, such as 207.120.67.30. Because the IP protocol must use a data link layer protocol to send packets to devices, IP must know how to translate the IP address of a device to the device's MAC address.

REMEMBER

You can use the `ipconfig` command (shown earlier in Figure 1-2) to see the IP address of your computer. The IP address shown in that figure is 172.16.0.19. Another way to display this information is to use the System Information command, found on the Start menu under Start➪All Programs➪Accessories➪System Tools➪System Information. The IP address is highlighted in Figure 1-3. Notice that the System Information program displays a lot of other useful information about the network besides the IP address. For example, you can also see the MAC address and what protocols are being used.

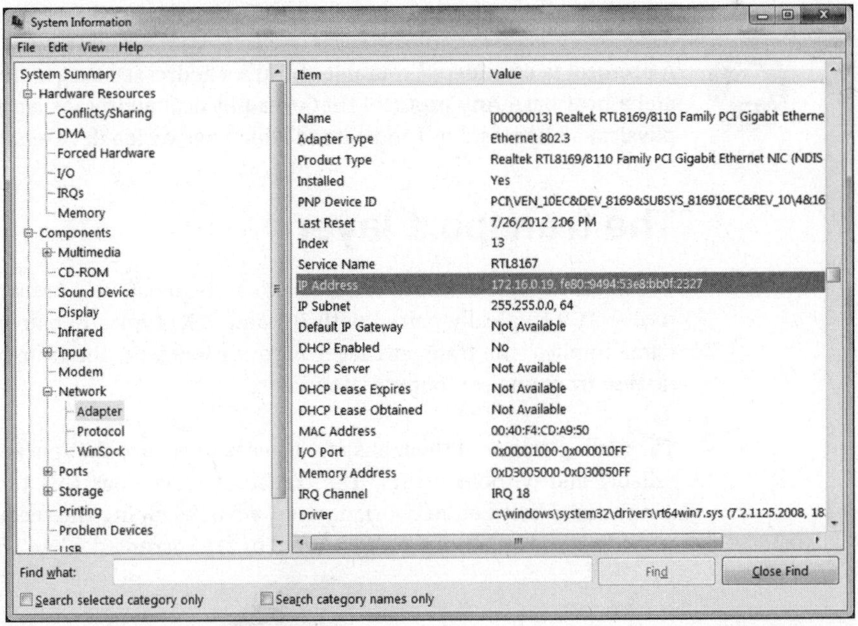

FIGURE 1-3:
Find network information from System Information.

Although the exact format of logical addresses varies depending on the protocol being used, most protocols divide the logical address into two parts:

>> **Network address:** Identifies which network the device resides on

>> **Device address:** Identifies the device on that network

In a typical IP address — say, 192.168.1.102 — the network address is 192.168.1, and the device address (called a *host address* in IP) is 102.

Similarly, IPX addresses consist of two parts: a network address and a node address. In an IPX address, the node address is the same as the MAC address. As a result, IPX doesn't have to translate between layer 2 and layer 3 addresses.

Routing

Routing comes into play when a computer on one network needs to send a packet to a computer on another network. In this case, a router is used to forward the packet to the destination network. In some cases, a packet may have to travel through several intermediate networks in order to reach its final destination network. You can find out more about routers in Chapter 4 of this minibook.

An important feature of routers is that you can use them to connect networks that use different layer 2 protocols. For example, a router can be used to send a packet from an Ethernet to a token ring network. As long as both networks support the same layer 3 protocol, it doesn't matter whether their layer 1 and layer 2 protocols are different.

TIP

A protocol is considered routable if it uses addresses that include a network part and a host part. Any protocol that uses physical addresses isn't routable because physical addresses don't indicate to which network a device belongs.

The transport layer

The *transport layer* is where you find two of the most well-known networking protocols: TCP (typically paired with IP) and SPX (typically paired with IPX). As its name implies, the transport layer is concerned with the transportation of information from one computer to another.

The main purpose of the transport layer is to ensure that packets are transported reliably and without errors. The transport layer does this task by establishing connections between network devices, acknowledging the receipt of packets, and resending packets that aren't received or are corrupted when they arrive.

In many cases, the transport layer protocol divides large messages into smaller packets that can be sent over the network efficiently. The transport layer protocol reassembles the message on the receiving end, making sure that all the packets that make up a single transmission are received so that no data is lost.

For some applications, speed and efficiency are more important than reliability. In such cases, a connectionless protocol can be used. As you can likely guess, a connectionless protocol doesn't go to the trouble of establishing a connection before sending a packet: It simply sends the packet. TCP is a connection-oriented transport layer protocol. The connectionless protocol that works alongside TCP is User Datagram Protocol (UDP).

You can view information about the status of TCP and UDP connections by running the Netstat command from a command window, as Figure 1-4 shows. In the figure, you can see that several TCP connections are established.

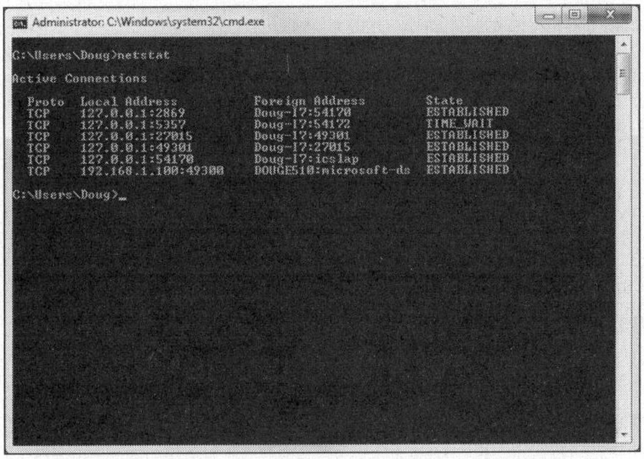

FIGURE 1-4:
See TCP and UDP connections.

In fact, you can use the command Netstat /N to see the numeric network addresses instead of the names. With the /N switch, the output in Figure 1-4 would look like this:

```
Active Connections
Proto Local Address Foreign Address State
TCP 127.0.0.1:2869 127.0.0.1:54170 ESTABLISHED
TCP 127.0.0.1:5357 127.0.0.1:54172 TIME_WAIT
TCP 127.0.0.1:27015 127.0.0.1:49301 ESTABLISHED
TCP 127.0.0.1:49301 127.0.0.1:27015 ESTABLISHED
TCP 127.0.0.1:54170 127.0.0.1:2869 ESTABLISHED
TCP 192.168.1.100:49300 192.168.1.101:445 ESTABLISHED
```

REMEMBER

TCP is a connection-oriented transport layer protocol. *UDP* is a connectionless transport layer protocol.

The session layer

The *session layer* establishes *conversations* — sessions — between networked devices. A *session* is an exchange of connection-oriented transmissions between two network devices. Each transmission is handled by the transport layer protocol. The session itself is managed by the session layer protocol.

A single session can include many exchanges of data between the two computers involved in the session. After a session between two computers has been established, it's maintained until the computers agree to terminate the session.

The session layer allows three types of transmission modes:

>> **Simplex:** Data flows in only one direction.

>> **Half-duplex:** Data flows in both directions, but only in one direction at a time.

>> **Full-duplex:** Data flows in both directions at the same time.

TIP

In actual practice, the distinctions in the session, presentation, and application layers are often blurred, and some commonly used protocols actually span all three layers. For example, SMB — the protocol that is the basis of file sharing in Windows networks — functions at all three layers.

The presentation layer

The *presentation layer* is responsible for how data is represented to applications. The most common representation for representing character data today is called UTF-8, which uses 8-bit sets to represent most characters found in western alphabets. UTF-8 is compatible with an older standard called ASCII.

TECHNICAL STUFF

UTF-8 is sometimes called *Unicode,* which is a standard for representing the characters found in most of the world's writing systems. Technically, UTF-8 is a particular method of implementing Unicode, so although the two terms are related, they are not identical.

TECHNICAL STUFF

Some computers, in particular IBM mainframe computers, use a different code called Extended Binary Coded Decimal Interchange Code (EBCDIC). ASCII and EBCDIC aren't compatible. To exchange information between a mainframe computer and a Windows computer, the presentation layer must convert the data from ASCII to EBCDIC, and vice versa.

Besides simply converting data from one code to another, the presentation layer can also apply sophisticated compression techniques so that fewer bytes of data are required to represent the information when it's sent over the network. At the other end of the transmission, the presentation layer then uncompresses the data.

The presentation layer can also scramble the data before it's transmitted and then unscramble it at the other end by using a sophisticated encryption technique that even Sherlock Holmes would have trouble breaking.

The application layer

The highest layer of the OSI model, the application layer deals with the techniques that application programs use to communicate with the network. The name of this layer is a little confusing. Application programs (such as Microsoft Office or QuickBooks) aren't a part of the application layer. Rather, the application layer represents the programming interfaces that application programs use to request network services.

Some of the better-known application layer protocols are

>> **Domain Name System (DNS):** For resolving Internet domain names

>> **File Transfer Protocol (FTP):** For file transfers

>> **Simple Mail Transfer Protocol (SMTP):** For email

>> **Server Message Block (SMB):** For file sharing in Windows networks

>> **Network File System (NFS):** For file sharing in Unix networks

>> **Telnet:** For terminal emulation

Following a Packet through the Layers

Figure 1-5 shows how a packet of information flows through the seven layers as it travels from one computer to another on the network. The data begins its journey when an end-user application sends data to another network computer. The data enters the network through an application layer interface, such as SMB. The data then works its way down through the protocol stack. Along the way, the protocol at each layer manipulates the data by adding header information, converting the data into different formats, combining packets to form larger packets, and so on. When the data reaches the physical layer protocol, it's placed on the network media (in other words, the cable) and sent to the receiving computer.

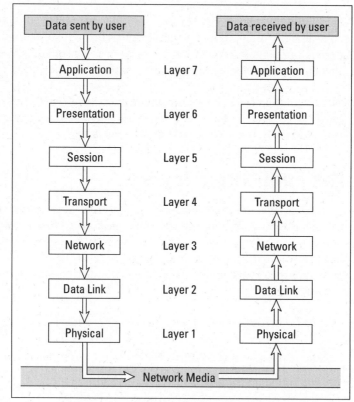

FIGURE 1-5:
How data travels through the seven layers.

When the receiving computer receives the data, the data works its way up through the protocol stack. Then, the protocol at each layer reverses the processing that was done by the corresponding layer on the sending computer. Headers are removed, data is converted back to its original format, packets that were split into smaller packets are recombined into larger messages, and so on. When the packet reaches the application layer protocol, it's delivered to an application that can process the data.

The Ethernet Protocol

As I mention earlier, the first two layers of the OSI model deal with the physical structure of the network and the means by which network devices can send information from one device on a network to another. By far, Ethernet is the most popular set of protocols for the physical and data link layers.

Ethernet has been around in various forms since the early 1970s. (For a brief history of Ethernet, see the sidebar, "Ethernet folklore and mythology.") The current incarnation of Ethernet is defined by the 802.3 IEEE standard. Various flavors of Ethernet operate at different speeds and use different types of media. However, all the versions of Ethernet are compatible with each other, so you can mix and match them on the same network by using devices such as bridges, hubs, and switches to link network segments that use different types of media.

TIP

The actual transmission speed of Ethernet is measured in millions of bits per second (Mbps) or billions of bits per second (Gbps). Ethernet comes in several different speed versions:

>> **Standard Ethernet:** 10 Mbps; rarely (if ever) used today.

>> **Fast Ethernet:** 100 Mbps; still used for devices where speed is not particularly important, such as printers or fax machines.

>> **Gigabit Ethernet and beyond:** 1,000 Mbps; the most common speed used to connect user computers to a network. Faster speeds, such as 10 Gbps, 100 Gbps, and even faster, are sometimes used in high-speed networks to connect servers and other critical devices to the network.

REMEMBER

Network transmission speed refers to the maximum speed that can be achieved over the network under ideal conditions. In reality, the actual throughput of an Ethernet network rarely reaches this maximum speed.

Ethernet operates at the first two layers of the OSI model — the physical and the data link layers. However, Ethernet divides the data link layer into two separate layers: the Logical Link Control (LLC) layer and the Medium Access Control (MAC) layer. Figure 1-6 shows how the various elements of Ethernet match up to the OSI model.

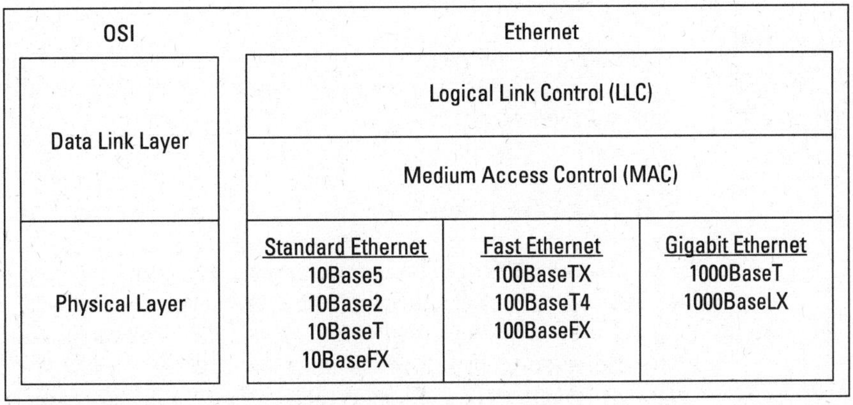

OSI	Ethernet		
	Logical Link Control (LLC)		
Data Link Layer	Medium Access Control (MAC)		
	Standard Ethernet 10Base5 10Base2 10BaseT 10BaseFX	Fast Ethernet 100BaseTX 100BaseT4 100BaseFX	Gigabit Ethernet 1000BaseT 1000BaseLX
Physical Layer			

FIGURE 1-6: Ethernet and the OSI model.

The following sections describe Standard Ethernet, Fast Ethernet, and Gigabit Ethernet in more detail.

Standard Ethernet

Standard Ethernet is the original Ethernet. It runs at 10 Mbps, which was considered fast in the 1970s but is excruciatingly slow by today's standards. Although plenty of existing Standard Ethernet is still in use, it's considered obsolete and should be replaced by Gigabit Ethernet as soon as possible.

Standard Ethernet came in three incarnations, depending on the type of cable used to string the network together:

>> **10Base5:** This original Ethernet cable was thick (about as thick as your thumb), heavy, and difficult to work with. It's seen today only in museum exhibits.

>> **10Base2:** This thinner type of coaxial cable (it resembles television cable) became popular in the 1980s and lingered into the early 1990s. Plenty of 10Base2 cable is still in use, but it's rarely installed in new networks. 10Base2 (like 10Base5) uses a bus topology, so wiring a 10Base2 network involves running cable from one computer to the next until all the computers are connected in a segment.

>> **10BaseT:** Unshielded twisted-pair (UTP) cable became popular in the 1990s because it's easier to install, lighter, and more reliable, and also it offers more flexibility in how networks are designed. 10BaseT networks use a star topology with hubs at the center of each star. Although the maximum length of 10BaseT cable is only 100 meters, hubs can be chained to extend networks well beyond the 100-meter limit.

10BaseT cable has four pairs of wires twisted together throughout the entire span of the cable. However, 10BaseT uses only two of these wire pairs, so the unused pairs are spares.

TIP

If you find yourself working with 10 Mbps Ethernet, spend a few moments enjoying your historical find. Then, as quickly as you can, update the entire network to Gigabit Ethernet.

Fast Ethernet

Fast Ethernet refers to Ethernet that runs at 100 Mbps, which is ten times the speed of Standard Ethernet. Although there are several varieties of Fast Ethernet, the most common is 100BaseTX, which transmits at 100 Mbps over just two pairs of a UTP cable. 100 Mbps Ethernet requires at least Cat-5 cable, but most networks are now wired with Cat-5e or Cat-6 cable, both of which are capable of gigabit speeds.

ETHERNET FOLKLORE AND MYTHOLOGY

Here's how Ethernet came to be so popular. The original idea for the Ethernet was hatched in the mind of Robert Metcalfe, a graduate computer science student at Harvard University. Looking for a thesis idea in 1970, he refined a networking technique used in Hawaii — the AlohaNet (actually a wireless network) — and developed a technique that would enable a network to efficiently use as much as 90 percent of its capacity. By 1973, he had his first Ethernet network up and running at the famous Xerox Palo Alto Research Center (PARC). Bob dubbed his network "Ethernet" in honor of the thick network cable, which he called "the ether." (Xerox PARC was busy in 1973. In addition to Ethernet, PARC developed the first personal computer that used a graphical user interface (GUI) complete with icons, windows, and menus, and the world's first laser printer.)

In 1979, Xerox began working with Intel and DEC (a once-popular computer company) to make Ethernet an industry standard networking product. Along the way, they enlisted the help of the IEEE, which formed committee number 802.3 and began the process of standardizing Ethernet in 1981. The 802.3 committee released the first official Ethernet standard in 1983.

Meanwhile, Bob Metcalfe left Xerox, turned down a job offer from Steve Jobs to work at Apple computers, and started a company called the Computer, Communication, and Compatibility Corporation — now known as 3Com. 3Com has since become one of the largest manufacturers of Ethernet equipment in the world.

Gigabit Ethernet

Gigabit Ethernet is Ethernet running at a 1,000 Mbps, or 1 Gbps. Gigabit Ethernet was once considerably more expensive than Fast Ethernet, so it was used only when the improved performance justified the extra cost. However, today Gigabit Ethernet is the standard for nearly all desktop and laptop PCs. Two grades of cable are commonly used: Cat-5e and Cat-6; Cat-6 is preferred because it can be used for even faster networks.

Beyond gigabit

Several varieties of Ethernet faster than 1 Gbps are available:

>> **2.5GBase-T:** 2.5 Gbps speed that can operate on Cat-5e cable.

>> **5GBase-T:** 5 Gbps speed that requires Cat-6 cable.

>> **10GBase-T:** 10 Gbps speed that requires Cat-6A cable. This is the fastest Ethernet variety commonly available that runs on copper cable; faster speeds typically require fiber cable.

>> **10GBase-LR and 10GBase-ER:** 10 Gbps speeds commonly used for wide-area networks on fiber cable, with distances of up to 10 km (10GBase-LR) and 40km (10Gbase-ER)

>> **Terabit Ethernet:** Speeds above 10 Gbps are still largely experimental; eventually, it is hoped that terabyte speeds — that is, 1,000 Gbps — can be achieved.

TECHNICAL
STUFF

Speeds higher than 10 Gbps can be achieved by combining several 10 Gbps circuits to form a single link. For example, 40 Gbps speed can be achieved using a connection called QSFP+, which combines four 10 Gbps connections to create a single 40 Gbps link.

The TCP/IP Protocol Suite

TCP/IP, the protocol on which the Internet is built, is not a single protocol but rather an entire suite of related protocols. TCP is even older than Ethernet. It was first conceived in 1969 by the Department of Defense. For more on the history of TCP/IP, see the sidebar, "The fascinating story of TCP/IP," later in this chapter. Currently, the Internet Engineering Task Force (IETF) manages the TCP/IP protocol suite.

The TCP/IP suite is based on a four-layer model of networking similar to the seven-layer OSI model. Figure 1-7 shows how the TCP/IP model matches up with the OSI model and where some of the key TCP/IP protocols fit into the model. As you can see, the lowest layer of the model, the network interface layer, corresponds to the OSI model's physical and data link layers. TCP/IP can run over a wide variety of network interface layer protocols, including Ethernet, as well as other protocols, such as token ring and FDDI (an older standard for fiber optic networks).

The application layer of the TCP/IP model corresponds to the upper three layers of the OSI model — the session, presentation, and application layers. Many protocols can be used at this level. A few of the most popular are HTTP, FTP, Telnet, SMTP, DNS, and SNMP.

In the following sections, I point out a few more details of the three most important protocols in the TCP/IP suite: IP, TCP, and UDP.

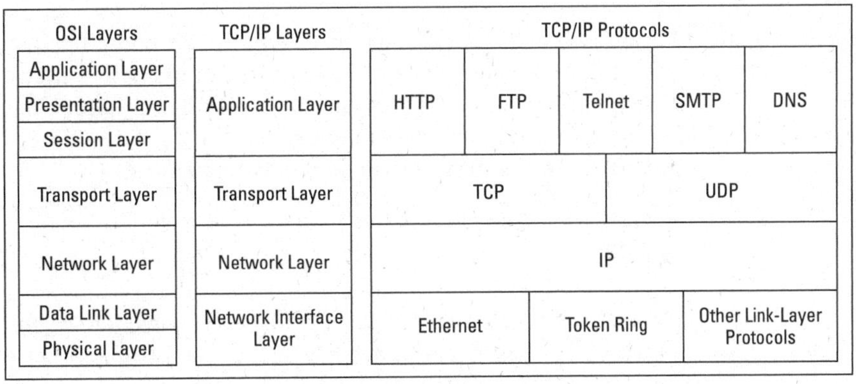

OSI Layers	TCP/IP Layers	TCP/IP Protocols				
Application Layer	Application Layer	HTTP	FTP	Telnet	SMTP	DNS
Presentation Layer						
Session Layer						
Transport Layer	Transport Layer	TCP			UDP	
Network Layer	Network Layer	IP				
Data Link Layer	Network Interface Layer	Ethernet		Token Ring		Other Link-Layer Protocols
Physical Layer						

FIGURE 1-7:
TCP/IP and the OSI model.

IP

Internet Protocol (IP) is a network layer protocol responsible for delivering packets to network devices. The IP protocol uses logical IP addresses to refer to individual devices rather than physical (MAC) addresses. Address Resolution Protocol (ARP) handles the task of converting IP addresses to MAC addresses.

TECHNICAL STUFF

10BASE WHAT?

The names of Ethernet cable standards resemble the audible signals a quarterback might shout at the line of scrimmage. In reality, the cable designations consist of three parts:

- The first number is the speed of the network in Mbps. So, 10BaseT is for 10 Mbps networks (Standard Ethernet), 100BaseTX is for 100 Mbps networks (Fast Ethernet), and 1000BaseT is for 1,000 Mbps networks (Gigabit Ethernet).

- "Base" (short for "baseband") indicates the type of network transmission that the cable uses. Baseband transmissions carry one signal at a time and are relatively simple to implement. The alternative to baseband is *broadband,* which can carry more than one signal at a time but is more difficult to implement. At one time, broadband incarnations of the 802.x networking standards existed, but they have all but fizzled due to lack of use.

- The tail end of the designation indicates the cable type. For coaxial cables, a number is used that roughly indicates the maximum length of the cable in hundreds of meters. 10Base5 cables can run up to 500 meters. 10Base2 cables can run up to 185 meters. (The IEEE rounded 185 up to 200 to come up with the name 10Base2.) If the designation ends with a T, twisted-pair cable is used. Other letters are used for other types of cables.

Because IP addresses consist of a network part and a host part, IP is a routable protocol. As a result, IP can forward a packet to another network if the host isn't on the current network. After all, the capability to route packets across networks is where IP gets its name. An *Internet* is a just a series of two or more connected TCP/IP networks that can be reached by routing.

TCP

Transmission Control Protocol (TCP) is a connection-oriented transport layer protocol. TCP lets a device reliably send a packet to another device on the same network or on a different network. TCP ensures that each packet is delivered, if at all possible, by establishing a connection with the receiving device and then sending the packets. If a packet doesn't arrive, TCP resends the packet. The connection is closed only after the packet has been successfully delivered or an unrecoverable error condition has occurred.

One key aspect of TCP is that it's always used for one-to-one communications. In other words, TCP allows a single network device to exchange data with another single network device. TCP isn't used to broadcast messages to multiple network recipients. Instead, UDP is used for that purpose.

Many well-known application layer protocols rely on TCP. For example, when a user running a web browser requests a page, the browser uses HTTP (Hyper-Text Transfer Protocol) to send a request via TCP to a web server. When that web server receives the request, it uses HTTP to send the requested web page back to the browser, again via TCP. Other application layer protocols that use TCP include Telnet (for terminal emulation), FTP (for file exchange), and SMTP (for email).

UDP

User Datagram Protocol (UDP) is a connectionless transport layer protocol used when the overhead of a connection isn't required. After UDP has placed a packet on the network (via the IP protocol), it forgets about it. UDP doesn't guarantee that the packet arrives at its destination. Most applications that use UDP simply wait for any replies expected as a result of packets sent via UDP. If a reply doesn't arrive within a certain period of time, the application either sends the packet again or gives up.

Probably the best-known application layer protocol that uses UDP is the Domain Name System (DNS). When an application needs to access a domain name (such as www.wiley.com), DNS sends a UDP packet to a DNS server to look up the domain. When the server finds the domain, it returns the domain's IP address in another UDP packet.

THE FASCINATING STORY OF TCP/IP

Some people are fascinated by history. They subscribe to cable TV just to get the History Channel. If you're one of those history buffs, you may be interested in the following chronicle of TCP/IP's humble origins. (For maximum effect, play some melancholy violin music in the background as you read the rest of this sidebar.)

In the summer of 1969, the four mop-topped singers from Liverpool were breaking up. The war in Vietnam was escalating. Astronauts Neil Armstrong and Buzz Aldrin walked on the moon. And the Department of Defense built a computer network called ARPANET to link its defense installations with several major universities throughout the United States.

By the early 1970s, ARPANET was becoming difficult to manage. So it was split into two networks: one for military use, called MILNET; and the other for nonmilitary use. The nonmilitary network retained the name ARPANET. To link MILNET with ARPANET, a new method of connecting networks — Internet Protocol (IP) — was invented.

The whole purpose of IP was to enable these two networks to communicate with each other. Fortunately, the designers of IP realized that it wouldn't be too long before other networks wanted to join in the fun, so they designed IP to allow for more than two networks. In fact, their ingenious design allowed for tens of thousands of networks to communicate via IP.

The decision was a fortuitous one, as the Internet quickly began to grow. By the mid-1980s, the original ARPANET reached its limits. Just in time, the National Science Foundation (NSF) decided to get into the game. NSF had built a network called NSFNET to link its huge supercomputers. NSFNET replaced ARPANET as the new background for the Internet. Around that time, such magazines as *Time* and *Newsweek* began writing articles about this new phenomenon called the Internet, and the *Net* (as it became nick-named) began to grow like wildfire. Soon NSFNET couldn't keep up with the growth, so several private commercial networks took over management of the Internet backbone. The Internet has grown at a dizzying rate ever since, and nobody knows how long this frenetic growth rate will continue. One thing is sure: TCP/IP is now the most popular networking protocol in the world.

Other Protocols Worth Knowing About

Although the vast majority of networks now use Ethernet and TCP/IP, a few other networking protocols are still in use and are therefore worth knowing about. In particular:

>> **Network Basic Input/Output System (NetBIOS):** The basic application programming interface for network services on Windows computers. It's installed automatically when you install TCP/IP, but doesn't show up as a separate protocol when you view the network connection properties. (Refer to Figure 1-1.) NetBIOS is a session layer protocol that can work with transport layer protocols, such as TCP, SPX, or NetBEUI.

>> **Network BIOS Extended User Interface (NetBEUI):** A transport layer protocol designed for early IBM and Microsoft networks. NetBEUI is now considered obsolete.

>> **IPX/SPX:** A protocol suite made popular in the 1980s by Novell for use with its NetWare servers. TCP/IP has become so dominant that IPX/SPX is rarely used now.

>> **AppleTalk:** An obsolete suite of network protocols introduced by Apple in the 1980s and finally abandoned in 2009. The AppleTalk suite included a physical and data link layer protocol called LocalTalk, but could also work with standard lower-level protocols, including Ethernet and token ring.

>> **Systems Network Architecture (SNA):** An IBM networking architecture dating back to the 1970s, when mainframe computers roamed the earth and PCs had barely emerged from the primordial computer soup. SNA was designed primarily to support huge terminals such as airline reservations and banking systems, with tens of thousands of terminals attached to central host computers. Now that IBM mainframes support TCP/IP and mainframe terminal systems have all but vanished, SNA is beginning to fade away. Still, many networks that incorporate mainframe computers have to contend with SNA.

Chapter **2**

TCP/IP and the Internet

any years ago, Transmission Control Protocol/Internet Protocol (TCP/IP) was known primarily as the protocol of the Internet. The biggest challenge of getting a local area network (LAN) connected to the Internet was figuring out how to mesh TCP/IP with the proprietary protocols that were the basis of the LANs — most notably Internetwork Packet Exchange/Sequenced Packet Exchange (IPX/SPX) and NetBIOS Extended User Interface (NetBEUI).

But then, some years ago, network administrators realized that they could save the trouble of combining TCP/IP with IPX/SPX and NetBEUI by eliminating IPX/SPX and NetBEUI from the equation altogether. As a result, TCP/IP is not just the protocol of the Internet now, but it's also the protocol on which most LANs are based.

This chapter is a gentle introduction to the Internet in general and the TCP/IP suite of protocols in particular. After I get the introductions out of the way, you'll be able to focus more in-depth on the detailed TCP/IP information given in the remaining chapters of Book 3.

What Is the Internet?

The Goliath of all computer networks, the Internet links hundreds of millions of computer users throughout the world. Strictly speaking, the Internet is a network of networks. It consists of hundreds of thousands of separate computer networks, all interlinked, so that a user on any of those networks can reach out and potentially touch a user on any of the other networks. This network of networks connects more than a billion computers to each other. (That's right, *billion* with a *b*.)

One of the official documents (RFC 2026) of the Internet Engineering Task Force (IETF) defines the Internet as "a loosely organized international collaboration of autonomous, interconnected networks." Broken down piece by piece, this definition encompasses several key aspects of what the Internet is:

>> **Loosely organized:** No single organization has authority over the Internet. As a result, the Internet is not highly organized. Online services, such as America Online or MSN, are owned and operated by individual companies that control exactly what content appears on the service and what software can be used with the service. No one exercises that kind of control over the Internet. As a result, you can find just about any kind of material imaginable on the Internet. No one guarantees the accuracy of information that you find on the Internet, so you have to be careful as you work your way through the labyrinth.

>> **International:** Nearly 200 countries are represented on the Internet, from Afghanistan to Zimbabwe.

>> **Collaboration:** The Internet exists only because many different organizations cooperate to provide the services and support needed to sustain it. For example, much of the software that drives the Internet is open source software that's developed collaboratively by programmers throughout the world, who constantly work to improve the code.

TECHNICAL STUFF

JUST HOW BIG IS THE INTERNET?

Because the Internet is not owned or controlled by any one organization, no one knows how big the Internet really is. Several organizations do attempt to periodically determine the size of the Internet, including the Internet Systems Consortium (ISC), which completed its last survey in July 2017 and found that well over a billion host computers are connected to the Internet. The first year the ISC did the survey (1993), it found only 1.3 million host computers. It passed 10 million hosts in 1996, 100 million hosts in 2000, and edged over 1 billion hosts in 2014.

Unfortunately, no one knows how many actual users are on the Internet. Each host can support a single user — or in the case of domains, hundreds of thousands or perhaps even millions of users. No one really knows. Still, the indisputable point is that the Internet is big and growing every day.

You can check the latest Internet statistics from ISC by visiting its website at www.isc.org/network/survey.

>> **Autonomous:** The Internet community respects that organizations that join the Internet are free to make their own decisions about how they configure and operate their networks. Although legal issues sometimes boil up, for the most part, each player on the Internet operates independently.

>> **Interconnected:** The whole key to the Internet is the concept of *interconnection,* which uses standard protocols that enable networks to communicate with each other. Without the interconnection provided by the TCP/IP protocol, the Internet would not exist.

>> **Networks:** The Internet would be completely unmanageable if it consisted of half a billion individual users, all interconnected. That's why the Internet is often described as a network of networks. Most individual users on the Internet don't access the Internet directly. Instead, they access the Internet indirectly through another network, which may be a LAN in a business or academic environment, or a dialup or broadband network provided by an Internet service provider (ISP). In each case, however, the users of the local network access the Internet via a gateway IP router.

The Internet is composed of several distinct types of networks: Government agencies, such as the Library of Congress and the White House; military sites (did you ever see *War Games* or any of the *Terminator* movies?); educational institutions, such as universities and colleges (and their libraries); businesses, such as Microsoft and IBM; ISPs, which allow individuals to access the Internet; and commercial online services, such as America Online and MSN.

A Little Internet History

The Internet has a fascinating history, if such things interest you. There's no particular reason why you should be interested in such things, of course, except that a superficial understanding of how the Internet got started may help you to understand and cope with the way this massive computer network exists today. So here goes.

The Internet traces its beginnings back to a small network called ARPANET, built by the Department of Defense in 1969 to link defense installations. ARPANET soon expanded to include not only defense installations but universities as well. In the 1970s, ARPANET was split into two networks: one for military use (renamed MIL-NET) and the original ARPANET (for nonmilitary use). The two networks were connected by a networking link called IP — the *Internet protocol* — so called because it allowed communication between two networks.

The good folks who designed IP had the foresight to realize that soon, more than two networks would want to be connected. In fact, they left room for tens of thousands of networks to join the game, which is a good thing because it wasn't long before the Internet began to take off.

By the mid-1980s, ARPANET was beginning to reach the limits of what it could do. Enter the National Science Foundation (NSF), which set up a nationwide network designed to provide access to huge *supercomputers,* those monolithic computers used to discover new prime numbers and calculate the orbits of distant galaxies. The supercomputers were never put to much use, but the network that was put together to support the supercomputers — NSFNET — was used. In fact, NSFNET replaced ARPANET as the new backbone for the Internet.

Then, out of the blue, it seemed as if the whole world became interested in the Internet. Stories about it appeared in *Time* and *Newsweek.* Any company that had "dot com" in its name practically doubled in value every month. Al Gore claimed he invented the Internet. The Net began to grow so fast that even NSFNET couldn't keep up, so private commercial networks got into the game. The size of the Internet nearly doubled every year for most of the 1990s. Then, in the first few years of the millennium, the growth rate slowed a bit. However, the Internet still seems to be growing at the phenomenal rate of about 30 to 50 percent per year, and who knows how long this dizzying rate of growth will continue.

TCP/IP Standards and RFCs

The TCP/IP protocol standards that define how the Internet works are managed by the IETF. However, the IETF doesn't impose standards. Instead, it simply oversees the process by which ideas are developed into agreed-upon standards.

An Internet standard is published in the Request for Comments (RFC) document. When a document is accepted for publication, it is assigned an RFC number by the IETF. The RFC is then published. After it's published, an RFC is never changed. If a standard is enhanced, the enhancement is covered in a separate RFC.

Thousands of RFCs are available from the IETF website (www.ietf.org). The oldest RFC is RFC 0001, published in April 1969. It describes how the host computers communicated with each other in the original ARPANET. The most recent proposed standard (as of January 2018) is RFC 8311, entitled "Relaxing Restrictions on Explicit Congestion Notification (ECN) Experimentation."

Not all RFCs represent Internet standards. The following paragraphs summarize the various types of RFC documents:

>> **Internet Standards Track:** This type of RFC represents an Internet standard. Standards Track RFCs have one of three maturity levels, as described in Table 2-1. An RFC enters circulation with Proposed Standard status but may be elevated to Draft Standard status — and, ultimately, to Internet Standard status.

>> **Experimental specifications:** These are a result of research or development efforts. They're not intended to be standards, but the information they contain may be of use to the Internet community.

>> **Informational specifications:** These simply provide general information for the Internet community.

>> **Historic specifications:** These RFCs have been superseded by a more recent RFC and are thus considered obsolete.

>> **Best Current Practice (BCP):** RFCs are documents that summarize the consensus of the Internet community's opinion on the best way to perform an operation or procedure. BCPs are guidelines, not standards.

TABLE 2-1   **Maturity Levels for Internet Standards Track RFCs**

Maturity Level	Description
Proposed Standard	Generally stable, have resolved known design choices, are believed to be well understood, have received significant community review, and appear to enjoy enough community interest to be considered valuable.
Draft Standard	Well understood and known to be quite stable. At least two interoperable implementations must exist, developed independently from separate code bases. The specification is believed to be mature and useful.
Internet Standard	Have been fully accepted by the Internet community as highly mature and useful standards.

Table 2-2 summarizes the RFCs that apply to the key Internet standards described in this book.

TIP

My favorite RFC is 1149, an experimental specification for the "Transmission of IP datagrams on avian carriers." The specification calls for IP datagrams to be written in hexadecimal on scrolls of paper and secured to "avian carriers" with duct tape. (Not surprisingly, it's dated April 1, 1990. Similar RFCs are frequently submitted on April 1.)

TABLE 2-2   **RFCs for Key Internet Standards**

RFC	Date	Description
768	August 1980	User Datagram Protocol (UDP)
791	September 1981	Internet Protocol (IP)
792	September 1981	Internet Control Message Protocol (ICMP)
793	September 1981	Transmission Control Protocol (TCP)
826	November 1982	Ethernet Address Resolution Protocol (ARP)
950	August 1985	Internet Standard Subnetting Procedure
959	October 1985	File Transfer Protocol (FTP)
1034	November 1987	Domain Names — Concepts and Facilities (DNS)
1035	November 1987	Domain Names — Implementation and Specification (DNS)
1939	May 1996	Post Office Protocol Version 3 (POP3)
2131	March 1997	Dynamic Host Configuration Protocol (DHCP)
3376	November 1997	Internet Group Management Protocol (IGMP) (Updates RFC 2236 and 1112)
7230 through 7235	June 2014	Hypertext Transfer Protocol – HTTP/1.1
5321	October 2008	Simple Mail Transfer Protocol (SMTP)

The TCP/IP Protocol Framework

Like the seven-layer OSI Reference Model, TCP/IP protocols are based on a layered framework. TCP/IP has four layers, as shown in Figure 2-1. These layers are described in the following sections.

Network interface layer

The lowest level of the TCP/IP architecture is the network interface layer. It corresponds to the OSI physical and data link layers. You can use many different TCP/IP protocols at the network interface layer, including Ethernet and token ring for LANs and protocols such as X.25, Frame Relay, and ATM for wide area networks (WANs).

The network interface layer is assumed to be unreliable.

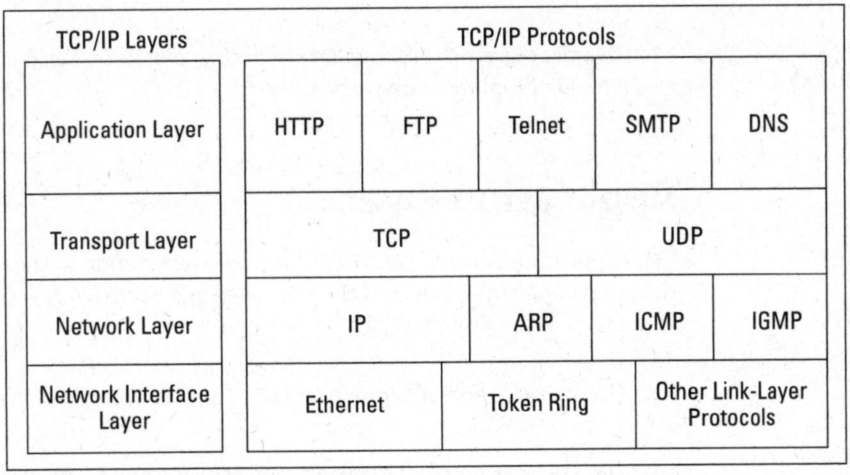

FIGURE 2-1
The four layers of the TCP/IP framework.

TCP/IP Layers	TCP/IP Protocols				
Application Layer	HTTP	FTP	Telnet	SMTP	DNS
Transport Layer	TCP			UDP	
Network Layer	IP		ARP	ICMP	IGMP
Network Interface Layer	Ethernet		Token Ring	Other Link-Layer Protocols	

Network layer

The network layer is where data is addressed, packaged, and routed among networks. Several important Internet protocols operate at the network layer:

>> **Internet Protocol (IP):** A routable protocol that uses IP addresses to deliver packets to network devices. IP is an intentionally unreliable protocol, so it doesn't guarantee delivery of information.

>> **Address Resolution Protocol (ARP):** Resolves IP addresses to hardware Media Access Control (MAC) addresses, which uniquely identify hardware devices.

>> **Internet Control Message Protocol (ICMP):** Sends and receives diagnostic messages. ICMP is the basis of the ubiquitous ping command.

>> **Internet Group Management Protocol (IGMP):** Used to multicast messages to multiple IP addresses at once.

Transport layer

The transport layer is where sessions are established and data packets are exchanged between hosts. Two core protocols are found at this layer:

>> **Transmission Control Protocol (TCP):** Provides reliable connection-oriented transmission between two hosts. TCP establishes a session between hosts, and then ensures delivery of packets between the hosts.

>> **User Datagram Protocol (UDP):** Provides connectionless, unreliable, one-to-one or one-to-many delivery.

Application layer

The application layer of the TCP/IP model corresponds to the session, presentation, and application layers of the OSI Reference Model. A few of the most popular application layer protocols are

>> **HyperText Transfer Protocol (HTTP):** The core protocol of the World Wide Web.

>> **File Transfer Protocol (FTP):** A protocol that enables a client to send and receive complete files from a server.

>> **Telnet:** The protocol that lets you connect to another computer on the Internet in a terminal emulation mode.

>> **Simple Mail Transfer Protocol (SMTP):** One of several key protocols that are used to provide email services.

>> **Domain Name System (DNS):** The protocol that allows you to refer to other host computers by using names rather than numbers.

Chapter **3**

IP Addresses

One of the most basic components of TCP/IP is IP addressing. Every device on a TCP/IP network must have a unique IP address. In this chapter, I describe the ins and outs of these IP addresses. Enjoy!

Understanding Binary

Before you can understand the details of how IP addressing works, you need to understand how the binary numbering system works because binary is the basis of IP addressing. If you already understand binary, please skip to the section "Introducing IP Addresses." I don't want to bore you with stuff that's too basic.

Counting by ones

Binary is a counting system that uses only two numerals: 0 and 1. In the decimal system (with which most people are accustomed), you use ten numerals: 0–9. In an ordinary decimal number — such as 3,482 — the rightmost digit represents ones; the next digit to the left, tens; the next, hundreds; the next, thousands; and so on. These digits represent powers of ten: first 10^0 (which is 1); next, 10^1 (10); then 10^2 (100); then 10^3 (1,000); and so on.

In binary, you have only two numerals rather than ten, which is why binary numbers look somewhat monotonous, as in 110011, 101111, and 100001.

The positions in a binary number (called *bits* rather than *digits*) represent powers of two rather than powers of ten: 1, 2, 4, 8, 16, 32, and so on. To figure the decimal value of a binary number, you multiply each bit by its corresponding power of two and then add the results. The decimal value of binary 10111, for example, is calculated as follows:

$$1 \times 2^0 = 1 \times 1 = 1$$

$$1 \times 2^1 = 1 \times 2 = 2$$

$$1 \times 2^2 = 1 \times 4 = 4$$

$$0 \times 2^3 = 0 \times 8 = 0$$

$$1 \times 2^4 = 1 \times 16 = 16$$

$$\text{Total} = 1 + 2 + 4 + 0 + 16 = 23$$

Fortunately, converting a number between binary and decimal is something a computer is good at — so good, in fact, that you're unlikely ever to need to do any conversions yourself. The point of learning binary is not to be able to look at a number such as 1110110110110 and say instantly, "Ah! Decimal 7,606!" (If you could do that, Piers Morgan would probably interview you, and they would even make a movie about you.)

Instead, the point is to have a basic understanding of how computers store information and — most important — to understand how the binary counting system works, which I describe in the following section.

Here are some of the more interesting characteristics of binary and how the system is similar to and differs from the decimal system:

» **In decimal, the number of decimal places allotted for a number determines how large the number can be.** If you allot six digits, for example, the largest number possible is 999,999. Because 0 is itself a number, however, a six-digit number can have any of 1 million different values.

   Similarly, the number of bits allotted for a binary number determines how large that number can be. If you allot eight bits, the largest value that number can store is 11111111, which happens to be 255 in decimal.

TIP

» **To quickly figure how many different values you can store in a binary number of a given length, use the number of bits as an exponent of two.** An eight-bit binary number, for example, can hold 2^8 values. Because 2^8 is 256, an eight-bit number can have any of 256 different values. This is why a *byte* — eight bits — can have 256 different values.

>> **This "powers of two" thing is why computers don't use nice, even, round numbers in measuring such values as memory or disk space.** A value of 1K, for example, is not an even 1,000 bytes: It's actually 1,024 bytes because 1,024 is 2^{10}. Similarly, 1MB is not an even 1,000,000 bytes but instead 1,048,576 bytes, which happens to be 2^{20}.

REMEMBER

One basic test of computer nerddom is knowing your powers of two because they play such an important role in binary numbers. Just for the fun of it, but not because you really need to know, Table 3-1 lists the powers of two up to 32.

Table 3-1 also shows the common shorthand notation for various powers of two. The abbreviation *K* represents 2^{10} (1,024). The *M* in *MB* stands for 2^{20}, or 1,024K, and the *G* in *GB* represents 2^{30}, which is 1,024MB. These shorthand notations don't have anything to do with TCP/IP, but they're commonly used for measuring computer disk and memory capacities, so I thought I'd throw them in at no charge because the table had extra room.

TABLE 3-1   **Powers of Two**

Power	Bytes	Kilobytes	Power	Bytes	K, MB, or GB
2^1	2		2^{17}	131,072	128K
2^2	4		2^{18}	262,144	256K
2^3	8		2^{19}	524,288	512K
2^4	16		2^{20}	1,048,576	1MB
2^5	32		2^{21}	2,097,152	2MB
2^6	64		2^{22}	4,194,304	4MB
2^7	128		2^{23}	8,388,608	8MB
2^8	256		2^{24}	16,777,216	16MB
2^9	512		2^{25}	33,554,432	32MB
2^{10}	1,024	1K	2^{26}	67,108,864	64MB
2^{11}	2,048	2K	2^{27}	134,217,728	128MB
2^{12}	4,096	4K	2^{28}	268,435,456	256MB
2^{13}	8,192	8K	2^{29}	536,870,912	512MB
2^{14}	16,384	16K	2^{30}	1,073,741,824	1GB
2^{15}	32,768	32K	2^{31}	2,147,483,648	2GB
2^{16}	65,536	64K	2^{32}	4,294,967,296	4GB

Doing the logic thing

One of the great things about binary is that it's very efficient at handling special operations: namely, logical operations. Four basic logical operations exist although additional operations are derived from the basic four operations. Three of the operations — AND, OR, and XOR — compare two binary digits (bits). The fourth (NOT) works on just a single bit.

The following list summarizes the basic logical operations:

>> **AND:** Compares two binary values. If both values are 1, the result of the AND operation is 1. If one or both of the values are 0, the result is 0.

>> **OR:** Compares two binary values. If at least one value is 1, the result of the OR operation is 1. If both values are 0, the result is 0.

>> **XOR:** Compares two binary values. If one of them is 1, the result is 1. If both values are 0 or if both values are 1, the result is 0.

>> **NOT:** Doesn't compare two values but simply changes the value of a single binary value. If the original value is 1, NOT returns 0. If the original value is 0, NOT returns 1.

Table 3-2 summarizes how AND, OR, and XOR work.

TABLE 3-2 **Logical Operations for Binary Values**

First Value	Second Value	AND	OR	XOR
0	0	0	0	0
0	1	0	1	1
1	0	0	1	1
1	1	1	1	0

Logical operations are applied to binary numbers that have more than one binary digit by applying the operation one bit at a time. The easiest way to do this manually is to line the two binary numbers on top of one another and then write the result of the operation beneath each binary digit. The following example shows how you would calculate 10010100 AND 11011101:

```
10010100
AND 11011101
10010100
```

As you can see, the result is 10010100.

Working with the binary Windows Calculator

The Calculator program that comes with all versions of Windows has a special Programmer mode that many users don't know about. When you flip the Calculator into this mode, you can do instant binary and decimal conversions, which can occasionally come in handy when you're working with IP addresses.

To use the Windows Calculator in Programmer mode, launch the Calculator by choosing Start➪All Programs➪Accessories➪Calculator. Then, choose the View➪Programmer command from the Calculator menu. The Calculator changes to a fancy programmer model in which all kinds of buttons appear, as shown in Figure 3-1.

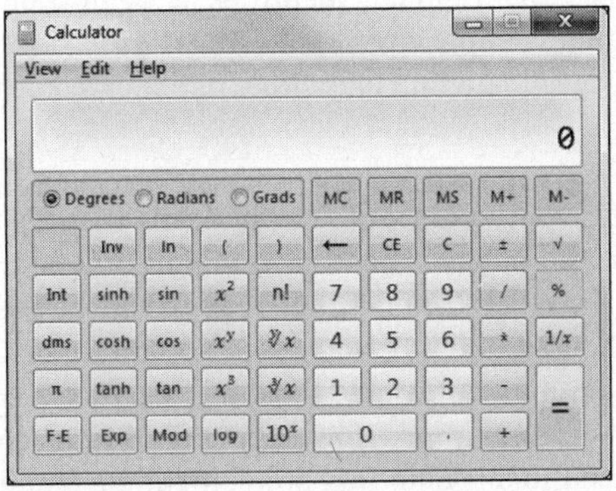

FIGURE 3-1:
The free Windows Programmer Calculator.

You can switch the number base by using the Hex, Dec, Oct, and Bin radio buttons to convert values between base 16 (hexadecimal), base 10 (decimal), base 8 (octal), and base 2 (binary). For example, to find the binary equivalent of decimal 155, enter **155** and then select the Bin radio button. The value in the display changes to 10011011.

Here are a few other things to note about the Programmer mode of the Calculator:

>> Although you can convert decimal values to binary values with the programmer Calculator, the Calculator can't handle the dotted-decimal IP address format that's described later in this chapter. To convert a dotted-decimal address to binary, just convert each octet separately. For example, to convert

172.65.48.120 to binary, first convert 172; then convert 65; then convert 48; and finally, convert 120.

>> The Programmer Calculator has several features that are designed specifically for binary calculations, such as AND, OR, XOR, and so on.

>> The Calculator program in Windows versions prior to Windows 7 does not have the programmer mode. However, those versions do offer a scientific mode that provides binary, hexadecimal, and decimal conversions.

Introducing IP Addresses

An *IP address* is a number that uniquely identifies every host on an IP network. IP addresses operate at the network layer of the TCP/IP protocol stack, so they are independent of lower-level data link layer MAC addresses, such as Ethernet MAC addresses.

IP addresses are 32-bit binary numbers, which means that theoretically, a maximum of something in the neighborhood of 4 billion unique host addresses can exist throughout the Internet. You'd think that would be enough, but TCP/IP places certain restrictions on how IP addresses are allocated. These restrictions severely limit the total number of usable IP addresses. Many experts predict that we will run out of IP addresses soon. However, new techniques for working with IP addresses have helped to alleviate this problem, and a standard for 128-bit IP addresses has been adopted, though it still is not yet in widespread use.

Networks and hosts

IP stands for *Internet Protocol*, and its primary purpose is to enable communications between networks. As a result, a 32-bit IP address actually consists of two parts:

>> **The network ID (or network address):** Identifies the network on which a host computer can be found

>> **The host ID (or host address):** Identifies a specific device on the network indicated by the network ID

Most of the complexity of working with IP addresses has to do with figuring out which part of the complete 32-bit IP address is the network ID and which part is the host ID, as described in the following sections.

TECHNICAL STUFF

As I describe the details of how host IDs are assigned, you may notice that two host addresses seem to be unaccounted for. For example, the Class C addressing scheme, which uses eight bits for the host ID, allows only 254 hosts — not the 256 hosts you'd expect. The host ID can't be 0 (the host ID is all zeros) because that address is always reserved to represent the network itself. And the host ID can't be 255 (the host ID is all ones) because that host ID is reserved for use as a broadcast request that's intended for all hosts on the network.

The dotted-decimal dance

IP addresses are usually represented in a format known as *dotted-decimal notation*. In dotted-decimal notation, each group of eight bits — an *octet* — is represented by its decimal equivalent. For example, consider the following binary IP address:

```
11000000101010001000100000011100
```

To convert this value to dotted-decimal notation, first divide it into four octets, as follows:

```
11000000 10101000 10001000 00011100
```

Then, convert each of the octets to its decimal equivalent:

```
11000000 10101000 10001000 00011100
192      168      136      28
```

Then, use periods to separate the four decimal numbers, like this:

```
192.168.136.28
```

This is the format in which you'll usually see IP addresses represented.

Figure 3-2 shows how the 32 bits of an IP address are broken down into four octets of eight bits each. As you can see, the four octets of an IP address are often referred to as *w*, *x*, *y*, and *z*.

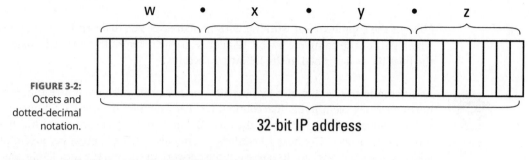

FIGURE 3-2:
Octets and
dotted-decimal
notation.

32-bit IP address

Classifying IP Addresses

When the original designers of the IP protocol created the IP addressing scheme, they could have assigned an arbitrary number of IP address bits for the network ID. The remaining bits would then be used for the host ID. For example, suppose that the designers decided that half of the address (16 bits) would be used for the network, and the remaining 16 bits would be used for the host ID. The result of that scheme would be that the Internet could have a total of 65,536 networks, and each of those networks could have 65,536 hosts.

In the early days of the Internet, this scheme probably seemed like several orders of magnitude more than would ever be needed. However, the IP designers realized from the start that few networks would actually have tens of thousands of hosts. Suppose that a network of 1,000 computers joins the Internet and is assigned one of these hypothetical network IDs. Because that network will use only 1,000 of its 65,536 host addresses, more than 64,000 IP addresses would be wasted.

As a solution to this problem, the idea of IP address classes was introduced. The IP protocol defines five different address classes: A, B, C, D, and E. Each of the first three classes, A–C, uses a different size for the network ID and host ID portion of the address. Class D is for a special type of address called a *multicast address.* Class E is an experimental address class that isn't used.

The first four bits of the IP address are used to determine into which class a particular address fits, as follows:

>> **Class A:** The first bit is zero.

>> **Class B:** The first bit is one, and the second bit is zero.

>> **Class C:** The first two bits are both one, and the third bit is zero.

>> **Class D:** The first three bits are all one, and the fourth bit is zero.

>> **Class E:** The first four bits are all one.

WHAT ABOUT IPv6?

Most of the current Internet is based on version 4 of the Internet Protocol, also known as IPv4. IPv4 has served the Internet well for more than 30 years. However, the growth of the Internet has put a lot of pressure on IPv4's limited 32-bit address space. This chapter describes how IPv4 has evolved to make the best possible use of 32-bit addresses. Eventually, though, all the addresses will be assigned, and the IPv4 address space will be filled to capacity. When that happens, the Internet will have to migrate to the next version of IP, known as IPv6.

IPv6 is also called *IP next generation,* or *IPng,* in honor of the favorite television show of most Internet gurus, *Star Trek: The Next Generation.*

IPv6 offers several advantages over IPv4, but the most important is that it uses 128 bits for Internet addresses instead of 32 bits. The number of host addresses possible with 128 bits is a number so large that it would have made Carl Sagan proud. It doesn't just double or triple the number of available addresses, or even a thousand-fold or even a million-fold. Just for the fun of it, here is the number of unique Internet addresses provided by IPv6:

340,282,366,920,938,463,463,374,607,431,768,211,456

This number is so large it defies understanding. If the Internet Assigned Numbers Authority (IANA) had been around at the creation of the universe and started handing out IPv6 addresses at a rate of one per millisecond — that is, 1,000 addresses every second — it would now, 15 billion years later, have not yet allocated even 1 percent of the available addresses.

The transition from IPv4 to IPv6 has been slow. IPv6 is available on all new computers and has been supported on Windows since Windows XP Service Pack 1 (released in 2002). However, most ISPs still base their service on IPv4. Thus, the Internet will continue to be driven by IPv4 for at least a few more years.

Note: This is now the sixth edition of this book. Every previous edition of this book, all the way back to the very first edition published in 2004, has had this very sidebar. In 2004, I said that the Internet would continue to be driven by IPv4 for at least a few more years. "A few more years" has morphed into 14 years, and we're still living in the world of IPv4. Make no mistake: The world will eventually run out of IPv4 addresses, and we'll have to migrate to IPv6 . . . in a few years, whatever that means.

Because Class D and E addresses are reserved for special purposes, I focus the rest of the discussion here on Class A, B, and C addresses. Table 3-3 summarizes the details of each address class.

TABLE 3-3   **IP Address Classes**

Class	Address Number Range	Starting Bits	Length of Network ID	Number of Networks	Hosts
A	1–126.x.y.z	0	8	126	16,777,214
B	128–191.x.y.z	10	16	16,384	65,534
C	192–223.x.y.z	110	24	2,097,152	254

Class A addresses

Class A addresses are designed for very large networks. In a Class A address, the first octet of the address is the network ID, and the remaining three octets are the host ID. Because only eight bits are allocated to the network ID and the first of these bits is used to indicate that the address is a Class A address, only 126 Class A networks can exist in the entire Internet. However, each Class A network can accommodate more than 16 million hosts.

Only about 40 Class A addresses are actually assigned to companies or organizations. The rest are either reserved for use by the Internet Assigned Numbers Authority (IANA) or are assigned to organizations that manage IP assignments for geographic regions such as Europe, Asia, and Latin America.

Just for fun, Table 3-4 lists some of the better-known Class A networks (as of January 2018 — these change frequently). You'll probably recognize many of them. In case you're interested, you can find a complete list of all the Class A address assignments at `www.iana.org/assignments/ipv4-address-space/ipv4-address-space.xml`.

You may have noticed in Table 3-3 that Class A addresses end with 126.x.y.z, and Class B addresses begin with 128.x.y.z. What happened to 127.x.y.z? This special range of addresses is reserved for loopback testing, so these addresses aren't assigned to public networks.

TABLE 3-4   **Some Well-Known Class A Networks**

Network	Description	Network	Description
3	General Electric Company		
4	Level 3 Communications	22	Defense Information Systems Agency
6	Army Information Systems Center	25	UK Ministry of Defense
8	Level-3 Communications	26	Defense Information Systems Agency
9	IBM	28	Decision Sciences Institute (North)
11	DoD Intel Information Systems	29–30	Defense Information Systems Agency
12	AT&T Bell Laboratories	33	DLA Systems Automation Center
15	Hewlett-Packard Company	44	44Amateur Radio Digital Communications
16	Digital Equipment Corporation	48	Prudential Securities, Inc.
17	Apple Computer, Inc.	53	Daimler
18	MIT	55	DoD Network Information Center
19	Ford Motor Company	56	U.S. Postal Service
20	Computer Sciences Corporation		

Class B addresses

In a Class B address, the first two octets of the IP address are used as the network ID, and the second two octets are used as the host ID. Thus, a Class B address comes close to my hypothetical scheme of splitting the address down the middle, using half for the network ID and half for the host ID. It isn't identical to this scheme, however, because the first two bits of the first octet are required to be 10, in order to indicate that the address is a Class B address. As a result, a total of 16,384 Class B networks can exist. All Class B addresses fall within the range $128.x.y.z$ to $191.x.y.z$. Each Class B address can accommodate more than 65,000 hosts.

The problem with Class B networks is that even though they are much smaller than Class A networks, they still allocate far too many host IDs. Very few networks have tens of thousands of hosts. Thus, careless assignment of Class B addresses can lead to a large percentage of the available host addresses being wasted on organizations that don't need them.

Class C addresses

In a Class C address, the first three octets are used for the network ID, and the fourth octet is used for the host ID. With only eight bits for the host ID, each Class C network can accommodate only 254 hosts. However, with 24 network ID bits, Class C addresses allow for more than 2 million networks.

The problem with Class C networks is that they're too small. Although few organizations need the tens of thousands of host addresses provided by a Class B address, many organizations need more than a few hundred. The large discrepancy between Class B networks and Class C networks is what led to the development of *subnetting*, which I describe in the next section.

Subnetting

Subnetting is a technique that lets network administrators use the 32 bits available in an IP address more efficiently by creating networks that aren't limited to the scales provided by Class A, B, and C IP addresses. With subnetting, you can create networks with more realistic host limits.

Subnetting provides a more flexible way to designate which portion of an IP address represents the network ID and which portion represents the host ID. With standard IP address classes, only three possible network ID sizes exist: 8 bits for Class A, 16 bits for Class B, and 24 bits for Class C. Subnetting lets you select an arbitrary number of bits to use for the network ID.

Two reasons compel people to use subnetting. The first is to allocate the limited IP address space more efficiently. If the Internet were limited to Class A, B, or C addresses, every network would be allocated 254, 64 thousand, or 16 million IP addresses for host devices. Although many networks with more than 254 devices exist, few (if any) exist with 64 thousand, let alone 16 million. Unfortunately, any network with more than 254 devices would need a Class B allocation and probably waste tens of thousands of IP addresses.

The second reason for subnetting is that even if a single organization has thousands of network devices, operating all those devices with the same network ID would slow the network to a crawl. The way TCP/IP works dictates that all the computers with the same network ID must be on the same physical network. The physical network comprises a single *broadcast domain,* which means that a single network medium must carry all the traffic for the network. For performance reasons, networks are usually segmented into broadcast domains that are smaller than even Class C addresses provide.

Subnets

A *subnet* is a network that falls within a Class A, B, or C network. Subnets are created by using one or more of the Class A, B, or C host bits to extend the network ID. Thus, instead of the standard 8-, 16-, or 24-bit network ID, subnets can have network IDs of any length.

Figure 3-3 shows an example of a network before and after subnetting has been applied. In the unsubnetted network, the network has been assigned the Class B address 144.28.0.0. All the devices on this network must share the same broadcast domain.

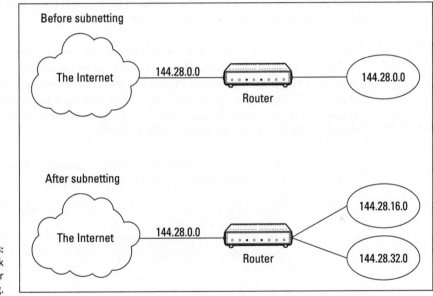

FIGURE 3-3:
A network before and after subnetting.

In the second network, the first four bits of the host ID are used to divide the network into two small networks, identified as subnets 16 and 32. To the outside world (that is, on the other side of the router), these two networks still appear to be a single network identified as 144.28.0.0. For example, the outside world considers the device at 144.28.16.22 to belong to the 144.28.0.0 network. As a result, a packet sent to this device will be delivered to the router at 144.28.0.0. The router then considers the subnet portion of the host ID to decide whether to route the packet to subnet 16 or subnet 32.

Subnet masks

For subnetting to work, the router must be told which portion of the host ID should be used for the subnet network ID. This little sleight of hand is accomplished by using another 32-bit number, known as a *subnet mask.* Those IP address bits that represent the network ID are represented by a 1 in the mask, and those bits that represent the host ID appear as a 0 in the mask. As a result, a subnet mask always has a consecutive string of ones on the left, followed by a string of zeros.

For example, the subnet mask for the subnet shown in Figure 3-3, where the network ID consists of the 16-bit network ID plus an additional 4-bit subnet ID, would look like this:

```
11111111 11111111 11110000 00000000
```

In other words, the first 20 bits are ones, and the remaining 12 bits are zeros. Thus, the complete network ID is 20 bits in length, and the actual host ID portion of the subnetted address is 12 bits in length.

To determine the network ID of an IP address, the router must have both the IP address and the subnet mask. The router then performs a bitwise operation called a *logical AND* on the IP address in order to extract the network ID. To perform a logical AND, each bit in the IP address is compared with the corresponding bit in the subnet mask. If both bits are 1, the resulting bit in the network ID is set to 1. If either of the bits are 0, the resulting bit is set to 0.

For example, here's how the network address is extracted from an IP address using the 20-bit subnet mask from the previous example:

```
144 . 28 . 16 . 17
IP address: 10010000 00011100 00010000 00010001
Subnet mask: 11111111 11111111 11110000 00000000
Network ID: 10010000 00011100 00010000 00000000
 144  .  28 . 16 . 0
```

Thus, the network ID for this subnet is 144.28.16.0.

The subnet mask itself is usually represented in dotted-decimal notation. As a result, the 20-bit subnet mask used in the previous example would be represented as 255.255.240.0:

```
Subnet mask: 11111111 11111111 11110000 00000000
 255  .  255 .  240 . 0
```

TIP

Don't confuse a subnet mask with an IP address. A subnet mask doesn't represent any device or network on the Internet. It's just a way of indicating which portion of an IP address should be used to determine the network ID. (You can spot a subnet mask right away because the first octet is always 255, and 255 is not a valid first octet for any class of IP address.)

Network prefix notation

Because a subnet mask always begins with a consecutive sequence of ones to indicate which bits to use for the network ID, you can use a shorthand notation — a *network prefix* — to indicate how many bits of an IP address represent the network ID. The network prefix is indicated with a slash immediately after the IP address, followed by the number of network ID bits to use. For example, the IP address 144.28.16.17 with the subnet mask 255.255.240.0 can be represented as 144.28.16.17/20 because the subnet mask 255.255.240.0 has 20 network ID bits.

Network prefix notation is also called *classless interdomain routing* notation (*CIDR*, for short) because it provides a way of indicating which portion of an address is the network ID and which is the host ID without relying on standard address classes.

Default subnets

The *default subnet masks* are three subnet masks that correspond to the standard Class A, B, and C address assignments. These default masks are summarized in Table 3-5.

TABLE 3-5   **The Default Subnet Masks**

Class	Binary	Dotted-Decimal	Network Prefix
A	11111111 00000000 00000000 00000000	255.0.0.0	/8
B	11111111 11111111 00000000 00000000	255.255.0.0	/16
C	11111111 11111111 11111111 00000000	255.255.255.0	/24

TIP

Keep in mind that a subnet mask is not actually required to use one of these defaults because the IP address class can be determined by examining the first three bits of the IP address. If the first bit is 0, the address is Class A, and the subnet mask 255.0.0 is applied. If the first two bits are 10, the address is Class B, and 255.255.0.0 is used. If the first three bits are 110, the Class C default mask 255.255.255.0 is used.

The great subnet roundup

You should know about a few additional restrictions that are placed on subnets and subnet masks. In particular

> » **The minimum number of network ID bits is eight.** As a result, the first octet of a subnet mask is always 255.

>> **The maximum number of network ID bits is 30.** You have to leave at least two bits for the host ID portion of the address to allow for at least two hosts. If you use all 32 bits for the network ID, that leaves no bits for the host ID. Obviously, that won't work. Leaving just one bit for the host ID won't work, either, because a host ID of all ones is reserved for a broadcast address, and all zeros refers to the network itself. Thus, if you use 31 bits for the network ID and leave only 1 for the host ID, host ID 1 would be used for the broadcast address, and host ID 0 would be the network itself, leaving no room for actual hosts. That's why the maximum network ID size is 30 bits.

>> **Because the network ID portion of a subnet mask is always composed of consecutive bits set to 1, only eight values are possible for each octet of a subnet mask:** 0, 128, 192, 224, 248, 252, 254, and 255.

>> **A subnet address can't be all zeros or all ones.** Thus, the number of unique subnet addresses is two less than two raised to the number of subnet address bits. For example, with three subnet address bits, six unique subnet addresses are possible ($2^3 - 2 = 6$). This implies that you must have at least two subnet bits. (If a single-bit subnet mask were allowed, it would violate the "can't be all zeros or all ones" rule because the only two allowed values would be 0 or 1.)

IP block parties

A subnet can be thought of as a range or block of IP addresses that have a common network ID. For example, the CIDR 192.168.1.0/28 represents the following block of 14 IP addresses:

```
192.168.1.1 192.168.1.2 192.168.1.3 192.168.1.4
192.168.1.5 192.168.1.6 192.168.1.7 192.168.1.8
192.168.1.9 192.168.1.10 192.168.1.11 192.168.1.12
192.168.1.13 192.168.1.14
```

Given an IP address in CIDR notation, it's useful to be able to determine the range of actual IP addresses that the CIDR represents. This matter is straightforward when the octet within which the network ID mask ends happens to be 0, as in the preceding example. You just determine how many host IDs are allowed based on the size of the network ID and count them off.

However, what if the octet where the network ID mask ends is not 0? For example, what are the valid IP addresses for 192.168.1.100 when the subnet mask is 255.255.255.240? In that case, the calculation is a little harder. The first step is to determine the actual network ID. You can do that by converting both the IP address and the subnet mask to binary and then extracting the network ID as in this example:

```
  192 . 168 . 1 . 100
IP address: 11000000 10101000 00000001 01100100
Subnet mask: 11111111 11111111 11111111 11110000
Network ID: 11000000 10101000 00000001 01100000
  192 . 168 . 1 . 96
```

As a result, the network ID is 192.168.1.96.

Next, determine the number of allowable hosts in the subnet based on the network prefix. You can calculate this by subtracting the last octet of the subnet mask from 254. In this case, the number of allowable hosts is 14.

To determine the first IP address in the block, add 1 to the network ID. Thus, the first IP address in my example is 192.168.1.97. To determine the last IP address in the block, add the number of hosts to the network ID. In my example, the last IP address is 192.168.1.110. As a result, the 192.168.1.100 with subnet mask 255.255.255.240 designates the following block of IP addresses:

```
192.168.1.97 192.168.1.98 192.168.1.99 192.168.1.100
192.168.1.101 192.168.1.102 192.168.1.103 192.168.1.104
192.168.1.105 192.168.1.106 192.168.1.107 192.168.1.108
192.168.1.109 192.168.1.110
```

Private and public addresses

Any host with a direct connection to the Internet must have a globally unique IP address. However, not all hosts are connected directly to the Internet. Some are on networks that aren't connected to the Internet. Some hosts are hidden behind firewalls, so their Internet connection is indirect.

Several blocks of IP addresses are set aside just for this purpose, for use on private networks that are not connected to the Internet or to use on networks that are hidden behind a firewall. Three such ranges of addresses exist, summarized in Table 3-6. Whenever you create a private TCP/IP network, you should use IP addresses from one of these ranges.

TABLE 3-6   **Private Address Spaces**

CIDR	Subnet Mask	Address Range
10.0.0.0/8	255.0.0.0	10.0.0.1–10.255.255.254
172.16.0.0/12	255.240.0.0	172.16.1.1–172.31.255.254
192.168.0.0/16	255.255.0.0	192.168.0.1–192.168.255.254

Network Address Translation

Many firewalls use a technique called *network address translation* (NAT) to hide the actual IP address of a host from the outside world. When that's the case, the NAT device must use a globally unique IP to represent the host to the Internet. Behind the firewall, though, the host can use any IP address it wants. When packets cross the firewall, the NAT device translates the private IP address to the public IP address and vice versa.

One of the benefits of NAT is that it helps to slow down the rate at which the IP address space is assigned. That's because a NAT device can use a single public IP address for more than one host. It does so by keeping track of outgoing packets so that it can match incoming packets with the correct host. To understand how this works, consider the following sequence of steps:

1. A host whose private address is 192.168.1.100 sends a request to 216.239.57.99, which as of January 2018 happens to be www.google.com. The NAT device changes the source IP address of the packet to 208.23.110.22, the IP address of the firewall. That way, Google will send its reply back to the firewall router. The NAT records that 192.168.1.100 sent a request to 216.239.57.99.

2. Now another host, at address 192.168.1.107, sends a request to 207.46.134.190, which happens to be www.microsoft.com. The NAT device changes the source of this request to 208.23.110.22 so that Microsoft will reply to the firewall router. The NAT records that 192.168.1.107 sent a request to 207.46.134.190.

3. A few seconds later, the firewall receives a reply from 216.239.57.99. The destination address in the reply is 208.23.110.22, the address of the firewall. To determine to whom to forward the reply, the firewall checks its records to see who is waiting for a reply from 216.239.57.99. It discovers that 192.168.1.100 is waiting for that reply, so it changes the destination address to 192.168.1.100 and sends the packet on.

Actually, the process is a little more complicated than that, because it's very likely that two or more users may have pending requests from the same public IP. In that case, the NAT device uses other techniques to figure out to which user each incoming packet should be delivered.

Chapter **4**

Routing

I n the simplest terms, a *router* is a device that works at layer 3 of the OSI Reference Model. Layer 3 is the network layer, which means that layer 3 is responsible for exchanging information between distinct networks. And that's exactly the function of a router: Connecting two or more networks so that packets can flow freely between them.

Routing is the general term that describes what routers do. In short, when a router receives a packet from one network that is destined for a device on another network, the router determines the best way to get the packet to its destination.

In a way, routers are the post offices of the Internet. When you drop a letter into a public mailbox, a mail carrier collects the mail and delivers it to a nearby post office. There, the mail is sorted and sent off to a regional post office, where the mail is sorted again and maybe sent off to yet another regional post office, and so on until the mail finally arrives at a post office close to the delivery address, where the mail is sorted one last time and given to a mail carrier who delivers the letter to the correct address.

At each step of the way, the best route to move the mail closer to its destination is determined, and the mail is sent along its way. Routers work pretty much just like that.

In this chapter, you learn about three of the most important uses for routers: connecting to the Internet, connecting remote offices to each other via the Internet, and managing traffic in extremely large networks such as large campuses, huge office buildings, or the Internet itself.

Considering the Usefulness of Routers

Routers are an indispensable part of any network. In fact, virtually all networks require at least one router. The following sections describe the most common reasons for introducing a router into your network.

Connecting to the Internet

A router is required for any network that needs access to the Internet. Such a device is known as an *Internet gateway* because it serves as a "gateway" to the Internet.

Strictly speaking, the Internet isn't a network — it's an enormous collection of millions of networks, all tied together via millions of individual routers. Your Internet service provider (ISP) is just one of those millions of networks, and your Internet gateway connects your private network to your ISP's network. Your ISP, in turn, provides the routers that connect the ISP's network to other networks, which ultimately connects to the Internet backbone and the rest of the world.

For a home network or a very small business network, you can use an inexpensive *residential gateway* device that you can buy at a consumer electronics store such as Best Buy. A residential gateway typically includes five distinct components, all bundled into one neat package:

» A router, used to connect your private network to your ISP's network

» A small switch, typically providing from three to eight ports to connect wired devices such as computers and printers

» A wireless access point (WAP) to connect wireless devices such as laptops or smartphones

» A firewall to provide protection from intruders seeking to compromise your network

» A DHCP server to provide IP addresses for the computers and other devices on your network

Figure 4-1 shows an example of this type of setup. In this example, an ISP provides a cable feed into your house that connects to a *cable modem*, which provides a single Ethernet port to which you can connect a residential gateway. Computers on the home network are connected to the gateway's switch ports, and wireless devices connect via the Wi-Fi network. The gateway's DHCP server hands out IP addresses to any devices connected to the network.

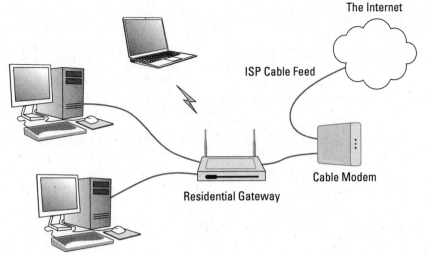

The Internet

ISP Cable Feed

Cable Modem

Residential Gateway

FIGURE 4-1:
Connecting to
the Internet via
a residential
gateway.

Figure 4-2 shows the type of Internet gateway typically used in a larger network. Here, the ISP delivers a high-speed fiber-optic feed to the customer's location and provides an *Ethernet handoff,* which is simply one or more Ethernet ports that the customer can connect to.

The Ethernet handoff establishes what is called the *demarcation point,* usually called simply the *demark.* The demark is simply the dividing line that establishes who is responsible for what: The ISP is responsible for everything between the Internet and the demark; the customer is responsible for everything on the private network side of the demark.

A *gateway router* is used to connect the private network to the Ethernet handoff. Much like a residential gateway, a gateway router typically provides several features into one combined device, including a router, a small switch, and a firewall. However, most business-class gateway routers don't provide Wi-Fi — the wireless network is provided by dedicated WAPs. And the small switch provided by the gateway doesn't serve the entire network; instead, it is connected to a network of switches that in turn connect the network's computers together.

One of the distinguishing characteristics of a gateway router is that it has a small number of network interfaces. At the minimum, a gateway router needs just two interfaces: an external interface and an internal interface. The *external interface,* often labeled *WAN* on the device, connects to the ISP's feed. The *internal interface* connects to the private network. (If the device includes a switch, it will have more than one internal interface.)

For more information about using a router to connect to the Internet, refer to Book 2, Chapter 2.

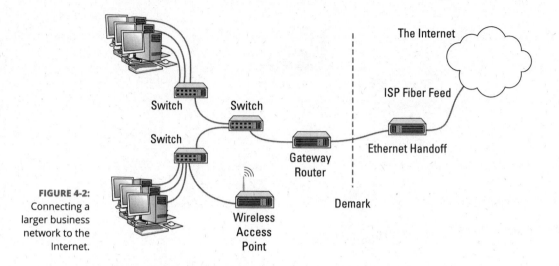

FIGURE 4-2:
Connecting a
larger business
network to the
Internet.

Connecting remote locations

Another common use for routers is to connect geographically separated offices to form a single network that spans multiple locations. You can do this by using a pair of gateway routers to create a secure virtual private network (VPN) between the two networks. Each network uses its gateway router to connect to the Internet, and the routers establish a secure tunnel between themselves to exchange private information.

Figure 4-3 shows how a VPN can be used to establish a site-to-site tunnel between offices in Los Angeles and Las Vegas. As you can see, each site has its own gateway router that connects to the Internet. The routers are configured to provide a VPN that securely connects the two networks.

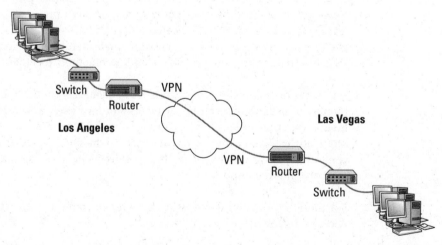

FIGURE 4-3:
Connecting two
networks via VPN.

Note that the need for a VPN tunnel between networks is not related to the size of the network, at least not in terms of how many users are on the network. Instead, it's simply a function of geography. A small-town company that has two three-person offices on opposite sides of the same street can benefit from a VPN tunnel just as much as a company that has a 200-person office in Dallas and a second 200-person office in Houston.

Splitting up large networks

Large networks often have need for routers that are internal to the network itself. For example, consider a company that employs several thousand employees on a single campus that consists of several dozen buildings. For a network like this, routers are used to manage the network by dividing it into smaller, more manageable networks all connected with routers.

Figure 4-4 shows a simplified version of how this works. Here, a large network is segmented into two smaller networks, each on a different subnet: one on 10.0.100.x (subnet mask 255.255.255.0), the other on 10.0.200.x (also 255.255.255.0). A router is used to provide a link between the two subnets, so packets can flow from one subnet to the other.

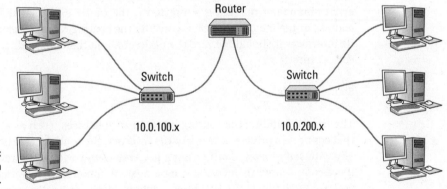

FIGURE 4-4:
Using an internal router.

A router used in this way is called an *internal router* because it doesn't connect a private network to a public network. Instead, it connects two portions of a larger network.

TECHNICAL STUFF

If you've read the preceding chapter (Book 2, Chapter 3) on IP addressing and Book 1, Chapter 2, which introduces network infrastructure, you may be wondering why a router would be necessary in this situation. After all, an advanced switch can handle the connection between subnets via a trunk port, so technically a router isn't necessary to connect subnets.

Well, yes and no. Subnets are separate networks, and any device that sends packets from one subnet to another must operate at layer 3 of the OSI model because the device must know about IP addresses. That technically makes the device a router. So, switches that can manage traffic between subnets are acting as routers when they do so.

Most advanced switches today actually operate at both layer 2 and layer 3. Because of this, separate routers are used much less than they used to be.

Still, very large networks still require routers to handle the large amount of traffic that must flow between networks. Picture a large college campus, in which each department has its own network each with dozens or possibly hundreds of devices. Each of those networks would have a relatively small departmental router, but a larger internal router would be used in the data center to connect all the departmental routers.

Understanding Routing Tables

Routers work by maintaining an internal list of networks that can be reached via each of the router's interfaces. This list is called a *routing table.* When a packet arrives on one of the router's interfaces, the router examines the destination IP address of the incoming packet, consults the routing table to determine which of its interfaces it should forward the packet to, and then forwards the packet to the correct interface.

Sounds simple enough.

The trick is building the routing table. In simple cases, such as a gateway router that connects a private network to the Internet, the routing table is created manually with *static routes.* Configuring a gateway router with static routes isn't much more complicated than configuring a host computer with a static IP address. All you need to know is the IP address, subnet mask, and gateway address provided by your ISP for the external interface and the network address and subnet mask of the private network for the internal interface.

For more complicated environments, where multiple routers are used on the private network, special *routing protocols* are used to build *dynamic routes.* These routing protocols are designed to discover the topology of the network by finding out which routers are present on the network and which networks each router can reach.

Refer back to Figure 4-2, which depicts a small business network that has a fiber-optic connection to the Internet provided by an ISP and a gateway router that connects to the Ethernet handoff.

Let's assume that the private network for this business operates on a single subnet, and the IP address for the network is 10.0.1.0 with the subnet mask 255.255.255.0. The six computers in the private network have IP addresses 10.0.101.1 through 10.0.101.6. And the internal interface on the gateway will be configured with the IP address 10.0.1.254.

Now let's assume that the ISP provides you with the following information for your Ethernet handoff:

IP address: 205.186.181.97

Subnet mask: 255.255.255.255

Default gateway: 107.0.65.31

In this example, the gateway router would have the following entries in its routing table:

Entry	Destination Network IP	Subnet Mask	Gateway	Interface
1	10.0.1.0	255.255.255.0	10.0.1.254	Internal
2	205.186.181.97	255.255.255.255	205.186.181.97	External
3	107.0.65.31	255.255.255.255	107.0.65.31	External
4	0.0.0.0	0.0.0.0	107.0.65.31	External

First, let's have a look at each of the columns in the routing table:

>> **Entry:** The entry number.

>> **Destination network IP:** This is the IP address of the destination network. This column is used in conjunction with the subnet mask column to determine the network to which that packet's destination IP address belongs.

>> **Subnet mask:** The subnet mask that is applied to the destination IP address to determine the destination network.

>> **Gateway:** The address of the router that the packet should be forwarded to.

>> **Interface:** The interface that the packet should be forwarded through. Here, *internal* means the interface to which the internal private network is connected and *external* means the interface on which the ISP's handoff is connected. (In many gateway devices, these interfaces are labeled LAN and WAN, respectively.)

Now let's have a look at the four entries in this routing table:

>> **Entry 1:** This entry tells the router what to do with packets whose destination is on the internal network (10.0.1.x). The IP address of the internal network is 10.0.1.0 and the subnet mask is 255.255.255.0. These packets will be sent to the internal interface, whose IP address is 10.0.1.254.

>> **Entry 2:** This entry handles packets whose destination is the ISP's gateway (107.0.65.31). The 255.255.255.255 subnet mask means that the destination is a specific IP address, not a network. These packets are forwarded to the ISP's gateway on the external interface.

>> **Entry 3:** This entry handles packets whose destination is the gateway's external interface, which has been assigned the IP address 205.186.181.97 by the ISP. These packets are forwarded to the gateway address on the external interface.

>> **Entry 4:** This entry handles everything else. The network IP address 0.0.0.0 with no subnet mask means that all packets that aren't caught by any of the other rules are forwarded out to the ISP's gateway router (107.0.65.31) on the external interface.

The entries in the routing table are evaluated against each packet's destination IP address to determine where the packet should be sent. The entries are evaluated in order, and the first one that matches is used to send the packet along its way.

For example, suppose a packet is received on the external interface and the destination address is 10.0.1.5. The router will first consider entry 1, applying the subnet mask 255.255.255.0 to consider the 10.0.1.0. Because this matches the network ID in entry 1, the packet will be forwarded over the internal interface, where the switch can hand the packet off to the correct computer.

On the other hand, suppose a packet is received on the internal interface and the destination IP address is 108.211.23.42. When the router tries the first entry, the subnet mask extracts the network address 108.211.23.42. This doesn't match 10.0.1.0, so the router considers the second entry. The subnet mask 255.255.255.255 tells the router to compare the entire destination address with the IP address 107.0.65.31. Because that address doesn't match, the router tries the third entry.

Again, the subnet mask 255.255.255.255 tells the router to compare the entire destination address, this time with the IP address 205.186.181.97. Again, the addresses don't match, so the router moves to the fourth and final entry in the router table. The subnet mask 0.0.0.0 reduces the entire destination address to 0.0.0.0, which matches the destination network 0.0.0.0. Therefore, the router forwards the packet on to the ISP's router at 107.0.65.31 via the external interface.

It sounds pretty simple, but in reality there is a lot more going on under the hood. In more complicated networks, there are a lot more than just four entries in the routing table. And in a busy network, a router is likely handling hundreds or even thousands of packets per second. For example, if you have 100 users on your network, all of them browsing the web, accessing email, and using other applications that cross the router, the router has an enormous workload.

Chapter **5**

DHCP

E very host on a Transmission Control Protocol/Internet Protocol (TCP/IP) network must have a unique IP address. Each host must be properly configured so that it knows its IP address. When a new host comes online, it must be assigned an IP address that's within the correct range of addresses for the subnet but not already in use. Although you can manually assign IP addresses to each computer on your network, that task quickly becomes overwhelming if the network has more than a few computers.

That's where DHCP — Dynamic Host Configuration Protocol — comes into play. *DHCP* automatically configures the IP address for every host on a network, thus assuring that each host has a valid, unique IP address. DHCP even automatically reconfigures IP addresses as hosts come and go. As you can imagine, DHCP can save a network administrator many hours of tedious configuration work.

In this chapter, you discover the ins and outs of DHCP: what it is, how it works, and how to set it up.

Understanding DHCP

DHCP allows individual computers on a TCP/IP network to obtain their configuration information — in particular, their IP address — from a server. The DHCP server keeps track of which IP addresses are already assigned so that when a computer requests an IP address, the DHCP server offers it an IP address that's not already in use.

Configuration information provided by DHCP

Although the primary job of DHCP is to dole out IP addresses and subnet masks, DHCP actually provides more configuration information than just the IP address to its clients. The additional configuration information consists of DHCP options. The following is a list of some common DHCP options that can be configured by the server:

» The router address, also known as the Default Gateway address

» The expiration time for the configuration information

» Domain name

» Domain Name Server (DNS) server address

» Windows Internet Name Service (WINS) server address

DHCP servers

A DHCP server can be a server computer located on the TCP/IP network. All modern server operating systems have a built-in DHCP server. To set up DHCP on a network server, all you have to do is enable the server's DHCP function and configure its settings. In the upcoming section, "Working with a DHCP Server," I show you how to configure a DHCP server for Windows Server 2016. (The procedure for Windows Server 2012 and 2008 is similar.)

A server computer running DHCP doesn't have to be devoted entirely to DHCP unless the network is very large. For most networks, a file server can share duty as a DHCP server. This is especially true if you provide long leases for your IP addresses. (*Lease* is the term used by DHCP to indicate that an IP address has been temporarily given out to a particular computer or other device.)

Many multifunction routers also have built-in DHCP servers. If you don't want to burden one of your network servers with the DHCP function, you can enable the router's built-in DHCP server. An advantage of allowing the router to be your network's DHCP server is that you rarely need to power-down a router. In contrast, you occasionally need to restart or power-down a file server to perform system maintenance, apply upgrades, or perform troubleshooting.

TIP

Most networks require only one DHCP server. Setting up two or more servers on the same network requires that you carefully coordinate the IP address ranges (known as *scopes*) for which each server is responsible. If you accidentally set up two DHCP servers for the same scope, you may end up with duplicate address assignments if the servers attempt to assign the same IP address to two different hosts. To prevent this from happening, just set up one DHCP server unless your network is so large that one server can't handle the workload.

How DHCP actually works

You can configure and use DHCP without knowing the details of how DHCP client configuration actually works. However, a basic understanding of the process can help you to understand what DHCP is actually doing. Not only is this understanding enlightening, but it can also help when you're troubleshooting DHCP problems.

The following paragraphs contain a blow-by-blow account of how DHCP configures TCP/IP hosts. This procedure happens every time you boot up a host computer. It also happens when you release an IP lease and request a fresh lease.

1. **When a host computer starts up, the DHCP client software sends a special broadcast packet, known as a *DHCP Discover message*.**

   This message uses the subnet's broadcast address (all host ID bits set to one) as the destination address and 0.0.0.0 as the source address.

TIP

   The client has to specify 0.0.0.0 as the source address because it doesn't yet have an IP address, and it specifies the broadcast address as the destination address because it doesn't know the address of any DHCP servers. In effect, the DHCP Discover message is saying, "Hey! I'm new here. Are there any DHCP servers out there?"

2. **The DHCP server receives the broadcast DHCP Discover message and responds by sending a *DHCP Offer* message.**

   The DHCP Offer message includes an IP address that the client can use.

   Like the DHCP Discover message, the DHCP Offer message is sent to the broadcast address. This makes sense because the client to which the message is being sent doesn't yet have an IP address and won't have one until it accepts the offer. In effect, the DHCP Offer message is saying, "Hello there, whoever you are. Here's an IP address you can use, if you want it. Let me know."

   What if the client never receives a DHCP Offer message from a DHCP server? In that case, the client waits for a few seconds and tries again. The client will try four times — at 2, 4, 8, and 16 seconds. If it still doesn't get an offer, it will try again after five minutes.

3. **The client receives the DHCP Offer message and sends back a message known as a *DHCP Request message*.**

    At this point, the client doesn't actually own the IP address: It's simply indicating that it's ready to accept the IP address that was offered by the server. In effect, the DHCP Request message says, "Yes, that IP address would be good for me. Can I have it, please?"

4. **When the server receives the DHCP Request message, it marks the IP address as assigned to the client and broadcasts a *DHCP Ack message*.**

    The DHCP Ack message says, in effect, "Okay, it's all yours. Here's the rest of the information you need to use it."

5. **When the client receives the DHCP Ack message, it configures its TCP/IP stack by using the address it accepted from the server.**

Understanding Scopes

A *scope* is simply a range of IP addresses that a DHCP server is configured to distribute. In the simplest case, where a single DHCP server oversees IP configuration for an entire subnet, the scope corresponds to the subnet. However, if you set up two DHCP servers for a subnet, you can configure each with a scope that allocates only one part of the complete subnet range. In addition, a single DHCP server can serve more than one scope.

You must create a scope before you can enable a DHCP server. When you create a scope, you can provide it with the following properties:

>> A **scope name,** which helps you to identify the scope and its purpose

>> A **scope description,** which lets you provide additional details about the scope and its purpose

>> A **starting IP address** for the scope

>> An **ending IP address** for the scope

>> A **subnet mask** for the scope

   You can specify the subnet mask with dotted-decimal notation or with network prefix notation.

>> **One or more ranges of excluded addresses**

   These addresses won't be assigned to clients. For more information, see the section "Feeling excluded?" later in this chapter.

» **One or more reserved addresses**

These are addresses that will always be assigned to particular host devices. For more information, see the section "Reservations suggested" later in this chapter.

» The **lease duration,** which indicates how long the host will be allowed to use the IP address

The client will attempt to renew the lease when half of the lease duration has elapsed. For example, if you specify a lease duration of eight days, the client will attempt to renew the lease after four days. This allows the host plenty of time to renew the lease before the address is reassigned to some other host.

» The **router address** for the subnet

This value is also known as the Default Gateway address.

» The **domain name** and the **IP address** of the network's DNS servers and WINS servers

TIP

Feeling excluded?

Everyone feels excluded once in awhile. With a wife, three daughters, and a female dog, I know how it feels. Sometimes, however, being excluded is a good thing. In the case of DHCP scopes, exclusions can help you to prevent IP address conflicts and can enable you to divide the DHCP workload for a single subnet among two or more DHCP servers.

An *exclusion* is a range of addresses that are not included in a scope. The exclusion range falls within the range of the scope's starting and ending addresses. In effect, an exclusion range lets you punch a hole in a scope. The IP addresses that fall within the hole won't be assigned.

Here are a few reasons for excluding IP addresses from a scope:

» **The computer that runs the DHCP service itself must usually have a static IP address assignment.** As a result, the address of the DHCP server should be listed as an exclusion.

» **Some hosts, such as a server or a printer, may need to have a predictable IP address.** In that case, the host will require a static IP address. By excluding its IP address from the scope, you can prevent that address from being assigned to any other host on the network.

Reservations suggested

In some cases, you may want to assign a particular IP address to a particular host. One way to do this is to configure the host with a static IP address so that the host doesn't use DHCP to obtain its IP configuration. However, here are two major disadvantages to that approach:

>> **TCP/IP configuration supplies more than just the IP address.** If you use static configuration, you must manually specify the subnet mask, the Default Gateway address, the DNS server address, and other configuration information required by the host. If this information changes, you have to change it not only at the DHCP server, but also at each host that you configured statically.

>> **You must remember to exclude the static IP address from the DHCP server's scope.** Otherwise, the DHCP server won't know about the static address and may assign it to another host. Then, you'll have two hosts with the same address on your network.

A better way to assign a fixed IP address to a particular host is to create a DHCP reservation. A *reservation* simply indicates that whenever a particular host requests an IP address from the DHCP server, the server should provide it the address that you specify in the reservation. The host won't receive the IP address until the host requests it from the DHCP server, but whenever the host does request IP configuration, it will always receive the same address.

WHAT ABOUT BootP?

BootP — Bootstrap Protocol — is an Internet protocol that enables diskless workstations to boot themselves over the Internet or local network. Like DHCP, BootP allows a computer to receive an IP address assigned from a server. However, unlike DHCP, BootP also enables the computer to download a *boot image file,* which the computer can then use to boot itself from. A significant difference between BootP and DHCP is that BootP comes into play before the computer actually loads an operating system. In contrast, DHCP is used after an operating system has been loaded, during the configuration of network devices.

Most DHCP servers can also support BootP. If your network has diskless workstations, you can use the DHCP server's BootP support to boot those computers. At one time, diskless workstations were all the rage because network administrators thought they'd be easier to manage. Users hated them, however. Most diskless workstations have now been buried in landfills, and BootP isn't used much.

TIP

To create a reservation, you associate the IP address that you want assigned to the host with the host's Media Access Control (MAC) address. As a result, you need to get the MAC address from the host before you create the reservation. You can get the MAC address by running the command `ipconfig /all` from a command prompt.

REMEMBER

If you set up more than one DHCP server, each should be configured to serve a different range of IP addresses. Otherwise, the servers might assign the same address to two different hosts.

How long to lease?

One of the most important decisions that you'll make when you configure a DHCP server is the length of time to specify for the lease duration. The default value is eight days, which is appropriate in many cases. However, you may encounter situations in which a longer or shorter interval may be appropriate:

>> **The more stable your network,** the longer the lease duration can safely exist. If you only periodically add new computers to the network or replace existing computers, you can safely increase the lease duration past eight days.

>> **The more volatile the network,** the shorter the lease duration should be. For example, a wireless network in a university library is used by students who bring their laptop computers into the library to work for a few hours at a time. For this network, a duration such as one hour may be appropriate.

WARNING

Don't configure your network to allow infinite duration leases. Some administrators feel that this cuts down the workload for the DHCP server on stable networks. However, no network is permanently stable. Whenever you find a DHCP server that's configured with infinite leases, look at the active leases. I guarantee you'll find IP leases assigned to computers that no longer exist.

Working with a DHCP Server

Usually, the best way to understand abstract concepts is to see how they work in the real world. To that end, the next few sections show you a brief overview of how DHCP is managed in a Windows network. First, you see how a DHCP server is installed in Windows Server 2016. Then you see how a DHCP server is configured.

Installing a Windows Server 2016 DHCP server

To install the DHCP server role on Windows Server 2016, follow these steps:

1. **Click Server Manager in the taskbar.**

   The Server Manager application appears.

2. **Click Manage Roles & Features.**

   The Before You Begin page of the Add Roles and Features Wizard appears.

3. **Click Next.**

   The Installation Type page appears.

4. **Choose Role-Based or Feature-Based Installation and then click Next.**

   The wizard displays a list of available servers.

5. **Select the server on which you want to install the DHCP role on; then click Next.**

   The wizard displays a list of available server roles.

6. **Select DHCP Server from the list of roles and then click Next.**

   The wizard displays a list of required features that must also be installed to support DHCP.

7. **Click Add Features, and then click Next.**

   The wizard displays a page describing what the DHCP role entails.

8. **Click Next.**

   The wizard displays a list of available server features; the features required to support the DHCP role are already selected.

9. **Click Next.**

   The wizard displays a summary of what the DHCP role does.

10. **Click Next.**

    The wizard displays a confirmation page.

11. **Click Install.**

    The wizard installs the DHCP role, which may take a few minutes. When the installation completes, a results page is displayed to summarize the results of the installation.

12. **Click Close.**

    You're done!

Configuring a new scope

After you install the DHCP role on Windows Server 2016, you'll need to create at least one scope so the server can start handing out IP addresses. Here are the steps:

1. **In Server Manager, choose Tools⇨Serve**

This brings up the DHCP management console, shown in Figure 5-1.

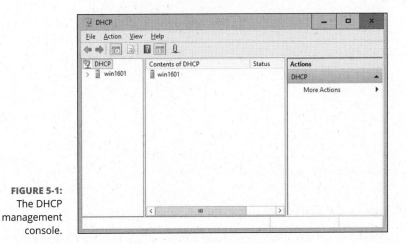

FIGURE 5-1:
The DHCP management console.

2. **Select the DHCP server you want to define the scope for, click IPv4, and then click the New Scope button on the toolbar.**

This brings up the New Scope Wizard dialog box, as shown in Figure 5-2.

FIGURE 5-2:
The New Scope Wizard comes to life.

3. Click Next.

You're prompted for the name of the scope, as shown in Figure 5-3.

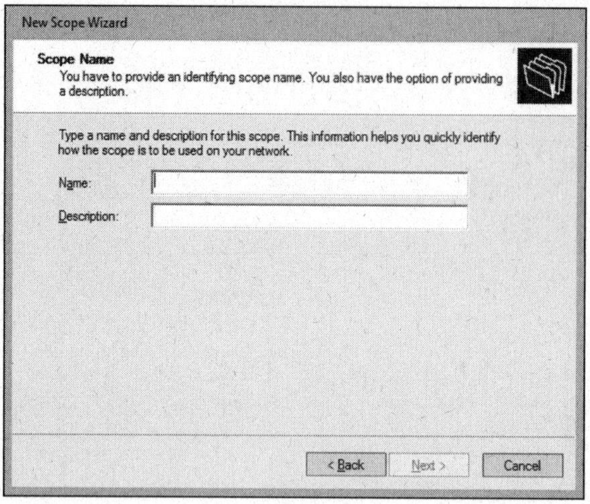

FIGURE 5-3: The wizard asks for a name for the new scope.

4. Enter a name and optional description, and then click Next.

The wizard asks for information required to create the scope, as shown in Figure 5-4.

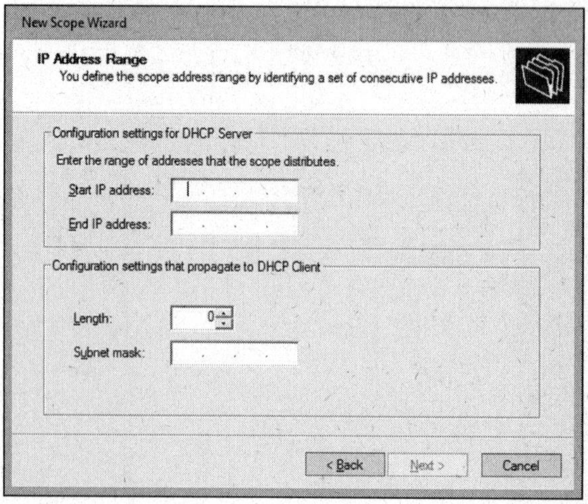

FIGURE 5-4: The wizard asks for scope information.

5. Enter the information for the new scope.

You must enter the following information:

- *Start IP Address:* This is the lowest IP address that will be issued for this scope.

- *End IP Address:* This is the highest IP address that will be issued for this scope.

- *Subnet Mask:* This is the subnet mask issued for IP addresses in this scope.

6. Click Next.

The wizard asks whether you want to exclude any ranges from the scope range, as shown in Figure 5-5.

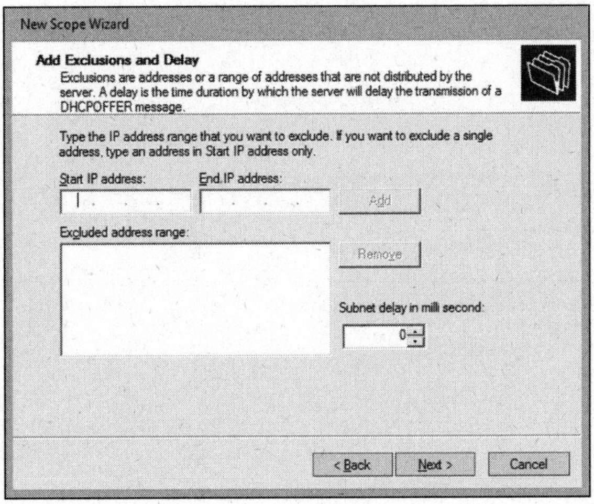

FIGURE 5-5:
Do you want
to create
exclusions?

7. (Optional) To create an exclusion, enter the IP address range to exclude and then click Add.

You can repeat this step as many times as necessary to add any excluded addresses.

8. Click Next.

The wizard asks for the lease duration, as shown in Figure 5-6.

9. (Optional) Change the lease duration; then click Next.

When the wizard asks whether you want to configure additional DHCP options, leave this option set to Yes to complete your DHCP configuration now.

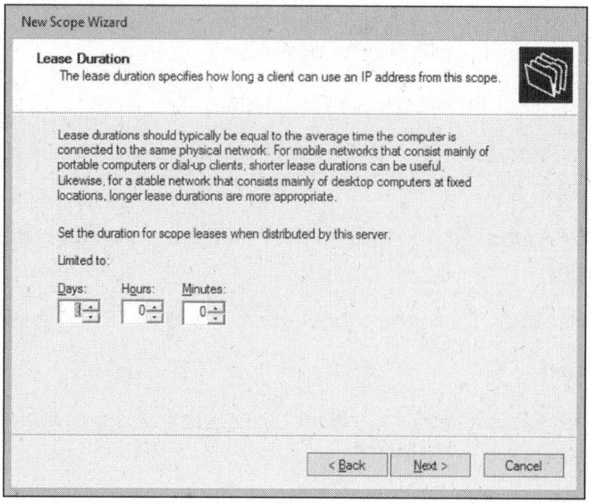

FIGURE 5-6:
Set the lease
duration.

10. **Click Next.**

The wizard asks for the default gateway information, as shown in Figure 5-7.

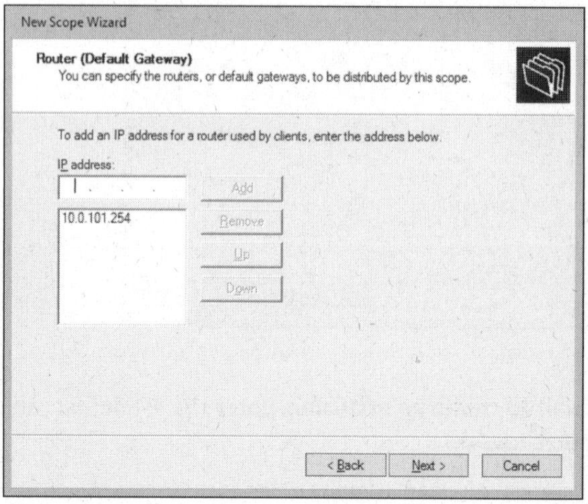

FIGURE 5-7:
Provide the
Default Gateway
address.

11. **Enter the address of your network's router and click Add; then click Next.**

The wizard now asks for additional DNS information, as shown in Figure 5-8.

12. **(Optional) If you want to add a DNS server, enter its address and then click Add.**

Repeat this step as many times as necessary to add any additional DNS servers.

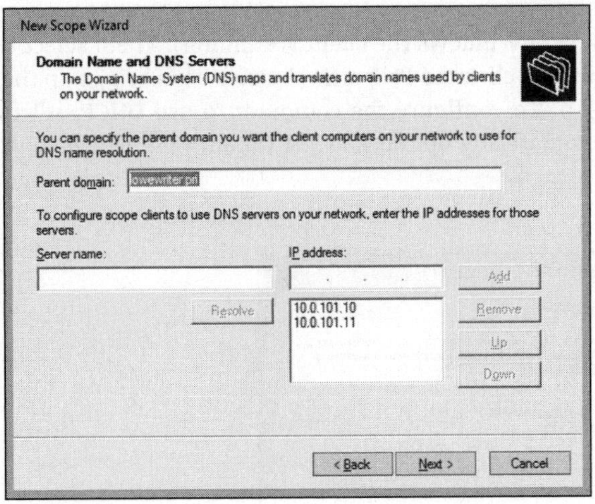

FIGURE 5-8:
Provide
additional DNS
information.

13. Click Next.

The wizard next asks for WINS configuration information.

14. (Optional) If you want to enable WINS, enter the WINS server configuration.

WINS isn't required for most modern networks, so you can usually just leave this page blank.

15. Click Next.

The wizard now asks whether you want to activate the scope.

16. Select Yes, I Want to Activate This Scope and then click Next.

A final confirmation page is displayed.

17. Click Finish.

The scope is created.

How to Configure a Windows DHCP Client

Configuring a Windows client for DHCP is easy. The DHCP client is automatically included when you install the TCP/IP protocol, so all you have to do is configure TCP/IP to use DHCP. And in nearly all cases, DHCP is configured automatically when you install Windows.

If you must configure DHCP manually, bring up the Network Properties dialog box by choosing Network or Network Connections from Control Panel (depending on which version of Windows the client is running). Then, select the Internet Protocol Version 4 and click the Properties button. This brings up the dialog box shown in Figure 5-9. To configure the computer to use DHCP, select the Obtain an IP Address Automatically option and the Obtain DNS Server Address Automatically option.

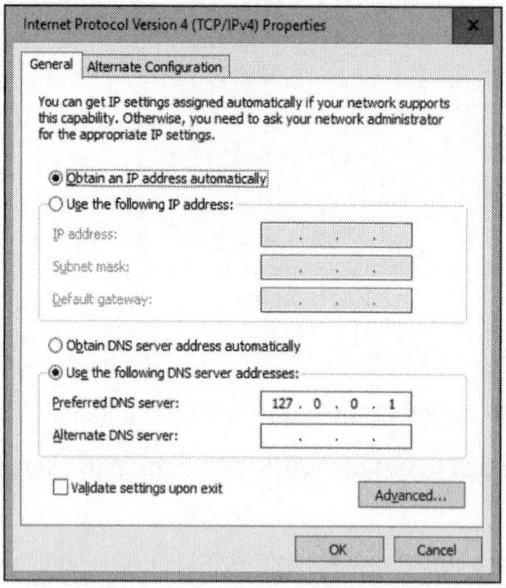

FIGURE 5-9:
Configuring a
Windows client to
use DHCP.

Automatic private IP addressing

If a Windows computer is configured to use DHCP but the computer can't obtain an IP address from a DHCP server, the computer automatically assigns itself a private address by using a feature called Automatic Private IP Addressing (APIPA). APIPA assigns a private address from the 169.254.x.x range and uses a special algorithm to ensure that the address is unique on the network. As soon as the DHCP server becomes available, the computer requests a new address, so the APIPA address is used only while the DHCP server is unavailable.

Renewing and releasing leases

Normally, a DHCP client attempts to renew its lease when the lease is halfway to the point of being expired. For example, if a client obtains an eight-day lease, it attempts to renew the lease after four days. However, you can renew a lease sooner by issuing the ipconfig /renew command at a command prompt. You may want to do this if you changed the scope's configuration or if the client's IP configuration isn't working correctly.

You can also release a DHCP lease by issuing the `ipconfig /release` command at a command prompt. When you release a lease, the client computer no longer has a valid IP address. This is shown in the output from the `ipconfig /release` command:

```
C:\>ipconfig /release
Windows IP Configuration
Ethernet adapter Local Area Connection:
Connection-specific DNS Suffix . :
IP Address... ... ... ... : 0.0.0.0
Subnet Mask ... ... ... . . : 0.0.0.0
Default Gateway ... ... ... :
```

Here, you can see that the IP address and subnet masks are set to `0.0.0.0` and that the Default Gateway address is blank. When you release an IP lease, you can't communicate with the network by using TCP/IP until you issue an `ipconfig /renew` command to renew the IP configuration or restart the computer.

Chapter **6**

DNS

Domain Name Server — DNS — is the TCP/IP facility that lets you use names rather than numbers to refer to host computers. Without DNS, you'd buy books from 176.32.103.205 instead of from www.amazon.com, you'd sell your used furniture at 66.135.216.190 instead of on www.ebay.com, and you'd search the web at 173.194.43.64 instead of at www.google.com.

Understanding how DNS works and how to set up a DNS server is crucial to setting up and administering a Transmission Control Protocol/Internet Protocol (TCP/IP) network. (For more on that, see Chapter 1 of this minibook.) This chapter introduces you to the basics of DNS, including how the DNS naming system works and how to set up a DNS server.

TECHNICAL STUFF

If you want to review the complete official specifications for DNS, look up RFC 1034 and 1035 at www.ietf.org/rfc/rfc1034.txt and www.ietf.org/rfc/rfc1035.txt, respectively.

Understanding DNS Names

DNS is a name service that provides a standardized system for providing names to identify TCP/IP hosts as well as a way to look up the IP address of a host, given the host's DNS name. For example, if you use DNS to look up the name www.ebay.com, you get the IP address of the eBay web host: 66.135.216.190. Thus, DNS allows you to access the eBay website by using the DNS name `www.ebay.com` instead of the site's IP address.

The following sections describe the basic concepts of DNS.

Domains and domain names

To provide a unique DNS name for every host computer on the Internet, DNS uses a time-tested technique: Divide and conquer. DNS uses a hierarchical naming system that's similar to how folders are organized hierarchically on a Windows computer. Instead of folders, however, DNS organizes its names into domains. Each domain includes all the names that appear directly beneath it in the DNS hierarchy.

For example, Figure 6-1 shows a small portion of the DNS domain tree. At the very top of the tree is the *root domain,* which is the anchor point for all domains. Directly beneath the root domain are four top-level domains, named `edu`, `com`, `org`, and `gov`.

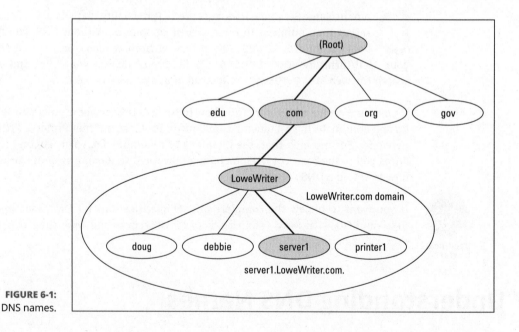

FIGURE 6-1:
DNS names.

In reality, many more top-level domains than this exist in the Internet's root domain. For more information, see the section "Top-Level Domains," later in this chapter.

Beneath the `com` domain in Figure 6-1 is another domain called `LoweWriter`, which happens to be my own personal domain. (Pretty clever, eh?) To completely identify this domain, you have to combine it with the name of its *parent domain* (in this case, `com`) to create the complete domain name: `LoweWriter.com`. Notice that the parts of the domain name are separated from each other with periods, which are called dots. As a result, when you read this domain name, you pronounce it *LoweWriter dot com*.

Beneath the `LoweWriter` node are four host nodes, named `doug`, `debbie`, `server1`, and `printer1`. Respectively, these correspond to three computers and a printer on my home network. You can combine the host name with the domain name to get the complete DNS name for each of my network's hosts. For example, the complete DNS name for my server is `server1.LoweWriter.com`. Likewise, my printer is `printer1.LoweWriter.com`.

Here are a few additional details that you need to remember about DNS names:

» **DNS names are not case sensitive.** As a result, `LoweWriter` and `Lowewriter` are treated as the same name, as are `LOWEWRITER`, `LOWEwriter`, and `LoWeWrItEr`. When you use a domain name, you can use capitalization to make the name easier to read, but DNS ignores the difference between capital and lowercase letters.

» **The name of each DNS node can be up to 63 characters long (not including the dot) and can include letters, numbers, and hyphens.**

WARNING

No other special characters are allowed.

» **A *subdomain* is a domain that's beneath an existing domain.** For example, the `com` domain is actually a subdomain of the root domain. Likewise, `LoweWriter` is a subdomain of the `com` domain.

» **DNS is a hierarchical naming system that's similar to the hierarchical folder system used by Windows.**

TIP

However, one crucial difference exists between DNS and the Windows naming convention. When you construct a complete DNS name, you start at the bottom of the tree and work your way up to the root. Thus, `doug` is the lowest node in the name `doug.LoweWriter.com`. In contrast, Windows paths are the opposite: They start at the root and work their way down. For example, in the path `\Windows\System32\dns`, `dns` is the lowest node.

» **The DNS tree can be up to 127 levels deep.** However, in practice, the DNS tree is pretty shallow. Most DNS names have just three levels (not counting the root). And although you'll sometimes see names with four or five levels, you'll rarely see more levels than that.

>> **Although the DNS tree is shallow, it's very broad.** In other words, each of the top-level domains has a huge number of second-level domains immediately beneath it. For example, at the time of this writing, the com domain had well over 100 million second-level domains beneath it.

Fully qualified domain names

If a domain name ends with a trailing dot, that trailing dot represents the root domain, and the domain name is said to be a *fully qualified domain name* (also known as an FQDN). A fully qualified domain name is also called an *absolute name*. A fully qualified domain name is unambiguous because it identifies itself all the way back to the root domain. In contrast, if a domain name doesn't end with a trailing dot, the name may be interpreted in the context of some other domain. Thus, DNS names that don't end with a trailing dot are called *relative names*.

This is similar to how relative and absolute paths work in Windows. For example, if a path begins with a backslash, such as \Windows\System32\dns, the path is absolute. However, a path that doesn't begin with a backslash, such as System32\dns, uses the current directory as its starting point. If the current directory happens to be \Windows, then \Windows\System32\dns and System32\dns refer to the same location.

In many cases, relative and fully qualified domain names are interchangeable because the software that interprets them always interprets relative names in the context of the root domain. That's why, for example, you can type www.wiley.com (without the trailing dot) — not www.wiley.com. — to go to the Wiley home page in a web browser. Some applications, such as DNS servers, may interpret relative names in the context of a domain other than the root.

Top-Level Domains

A *top-level domain* appears immediately beneath the root domain. Top-level domains come in two categories: generic domains and geographic domains. These categories are described in the following sections. (Actually, a third type of top-level domain exists, which is used for reverse lookups. I describe it later in this chapter, in the section "Reverse Lookup Zones.")

Generic domains

Generic domains are the popular top-level domains that you see most often on the Internet. Originally, seven top-level organizational domains existed. In 2002, seven more were added to help ease the congestion of the original seven — in particular, the com domain.

Table 6-1 summarizes the original seven generic top-level domains. Of these, you can see that the com domain is far and away the most populated, with nearly 119 million second-level domains beneath it.

TABLE 6-1

The Original Seven Top-Level Domains

Domain	Description	Size
com	Commercial organizations	130,992,926
edu	Educational institutions	7,488
gov	Government institutions	5,659
int	International treaty organizations	200
mil	Military institutions	1,606
net	Network providers	14,919,762
org	Noncommercial organizations	10,432,712

TIP

The Size column in this table indicates approximately how many second-level domains existed under each top-level domain as of January 2018, according to www.domaintools.com.

Because the com domain ballooned to an almost unmanageable size in the late 1990s, the Internet authorities approved seven new top-level domains in an effort to take some of the heat off of the com domain. Most of these domains, listed in Table 6-2, became available in 2002. As you can see, they haven't really caught on yet even though they've been around for several years.

Geographic domains

Although the top-level domains are open to anyone, U.S. companies and organizations dominate them. An additional set of top-level domains corresponds to international country designations. Organizations outside the United States often use these top-level domains to avoid the congestion of the generic domains.

TABLE 6-2

The New Seven Top-Level Domains

Domain	Description	Size
aero	Aerospace industry	34,461
biz	Business	2,106,466
coop	Cooperatives	7,670
info	Informational sites	6.156,488
museum	Museums	1,204
name	Individual users	147,207
pro	Professional organizations	274,565

Table 6-3 lists those geographic top-level domains with more than 200 registered subdomains at the time of this writing, in alphabetical order. In all, about 150 geographic top-level domains exist. The exact number varies from time to time as political circumstances change.

TABLE 6-3

Geographic Top-Level Domains with More Than 200 Subdomains

Domain	Description	Domain	Description
ac	Ascension Island	ie	Ireland
ae	United Arab Emirates	in	India
ag	Antigua and Barbuda	is	Iceland
am	Armenia	it	Italy
an	Netherlands Antilles	jp	Japan
as	American Samoa	kz	Kazakhstan
at	Austria	la	Lao People's Democratic Republic
be	Belgium	li	Liechtenstein
bg	Bulgaria	lk	Sri Lanka
br	Brazil	lt	Lithuania
by	Belarus	lu	Luxembourg
bz	Belize	lv	Latvia
ca	Canada	ma	Morocco

Domain	Description	Domain	Description
cc	Cocos (Keeling) Islands	md	Moldova
ch	Switzerland	nl	Netherlands
cl	Chile	no	Norway
cn	China	nu	Niue
cx	Christmas Island	pl	Poland
cz	Czech Republic	pt	Portugal
de	Germany	ro	Romania
dk	Denmark	ru	Russian Federation
ee	Estonia	se	Sweden
es	Spain	si	Slovenia
eu	European Union	sk	Slovakia
fi	Finland	st	São Tomé and Principe
fm	Micronesia	su	Soviet Union
fo	Faroe Islands	to	Tonga
fr	France	tv	Tuvalu
ge	Georgia	tw	Taiwan
gr	Greece	ua	Ukraine
hr	Croatia	us	United States
hu	Hungary	ws	Samoa

The Hosts File

Long ago, in a network far, far away, the entire Internet was small enough that network administrators could keep track of it all in a simple text file. This file, called the *Hosts file*, simply listed the name and IP address of every host on the network. Each computer had its own copy of the Hosts file. The trick was keeping all those Hosts files up to date. Whenever a new host was added to the Internet, each network administrator would manually update his copy of the Hosts file to add the new host's name and IP address.

As the Internet grew, so did the Hosts file. In the mid-1980s, it became obvious that a better solution was needed. Imagine trying to track the entire Internet today by using a single text file to record the name and IP address of the millions of hosts on the Internet! DNS was invented to solve this problem.

Understanding the Hosts file is important for two reasons:

» **The Hosts file is not dead.** For small networks, a Hosts file may still be the easiest way to provide name resolution for the network's computers. In addition, a Hosts file can coexist with DNS. The Hosts file is always checked before DNS is used, so you can even use a Hosts file to override DNS if you want.

» **The Hosts file is the precursor to DNS.** DNS was devised to circumvent the limitations of the Hosts file. You'll be in a better position to appreciate the benefits of DNS when you understand how the Hosts file works.

The Hosts file is a simple text file that contains lines that match IP addresses with host names. You can edit the Hosts file with any text editor, including Notepad. The exact location of the Hosts file depends on the client operating system, as listed in Table 6-4.

TABLE 6-4

Location of the Hosts File

Operating System	Location of Hosts File
Windows	c:\windows\system32\drivers\etc
Unix/Linux	/etc/hosts

All TCP/IP implementations are installed with a starter Hosts file. For example, Listing 6-1 shows a typical Windows TCP/IP Hosts file. As you can see, the starter file begins with some comments that explain the purpose of the file.

The Hosts file ends with comments, which show the host mapping commands used to map for the host name localhost, mapped to the IP address 127.0.0.1. The IP address 127.0.0.1 is the standard loopback address. As a result, this entry allows a computer to refer to itself by using the name localhost.

Note that after the 127.0.0.1 localhost entry, another localhost entry defines the standard IPv6 loopback address (::1). This is required because all versions of Windows since Vista provide built-in support for IPv6.

Prior to Windows 7, these lines were not commented out in the Hosts file. But beginning with Windows 7, the name resolution for localhost is handled by DNS itself, so its definition isn't required in the Hosts file.

LISTING 6-1: **A Sample Hosts File**

```
# Copyright (c) 1993-2009 Microsoft Corp.
#
# This is a sample HOSTS file used by Microsoft TCP/IP for Windows.
#
# This file contains the mappings of IP addresses to host names. Each
# entry should be kept on an individual line. The IP address should
# be placed in the first column followed by the corresponding host name.
# The IP address and the host name should be separated by at least one
# space.
#
# Additionally, comments (such as these) may be inserted on individual
# lines or following the machine name denoted by a '#' symbol.
#
# For example:
#
# 102.54.94.97 rhino.acme.com # source server
# 38.25.63.10 x.acme.com # x client host

# localhost name resolution is handled within DNS itself.
#127.0.0.1 localhost
#::1 localhost
```

To add an entry to the Hosts file, simply edit the file in any text editor. Then, add a line at the bottom of the file, after the localhost entry. Each line that you add should list the IP address and the host name that you want to use for the address. For example, to associate the host name server1.LoweWriter.com with the IP address 192.168.168.201, you add this line to the Hosts file:

```
192.168.168.201 server1.LoweWriter.com
```

Then, whenever an application requests the IP address of the host name server1.LoweWriter.com, the IP address 192.168.168.201 is returned.

You can also add an alias to a host mapping. This enables users to access a host by using the alias as an alternative name. For example, consider the following line:

```
192.168.168.201 server1.LoweWriter.com s1
```

Here, the device at address `192.168.168.201` can be accessed as `server1.LoweWriter.com` or just `s1`.

Listing 6-2 shows a Hosts file with several hosts defined.

LISTING 6-2: **A Hosts File with Several Hosts Defined**

```
# Copyright (c) 1993-2009 Microsoft Corp.
#
# This is a sample HOSTS file used by Microsoft TCP/IP for Windows.
#
# This file contains the mappings of IP addresses to host names. Each
# entry should be kept on an individual line. The IP address should
# be placed in the first column followed by the corresponding host name.
# The IP address and the host name should be separated by at least one
# space.
#
# Additionally, comments (such as these) may be inserted on individual
# lines or following the machine name denoted by a '#' symbol.
#
# For example:
#
# 102.54.94.97 rhino.acme.com # source server
# 38.25.63.10 x.acme.com # x client host
# localhost name resolution is handled within DNS itself.
# 127.0.0.1 localhost
# ::1 localhost
192.168.168.200 doug.LoweWriter.com #Doug's computer
192.168.168.201 server1.LoweWriter.com s1 #Main server
192.168.168.202 kristen.LoweWriter.com #Kristen's computer
192.168.168.203 printer1.LoweWriter.com p1 #HP Laser Printer
```

Even if your network uses DNS, every client still has a Hosts file that defines at least `localhost`.

Understanding DNS Servers and Zones

A *DNS server* is a computer that runs DNS server software, helps to maintain the DNS database, and responds to DNS name resolution requests from other computers. Although many DNS server implementations are available, the two most popular are

BIND and the Windows DNS service. BIND runs on Unix-based computers (including Linux computers), and Windows DNS (naturally) runs on Windows computers. Both provide essentially the same services and can interoperate.

The key to understanding how DNS servers work is to realize that the DNS database — that is, the list of all the domains, subdomains, and host mappings — is a massively distributed database. No single DNS server contains the entire DNS database. Instead, authority over different parts of the database is delegated to different servers throughout the Internet.

For example, suppose that I set up a DNS server to handle name resolutions for my LoweWriter.com domain. Then, when someone requests the IP address of doug.LoweWriter.com, my DNS server can provide the answer. However, my DNS server wouldn't be responsible for the rest of the Internet. Instead, if someone asks my DNS server for the IP address of some other computer, such as coyote.acme.com, my DNS server will have to pass the request on to another DNS server that knows the answer.

Zones

To simplify the management of the DNS database, the entire DNS namespace is divided into zones, and the responsibility for each zone is delegated to a particular DNS server. In many cases, zones correspond directly to domains. For example, if I set up a domain named LoweWriter.com, I can also set up a DNS zone called LoweWriter.com that's responsible for the entire LoweWriter.com domain.

However, the subdomains that make up a domain can be parceled out to separate zones, as shown in Figure 6-2. Here, a domain named LoweWriter.com has been divided into two zones. One zone, us.LoweWriter.com, is responsible for the entire us.LoweWriter.com subdomain. The other zone, LoweWriter.com, is responsible for the entire LoweWriter.com domain except for the us.LoweWriter.com subdomain.

Why would you do that? The main reason is to delegate authority for the zone to separate servers. For example, Figure 6-2 suggests that part of the LoweWriter.com domain is administered in the United States and that part of it is administered in France. The two zones in the figure allow one server to be completely responsible for the U.S. portion of the domain, and the other server handles the rest of the domain.

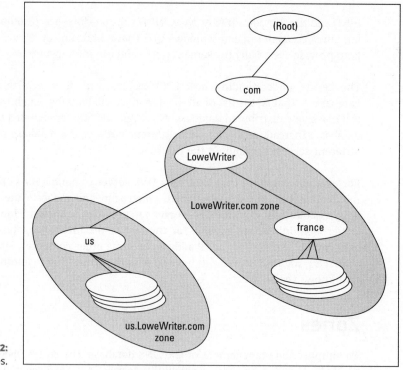

FIGURE 6-2:
DNS zones.

The following are the two basic types of zones:

>> A **primary zone** is the master copy of a zone. The data for a primary zone is stored in the local database of the DNS server that hosts the primary zone. Only one DNS server can host a particular primary zone. Any updates to the zone must be made to the primary zone.

>> A **secondary zone** is a read-only copy of a zone. When a server hosts a secondary zone, the server doesn't store a local copy of the zone data. Instead, it obtains its copy of the zone from the zone's primary server by using a process called *zone transfer*. Secondary servers must periodically check primary servers to see whether their secondary zone data is still current. If not, a zone transfer is initiated to update the secondary zone.

Primary and secondary servers

Each DNS server is responsible for one or more zones. The following are the two different roles that a DNS server can take:

THE OLD PHONY HOSTS FILE TRICK

The Hosts file can be the basis of a fun, practical joke. Of course, neither I nor my editors or publishers recommend that you actually do this. If it gets you into trouble, don't send your lawyers to me. This sidebar is here only to let you know what to do if it happens to you.

The idea is to edit your poor victim's Hosts file so that whenever the user tries to access his favorite website, a site of your choosing comes up instead. For example, if you're trying to get your husband to take you on a cruise, add a line to his Hosts file that replaces his favorite website with the website for a cruise line. For example, this line should do the trick:

```
23.10.137.106 www.espn.com
```

Now, whenever your husband tries to call up the ESPN website, he'll get the Carnival Cruise Lines home page instead. (To find out the IP address of the website you want displayed, open a command prompt and type **ping** followed by a space and the URL of the desired website. This will display the correct IP address.)

Of course, to actually pull a stunt like this would be completely irresponsible, especially if you didn't first make a backup copy of the Hosts file, just in case it somehow gets messed up.

Be warned: If the wrong websites suddenly start coming up, check your Hosts file to see whether it's been tampered with.

DNS

>> **Primary server for a zone,** which means that the DNS server hosts a primary zone. The data for the zone is stored in files on the DNS server. Every zone must have one primary server.

>> **Secondary server for a zone,** which means that the DNS server obtains the data for a secondary zone from a primary server. Every zone should have at least one secondary server. That way, if the primary server goes down, the domain defined by the zone can be accessed via the secondary server or servers.

WARNING

A secondary server should be on a different subnet than the zone's primary server. If the primary and secondary servers are on the same subnet, both servers will be unavailable if the router that controls the subnet goes down.

Note that a single DNS server can be the primary server for some zones and a secondary server for other zones. A server is said to be *authoritative* for the primary and secondary zones that it hosts because it can provide definitive answers for queries against those zones.

Root servers

The core of DNS comprises the *root servers*, which are authoritative for the entire Internet. The main function of the root servers is to provide the address of the DNS servers that are responsible for each of the top-level domains. These servers, in turn, can provide the DNS server address for subdomains beneath the top-level domains.

The root servers are a major part of the glue that holds the Internet together. As you can imagine, they're swamped with requests day and night. A total of 13 root servers are located throughout the world. Table 6-5 lists the IP address and the organization that oversees the operation of each of the 13 root servers.

TABLE 6-5

The 13 Root Servers

Server	IP Address	Operator
A	198.41.0.4	VeriSign Global Registry Services
B	192.228.79.201	Information Sciences Institute
C	192.33.4.12	Cogent Communications
D	128.8.10.90	University of Maryland
E	192.203.230.10	NASA Ames Research Center
F	192.5.5.241	Internet Systems Consortium
G	192.112.36.4	U.S. DOD Network Information
H	128.63.2.53	U.S. Army Research Lab
I	192.36.148.17	Netnod
J	192.58.128.30	Verisign, Inc.
K	193.0.14.129	RIPE NCC
L	199.7.83.42	ICANN
M	202.12.27.33	WIDE Project

DNS servers learn how to reach the root servers by consulting a *root hints* file that's located on the server. In the Unix/Linux world, this file is known as `named.root` and can be found at `/etc/named.root`. For Windows, the root hints are stored within Active Directory rather than as a separate file. Listing 6-3 shows a typical `named.root` file.

LISTING 6-3: **The `named.root` File**

```
; This file holds the information on root name servers needed to
; initialize cache of Internet domain name servers
; (e.g. reference this file in the "cache . <file>"
; configuration file of BIND domain name servers).
;
; This file is made available by InterNIC
; under anonymous FTP as
; file /domain/named.root
; on server FTP.INTERNIC.NET
; -OR- RS.INTERNIC.NET
;
; last update: Dec 12, 2008
; related version of root zone: 2008121200
;
; formerly NS.INTERNIC.NET
;
.                        3600000  IN  NS  A.ROOT-SERVERS.NET.
A.ROOT-SERVERS.NET.      3600000      A   198.41.0.4
A.ROOT-SERVERS.NET.      3600000      AAAA 2001:503:BA3E::2:30
;
; FORMERLY NS1.ISI.EDU
;
.                        3600000      NS  B.ROOT-SERVERS.NET.
B.ROOT-SERVERS.NET.      3600000      A   192.228.79.201
;
; FORMERLY C.PSI.NET
;
.                        3600000      NS  C.ROOT-SERVERS.NET.
C.ROOT-SERVERS.NET.      3600000      A   192.33.4.12
;
; FORMERLY TERP.UMD.EDU
;
.                        3600000      NS  D.ROOT-SERVERS.NET.
D.ROOT-SERVERS.NET.      3600000      A   128.8.10.90
;
; FORMERLY NS.NASA.GOV
;
.                        3600000      NS  E.ROOT-SERVERS.NET.
```

(continued)

LISTING 6-3: *(continued)*

```
E.ROOT-SERVERS.NET. 3600000 A 192.203.230.10
;
; FORMERLY NS.ISC.ORG
;
. 3600000 NS F.ROOT-SERVERS.NET.
F.ROOT-SERVERS.NET. 3600000 A 192.5.5.241
F.ROOT-SERVERS.NET. 3600000 AAAA 2001:500:2F::F
;
; FORMERLY NS.NIC.DDN.MIL
;
. 3600000 NS G.ROOT-SERVERS.NET.
G.ROOT-SERVERS.NET. 3600000 A 192.112.36.4
;
; FORMERLY AOS.ARL.ARMY.MIL
;
. 3600000 NS H.ROOT-SERVERS.NET.
H.ROOT-SERVERS.NET. 3600000 A 128.63.2.53
H.ROOT-SERVERS.NET. 3600000 AAAA 2001:500:1::803F:235
;
; FORMERLY NIC.NORDU.NET
;
. 3600000 NS I.ROOT-SERVERS.NET.
I.ROOT-SERVERS.NET. 3600000 A 192.36.148.17
;
; OPERATED BY VERISIGN, INC.
;
. 3600000 NS J.ROOT-SERVERS.NET.
J.ROOT-SERVERS.NET. 3600000 A 192.58.128.30
J.ROOT-SERVERS.NET. 3600000 AAAA 2001:503:C27::2:30
;
; OPERATED BY RIPE NCC
;
. 3600000 NS K.ROOT-SERVERS.NET.
K.ROOT-SERVERS.NET. 3600000 A 193.0.14.129
K.ROOT-SERVERS.NET. 3600000 AAAA 2001:7FD::1
;
; OPERATED BY ICANN
;
. 3600000 NS L.ROOT-SERVERS.NET.
L.ROOT-SERVERS.NET. 3600000 A 199.7.83.42
L.ROOT-SERVERS.NET. 3600000 AAAA 2001:500:3::42
;
; OPERATED BY WIDE
;
. 3600000 NS M.ROOT-SERVERS.NET.
M.ROOT-SERVERS.NET. 3600000 A 202.12.27.33
M.ROOT-SERVERS.NET. 3600000 AAAA 2001:DC3::35
; End of File
```

Caching

DNS servers don't really like doing all that work to resolve DNS names, but they're not stupid. They know that if a user visits www.wiley.com today, he'll probably do it again tomorrow. As a result, name servers keep a cache of query results. The next time the user visits www.wiley.com, the name server is able to resolve this name without having to query all those other name servers.

The Internet is constantly changing, however, so cached data can quickly become obsolete. For example, suppose that John Wiley & Sons, Inc., switches its website to a different server. It can update its name servers to reflect the new IP address, but any name servers that have a cached copy of the query will be out of date.

To prevent this from being a major problem, DNS data is given a relatively short expiration time. The expiration value for DNS data is called the *TTL* (Time to Live). TTL is specified in seconds. Thus, a TTL of 60 means the data is kept for one minute.

Understanding DNS Queries

When a DNS client needs to resolve a DNS name to an IP address, it uses a library routine — a *resolver* — to handle the query. The resolver takes care of sending the query message over the network to the DNS server, receiving and interpreting the response, and informing the client of the results of the query.

A DNS client can make two basic types of queries: recursive and iterative. The following list describes the difference between these two query types. (The following discussion assumes that the client is asking the server for the IP address of a host name, which is the most common type of DNS query. You find out about other types of queries later; they, too, can be either recursive or iterative.)

>> **Recursive queries:** When a client issues a *recursive DNS query,* the server must reply with either the IP address of the requested host name or an error message indicating that the host name doesn't exist. If the server doesn't have the information, it asks another DNS server for the IP address. When the first server finally gets the IP address, it sends it back to the client. If the server determines that the information doesn't exist, it returns an error message.

>> **Iterative queries:** When a server receives an iterative query, it returns the IP address of the requested host name if it knows the address. If the server doesn't know the address, it returns a *referral,* which is simply the address of a DNS server that should know. The client can then issue an iterative query to the server to which it was referred.

Normally, DNS clients issue recursive queries to DNS servers. If the server knows the answer to the query, it replies directly to the client. If not, the server issues an iterative query to a DNS server that it thinks should know the answer. If the original server gets an answer from the second server, it returns the answer to the client. If the original server gets a referral to a third server, the original server issues an iterative query to the third server. The original server keeps issuing iterative queries until it either gets the answer or an error occurs. It then returns the answer or the error to the client.

A real-life DNS example

Confused? I can understand why. An example may help to clear things up. Suppose that a user wants to view the web page www.wiley.com. The following sequence of steps occurs to resolve this address:

1. **The browser asks the client computer's resolver to find the IP address of www.wiley.com.**

2. **The resolver issues a recursive DNS query to its name server.**

   In this case, I'll call the name server ns1.LoweWriter.com.

3. **The name server ns1LoweWriter.com checks whether it knows the IP address of www.wiley.com.**

   It doesn't, so the name server issues an iterative query to one of the root name servers to see whether it knows the IP address of www.wiley.com.

4. **The root name server doesn't know the IP address of www.wiley.com, so it returns a list of the name servers that are authoritative for the com domain.**

5. **The ns1.LoweWriter.com name server picks one of the com domain name servers and sends it an iterative query for www.wiley.com.**

6. **The com name server doesn't know the IP address of www.wiley.com, so it returns a list of the name servers that are authoritative for the wiley.com domain.**

7. **The ns1.LoweWriter.com name server picks one of the name servers for the wiley.com domain and sends it an iterative query for www.wiley.com.**

8. **The wiley.com name server knows the IP address for www.wiley.com, so the name server returns it.**

9. The `ns1.LoweWriter.com` name server shouts with joy for having finally found the IP address for `www.wiley.com`. It gleefully returns this address to the client. It also caches the answer so that the next time the user looks for `www.wiley.com`, the name server won't have to contact other name servers to resolve the name.

10. The client also caches the results of the query.

   The next time the client needs to look for `www.wiley.com`, the client can resolve the name without troubling the name server.

Zone Files and Resource Records

Each DNS zone is defined by a *zone file* (also known as a *DNS database* or a *master file*). For Windows DNS servers, the name of the zone file is `domain.zone`. For example, the zone file for the `LoweWriter.com` zone is named `LoweWriter.com.zone`. For BIND DNS servers, the zone files are named `db.domain`. Thus, the zone file for the `LoweWriter.com` domain would be `db.LoweWriter.com`. The format of the zone file contents is the same for both systems, however.

A zone file consists of one or more resource records. Creating and updating the resource records that comprise the zone files is one of the primary tasks of a DNS administrator. The Windows DNS server provides a friendly graphical interface to the resource records. However, you should still be familiar with how to construct resource records.

Resource records are written as simple text lines, with the following fields:

```
Owner TTL Class Type RDATA
```

These fields must be separated from each other by one or more spaces. The following list describes the five resource record fields:

>> **Owner:** The name of the DNS domain or the host that the record applies to. This is usually specified as a fully qualified domain name (with a trailing dot) or as a simple host name (without a trailing dot), which is then interpreted in the context of the current domain.

   You can also specify a single @ symbol as the owner name. In that case, the current domain is used.

TIP

>> **TTL:** Also known as *Time to Live;* the number of seconds that the record should be retained in a server's cache before it's invalidated. If you omit the TTL value for a resource record, a default TTL is obtained from the Start of Authority (SOA) record.

» **Class:** Defines the protocol to which the record applies. You should always specify IN, for the Internet protocol. If you omit the class field, the last class field that you specified explicitly is used. As a result, you'll sometimes see zone files that specify IN only on the first resource record (which must be an SOA record) and then allow it to default to IN on all subsequent records.

» **Type:** The resource record type. The most commonly used resource types are summarized in Table 6-6 and are described separately later in this section. Like the Class field, you can also omit the Type field and allow it to default to the last specified value.

» **RDATA:** Resource record data that is specific to each record type.

TABLE 6-6   ## Common Resource Record Types

Type	Name	Description
SOA	Start of Authority	Identifies a zone
NS	Name Server	Identifies a name server that is authoritative for the zone
A	Address	Maps a fully qualified domain name to an IP address
CNAME	Canonical Name	Creates an alias for a fully qualified domain name
MX	Mail Exchange	Identifies the mail server for a domain
PTR	Pointer	Maps an IP address to a fully qualified domain name for reverse lookups

REMEMBER

Most resource records fit on one line. If a record requires more than one line, you must enclose the data that spans multiple lines in parentheses.

TIP

You can include comments to clarify the details of a zone file. A comment begins with a semicolon and continues to the end of the line. If a line begins with a semi-colon, the entire line is a comment. You can also add a comment to the end of a resource record. You see examples of both types of comments later in this chapter.

SOA records

Every zone must begin with an SOA record, which names the zone and provides default information for the zone. Table 6-7 lists the fields that appear in the RDATA section of an SOA record. Note that these fields are positional, so you should include a value for all of them and list them in the order specified. Because the SOA record has so many RDATA fields, you'll probably need to use parentheses to continue the SOA record onto multiple lines.

TABLE 6-7 **RDATA Fields for an SOA Record**

Name	Description
MNAME	The domain name of the name server that is authoritative for the zone.
RNAME	An email address (specified in domain name format; not regular email format) of the person responsible for this zone.
SERIAL	The serial number of the zone. Secondary zones use this value to determine whether they need to initiate a zone transfer to update their copy of the zone.
REFRESH	A time interval that specifies how often a secondary server should check whether the zone needs to be refreshed. A typical value is 3600 (one hour).
RETRY	A time interval that specifies how long a secondary server should wait after requesting a zone transfer before trying again. A typical value is 600 (ten minutes).
EXPIRE	A time interval that specifies how long a secondary server should keep the zone data before discarding it. A typical value is 86400 (one day).
MINIMUM	A time interval that specifies the TTL value to use for zone resource records that omit the TTL field. A typical value is 3600 (one hour).

Note two things about the SOA fields:

>> **The email address of the person responsible for the zone is given in DNS format, not in normal email format.** Thus, you separate the user from the mail domain with a dot rather than an @ symbol. For example, doug@ LoweWriter.com would be listed as doug.lowewriter.com.

>> **The serial number should be incremented every time you change the zone file.** If you edit the file via the graphic interface provided by Windows DNS, the serial number is incremented automatically. However, if you edit the zone file via a simple text editor, you have to manually increment the serial number.

Here's a typical example of an SOA record, with judicious comments to identify each field:

```
lowewriter.com. IN SOA (
ns1.lowewriter.com ; authoritative name server
doug.lowewriter.com ; responsible person
148 ; version number
3600 ; refresh (1 hour)
600 ; retry (10 minutes)
86400 ; expire (1 day)
3600 ) ; minimum TTL (1 hour)
```

NS records

Name server (NS) records identify the name servers that are authoritative for the zone. Every zone must have at least one NS record. Using two or more NS records is better so that if the first name server is unavailable, the zone will still be accessible.

The owner field should either be the fully qualified domain name for the zone, with a trailing dot, or an @ symbol. The RDATA consists of just one field: the fully qualified domain name of the name server.

The following examples show two NS records that serve the `lowewriter.com` domain:

```
lowewriter.com.  IN NS ns1.lowewriter.com.
lowewriter.com.  IN NS ns2.lowewriter.com.
```

A records

Address (A) records are the meat of the zone file: They provide the IP addresses for each of the hosts that you want to make accessible via DNS. In an A record, you usually list just the host name in the owner field, thus allowing DNS to add the domain name to derive the fully qualified domain name for the host. The RDATA field for the A record is the IP address of the host.

The following lines define various hosts for the `LoweWriter.com` domain:

```
doug IN A 192.168.168.200
server1 IN A 192.168.168.201
debbie IN A 192.168.168.202
printer1 IN A 192.168.168.203
router1 IN A 207.126.127.129
www IN A 64.71.129.102
```

Notice that for these lines, I don't specify the fully qualified domain names for each host. Instead, I just provide the host name. DNS will add the name of the zone's domain to these host names in order to create the fully qualified domain names.

If I wanted to be more explicit, I could list these A records like this:

```
doug.lowewriter.com.  IN A 192.168.168.200
server1.lowewriter.com.  IN A 192.168.168.201
debbie.lowewriter.com.  IN A 192.168.168.202
printer1.lowewriter.com.  IN A 192.168.168.203
router1.lowewriter.com IN A 207.126.127.129
www.lowewriter.com.  IN A 64.71.129.102
```

However, all this does is increase the chance for error. Plus, it creates more work for you later if you decide to change your network's domain.

CNAME records

A *Canonical Name* (CNAME) record creates an alias for a fully qualified domain name. When a user attempts to access a domain name that is actually an alias, the DNS system substitutes the real domain name — known as the *Canonical Name* — for the alias. The owner field in the CNAME record provides the name of the alias that you want to create. Then, the RDATA field provides the Canonical Name — that is, the real name of the host.

For example, consider these resource records:

```
ftp.lowewriter.com. IN A 207.126.127.132
files.lowewriter.com. IN CNAME www1.lowewriter.com.
```

Here, the host name of an FTP server at 207.126.127.132 is ftp.lowewriter.com. The CNAME record allows users to access this host as files.lowewriter.com if they prefer.

PTR records

A *Pointer* (PTR) record is the opposite of an address record: It provides the fully qualified domain name for a given address. The owner field should specify the reverse lookup domain name, and the RDATA field specifies the fully qualified domain name. For example, the following record maps the address 64.71.129.102 to www.lowewriter.com:

```
102.129.71.64.in-addr.arpa. IN PTR www.lowewriter.com.
```

PTR records don't usually appear in normal domain zones. Instead, they appear in special reverse lookup zones. For more information, see the section "Reverse Lookup Zones," later in this chapter.

MX records

Mail Exchange (MX) records identify the mail server for a domain. The owner field provides the domain name that users address mail to. The RDATA section of the record has two fields. The first is a priority number used to determine which mail servers to use when several are available. The second is the fully qualified domain name of the mail server itself.

For example, consider the following MX records:

```
lowewriter.com. IN MX 0 mail1.lowewriter.com.
lowewriter.com. IN MX 10 mail2.lowewriter.com.
```

In this example, the `lowewriter.com` domain has two mail servers, named `mail1.lowewriter.com` and `mail2.lowewriter.com`. The priority numbers for these servers are 0 and 10. Because it has a lower priority number, mail will be delivered to `mail1.lowewriter.com` first. The `mail2.lowewriter.com` server will be used only if `mail1.lowewriter.com` isn't available.

TIP

The server name specified in the RDATA section should be an actual host name, not an alias created by a CNAME record. Although some mail servers can handle MX records that point to CNAMEs, not all can. As a result, you shouldn't specify an alias in an MX record.

WARNING

Be sure to create a reverse lookup record (PTR, described in the next section) for your mail servers. Some mail servers won't accept mail from a server that doesn't have valid reverse lookup entries.

Reverse Lookup Zones

Normal DNS queries ask a name server to provide the IP address that corresponds to a fully qualified domain name. This kind of query is a *forward lookup*. A *reverse lookup* is the opposite of a forward lookup: It returns the fully qualified domain name of a host based on its IP address.

Reverse lookups are possible because of a special domain called the `in-addr.arpa` domain, which provides a separate fully qualified domain name for every possible IP address on the Internet. To enable a reverse lookup for a particular IP address, all you have to do is create a PTR record in a reverse lookup zone (a zone that is authoritative for a portion of the `in-addr.arpa` domain). The PTR record maps the `in-addr.arpa` domain name for the address to the host's actual domain name.

The technique used to create the reverse domain name for a given IP address is pretty clever. It creates subdomains beneath the `in-addr.arpa` domain by using the octets of the IP address, listing them in reverse order. For example, the reverse domain name for the IP address `207.126.67.129` is `129.67.126.207.in-addr.arpa`.

Why list the octets in reverse order? Because that correlates the network portions of the IP address (which work from left to right) with the subdomain structure of DNS names (which works from right to left). The following description should clear this up:

>> The 255 possible values for the first octet of an IP address each have a subdomain beneath the `in-addr.arpa` domain. For example, any IP address that begins with 207 can be found in the `207.in-addr.arpa` domain.

>> Within this domain, each of the possible values for the second octet can be found as a subdomain of the first octet's domain. Thus, any address that begins with `207.126` can be found in the `126.207.in-addr.arpa` domain.

>> The same holds true for the third octet, so any address that begins with `207.126.67` can be found in the `67.126.207.in-addr.arpa` domain.

>> By the time you get to the fourth octet, you've pinpointed a specific host. The fourth octet completes the fully qualified reverse domain name. Thus, `207.126.67.129` is mapped to `129.67.126.207.in-addr.arpa`.

As a result, to determine the fully qualified domain name for the computer at `207.126.67.129`, the client queries its DNS server for the FQDN that corresponds to `129.67.126.207.in-addr.arpa`.

Working with the Windows DNS Server

Installing and managing a DNS server depends on the network operating system (NOS) that you're using. The following sections are specific to working with a DNS server in Windows Server 2012. Working with BIND in a Unix/Linux environment is similar but without the help of a graphical user interface (GUI), and working with Windows Server 2016 is similar.

You can install the DNS server on a Windows server from the Server Manager application. Open the Server Manager and choose Manage⇨Add Roles and Features. Then, follow the wizard's instructions to add the DNS Role.

After you set up a DNS server, you can manage the DNS server from the DNS management console, as shown in Figure 6-3. From this management console, you can perform common administrative tasks, such as adding additional zones, changing zone settings, adding A or MX records to an existing zone, and so on. The DNS management console hides the details of the actual resource records from you, thus allowing you to work with a friendly GUI instead.

To add a new host (that is, an A record) to a zone, right-click the zone in the DNS management console and choose the Add New Host command. This brings up the New Host dialog box, as shown in Figure 6-4. From this dialog box, specify the following information.

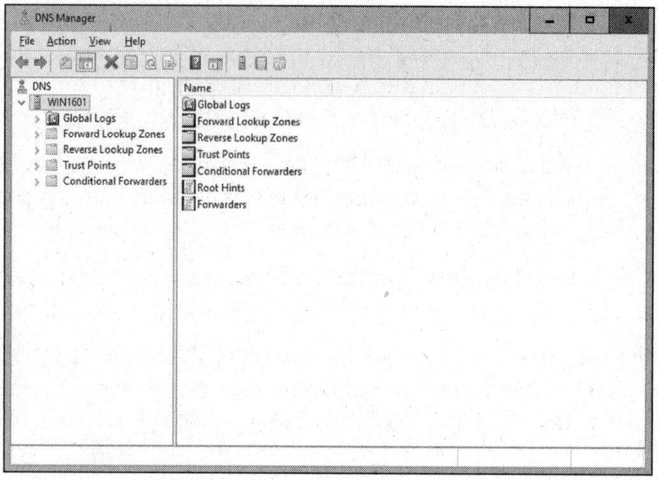

FIGURE 6-3:
The DNS management console.

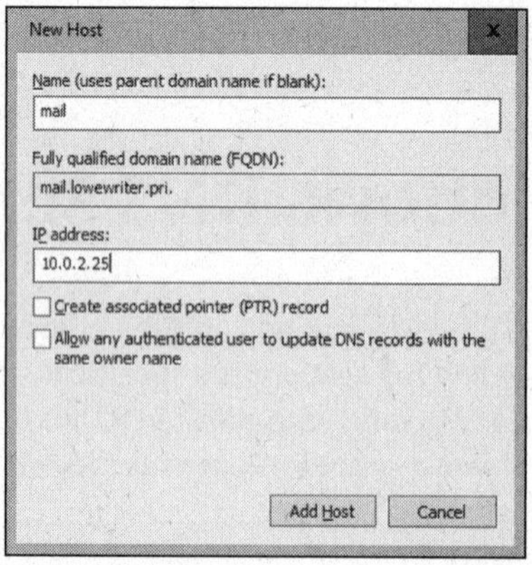

FIGURE 6-4:
The New Host dialog box.

>> **Name:** The host name for the new host.

>> **IP Address:** The host's IP address.

>> **Create Associated Pointer (PTR) Record:** Automatically creates a PTR record in the reverse lookup zone file. Select this option if you want to allow reverse lookups for the host.

You can add other records, such as MX or CNAME records, in the same way.

How to Configure a Windows DNS Client

Client computers don't need much configuration in order to work properly with DNS. The client must have the address of at least one DNS server. Usually, this address is supplied by DHCP, so if the client is configured to obtain its IP address from a DHCP server, it will also obtain the DNS server address from DHCP.

To configure a client computer to obtain the DNS server location from DHCP, bring up the Network Properties dialog box by choosing Network or Network Connections in Control Panel (depending on which version of Windows the client is running). Then, select the Internet Protocol Version 4 (TCP/IPv4) protocol and click the Properties button. This summons the dialog box shown in Figure 6-5. To configure the computer to use Dynamic Host Configuration Protocol (DHCP), select the Obtain an IP Address Automatically and the Obtain DNS Server Address Automatically options.

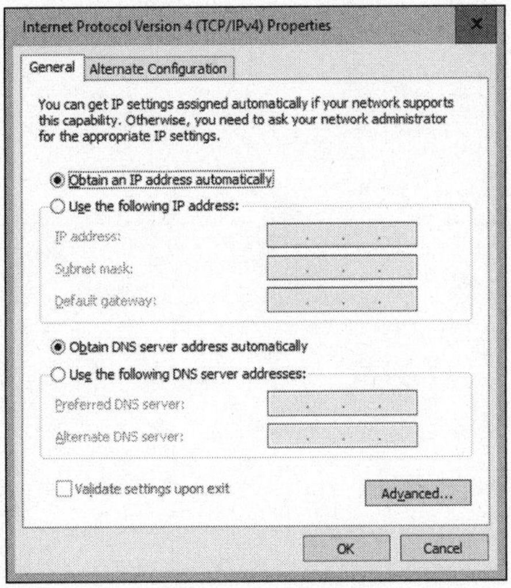

FIGURE 6-5:
Configuring a Windows client to obtain its DNS address from DHCP.

If the computer doesn't use DHCP, you can use this same dialog box to manually enter the IP address of your DNS server.

Chapter **7**

TCP/IP Tools and Commands

M ost client and server operating systems that support Transmission Control Protocol/Internet Protocol (TCP/IP) come with a suite of commands and tools that are designed to let you examine TCP/IP configuration information and diagnose and correct problems. Although the exact form of these commands varies between Windows and Unix/Linux, most are surprisingly similar. This chapter is a reference to the most commonly used TCP/IP commands.

Using the arp Command

Using the arp command allows you to display and modify the Address Resolution Protocol (ARP) cache, which is a simple mapping of IP addresses to MAC addresses. Each time a computer's TCP/IP stack uses ARP to determine the Media Access Control (MAC) address for an IP address, it records the mapping in the ARP cache so that future ARP lookups go faster.

If you use the arp command without any parameters, you get a list of the command's parameters. To display the ARP cache entry for a specific IP address, use an –a switch followed by the IP address. For example:

```
C:\>arp -a 192.168.168.22
Interface: 192.168.168.21 --- 0x10004
```

```
Internet Address Physical Address Type
192.168.168.22 00-60-08-39-e5-a1 dynamic
C:\>
```

You can display the complete ARP cache by using –a without specifying an IP address, like this:

```
C:\>arp -a
Interface: 192.168.168.21 --- 0x10004
Internet Address Physical Address Type
192.168.168.9 00-02-e3-16-e4-5d dynamic
192.168.168.10 00-50-04-17-66-90 dynamic
192.168.168.22 00-60-08-39-e5-a1 dynamic
192.168.168.254 00-40-10-18-42-49 dynamic
C:\>
```

TIP

ARP is sometimes useful when diagnosing duplicate IP assignment problems. For example, suppose you can't access a computer that has an IP address of 192.168.168.100. You try to ping the computer, expecting the ping to fail, but lo and behold — the ping succeeds. One possible cause for this may be that two computers on the network have been assigned the address 192.168.168.100, and your ARP cache is pointing to the wrong one. The way to find out is to go to the 192.168.168.100 computer that you want to access, run ipconfig /all, and make a note of the physical address. Then return to the computer that's having trouble reaching the 192.168.168.100 computer, run arp –a, and compare the physical address with the one you noted. If they're different, two computers are assigned the same IP address. You can then check the Dynamic Host Configuration Protocol (DHCP) or static TCP/IP configuration of the computers involved to find out why.

Using the hostname Command

The hostname command is the simplest of all the TCP/IP commands presented in this chapter. It simply displays the computer's host name. For example:

```
C:\>hostname
doug
C:\>
```

Here, the host name for the computer is doug. The Windows version of the host-name command has no parameters. However, the Unix/Linux versions of hostname let you set the computer's host name as well as display it. You do that by specifying the new host name as an argument.

Using the ipconfig Command

Using the `ipconfig` command displays information about a computer's TCP/IP configuration. It can also be used to update DHCP and Domain Name Server (DNS) settings.

Displaying basic IP configuration

To display the basic IP configuration for a computer, use the `ipconfig` command without any parameters, like this:

```
C:\>ipconfig
Windows IP Configuration
Ethernet adapter Local Area Connection:
Connection-specific DNS Suffix . :
Link-local IPv6 Address ... . . . : fe80::cca:9067:9427:a911%8
IPv4 Address... ... ... . . . : 192.168.1.110
Subnet Mask ... ... ... . . : 255.255.255.0
Default Gateway ... ... ... : 192.168.1.1
Tunnel adapter Local Area Connection* 6:
Connection-specific DNS Suffix . :
IPv6 Address... ... ... . . : 2001:0:4136:e38c:2c6c:670:3f57:fe91
Link-local IPv6 Address ... . . : fe80::2c6c:670:3f57:fe91%9
Default Gateway ... ... ... : ::
Tunnel adapter Local Area Connection* 7:
Connection-specific DNS Suffix . :
Link-local IPv6 Address ... . . : fe80::5efe:192.168.1.110%10
Default Gateway ... ... ... :
C:\>
```

When you use `ipconfig` without parameters, the command displays the name of the adapter, the domain name used for the adapter, the IP address, the subnet mask, and the default gateway configuration for the adapter. This is the easiest way to determine a computer's IP address.

TIP

If your computer indicates an IP address in the 169.254.*x*.*x* block, odds are good that the DHCP server isn't working. 169.254.*x*.*x* is the Class B address block that Windows uses when it resorts to IP Autoconfiguration. This usually happens only when the DHCP server can't be reached or isn't working.

Displaying detailed configuration information

You can display detailed IP configuration information by using an `/all` switch with the `ipconfig` command, like this:

```
C:\>ipconfig /all
Windows IP Configuration
```

```
Host Name ... .. ... .. : WK17-001
Primary Dns Suffix .. .. . :
Node Type ... .. ... .. : Hybrid
IP Routing Enabled.. ... : No
WINS Proxy Enabled... ... : No
Ethernet adapter Local Area Connection:
Connection-specific DNS Suffix . :
Description ... .. ... .. . : Intel(R) PRO/100 VE Network Connection
Physical Address... .. ... : 00-12-3F-A7-17-BA
DHCP Enabled... .. ... . : No
Autoconfiguration Enabled ... . : Yes
Link-local IPv6 Address ... . . : fe80::cca:9067:9427:a911%8(Preferred)
IPv4 Address... ... ... . : 192.168.1.110(Preferred)
Subnet Mask ... .. ... . : 255.255.255.0
Default Gateway ... .. ... : 192.168.1.1
DNS Servers ... .. ... . : 192.168.1.10
68.87.76.178
NetBIOS over Tcpip... .. ... : Enabled
C:\>
```

You can determine a lot of information about the computer from the `ipconfig /all` command. For example:

>> The computer's host name is WK17-001.

>> The computer's IPv4 address is 192.168.1.110, and the subnet mask is 255.255.255.0.

>> The default gateway is a router located at 192.168.1.1.

>> The DNS servers are at 192.168.1.10 and 68.87.76.178.

Renewing an IP lease

If you're having an IP configuration problem, you can often solve it by renewing the computer's IP lease. To do that, use a /renew switch, like this:

```
C:\>ipconfig /renew
Windows IP Configuration
Ethernet adapter Local Area Connection:
Connection-specific DNS Suffix . :
IP Address... .. ... .. : 192.168.1.110
Subnet Mask ... .. ... . : 255.255.255.0
Default Gateway ... .. ... : 192.168.1.1
C:\>
```

When you renew an IP lease, the `ipconfig` command displays the new lease information.

WARNING

This command won't work if you configured the computer to use a static IP address.

Releasing an IP lease

You can release an IP lease by using an `ipconfig` command with the `/release` parameter, like this:

```
C:\>ipconfig /release
Windows IP Configuration
Ethernet adapter Local Area Connection:
Connection-specific DNS Suffix . :
IP Address ... ... ... .. : 0.0.0.0
Subnet Mask... ... ... .. : 0.0.0.0
Default Gateway ... ... ... :
C:\>
```

As you can see, the DNS suffix and default gateway for the computer are blank, and the IP address and subnet mask are set to `0.0.0.0`.

After you release the DHCP lease, you can use an `ipconfig /renew` command to obtain a new DHCP lease for the computer.

Flushing the local DNS cache

You probably won't need to do this unless you're having DNS troubles. If you've been tinkering with your network's DNS configuration, though, you may need to flush the cache on your DNS clients so that they'll be forced to reacquire information from the DNS server. You can do that by using a `/flushdns` switch:

```
C:\>ipconfig /flushdns
Windows IP Configuration
Successfully flushed the DNS Resolver Cache.
C:\>
```

TIP

Even if you don't need to do this, it's fun just to see the computer read `flushed`. If I worked at Microsoft, you'd be able to revert Windows Vista computers back to XP by using a `/flushVista` switch.

Using the nbtstat Command

nbtstat is a Windows-only command that can help solve problems with Net-BIOS name resolution. (*nbt* stands for *NetBIOS over TCP/IP.*) You can use any of the switches listed in Table 7-1 to specify what nbtstat output you want to display. For example, you can use an –a switch to display the cached name table for a specified computer, like this:

```
C:\>nbtstat -a WK07-001
Local Area Connection:
Node IpAddress: [192.168.1.110] Scope Id: []
NetBIOS Remote Machine Name Table
Name Type Status
_____
WK07-001    <00>  UNIQUE Registered
WORKGROUP   <00>  GROUP  Registered
WK07-001    <20>  UNIQUE Registered
WORKGROUP   <1E>  GROUP  Registered
WORKGROUP   <1D>  UNIQUE Registered
..__MSBROWSE__.<01>  GROUP Registered
MAC Address = 00-12-3F-A7-17-BAC:\>
C:\>
```

Table 7-1 lists the switches that you can use with nbtstat and explains the function of each switch.

TABLE 7-1   **nbtstat Command Switches**

Switch	What It Does
-a name	Lists the specified computer's name table given the computer's name
-A IP-address	Lists the specified computer's name table given the computer's IP address
-c	Lists the contents of the NetBIOS cache
-n	Lists locally registered NetBIOS names
-r	Displays a count of the names resolved by broadcast and via WINS
-R	Purges and reloads the cached name table from the LMHOSTS file
-RR	Releases and then reregisters all names
-S	Displays the sessions table using IP addresses
-s	Displays the sessions table and converts destination IP addresses to computer NetBIOS names

Using the netstat Command

Using the `netstat` command displays a variety of statistics about a computer's active TCP/IP connections. It's a useful tool to use when you're having trouble with TCP/IP applications, such as File Transfer Protocol (FTP), HyperText Transport Protocol (HTTP), and so on.

Displaying connections

If you run `netstat` without specifying any parameters, you get a list of active connections, something like this:

```
C:\>netstat
Active Connections
Proto Local Address Foreign Address State
TCP Doug:1463 192.168.168.10:1053 ESTABLISHED
TCP Doug:1582 192.168.168.9:netbios-ssn ESTABLISHED
TCP Doug:3630 192.168.168.30:9100 SYN_SENT
TCP Doug:3716 192.168.168.10:4678 ESTABLISHED
TCP Doug:3940 192.168.168.10:netbios-ssn ESTABLISHED
C:\>
```

This list shows all the active connections on the computer and indicates the local port used by the connection, as well as the IP address and port number for the remote computer.

You can specify the –n switch to display both local and foreign addresses in numeric IP form:

```
C:\>netstat –n
Active Connections
Proto Local Address Foreign Address State
TCP 192.168.168.21:1463 192.168.168.10:1053 ESTABLISHED
TCP 192.168.168.21:1582 192.168.168.9:139 ESTABLISHED
TCP 192.168.168.21:3658 192.168.168.30:9100 SYN_SENT
TCP 192.168.168.21:3716 192.168.168.10:4678 ESTABLISHED
TCP 192.168.168.21:3904 207.46.106.78:1863 ESTABLISHED
TCP 192.168.168.21:3940 192.168.168.10:139 ESTABLISHED
C:\>
```

Finally, you can specify the –a switch to display all TCP/IP connections and ports that are being listened to. I won't list the output from that command here because it would run several pages, and I want to do my part for the rainforests. Suffice it to say that it looks a lot like the `netstat` output shown previously, but a lot longer.

Displaying interface statistics

If you use an –e switch, netstat displays various protocol statistics, like this:

```
C:\>netstat -e
Interface Statistics
Received Sent
Bytes 672932849 417963911
Unicast packets 1981755 1972374
Non-unicast packets 251869 34585
Discards 0 0
Errors 0 0
Unknown protocols 1829
C:\>
```

REMEMBER

The items to pay attention to in this output are the Discards and Errors. These numbers should be zero, or at least close to it. If they're not, the network may be carrying too much traffic or the connection may have a physical problem. If no physical problem exists with the connection, try segmenting the network to see whether the error and discard rates drop.

You can display additional statistics by using an –s switch, like this:

```
C:\>netstat -s
IPv4 Statistics
Packets Received = 9155
Received Header Errors = 0
Received Address Errors = 0
Datagrams Forwarded = 0
Unknown Protocols Received = 0
Received Packets Discarded = 0
Received Packets Delivered = 14944
Output Requests = 12677
Routing Discards = 0
Discarded Output Packets = 71
Output Packet No Route = 0
Reassembly Required = 0
Reassembly Successful = 0
Reassembly Failures = 0
Datagrams Successfully Fragmented = 0
Datagrams Failing Fragmentation = 0
Fragments Created = 0
IPv6 Statistics
Packets Received = 3
Received Header Errors = 0
Received Address Errors = 0
Datagrams Forwarded = 0
```

```
Unknown Protocols Received = 0
Received Packets Discarded = 0
Received Packets Delivered = 345
Output Requests = 377
Routing Discards = 0
Discarded Output Packets = 0
Output Packet No Route = 0
Reassembly Required = 0
Reassembly Successful = 0
Reassembly Failures = 0
Datagrams Successfully Fragmented = 0
Datagrams Failing Fragmentation = 0
Fragments Created = 0
ICMPv4 Statistics
Received Sent
Messages 6 14
Errors 0 0
Destination Unreachable 6 14
Time Exceeded 0 0
Parameter Problems 0 0
Source Quenches 0 0
Redirects 0 0
Echo Replies 0 0
Echos 0 0
Timestamps 0 0
Timestamp Replies 0 0
Address Masks 0 0
Address Mask Replies 0 0
Router Solicitations 0 0
Router Advertisements 0 0
ICMPv6 Statistics
Received Sent
Messages 3 7
Errors 0 0
Destination Unreachable 0 0
Packet Too Big 0 0
Time Exceeded 0 0
Parameter Problems 0 0
Echos 0 0
Echo Replies 0 0
MLD Queries 0 0
MLD Reports 0 0
MLD Dones 0 0
Router Solicitations 0 6
Router Advertisements 3 0
Neighbor Solicitations 0 1
Neighbor Advertisements 0 0
Redirects 0 0
```

```
Router Renumberings 0 0
TCP Statistics for IPv4
Active Opens = 527
Passive Opens = 2
Failed Connection Attempts = 1
Reset Connections = 301
Current Connections = 1
Segments Received = 8101
Segments Sent = 6331
Segments Retransmitted = 301
TCP Statistics for IPv6
Active Opens = 1
Passive Opens = 1
Failed Connection Attempts = 0
Reset Connections = 1
Current Connections = 0
Segments Received = 142
Segments Sent = 142
Segments Retransmitted = 0
UDP Statistics for IPv4
Datagrams Received = 6703
No Ports = 0
Receive Errors = 0
Datagrams Sent = 6011
UDP Statistics for IPv6
Datagrams Received = 32
No Ports = 0
Receive Errors = 0
Datagrams Sent = 200
C:\>
```

Using the nslookup Command

The nslookup command is a powerful tool for diagnosing DNS problems. You know you're experiencing a DNS problem when you can access a resource by specifying its IP address but not its DNS name. For example, if you can get to www.ebay.com by typing **66.135.192.87** in your browser's address bar but not by typing www.ebay.com, you have a DNS problem.

Looking up an IP address

The simplest use of nslookup is to look up the IP address for a given DNS name. For example, how did I know that 66.135.192.87 was the IP address for www.ebay.com? I used nslookup to find out:

```
C:\>nslookup ebay.com
Server:  ns1.orng.twtelecom.net
Address:  168.215.210.50
Non-authoritative answer:
Name:  ebay.com
Address:  66.135.192.87
C:\>
```

As you can see, just type **nslookup** followed by the DNS name you want to look up, and nslookup issues a DNS query to find out. This DNS query was sent to the server named ns1.orng.twtelecom.net at 168.215.210.50. It then displayed the IP address that's associated with ebay.com: namely, 66.135.192.87.

TIP

In some cases, you may find that using an nslookup command gives you the wrong IP address for a host name. To know that for sure, of course, you have to know with certainty what the host IP address *should* be. For example, if you know that your server is 203.172.182.10 but nslookup returns a completely different IP address for your server when you query the server's host name, something is probably wrong with one of the DNS records.

GET ME OUT OF HERE!

One of my pet peeves is that it seems as if every program that uses subcommands chooses a different command to quit the application. I can never remember whether the command to get out of nslookup is quit, bye, or exit. I usually end up trying them all. And no matter what program I'm using, I always seem to choose the one that works for some other program first. When I'm in nslookup, I use bye first. When I'm in FTP, I try exit first. Arghh! If I were King of the Computer Hill, every program that had subcommands would respond to any of the following commands by exiting the program and returning to a command prompt:

Quit	Sayonara
Exit	Ciao
Bye	Mañana
Leave	Makelikeatree

Of course, the final command to try would be Andgetouttahere (in honor of Biff from the *Back to the Future* movies).

Using nslookup subcommands

If you use `nslookup` without any arguments, the `nslookup` command enters a subcommand mode. It displays a prompt character (>) to let you know that you're in `nslookup` subcommand mode rather than at a normal Windows command prompt. In subcommand mode, you can enter various subcommands to set options or to perform queries. You can type a question mark (?) to get a list of these commands. Table 7-2 lists the subcommands you'll use most.

TABLE 7-2   **The Most Commonly Used `nslookup` Subcommands**

Subcommand	What It Does
`name`	Queries the current name server for the specified name.
`server name`	Sets the current name server to the server you specify.
`root`	Sets the root server as the current server.
`set type=x`	Specifies the type of records to be displayed, such as A, CNAME, MX, NS, PTR, or SOA. Specify ANY to display all records.
`set debug`	Turns on Debug mode, which displays detailed information about each query.
`set nodebug`	Turns off Debug mode.
`set recurse`	Enables recursive searches.
`set norecurse`	Disables recursive searches.
`exit`	Exits the `nslookup` program and returns you to a command prompt.

Displaying DNS records

One of the main uses of `nslookup` is to examine your DNS configuration to make sure that it's set up properly. To do that, follow these steps:

1. **At a command prompt, type** nslookup **without any parameters.**

   nslookup displays the name of the default name server and displays the > prompt.

   ```
   C:\>nslookup
   Default Server: ns1.orng.twtelecom.net
   Address: 168.215.210.50

   >
   ```

2. **Type the subcommand** set type=any.

nslookup silently obeys your command and displays another prompt:

```
> set type=any
>
```

3. **Type your domain name.**

nslookup responds by displaying the name servers for your domain:

```
> lowewriter.com
Server: ns1.orng.twtelecom.net
Address: 168.215.210.50
Non-authoritative answer:
lowewriter.com nameserver = NS000.NS0.com
lowewriter.com nameserver = NS207.PAIR.com
lowewriter.com nameserver = NS000.NS0.com
lowewriter.com nameserver = NS207.PAIR.com
>
```

4. **Use a server command to switch to one of the domain's name servers.**

For example, to switch to the first name server listed in Step 3, type **server NS000.NS0.com**. nslookup replies with a message that indicates the new default server:

```
> server ns000.ns0.com
Default Server: ns000.ns0.com
Address: 216.92.61.61
>
```

5. **Type your domain name again.**

This time, nslookup responds by displaying the DNS information for your domain:

```
> lowewriter.com
Server: ns000.ns0.com
Address: 216.92.61.61
lowewriter.com
primary name server = ns207.pair.com
responsible mail addr = root.pair.com
serial = 2001121009
refresh = 3600 (1 hour)
retry = 300 (5 mins)
expire = 604800 (7 days)
default TTL = 3600 (1 hour)
```

```
lowewriter.com nameserver = ns000.ns0.com
lowewriter.com nameserver = ns207.pair.com
lowewriter.com MX preference = 50, mail exchanger = sasi.pair.com
lowewriter.com internet address = 209.68.34.15
>
```

6. **Type exit to leave the `nslookup` program.**

   You return to a command prompt.

   ```
   > exit
   C:\>
   ```

Wasn't that fun?

Locating the mail server for an email address

If you're having trouble delivering mail to someone, you can use `nslookup` to determine the IP address of the user's mail server. Then, you can use the `ping` command to see whether you can contact the user's mail server. If not, you can use the `tracert` command to find out where the communication breaks down. (See "Using the `tracert` Command" later in this chapter for more information.)

To find a user's mail server, start `nslookup` and enter the command **set type=MX**. Then, enter the domain portion of the user's email address. For example, if the user's address is Doug@LoweWriter.com, enter **LoweWriter.com**. `nslookup` will display the MX (Mail Exchange) information for the domain, like this:

```
C:\>nslookup
Default Server: ns7.attbi.com
Address: 204.127.198.19
> set type=mx
> lowewriter.com
Server: ns7.attbi.com
Address: 204.127.198.19
lowewriter.com MX preference = 50, mail exchanger = sasi.pair.com
lowewriter.com nameserver = ns000.ns0.com
lowewriter.com nameserver = ns207.pair.com
ns000.ns0.com internet address = 216.92.61.61
ns207.pair.com internet address = 209.68.2.52
>
```

Here, you can see that the name of the mail server for the LoweWriter.com domain is sasi.pair.com.

Taking a ride through DNS-Land

Ever find yourself wondering how DNS really works? I mean, how is it that you can type a DNS name like **www.disneyland.com** into a web browser and you're almost instantly transported to the Magic Kingdom? Is it really magic?

Nope. It isn't magic; it's DNS. In Book 2, Chapter 6, I present a somewhat dry and theoretical overview of DNS. After you have the nslookup command in your trusty TCP/IP toolbox, take a little trip through the Internet's maze of DNS servers to find out how DNS gets from www.disneyland.com to an IP address in just a matter of milliseconds.

DNS does its whole name resolution thing so fast that it's easy to take it for granted. If you follow this little procedure, you'll gain a deeper appreciation for what DNS does literally tens of thousands of times every second of every day.

1. **At a command prompt, type** nslookup **without any parameters.**

   nslookup displays the name of the default name server and displays the › prompt.

   ```
   C:\>nslookup
   Default Server: ns1.orng.twtelecom.net
   Address: 168.215.210.50
   >
   ```

2. **Type** root **to switch to one of the Internet's root servers.**

   nslookup switches to one of the Internet's 13 root servers and then displays the › prompt.

   ```
   > root
   Default Server: A.ROOT-SERVERS.NET
   Address: 198.41.0.4
   ```

3. **Type** www.disneyland.com.

   nslookup sends a query to the root server to ask whether it knows the IP address of www.disneyland.com. The root server answers with a referral, meaning that it doesn't know about www.disneyland.com, but you should try one of these servers because they know all about the com domain.

   ```
   > www.disneyland.com
   Server: A.ROOT-SERVERS.NET
   Address: 198.41.0.4
   Name: www.disneyland.com
   Served by:
   - A.GTLD-SERVERS.NET
   ```

```
192.5.6.30
com
   - G.GTLD-SERVERS.NET
192.42.93.30
com
   - H.GTLD-SERVERS.NET
192.54.112.30
com
   - C.GTLD-SERVERS.NET
192.26.92.30
com
   - I.GTLD-SERVERS.NET
192.43.172.30
com
   - B.GTLD-SERVERS.NET
192.33.14.30
com
   - D.GTLD-SERVERS.NET
192.31.80.30
com
   - L.GTLD-SERVERS.NET
192.41.162.30
com
   - F.GTLD-SERVERS.NET
192.35.51.30
com
   - J.GTLD-SERVERS.NET
192.48.79.30
Com
   >
```

4. **Type** server **followed by the name or IP address of one of the** com **domain name servers.**

   It doesn't really matter which one you pick. nslookup switches to that server. (The server may spit out some other information besides what I show here; I left it out for clarity.)

   ```
   > server 192.48.79.30
   Default Server: [192.5.6.30]
   Address: 192.5.6.30

   >
   ```

5. **Type** www.disneyland.com **again.**

   nslookup sends a query to the com server to ask whether it knows where the Magic Kingdom is. The com server's reply indicates that it doesn't know where www.disneyland.com is, but it does know which server is responsible for disneyland.com.

```
Server: [192.5.6.30]
Address: 192.5.6.30
Name: www.disney.com
Served by:
- huey.disney.com
204.128.192.10
disney.com
- huey11.disney.com
208.246.35.40
disney.com
>
```

TECHNICAL
STUFF

It figures that Disney's name server is huey.disney.com. There's probably also a dewey.disney.com and a louie.disney.com.

6. **Type** server **followed by the name or IP address of the second-level domain name server.**

   nslookup switches to that server:

   ```
   > server huey.disney.com
   Default Server: huey.disney.com
   Address: 204.128.192.10
   >
   ```

7. **Type** www.disneyland.com **again.**

   Once again, nslookup sends a query to the name server to find out whether it knows where the Magic Kingdom is. Of course, huey.disney.com *does* know, so it tells us the answer:

   ```
   > www.disneyland.com
   Server: huey.disney.com
   Address: 204.128.192.10
   Name: disneyland.com
   Address: 199.181.132.250
   Aliases: www.disneyland.com
   >
   ```

8. **Type** Exit, **and then shout like Tigger in amazement at how DNS queries work.**

   And be glad that your DNS resolver and primary name server do all this querying for you automatically.

Okay, maybe that wasn't an E Ticket ride, but it never ceases to amaze me that the DNS system can look up any DNS name hosted anywhere in the world almost instantly.

Using the pathping Command

pathping is an interesting command that's unique to Windows. It's sort of a cross between the ping command and the tracert command, combining the features of both into one tool. When you run pathping, it first traces the route to the destination address much the way tracert does. Then, it launches into a 25-second test of each router along the way, gathering statistics on the rate of data loss to each hop. If the route has a lot of hops, this can take a long time. However, it can help you to spot potentially unreliable hops. If you're having intermittent trouble reaching a particular destination, using pathping may help you pinpoint the problem.

The following command output is typical of the pathping command. Using an −n switch causes the display to use numeric IP numbers only, instead of DNS host names. Although fully qualified host names are convenient, they tend to be very long for network routers, which makes the pathping output very difficult to decipher.

```
C:\>pathping −n www.lowewriter.com
Tracing route to lowewriter.com [209.68.34.15]
over a maximum of 30 hops:
0 192.168.168.21
1 66.193.195.81
2 66.193.200.5
3 168.215.55.173
4 168.215.55.101
5 168.215.55.77
6 66.192.250.38
7 66.192.252.22
8 208.51.224.141
9 206.132.111.118
10 206.132.111.162
11 64.214.174.178
12 192.168.1.191
13 209.68.34.15
Computing statistics for 325 seconds...
               Source to Here This Node/Link
Hop RTT Lost/Sent = Pct Lost/Sent = Pct Address
0 192.168.168.21
                        0/ 100 = 0% |
1 1ms 0/ 100 = 0% 0/ 100 = 0% 66.193.195.81]
                        0/ 100 = 0% |
2 14ms 0/ 100 = 0% 0/ 100 = 0% 66.193.200.5
                        0/ 100 = 0% |
3 10ms 0/ 100 = 0% 0/ 100 = 0% 168.215.55.173
                        0/ 100 = 0% |
4 10ms 0/ 100 = 0% 0/ 100 = 0% 168.215.55.101
                        0/ 100 = 0% |
5 12ms 0/ 100 = 0% 0/ 100 = 0% 168.215.55.77
```

```
0/ 100 = 0% |
6 14ms 0/ 100 = 0% 0/ 100 = 0% 66.192.250.38
0/ 100 = 0% |
7 14ms 0/ 100 = 0% 0/ 100 = 0% 66.192.252.22
0/ 100 = 0% |
8 14ms 0/ 100 = 0% 0/ 100 = 0% 208.51.224.141
0/ 100 = 0% |
9 81ms 0/ 100 = 0% 0/ 100 = 0% 206.132.111.118
0/ 100 = 0% |
10 81ms 0/ 100 = 0% 0/ 100 = 0% 206.132.111.162]
0/ 100 = 0% |
11 84ms 0/ 100 = 0% 0/ 100 = 0% 64.214.174.178]
0/ 100 = 0% |
12 --- 100/ 100 =100% 100/ 100 =100% 192.168.1.191
0/ 100 = 0% |
13 85ms 0/ 100 = 0% 0/ 100 = 0% 209.68.34.15
Trace complete.
```

Using the ping Command

ping is probably the most basic TCP/IP command line tool. Its main purpose is to determine whether you can reach another computer from your computer. It uses Internet Control Message Protocol (ICMP) to send mandatory ECHO_REQUEST datagrams to the specified host computer. When the reply is received back from the host, the ping command displays how long it took to receive the response.

You can specify the host to ping by using an IP address, as in this example:

```
C:\>ping 192.168.168.10
Pinging 192.168.168.10 with 32 bytes of data:
Reply from 192.168.168.10: bytes=32 time<1ms TTL=128
Reply from 192.168.168.10: bytes=32 time<1ms TTL=128
Reply from 192.168.168.10: bytes=32 time<1ms TTL=128
Reply from 192.168.168.10: bytes=32 time<1ms TTL=128
Ping statistics for 192.168.168.10:
Packets: Sent = 4, Received = 4, Lost = 0 (0% loss),
Approximate round trip times in milli-seconds:
Minimum = 0ms, Maximum = 0ms, Average = 0ms
C:\>
```

By default, the ping command sends four packets to the specified host. It displays the result of each packet sent. Then it displays summary statistics: how many packets were sent, how many replies were received, the error loss rate, and the approximate round-trip time.

You can also ping by using a DNS name, as in this example:

```
C:\>ping www.lowewriter.com
Pinging lowewriter.com [209.68.34.15] with 32 bytes of data:
Reply from 209.68.34.15: bytes=32 time=84ms TTL=53
Reply from 209.68.34.15: bytes=32 time=84ms TTL=53
Reply from 209.68.34.15: bytes=32 time=84ms TTL=53
Reply from 209.68.34.15: bytes=32 time=84ms TTL=53
Ping statistics for 209.68.34.15:
Packets: Sent = 4, Received = 4, Lost = 0 (0% loss),
Approximate round trip times in milli-seconds:
Minimum = 84ms, Maximum = 84ms, Average = 84ms
C:\>
```

The ping command uses a DNS query to determine the IP address for the specified host, and then pings the host based on its IP address.

The ping command has a number of other switches that you'll use rarely, if ever. Some of these switches are available only for some operating systems. To find out which switches are available for your version of Ping, type **ping /?** (Windows) or **man ping** (Unix/Linux).

TECHNICAL STUFF

You can find a very interesting story about the creation of the ping command written by the command's author, Mike Muus, at his website at http://ftp.arl. mil/~mike/ping.html. (Sadly, Mr. Muus was killed in an automobile accident in November 2000.)

Using the route Command

Using the route command displays or modifies the computer's routing table. For a typical computer that has a single network interface and is connected to a local area network (LAN) that has a router, the routing table is pretty simple and isn't often the source of network problems. Still, if you're having trouble accessing other computers or other networks, you can use the route command to make sure that a bad entry in the computer's routing table isn't the culprit.

For a computer with more than one interface and that's configured to work as a router, the routing table is often a major source of trouble. Setting up the routing table properly is a key part of configuring a router to work.

Displaying the routing table

To display the routing table (both IPv4 and IPv6) in Windows, use the route print command. In Unix/Linux, you can just use route without any command line switches. The output displayed by the Windows and Unix/Linux commands are similar. Here's an example from a typical Windows client computer:

```
C:\>route print
===========================================================================
Interface List
8 ...00 12 3f a7 17 ba ...... Intel(R) PRO/100 VE Network Connection
1 ......................... Software Loopback Interface 1
9 ...02 00 54 55 4e 01 ...... Teredo Tunneling Pseudo-Interface
10 ...00 00 00 00 00 00 00 e0 isatap.{D0F85930-01E2-402F-B0FC-31DFF887F06F}
===========================================================================
IPv4 Route Table
===========================================================================
Active Routes:
Network Destination Netmask Gateway Interface Metric
0.0.0.0 0.0.0.0 192.168.1.1 192.168.1.110 276
127.0.0.0 255.0.0.0 On-link 127.0.0.1 306
127.0.0.1 255.255.255.255 On-link 127.0.0.1 306
127.255.255.255 255.255.255.255 On-link 127.0.0.1 306
192.168.1.0 255.255.255.0 On-link 192.168.1.110 276
192.168.1.110 255.255.255.255 On-link 192.168.1.110 276
192.168.1.255 255.255.255.255 On-link 192.168.1.110 276
224.0.0.0 240.0.0.0 On-link 127.0.0.1 306
224.0.0.0 240.0.0.0 On-link 192.168.1.110 276
255.255.255.255 255.255.255.255 On-link 127.0.0.1 306
255.255.255.255 255.255.255.255 On-link 192.168.1.110 276
===========================================================================
Persistent Routes:
Network Address Netmask Gateway Address Metric
0.0.0.0 0.0.0.0 192.168.1.1 Default
===========================================================================
IPv6 Route Table
===========================================================================
Active Routes:
If Metric Network Destination Gateway
9 18 ::/0 On-link
1 306 ::1/128 On-link
9 18 2001::/32 On-link
9 266 2001:0:4136:e38c:2c6c:670:3f57:fe91/128
On-link
8 276 fe80::/64 On-link
9 266 fe80::/64 On-link
10 281 fe80::5efe:192.168.1.110/128
On-link
8 276 fe80::cca:9067:9427:a911/128
On-link
9 266 fe80::2c6c:670:3f57:fe91/128
On-link
1 306 ff00::/8 On-link
```

TCP/IP Tools and Commands

```
9 266 ff00::/8 On-link
8 276 ff00::/8 On-link

==========================================================================
Persistent Routes:
None
C:\>
```

For each entry in the routing table, five items of information are listed:

>> **The destination IP address**

   Actually, this is the address of the destination subnet, and must be interpreted in the context of the subnet mask.

>> **The subnet mask that must be applied to the destination address to determine the destination subnet**

>> **The IP address of the gateway to which traffic intended for the destination subnet will be sent**

>> **The IP address of the interface through which the traffic will be sent to the destination subnet**

>> **The *metric*, which indicates the number of hops required to reach destinations via the gateway**

Each packet that's processed by the computer is evaluated against the rules in the routing table. If the packet's destination address matches the destination subnet for the rule, the packet is sent to the specified gateway via the specified network interface. If not, the next rule is applied.

The computer on which I ran the route command in this example is on a private 192.168.1.0 subnet. The computer's IP address is 192.168.1.100, and the default gateway is a router at 192.168.1.1.

Here's how the rules shown in this example are used. Notice that you have to read the entries from the bottom up:

>> **The first rule is for packets sent to 255.255.255.255, with subnet mask 255.255.255.255.** This special IP address is for broadcast packets. The rule specifies that these broadcast packets should be delivered to the local network interface (192.168.1.100).

>> **The next rule is for packets sent to 192.168.1.255, again with subnet mask 255.255.255.255.** These are also broadcast packets and are sent to the local network interface.

>> **The next rule is for packets sent to 192.168.1.100, again with subnet mask 255.255.255.255.** This is for packets that the computer is sending to

itself via its own IP address. This rule specifies that these packets will be sent to the local loopback interface on 127.0.0.1.

>> **The next rule is for packets sent to** 192.168.1.0, **with subnet mask** 255.255.255.0. These are packets intended for the local subnet. They're sent to the subnet via the local interface at 192.169.1.100.

>> **The next rule is for packets sent to the loopback address (**127.0.0.1, **subnet mask** 255.0.0.0**).** These packets are sent straight through to the loopback interface, 127.0.0.1.

>> **The last rule is for everything else.** All IP addresses will match the destination IP address 0.0.0.0 with subnet mask 0.0.0.0 and will be sent to the default gateway router at 192.168.1.1 via the computer's network interface at 192.168.1.100.

TIP

One major difference between the Windows version of route and the Unix/Linux version is the order in which they list the routing table. The Windows route command lists the table starting with the most general entry and works toward the most specific. The Unix/Linux version is the other way around: It starts with the most specific and works toward the more general. The Unix/Linux order makes more sense — the Windows route command displays the routing list upside down.

Modifying the routing table

Besides displaying the routing table, the route command also lets you modify it by adding, deleting, or changing entries.

WARNING

Don't try this unless you know what you're doing. If you mess up the routing table, your computer may not be able to communicate with anyone.

The syntax for the route command for adding, deleting, or changing a route entry is

```
route [-p] command dest [mask subnet] gateway [-if interface]
```

The following list describes each of the route command's parameters:

>> –p: Makes the entry persistent. If you omit –p, the entry will be deleted the next time you reboot. (Use this only with add commands.)

>> *command*: Add, delete, or change.

>> *dest*: The IP address of the destination subnet.

>> mask *subnet*: The subnet mask. If you omit the subnet mask, the default is 255.255.255.255, meaning that the entry will apply only to a single host rather than a subnet. You usually want to include the mask.

> » *gateway*: The IP address of the gateway to which packets will be sent.

> » if *interface*: The IP address of the interface through which packets will be sent. If your computer has only one network interface, you can omit this.

Suppose that your network has a second router that serves as a link to another private subnet, 192.168.2.0 (subnet mask 255.255.255.0). The interface on the local side of this router is at 192.168.1.200. To add a static route entry that sends packets intended for the 192.168.2.0 subnet to this router, use a command like this:

```
C:\>route -p add 192.168.2.0 mask 255.255.255.0 192.168.1.200
```

Now, suppose that you later change the IP address of the router to 192.168.1.222. You can update this route with the following command:

```
C:\>route change 192.168.2.0 mask 255.255.255.0 192.168.1.222
```

Notice that I specify the mask again. If you omit the mask from a route change command, the command changes the mask to 255.255.255.255!

Finally, suppose that you realize that setting up a second router on this network wasn't such a good idea after all, so you want to just delete the entry. The following command will do the trick:

```
C:\>route delete 192.168.2.0
```

Using the tracert Command

The tracert command (traceroute in Unix/Linux implementations) is one of the key diagnostic tools for TCP/IP. It displays a list of all the routers that a packet must go through to get from the computer where tracert is run to any other computer on the Internet. Each one of these routers is called a *hop*, presumably because the original designers of the IP protocol played a lot of hopscotch when they were young. If you can't connect to another computer, you can use tracert to find out exactly where the problem is occurring.

tracert makes three attempts to contact the router at each hop and displays the response time for each of these attempts. Then, it displays the DNS name of the router (if available) and the router's IP address.

To use tracert, type the tracert command followed by the host name of the computer to which you want to trace the route. For example, suppose that you're having trouble sending mail to a recipient at wiley.com. You've used nslookup to determine that the mail server for wiley.com is xmail.wiley.com, so now you can use tracert to trace the routers along the path from your computer to xmail.wiley.com:

```
C:\>tracert xmail.wiley.com
Tracing route to xmail.wiley.com [208.215.179.78]
over a maximum of 30 hops:
1 27 ms 14 ms 10 ms 10.242.144.1
2 11 ms 43 ms 10 ms bar01-p5-0-0.frsnhe4.ca.attbb.net [24.130.64.125]
3 9 ms 14 ms 12 ms bar01-p4-0-0.frsnhe1.ca.attbb.net [24.130.0.5]
4 25 ms 30 ms 29 ms bic01-p6-0.elsgrdc1.ca.attbb.net [24.130.0.49]
5 25 ms 29 ms 43 ms bic02-d4-0.elsgrdc1.ca.attbb.net [24.130.0.162]
6 21 ms 19 ms 20 ms bar01-p2-0.lsanhe4.ca.attbb.net [24.130.0.197]
7 37 ms 38 ms 19 ms bic01-p2-0.lsanhe3.ca.attbb.net [24.130.0.193]
8 20 ms 22 ms 21 ms 12.119.9.5
9 21 ms 21 ms 22 ms tbr2-p012702.la2ca.ip.att.net [12.123.199.241]
10 71 ms 101 ms 62 ms tbr2-p013801.sl9mo.ip.att.net [12.122.10.13]
11 68 ms 77 ms 71 ms tbr1-p012401.sl9mo.ip.att.net [12.122.9.141]
12 79 ms 81 ms 83 ms tbr1-cl4.wswdc.ip.att.net [12.122.10.29]
13 83 ms 107 ms 103 ms tbr1-p012201.n54ny.ip.att.net [12.122.10.17]
14 106 ms 85 ms 105 ms gbr6-p30.n54ny.ip.att.net [12.122.11.14]
15 104 ms 96 ms 88 ms gar3-p370.n54ny.ip.att.net [12.123.1.189]
16 98 ms 86 ms 83 ms 12.125.50.162
17 85 ms 90 ms 87 ms xmail.wiley.com [208.215.179.78]
Trace complete.
```

Wow, when I send mail to my editors at Wiley, the mail travels through 17 routers along the way. No wonder I'm always missing deadlines!

The most likely problem that you'll encounter when you use tracert is a timeout during one of the hops. Timeouts are indicated by asterisks where you'd expect to see a time. For example, the following tracert output shows the fourth hop timing out on all three attempts:

```
C:\>tracert xmail.wiley.com
Tracing route to xmail.wiley.com [208.215.179.78]
over a maximum of 30 hops:
1 27 ms 14 ms 10 ms 10.242.144.1
2 11 ms 43 ms 10 ms bar01-p5-0-0.frsnhe4.ca.attbb.net [24.130.64.125]
3 9 ms 14 ms 12 ms bar01-p4-0-0.frsnhe1.ca.attbb.net [24.130.0.5]
4 * * * Request timed out.
```

Sometimes, timeouts are caused by temporary problems, so you should try the tracert again to see if the problem persists. If you keep getting timeouts at the same router, the router could be having a genuine problem.

UNDERSTANDING HOW TRACERT WORKS

Understanding how `tracert` works can provide some insight that may help you to interpret the results it provides. Plus, you can use this knowledge to impress your friends, who probably don't know how it works.

The key to `tracert` is a field that's a standard part of all IP packets called TTL, which stands for *Time to Live*. In most other circumstances, a value called TTL would be a time value — not in IP packets, however. In an IP packet, the TTL value indicates how many routers a packet can travel through on its way to its destination. Every time a router forwards an IP packet, it subtracts one from the packet's TTL value. When the TTL value reaches zero, the router refuses to forward the packet.

The `tracert` command sends a series of special messages called ICMP Echo Requests to the destination computer. The first time it sends this message, it sets the TTL value of the packet to 1. When the packet arrives at the first router along the path to the destination, that router subtracts one from the TTL value, sees that the TTL value has become 0, so it sends a Time Exceeded message back to the original host. When the `tracert` command receives this Time Exceeded message, it extracts the IP address of the router from it, calculates the time it took for the message to return, and displays the first hop.

Then the `tracert` command sends another Echo Request message: this time, with the TTL value set to 2. This message goes through the first router to the second router, which sees that the TTL value has been decremented to 0 and then sends back a Time Exceeded message. When `tracert` receives the Time Exceeded message from the second router, it displays the line for the second hop. This process continues, each time with a greater TTL value, until the Echo Request finally reaches the destination.

Pretty clever, eh?

(Note that the Unix/Linux `traceroute` command uses a slightly different set of TCP/IP messages and responses to accomplish the same result.)

3

Planning a Network

Contents at a Glance

Chapter 1

Local Area Networks

Okay, so you're convinced that you need to network your computers. What now? Do you stop by Computers-R-Us on the way to work, install the network before drinking your morning coffee, and expect the network to be fully operational by noon?

I don't think so.

Networking your computers is just like any other worthwhile endeavor: Doing it right requires a bit of planning. This chapter helps you to think through your network before you start spending money. It shows you how to come up with a networking plan that's every bit as good as the plan that a network consultant would charge thousands of dollars for. See? This book is already saving you money!

Making a Network Plan

Before you begin any networking project, whether a new network installation or an upgrade of an existing network, make a detailed plan *first*. If you make technical decisions too quickly, before studying all the issues that affect the project, you'll regret it. You'll discover too late that a key application won't run over the network, the network has unacceptably slow performance, or key components of the network don't work together.

Here are some general thoughts to keep in mind while you create your network plan:

>> **Don't rush the plan.** The most costly networking mistakes are the ones that you make before you install the network. Think things through and consider alternatives.

>> **Write down the network plan.** The plan doesn't have to be a fancy, 500-page document. If you want to make it look good, pick up a ½-inch three-ring binder, which is big enough to hold your network plan with plenty of room to spare.

>> **Ask someone else to read your network plan before you buy anything.** Preferably, ask someone who knows more about computers than you do.

>> **Keep the plan up to date.** If you add to the network, dig up the plan, dust it off, and update it.

TIP

"The best laid schemes of mice and men gang aft agley, and leave us naught but grief and pain for promised joy." Robert Burns lived a few hundred years before computer networks, but his famous words ring true. A network plan isn't chiseled in stone. If you discover that something doesn't work the way you thought it would, that's okay. Just change your plan.

Being Purposeful

One of the first steps in planning your network is making sure that you understand why you want the network in the first place. Here are some of the more common reasons for needing a network, all of them quite valid:

>> **My co-worker and I exchange files using flash drives just about every day.** With a network, trading files is easier.

>> **I don't want to buy everyone a color laser printer when I know the one we have now just sits there taking up space most of the day.** So wouldn't buying a network be better than buying a color laser printer for every computer?

>> **I want everyone to be able to access the Internet.** Many networks, especially smaller ones, exist solely for the purpose of sharing an Internet connection.

>> **Business is so good that one person typing in orders eight hours each day can't keep up.** With a network, more than one person can enter orders, which expedites orders and possibly saves on overtime expenses.

>> **My brother-in-law just put in a network at his office.** No one wants to be behind the times.

>> **I already have a network, but it's so old that it may as well be made of kite string and tin cans.** An improved network speeds up access to shared files, provides better security, is easier to manage, and is more reliable.

REMEMBER

After you identify all the reasons why you think you need a network, write them down. Don't worry about winning the Pulitzer Prize for your stunning prose. Just make sure that you write down what you expect a network to do for you. If you were making a 500-page networking proposal, you'd place the description of why a network is needed in a tabbed section labeled Justification. In your ½-inch network binder, file the description under Purpose.

TIP

As you consider the reasons why you need a network, you may conclude that you don't need a network after all. That's okay. You can always use the binder for your stamp collection.

Taking Stock

One of the initial challenges of planning a network is figuring out how to work with the computers that you already have. In other words, how do you get from here to there? Before you can plan how to get "there," you have to know where "here" is. In other words, you have to take a thorough inventory of your current computers.

What you need to know

You need to know the following information about each of your computers:

>> **The processor type and, if possible, its clock speed:** It would be nice if each of your computers had a shiny new i7 10-Core processor. In most cases, though, you find a mixture of computers: some new, some old, some borrowed, some blue. You may even find a few archaic Pentium computers.

TIP

You can't usually tell what kind of processor a computer has just by looking at the computer's case. But you can easily find out by right-clicking Computer on the Start menu and choosing Properties.

» **The size of the hard drive and the arrangement of its partitions:** To find the size of your computer's hard drive, open the Computer window, right-click the drive icon, and choose the Properties command from the shortcut menu that appears. Figure 1-1 shows the Properties dialog box for a 922GB hard drive that has about 867GB of free space.

If your computer has more than one hard drive, Windows lists an icon for each drive in the Computer window. Jot down the size and amount of free space available on each drive.

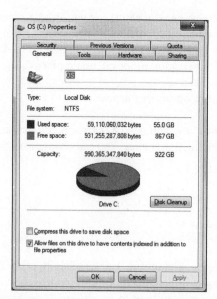

FIGURE 1-1:
The Properties
dialog box for a
disk drive.

» **The amount of memory:** To find this information in Windows, right-click Computer from the Start menu and choose the Properties command. The amount of memory on your computer is shown in the dialog box that appears. For example, Figure 1-2 shows the System Properties dialog box for a computer with 8GB of RAM.

» **The operating system version:** This you can also deduce from the System Properties dialog box. For example, the Properties page shown in Figure 1-2 indicates that the computer is running Windows 7 Ultimate.

» **What kind of printer, if any, is attached to the computer:** Usually, you can tell just by looking at the printer. You can also tell by double-clicking the Printers icon in Control Panel.

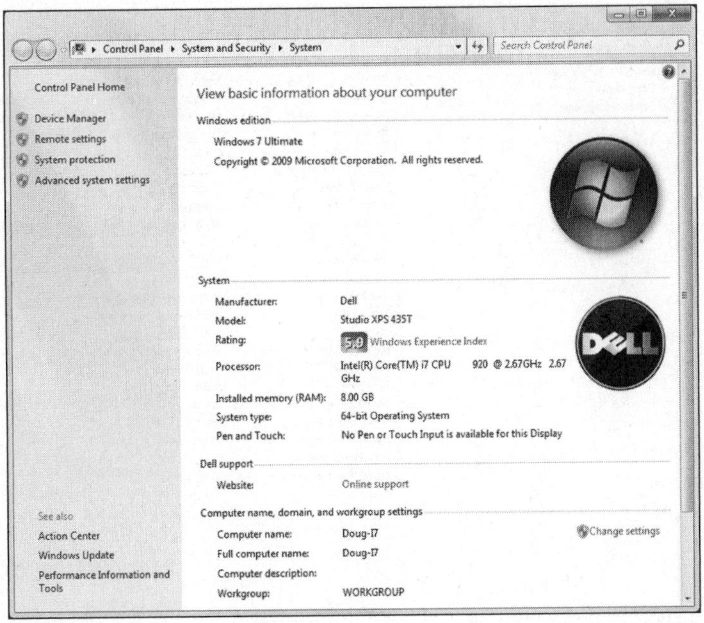

FIGURE 1-2:
The Properties page for a computer with 8GB of RAM.

>> **Any other devices connected to the computer:** A DVD or Blu-ray drive? Scanner? External disk? Webcam? Battle droid? Hot tub?

>> **What software is used on the computer:** Microsoft Office? AutoCAD? QuickBooks? Make a complete list and include version numbers.

Programs that gather information for you

Gathering information about your computers is a lot of work if you have more than a few computers to network. Fortunately, several software programs are available that can automatically gather the information for you. These programs inspect various aspects of a computer, such as the CPU type and speed, amount of RAM, and the size of the computer's hard drives. Then they show the information on the screen and give you the option of saving the information to a hard drive file or printing it.

Windows comes with just such a program: Microsoft System Information. Choose Start⇨All Programs⇨Accessories⇨System Tools⇨System Information.

When you fire up Microsoft System Information, you see a window similar to the one shown in Figure 1-3. Initially, Microsoft System Information displays basic information about your computer, such as your version of Microsoft Windows, the processor type, the amount of memory on the computer, and so on. You can obtain more detailed information by clicking Hardware Resources, Components, or other categories in the left side of the window.

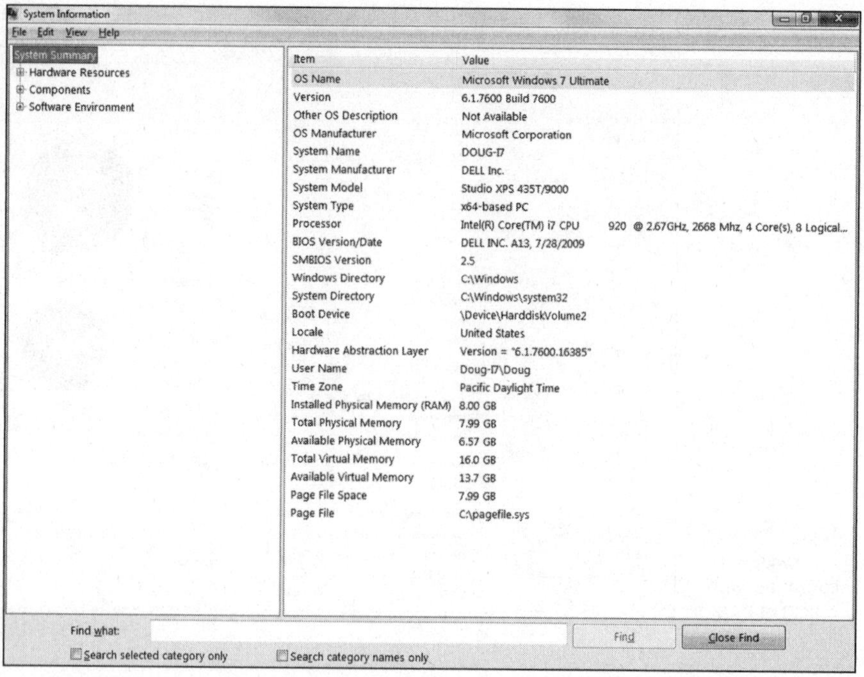

FIGURE 1-3:
Let the System Information program gather the data you need.

Considering Cable

Over the years, several different types of cables have been used for networking. But today, almost all cabled networks are built using simple copper-based Unshielded Twisted-Pair (UTP) cable. Figure 1-4 shows a twisted-pair cable.

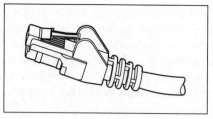

FIGURE 1-4:
Twisted-pair cable.

When you use UTP cable to construct an Ethernet network, you connect the computers in a star-like arrangement, in which each computer is connected to a central point. At the center of the stars are switches (see Book 1, Chapter 3). Depending on the model, a single switch can connect from 4 to 48 or more devices.

Here are a few additional details that you should know about twisted-pair cabling:

>> UTP cable consists of four pairs of thin wire twisted around each other; several such pairs are gathered up inside an outer insulating jacket. Ethernet uses two pairs of wires, or four wires altogether.

>> UTP cable comes in various grades known as *categories.* Don't use anything less than Category 5e cable for your network; Category 6 is better yet. Although lower-category cables may be less expensive, they won't be able to support faster networks.

TIP

Be prepared for the future. Although higher-category cables are more expensive than lower-category cables, the real cost of installing Ethernet cabling is the labor required to actually pull the cables through the walls. As a result, I recommend that you invest in Category 6.

>> UTP cable connectors look like modular phone connectors but are a bit larger. UTP connectors are officially called RJ-45 connectors.

>> UTP cable can be purchased in prefabricated lengths, but for most jobs you'll want to purchase the cable in bulk and have a professional installer attach the connectors. Or, you can attach the connectors yourself using a simple crimping tool you can purchase for about $50.

>> The maximum allowable cable length between the switch and the computer is 100 meters (about 328 feet). That should be more than enough for most circumstances, but don't forget that the distance includes the vertical distance required for getting from the floor up to the ceiling, and back down again.

>> Always leave at least 5 feet or more of extra cable neatly coiled up in the ceiling space above each location where the cable drops through the wall to floor level. That way, you'll have some flexibility to re-route the cable later on if necessary.

Surmising Switches

As I mention in the previous section, computers and other devices are connected to a network in a starlike configuration, with switches at the center of the star. Figure 1-5 shows a switch with five computers connected to it.

A switch contains a number of *ports,* each of which is a receptacle that can accommodate an RJ-45 jack connected to a UTP cable. In Figure 1-5, there are five UTP cables. One end of each of these cables is plugged into a port on the switch, and the other end is plugged into the computer's network adapter.

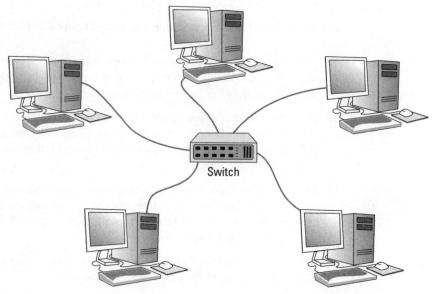

FIGURE 1-5:
A switch with
five computers
connected.

Although it may not be obvious from the figure, the switch does not have to be in the same room as the computers. In fact, ideally the switch will be in a separate room from the computers. The cables run through the ceilings and the walls from the location of the switch to the location of the computers, within the 100–meter limit of UTP cable. (The switches are generally located in the same room as the servers.)

Here are some additional ins and outs for working with switches:

>> Because you must run a cable from each computer to the switch, find a central location for the switch to which you can easily route the cables.

>> The switch requires electrical power, so make sure that an electrical outlet is handy.

>> As a general rule, purchase twice as many switch ports as you currently need. Don't buy an eight-port switch if you want to network eight computers because when (not *if*) you add the ninth computer, you'll have to buy another switch.

>> You can connect — or *daisy-chain* — switches to one another, as shown in Figure 1-6. You connect one end of a cable to a port on one switch and the other end to a port on the other switch.

WARNING

>> Although you can daisy-chain as many switches together as you want, in actual practice you should limit the number of daisy chains in your switch configuration. Daisy-chaining can slow down a network a bit because each switch must fully receive each packet before it begins to forward the packet to the next switch. (However, some switches actually start the packet forwarding before the entire packet is received, which reduces the performance hit a bit.)

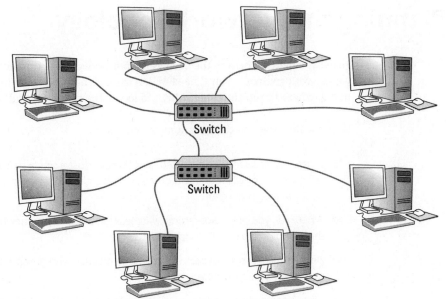

FIGURE 1-6:
Daisy-chaining
switches.

>> If you need more ports than a single switch can provide, you can use *stackable switches.* Stackable switches have high-speed direct connections that enable two or more switches to be connected in such a way that they behave as if they were a single switch.

This type of connection is sometimes called a *back-plane connection* because the interconnect may be on the back of the switch, but that's not always the case. If a single switch will suffice for you now, but there is a reasonable chance that you might outgrow it and need a second switch, I suggest you invest in a stackable switch so that you can expand your network later without daisy-chaining.

>> Another way to provide a high-speed interconnect between switches is to purchase switches that have a few high-speed SFP ports. You can then equip those ports with 10 Gb connections to route traffic between the switches. (These high-speed connections can also be used to connect switches to servers.)

>> Yet another way to create high-speed interconnects between switches is to use a feature called *link aggregation.* If your switches provide this feature, you simply run two or more cables between the switches, using two or more ports on each switch. Then, you use the switch's configuration software to bond the two ports together to create one link with double the port speed.

Professional-quality network switches have network-management features that allow you to log in to the switch, usually via a web interface, to monitor and configure the switch. Such switches are called *managed switches.* Consumer-grade switches, also called *unmanaged switches,* are less expensive primarily because they do not support this feature. If you have more than a few dozen users, you'll want to invest in managed switches.

Planning the Network Topology

Topology refers to the way the devices in your network are connected to each other via network switches. You'll need to determine what kind of switches to use, how many, where to run the cable, where to locate the switches, and so on.

Here are just a few of the questions to consider:

>> Where will the servers be located? Will there be just a single switch in the server room, or will there be a central switch with workgroup switches located closer to the computers?

>> Where will you place workgroup switches? On a desktop somewhere within the group or in a small wiring closet?

>> How many client computers will you place on each workgroup switch, and how many switches will you need?

>> If you need more than one switch, how will you connect the switches to each other?

>> If you need wireless networking, what kind of wireless networking devices will you need, where will you put them, and how will you connect them to the network?

For midsized networks (say, 50 to 200 users), a common way to design the network topology is to use a two-layer switch architecture as shown in Figure 1-7:

>> **Core layer:** The *core layer* contains high-performance switches that connect to the servers, the Internet gateway, and to each other. These connections should be as fast as possible — ideally, 10 Gbps fiber or copper connections using SFP ports.

>> **Access layer:** The *access layer* consists of switches that are connected to the core layer and to the end-user computers.

In Figure 1-7, there are two switches at the core layer and four switches at the access layer. The two core switches are connected to each other, to the servers, and to the access layer switches using 10 Gbps fiber SFP connections. The access switches connect to the computers using standard 1 Gb Ethernet connections.

For even larger networks, a three-tier design can be used. In that case, a *distribution layer* is added between the access and core layers. The servers are moved to the distribution layer and the core layer using specialized high-speed switches whose sole purpose is to move large amounts of data between the distribution switches as quickly as possible.

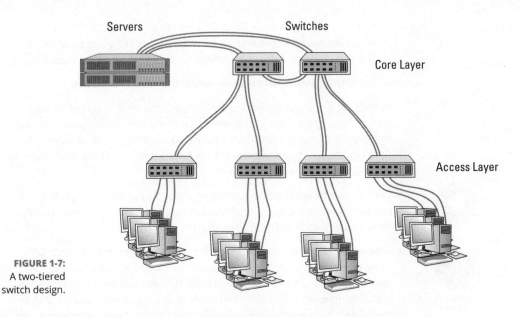

FIGURE 1-7:
A two-tiered
switch design.

Planning the TCP/IP Implementation

In addition to planning for the physical parts of your network infrastructure (cables, switches, ports, and so on), you'll also need to plan the details of how you'll implement TCP/IP for your network. TCP/IP is the basic networking protocol that your network uses to keep track of the individual computers and other devices on the network. Each computer or device will need an IP address (for example, 10.0.101.65). You'll need to devise a plan for how these addresses will be allocated.

You learn everything you need to know about TCP/IP in Book 2, Chapter 3, so make sure you understand the information in that chapter before you complete this part of your plan. For now, here are some of the main points your plan should address:

» **The subnet structure of your network:** Will everything be on a single subnet, or will you use two or more subnets to separate different types of devices?

Although it isn't impossible, dividing an existing network into separate subnets later on is a bit of a pain. So unless your network is very small, I suggest you plan on using subnets from the very start. In particular, you should consider using separate subnets for the following:

• **Wireless networks:** In fact, if you create two or more wireless networks (for example, a corporate network for company-owned mobile devices, an employee network for personal smartphones, and a guest network for visitors), I suggest a separate subnet for each of the wireless networks.

- **Remote locations that will be connected via a VPN tunnel.**

In addition, if you use IP phones, definitely put the phones on their own subnet. And if your organization has more than a few dozen users, consider dividing them among two or more subnets according to their work groups. For example, you might use one subnet for the sales department and another one for the production department.

Don't go overboard with the subnets, however. Try to find the right balance between running the entire organization on a single subnet versus creating a lot of subnets, each with just a few users.

Why bother with the subnets? The main reason is to avoid issues that will come up when your organization grows. You may have just 20 employees now, but years from now, when you have 100, and everyone starts bringing their smartphones and tablets and connecting to your Wi-Fi, you'll find that the limit of 253 devices per subnet on a 255.255.255.0 network is simply not enough. When you run out of DHCP space and your users can't get on the network, you'll wish you had spread things out over a couple of subnets.

>> **The DHCP structure:** Speaking of DHCP, what server will be responsible for DHCP? What will be the DHCP scope — that is, the range of addresses that are given out by DHCP? How will the size of your scope accommodate all the devices that will require DHCP on the subnet, with plenty of room for growth? (Again, be especially careful if you connect a wireless access point to the same subnet that your cabled network is on. You'll be surprised how quickly you can run out of IP addresses when every one of your users brings an iPhone and an iPad. Subnets are the best answer to that problem.)

>> **The static IP addresses of devices whose IP should never change:** These devices may include servers, printers, firewalls, and other managed devices. You'll be surprised how quickly these can add up, as well. You'll need static IP addresses for each of the network interfaces on your servers, for your switches, printers, copiers, fax machines, firewalls, routers, tape backup devices, and network storage devices. If you use virtualization software, the host processors will also need an IP address for each network interface. Even your UPS battery backups may want an IP address. The list goes on and on.

It is absolutely imperative that you keep a good record of what static IP addresses you have assigned in your network, and that you configure your DHCP server properly so that it doesn't step on top of static IP addresses. Every time you add a device with a static IP address, be sure to update your list. And, just as important, whenever you retire a device that uses a static IP address, update your master list to remove the IP address.

Drawing Diagrams

One of the most helpful techniques for creating a network plan is to draw a picture of it. The diagram can be a detailed floor plan, showing the actual location of each network component: a *physical map.* If you prefer, the diagram can be a *logical map,* which is more abstract and Picasso-like. Any time you change the network layout, update the diagram. Also include a detailed description of the change, the date that the change was made, and the reason for the change.

You can diagram very small networks on the back of a napkin, but if the network has more than a few computers, you'll want to use a drawing program to help you create the diagram. One of the best programs for this purpose is Microsoft Visio, shown in Figure 1-8.

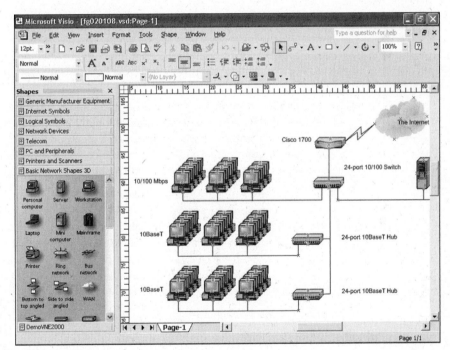

FIGURE 1-8:
Using Visio to draw a network diagram.

Here's a rundown of some of the features that make Visio so useful:

>> Smart shapes and connectors maintain the connections drawn between network components, even if you rearrange the layout of the components on the page.

>> Stencils provide dozens of useful shapes for common network components — not just for client and server computers, but for routers, hubs, switches, and

just about anything else you can imagine. If you're really picky about the diagrams, you can even purchase stencil sets that have accurate drawings of specific devices, such as Cisco routers or IBM mainframe computers.

>> You can add information to each computer or device in the diagram, such as the serial number or physical location. Then, you can quickly print an inventory that lists this information for each device in the diagram.

>> You can easily create large diagrams that span multiple pages.

More Questions Your Network Plan Should Address

In addition to the basic questions of why you need a network, what kind of servers you need to provide, and what kind of infrastructure your network will require, your network plan should address the following questions:

>> **Does it allow for growth?** What growth areas do you anticipate over the next few years? Does this network plan provide for such growth? For example, if you currently have 20 devices on the network, a 24-port switch may be adequate for today. But you should consider a 48-port switch instead. It will cost more now, but will simplify your expansion down the road.

Similarly, if you anticipate that each office will have just one employee, consider what you'll have to do if you run out of offices and end up putting two employees in each office. If you run a single cable to each office now, you'll have to pay to have a second cable run later. Better to spend a little more for extra cable and have the installer pull two cables to each office. (Better yet, have the installer pull three cables to each office: When you move a second employee into the office, you may also put a printer in there.)

>> **How will you secure it?** What kind of safety precautions will you take to keep unwanted visitors off your network? You'll need a strong, well-configured firewall to keep intruders from breaking in to your network via your Internet connection. If you're installing wireless access points, you'll have to take precautions to secure the wireless networks. And you'll need strong password policies to prevent hackers who do manage to get on to your network from getting at any valuable data.

For more information about network security, refer to the chapters in Book 9.

>> **How will you back it up?** You'll need to include a solid plan to back up your servers and the data that resides on them. That plan will probably require additional hardware, such as separate disk storage to hold the first level of backup data, as well as a means to get the backed up files off-site so they can survive a true disaster such as a fire or flood.

You'll also need to be certain that you provide adequate network disk storage so that all users can put all their work on the network, where it can be backed up. In lieu of that, you'll need a plan that backs up not only your servers, but also the client computers.

For more information about backing up your network, refer to Book 9, Chapter 4.

>> **How will you recover from failures?** Make sure you have a plan in place that will protect you from the commonplace maladies of daily life such as occasional power failures, as well as from the unforeseen, such as vandalism, theft, or fire. Every device on your network, no matter how insignificant, should be protected by battery backup. When possible, you should have spares of critical components.

For more information about disaster recovery, see Book 9, Chapter 5.

Chapter **2**

Wide Area Networks

O bviously, your network needs to be connected to the Internet. But that's easy, right? All you have to do is call the cable company and have them send someone out. They'll get you hooked up in a jiffy.

Wrong. Unfortunately, connecting to the Internet involves more than just calling the cable company. For starters, you have to make sure that cable is the right way to connect. Then you have to select and configure the right device to connect your network to the Internet. And, in all likelihood, you have to figure out how to provide remote access to your network so you can connect from a hotel room on a business trip or link up with the branch office in Albuquerque. And finally, you have to lie awake at night worrying whether hackers are breaking into your network via its Internet connection.

Not to worry. The advice in this chapter helps you decide how to design your wide area network (WAN) architecture. This includes your Internet connection, as well as remote access options.

Connecting to the Internet

Connecting to the Internet isn't free. For starters, you have to purchase the computer equipment necessary to make the connection. Then you have to obtain a connection from an Internet service provider (ISP). The ISP charges you a monthly fee that depends on the speed and capacity of the connection.

Choosing an ISP and negotiating a contract is a basic first step in setting up a WAN connection for your private network. The following sections describe the most commonly used methods of connecting network users to the Internet.

Connecting with cable or DSL

For small and home offices, the two most popular methods of connecting to the Internet are cable and digital subscriber line (DSL). Cable and DSL connections are often called *broadband connections* for technical reasons you don't really want to know.

Cable Internet access works over the same cable that brings 40 billion TV channels into your home, whereas DSL is a digital phone service that works over a standard phone line. Both offer three major advantages over old-fashioned dialup connections:

>> **Cable and DSL are much faster than dialup connections.** A cable connection can be anywhere from 10 to 200 times faster than a dialup connection, depending on the service you get. And the speed of a DSL line is comparable with cable. (Although DSL is a dedicated connection, cable connections are shared among several subscribers. The speed of a cable connection may slow down when several subscribers use the connection simultaneously.)

>> **With cable and DSL, you're always connected to the Internet.** You don't have to connect and disconnect each time you want to go online like you would if you use a modem. No more waiting for the modem to dial your service provider and listening to the annoying modem shriek while it attempts to establish a connection.

>> **Cable and DSL don't tie up a phone line while you're online.** With cable, your Internet connection works over TV cables, not over phone cables. With DSL, the phone company installs a separate phone line for the DSL service, so your regular phone line isn't affected.

Unfortunately, there's no such thing as a free lunch, and the high-speed, always-on connections offered by cable and DSL don't come without a price. For starters, you can expect to pay a higher monthly access fee for cable or DSL. In most areas of the United States, cable runs about $50 per month for residential users; business users can expect to pay two to three times that for the same speeds, primarily because the providers expect a higher level of usage and offer a slightly better service level for business connections.

The cost for DSL service depends on the access speed you choose. In some areas, residential users can get a relatively slow DSL connection for as little as $30 per month. For higher access speeds or for business users, DSL can cost substantially more.

Besides the cost, there are a few inherent disadvantages with DSL and cable providers:

>> **Cable and DSL are *asymmetrical* technologies, which means that their download speeds are much faster than their upload speeds.** For example, a circuit that can download at 100 Mbps is probably limited to about 10 Mbps for upload speeds. For many users, this is acceptable. But if you need to upload data as often as you need to download, the asymmetrical nature of cable and DSL will be a drawback.

>> **Business-class cable and DSL provides "best effort" service levels.** The provider will do its best to keep the connection up and respond to issues, but there is no guaranteed service level. When the service goes down, it can be down for a few hours or a few days.

And it will go down. Most users find that business-class cable and DSL are unreliable. Some users find that short service interruptions are an almost daily experience. The reason is that both cable and DSL service are shared services. The performance you get depends on what else is happening nearby. If all your neighbors suddenly start streaming the latest big thing on Netflix, your performance will suffer. Business-class cable and DSL don't claim to be 100 percent reliable — and they aren't.

>> **Cable and DSL access aren't available everywhere.** But if you live in an area where cable or DSL isn't available, you can still get high-speed Internet access by using a satellite hookup or a cellular network.

Connecting with T1 lines

Telephone providers such as AT&T, Time Warner, and others offer Internet service over dedicated copper phone lines using a time-proven technology called T1. I say "time-proven" because the original T1 service was developed in the 1960s, decades before the Internet even existed. T1 is not particularly fast — a single T1 line carries data at a paltry 1.44 Mbps. You can bond multiple T1 lines together to increase the speed, but you'd have to use 35 T1 lines to get 50 Mbps service. Newer versions such as T3 provide faster service (44.184 Mbps) but cost considerably more.

Although T1 is not the best type of service available (see the next section, "Connecting with fiber"), it's an improvement over business-class cable or DSL from a service and reliability perspective. Your carrier will provide a guaranteed service-level agreement (SLA) with a T1 line and will give you priority service if a problem occurs.

In addition, T1 service is symmetrical and predictable. Upload and download speeds are the same, so if you have ten T1 circuits that aggregate to 14.4 Mbps, you'll get that performance level for both uploads and downloads. And because the circuits are dedicated to your network, the performance will be consistent — it won't slow down in the afternoon when school gets out and kids start gaming over the Internet with their home cable or DSL connections.

If you don't have enough users to justify the expense of an entire T1 or T3 line, you can lease just a portion of the line. With a fractional T1 line, you can get connections with speeds of 128 Kbps to 768 Kbps; with a fractional T3 line, you can choose speeds ranging from 4.6 Mbps to 32 Mbps.

TIP

You may be wondering whether T1 or T3 lines are really any faster than cable or DSL connections. After all, T1 runs at 1.544 Mbps and T3 runs at 44.184 Mbps, and cable and DSL claim to run at much faster speeds, at least for downloads. But there are many differences that justify the substantial extra cost of a T1 or T3 line. In particular, a T1 or T3 line is a *dedicated* line — not shared by any other users. T1 and T3 are higher-quality connections, so you actually get the 1.544 or 44.184 connection speeds. In contrast, both cable and DSL connections usually run at substantially less than their advertised maximum speeds because of poor-quality connections and because the connections are often shared with other users.

Connecting with fiber

The fastest, most reliable, best, and of course most expensive form of Internet connection is fiber-optic. Fiber-optic cable uses strands of glass to transmit data over light signals at very high speeds. Because the light signals traveling within the fiber cables are not subject to electromagnetic interference, fiber connections are extremely reliable; about the only thing that can interrupt a fiber connection is if someone physically cuts the wire.

Fiber connections are typically available starting at 20 Mbps and ranging up to 1 Gbps. Obviously, the 1 Gbps service will cost a lot more than the 20 Mbps. But the cost of increased speed is incremental. For example, 20 Mbps might cost $800 per month, but 50 Mbps might be $1,000 per month and 100 Mbps might be $1,200 per month. In other words, the cost per megabit per second goes down as the speed increases.

Costs vary greatly depending on your location, so the only way to find out for sure is to get quotes from providers in your area.

In most major communities throughout the United States, providers are still building out their fiber-optic networks. The cost to bring fiber to your location may be prohibitive if you're in an area that isn't yet developed. If a provider already has fiber under the street running right past your building, getting fiber to your business will be relatively inexpensive. But if the nearest fiber is 5 miles away, the cost may be prohibitive.

You may be able to negotiate with the provider if you're willing to commit to a longer term of service, such as three, four, or even five years. That will make their investment more worthwhile. It also helps if you're in a business area where you'll be the first fiber customer but there is a potential customer pool nearby that the provider can tap into. If you're the only business out on the edge of town, you may not be able to convince anyone to bring fiber to you.

TIP

Phone service can be delivered via a fiber connection and bundled for one price. That can work to your advantage, because the provider will be more willing to bargain on the overall deal if the phone service is included.

Connecting with a cellular network

In areas where wired service (such as cable or fiber) is not available, you may be able to find wireless service, which provides Internet access using cellular or other wireless technology.

Cellular connections are not particularly fast, but they're getting faster all the time. The current generation of cellular technology (4G) can consistently achieve speeds in the neighborhood of 10 to 12 Mbps for download, with peak speeds approaching 50 Mbps. Upload is a bit slower, usually in the 5 Mbps range.

However, actual performance depends a lot on your location. I've seen 4G service as bad as 0.1 Mbps. You should use a smartphone to test the upload and download speed in your area before committing to a cellular solution.

The next-generation cellular technology (5G) hasn't rolled out yet, but it promises to be much faster, with speeds as much as 100 Mbps in major metropolitan areas.

With a cellular connection, the cost isn't so much the speed but the amount of data transferred. Individual cellular contracts run about $50 to $100 per month, but they typically limit the amount of data to about 5GB or 10GB per month. You can expect to pay considerably more than that if you need more data.

Choosing a Router

After you choose a method to connect to the Internet, you can turn your attention to setting up the connection so that your private network can access the Internet. The provider you select for your Internet connection will give you an

Ethernet handoff, which is simply an Ethernet port that you can use to connect to your private network. You'll need a router to make that connection. The router is the device that provides the link between your private network and the Ethernet handoff that leads to the Internet. (For more information about routers, refer to Book 1, Chapters 2 and 3, and Book 2, Chapter 4.)

Because all communications between your network and the Internet must go through the router, the router is a natural place to provide the security measures necessary to keep your network safe from the many perils of the Internet. As a result, a router used for Internet connections often doubles as a firewall, as described in the "Securing Your Connection with a Firewall" section, later in this chapter.

Choosing a small office router

For a small office, you can probably get by with a consumer-grade router that you can purchase at a local electronics retailer such as Best Buy. Figure 2-1 shows one such router, a Linksys WRT1900AC. This router has the following specifications:

» A WAN connection that lets you connect to your ISP's Ethernet handoff.

» A four-port 1 Gbps Ethernet switch. You can use this to connect up to four PCs, or to connect to an external switch for additional computers.

» A Wi-Fi Access Point that works with most 802.11 Wi-Fi standards, including 802.11ac.

» A USB 3.0 port that lets you connect a USB disk drive to provide storage accessible throughout your network.

» Built-in firewall capability.

To learn more about this router and other routers offered by Linksys, visit www.linksys.com.

FIGURE 2-1:
A Linksys
WRT1900AC
router.

Courtesy of Linksys

Choosing an enterprise router

For larger networks where greater throughput and more control is needed, you'll want to select an enterprise-grade router. There are many brands to choose from, but most professionals select a Cisco router. Figure 2-2 shows several models of one of their popular routers, the ASA 5500-X series.

These routers range from small tabletop units to powerful rack-mounted units that are capable of serving networks of all sizes. *ASA* stands for *Adaptive Security Appliance;* as the name suggests, these devices aren't just routers but incorporate state-of-the-art firewall capabilities.

Table 2-1 outlines the basic capabilities of six models of the ASA 5500-X that are appropriate for most networks.

TABLE 2-1

ASA 5500-X Models

Model	Throughput	1 Gb Ports	Form Factor
5506-X	300 Mbps	8	Desktop
5508-X	500 Mbps	8	1U Rackmount
5516-X	900 Mbps	8	1U Rackmount
5525-X	1 Gbps	8	1U Rackmount
5545-X	1.5 Gbps	8	1U Rackmount
5555-X	2 Gbps	8	1U Rackmount

As you can see, the main difference between these models is the total throughput that can be supported. To support the higher bandwidth, the higher model numbers have faster CPUs and more RAM than the lower model numbers. Additional models of the ASA series can support substantially more bandwidth, but these models are sufficient for nearly all midsize networks.

The ASA 5506-X is designed primarily as a small branch router, where a dedicated equipment room with a 19-inch rack may not be available. The other models are rack-mountable and more appropriate for larger networks where a dedicated equipment room is available.

These routers are not cheap — the list prices range from just under $1,000 to almost $45,000, depending on the exact options selected. But the performance, reliability, and flexibility they afford are well worth the cost.

For more information about the ASA 5500-X series, browse to www.cisco.com/c/en/us/products/security/asa-firepower-services/index.html.

Choosing a cellular router

If you opt to use a cellular connection for Internet, either as your office's primary connection or as a fail-over connection in case your primary connection goes down, you'll need a router that can interface with a cellular modem. Cellular modems are usually USB devices, so your router will need to provide a USB external port to connect the cellular modem to.

Securing Your Connection with a Firewall

If your network is connected to the Internet, a whole host of security issues bubbles to the surface. You probably connected your network to the Internet so that your network's users can get out to the Internet. Unfortunately, however, your Internet connection is a two-way street. It not only enables your network's users to step outside the bounds of your network to access the Internet, but it also enables others to step in and access your network.

And step in they will. The world is filled with hackers who are looking for networks like yours to break into. They may do it just for the fun of it, or they may do it to steal your customers' credit card numbers or to coerce your mail server into sending thousands of spam messages on behalf of the bad guys. Whatever their motive, rest assured that your network will be broken into if you leave it unprotected.

A *firewall* is a security-conscious router that sits between the Internet and your network with a single-minded task: preventing *them* from getting to *us*. The firewall acts as a security guard between the Internet and your private network. All network traffic into and out of the private network must pass through the firewall, which prevents unauthorized access to the network.

Some type of firewall is an absolute must if your network has a connection to the Internet, whether that connection is broadband (cable modem or DSL), T1, fiber, cellular modem, smoke signals, carrier pigeon, or anything else. Without it, sooner or later a hacker will discover your unprotected network and tell his friends about it, and within a few hours, your network will be toast.

You can set up a firewall in two basic ways:

>> **Firewall appliance:** The easiest way, and usually the best choice. A firewall appliance is basically a self-contained router with built-in firewall features.

Most firewall appliances include web-based interfaces that enable you to connect to the firewall from any computer on your network by using a browser. You can then customize the firewall settings to suit your needs.

>> **Server computer:** Can be set up to function as a firewall computer.

The server can run just about any network operating system, but most dedicated firewall systems run Linux.

Whether you use a firewall appliance or a firewall computer, the firewall must be located between your network and the Internet, as shown in Figure 2-3. Here, one end of the firewall is connected to a network switch, which is, in turn, connected to the other computers on the network. The other end of the firewall is connected to the Internet. As a result, all traffic from the LAN to the Internet (and vice versa) must travel through the firewall.

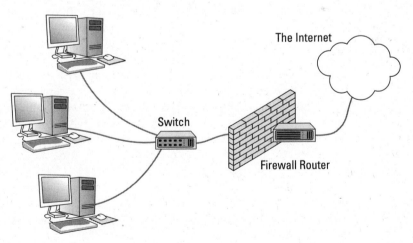

FIGURE 2-3: A firewall router creates a secure link between a network and the Internet.

The term *perimeter* or *edge* is sometimes used to describe the location of a firewall on your network. In short, a firewall is like a perimeter fence that completely surrounds and protects the edge of your property and forces all visitors to enter through the front gate.

WARNING

In large networks, figuring out exactly where the perimeter is located can be a little difficult. If your network has two or more Internet connections, make sure that every one of those connections connects to a firewall — and not directly to the network. You can do this by providing a separate firewall for each Internet connection or by using a firewall with more than one Internet port.

TIP

Some firewall routers can also enforce virus protection for your network. For more information about virus protection, see Book 9, Chapter 2.

Providing Redundancy for Your Internet Connection

Important considerations when designing how your private network will connect to the Internet are the reliability of your Internet connection and the importance to your company for having that connection be reliable. For some companies, an occasional disruption in Internet connectivity is acceptable. For others, it isn't — business grinds to a halt, and money is lost for every minute the Internet is down.

If that's the case, you'll want to provide at least two pathways to the Internet: a primary Internet connection and a backup Internet connection. The backup connection is often called a *fail-over connection,* because it comes into play only when the primary connection fails. With the right setup (and proper configuration), fail-over can happen automatically. When the primary Internet connection drops, the gateway router can instantly switch over to the backup connection. Then, when the primary connection is re-established, the gateway router can revert to it.

In most cases, you can get away with a slower and less reliable connection for the backup. For example, you might have a fiber-optic connection as your primary connection and use business-class cable as the backup. Fiber-optic connections are very reliable, but they do go down from time to time. Especially when a back-hoe operator doesn't realize that he or she is digging in the middle of a street where your provider's fiber run lies buried.

Business-class cable isn't nearly as reliable as fiber, but what are the odds that both will be down at the same time? Not likely, because most providers use separate routes for their fiber and cable runs. So, a single mishap with a back-hoe is unlikely to take out both.

If you do use a backup Internet service, you'll need to ensure that your router can support automatic fail-over. That means you'll need to use an enterprise-grade router such as the Cisco ASA 5500-X series described earlier in this chapter.

TIP

If you use a backup Internet service with automatic fail-over, be sure to test it periodically. The easiest way to do that is simply to unplug the cable from the primary Internet Ethernet handoff to the router, and then see if your router has switched over to the backup connection. If you can still reach the Internet, your fail-over is working. (If you want to keep what friends you have at your company, I suggest conducting this test after hours.)

Securing Connections to Remote Locations and Users

One final topic for this chapter is providing secure connections for remote users. These can be individuals who need to occasionally work from home or from the road, telecommuters who have convinced their boss to let them work from a home office, or branch offices that need a permanent connection to the main office network.

The solution to all these situations is a virtual private network. A VPN works by establishing a secure *tunnel* between two devices that are connected to the Internet. For the private network at your main office, the gateway router will provide the VPN capability. Remote users can run VPN software on their computers to connect to the main office VPN; remote sites such as branch offices should use gateway routers that can permanently (and transparently) connect to the VPN.

As part of your WAN network planning, you should identify all the VPN capabilities that your network will require. This will help you choose appropriate routers, because less expensive routers don't usually provide VPN features.

Figure 2-4 shows an example of a network drawing that shows four VPN tunnels — three to remote offices and one for mobile users. To support this network, you'd need a router that can let you create at least four separate VPNs. So, a consumer-grade gateway won't be sufficient for this network. In the figure, I specify various Cisco ASA routers to use for the VPN connections.

For more information about VPN, refer to Book 4, Chapter 6.

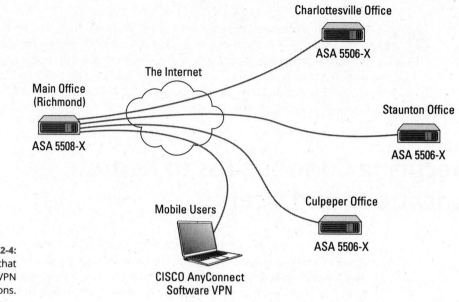

Charlottesville Office

ASA 5506-X

The Internet

Main Office
(Richmond)

ASA 5508-X

Staunton Office

ASA 5506-X

Mobile Users

Culpeper Office

ASA 5506-X

CISCO AnyConnect
Software VPN

FIGURE 2-4:
A network that
requires four VPN
connections.

Chapter **3**

Server Architecture

This chapter presents the task of planning the servers that your network will require. Over time, most networks gather servers like squirrels collect nuts. You start with just a few, and within a few years you have dozens of servers. In this chapter, you take stock of what servers you need, consider whether you should combine some of your servers, and look briefly at how to connect all the servers.

In the end, you'll find that the best way to manage your servers is to virtualize them. I look more closely at that topic in the next chapter.

Deciding How Many Servers You Need

A basic decision that you must make when planning a network is determining how many servers your network will require. At a minimum, all but the smallest networks require at least two domain controllers, plus additional servers to satisfy the needs of your users.

When setting up servers, you have the option of creating a bunch of single-purpose servers or a smaller number of multipurpose servers. For example, if you need a printer server and a file server, you can create a separate server for each function, or you can use a single server to perform both functions. There are advantages and disadvantages to both approaches:

>> Consolidating server functions into a smaller number of servers can save in licensing and administration costs. For example, if you can support all your functions on 6 servers rather than 12, you only need to purchase 6 licenses of Windows Server and you only need to keep 6 servers up to date rather than 12.

>> On the other hand, overloading several functions on a single server increases risk. For one thing, the more complicated a server is, the more likely it is to malfunction. And if you need to reboot the server or take the server down for repairs, you'll have downtime on multiple functions.

The trick is finding the right balance, and doing so is tricky. As a general rule, mission-critical functions such as Active Directory and email should be isolated on their own servers. Other server functions can be combined, as long as you take into consideration the risks and complexities of doing so.

Note that throughout this chapter, I'm ignoring the implications of virtualization. If you're running a virtual environment, you still need the same servers in place. Yes, virtualization makes it much easier to create more servers with fewer responsibilities on each server. In fact, that's one of the main reasons to virtualize your servers — if you don't, you have to purchase actual server hardware to bring up a new server. Even so, if a server function deserves to be isolated on its own server, it deserves its own server, regardless of whether you virtualize the server or run it on dedicated hardware. I look more closely at the question of virtualization in Chapter 4 of this minibook.

Deciding Which Servers You Need

At the outset, you should make a list of the various servers you think your network will need. The following sections describe some of the basic server functions you're likely to require. You may be surprised how many servers you end up with!

Domain controllers

Your Active Directory infrastructure should have at least two domain controllers. You can technically get by with just one, but if it fails, your entire network will be down until you get it fixed. Running two domain controllers provides an essential safety net.

In addition, you should isolate the domain controller function to single-purpose servers to minimize any required downtime. For example, if a domain controller doubles as a file server, you may have to take the server down to add disk space. That's a routine operation for a file server, but you don't want to impose the need to take down Active Directory just to increase disk space on a file server. Best to keep the domain controllers on separate servers.

Note that DNS and Active Directory are pretty much intertwined and dependent on one another, so it's common to enable DNS on a domain controller. In fact, Microsoft actually recommends that you combine DNS and Active Directory on your domain controllers, because Active Directory depends on DNS for name resolution.

DHCP servers

DHCP is a core service that is required for every network to run smoothly. Without DHCP, your users won't be able to connect to the network unless they all have static IP addresses, which is not a good idea, even on really small networks.

DHCP can run in several different locations, depending on your needs. For small networks, you can configure your router as the network's DHCP server. However, most DHCP implementations on routers aren't suitable for larger networks.

Technically, you can run DHCP on one of your domain controllers, but Microsoft recommends against it for two reasons:

>> **Performance:** On a large network, DHCP can suck a lot of performance from a server, which can slow down Active Directory.

>> **Security:** Running DHCP on a domain controller can potentially compromise the security of the domain controller.

So, if you can, I recommend you set up a separate server devoted to DHCP. And if you can't, double up DHCP on some other server rather than on a domain controller.

Mail servers

A *mail server* is a server that handles the network's email needs. It's configured with email server software, such as Microsoft Exchange Server. Exchange Server is designed to work with Microsoft Outlook, the email client software that comes with Microsoft Office.

Most mail servers actually do much more than just send and receive email. For example, here are some of the features that Exchange Server offers beyond simple email:

>> Calendaring and scheduling meetings

>> Collaboration features that simplify the management of collaborative projects

>> Audio and video conferencing

>> Chat rooms and instant messaging (IM) services

>> Microsoft Exchange Forms Designer, which lets you develop customized forms for applications such as vacation requests or purchase orders

Microsoft Exchange is a major piece of software that requires careful administration and, depending on how many users you have and how long you retain email, tons of disk storage. It is *always* a mistake to combine Exchange with any other server role — email should always be installed on its own dedicated server.

Many organizations are not installing Exchange on their own servers and instead using Office 365 for their email. In essence, this puts the burden of maintaining Exchange on Microsoft's Azure cloud services. For more information about this, refer to Book 5, Chapter 3.

File servers

File servers provide centralized disk storage that can be conveniently shared by client computers on the network. The most common task of a file server is to store shared files and programs. For example, members of a small workgroup can use disk space on a file server to store their Microsoft Office documents.

File servers must ensure that two users don't try to update the same file at the same time. The file servers do this by *locking* a file while a user updates the file so that other users can't access the file until the first user finishes. For document files (for example, word processing or spreadsheet files), the whole file is locked. For database files, the lock can be applied just to the portion of the file that contains the record(s) being updated.

Most organizations will have at least one file server, and some may have many file servers to support different applications or departments.

Print servers

Although it isn't necessary, a server computer can be dedicated for use as a *print server*, the sole purpose of which is to collect information being sent to a shared printer by client computers and print it in an orderly fashion.

A single computer may double as both a file server and a print server, but performance is better if you use separate print and file server computers.

With inexpensive inkjet printers running about $100 each, just giving each user his or her own printer is tempting. But you get what you pay for. Instead of buying $100 printers for 15 users, you may be better off buying one high-speed $1,500 color laser printer and sharing it. The $1,500 laser printer will be much faster, will probably produce better-looking output, and will be less expensive to operate.

Better yet, lease a high-speed multifunction copier from a copier vendor. That way, the copier vendor will be responsible for keeping the beast working, and you'll be able to get a high-performance machine in the bargain. The printer function of a multifunction copier can be managed through a print server.

You can get by without setting up a print server. Instead, each user on your network can connect directly to the printer via its IP address. There are several disadvantages to that, however:

>> **You have to manage drivers for each computer separately.** If you have 50 users connected to a printer and you need to update the driver, you'll have to update 50 computers.

>> **Some users will inevitably mess up their print driver configuration.** You'll get called to fix it.

>> **You lose overall control of the printer.** There is no centralized print queue and no ability to manage all your printers from a single point.

For more information about managing network printers, refer to Book 4, Chapter 5.

Web servers

A *web server* is a server computer that runs software that enables the computer to host an Internet website. The two most popular web server programs are Microsoft's Internet Information Services (IIS) and Apache, an open-source web server managed by the Apache Software Foundation.

If you're going to use an internal web server to provide external users access to your corporate website, you need to carefully manage the security configuration of both the web server and your firewall to ensure that intruders can't use the website as a way to gain access to your entire network. For that reason, it's a good idea to host your website on a completely separate network if possible. Many companies use web hosting services for that purpose, so the web server for their company's website isn't part of their network at all.

However, it's very common to set up internal web servers for your company's intranet — that is, for web pages that are meant to be used within your company, not by users outside your company. If you intend to support a company intranet, you'll need to set up a separate web server for it.

For more information about web servers, see Book 6, Chapter 7, and Book 7, Chapter 6.

Database servers

A *database server* is a server computer that runs database software, such as Microsoft's SQL Server 2017. Database servers are usually used along with customized business applications, such as accounting or marketing systems.

Like Exchange, SQL Server is a complicated enough piece of software that you should run it on a dedicated server. For more information, see Book 6, Chapter 9.

Application servers

An *application server* is a server computer that runs a specific application. For example, you might use an accounting application that requires its own server. In that case, you'll need to dedicate a server to the accounting application.

Again, application servers are typically complicated enough and important enough to merit their own servers. It's not a good idea to bundle your accounting server with your print server; you don't want the entire accounting department calling your desk if you need to reboot the print server.

Backup servers

Depending on the backup software you use, you may need to provide a separate server that is devoted strictly to backing up your other servers. This is especially true if you back up to tape, as most tape devices don't connect via the network, but instead connect directly to a server. Isolating the important backup functions to a separate server is a great idea so backups don't interfere with other server processes, and vice versa.

For more information on different approaches to backing up your network, refer to Book 9, Chapter 4.

License servers

Some organizations use software that requires licenses that are distributed from a centralized license server. For example, engineering firms often use computer-aided design (CAD) software such as AutoCAD, which requires a license server. In that case, you'll need to set up a server to handle the licensing function.

You'll find more detailed information about managing software licensing in Book 8, Chapter 6.

Deployment servers

A *deployment server* is a server dedicated to the task of automatically installing Windows images on network computers. You probably don't need this on a small network, but when your network gets to more than 50 or 100 computers, it's nice to have an automated way to deploy images to new computers or to redeploy images to computers that are having difficulty.

Microsoft provides support for this capability built in to Windows Server though a server role called Windows Deployment Services. Other companies that provide similar services that are more comprehensive and easier to use include Symantec Ghost and Acronis Snap Deploy. Search the web for more information about these tools, and consider setting up a deployment server if your network is large enough to merit it.

Update servers

An *update server* is a server devoted to managing updates to Windows computers. If you have just a few computers on your network, you can simply turn on automatic updates for the computers and let them update themselves. However, imagine how much network traffic will be wasted if you have 100 computers, all of them downloading updates directly from Microsoft's servers. With an update server, the updates are downloaded from Microsoft's servers to your update server. Then your computers are directed to your server for their updates, cutting down significantly on the Internet traffic required to keep your computers up to date.

The simplest and easiest way to set up an update server is to use Windows Server Update Services (WSUS), a built-in component of all Windows Server operating systems. Simply devote a server computer to the task, install Windows Server, and then activate and configure the WSUS role.

An alternative is to use a third-party patch management tool such as Patch from Ivanti (www.ivanti.com) or LanGuard from GFI (www.gfi.com).

Virtualization management platform

If you're using a virtualizing platform (and you should be!), you'll need a server dedicated to managing all your virtual servers, network, and storage. For VMware, this management server is called vCenter. For Hyper-V, it's System Center Virtual Machine Manager. Either way, you'll want to devote one server to the management of your virtualization environment.

Connecting Your Servers

After you've determined just how many servers you need, it's time to figure out how you'll connect all those servers to your network.

If you aren't using virtualization, and instead you're implementing each of your servers as a separate physical server, you're bound to have a mess on your hands. It's generally a good idea to double up the network connection on each server for redundancy's sake (in other words, provide at least two paths to each server in case one path goes down). And it's also best to use the fastest connection speed possible for each server.

Figure 3-1 shows a simplified version of how you might connect seven servers (two domain controllers, two file servers, an Exchange server, a web server, and an update server) to a network. In this example, I'm using two core switches for all the servers and providing a separate connection from each server to each of the core switches. To keep the figure simple, I've omitted any access switches or end-user computers. As you can see, the figure is a rat's nest as it is.

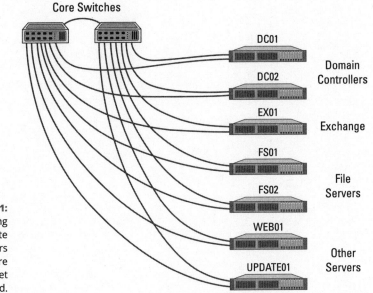

FIGURE 3-1:
Connecting
separate
physical servers
to multiple core
switches can get
complicated.

Imagine how much more complex the diagram would be if there were 15 servers! One of the many reasons for using virtualization is to reduce the complexity of the network connections required to integrate all your servers into the network. I take a more detailed look at virtualization and what it has to offer in the next chapter.

Server Architecture

Chapter **4**

Virtualization Architecture

Virtualization is one of the hottest trends in networking today. According to some industry pundits, virtualization is the best thing to happen to computers since the invention of the transistor. If you haven't already begun to virtualize your network, you're standing on the platform watching as the train is pulling out.

This chapter introduces you to the basic concepts of virtualization, with an emphasis on using it to leverage your network server hardware to provide more servers using less hardware. Virtualization can dramatically simplify the design of your network — you can support more servers on less hardware, and with less hardware, your network will have fewer interconnects that link servers to the private network. Win, win!

TIP

Mastering a virtualization environment calls for a book of its own. I recommend two titles, both from John Wiley & Sons, Inc.: *Virtualization For Dummies*, by Bernard Golden, and *VMware Infrastructure 3 For Dummies*, by William Lowe (no relation, honest).

Understanding Virtualization

The basic idea behind virtualization is to use software to simulate the existence of hardware. This powerful idea enables you to run more than one independent computer system on a single physical computer system. Suppose that your organization requires a total of 12 servers to meet its needs. You could run each of these 12 servers on a separate computer, in which case you would have 12 computers in your server room. Or, you could use virtualization to run these 12 servers on just two computers. In effect, each of those computers would simulate six separate computer systems, each running one of your servers.

Each of the simulated computers is called a *virtual machine* (VM). For all intents and purposes, each VM appears to be a complete, self-contained computer system with its own processor (or, more likely, processors), memory, disk drives, CD-ROM/DVD drives, keyboard, mouse, monitor, network interfaces, USB ports, and so on.

Like a real computer, each virtual machine requires an operating system to do productive work. In a typical network server environment, each virtual machine runs its own copy of Windows Server. The operating system has no idea that it's running on a virtual machine rather than on a real machine.

Here are a few terms you need to be familiar with if you expect to discuss virtualization intelligently:

>> **Host:** The actual physical computer on which one or more virtual machines run. Admittedly, this term is kind of confusing, because it's also used to refer to any device that is connected to the network, such as an end-user computer. Context is everything — when discussing servers, *host* usually means the physical computer that virtual servers run on.

>> **Bare metal:** Another term for the host computer that runs one or more virtual machines.

>> **Guest:** Another term for a virtual machine running on a host.

» **Guest operating system:** An operating system that runs within a virtual machine. By itself, a guest is just a machine; it requires an operating system to run. The guest operating system is what brings the guest to life.

As far as licensing is concerned, Microsoft treats each virtual machine as a separate computer. Thus, if you run six guests on a single host, and each guest runs Windows Server, you need licenses to run six servers. Unfortunately, figuring out how to ensure that you have the right number of licenses can be a bit complicated; see the section "Understanding Windows Server 2016 Licensing" later in this chapter for an explanation.

» **Hypervisor:** The virtualization operating system that creates and runs virtual machines. For more information about hypervisors, read the next section, "Understanding Hypervisors."

» **Hardware Abstraction Layer (HAL):** A layer of software that acts as a go-between to separate actual hardware from the software that interacts with it. An operating system provides a hardware abstraction layer, because it uses device drivers to communicate with actual hardware devices so that software running in the operating system doesn't have to know the details of the specific device it's interacting with. A hypervisor also provides a hardware abstraction layer that enables the guest operating systems in virtual machines to interact with virtualized hardware.

Understanding Hypervisors

At the core of virtualization is a *hypervisor*, a layer of software that manages the creation and execution of virtual machines. A hypervisor provides several core functions:

» It provides a HAL, which virtualizes all the hardware resources of the host computer on which it runs. This includes processor cores, RAM, and I/O devices such as disk drives, keyboards, mice, monitors, USB devices, and so on.

» It creates pools of these abstracted hardware resources that can be allocated to virtual machines.

» It creates virtual machines, which are complete implementations of an idealized computer system that has the hardware resources of the host available to it. The hardware for each virtual machine is drawn from the pools of available hardware resources managed by the hypervisor.

» It manages the execution of its virtual machines, allocating host hardware resources as needed to each virtual machine and starting and stopping virtual machines when requested by users.

>> It ensures that each virtual machine is completely isolated from all other virtual machines, so that if a problem develops in one virtual machine, none of the other virtual machines is affected.

>> It manages communication among the virtual machines over virtual networks, enabling the virtual machines to connect with each other and with a physical network that reaches beyond the host.

THE LONG TREK OF VIRTUALIZATION

Kids these days think they invented everything, including virtualization.

Little do they know.

Virtualization was developed for PC-based computers in the early 1990s, around the time Captain Picard was flying the Enterprise around in *Star Trek: The Next Generation*.

But the idea is much older than that.

The first virtualized server computers predate Captain Picard by about 20 years. In 1972, IBM released an operating system called simply VM, which had nearly all the basic features found in today's virtualization products.

VM allowed the administrators of IBM's System/370 mainframe computers to create multiple independent virtual machines, each of which was called (you guessed it) a virtual machine, or VM. This terminology is still in use today.

Each VM could run one of the various guest operating systems that were compatible with the System/370 and appeared to this guest operating system to be a complete, independent System/370 computer with its own processor cores, virtual memory, disk partitions, and input/output devices.

The core of the VM system itself was called the *hypervisor* — another term that persists to this day.

The VM product that IBM released in 1972 was actually based on an experimental product that IBM released on a limited basis in 1967.

So whenever someone tells you about this new technology called *virtualization,* you can tell him or her that it was invented when *Star Trek* was on TV. When someone asks, "You mean the one with Picard?" you can say, "No, the one with Kirk."

There are two basic types of hypervisors you should know about:

>> **Type-1:** A type-1 hypervisor runs directly on the host computer, with no intervening operating system. This is the most efficient type of hypervisor because it has direct access to the hardware resources of the host system.

The two best-known examples of type-1 hypervisors are VMware's ESXi and Microsoft's Hyper-V. ESXi is part of a suite of popular virtualization products from VMware, and Hyper-V is the built-in virtualization platform that is included with recent versions of Windows Server.

>> **Type-2:** A type-2 hypervisor runs as an application within an operating system that runs directly on the host computer. Type-2 hypervisors are less efficient than type-1 hypervisors because when you use a type-2 hypervisor, you add an additional layer of hardware abstraction: the first provided by the operating system that runs natively on the host, and the second by the hypervisor that runs as an application on the host operating system.

TIP

For production use, you should always use type-1 hypervisors because they're much more efficient than type-2 hypervisors. Type-1 hypervisors are considerably more expensive than type-2 hypervisors, however. As a result, many people use inexpensive or free type-2 hypervisors to experiment with virtualization before making a commitment to purchase an expensive type-1 hypervisor.

Understanding Virtual Disks

Computers aren't the only things that are virtualized in a virtual environment. In addition to creating virtual computers, virtualization also creates virtual disk storage. Disk virtualization lets you combine a variety of physical disk storage devices to create pools of disk storage that you can then parcel out to your virtual machines as needed.

Virtualization of disk storage is nothing new. In fact, there are actually several layers of virtualization involved in any disk storage environment. At the lowest level are the actual physical disk drives. Physical disk drives are usually bundled together in arrays of individual drives. This bundling is a type of virtualization in that it creates the image of a single large disk drive that isn't really there. For example, four 2TB disk drives might be combined in an array to create a single 8TB disk drive.

Note that disk arrays are usually used to provide data protection through redundancy. This is commonly called RAID, which stands for *Redundant Array of Inexpensive Disks.*

One common form of RAID, called RAID-10, lets you create mirrored pairs of disk drives so that data is always written to both of the drives in a mirror pair. So, if one of the drives in a mirror pair fails, the other drive can carry the load. With RAID-10, the usable capacity of the complete array is equal to one-half of the total capacity of the drives in the array. For example, a RAID-10 array consisting of four 2TB drives contains two pairs of mirrored 2TB disk drives, for a total usable capacity of 4TB.

Another common form of RAID is RAID-5, in which disk drives are combined and one of the drives in the group is used for redundancy. Then, if any one of the drives in the array fails, the remaining drives can be used to re-create the data that was on the drive that failed. The total capacity of a RAID-5 array is equal to the sum of the capacities of the individual drives, minus one of the drives. For example, an array of four 2TB drives in a RAID-5 configuration has a total usable capacity of 6TB.

In a typical virtual environment, the host computers can be connected to disk storage in several distinct ways:

>> **Local disk storage:** In local disk storage, disk drives are mounted directly into the host computer and are connected to the host computer via its internal disk drive controllers. For example, a host computer might include four 1TB disk drives mounted within the same chassis as the computer itself. These four drives might be used to form a RAID-10 array with a usable capacity of 2TB.

The main drawbacks of local disk storage is that it's limited to the physical capacity of the host computers and is available only to the host computer that it's installed in.

>> **Storage Area Network (SAN):** In a SAN, disk drives are contained in a separate device that is connected to the host via a high-speed controller. The difference between a SAN and local storage is that the SAN is a separate device. Its high-speed connection to the host is often just as fast as the internal connection of local disk storage, but the SAN includes a separate storage controller that is responsible for managing the disk drives.

A typical SAN can hold a dozen or more disk drives and can allow high-speed connections to more than one host. A SAN can often be expanded by adding one or more expansion chassis, which can contain a dozen or more disk drives each. Thus, a single SAN can manage hundreds of terabytes of disk data.

>> **Network Accessible Storage (NAS):** This type of storage is similar to a SAN, but instead of connecting to the hosts via a high-speed controller, a NAS connects to the host computers via standard Ethernet connections and TCP/IP. NAS is the least expensive of all forms of disk storage, but it's also the slowest.

Regardless of the way the storage is attached to the host, the hypervisor consolidates its storage and creates virtual pools of disk storage typically called *data stores*. For example, a hypervisor that has access to three 2TB RAID-5 disk arrays might consolidate them to create a single 6TB data store.

From this data store, you can create *volumes*, which are essentially virtual disk drives that can be allocated to a particular virtual machine. Then, when an operating system is installed in a virtual machine, the operating system can mount the virtual machine's volumes to create drives that the operating system can access.

For example, let's consider a virtual machine that runs Windows Server. If you were to connect to the virtual machine, log in, and use Windows Explorer to look at the disk storage that's available to the machine, you might see a C: drive with a capacity of 100GB. That C: drive is actually a 100GB volume that is created by the hypervisor and attached to the virtual machine. The 100GB volume, in turn, is allocated from a data store, which might be 4TB in size. The data store is created from disk storage contained in a SAN attached to the host, which might be made up of a RAID-10 array consisting of four 2TB physical disk drives.

So, you can see that there are at least four layers of virtualization required to make the raw storage available on the physical disk drives available to the guest operating system:

>> Physical disk drives are aggregated using RAID-10 to create a unified disk image that has built-in redundancy. RAID-10 is, in effect, the first layer of virtualization. This layer is managed entirely by the SAN.

>> The storage available on the SAN is abstracted by the hypervisor to create data stores. This is, effectively, a second level of virtualization.

>> Portions of a data store are used to create volumes that are then presented to virtual machines. Volumes represent a third layer of virtualization.

>> The guest operating system sees the volumes as if they're physical devices, which can be mounted and then formatted to create usable disk storage accessible to the user. This is the fourth layer of virtualization.

Although it may seem overly complicated, these layers of virtualization give you a lot of flexibility when it comes to storage management. New disk arrays can be added to a SAN, or a new NAS can be added to the network, and then new data stores can be created from them without disrupting existing data stores. Volumes can be moved from one data store to another without disrupting the virtual machines they're attached to. In fact, you can increase the size of a volume on the fly, and the virtual machine will immediately see the increased storage capacity of its disk drives, without even requiring so much as a reboot.

Understanding Network Virtualization

When you create one or more virtual machines on a host system, you need to provide a way for those virtual machines to communicate not only with each other but also with the other physical computers on your network. To enable such connections, you must create a *virtual network* within your virtualization environment. The virtual network connects the virtual machines to each other and to the physical network.

To create a virtual network, you must create a *virtual switch,* which connects the virtual machines to each other and to a physical network via the host computer's network interfaces. Like a physical switch, a virtual switch has ports. When you create a virtual switch, you connect the virtual switch to one or more of the host computer's network interfaces. These interfaces are then connected with network cable to physical switches, which effectively connects the virtual switch to the physical network.

Then, when you create virtual machines, you connect each virtual machine to a port on the virtual switch. When all the virtual machines are connected to the switch, the VMs can communicate with each other via the switch. And they can communicate with devices on the physical network via the connections through the host computer's network interfaces.

Considering the Benefits of Virtualization

You might suspect that virtualization is inefficient because a real computer is inherently faster than a simulated computer. Although it's true that real computers are faster than simulated computers, virtualization technology has become so advanced that the performance penalty for running on a virtualized machine rather than a real machine is only a few percent.

The small amount of overhead imposed by virtualization is usually more than made up for by the simple fact that even the most heavily used servers spend most of their time twiddling their digital thumbs, waiting for something to do. In fact, many servers spend nearly *all* their time doing nothing. As computers get faster and faster, they spend even more of their time with nothing to do.

Virtualization is a great way to put all this unused processing power to good use.

Besides this basic efficiency benefit, virtualization has several compelling benefits:

» **Hardware cost:** You typically can save a lot of money by reducing hardware costs when you use virtualization. Suppose that you replace ten servers that cost $4,000 each with one host server. Granted, you'll probably spend more than $4,000 on that server, because it needs to be maxed out with memory, processor cores, network interfaces, and so on. So you'll probably end up spending $15,000 or $20,000 for the host server. Also, you'll end up spending something like $5,000 for the hypervisor software. But that's still a lot less than the $40,000 you would have spent on ten separate computers at $4,000 each.

» **Energy costs:** Many organizations have found that going virtual has reduced their overall electricity consumption for server computers by 80 percent. This savings is a direct result of using less computer hardware to do more work. One host computer running ten virtual servers uses approximately one-tenth the energy that would be used if each of the ten servers ran on separate hardware.

» **Reduced downtime:** Virtual environments typically have less downtime than nonvirtual environments. For example, suppose you need to upgrade the BIOS on one of your server computers. With physical servers, this type of upgrade will ordinarily require that you shut down the operating system that runs on the server, upgrade the BIOS, and then restart the server. During the upgrade, the server will be unavailable.

In a virtual environment, you don't need to shut down the servers to upgrade the BIOS on the host computer that runs the server. Instead, all you do is move the servers that run on the host that needs the upgrade to another host. When the servers are moved (an operation that can be done without shutting them down), you can shut down the host and upgrade its BIOS. Then, after you restart the host, you can move the servers back to the host — again, without shutting down the servers.

» **Recoverability:** One of the biggest benefits of virtualization isn't the cost savings, but the ability to recover quickly from hardware failures. Suppose that your organization has ten servers, each running on separate hardware. If any one of those servers goes down due to a hardware failure — say, a bad motherboard — that server will remain down until you can fix the computer. On the other hand, if those ten servers are running as virtual machines on two different hosts, and one of the hosts fails, the virtual machines that were running on the failed host can be brought up on the other host in a matter of minutes.

Granted, the servers will run less efficiently on a single host than they would have on two hosts, but the point is that they'll all be running after only a short downtime.

Virtualization
Architecture

In fact, with the most advanced hypervisors available, the transfer from a failing host to another host can be done automatically and instantaneously, so downtime is all but eliminated.

>> **Disaster recovery:** Besides the benefit of recoverability when hardware failures occur, an even bigger benefit of virtualization comes into play in a true disaster-recovery situation. Suppose that your organization's server infrastructure consists of 20 separate servers. In the case of a devastating disaster, such as a fire in the server room that destroys all hardware, how long will it take you to get all 20 of those servers back up and running on new hardware? Quite possibly, the recovery time will be measured in weeks.

By contrast, virtual machines are actually nothing more than files that can be backed up onto tape. As a result, in a disaster-recovery situation, all you have to do is rebuild a single host computer and reinstall the hypervisor software. Then you can restore the virtual-machine backups from tape, restart the virtual machines, and get back up and running in a matter of days instead of weeks.

Choosing Virtualization Hosts

Having made the decision to virtualize your servers, you're next faced with the task of selecting the host computers on which you'll run your virtual servers. The good news is that you need to purchase fewer servers than if you use physical servers. The not-so-good news is that you need to purchase really good servers to act as hosts, because each host will support multiple virtual servers. Here are some tips to get you started:

>> **If possible, purchase at least two hosts, and make sure that each host is independently capable of running all your virtual servers.** That way, if one of the hosts goes down, you can temporarily move all your servers to the good host while the bad one is being repaired. When both hosts are up, you can spread the workload across the two hosts for better performance.

>> **Add up the amount of memory you intend to allocate for each server to determine the amount of RAM for each host.** Then give yourself plenty of cushion. If your servers will require a total of 50GB of RAM, get 72GB on each host, for a total of 144GB if you have two hosts. That will give you plenty of room to grow.

>> **Do a similar calculation for processor cores.** It's easier to oversubscribe processor cores on hosts than it is to oversubscribe memory. Like most computers, servers spend an enormous percentage of their time idling. Virtualization makes very efficient use of processor cores for a large number of servers.

>> **Get the best network connections you can afford.** Ideally, each host should have a pair of small form-factor pluggable (SFP) ports that you can run 10 Gb fiber over. That way, your hosts can communicate with the core switches at top speed.

>> **Provide redundancy in the host's subcomponents.** Most hosts support two processors, two memory banks, two network interfaces, and two power supplies. That provides for a maximum of uptime.

Understanding Windows Server 2016 Licensing

When planning your server architecture, you'll need to account for the fact that you must purchase sufficient licenses of Windows Server to cover all the servers you're running. Before virtualization, this was easy: Each server required its own license. With virtualization, things get tricky — and Microsoft doesn't make it easier by trying to simplify things.

Windows Server 2016 comes in three editions. These editions are as follows:

>> **Standard Edition:** Ideal for customers who aren't virtualized or who are virtualized but have a relatively small number of servers (approximately 12 per host). Standard Edition costs $882 per license. Each license entitles you run two virtual machines, which seems like a heck of a deal. However, a major drawback is that the license is also limited to hosts that have a maximum of 8 cores per processor and two processors, for a total of 16 cores. If your host has more than 8 cores per processor or more than two processors, you'll need additional licenses.

>> **Datacenter Edition:** Ideal for customers who are virtualized and have a large number of servers. Datacenter Edition costs $6,155 per license. Each license lets you run an unlimited number of virtual machines on a single host. Again, each host is limited to 8 cores per processor and two processors, for a total of 16 cores. If your host has more than 8 cores per processor or more than two processors, you'll need additional licenses.

>> **Essentials Edition:** Designed for small businesses setting up their first server. It's limited to just 25 users. I won't consider this edition further here.

So, you've got to do some real math to figure out which licenses you'll need. Let's say you need to run a total of 16 servers on two hosts. Here are two licensing scenarios that would be permissible:

>> Purchase eight Standard Edition licenses, for a total of $7,056. That works out to just $441 per server. These licenses will allow you to run 16 virtual machines (two per license), as long as your hosts have fewer than 8 processors per core and two processors per host. If your hosts have more than that — say, 12 processors per core, you'll need to purchase 16 Standard Edition licenses, for a total of $14,112, or $882 per server.

>> Purchase two Datacenter Edition licenses, for a total of $12,310. That works out to about $769 per server. This is more than the Standard Edition licenses would cost, but it allows you to run an unlimited number of servers. In contrast, additional Standard Edition servers will require additional licenses. As with Standard Edition, if your hosts have more than 8 cores per processor or two processors per host, you'll have to purchase an additional license for each host, bringing the total to $24,620. That works out to about $1,539 per server.

It's obvious that Microsoft charges more to run Windows Server on more powerful hosts, which makes for an interesting pricing strategy. As it turns out, over the next few years, you'll be hard pressed to purchase hosts that fall below the single-license core limit of 8 cores per processor or two processors per host. That's because Intel's dual-socket Xeon processors are getting more and more cores with each successive generation. The current generation of Xeon processors sports up to 18 cores per processor. While Intel still makes 4-, 6-, and 8-core versions of the Xeon processor, who knows what the future will bring.

In any event, the per-core nature of Microsoft's licensing encourages you to purchase host processors with cores as close to but below 8 per processor increments. In other words, use 8- or 16-core processors in your hosts; avoid 10- or 18-core processors, because they nudge you just over the core limits for licensing.

Chapter **5**

Storage Architecture

There's never enough storage, right? What may seem huge today will be laughably small in just a few years. Disk storage is like closet space: No matter how big the space, people find a way to fill it up.

In this chapter, I look at the most important things you need to consider when planning the storage side of your network. I cover various technologies for providing that disk storage, including various types of disk drives, different drive interfaces, and several ways to connect storage to your servers.

Considering Disk Space

The first basic decision you need to make when planning your network storage is the most obvious: How much storage do you need?

Unfortunately, that's not an easy decision to make. You can easily add up how much disk storage you currently have, and you can calculate how much is actually in use and how much free capacity you have. But predicting the future is hard.

One thing is for certain: The increase in your disk usage is not a linear function. In other words, you can't calculate some number — let's randomly pick 5TB — and assume that your company will use that much additional storage every year for the next five years. If it were true, your life would be simple. You'd just need to provide 25TB of free space to last for five years.

Unfortunately, experience suggests that disk usage is an exponential function, not a linear function. It's more like, "Every few years we need twice as much as we needed just a few years ago."

Experience bears that out. Most of us old folks remember the first 10MB hard disks in 1981. Soon it was 100MB, then gigabytes. Now terabytes. When will it be petabytes? Over the course of my career, disk capacity on my desktop has increased a million-fold, at a rate of about 1.4 times per year!

The point is, don't underestimate how much your disk needs will grow. Make sure your network plan can accommodate growth.

Here are a few general rules:

>> **Plan on about 100GB of disk space for the root drives of all your servers, and allow for twice as many servers as you currently have.** So if you have ten servers now, plan on 2TB of disk space to support server root drives (20 servers times 100GB each).

>> **If possible, choose expandable disk subsystems, and don't load them up to capacity.** Make sure the disk subsystem you purchase can be expanded to at least double its current capacity, either by adding additional drives or adding additional enclosures to accommodate more drives.

    Also, make sure you leave some room in your rack (or racks) to accommodate additional storage devices, and plan your rack layout in a way that leaves empty space below your current disk subsystem.

>> **Be wary of the desire to increase capacity at the risk of performance or reliability.** For example, always use RAID to provide the protection of redundancy for your server storage. And resist the temptation to use RAID 5 rather than RAID 10 for critical data simply because RAID 5 gives you more space. Opt for more drives instead, and use the best level of protection.

>> **Don't be tempted by huge drive capacities.** Yes, you can use 10TB drives to build out a huge storage network, but that's a lot of data to commit to a single drive. I'd rather use five 2TB drives, which spreads out the risks and simplifies recovery when failures occur (and they will!).

>> **Don't put too much faith in manufacturer claims of the benefits of tricks like compression or deduplication.** These techniques can (and do) work, but not always at the rate that the manufacturers claim.

>> **Don't neglect data retention policies and archiving strategies.** They can help keep unneeded files off your server storage.

Considering Disk Drive Types

The next basic decision in planning your disk storage is deciding what type of disk drives to use. There are two basic types of storage to choose from:

Hard disk drives

Hard disk drives (HDDs), also known as *spinning drives,* are traditional magnetic disks drives. Capacities of modern HDDs range anywhere from 500GB to 6TB or more.

HDDs include mechanical components such as the motor that spins the disk platters and the servos that move the read/write heads over the spinning platters to read and write data.

The performance of an HDD depends in large part on how fast the disk platters spin. Disk speed is measured in revolutions per minute (RPM), with three speeds being common: 7.2K, 10K, and 15K. The higher-RPM drives have better performance because the read/write heads must wait less time for data to arrive under the heads. In addition, when the data does arrive at the read/write heads, it can be read or written faster because the magnetic medium of the disk platter travels past the heads at a higher rate of speed.

Higher-RPM drives are also more expensive than slower-spinning drives because greater engineering care is needed to safely spin the platters at higher speeds.

Solid state drives

Solid state drives (SSDs) are all-electronic devices with no moving parts. They're based on memory technology, and they're considerably faster than HDDs. They're also considerably more expensive, and they tend to have smaller capacity — typically 100GB to 1TB.

SSD storage is significantly faster than HDD storage because no moving parts are involved. SSD technology is on the order of a thousand times faster than HDD technology, though that doesn't necessarily mean a given SSD drive is 1,000 times faster than a given HDD; many other factors combine to determine the overall performance of a storage device. Still, SSD is several orders of magnitude faster than HDD storage. (HDD access speed is measured in milliseconds — thousands of a second — while SSD storage is measured in microseconds — *millionths* of a second.)

FORM FACTORS

Form factor refers to the size of the disk drives you will use. Both HDDs and SSDs come in two basic form factors: 3.5-inch, called *LFF* (for *large form factor*) and 2.5-inch, called *SFF* (for *small form factor*). Because 3.5-inch disk drives are larger, they have potentially higher capacity. At the time I wrote this, the largest 3.5-inch enterprise-class HDD drives held 10TB.

The smaller 2.5-inch drives have smaller capacity (the maximum is currently 2.4TB). However, more 2.5-inch drives can be accommodated in a single enclosure. Typically, a rack enclosure of a given size can hold twice as many 2.5-inch drives as 3.5-inch drives.

SSD storage devices are based on *flash memory*, similar to the memory that is used in USB flash drives, but more reliable and considerably faster.

SSDs are considerably more expensive than HDDs of similar capacity, so for the time being, HDD is more likely to fit within your budget. Most networks include a combination of both SSDs and HDDs, reserving SSDs for data in which the speed benefit of HDD outweighs the price penalty.

Considering Drive Interfaces

Another factor to consider when planning your storage environment is which drive interfaces to use. The drive interface manages the connection between the disk drive itself and the control unit that the drive is attached to. In a desktop or laptop computer, the disk controller is built into the motherboard, and it's almost always the first variety, known as *SATA*. In a network server, the disk controller is often a separate card installed into the server's chassis — or, sometimes, in a separate chassis. In that case, either the SATA interface or the more advanced SAS interface can be used.

The following paragraphs describe the differences between SATA and SAS.

SATA

SATA is the most popular interface for consumer devices. It's an evolution of the original disk interface that was used when hard drives were first introduced on IBM PCs. That interface was originally called *IDE*, which stood for *integrated device electronics*. That was soon replaced by an improved interface called *ATA*, which stood for *AT attachment* because it was designed to work with IBM's PC-AT line of personal computers.

The original IDE and ATA interfaces were *parallel interfaces*, which meant that they transmitted and received 16 bits of data at a time. This arrangement required a total of 40 separate wires on the cables that connected the disk drives to the controllers, and complicated circuitry that kept the data synchronized on all the wires.

Parallel interfaces were increasingly difficult to keep up with increasing disk transfer speeds, so IDE and ATA evolved into a serial interface called *SATA*, which stands for *serial ATA*. In a serial interface, data is transmitted one bit at a time. Intuitively, that sounds less efficient than transmitting data 16 bits at a time, but in reality it's possible to send and receive data much faster using serial transmission than using parallel transmission because of the difficulty of keeping parallel transmission lines in sync.

Today, SATA is used on nearly all desktop and laptop computers and on many low-end server computers. Most SATA disks can transmit data at 6 Gbps (6 billion bits per second).

You also need to be aware that there are actually two classes of SATA disk devices: consumer and enterprise. Consumer-class SATA disks are found in desktop and laptop computers and are the least expensive disk drives available. Enterprise-class SATA drives are preferred for server storage, because they're about ten times as reliable as consumer-class drives. They're a bit more expensive, but the additional cost is well worth it.

SAS

SAS is the preferred drive interface for network storage. It's an evolution of an older drive interface called *SCSI*, which stands for *small computer system interface*. Like IDE and ATA, the original SCSI interface was a parallel interface. *SAS* is the serial version of SCSI; it stands for *Serial Attached SCSI*. (Incidentally, *SCSI* is pronounced "scuzzy.")

The SAS interface is faster than the SATA interface. Most SAS devices transfer data from the disk to the controller at either 6 Gbps or 12 Gbps.

The ability to work at 12 Gbps is one of the main benefits of SAS or SATA, but reliability is another important factor: Enterprise-class SAS drives are about ten times more reliable than enterprise-class SATA drives. (Because enterprise SATA is about ten times more reliable than consumer-class SATA, that makes enterprise-class SAS about 100 times more reliable than consumer-class SATA.)

Other than price, performance, and reliability, there's not much practical difference between SATA and SAS. But because performance and reliability are important considerations for network storage, I recommend you go with 12 Gbps SAS drives whenever your budget will allow.

Considering RAID

Reliability is one of the most important considerations when planning your network storage. All disk devices will eventually fail. This includes SSDs as well as HDDs. In fact, SSDs and HDDs have about the same reliability; both fail at about the same rate.

As a general rule, about 2 percent of your disk drives will fail every year. So if you have 25 disk drives in your server room, you can expect one to fail about every two years. If you have 100 disk drives, expect one to fail every six months. You can do the math: Drive failures are not uncommon.

Fortunately, we have ways to survive disk drive failures. The first line of defense is to use *RAID*, which groups disk drives together into arrays that have built-in redundancy and automatic recovery when one of the drives in an array fails.

Although there are many different types of RAID configurations, only three are in widespread use: RAID 10, RAID 5, and RAID 6.

RAID 10

In a RAID 10 array, the disks in the array are paired into mirror sets, in which both disks in each set contain the same data. Whenever data is written to one disk in a set, the exact same data is written to the other disk. Thus, if either of the two disks in the set fails, the other disk in the set has a backup copy of the data.

For example, suppose a RAID-10 array has six drives with a capacity of 1TB each. The array has a total of 6TB of disk storage, but because the drives are paired into mirror sets, only 3TB of data can be stored on the array. If any one drive fails, nothing is lost — the data can be retrieved from the surviving drive in the mirror set. When the drive that failed is replaced, the array can heal itself by copying all the data from the surviving disk to the replacement disk.

RAID 10 is generally considered the safest form of RAID, but it's vulnerable to a loss of two disks in the array. If two disks fail at the same time, only luck will determine whether the entire array is lost. If the failing disks are in separate mirror sets, the array will survive. But if both disks in a single mirror set are lost, the entire array will be lost.

RAID 5

In a RAID 5 array, multiple disks are combined into a single array, but the equivalent of one disk's worth of space is set aside for redundancy. (The redundancy data is actually spread across all the disks in the array, but the total amount of disk space needed for the redundancy is equivalent to one full disk in the array.)

If any disk in the array fails, the contents of that disk can be recovered to a new disk by calculating the data that was on the failed disk using the data that is on the surviving disks.

The usable capacity of the array is one drive less than the total number of drives in the array. For example, if you create a RAID 5 array using six 1TB drives, the usable capacity of the array will be 5TB. The sixth terabyte is used for redundancy.

The basic principle of how a RAID 5 array works is actually pretty simple to understand. Suppose I tell you to write down a list of five numbers. For example:

```
22
37
16
81
53
```

If I were to then erase one of the numbers at random, could you reconstruct the list? Not unless you have a really good memory!

But if you know in advance that I might erase one of the numbers, there's an easy trick that will help you recover the erased number: Just add all the numbers up, and write down the sum:

```
22
37
16
81
53
209
```

Now, if I erase any of the original five numbers, you can easily figure out what it was by subtracting the surviving four numbers from the sum.

That's essentially how RAID 5 works. The math is a bit more complicated than that, but the principle is the same. (It's also worth noting that RAID 5 doesn't simply designate one of the drives in the array to hold all the calculated redundancy data; instead, the redundancy data is spread across all the drives in the array.)

RAID 5 is more efficient than RAID 10 in terms of disk capacity. For example, a RAID 10 array of six 1TB drives has a usable capacity of just 3TB, while a RAID 5 array of the same six 1TB drives has a usable capacity of 5TB.

But from a performance perspective, RAID 5 is considerably slower than RAID 10 when writing data to the disk. To write data to a RAID 5 array, first the redundancy data must be calculated. Then both the data initially to be written as well as the redundancy data must be written to the array. The RAID 5 is less efficient because of the calculation and because of the need for multiple writes.

And finally, when one of the drives in a RAID 5 array fails, the array will take much longer to rebuild than when a drive in a RAID 10 array fails. In a RAID 10 rebuild, data from the surviving mirror pair is simply copied to the replacement drive. But in a RAID 5 rebuild, all the data from all the surviving drives must be read. Then the data for the replacement drive must be written. In our six 1TB-drive array examples, recovering a RAID 10 array requires that 1TB of data be read and 1TB of data be written. But for a RAID 5 array, 5TB of data must be read, 1TB of data must be calculated, and 1TB of data must be written.

In short, the rebuild of a failed RAID 5 array often requires several *days*.

In fact, many experts and most disk drive manufacturers recommend against RAID 5 altogether because of how long it takes to rebuild a failed drive. The problem with RAID 5 is that disk drive capacity has increased much faster than disk drive speed. We've been stuck at 6 Gbps or 12 Gbps for many years now, but disk capacity has soared. That means that rebuild times for RAID 5 arrays have also soared. Unfortunately, there's a not unreasonable chance that a *second* drive in a RAID 5 will fail during a rebuild operation. If that happens, the entire array will be lost.

You may think it unlikely that a second drive failure will happen during a rebuild, but keep in mind that most RAID arrays are populated with disk drives that were purchased at the same time from a single manufacturer. There's a good chance all the drives came from a single manufacturing lot, will have a similar expected lifetime, and have about the same amount of usage on them. The odds are better than you think. Because of this, most experts now recommend you use RAID 6 instead of RAID 5, as explained in the next section.

RAID 6

RAID 6 is one step more secure than RAID 5. Instead of calculating one set of redundancy data for the entire array, in RAID 6 two sets of redundancy information are calculated. Effectively, two of the disks in the array are set aside for redundancy. This allows the array to survive the loss of any two disks in the array, not just a single disk.

Of course, RAID 6 imposes a greater space penalty than RAID 5. A RAID 6 array of six 1TB drives will have a usable space of 4TB. In addition, RAID 6 is a bit slower than RAID 5 because two sets of redundancy data must be calculated rather than just one.

But RAID 6 is considerably safer than RAID 5.

Considering Attachment Types

To be useful, disk storage must be attached to your servers. It will do you no good to populate your rack with terabytes of disk storage if your users can't access it!

The following sections describe four basic approaches to attaching storage to your servers.

Direct attached storage

Direct attached storage (DAS) is the simplest and most obvious way to attach storage to a server. With DAS, storage is directly connected to a hard disk controller within the server. This provides the fastest possible connection to the computer, but it's also the most limited because the storage can be used only by the computer to which it is directly attached.

In a normal workstation computer, the hard disk controller is on the motherboard, and the disk drive or drives are mounted inside the computer's case in internal drive bays. In a typical rack-mounted server computer, drive bays for DAS are also built into the case, but they're usually accessible from the front of the server and they're usually hot-swappable, which means they can be removed and replaced while the server is powered up.

Most server computers need at least a small amount of DAS installed directly in the server chassis. You can use this storage for the server's operating system — or, if you use virtualization, for the server's hypervisor. Typically, a pair of 72 or 100GB SAS drives in a RAID 10 array are appropriate.

It is generally *not* a good idea to install large amounts of storage directly into a server chassis, because that storage will be accessible only to that server. This doesn't mean that you can't use DAS for large amounts of storage to be shared by several host servers; it just means you shouldn't install that storage in the chassis of one of the servers. Instead, you can use an external storage subsystem that has the ability to directly attach to more than one host. Such systems can typically be attached to anywhere from two to four host servers. The attachments are usually made with external SAS cables. This arrangement requires external SAS adapters on both the host servers and the external storage subsystem.

Figure 5-1 shows how two host servers might be connected to a single storage subsystem. In this case, the storage subsystem contains three enclosures that each hold 12 disks, so a total of 36 disk drives are available via this subsystem. Each of the two host computers has an external SAS adapter that is used to connect to the disk subsystem via external SAS cables.

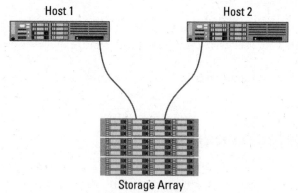

FIGURE 5-1:
Two hosts directly attached to a storage subsystem.

Storage area networks

A *storage area network* (SAN) is used when the number of storage devices or host computers makes it impossible to directly connect the storage to the hosts. Instead, a separate network of storage devices is created using a networking technology called *Fibre Channel*. Fibre Channel is similar in many ways to other networking technologies such as Ethernet, but it's designed specifically for connecting huge numbers of storage devices to servers. Fibre Channel networks can support thousands of storage devices.

Fibre Channel is also very fast, with top speeds of up to 128 Gbps. However, most Fibre Channel networks run at a more modest 16 Gbps. Fibre Channel usually operates over fiber-optic cable, but it can also run on copper cable at slower speeds.

Like Ethernet, Fibre Channel relies on switches to interconnect storage devices and hosts. Figure 5-2 shows a small Fibre Channel network in which six hosts are connected to three storage subsystems via a Fibre Channel switch. The cables and connectors for this network are 16 Gbps fiber-optic.

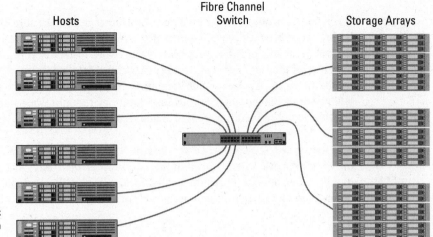

FIGURE 5-2:
A Storage Area Network.

TECHNICAL STUFF

Why the British spelling of *Fibre* rather than the American spelling *Fiber*? Originally, the American spelling was used, and Fiber Channel networks could be implemented only using fiber-optic cables. When copper cabling was added to the specification, the spelling was changed to the British variant just for fun.

Network attached storage

One final form of attaching storage in a network is called *network attached storage* (NAS). When NAS is used, storage devices are connected directly to the existing Ethernet network and data is accessed over TCP/IP using a variety of protocols that enable normal disk and file handling operations to be encapsulated in IP packets. NAS is one of the easiest ways to add large amounts of storage to a network, but NAS doesn't have nearly the performance that SAN or DAS does. In effect, data accessed via NAS devices is limited to the speed of the underlying network, which is typically 1 Gbps. Figure 5-3 shows how a NAS device can be attached to a network.

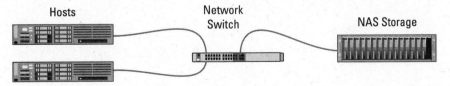

FIGURE 5-3:
A NAS system connected to a network.

The most common form of NAS consists of appliance-like devices that are essentially a small computer running as a file server with a large amount of disk storage. Users can access data on a NAS appliance as if it were any other file server on the network. The NAS appliances usually have a web-based administrative console that can be used to set up shares, manage permissions, and so on.

TIP

When you incorporate NAS into your overall storage plan, be sure to account for the backup and recovery requirements of the NAS. It's temptingly easy to add inexpensive terabytes of NAS storage to your network to satisfy your users' increasing appetite for storage. But don't forget that if the data is important enough to save on the network, it's important enough to back up on a regular basis. Your users will be sorely disappointed if they lose data they thought was safely ensconced on NAS if you fail to incorporate it into your backup plans.

WARNING

Another issue to be concerned about with NAS is that it can just randomly appear on your network when a user decides to stop at Best Buy on the way to work one day. Inexpensive, consumer-quality NAS is readily available and can easily be plugged in to any available network port. Keep on the lookout for rogue NAS devices.

4

Implementing a Network

Contents at a Glance

Chapter **1**

Network Hardware

After you plan your network, then comes the fun of actually putting every-thing together. In this chapter, I describe some of the important details for installing network hardware, including cables and switches, as well as professional touches like patch panels and cable management.

Working with Cable

Most Ethernet networks are built using twisted-pair cable (also known as UTP cable), which resembles phone cable but isn't the same. For more information about the general characteristics of twisted-pair cable, see of Book 3, Chapter 1.

In the following sections, you find out what you need to know to select and install twisted-pair cable.

Cable categories

Twisted-pair cable comes in various grades, or *categories.*

Higher-category cables are more expensive than lower-category cables, but the real cost of installing Ethernet cabling is the labor required to actually pull the cables through the walls. You should never install anything less than Category 5 cable. And if at all possible, invest in Category 5e (the *e* stands for enhanced) or even Category 6 cable to allow for upgrades to your network.

CAT GOT YOUR TONGUE?

Twisted-pair cable grades are categories specified by the ANSI/TIA standard 568. ANSI stands for American National Standards Institute; TIA stands for Telecommunications Industries Association. The higher the number, the faster the data transfer rate, so Cat-5 is faster than Cat-2. If you want to sound like you know what you're talking about, say "Cat 5e" instead of "Category 5e." Twisted pair is often referred to as UTP (unshielded twisted pair). Now you're hip.

Table 1-1 lists the various categories of twisted-pair cable.

TABLE 1-1

Twisted-Pair Cable Categories

Category	Maximum Data Rate	Intended Use
1	1 Mbps	Voice only
2	4 Mbps	4 Mbps token ring
3	16 Mbps	10BaseT Ethernet
4	20 Mbps	16 Mbps token ring
5	100 Mbps (2 pair)	100BaseT Ethernet
	1,000 Mbps (4 pair)	Gigabit Ethernet
5e	1,000 Mbps (2 pair)	Gigabit Ethernet
6	1,000 Mbps (2 pair)	Gigabit Ethernet
6a	10,000 Mbps	10 gigabit (experimental)
7	10,000 Mbps	10 gigabit (experimental)

What's with the pairs?

Most twisted-pair cable has four pairs of wires, for a total of eight wires. Standard Ethernet actually uses only two of the pairs, so the other two pairs are unused. You may be tempted to save money by purchasing cable with just two pairs of wires, but that's a bad idea. If a network cable develops a problem, you can sometimes fix it by switching over to one of the extra pairs. If you try to carry a separate connection over the extra pairs, though, electrical interference will prevent the signals from getting through.

WARNING

Don't give in to temptation to use the extra pairs for some other purpose, such as for a voice line. The electrical noise generated by voice signals in the extra wires can interfere with your network.

To shield or not to shield

Unshielded twisted-pair cable (UTP) is designed for normal office environments. When you use UTP cable, you must be careful not to route cable close to fluorescent light fixtures, air conditioners, or electric motors (such as automatic door motors or elevator motors). UTP is the least expensive type of cable.

In outdoor environments or other environments with a lot of electrical interference, such as factories, you may want to use shielded twisted-pair cable (STP). STP can cost up to three times more than regular UTP, so you won't want to use STP unless you have to. With a little care, UTP can withstand the amount of electrical interference found in a normal office environment.

Most STP cable is shielded by a layer of aluminum foil. For buildings with unusually high amounts of electrical interference, you can use more expensive, braided copper shielding for even more protection.

When to use plenum cable

The outer sheath of both shielded and unshielded twisted-pair cable comes in two varieties:

>> **PVC:** The most common and least expensive type.

>> **Plenum:** A special type of fire-retardant cable designed for use in the plenum space of a building (typically, in the hollows below a floor or above a ceiling).

Plenum cable has a special Teflon coating that not only resists heat, but also gives off fewer toxic fumes if it does burn. Unfortunately, plenum cable costs more than twice as much as ordinary PVC cable.

WARNING

Most local building codes require that you use plenum cable whenever the wiring is installed within the plenum space of the building.

Sometimes solid, sometimes stranded

The actual copper wire that composes the cable comes in two varieties: solid and stranded. Your network will have some of each.

>> **Stranded cable:** Each conductor is made from a bunch of very small wires twisted together. Stranded cable is more flexible than solid cable, so it doesn't break as easily. However, stranded cable is more expensive than solid cable and isn't very good at transmitting signals over long distances. Stranded cable is best used for patch cables, such as the cable used to connect a computer to a wall jack or the cable used to connect patch panels to hubs and switches.

>> Strictly speaking, the cable that connects your computer to the wall jack is a *station cable* — not a patch cable. Patch cables are used in the wiring closet, usually to connect patch panels to switches. However, in common practice, the terms *station cable* and *patch cable* are used interchangeably.

>> **Solid cable:** Each conductor is a single solid strand of wire. Solid cable is less expensive than stranded cable and carries signals farther, but it isn't very flexible. If you bend it too many times, it will break. Solid cable is usually used for permanent wiring within the walls and ceilings of a building.

Installation guidelines

The hardest part about installing network cable is the physical task of pulling the cable through ceilings, walls, and floors. This job is just tricky enough that I recommend that you don't attempt it yourself except for small offices. For large jobs, hire a professional cable installer. You may even want to hire a professional for small jobs if the ceiling and wall spaces are difficult to access.

Here are some general pointers to keep in mind if you decide to install cable yourself:

>> You can purchase twisted-pair cable in prefabricated lengths, such as 50 feet, 75 feet, or 100 feet. You can also special-order prefabricated cables in any length you need. However, attaching connectors to bulk cable isn't that difficult. I recommend that you use prefabricated cables only for very small networks and only when you don't need to route the cable through walls or ceilings.

>> Always use a bit more cable than you need, especially if you're running cable through walls. For example, when you run a cable up a wall, leave a few feet of slack in the ceiling above the wall. That way, you'll have plenty of cable if you need to make a repair later on.

>> When running cable, avoid sources of interference, such as fluorescent lights, big motors, x-ray machines, and so on. The most common source of interference for cables that are run behind dropped ceiling panels are fluorescent lights; be sure to give light fixtures a wide berth as you run your cable. Three feet should do it.

>> The maximum allowable cable length between a hub and the computer is 100 meters (about 328 feet).

>> If you must run cable across the floor where people walk, cover the cable so that no one trips over it. Inexpensive cable protectors are available at most hardware stores.

>> When running cables through walls, label each cable at both ends. Most electrical supply stores carry pads of cable labels that are perfect for the job. These pads contain 50 sheets or so of precut labels with letters and numbers. They look much more professional than wrapping a loop of masking tape around the cable and writing on the tape with a marker.

>> If nothing else, use a permanent marker to write directly on the cable.

>> When several cables come together, tie them with plastic cable ties or — better yet — strips of Velcro. Don't use masking tape or duct tape; the tape doesn't last, but the sticky glue stuff does. It's a mess a year later. Cable ties are available at electrical supply stores. You can purchase rolls of Velcro that you can cut to the desired lengths from online suppliers.

>> Cable ties have all sorts of useful purposes. Once on a backpacking trip, I used a pair of cable ties to attach an unsuspecting buddy's hat to a high tree limb. He wasn't impressed with my innovative use of the cable ties, but my other hiking companions were.

>> When you run cable above suspended ceiling panels, use cable ties, J-hooks, or clamps to secure the cable to the actual ceiling or to the metal frame that supports the ceiling tiles. Don't just lay the cable on top of the tiles.

Getting the tools that you need

Of course, to do a job right, you must have the right tools.

Start with a basic set of computer tools, which you can get for about $15 from any computer store or large office-supply store. These kits include the right screwdrivers and socket wrenches to open up your computers and insert adapter cards. (If you don't have a computer toolkit, make sure that you have several flat-head and Phillips screwdrivers of various sizes.)

If all your computers are in the same room and you're going to run the cables along the floor and you're using prefabricated cables, the computer tool kit should contain everything that you need.

If you're using bulk cable and plan on attaching your own connectors, you need the following tools in addition to the tools that come with the basic computer toolkit:

>> **Wire cutters:** You need decent wire cutters to cut UTP cable.

>> **Crimp tool:** Use this tool to attach the connectors to the cable. Don't use a cheap $10 crimp tool. A good one will cost $100 but will save you many headaches in the long run. Remember this adage: When you crimp, you mustn't scrimp.

>> **Wire stripper:** You need this only if the crimp tool doesn't include a wire stripper.

If you plan on running cables through walls, you need these additional tools:

>> **A hammer**

>> **A keyhole saw:** This is useful if you plan on cutting holes through walls to route your cable.

>> **A flashlight**

>> **A ladder**

>> **Someone to hold the ladder**

>> **Possibly a fish tape:** A *fish tape* is a coiled-up length of stiff metal tape. To use it, you feed the tape into one wall opening and fish it toward the other opening, where a partner is ready to grab it when the tape arrives. Next, your partner attaches the cable to the fish tape and yells something like, "Let 'er rip!" or "Bombs away!" Then you reel in the fish tape and the cable along with it. (You can find fish tape in the electrical section of most well-stocked hardware stores.)

If you plan on routing cable through a concrete subfloor, you need to rent a jack-hammer and a back-hoe and hire someone to hold a yellow flag while you work.

Pinouts for twisted-pair cables

Each pair of wires in a twisted-pair cable is one of four colors: orange, green, blue, or brown. The two wires that make up each pair are complementary: One is a solid color, and the other is white with a stripe of the corresponding color. For example, the orange pair has an orange wire and then a white wire with an orange stripe. Likewise, the blue pair has a blue wire and a white wire with a blue stripe.

When you attach a twisted-pair cable to a modular connector or jack, you must match up the right wires to the right pins. You can use several different standards to wire the connectors. To confuse matters, you can use one of the two popular standard ways of hooking up the wires. One is known as ANSI/TIA 568A; the other is ANSI/TIA 568B, also known as AT&T 258A. Table 1-2 shows both wiring schemes.

TABLE 1-2   **Pin Connections for Twisted-Pair Cable**

Pin Number	Function	EIA/TIA 568A	EIA/TIA 568B AT&T 258A
Pin 1	Transmit +	White/green	White/orange
Pin 2	Transmit –	Green	Orange
Pin 3	Receive +	White/orange	White/green
Pin 4	Unused	Blue	Blue
Pin 5	Unused	White/blue	White/blue
Pin 6	Receive –	Orange	Green
Pin 7	Unused	White/brown	White/brown
Pin 8	Unused	Brown	Brown

WARNING

It doesn't matter which of these wiring schemes you use, but pick one and stick with it. If you use one wiring standard on one end of a cable and the other standard on the other end, the cable won't work.

The only difference between the two wiring standards is which pair is used to transmit data and which pair is used to receive data. In the EIA/TIA 568A standard, the green pair is used to transmit and the orange pair is used to receive. In the EIA/TIA 568B and AT&T 258A standards, the orange pair is used to transmit and the green pair to receive.

Attaching RJ-45 connectors

RJ-45 connectors for twisted-pair cables aren't too difficult to attach if you have the right crimping tool. The trick is in both making sure that you attach each wire to the correct pin and pressing the tool hard enough to ensure a good connection.

Here's the procedure for attaching an RJ-45 connector:

1. **Cut the end of the cable to the desired length.**

   Make sure that you make a square cut — not a diagonal cut.

2. **Insert the cable into the stripper portion of the crimp tool so that the end of the cable is against the stop.**

   Squeeze the handles and slowly pull the cable out, keeping it square. This strips off the correct length of outer insulation without puncturing the insulation on the inner wires.

3. **Arrange the wires so that they lay flat and line up according to Table 1-2.**

   You'll have to play with the wires a little bit to get them to lay out in the right sequence.

4. **Slide the wires into the pinholes on the connector.**

   Double-check to make sure that all the wires slip into the correct pinholes.

5. **Insert the plug and wire into the crimping portion of the tool and then squeeze the handles to crimp the plug.**

   Squeeze it tight!

6. **Remove the plug from the tool and double-check the connection.**

   You're done!

Here are a few other points to remember when dealing with RJ-45 connectors and twisted-pair cable:

TIP

>> The pins on the RJ-45 connectors aren't numbered, but you can tell which is pin 1 by holding the connector so that the metal conductors are facing up, as shown in Figure 1-1. Pin 1 is on the left.

>> Be extra careful to follow the rules of Cat-5 cabling. That means, among other things, making sure that you use Cat-5 components throughout. The cable and all the connectors must be up to Cat-5 specs. When you attach the connectors, don't untwist more than one-half inch of cable. And don't try to stretch the cable runs beyond the 100m maximum. When in doubt, have cable for a 100 Mbps Ethernet system professionally installed.

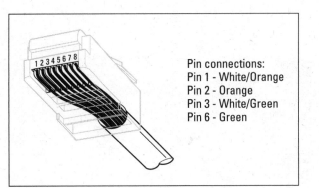

Pin connections:
Pin 1 - White/Orange
Pin 2 - Orange
Pin 3 - White/Green
Pin 6 - Green

FIGURE 1-1:
Attaching an
RJ-45 connector
to twisted-pair
cable.

Wall jacks and patch panels

From the files of "Sure, You Could Do This, But Here's Why This Is a Bad Idea," you could run a single length of cable from a network switch in a wiring closet through a hole in the wall, up the wall to the space above the ceiling, through the ceiling space to the wall in an office, down the wall, through a hole, and all the way to a desktop computer. Here's the pitfall, though: Every time someone moves the computer or even cleans behind it, the cable will get moved a little bit. Eventually, the connection will fail, and the RJ-45 plug will have to be replaced. Then the cables in the wiring closet will quickly become a tangled mess.

The smarter path is to put a wall jack at the user's end of the cable and connect the other end of the cable to a patch panel. Then, the cable itself is completely contained within the walls and ceiling spaces. To connect a computer to the network, you plug one end of a patch cable (properly called a *station cable*) into the wall jack and plug the other end into the computer's network interface. In the wiring closet, you use a patch cable to connect the wall jack to the network switch. Figure 1-2 shows how this arrangement works.

Connecting a twisted-pair cable to a wall jack or a patch panel is similar to connecting it to an RJ-45 plug. However, you don't usually need any special tools. Instead, the back of the jack has a set of slots that you lay each wire across. You then snap a removable cap over the top of the slots and press it down. This forces the wires into the slots, where little metal blades pierce the insulation and establish the electrical contact.

TIP

When you connect the wire to a jack or patch panel, be sure to carefully follow the color-code label on the jack, and to untwist as little of the wire as possible. If you untwist too much of the wire, the signals that pass through the wire may become unreliable.

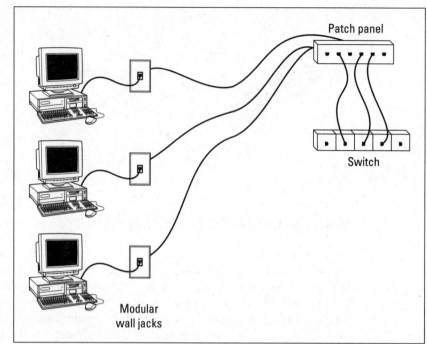

FIGURE 1-2:
Using wall jacks
and patch panels.

Installing Switches

Setting up a network switch is remarkably simple. In fact, you need to know only a few details:

» Installing a switch is usually very simple. Just plug in the power cord and then plug in patch cables to connect the network.

» Each port on the switch has an RJ-45 jack and an LED indicator that lights up when a connection has been established on the port. If you plug one end of a cable into the port and the other end into a computer or other network device, the Link light should come on. If it doesn't, something is wrong with the cable, the hub (or switch port), or the device on the other end of the cable.

» Each port may also have an LED indicator that flashes to indicate network activity. If you stare at a switch for awhile, you can find out who uses the network most by noting which activity indicators flash the most.

» The ports may also have an LED that indicates the speed of the connection that has been established. For example, the LED might be light green for a 1GB connection but amber for a 100MB connection. You can use this LED to identify ports that have potential cabling problems, as computers that should connect at 1GB will often connect at 100MB instead if the cable is suspect.

Daisy-Chaining Switches

If a single switch doesn't have enough ports for your entire network, you can connect switches together by *daisy-chaining* them. On older switches, you sometimes had to use special cables (called *crossover cables*) or designated ports (called *uplink ports*) to daisy-chain switches together. Modern switches don't require this extra consideration. Instead, you can daisy-chain two switches simply by connecting any port on the first switch to any port on the second switch.

Note that you should not chain more than three switches together. As explained in Book 3, Chapter 1, you can get around this rule by using stackable switches. Stackable switches have a special type of cable connector that connects two or more switches in a way that lets them function as if they were a single switch. Stackable switches are a must for large networks.

WARNING

When you daisy-chain switches, be careful to avoid creating a loop. For example, suppose you have three switches, called SW1, SW2, and SW3. If you daisy-chain SW1 to SW2, and then daisy-chain SW2 to SW3, and then finally daisy-chain SW3 to SW1, you will have created a loop. When that happens, all insanity will break loose and your network will grind to a halt. (A good reason to use managed switches instead of inexpensive consumer-grade switches is that managed switches can detect such loops and quickly shut them down.)

Chapter **2**

Wireless Networks

N early all modern networks include wireless access. In Book 1, Chapter 3, you learn the basics of how wireless network works and how to incorporate wireless access in your networking plan. In this chapter, you learn the basics of configuring and securing a wireless network.

Installing a Wireless Access Point

The physical setup for a wireless access point is pretty simple: You take it out of the box, mount it in its desired location, and plug it in. You can place the access point on top of a bookcase or shelf, or you can mount it to a wall or the ceiling. Many access points come with mounting hardware designed to hang the access point from a suspended ceiling.

The most important part of installing the access point is choosing the location. Ideally, it should be centrally located within the space it needs to provide access to. And it will need to have access to both power and the wired network. That's why it's important that you plan for wireless installation when you create the network's cabling plan.

If you don't have an electrical outlet at the location where you want to place the access point, you can use a Power over Ethernet (PoE) switch, which injects power on the Ethernet cable. That way, the power and network access are delivered to the access point over a single cable. Of course, you'll need to make sure that your access point is compatible with PoE to use this solution.

An alternative to using a PoE switch is to use a device called a *PoE injector.* A PoE injector has two Ethernet jacks — an input and an output — plus a power cable. The input jack accepts a standard Ethernet cable coming from a switch. You can then connect one end of an Ethernet cable to the injector's output jack and the other end to the access point. The PoE injector adds power to the output jack to provide power for the access point.

Configuring a Wireless Access Point

The software configuration for an access point is a little more involved but still not very complicated. It's usually done via a web interface. To get to the configuration page for the access point, you need to know the access point's IP address. Then you just type that address in the address bar of a browser on any computer on the network.

Multifunction access points usually provide DHCP and NAT services for the networks and double as the network's gateway router. As a result, they typically have a private IP address that's at the beginning of one of the Internet's private IP address ranges, such as 192.168.0.1 or 10.0.0.1. Consult the documentation that came with the access point to find out more.

TIP

If you use a multifunction access point that is both your wireless access point and your Internet router, and you can't remember the IP address, run the ipconfig command at a command prompt on any computer on the network. The Default Gateway IP address should be the IP address of the access point.

Basic configuration options

Figure 2-1 shows the main configuration screen for a typical wireless access point router. I called up this configuration page by entering **192.168.1.1** in the address bar of a web browser and then supplying the login password when prompted.

The main setup page of this router lets you figure information such as the host-name and IP address of the router and whether the router's DHCP server should be enabled. Options that are found on additional tabs let you configure wireless settings such as the network name (also called the SSID), the type of security to enforce, and a variety of other settings

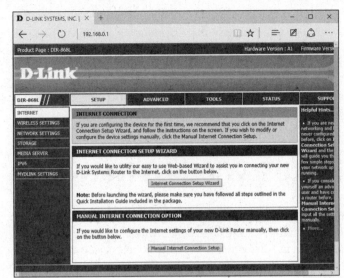

FIGURE 2-1:
The main
configuration
page for a typical
wireless router.

DHCP configuration

You can configure most multifunction access points to operate as a DHCP server. For small networks, it's common for the access point to also be the DHCP server for the entire network. In that case, you need to configure the access point's DHCP server. Figure 2-2 shows the DHCP configuration page for the Linksys WAP router. To enable DHCP, you select the Enable option and then specify the other configuration options to use for the DHCP server.

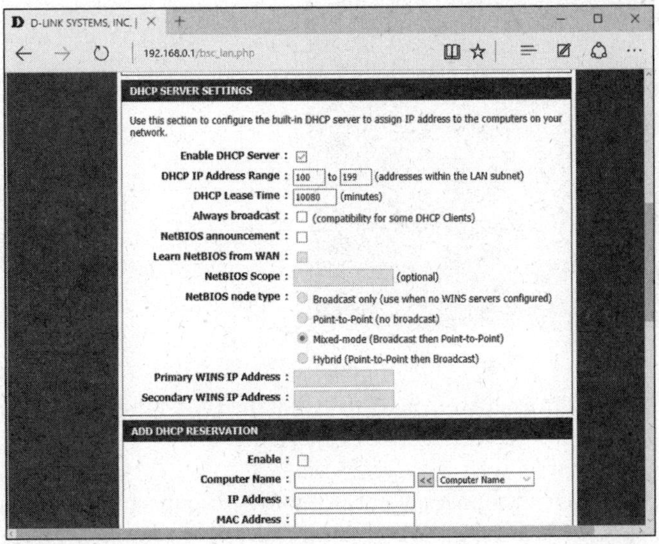

FIGURE 2-2:
Configuring DHCP
for a D-Link
wireless router.

Larger networks that have more demanding DHCP requirements are likely to have a separate DHCP server running on another computer. In that case, you can defer to the existing server by disabling the DHCP server in the access point.

For more information on configuring a DHCP server, please refer to Book 2, Chapter 5.

Connecting to a Wireless Network

Connecting to a wireless network on a Windows computer is straightforward. Windows automatically detects any wireless networks that are in range and displays them in a list when you tap the Wireless icon at the bottom of the screen, as shown in Figure 2-3.

FIGURE 2-3:
Choosing a wireless network in Windows 10.

To connect to a network, just tap it, and then enter the security key when prompted. If the key is correct, you'll be connected.

At the time you connect, you can choose to connect to the network automatically whenever it's in range. If you select this option, you won't have to select the network manually or enter the security key; you'll just be connected automatically.

Windows remembers every network you connect to, which is a plus for networks you frequently use but a drawback for networks you'll likely never use again. To tell Windows to forget a network, follow these steps:

1. **Click Start, and then tap Settings.**

   The Settings window appears.

2. **Click Network & Internet.**

   This brings up the Network & Internet page, which lists the known networks.

3. **Scroll to the bottom of the list of known networks, and then click Manage Wi-Fi Settings.**

   This brings up the Manage Wi-Fi Settings page, which includes a section titled Manage Known Networks.

4. **In the Manage Known Networks section, click the network you want to forget.**

   The network is selected, as shown in Figure 2-4.

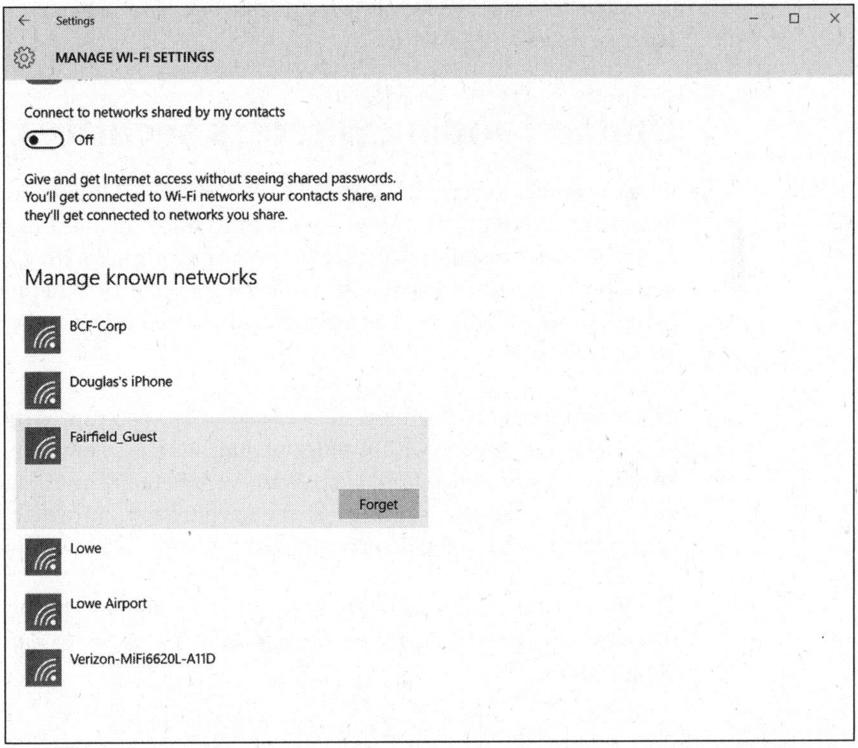

FIGURE 2-4:
Forgetting a wireless network in Windows 10.

5. **Tap Forget.**

   The network will be forgotten. To log into this network again, you'll have to enter the security key.

Paying Attention to Wireless Network Security

Before you dive headfirst into the deep end of the wireless networking pool, you should consider the inherent security risks in setting up a wireless network. With a cabled network, the best security tool that you have is the lock on the front door of your office. Unless someone can physically get to one of the computers on your network, he or she can't get into your network.

If you go wireless, an intruder doesn't have to get into your office to hack into your network. He or she can do it from the office next door. Or the lobby. Or the parking garage below your office. Or the sidewalk outside. In short, when you introduce wireless devices into your network, you usher in a whole new set of security issues to deal with.

Understanding wireless security threats

Wireless networks have the same basic security considerations as wired networks. As a network administrator, you need to balance the need of legitimate users to access network resources against the risk of illegitimate users breaking into your network. That's the basic dilemma of network security. Whether the network uses cables, wireless devices, kite strings and tin cans, or smoke signals, the basic issues are the same.

At one extreme of the wireless network security spectrum is the totally open network, in which anyone within range of your wireless transmissions can log on as an administrator and gain full access to every detail of your network. At the other end is what I call the "cone-of-silence syndrome," in which the network is so secure that no one can gain access to the network — not even legitimate users.

The goal of securing a wireless network is to find the happy medium between these two extremes that meets the access and risk-management needs of your organization.

The following sections describe the types of security threats that wireless networks are most likely to encounter. You should take each of these kinds of threats into consideration when you plan your network's security.

Intruders

With a wired network, an intruder usually must gain access to your facility to physically connect to your network. That's not so with a wireless network. In fact, hackers equipped with notebooks that have wireless network capability can gain access to your network if they can place themselves physically within range of your network's radio signals. Consider these possibilities:

>> If you share a building with other tenants, the other tenants' offices may be within range.

>> If you're in a multifloor building, the floor immediately above or below you may be in range.

>> The lobby outside your office may be within range of your network.

>> The parking lot outside or the parking garage in the basement may be in range.

>> If a would-be intruder can't get within normal broadcast range, he or she may try one of several tricks to increase the range:

>> A would-be intruder can switch to a bigger antenna to extend the range of his or her wireless computer. Some experiments have shown that big antennas can receive signals from wireless networks miles away. In fact, I once read about someone who listened in on wireless networks based in San Francisco from the Berkeley hills, across San Francisco Bay.

>> If a would-be intruder is serious about breaking into your network, he or she may smuggle a wireless repeater device into your facility — or near it — to extend the range of your wireless network to a location that he or she *can* get to.

REMEMBER

A *physical* connection to your network isn't the only way an intruder can gain access, of course. You must still take steps to prevent an intruder from sneaking into your network through your Internet gateway. In most cases, this means that you need to set up a firewall to block unwanted and unauthorized traffic.

Freeloaders

Freeloaders are intruders who want to piggyback on your wireless network to get free access to the Internet. If they manage to gain access to your wireless network, they probably won't do anything malicious: They'll just fire up their web browsers and surf the Internet. These are folks who are too cheap to spend $40 per month on their own broadband connection at home, so they'd rather drive into your parking lot and steal yours.

Even though freeloaders may be relatively benign, they can be a potential source of trouble. In particular:

>> Freeloaders use bandwidth that you're paying for. As a result, their mere presence can slow down Internet access for your legitimate users.

>> After freeloaders gain Internet access through your network, they can potentially cause trouble for you or your organization. They may use your network to download illegal pornography, or they may try to send spam via your mail server. Most ISPs will cut you off cold if they catch you sending spam, and they won't believe you when you tell them that the spam came from a kid parked in a Pinto out in your parking lot.

>> If you're in the business of *selling* access to your wireless network, obviously, freeloaders are a problem.

>> Freeloaders may start out innocently looking for free Internet access. Once they get in, though, curiosity may get the better of them, leading them to snoop around your network.

>> If freeloaders can get in, so can malicious intruders.

Eavesdroppers

Eavesdroppers just like to listen to your network traffic. They don't actually try to gain access via your wireless network — at least, not at first. They just listen.

Unfortunately, wireless networks give them plenty to listen to:

>> Most wireless access points regularly broadcast their Service Set Identifiers (SSIDs) to anyone who's listening.

>> When a legitimate wireless network user joins the network, an exchange of packets occurs as the network authenticates the user. An eavesdropper can capture these packets and, if security isn't set up right, determine the user's logon name and password.

>> An eavesdropper can steal files that are opened from a network server. If a wireless user opens a confidential sales report that's saved on the network, the sales-report document is broken into packets that are sent over the wireless network to the user. A skilled eavesdropper can copy those packets and reconstruct the file.

> » When a wireless user connects to the Internet, an eavesdropper can see any packets that the user sends to or receives from the Internet. If the user purchases something online, the transaction may include a credit card number and other personal information. (Ideally, these packets will be encrypted so that the eavesdropper won't be able to decipher the data.)

Spoilers

A *spoiler* is a hacker who gets kicks from jamming networks so that they become unusable. A spoiler usually accomplishes this act by flooding the network with meaningless traffic so that legitimate traffic gets lost in the flow. Spoilers may also try to place viruses or worm programs on your network via an unsecured wireless connection.

Rogue access points

One of the biggest problems that network administrators have to deal with is the problem of rogue access points. A *rogue access point* is an access point that suddenly appears on your network out of nowhere. What usually happens is that an employee decides to connect a notebook computer to the network via a wireless computer. So this user stops at Computers R Us on the way home from work one day, buys a Fisher-Price wireless access point for $25, and plugs it into the network without asking permission.

Now, in spite of all the elaborate security precautions you've taken to fence in your network, this well-meaning user has opened the barn door. It's *very* unlikely that the user will enable the security features of the wireless access point; in fact, he or she probably isn't even aware that wireless access devices *have* security features.

Unless you take some kind of action to find it, a rogue access point can operate undetected on your network for months or even years. You may not discover it until you report to work one day and find that your network has been trashed by an intruder who found his or her way into your network via an unprotected wireless access point that you didn't even know existed.

TIP

Here are some steps you can take to reduce the risk of rogue access points appearing on your system:

> » Establish a policy prohibiting users from installing wireless access points on their own. Then make sure that you inform all network users of the policy, and let them know why installing an access point on their own can be such a major problem.

>> If possible, establish a program that quickly and inexpensively grants wireless access to users who want it. Rogue access points show up in the first place for two reasons:

>> Users need the access.

>> The access is hard to get through existing channels.

>> If you make it easier for users to get legitimate wireless access, you're less likely to find wireless access points hidden behind file cabinets or in flower pots.

>> Once in a while, take a walk through the premises, looking for rogue access points. Take a look at every network outlet in the building; see what's connected to it.

>> Turn off all your wireless access points and then walk around the premises with a wireless-equipped mobile device such as a smartphone and look for wireless networks that pop up. Just because you detect a wireless network, of course, doesn't mean you've found a rogue access point; you may have stumbled onto a wireless network in a nearby office or home. But knowing what wireless networks are available from within your office will help you determine whether or not any rogue access points exist.

Securing your wireless network

I hope you're convinced that wireless networks do, indeed, pose many security risks. In the following sections, I describe some steps that you can take to help secure your wireless network.

Changing the password

Probably the first thing you should do when you install a wireless access point is change its administrative password. Most access points have a built-in, web-based setup page that you can access from any web browser to configure the access point's settings. The setup page is protected by a username and password, but the username and password are initially set to default values that are easy to guess.

For Linksys access points, for example, the default username is usually either blank or admin, and the password is admin. If you leave the username and password set to their default values, anyone can access the access point and change its configuration settings, thus bypassing any other security features that you enable for the access point.

So, the first step in securing your wireless access point is changing the setup password to a value that can't be guessed. I suggest that you use a random combination of numerals and both uppercase and lowercase letters. Be sure to store the password in a secure location. (If you forget the password, you can press the Reset button on the router to restore it to its factory default. Then you can log on by using the default password, which you can find with the documentation that came with the router.)

Securing the SSID

The next step is to secure the SSID that identifies the network. A client must know the access point's SSID to join the wireless network. If you can prevent unauthorized clients from discovering the SSID, you can prevent them from accessing your network.

WARNING

Securing the SSID isn't a complete security solution, so you shouldn't rely on it as your only security mechanism. SSID security can slow down casual intruders who are just looking for easy and free Internet access, but it isn't possible to prevent serious hackers from discovering your SSID.

TIP

You can do three things to secure your SSID:

>> **Change the SSID from the default.** Most access points come preconfigured with well-known default SSIDs, such as those listed in Table 2-1. By changing your access point's SSID, you can make it more difficult for an intruder to determine your SSID and gain access.

>> **Disable SSID broadcast.** Most access points frequently broadcast their SSIDs so that clients can discover the network when they come within range. Clients that receive this SSID broadcast can use the SSID to join the network.

You can increase network security somewhat by disabling the SSID broadcast feature. That way, clients won't automatically learn the access point's SSID. To join the network, a client computer must figure out the SSID on its own. Then you can tell your wireless network users the SSID to use when they configure their clients.

WARNING

Unfortunately, when a client computer connects to a wireless network, it sends the SSID to the access point in an unencrypted packet. So a sophisticated intruder who's using a packet sniffer to eavesdrop on your wireless network can determine your SSID as soon as any legitimate computer joins the network.

>> **Disable guest mode.** Many access points have a guest-mode feature that enables client computers to specify a blank SSID or to specify "any" as the SSID. If you want to ensure that only clients that know the SSID can join the network, you must disable this feature.

TABLE 2-1

Common Default SSID Values

SSID	Manufacturer
3com	3Com
Compaq	Compaq
Linksys	Linksys
Tsunami	Cisco
Wireless	NetGear
WLAN	D-Link
WLAN	SMC

Enabling WEP

WEP stands for *wired equivalent privacy* and is designed to make wireless transmission as secure as transmission over a network cable. WEP encrypts your data by using either a 40-bit key or a 128-bit key. Keep in mind that 40-bit encryption is faster than 128-bit encryption and is adequate for most purposes. So unless you work for the Central Intelligence Agency, I suggest that you enable 40-bit encryption.

Note: WEP is less secure than other security methods such as WPA and WPA2. You should use WEP only if you need to connect to devices that do not support WPA or WPA2.

To use WEP, both the client and the server must know the encryption keys being used. A client that doesn't know the access point's encryption keys won't be able to join the network.

You can specify encryption keys for WEP in two ways. The first way is to create the ten-digit key manually by making up a random number. The second method, which I prefer, is to use a *passphrase,* which can be any word or combination of numerals and letters that you want. WEP automatically converts the passphrase to the numeric key used to encrypt data. If the client knows the passphrase used to generate the keys on the access point, the client will be able to access the network.

WARNING

As it turns out, security experts have identified several flaws in WEP that compromise its effectiveness. As a result, with the right tools, a sophisticated intruder can get past WEP. So although it's a good idea to enable WEP, you shouldn't count on it for complete security.

Besides just enabling WEP, you should take two steps to increase its effectiveness:

>> **Make WEP mandatory.** Some access points have a configuration setting that enables WEP but makes it optional. This setting may prevent eavesdroppers from viewing the data transmitted on WEP connections, but it doesn't prevent clients that don't know your WEP keys from accessing your network.

>> **Change the encryption keys.** Most access points come preconfigured with default encryption keys that make it easy for even casual hackers to defeat your WEP security. You should change the default keys, either by using a passphrase or by specifying your own key. Figure 2-5 shows the WEP key configuration page for a typical access point (in this case, a D-Link DIR-868L).

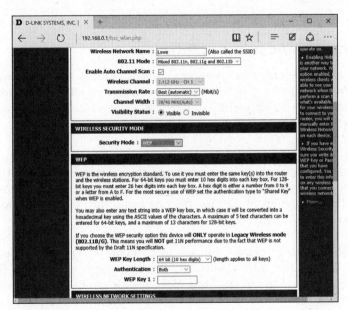

FIGURE 2-5:
Changing the
WEP settings
on a D-Link
wireless router.

Using WPA and WPA2

WPA, which stands for *Wi-Fi Protected Access*, is a newer form of security for wireless networks that's designed to plug some of the holes of WEP. WPA is similar in many ways to WEP. The big difference is that when you use WPA, the encryption key is automatically changed at regular intervals, thus thwarting all but the most sophisticated efforts to break the key. Most newer wireless devices support WPA. If your equipment supports it, I suggest that you use it.

Here are a few additional things to know about WPA:

>> A small office and home version of WPA, called WPA-PSK, bases its encryption keys on a passkey value that you supply. True WPA devices, however, rely on a special authentication server to generate the keys.

>> All versions of Windows since Windows XP Service Pack 2 have built-in support for WPA.

>> The official IEEE standard for WPA is 802.11i. However, WPA devices were widely available before the 802.11i standard was finalized; as a result, not all WPA devices implement every aspect of 802.11i.

>> The original version of WPA has been superseded by a newer version, named WPA2.

Using MAC address filtering

MAC address filtering allows you to specify a list of MAC addresses for the devices that are allowed to access the network or are prohibited from accessing the network. If a computer with a different MAC address tries to join the network via the access point, the access point will deny access.

MAC address filtering is a great idea for wireless networks with a fixed number of clients. If you set up a wireless network at your office so that a few workers can connect their notebook computers, you can specify the MAC addresses of those computers in the MAC filtering table. Then other computers won't be able to access the network via the access point.

WARNING

Unfortunately, it isn't difficult to configure a computer to lie about its MAC address. Thus, after a potential intruder determines that MAC filtering is being used, he or she can just sniff packets to determine an authorized MAC address and then configure his or her computer to use that address. (This practice is called *MAC spoofing*.) So you shouldn't rely on MAC address filtering as your only means of security.

Figure 2-6 shows the screen used to edit the MAC address table for a D-Link wireless access point.

Placing your access points outside the firewall

The most effective security technique for wireless networking is placing all your wireless access points *outside* your firewall. That way, all network traffic from wireless users will have to travel through the firewall to access the network.

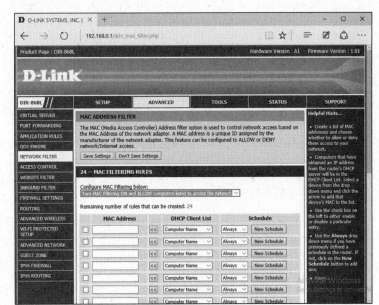

FIGURE 2-6:
A MAC address table for a D-Link wireless router.

As you can imagine, doing this can significantly limit network access for wireless users. To get around those limitations, you can enable a virtual private network (VPN) connection for your wireless users. The VPN will allow full network access to authorized wireless users.

DON'T NEGLECT THE BASICS

The security techniques described in this chapter are specific to wireless networks. They should be used alongside the basic security techniques that are presented in Book 3. In other words, don't forget the basics, such as these:

- Use strong passwords for your user accounts.

- Apply security patches to your servers.

- Change default server account information (especially the administrator password).

- Disable unnecessary services.

- Check your server logs regularly.

- Install virus protection.

- Back up!

Obviously, this solution requires a bit of work to set up and can be a little inconvenient for your users, but it's an excellent way to fully secure your wireless access points.

Troubleshooting a wireless network

Wireless networks are great until something goes haywire. When a regular network doesn't work, you usually know about it right away because the network simply becomes unavailable. You can't display web pages, read email, or access files on shared drives.

The troubleshooting chapters in Book 2 address the most common problems encountered on cabled networks. But wireless networks can cause problems of their own. And to add to the frustration, wireless networks tend to degrade rather than completely fail. Performance gets slower. Web pages that usually pop up in a second or two take 15 to 20 seconds to appear. Or sometimes they don't appear at all, but if you try again a few minutes later, they download fine.

This following sections offer some troubleshooting tips that can help you restore normalcy to a failing wireless network.

Checking for obvious problems

Before you roll up your sleeves and take drastic corrective action, you should check for a few obvious things if you're having wireless network trouble. The following list highlights some basic things you should check for:

>> Is everything turned on? Make sure you have lights on your wireless access point/router, as well as on your cable or DSL modem.

>> Many access point/routers use a power supply transformer that plugs into the wall. Make sure that the transformer is plugged into the wall outlet and that the small cable that comes out of the transformer is plugged into the power connector on the access point/router.

>> Are the cables connected? Check the network cable that connects your access point/router to the cable or DSL modem.

>> Try restarting everything. Turn off the computer, the access point/router, and your cable or DSL modem. Leave everything off for at least two minutes. Then turn everything back on. Sometimes, simply cycling the power off and back on clears up a connection problem.

Pinpointing the problem

If you can't connect to the Internet, one of the first steps (after you've made sure that everything is turned on) is finding out whether the problem is with your access point/router or with your broadband connection. Here is one way you can check to find out whether your wireless connection is working:

1. **Open a command prompt window by choosing Start⇨cmd, and pressing Enter.**

2. **At the command prompt, type** ipconfig, **and press Enter.**

    You should get a display similar to this:

    ```
    Ethernet adapter Wireless Network Connection:
    Connection-specific DNS Suffix . : hsd1.ca.comcast.net)).
    IP Address... ... ... ... : 192.168.1.101
    Subnet Mask ... ... ... . . : 255.255.255.0
    Default Gateway ... ... ... : 192.168.1.1
    ```

If the display resembles this but with different numbers, you're connected to the wireless network, and the problem most likely lies with your broadband modem.

But if the IP Address, Subnet Mask, and Default Gateway indicate 0.0.0.0 instead of valid IP addresses, you have a problem with your wireless network.

Changing channels

One of the most common sources of wireless network trouble is interference from other wireless devices. The culprit might be a cordless phone, or it could be a neighbor who also has a wireless network.

The simplest solution to this type of interference is changing channels. 802.11b access points let you select 1 of 11 different channels to broadcast on. If you're having trouble connecting to your access point, try changing the channel. To do that, you must log on to the router with the administrator password. Then hunt around the router's administrator pages until you find the controls that let you change the channel.

You may have to try changing the channel several times before you solve the problem. Unfortunately, 802.11b channels overlap slightly, which means that broadcasts on one channel may interfere with broadcasts on adjacent channels. Thus, if you're having trouble connecting on channel 1, don't bother switching to channel 2. Instead, try switching to channel 5 or 6. If that doesn't work, switch to channel 10 or 11.

Fiddling with the antennas

Sometimes, you can fix intermittent connection problems by fiddling with the antennas on the access point and your computer's wireless adapter. This procedure is similar to playing with old-fashioned rabbit-ear antennas on a TV to get the best reception.

The angles of the antennas sometimes make a difference, so try adjusting the antenna angles. In addition, you usually have better results if you place the access point at a high location, such as on top of a bookshelf.

In some cases, you may actually need to add a high-gain antenna to the access point to increase its range. A high-gain antenna simply snaps or screws onto the access point to provide a bigger antenna. Figure 2-7 shows high-gain antennas that are designed to work with Linksys access points. Antennas such as these cost about $70 for the pair.

FIGURE 2-7:
High-gain antennas for a Linksys wireless router.

Courtesy of Linksys

A more drastic fix is to add a signal booster to your access point. A *signal booster* is a power amplifier that increases the transmission power of most wireless devices by a factor of five. A typical signal booster costs about $100.

Adding another access point

If you have a computer that's out of range of your access point, one solution is to add a second access point closer to the problematic computer. Most likely, the only difficulty will be getting an Ethernet cable to the location where you want to put your second access point.

If possible, you can simply run a length of cable through your walls or attic to the second access point. If that solution isn't feasible, you can use a HomePlug or HomePNA network connection for the second access point.

An alternative to a second access point is simply adding a range extender such as the Linksys AC1200 Amplify shown in Figure 2-8. This handy device plugs directly into any electrical outlet and provides a pass-through outlet so you can still use your vacuum cleaner. Just plug this device midway between your access point and the computer that's having trouble connecting. (Note that using a range extender will slow down your Wi-Fi connection.)

FIGURE 2-8:
A wireless repeater such as this one from Linksys can help increase the range of your wireless network.

Courtesy of Linksys

Help! I forgot my router's password!

I mention many times throughout this book that you should always change the default passwords that come with computer and operating systems to more secure passwords, usually consisting of a random combination of letters, digits, and special symbols.

Ideally, you've already taken my sage advice and changed the password on your combination wireless access point/router. Good for you. But what if you forget the password later? Is there any way to get back into your access point/router then?

TIP

Fortunately, there is. Most access point/routers have a Reset button. It's usually located on the back or on the bottom of the router's case. Press this button to restore the access point/router to its factory default settings. That action resets the administrator password to the factory default — and also resets any other custom settings you've applied, so you may have to reconfigure your router to get it working again.

Chapter **3**

Windows Clients

B efore your network setup is complete, you must configure the network's client computers. In particular, you have to configure each client's network interface card so that it works properly, and you have to install the right protocols so that the clients can communicate with other computers on the network.

Fortunately, the task of configuring client computers for the network is child's play in Windows. For starters, Windows automatically recognizes your network interface card when you start up your computer. All that remains is to make sure that Windows properly installed the network protocols and client software.

With each version of Windows, Microsoft has simplified the process of configuring client network support. In this chapter, I describe the steps for configuring networking for Windows 10. The procedures for previous versions of Windows are similar.

Configuring Network Connections

Windows automatically detects and configures network adapters, so you don't have to manually install device drivers for your network adapters. When Windows detects that a network adapter is present on the system, Windows automatically creates a network connection and configures it to support basic networking protocols. You may need to change the configuration of a network connection manually, however.

The following steps show you how to configure your network adapter on a Windows 10 system:

1. **Click the Start icon (or press the Start button on the keyboard), and then tap or click Settings.**

    The Settings page appears, as shown in Figure 3-1.

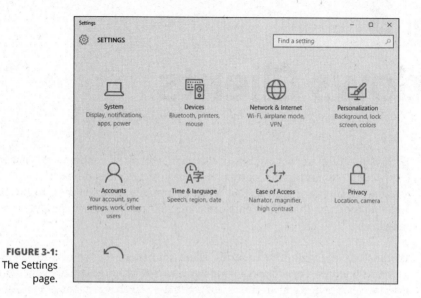

FIGURE 3-1: The Settings page.

2. **Click Network & Internet.**

    The Network & Internet page appears, as shown in Figure 3-2.

3. **Click Ethernet.**

    The Ethernet settings page appears, as shown in Figure 3-3.

4. **Click Change Adapter Options.**

    The Network Connections page appears, as shown in Figure 3-4. This page lists each of your network adapters. In this case, only a single wired Ethernet adapter is shown. If the device has more than one adapter, additional adapters will appear on this page.

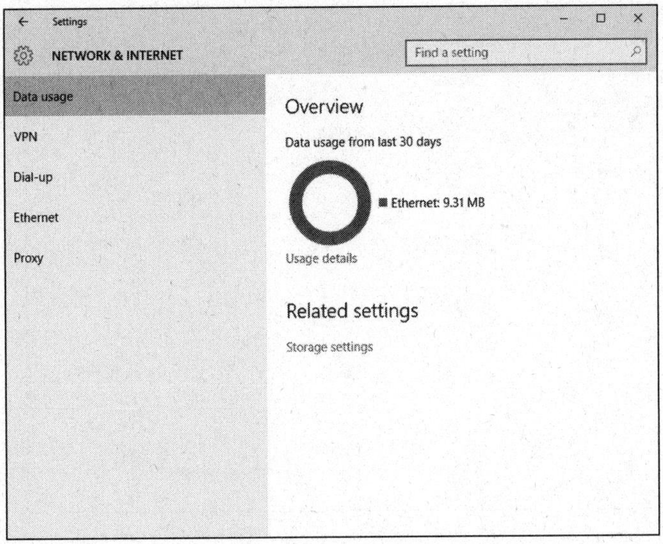

FIGURE 3-2:
The Network &
Internet page.

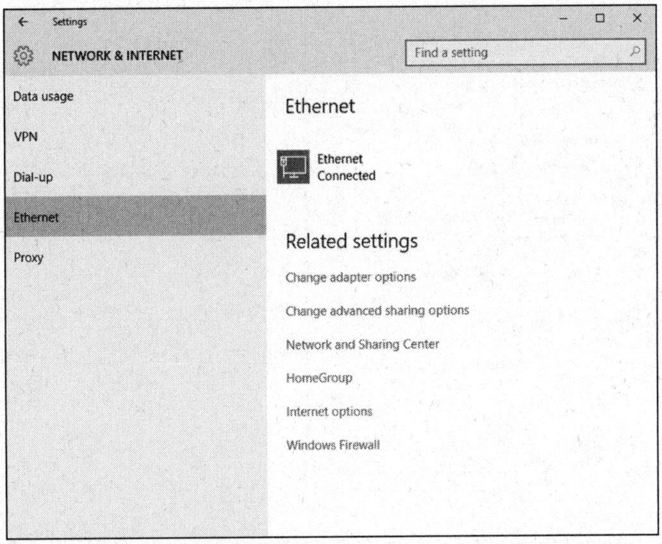

FIGURE 3-3:
The Ethernet
settings page.

5. **Right-click the connection that you want to configure and then choose Properties from the contextual menu that appears.**

This action opens the Properties dialog box for the network adapter, as shown in Figure 3-5.

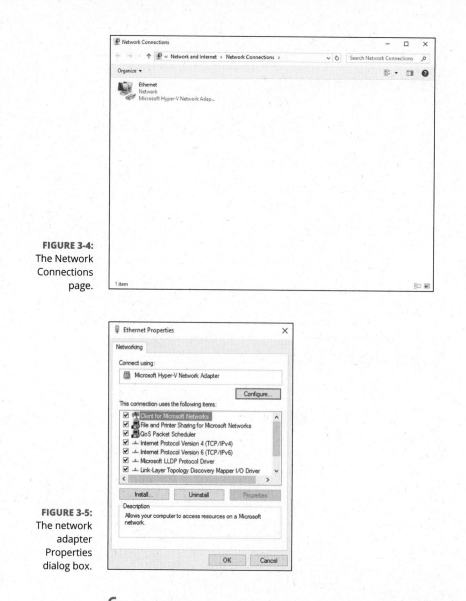

FIGURE 3-4:
The Network
Connections
page.

FIGURE 3-5:
The network
adapter
Properties
dialog box.

6. **To configure the network adapter card settings, click Configure.**

The Network Connection Properties dialog box appears, as shown in Figure 3-6. This dialog box has seven tabs that let you configure the adapter:

- *General:* This tab shows basic information about the adapter, such as the device type and status.

- *Advanced:* This tab lets you set a variety of device-specific parameters that affect the operation of the adapter.

- *About:* Displays information about the device's patent protection.

- *Driver:* This tab displays information about the device driver that's bound to the NIC and lets you update the driver to a newer version, roll back the driver to a previously working version, or uninstall the driver.
- *Details:* With this tab, you can inspect various properties of the adapter such as the date and version of the device driver. To view the setting of a particular property, select the property name from the drop-down list.
- *Events:* This tab lists recent events that have been logged for the device.
- *Power Management:* This tab lets you configure power management options for the device.

TIP

When you click OK to dismiss the Network Adapter Properties dialog box, the network connection's Properties dialog box closes and you are returned to the Network Connections page (refer to Figure 3-4). Right-click the network adapter and choose Properties again to continue the procedure.

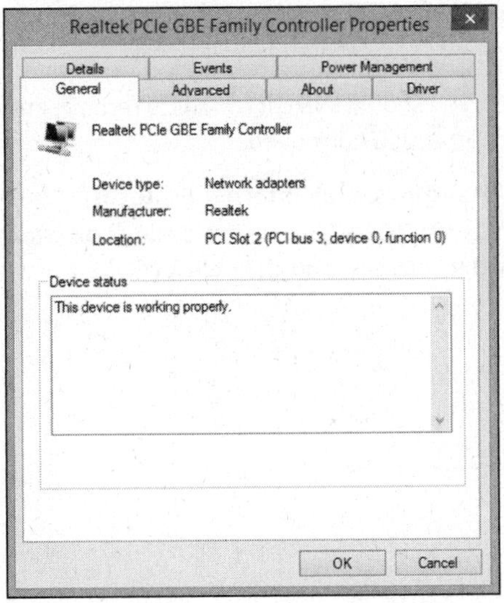

Realtek PCIe GBE Family Controller Properties
Details
Events
Power Management
General
Advanced
About
Driver
Realtek PCIe GBE Family Controller
Device type: Network adapters
Manufacturer: Realtek
Location: PCI Slot 2 (PCI bus 3, device 0, function 0)
Device status
This device is working properly.
OK
Cancel

FIGURE 3-6: The Properties dialog box for a network connection.

7. **Review the list of connection items listed in the Properties dialog box.**

   The most important items you commonly see are:

   - *Client for Microsoft Networks:* This item is required if you want to access a Microsoft Windows network. It should always be present.
   - *File and Printer Sharing for Microsoft Networks:* This item allows your computer to share its files or printers with other computers on the network.

TIP

This option is usually used with peer-to-peer networks, but you can use it even if your network has dedicated servers. If you don't plan to share files or printers on the client computer, however, you should disable this item.

Internet Protocol Version 4 (TCP/IPv4): This item enables the client computer to communicate by using the version 4 standard TCP/IP protocol.

Internet Protocol Version 6 (TCP/IPv6): This item enables version 6 of the standard TCP/IP protocol. Typically, both IP4 and IP6 are enabled, even though most networks rely primarily on IP4.

8. **If a protocol that you need isn't listed, click the Install button to add the needed protocol.**

A dialog box appears, asking whether you want to add a network client, protocol, or service. Click Protocol and then click Add. A list of available protocols appears. Select the one you want to add; then click OK.

9. **To remove a network item that you don't need (such as File and Printer Sharing for Microsoft Networks), select the item, and click the Uninstall button.**

For security reasons, you should make it a point to remove any clients, protocols, or services that you don't need.

10. **To configure TCP/IP settings, click Internet Protocol (TCP/IP); click Properties to display the TCP/IP Properties dialog box (shown in Figure 3-7); adjust the settings; and then click OK.**

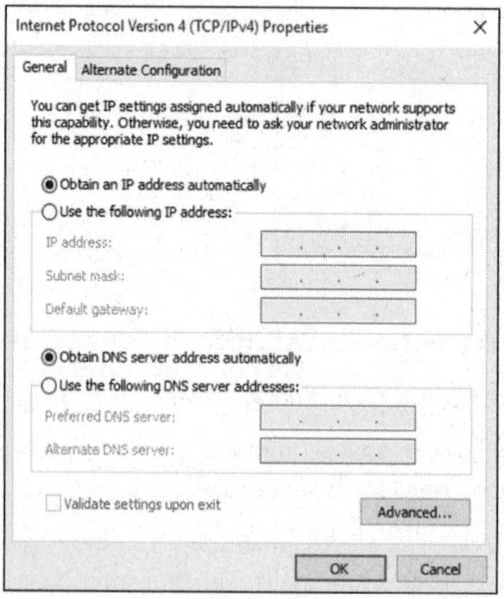

Internet Protocol Version 4 (TCP/IPv4) Properties ☒

General | Alternate Configuration

You can get IP settings assigned automatically if your network supports this capability. Otherwise, you need to ask your network administrator for the appropriate IP settings.

◉ Obtain an IP address automatically
○ Use the following IP address:

IP address:
Subnet mask:
Default gateway:

◉ Obtain DNS server address automatically
○ Use the following DNS server addresses:

Preferred DNS server:
Alternate DNS server:

☐ Validate settings upon exit   Advanced...

OK   Cancel

FIGURE 3-7:
Configuring
TCP/IP.

The TCP/IP Properties dialog box lets you choose among these options:

- *Obtain an IP Address Automatically:* Choose this option if your network has a DHCP server that assigns IP addresses automatically. Choosing this option dramatically simplifies administering TCP/IP on your network. (See Book 2, Chapter 5, and Book 3, Chapter 3, for more information about DHCP.)

- *Use the Following IP Address:* If your computer must have a specific IP address, choose this option and then type the computer's IP address, subnet mask, and default gateway address. (For more information about these settings, see Book 3, Chapter 3.)

- *Obtain DNS Server Address Automatically:* The DHCP server can also provide the address of the Domain Name System (DNS) server that the computer should use. Choose this option if your network has a DHCP server. (See Book 2, Chapter 6, for more information about DNS.)

- *Use the Following DNS Server Addresses:* Choose this option if a DNS server isn't available. Then type the IP addresses of the primary and secondary DNS servers.

Joining a Domain

When Windows first installs, it isn't joined to a domain network. Instead, it's available as part of a workgroup, which is an unmanaged network suitable only for the smallest of networks with just a few computers and without dedicated servers. To use a computer in a domain network, you must join the computer to the domain. Here are the steps for Windows 10:

1. **Click the Start icon (or press the Start button on the keyboard), and then tap or click Settings.**

   The Settings page appears (refer to Figure 3-1).

2. **Click System.**

   The System settings page appears, as shown in Figure 3-8.

3. **Click About.**

   The PC settings appear, as shown in Figure 3-9.

4. **(Optional) To change the name of the computer, click Rename PC.**

   You'll be prompted to enter a new name, and then reboot the computer.

   Before you join a domain, you should ensure that the computer's name won't be the same as the name of a computer that's already a member of the domain. If it is, you should first change the name.

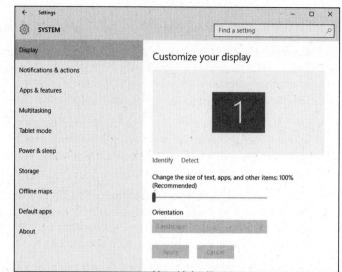

FIGURE 3-8:
The System
settings page.

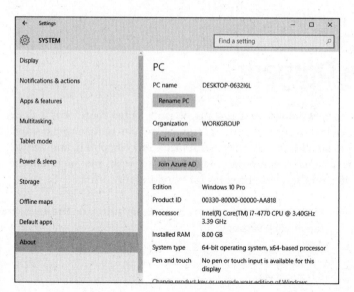

FIGURE 3-9:
The PC
settings page.

TIP

If you do change the computer's name, repeat the procedure from Step 1 after the reboot.

5. **Click Join a Domain.**

   The Join a Domain dialog box appears, as shown in Figure 3-10.

Join a domain

Join a domain
Domain name

Next   Cancel

FIGURE 3-10:
Joining a domain.

6. **Enter the domain name and click Next.**

   You're prompted for the username and password of a user who has administration privileges on the domain, as shown in Figure 3-11.

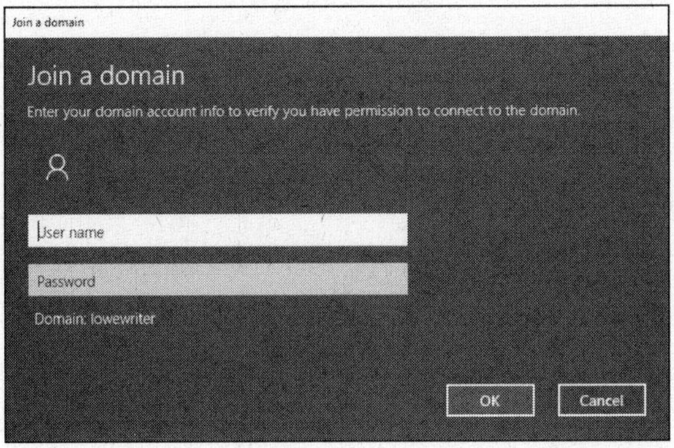

Join a domain

Join a domain
Enter your domain account info to verify you have permission to connect to the domain.

User name

Password

Domain: lowewriter

OK   Cancel

FIGURE 3-11:
You must
provide domain
administrator
credentials to
join a domain.

7. **Click OK.**

8. **Enter the username and password for an Administrator account when prompted.**

   You're asked to provide this information only if a computer account hasn't already been created for the client computer.

9. **When informed that you need to restart the computer, click Restart Now.**

   The computer is restarted and added to the domain.

Chapter **4**

Mac Networking

This book dwells on networking Windows-based computers, as though Microsoft were the only game in town. I'm sure plenty of people in Redmond, Washington (where Microsoft is headquartered) wished that it were so. But alas, there is an entirely different breed of computer: the Apple Macintosh, more commonly referred to simply as *Mac*.

Every Mac ever built, even an original 1984 model, includes networking support. Newer Mac computers have better built-in networking features than older Mac computers, of course. The newest Macs include either built-in Gigabit Ethernet connections or 802.11ac wireless connections, or both. Support for these network connections is pretty much automatic, so all you have to do is plug your Mac into a network or connect to a wireless network, and you're ready to go.

This chapter presents what you need to know to network Mac computers. You learn how to control basic Mac network options such as TCP/IP and file sharing. And you learn how to join a Mac to a Windows domain network.

Basic Mac Network Settings

Most network settings on a Mac are automatic. If you prefer, you can look at and change the default network settings by following these steps:

1. **Choose System Preferences, then choose Networking.**

The Network preferences page appears, as shown in Figure 4-1.

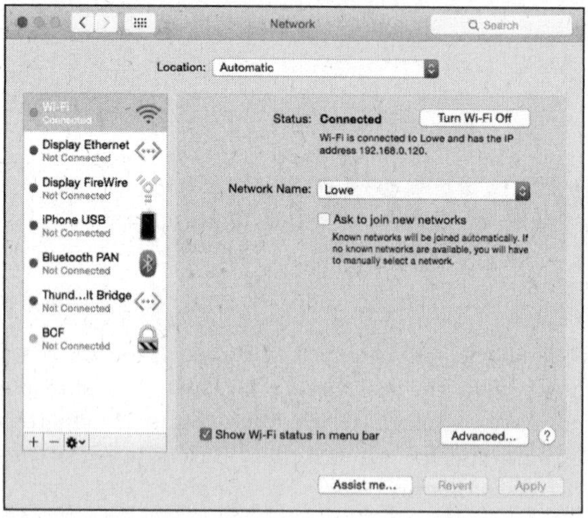

FIGURE 4-1:
Network
preferences.

2. **Click Advanced.**

The advanced network settings are displayed, as shown in Figure 4-2.

3. **Click the TCP/IP tab to view or change the TCP/IP settings.**

This brings up the TCP/IP settings, as shown in Figure 4-3. From this page, you can view the currently assigned IP address for the computer. And, if you want, you can assign a static IP address by changing the Configure IPv4 drop-down setting from Using DHCP to Manually. Then, you can enter your own IP address, subnet mask, and router address.

4. **Click the DNS tab to view or change the DNS settings.**

This brings up the DNS settings shown in Figure 4-4. Here, you can see the DNS servers currently being used, and you can add additional DNS servers if you want.

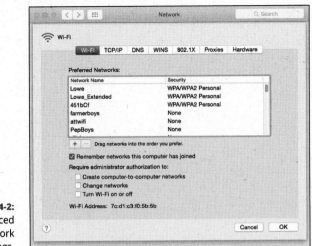

FIGURE 4-2:
Advanced
network
settings.

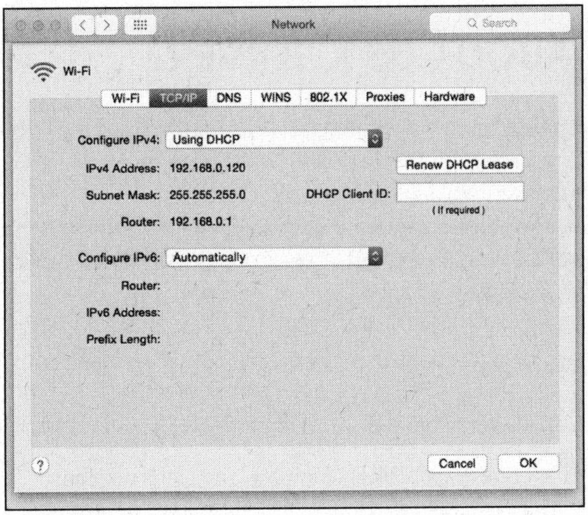

FIGURE 4-3:
TCP/IP settings.

5. **Click the Hardware tab to view hardware information.**

This brings up the settings shown in Figure 4-5. The most useful bit of information on this tab is the MAC address, which is sometimes needed to set up
wireless network security. (For more information, refer to Book 2, Chapter 1.)

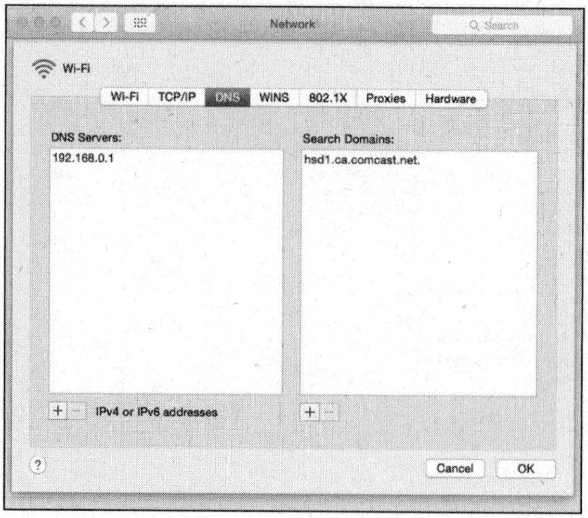

FIGURE 4-4:
DNS settings.

WHAT ABOUT OS X SERVER?

At one time, Apple offered a dedicated network operating system known as Mac OS X Server (the *X* is pronounced *Ten,* not *Ex*). In 2011, Apple merged Mac OS X Server with its desktop operating system and made the server components of the operating system available as an inexpensive add-on you can purchase from the App Store. For the latest version of OS X (10.8, released in July 2012), the Server App enhancement can be purchased for under $20.

The Server App download adds a variety of network server features to OS X, including:

- **Apache web server,** which also runs on Windows and Linux systems
- **MySQL,** which is also available in Windows and Linux versions
- **Wiki Server,** which lets you set up web-based wiki, blog, and calendaring sites
- **NetBoot,** a feature that simplifies the task of managing network client computers
- **Spotlight Server,** which lets you search for content on remote file servers
- **Podcast Producer,** which lets you create and distribute multimedia programs

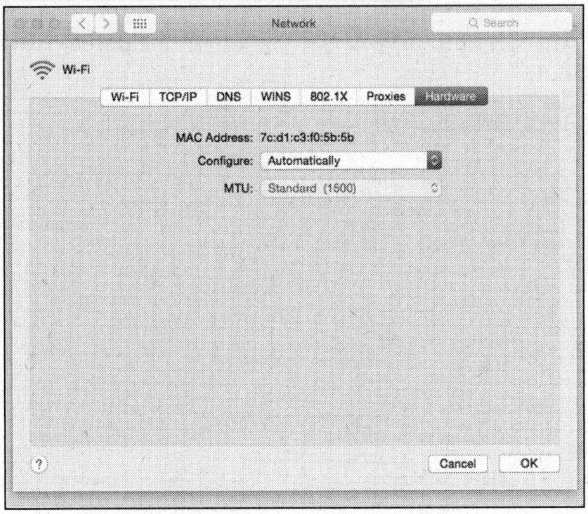

FIGURE 4-5:
Hardware
settings.

Joining a Domain

If you are using a Mac in a Windows domain environment, you can join the Mac to the domain by following these steps:

1. **Choose Settings, then choose Users & Groups.**

This brings up the Users & Groups page, as shown in Figure 4-6.

FIGURE 4-6:
Users & Groups.

2. **Select the user account you want to join to the domain, then click Login Options.**

The Login Options page appears, as shown in Figure 4-7.

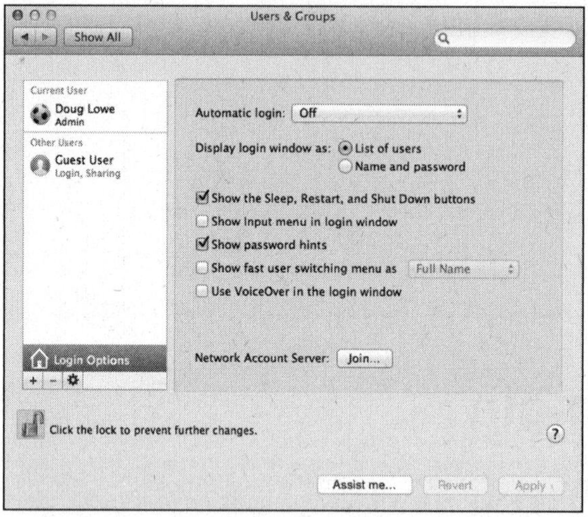

FIGURE 4-7:
Login Options.

3. **If the lock icon at the bottom-left corner of the page is locked, click it and enter your password when prompted.**

By default, the user login options are locked to prevent unauthorized changes. This step unlocks the settings so that you can join the domain.

4. **Click the Join button.**

You are prompted to enter the name of the domain you want to join, as shown in Figure 4-8.

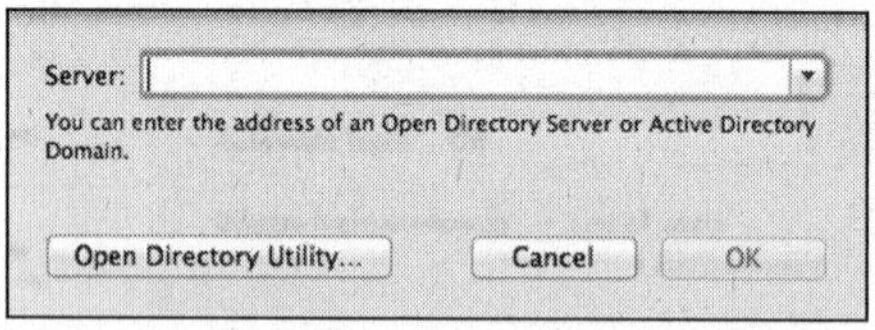

FIGURE 4-8:
Joining a domain.

5. **Enter the name of the domain you want to join.**

When you enter the domain name, the dialog box will expand to allow you to enter domain credentials to allow you to join the domain, as shown in Figure 4-9.

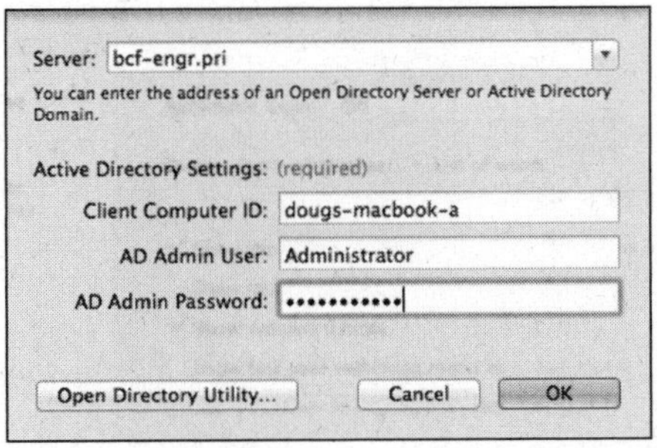

FIGURE 4-9:
Authenticating
with the domain.

6. **Enter the name and password of a domain administrator account, then click OK.**

You are returned to the Login Options page, which shows that you have successfully joined the domain, as shown in Figure 4-10.

7. **Close the Users & Groups window.**

FIGURE 4-10:
Congratulations!
You have now
joined the
domain.

Connecting to a Share

Once you have joined a domain, you can access its network shares via the Finder. Just follow these steps:

1. **Click Finder.**

This opens the Finder, as shown in Figure 4-11.

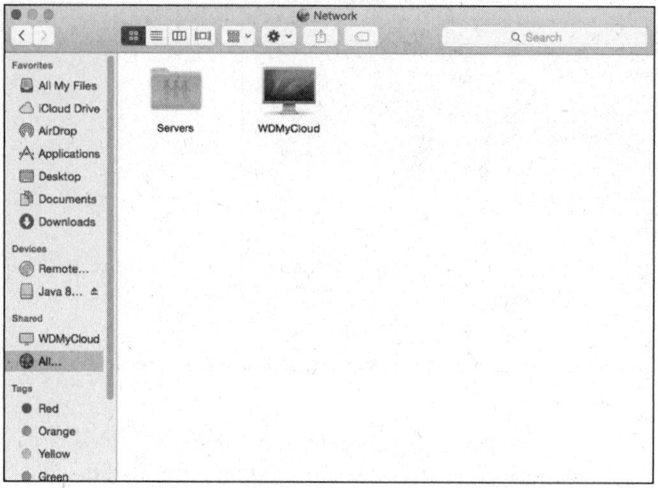

FIGURE 4-11:
Welcome to
the Finder.

2. **Choose Go⇨Finder.**

   The Connect to Server dialog box appears, as shown in Figure 4-12.

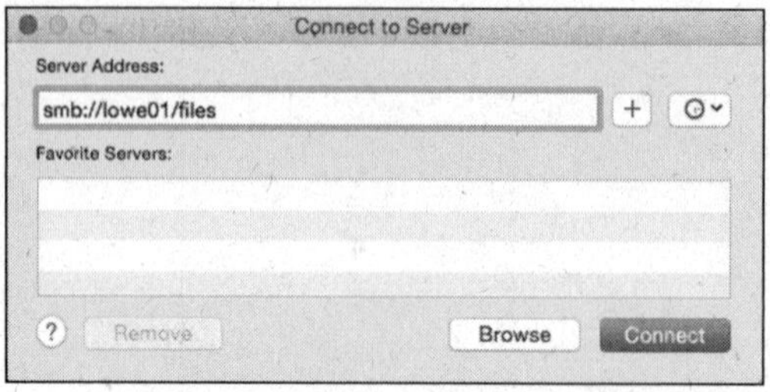

FIGURE 4-12:
The Connect to
Server dialog box.

3. **Type the smb path that leads to the server share you want to connect to.**

   To type a smb path, follow this syntax:

   smb://*server-name*/*share-name*

   Replace the *server–name* with the name of the server that contains the share and *share–name* with the name of the share. For example, to connect to a share named `files` on a server named `lowe01`, type `smb://lowe01/files`.

4. **Click Connect.**

   You'll be prompted for login credentials.

5. Enter a domain username and password, then click OK.

Precede the username with the domain name, separated by a backslash. For example, if the domain name is `lowewriter.pri` and the username is Doug, enter `lowewriter.pri\Doug` as the username.

Once connected, the files in the share will be displayed in the Finder window. You can then open files directly from the share (provided you have the right software, such as Microsoft Office, to read the files). You can also drag and drop files between the Mac and the file shares.

Chapter **5**

Network Printers

After you have your network servers and clients up and running, you still have many details to attend to before you can pronounce your network "finished." In this chapter, you discover a few more configuration chores that have to be done: configuring Internet access, setting up network printers, configuring email, and configuring mapped network drives.

Configuring Network Printers

Before network users can print on the network, the network's printers must be properly configured. For the most part, this task is a simple one. All you have to do is configure each client that needs access to the printer.

TIP

Before you configure a network printer to work with network clients, read the client configuration section of the manual that came with the printer. Many printers come with special software that provides more advanced printing and networking features than the standard features provided by Windows. If so, you may want to install the printer manufacturer's software on your client computers rather than use the standard Windows network printer support.

Adding a network printer

The exact procedure for adding a network printer varies a bit, depending on the Windows version that the client runs. The following steps describe the procedure for Windows 10; the procedure for previous versions of Windows is similar:

1. **Click the Start icon (or press the Start button on the keyboard), and then tap or click Settings.**

The Settings page appears, as shown in Figure 5-1.

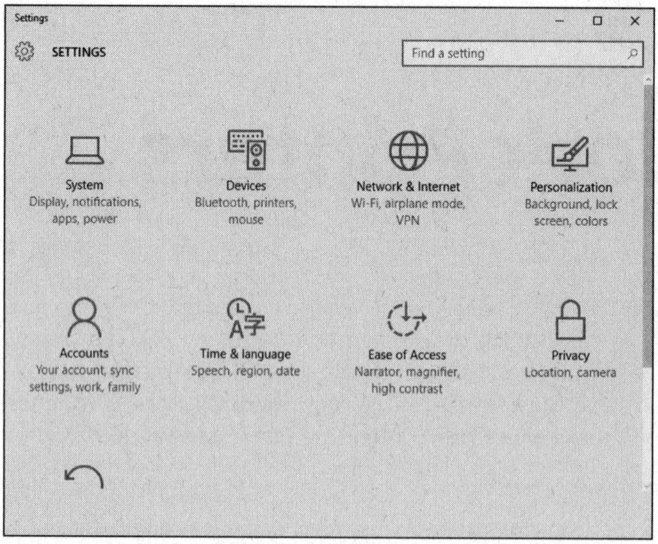

FIGURE 5-1:
The Settings page.

2. **Click Devices.**

The Devices page appears, as shown in Figure 5-2.

3. **Click Add a Printer or Scanner.**

The Printers & Scanners page appears, as shown in Figure 5-3. Windows scavenges your network looking for printers that are available for your use. Any printers that it finds are listed.

4. **Click the printer you want to use.**

If you can't find the printer you want to use, click The Printer That I Want Isn't Listed and enter the name of the printer or its IP address.

5. **Click Add Device.**

The wizard copies to your computer the correct printer driver for the network printer.

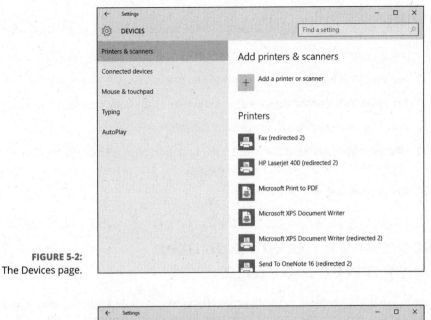

FIGURE 5-2:
The Devices page.

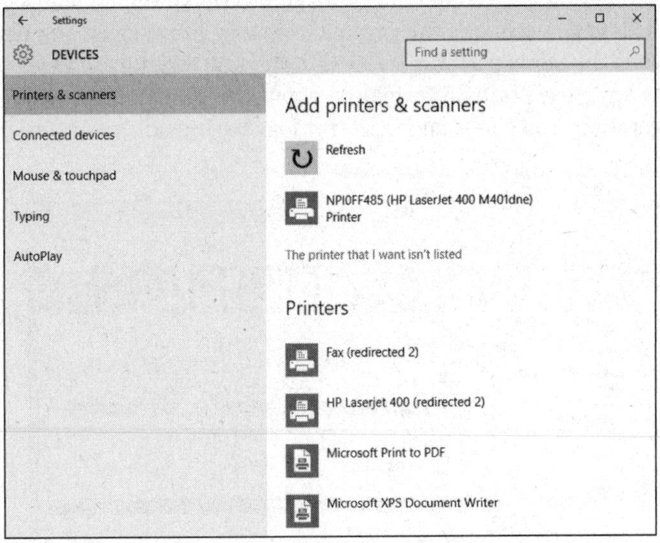

FIGURE 5-3:
Pick a printer.

You're done! The network printer has been added to the client computer.

TIP

If you're experienced with the Devices and Printers page from previous editions of Windows, you'll be happy to know that you can still get to that page. Just scroll down to the bottom of the Devices settings page (refer to Figure 5-2) and click Devices and Printers in the Related Settings section. This brings up the familiar Devices and Printers page, which lists the printers available on your computer.

From this page, you can right-click a printer and choose any of the following options:

>> **See What's Printing:** Displays the list of files that are currently being printed.

>> **Set as Default Printer:** Sets the selected printer as the default printer.

>> **Printing Preferences:** Sets the printing defaults for this printer.

>> **Printer Properties:** Displays and sets the basic printer properties, such as the printer's name, its port and driver, and so on.

>> **Remove Device:** Removes the printer.

Accessing a network printer using a web interface

TIP

Printers that have a direct network connection often include a built-in web server that lets you manage the printer from any browser on the network. Figure 5-4 shows the home page for an HP LaserJet 400 M401dne printer. This web interface lets you view status information about the printer and check the printer's configuration. You can even view error logs to find out how often the printer jams.

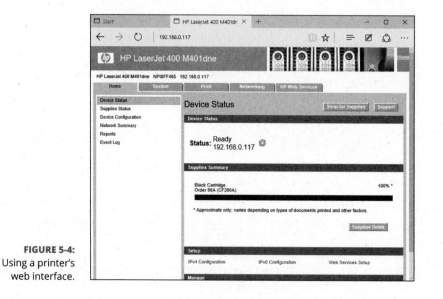

FIGURE 5-4:
Using a printer's web interface.

To call up a printer's web interface, enter its IP address or host name in the address bar of any web browser.

In addition to simply displaying information about the printer, you can adjust the printer's configuration from a web browser. Figure 5-5 shows the networking settings page for the HP printer. Here, you can view and change the network configuration details, such as the TCP/IP host name, IP address, subnet mask, domain name, and so on.

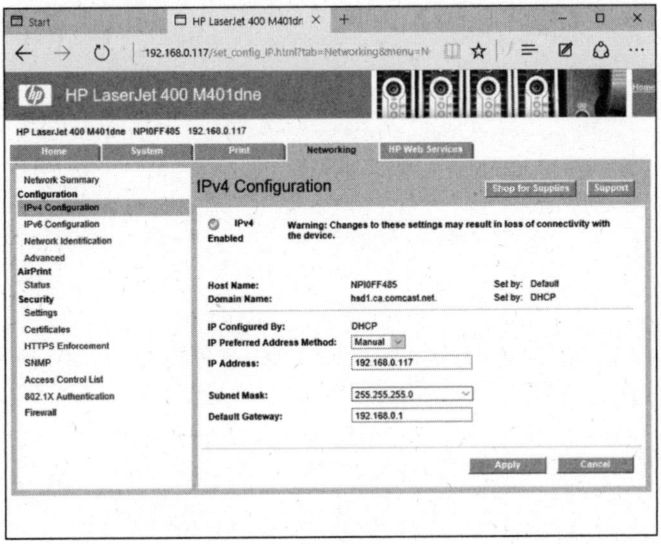

FIGURE 5-5:
Changing network settings via a printer's web interface.

As the network administrator, you may need to visit the printer's web page frequently. I suggest that you add it to your browser's Favorites menu so that you can get to it easily. If you have several printers, add them to a folder named Network Printers.

Chapter **6**

Virtual Private Networks

Today's network users frequently need to access their networks from remote locations: home offices, hotel rooms, beach villas, and their kid's soccer fields. In the early days of computer networking, the only real option for remotely accessing a network was to set up dialup access with telephone lines and modems, which was slow and unreliable. Today, enabling remote access to a local area network (LAN) is easily done with a virtual private network. Simply put, a virtual private network (VPN) enables remote users to access a LAN via any Internet connection.

This chapter is a short introduction to VPNs. You find out the basics of what a VPN is, how to set one up, and how to access one remotely. Enjoy!

Understanding VPN

A *virtual private network* (VPN) is a type of network connection that creates the illusion that you're directly connected to a network when in fact, you're not. For example, suppose you set up a LAN at your office, but you also occasionally work from home. But how will you access the files on your work computer from home?

> » You could simply copy whatever files you need from your work computer onto a flash drive and take them home with you, work on the files, copy the

updated files back to the flash drive, and take them back to work with you the next day.

>> You could email the files to your personal email account, work on them at home, and then email the changed files back to your work email account.

>> You could get a laptop and use the Windows Offline Files feature to automatically synchronize files from your work network with files on the laptop.

Or, you could set up a VPN that allows you to log on to your work network from home. The VPN uses a secured Internet connection to connect you directly to your work network, so you can access your network files as if you had a really long Ethernet cable that ran from your home computer all the way to the office and plugged directly into the work network.

There are at least three situations in which a VPN is the ideal solution:

>> One or more workers need to occasionally work from home (as in the scenario just described). In this situation, a VPN connection establishes a connection between the home computer and the office network.

ACCESSING YOUR COMPUTER REMOTELY

One of the most common reasons for setting up a VPN connection is to allow you to access a computer that is on your work network from a computer that is outside of your work network. For example, as a network administrator, you can use a VPN to connect to your work network from home. You can then use *Remote Desktop Connection* (RDC) to access your servers.

Before you can use RDC to connect remotely, you must enable remote access on the server computer. Right-click Computer on the Start menu and choose Properties, and then click Advanced System Settings. Click the Remote tab, and then select Allow Connections Only from Computers Running Remote Desktop with Network Level Authentication. This option lets you grant remote access only to specific users, whom you can designate by clicking the Select Users button.

After remote access has been granted, you can access the computer remotely by connecting to the network with a VPN. Then choose Start➪All Programs➪Remote Desktop Connection. Enter the name of the computer you want to connect to, and then click Connect. You're prompted for your Windows username and password. After it's all connected, you can access the remote computer's desktop in a window.

>> Mobile users — who may not ever actually show up at the office — need to connect to the work network from mobile computers, often from locations like hotel rooms, clients' offices, airports, or coffee shops. This type of VPN configuration is similar to the home user's configuration, except that the exact location of the remote user's computer is not fixed.

>> Your company has offices in two or more locations, each with its own LAN, and you want to connect the locations so that users on either network can access each other's network resources. In this situation, the VPN doesn't connect a single user with a remote network; instead, it connects two remote networks to each other.

Looking at VPN Security

The *V* in VPN stands for *virtual*, which means that a VPN creates the appearance of a local network connection when in fact the connection is made over a public network — the Internet. The term "tunnel" is sometimes used to describe a VPN because the VPN creates a tunnel between two locations, which can only be entered from either end. The data that travels through the tunnel from one end to the other is secure as long as it is within the tunnel — that is, within the protection provided by the VPN.

The *P* in VPN stands for *private*, which is the purpose of creating the tunnel. If the VPN didn't create effective security so that data can enter the tunnel only at one of the two ends, the VPN would be worthless; you may as well just open your network and your remote computer up to the Internet and let the hackers have their way.

Prior to VPN technology, the only way to provide private remote network connections was through actual private lines, which were (and still are) very expensive. For example, to set up a remote office you could lease a private T1 line from the phone company to connect the two offices. This private T1 line provided excellent security because it physically connected the two offices and could be accessed only from the two endpoints.

VPN provides the same point-to-point connection as a private leased line, but does it over the Internet instead of through expensive dedicated lines. To create the tunnel that guarantees privacy of the data as it travels from one end of the VPN to the other, the data is encrypted using special security protocols.

The most important of the VPN security protocols is *Internet Protocol Security* (IPSec), which is a collection of standards for encrypting and authenticating packets that travel on the Internet. In other words, it provides a way to encrypt the contents of a data packet so that only a person who knows the secret encryption keys can decode the data. And it provides a way to reliably identify the source of a packet so that the parties at either end of the VPN tunnel can trust that the packets are authentic.

TECHNICAL STUFF

Referring to the OSI Reference Model (see Book 2, Chapter 1), the IPSec protocol operates at layer 3 of the OSI model (the network layer). What that means is that the IPSec protocol has no idea what kind of data is being carried by the packets it encrypts and authenticates. The IPSec protocol concerns itself only with the details of encrypting the contents of the packets (sometimes called the *payload*) and ensuring the identity of the sender.

Another commonly used VPN protocol is Layer 2 Tunneling Protocol (L2TP). This protocol doesn't provide data encryption. Instead, it's designed to create end-to-end connections — *tunnels* — through which data can travel. L2TP is actually a combination of two older protocols: Layer 2 Forwarding Protocol (L2FP, from Cisco) and Point-to-Point Tunneling Protocol (PPTP, from Microsoft).

Many VPNs today use a combination of L2TP and IPSec: L2TP Over IPSec. This type of VPN combines the best features of L2TP and IPSec to provide a high degree of security and reliability.

Understanding VPN Servers and Clients

A VPN connection requires a VPN server — the gatekeeper at one end of the tunnel — and a VPN client at the other end. The main difference between the server and the client is that the client initiates the connection with the server, and a VPN client can establish a connection with just one server at a time. However, a server can accept connections from many clients.

Typically, the VPN server is a separate hardware device, most often a security appliance such as a Cisco ASA security appliance. VPN servers can also be implemented in software. For example, Windows Server 2008 includes built-in VPN capabilities even though they're not easy to configure. And a VPN server can be implemented in Linux as well.

Figure 6-1 shows one of the many VPN configuration screens for a Cisco ASA appliance. This screen provides the configuration details for an IPSec VPN connection. The most important item of information on this screen is the Pre-Shared Key, which is used to encrypt the data sent over the VPN. The client will need to provide the identical key in order to participate in the VPN.

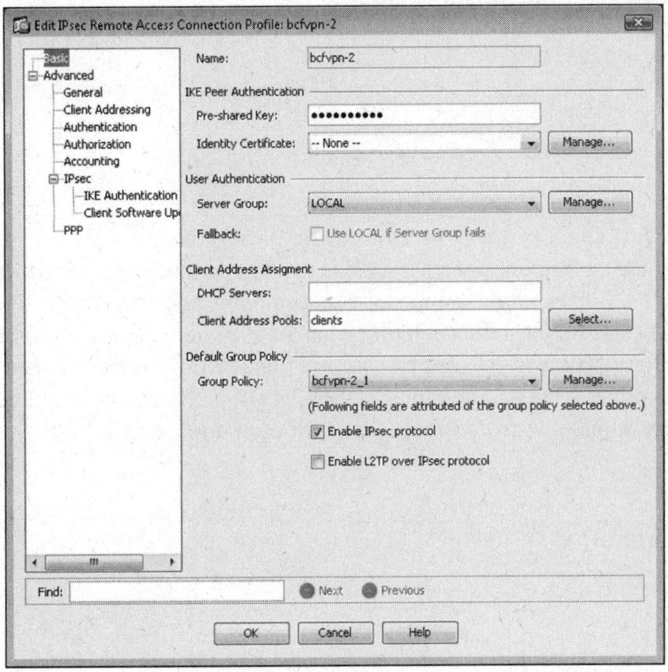

FIGURE 6-1:
An IPSec configuration page on a Cisco ASA security appliance.

REMEMBER

A VPN client is usually software that runs on a client computer that wants to connect to the remote network. The VPN client software must be configured with the IP address of the VPN server as well as authentication information such as a username and the Pre-Shared Key that will be used to encrypt the data. If the key used by the client doesn't match the key used by the server, the VPN server will reject the connection request from the client.

Figure 6-2 shows a typical VPN software client. When the client is configured with the correct connection information (which you can do by clicking the New button), you just click Connect. After a few moments, the VPN client will announce that the connection has been established and the VPN is connected.

Virtual Private Networks

FIGURE 6-2:
A VPN client.

A VPN client can also be a hardware device, like another security appliance. This is most common when the VPN is used to connect two networks at separate locations. For example, suppose your company has an office in Pixley and a second office in Hooterville. Each office has its own network with servers and client computers. The easiest way to connect these offices with a VPN would be to put an identical security appliance at each location. Then, you could configure the security appliances to communicate with each other over a VPN.

5

Implementing Virtualization

Contents at a Glance

Chapter **1**

Hyper-V

Hyper-V is a virtualization platform that comes as a standard part of all versions of Windows Server since version 2008 and all versions of desktop Windows since Windows 8.

On server versions of Windows, Hyper-V provides an enterprise-grade true Type-1 hypervisor that can manage huge virtualization farms with thousands of virtual machines. The version of Hyper-V that comes with desktop Windows is called Client Hyper-V. Client Hyper-V uses the same Type-1 hypervisor as the server-grade Hyper-V. However, it doesn't have the same enterprise-level management capabilities, because it's intended for use on client computers, not for production servers.

In this chapter, I first explain some of the details of how Hyper-V works. Then I show you how to set up virtual machines using the client version of Hyper-V. That way, you can build your own virtual machines to experiment with Hyper-V without the need for expensive hardware or server software.

Understanding the Hyper-V Hypervisor

Hyper-V is a built-in component of all modern versions of Windows. So, to use Hyper-V, you don't need to purchase any additional software from Microsoft. If you own a modern Microsoft operating system, you already own Hyper-V.

REMEMBER

Don't be confused by the fact that Hyper-V is an integral part of Windows: Although Hyper-V is built into Windows, Hyper-V is *not* a Type-2 hypervisor that runs as an application within Windows. Instead, Hyper-V is a true Type-1 hypervisor that runs directly on the host computer hardware. This is true even for the Client Hyper-V versions that are included with desktop versions of Windows.

In Hyper-V, each virtual machine runs within an isolated space called a *partition*. Each partition has access to its own processor, RAM, disk, network, and other virtual resources.

There are two types of partitions in Hyper-V: a *parent partition* and one or more *child partitions*. The parent partition is a special partition that hosts the Windows operating system that Hyper-V is associated with. Child partitions host additional virtual machines that you create as needed.

When you activate the Hyper-V feature, the hypervisor is installed and the existing Windows operating system is moved into a virtual machine that runs in the parent partition. Then, whenever you start the host computer, the hypervisor is loaded, the parent partition is created, and Windows is started in a virtual machine within the parent partition.

Although it may appear that the hypervisor is running within Windows, actually the reverse is true: Windows is running within the hypervisor.

In addition to the Windows operating system, the parent partition runs software that enables the management of virtual machines on the hypervisor. This includes creating new virtual machines, starting and stopping virtual machines, changing the resources allocated to existing virtual machines (for example, adding more processors, RAM, or disk storage), and moving virtual machines from one host to another.

Understanding Hyper-V Virtual Disks

Every Hyper-V virtual machine must have at least one virtual disk associated with it. A *virtual disk* is nothing more than a disk file that resides in the file system of the host operating system. The file has one of two file extensions, depending on which of two data formats you choose for the virtual disk:

>> **.vhd:** An older format that has a maximum virtual disk size of 2TB

>> **.vhdx:** A newer format that can support virtual disks up to 64TB

For either of these virtual disk formats, Hyper-V lets you create two different types of virtual disks:

» **Fixed-size disk:** A virtual disk whose disk space is preallocated to the full size of the drive when you create the disk. For example, if you create a 100GB fixed-size disk using the .vhdx format, a .vhdx file of 100GB will be allocated to the drive. Even if the drive contains only 10GB of data, it will still consume 100GB of space on the host system's disk drive.

» **Dynamically expanding disk:** A virtual disk that has a maximum disk space, but that actually consumes only the amount of disk space that is required to hold the data on the disk. For example, if you create a dynamically expanding disk with a maximum of 100GB but only put 10GB of data on it, the .vhdx file for the disk will occupy just 10GB of the host system's disk drive.

TECHNICAL
STUFF

Actually, there's a third type of disk called a *differencing disk*, which can be used to track changes made to another virtual disk. But this is an advanced topic that I don't cover in this chapter.

TIP

Don't be confused by the names *fixed-size* and *dynamically expanding*. Both types of disks can be expanded later if you run out of space. The main difference is whether the maximum amount of disk space allowed for the drive is allocated when the drive is first created or as needed when data is added to the drive. Allocating the space when the drive is created results in better performance for the drive, because Hyper-V doesn't have to grab more disk space every time data is added to the drive. Both types of drives can be expanded later if necessary.

Enabling Hyper-V

Hyper-V is not automatically enabled when you install Windows; you must first enable this feature before you can use Hyper-V.

To enable Hyper-V on a server version of Windows, call up the Server Manager and open the Add Roles and Features Wizard. Then enable the Hyper-V role. When you complete the wizard, Hyper-V will install the Type-1 hypervisor and move the existing Windows Server operating system into the parent partition. You can then start building virtual machines.

To enable Hyper-V on a desktop version of Windows, follow these steps:

1. **Open the Control Panel.**

2. **Choose Programs and Features.**

   The Programs and Features window comes to life.

Hyper-V

3. Click Turn Windows Features On or Off.

The Windows Features dialog box appears, as shown in Figure 1-1.

FIGURE 1-1:
Enabling
Hyper-V on a
desktop version
of Windows.

4. Select the Hyper-V feature and click OK.

The Client Hyper-V hypervisor is installed as an application on the existing desktop Windows operating system, and you can begin using Hyper-V.

5. When prompted, restart the computer.

The reboot is required to start the Hyper-V hypervisor. When your computer restarts, it's actually the Hyper-V hypervisor that starts, not Windows. The hypervisor then loads your desktop Windows into the parent partition.

Getting Familiar with Hyper-V

To manage Hyper-V, you use the Hyper-V Manager, shown in Figure 1-2. To start this program, click the Start button, type **Hyper-V**, and then choose Hyper-V Manager.

The Hyper-V Manager window is divided into five panes:

» **Navigation:** On the left side of the window is a navigation pane that lists the Hyper-V hosts, which Hyper-V calls *virtualization servers.* In Figure 1-2, just one host is listed: my Windows computer. In an enterprise environment where you have more than one host, each of the hosts will be listed in this pane.

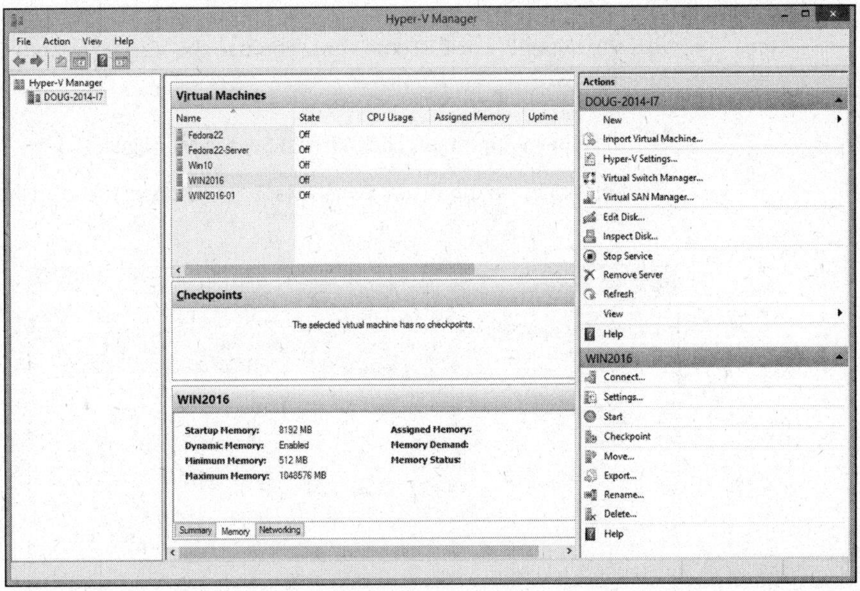

FIGURE 1-2:
Hyper-V Manager.

>> **Virtual Machines:** This pane lists the virtual machines that are defined for the selected host. In Figure 1-2, you can see several of the Hyper-V virtual machines that I created while I wrote this book — a couple of Linux machines, a Windows 10 machine, and a couple of Windows Server 2016 machines.

>> **Checkpoints:** In Hyper-V, a *checkpoint* is a recovery point for a virtual machine. You can create a checkpoint when you're going to make a modification to a virtual machine. Then, if something goes wrong, you can revert to the checkpoint.

>> **Virtual machine summary pane:** Below the Checkpoints pane is a pane that provides summary information for the virtual machine selected in the Virtual Machines pane. In Figure 1-2, you can see the summary information for one of the Windows Server 2016 machines. This pane has three tabs: Summary, Memory, and Networking. In the figure, the Memory tab is selected so you can see the memory that has been allocated to the machine.

>> **Actions:** The Actions tab contains buttons you can click to initiate actions for the selected host (DOUG-2014-I7) and the selected machine (WIN2016).

Creating a Virtual Switch

Before you start creating virtual machines in Hyper-V, you should create a virtual switch so that your virtual machines can communicate with each other and with the outside world. To do that, you use the Virtual Switch Manager. Here are the steps:

1. **In Hyper-V Manager, click Virtual Switch Manager.**

   This brings up the Virtual Switch Manager window, as shown in Figure 1-3.

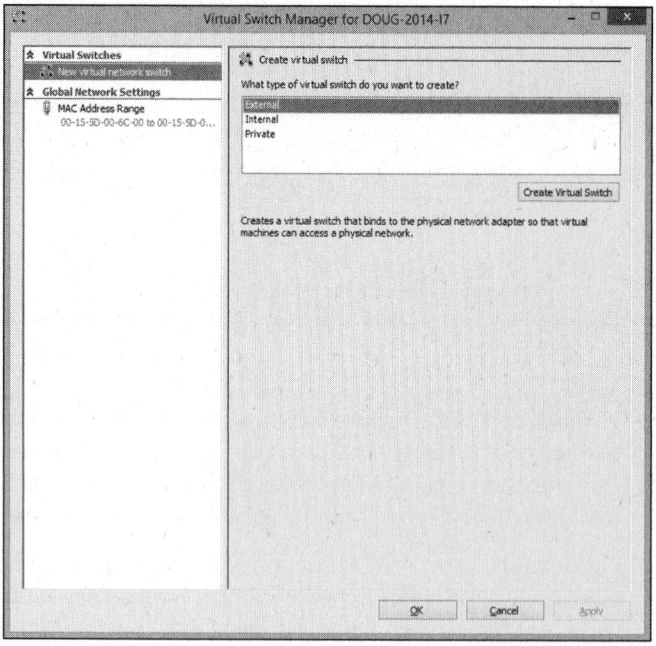

FIGURE 1-3:
The Virtual Switch
Manager window.

2. **Select the type of virtual switch you want to create.**

   Hyper-V lets you create three types of switches:

   - **External:** A virtual switch that binds to a physical network adapter, which allows virtual machines to communicate with each other, as well as with other computers on your physical network. This is usually the type of switch you should create.

   - **Internal:** A virtual switch that does not bind with a physical network adapter. This type of switch lets the virtual machines on this computer communicate with each other and with the host computer, but not with other computers on your physical network.

   - **Private:** A virtual switch that lets virtual machines communicate with each other but not with the host computer or with any computers on your physical network.

3. **Click Create Virtual Switch.**

   The settings for the new virtual switch appear, as shown in Figure 1-4.

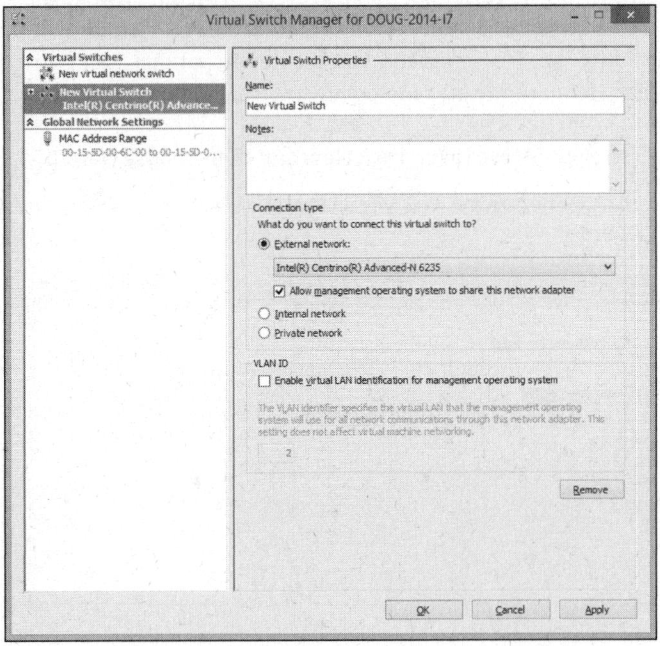

FIGURE 1-4:
Creating a new
virtual switch.

4. **Type a name for the new virtual switch in the Name field.**

   Use any name you want.

5. **Select the physical network adapter you want to bind the virtual switch to.**

   If your computer has more than one network adapter, select the one you want to use. Binding the virtual switch to a physical network adapter allows the virtual machines to communicate not only with each other but also with other computers connected via the adapter you select.

6. **If your network has multiple VLANs, click the Enable Virtual LAN Identification check box and enter the VLAN ID for the VLAN you want this switch to connect to.**

   If your network does not have multiple VLANs, you can skip this step.

7. **Click OK.**

   The virtual switch is created. Your Hyper-V environment now has a virtual network in place, so you can start creating virtual machines.

Hyper-V

Creating a Virtual Disk

Before you create a virtual machine, it's best to first create a virtual disk for the machine to use. Note that you can create a virtual disk at the same time that you create a virtual machine. However, creating the virtual disk first gives you more flexibility. So, I recommend you create virtual disks and virtual machines separately. Here are the steps to create a virtual disk:

1. **In Hyper-V Manager, click New and then choose Hard Disk.**

This brings up the New Virtual Hard Disk Wizard, as shown in Figure 1-5.

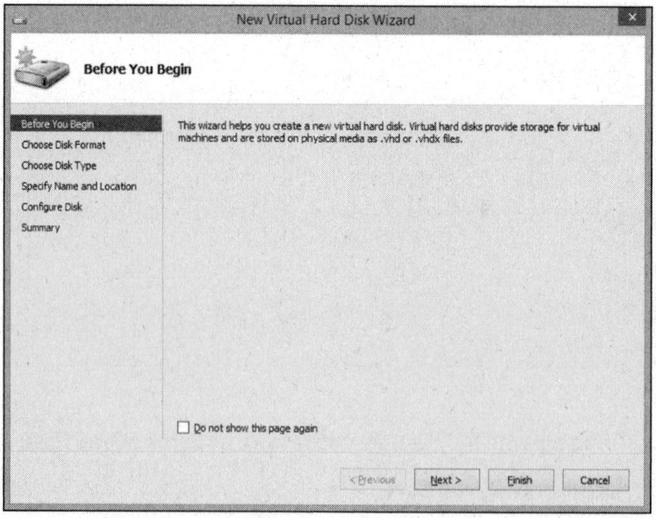

FIGURE 1-5:
The New Virtual Hard Disk Wizard.

2. **Click Next.**

You're asked which disk format to use, as shown in Figure 1-6.

3. **Select VHDX, and then click Next.**

I recommend you always use the VHDX format, which can support drives larger than 2TB.

When you click Next, the Choose Disk Type option page is displayed, as shown in Figure 1-7.

4. **Select the disk type you want to use.**

The options are Fixed Size, Dynamically Expanding, or Differencing. Choose Fixed Size if you're concerned about the performance of the disk; otherwise, choose Dynamically Expanding.

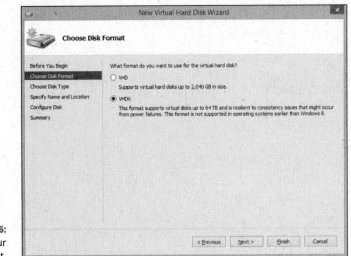

FIGURE 1-6:
Choose your
disk format.

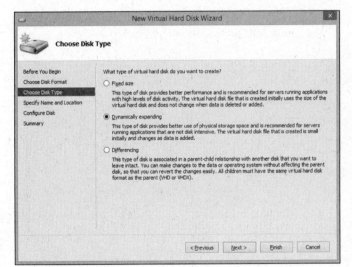

FIGURE 1-7:
Choose your
disk type.

5. **Click Next.**

   The page shown in Figure 1-8 appears.

6. **Specify the name and location of the new disk.**

   Type any name you want for the virtual disk drive. Then, click the Browse button to browse to the disk location where you want Hyper-V to create the .vhdx file.

   TIP

   Make sure you choose a location that has enough disk space to create the .vhdx file. If you're creating a dynamically expanding disk, you should ensure that the location has enough space to accommodate the drive as it grows.

Hyper-V

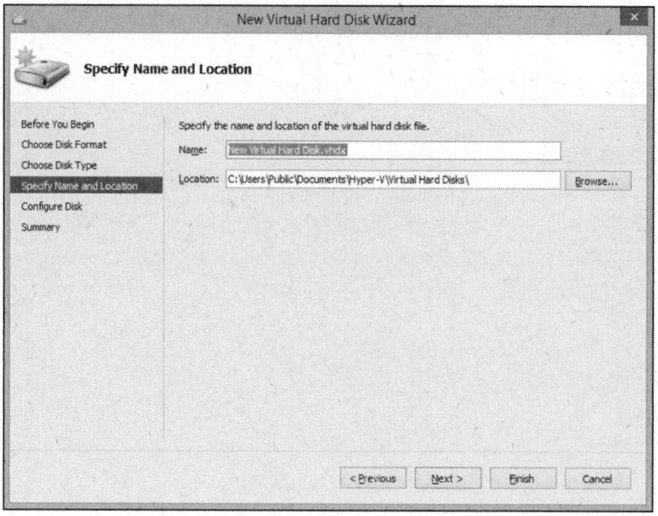

FIGURE 1-8:
Specify the name and location of the disk.

7. **Click Next.**

   The Configure Disk page appears, as shown in Figure 1-9.

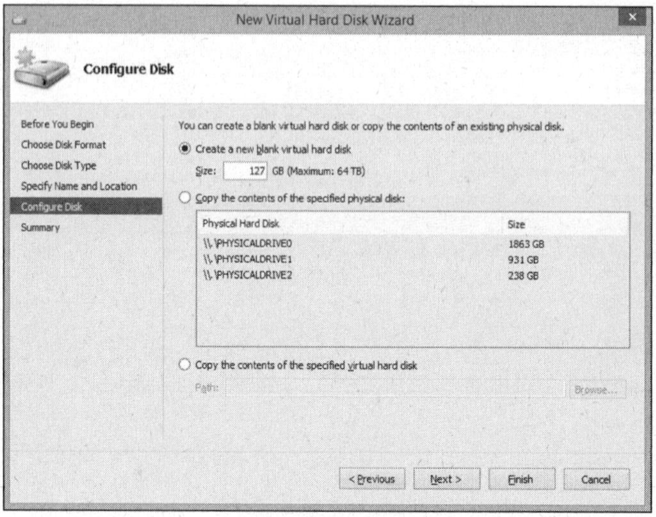

FIGURE 1-9:
Specify the size of the disk.

8. **Specify the maximum size for the disk drive.**

   This page also allows you to copy data either from an existing physical disk drive or from an existing virtual disk drive. Copying data from an existing physical drive is a quick way to convert a physical computer to a virtual computer; just copy the physical disk to a virtual disk, and then use the new virtual disk as the basis for a new virtual machine.

TIP

9. **Click Next.**

A confirmation screen appears, summarizing the options you've selected for your new disk.

10. **Click Finish.**

The new disk is created. Note that if you selected Fixed Disk as the disk type, creating the disk can take a while because the entire amount of disk storage you specified is allocated to the disk. Be patient.

You're done! You've now created a virtual disk that can be used as the basis for a new virtual machine.

Creating a Virtual Machine

After you've created a virtual disk, creating a virtual machine to use it is a straight-forward affair. Follow these steps:

1. **From Hyper-V Manager, choose New and then choose Virtual Machine.**

This brings up the New Virtual Machine Wizard, as shown in Figure 1-10.

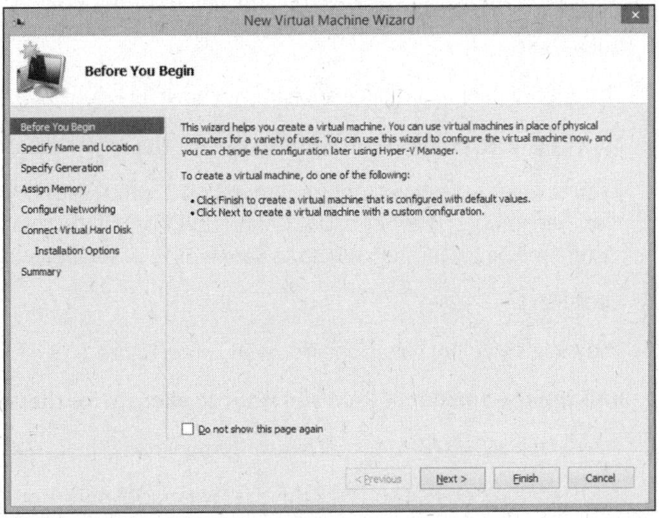

FIGURE 1-10:
Say hello to the New Virtual Machine Wizard.

2. **Click Next.**

The Specify Name and Location page appears, as shown in Figure 1-11.

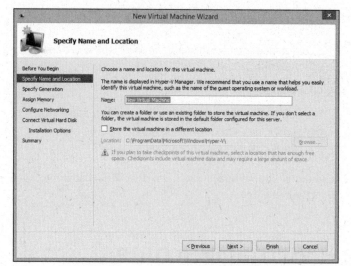

FIGURE 1-11:
Specify the name
and location
of the virtual
machine.

3. **Enter the name you want to use for your virtual machine.**

   You can choose any name you want here.

4. **Specify the location of the virtual machine's configuration file.**

   Every virtual machine has an XML file associated with it that defines the configuration of the virtual machine. You can allow this file to be stored in the default location, or you can override the default and specify a custom location.

5. **Click Next.**

   The Specify Generation page appears, as shown in Figure 1-12.

6. **Specify the generation you want to use for the new virtual machine.**

   In most cases, you should opt for Generation 2, which uses newer technology than Generation 1 machines. Use Generation 1 only if the guest operating system will be earlier than Windows Server 2012 or Windows 8.

7. **Click Next.**

   The Assign Memory page appears, as shown in Figure 1-13.

8. **Indicate the amount of RAM you want to allocate for the new machine.**

   The default is 512MB, but you'll almost certainly want to increase that.

   I also recommend that you click the Use Dynamic Memory for This Virtual Machine option, which improves memory performance.

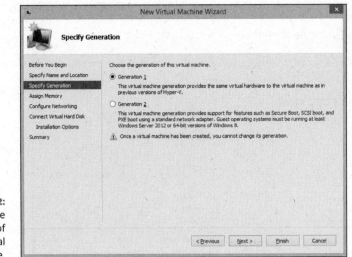

FIGURE 1-12:
Specify the
generation of
the new virtual
machine.

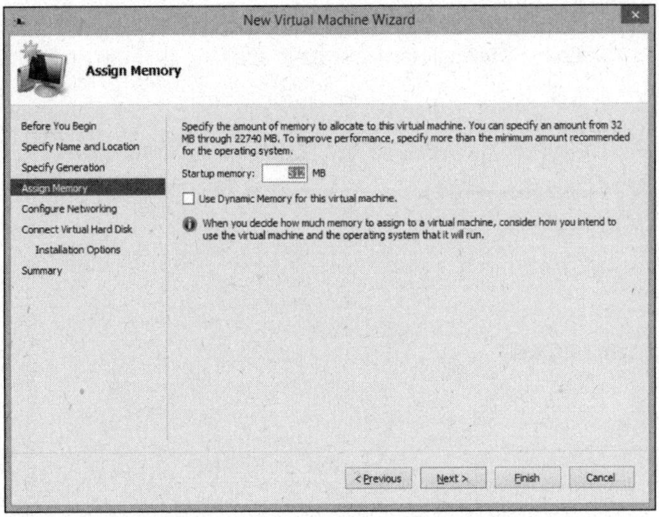

FIGURE 1-13:
Specify the
memory for
the new virtual
machine.

9. **Click Next.**

   The Configure Networking page appears, as shown in Figure 1-14.

10. **Select the virtual switch you want to use for the virtual machine.**

    This is the point where you realize why you needed to create a virtual switch
    before you start creating virtual machines. Use the Connection drop-down list
    to select the virtual switch you want to connect to this VM.

Hyper-V

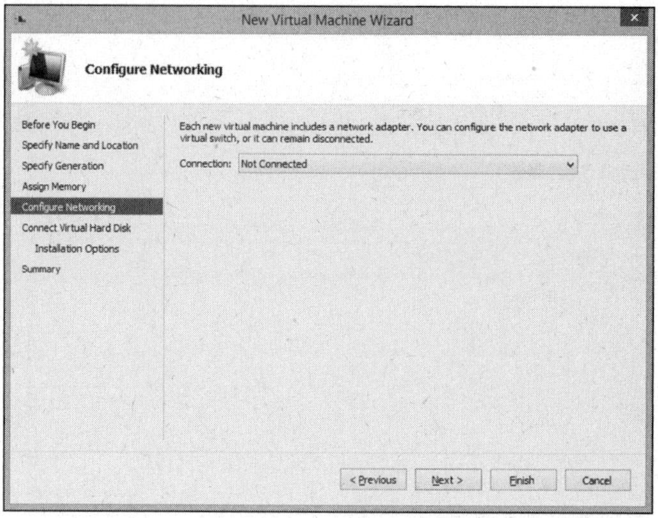

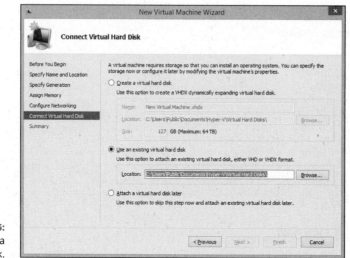

FIGURE 1-14:
Configure the
networking for
the new virtual
machine.

11. Click Next.

The Connect Virtual Hard Disk page appears, as shown in Figure 1-15.

FIGURE 1-15:
Connecting a
virtual disk.

Assuming you've already created a virtual disk for the virtual machine, choose the Use an Existing Virtual Hard Disk option, click Browse, and locate and select the virtual disk.

If you haven't already created a virtual disk, you can use the Create a Virtual Hard Disk option and create one now.

12. **Click Next.**

A summary page is displayed indicating the selections you've made.

13. **Click Finish.**

The virtual machine is created.

Installing an Operating System

After you've created a virtual machine, the next step is to configure it to install an operating system. First, you'll need to get the installation media in the form of an .iso file (an .iso file is a disk image of a CD or DVD drive). After you have the .iso file in place, follow these steps:

1. **From the Hyper-V Manager, choose the new virtual machine and click Settings.**

The Settings dialog box appears, as shown in Figure 1-16.

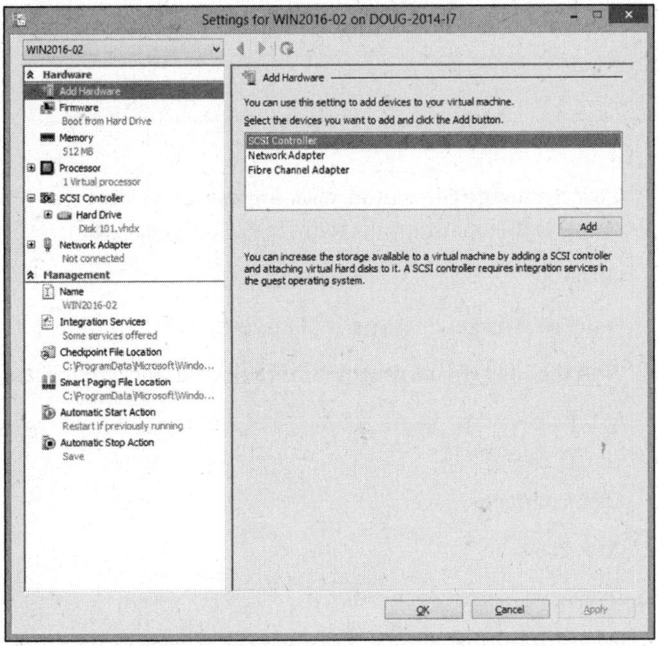

FIGURE 1-16: Editing the settings for a virtual machine.

2. **Click SCSI Controller in the Hardware list. Then select DVD Drive, and click Add.**

The configuration page shown in Figure 1-17 appears.

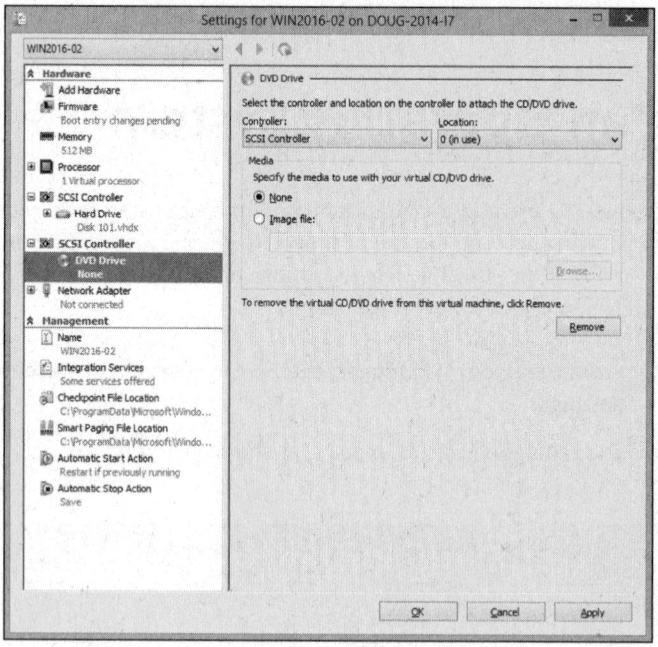

FIGURE 1-17:
Configuring a
DVD drive.

3. **Click the Image File option, click Browse, and select the .iso file that contains the operating system's installation program.**

4. **Click OK.**

You're returned to the Hyper-V Manager screen.

5. **With the new virtual machine still selected, click Connect.**

A console window opens, showing that the virtual machine is currently turned off (see Figure 1-18).

6. **Click Connect.**

7. **Click Start.**

The virtual machine powers up.

8. **When prompted to press a key to boot from the CD or DVD, press any key.**

The operating system's installation program starts.

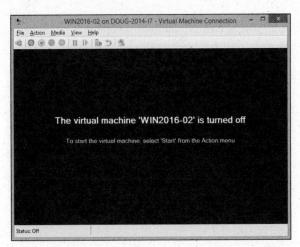

FIGURE 1-18:
Viewing a virtual
machine through
a console.

9. **Follow the instructions of the installation program to install the operating system.**

   That's all there is to it. You've now successfully created a Hyper-V virtual machine!

Hyper-V

Chapter **2**

VMware

Virtualization is a complex subject, and mastering the ins and outs of working with a full-fledged virtualization system like VMware Infrastructure is a topic that's beyond the scope of this book. You can dip your toes into the shallow end of the virtualization pond, however, by downloading and experimenting with VMware's free virtualization product, called VMware Player. You can download it from www.vmware.com.

This chapter is a brief introduction to VMware's virtualization platform and creating and using virtual machines with VMware Player.

Looking at vSphere

vSphere is an umbrella term for VMware's virtualization platform. The term *vSphere* encompasses several distinct products and technologies that work together to provide a complete infrastructure for virtualization. These products and technologies include the following:

» **ESXi:** ESXi is the core of vSphere; it is a Type-1 hypervisor that runs on host computers to manage the execution of virtual machines, allocating resources to the virtual machines as needed. ESXi comes in two basic flavors:

- *Installable:* The Installable version of software can be installed onto the hard drive on a host computer, much as any other operating system can be installed.

- *Embedded:* The Embedded version runs as firmware that is actually built into the host computer. It's preinstalled into read-only memory by the manufacturer of the host computer.

» **vCenter Server:** vCenter Server is a server application that runs on Windows Server installed in a virtual machine. vCenter is the central point for creating new virtual machines, starting and stopping virtual machines, and performing other management tasks in a vSphere environment.

» **vCenter Client:** vCenter Client is a Windows application that you use to access the features of a vCenter Server remotely. vCenter Client is the tool you'll work with most when you manage a vSphere environment.

» **VMFS:** VMFS, which stands for *Virtual Machine File System,* is the file system used by vSphere to manage disk resources that are made available to virtual machines. With VMFS, you can create *data stores* to access physical disk devices, and you can then create *volumes* on these data stores to make disk storage available to virtual machines.

Getting Started with VMware Player

VMware Player is a simplified version of the vSphere environment that provides many of vSphere's features but does not utilize the Type-1 ESXi hypervisor. Instead, VMware Player is a Type-2 hypervisor that runs within a Windows environment. VMware Player is useful for learning about virtualization and for simple desktop virtualization, but not for production use. I'm covering it here because experimenting with VMware Player is a great way to learn some of the basic concepts of virtualization.

Figure 2-1 shows VMware Player's main screen. From this screen, you can create a new virtual machine or run one of the virtual machines you've already created. As you can see in the figure, I've created several virtual machines: two that run various versions of Fedora (a popular Linux distribution) and one that runs Windows Server 2016.

You can run an existing virtual machine by selecting the virtual machine and clicking Play Virtual Machine. This launches the virtual machine, which opens in a new window, as shown in Figure 2-2. When you launch a virtual machine, the virtual machine behaves exactly as a real computer would when you power it up: First, it initializes its virtual hardware devices; then it loads the guest operating system that has been installed in the virtual machine.

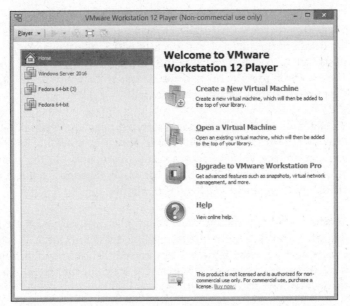

FIGURE 2-1:
VMware
Player lets you
experiment with
virtualization.

FIGURE 2-2:
A virtual machine
running Windows
Server 2016.

In Figure 2-2, Windows Server 2016 has booted up and is waiting for you to press
Ctrl+Alt+Del to log on.

The prompt to press Ctrl+Alt+Del shown in Figure 2-2 illustrates one of the peculiar details of running a virtual machine within a host operating system. When you press Ctrl+Alt+Del, which operating system — the host or the guest — responds? The answer is that the host operating system responds to the Ctrl+Alt+Del before the guest operating system ever sees it.

To get around this limitation, VMware uses the special keyboard shortcut Ctrl+Alt+End to send a Ctrl+Alt+Del to the guest operating system. Alternatively, you can use the VM drop-down menu that appears in the menu bar above the virtual machine menu. This menu lists several actions that can be applied to the virtual machine, including Send Ctrl+Alt+Del.

Another detail you should know about when working with a virtual machine is that when you click in the virtual machine's window, the VM captures your mouse and keyboard, so your input will be directed to the virtual machine rather than the host computer. If you want to break the bonds of the virtual machine and return to the host computer, press Ctrl+Alt.

Creating a Virtual Machine

Creating a new virtual machine in VMware Player is relatively easy. In fact, the most challenging part is getting hold of the installation disc for the operating system you want to install on the VM. Remember that a virtual machine is useless without a guest operating system, so you need to have the installation disc available before you create the virtual machine.

If you just want to experiment with virtualization and don't have extra licenses of a Windows Server operating system, you can always download an evaluation copy of Windows Server 2016 from www.microsoft.com. The evaluation period is six months, so you'll have plenty of time to experiment.

The downloadable trial version of Windows Server 2016 comes in the form of an .iso file, which is an image of a DVD file that you can mount within your virtual machine as though it were a real disc.

When you have your .iso file or installation disc ready to go, you can create a new virtual machine by following these steps:

1. **Click Create a New Virtual Machine on the VMware Player home screen (refer to Figure 2-1).**

   This brings up the New Virtual Machine Wizard, shown in Figure 2-3.

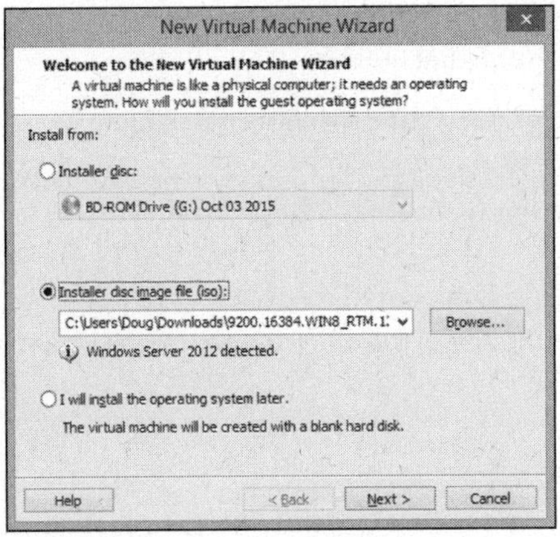

FIGURE 2-3:
The first page of
the New Virtual
Machine Wizard.

2. **Choose the installation option you want to use.**

You have three choices:

- *Installer Disc:* Select this option and then choose from the drop-down list
  the drive you'll install from if you want to install from an actual CD or DVD.

- *Install Disc Image File (iso):* Select this option, click the Browse button, and
  browse to the .iso file that contains the installation image.

- *I Will Install the Operating System Later:* Select this option if you want to
  create the virtual machine now but install the operating system later.

Note that the remaining steps in this procedure assume that you select a
Windows Server 2016 .iso file as the installation option.

3. **Click Next.**

The screen shown in Figure 2-4 appears.

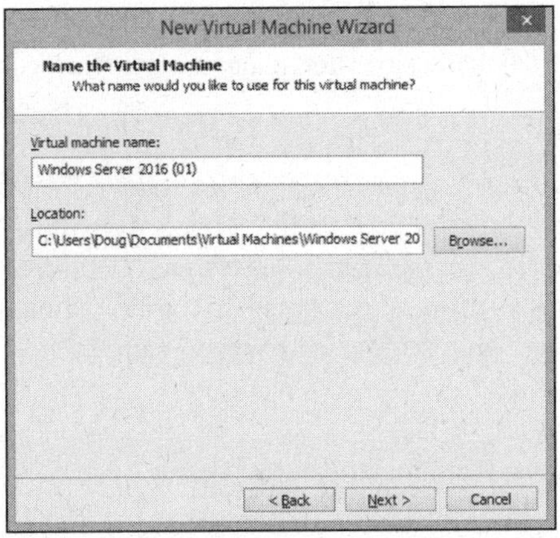

FIGURE 2-4:
Creating a name
and specifying
the virtual
machine disk
location.

4. **Enter a name for the virtual machine.**

5. **Enter the location of the virtual machine's disk file.**

If you want, you can click the Browse button and browse to the folder where you want to create the file.

6. **Click Next.**

The wizard asks for the size of the disk to create for the virtual machine, as shown in Figure 2-5.

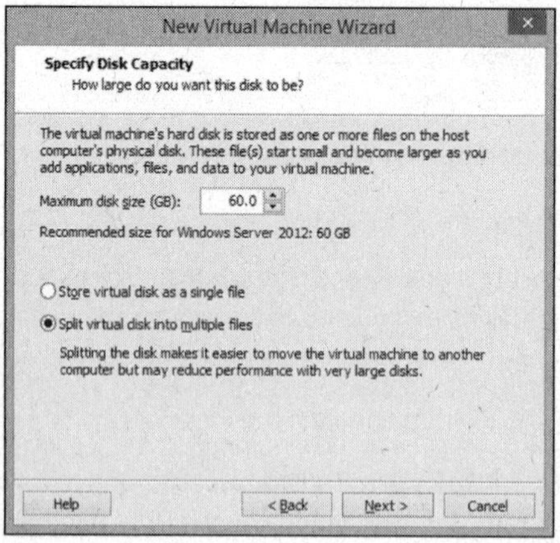

New Virtual Machine Wizard

Specify Disk Capacity
How large do you want this disk to be?

The virtual machine's hard disk is stored as one or more files on the host computer's physical disk. These file(s) start small and become larger as you add applications, files, and data to your virtual machine.

Maximum disk size (GB): 60.0

Recommended size for Windows Server 2012: 60 GB

○ Store virtual disk as a single file

● Split virtual disk into multiple files

Splitting the disk makes it easier to move the virtual machine to another computer but may reduce performance with very large disks.

Help   < Back   Next >   Cancel

FIGURE 2-5:
Specifying the virtual machine disk size.

7. **Set the size of the virtual machine's hard drive.**

The default setting is 40GB, but you can change it depending on your needs. Note that you must have sufficient space available on the host computer's disk drive.

8. **Click Next.**

The wizard displays a final confirmation page, as shown in Figure 2-6.

9. **Click Finish.**

The wizard creates the virtual machine and then starts it. Because the machine doesn't have an operating system installed, it boots from the CD/DVD installation image you specified back in Step 2. In this case, I booted with the Windows Server 2016 evaluation software disk image, so the new virtual machine displays the Windows Setup screen, as shown in Figure 2-7.

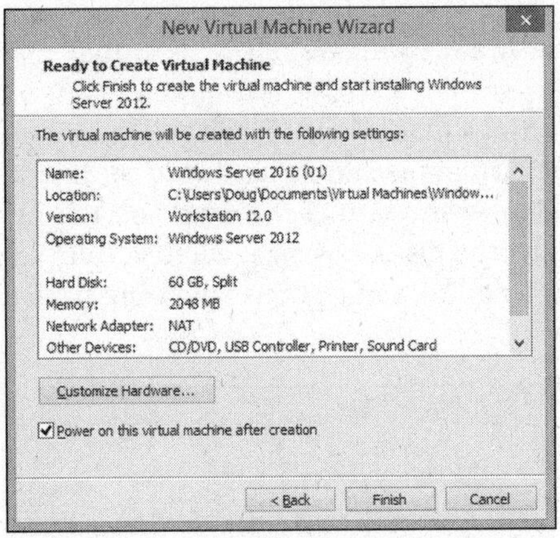

FIGURE 2-6:
VMware is ready
to create the
virtual machine.

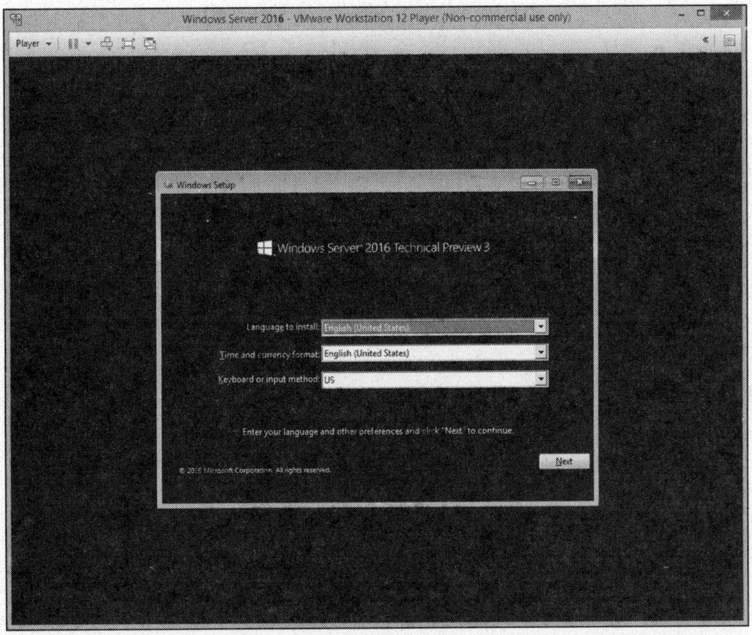

FIGURE 2-7:
Installing
Windows
Server 2016
on a virtual
machine.

10. Follow the steps to install the operating system.

Installing an operating system on a virtual machine is exactly the same as installing it on a physical computer, except that the installation screens appear within a virtual machine window.

When the operating system is installed, you're done! You can start using the virtual machine.

You can adjust the hardware configuration of a virtual machine by choosing VM⇨Settings while the virtual machine is running. This command brings up the Virtual Machine Settings dialog box, shown in Figure 2-8. From this dialog box, you can adjust the virtual machine's hardware configuration, including the amount of RAM available to the virtual machine and the number of processor cores. You can also adjust the disk drive size; add CD, DVD, or floppy drives; and configure network adapters, USB connections, and sound and display settings.

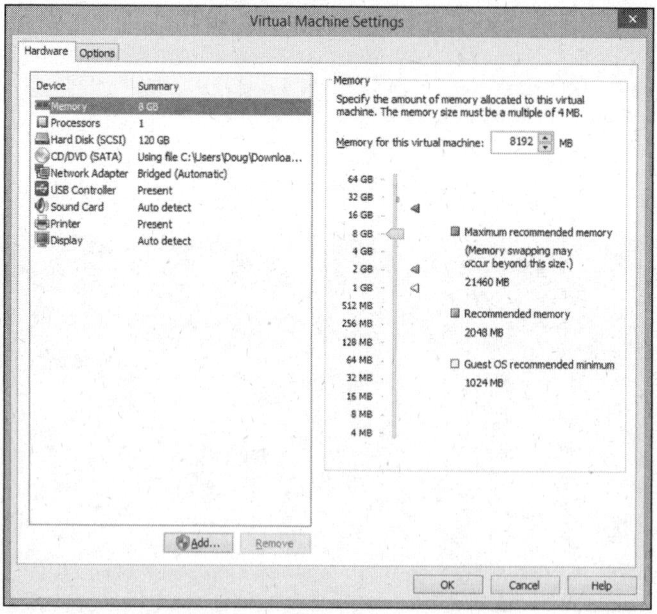

FIGURE 2-8:
Configuring
virtual machine
settings.

Installing VMware Tools

When you've installed an operating system into a VMware virtual machine, you should install an important application called *VMware Tools* before you do anything else. VMware Tools provides a variety of important functions for a VMware virtual machine:

>> Significantly improved graphics performance

>> Shared folders, which lets you share folders between the virtual machine and the host, making it easy to exchange files between the two

» A shared clipboard, which lets you copy and paste between the virtual machine and the host

» Synchronized time between the guest and host

» Better control of the mouse between guest and host

To install VMware Tools, follow this procedure:

1. Start the virtual machine.

2. On the menu of the VMware console window, choose Player⇨Manage⇨Install VMware Tools.

The dialog box shown in Figure 2-9 appears.

FIGURE 2-9:
Installing VMware
Tools.

3. Click Download and Install.

The VMware Tools are downloaded to the guest operating system. The Setup program displays the Welcome screen, shown in Figure 2-10.

FIGURE 2-10:
Installing VMware
Tools.

TIP

If the Setup program doesn't automatically start, press Windows+R, type **d:\setup.exe**, and press Enter. This will manually start the Setup program.

4. **Follow the instructions in the Setup program to install the VMware Tools.**

When the tools are installed, you'll be prompted to restart the virtual machine.

Chapter **3**

Azure

Microsoft Azure is a cloud computing service that provides a ton of alternatives for virtualizing your IT infrastructure in the cloud. Azure has been around since 2010 and is now one of the most robust platforms for building IT in the cloud.

Azure provides three basic types of cloud services:

» **Infrastructure as a Service (IaaS):** Cloud-hosted versions of the most basic types of virtual infrastructure components, including virtual machines, virtual disk storage, and virtual networks. With IaaS, Microsoft provides the physical hardware needed to run basic Hyper-V components.

» **Platform as a Service (PaaS):** A step up from IaaS, PaaS provides cloud-based platforms on which you can run applications. For example, you can deploy web-based ASP.NET applications to Azure and let Microsoft worry about managing the infrastructure needed to run the application.

» **Software as a Service (SaaS):** Fully functional software applications that you simply subscribe to.

In this chapter, I provide a brief overview of the most important services provided by Azure. Then I cover the nuts and bolts of setting up an Azure account and creating a virtual machine in Azure's cloud.

In case you're interested, the color *azure* is technically midway between blue and cyan. It's generally thought of as the color of the sky on a beautiful clear day. It gets its name from the mineral lapis lazuli, which has a striking blue color. The first use of the word *azure* in English came from none other than Geoffrey Chaucer in his 1374 poem *Troilus and Criseyde*.

Looking at Azure Services

At the time of this writing, Microsoft lists more than 600 distinct services provided by Azure. Here are the most popular and useful of these services:

» **Virtual machines (VMs):** Allows you to create and run fully functional VMs on Azure's cloud platform. The VMs can run Microsoft Windows Server operating systems or Linux. For Windows Server machines, the operating system license cost is included in the price of the VM.

When you provision an Azure VM, you select the size of the machine in terms of the number of processors, RAM, and disk space. You can easily adjust these settings later if your needs change.

You can also select a preconfigured disk image to use for the machine. This means that you don't have to go through the steps of installing an operating system; instead, you just choose an image that has the correct operating system already installed. You can also download server images from the Azure marketplace that are preconfigured by third-party vendors.

Pricing is based on actual usage at rates that vary depending on the class of service provided. The pricing structure is a bit complicated, so you'll want to explore it in depth to get an accurate understanding of what your VMs will actually cost. Fortunately, Microsoft has a nice estimating tool that can help you eliminate surprises.

» **Storage:** Allows you to create various types of storage resources, including simple disks, file systems, network-attached storage (NAS), and backup storage.

» **Networking:** Lets you create virtual networks that enable your Azure cloud components to communicate with one another and also with your physical network.

» **Web applications:** Azure can host complete web apps that can be developed using many popular programming platforms, including ASP.NET, Java, PHP, Node.js, Python, and HTML5. When you deploy an Azure Web App, Azure takes care of the details of managing the web server VM, so you can focus on the application itself.

>> **Mobile applications:** Enables you to create and deploy native or cross-platform mobile apps for iOS and Android. If you're looking for a way to create custom mobile applications for your company, the Azure Mobile App service is a good place to start.

>> **SQL database:** Allows you to create a SQL Server database without setting up a dedicated VM to run SQL Server. (For more information about SQL Server, refer to Book 6, Chapter 9.)

Creating an Azure Account

Before you can begin using Azure, you must set up an Azure account. Microsoft offers a free account that's designed to let you familiarize yourself with Azure's capabilities and learn how it works. Setting up the free account is easy, but you have to provide your credit card information. Don't worry — Microsoft won't actually charge your card until you upgrade to paid features.

To set up your account, go to `http://azure.microsoft.com`, click the link for a free account, and follow the instructions that appear on the screen.

Here's a general overview of what's available with a free account:

>> 750 hours of Windows Server General Purpose machines (known as Azure B1S), both Windows and Linux

>> 128GB of managed disk space

>> 250GB of SQL database

>> 15GB of outbound data bandwidth per month (unlimited inbound)

>> 10 web or mobile apps

>> An assortment of other free services, too detailed to list here

REMEMBER

Note that all these services are free for a period of one year. After the first year, normal charges are incurred.

When you set up your free account, Microsoft also gives you a $200 credit against any services that aren't included with the free services; this credit must be used within the first 30 days.

TIP

The nuances of what services are free under the free account are detailed and, of course, subject to change. So check out the FAQ available during the signup process to be sure you understand what's free and what isn't.

Examining the Azure Portal

After you've created your free Azure account, you can access the Azure portal by browsing to `http://azure.microsoft.com` and clicking the Portal link in the upper right. After you enter your username and password, the portal page will appear, as shown in Figure 3-1.

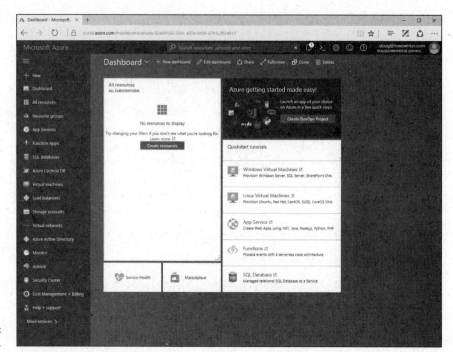

FIGURE 3-1:
The Azure Portal.

The center portion of the Portal initially displays the Dashboard, which summarizes the current status of your Azure account. Initially, the Dashboard isn't very interesting, because you haven't yet created any Azure resources. The All Resources area of the Dashboard indicates that you have "No resources to display." However, the Dashboard will get more interesting as you create Azure resources.

Next to the All Resources area, you can see some links to quick-start tutorials for common tasks such as creating new Windows or Linux VMs or other types of resources. If you want, you can view these quick-start tutorials now. I show you how to create a Windows VM later in this chapter, in the "Creating a Windows Virtual Machine" section.

Across the top of the Azure portal is a toolbar that contains a search box, as well as several useful icons:

» **Notifications:** Displays any recent notifications generated by Azure

» **Shell:** Displays the Azure command shell, which lets you manage Azure using PowerShell or Linux Bash commands

» **Settings:** Lets you configure portal settings

» **Feedback:** Allows you to send feedback to the Azure team

» **Help:** Provides access to useful Azure Help pages

Your username appears to the right of these icons. You can hover the mouse over your username to see more specific details about your user account (such as your email address and domain name), or you can click your username to display a drop-down menu that, among other things, lets you sign out or change your password.

On the left side of the Portal page is a menu featuring additional pages you can display in the portal. For example, +New lets you create new resources in Azure, and All Resources displays a list of all the resources you've created in Azure. I recommend you spend some time exploring this menu to familiarize yourself with the range of features that are available in Azure.

TIP

You can always return to the Dashboard by clicking the Dashboard link at the top of the Portal menu.

Creating a Windows Virtual Machine

After you've had some fun exploring the various pages available within the Azure portal, you're ready to get down to business by creating your first VM. Follow these steps:

1. **Click +New.**

The Azure Marketplace page is displayed, as shown in Figure 3-2. This page lists the range of Azure resources you can create. The menu on the left lists marketplace categories; specific resource types within the selected category are listed on the right.

2. **Click Get Started.**

TIP

The Get Started category lists the resources you're most likely to create when you're first getting started with Azure. At the top of that list is Windows Server 2016 VM, which you can use to create a Windows Server 2016 VM.

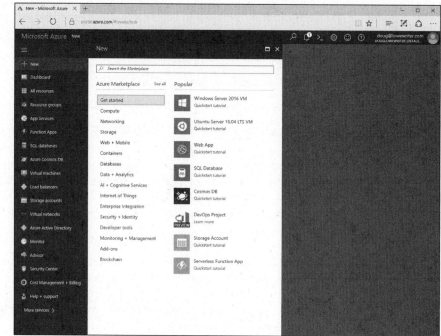

FIGURE 3-2:
The Azure
Marketplace.

3. **Click Windows Server 2016 VM.**

You're taken to the Create Virtual Machine page, shown in Figure 3-3.

4. **Enter the basic configuration information.**

The Basics tab of the Create Virtual Machine page requires that you enter the following information:

- *Name:* Enter the computer name you want to use for this VM.

- *VM Disk Type:* Select whether you want the VM to use solid state drives (SSDs) or hard disk drives (HDDs). Microsoft charges more for SSD storage, so choose HDD unless you need the added performance that SSD drives provide.

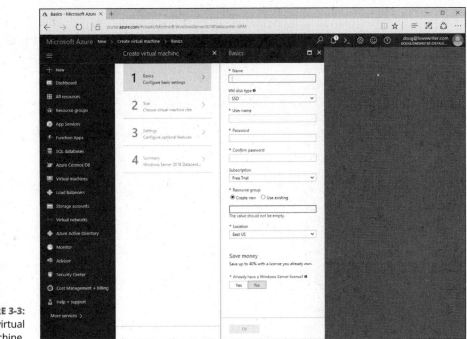

FIGURE 3-3:
Creating a virtual
machine.

- *Username:* The username for the administrator account.

- *Password:* The password for the administrator account. (This password must meet standard Windows complexity requirements.)

- *Resource group:* A *resource group* is simply a grouping by which Azure resources can be managed. Your account must contain at least one resource group. Because you haven't created one yet, you'll need to check the Create New option and enter a name for your new resource group.

- *Location:* The region where you would like your VM to be located. Scroll through the list to see the available options. In most cases, you'll want to choose the location that best describes your own location.

5. **Click OK.**

The Size tab of the Create Virtual Machine page appears, as shown in Figure 3-4.

6. **Select the size appropriate for your VM.**

The Size tab lists the recommended sizes for your VM; simply click the size you want to use to select it.

FIGURE 3-4:
Selecting
the virtual
machine size.

Each size option indicates the following aspects of the VM's specifications:

- The number of virtual CPUs

- The VM's RAM capacity

- The number of disk drives allocated to the machine

- The maximum I/O speed of the machine

- The size and type of the disks

- Whether the Load Balancing feature is used, which can improve performance

In addition, each size option includes the estimated price per month.

TIP

Notice that the default selection, identified as type D1_V2, has an estimated cost of around $100 per month. This VM option is *not* eligible for the free 12-month usage allowance provided with your free account. To choose a machine that is eligible for the one-year free usage, click View All. Then scroll down the list of all VM size options to the B1S type and select it. As you can see, this machine has one CPU and just 1GB of RAM.

7. Click Select.

The Settings tab of the Create Virtual Machine page appears, as shown in Figure 3-5.

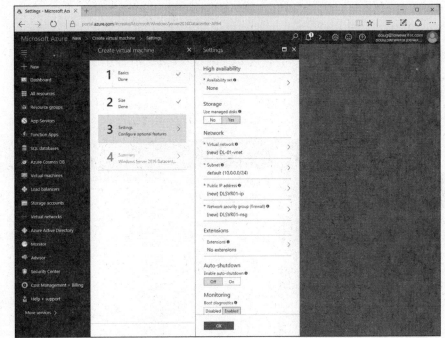

FIGURE 3-5:
Configuring the virtual machine settings.

8. Configure the VM settings.

In most cases, you can leave the settings at their defaults. Here's a rundown on the settings in case you'd like to change them:

- *High availability:* Use this option to configure high availability settings if you want to use it. I recommend you consult Azure Help on the topic before configuring this option. You don't need to use it for a simple test machine such as you're creating now.

- *Storage:* This option lets you disable Azure's Managed Disks feature, which provides redundancy and fault tolerance. In most cases, you should leave this feature enabled.

- *Network:* This set of options lets you customize the IP settings used by the new machine. Change these settings only if you're not satisfied with the choices Azure recommends.

- *Extensions:* You can use this option to add additional features to your VM, such as anti-malware protection. You can skip the extensions for a test machine.

9. **Click OK.**

   The Summary tab of the Create Virtual Machine page appears, as shown in Figure 3-6.

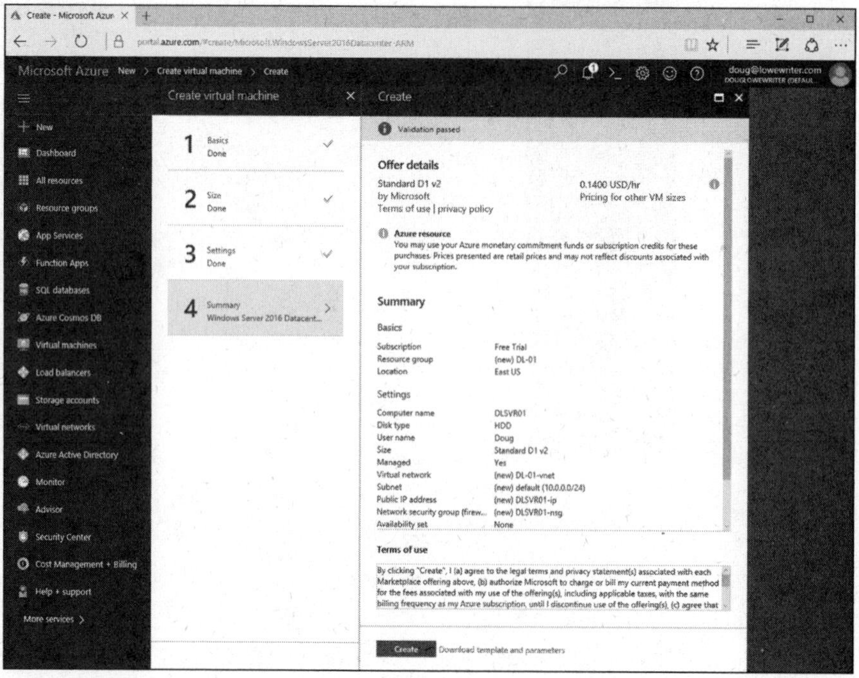

FIGURE 3-6: Azure is ready to create the server.

10. **Review the summary to make sure everything looks right.**

11. **Click Create.**

    Azure proceeds to deploy the server. This might take a few minutes, but eventually the new server will appear on the Dashboard, as shown in Figure 3-7.

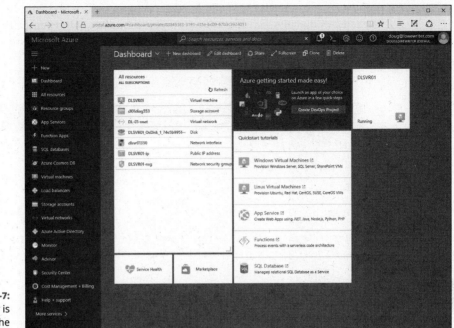

FIGURE 3-7:
The new server is available on the Dashboard.

Managing an Azure Virtual Machine

When you create an Azure VM, the machine is automatically pinned to the Dashboard, which means that it appears in a box at the right side of the page (refer to Figure 3-7); the box indicates that the server is running.

In addition, new resources associated with the new server are added to the list of resources, which was previously empty:

>> **DLSVR01:** The VM that was just created

>> **dl01diag553:** A storage account that was automatically created to manage the server's storage

>> **DL-01-vnet:** A virtual network that was created and to which the VM was added

>> **DLSVR01_OsDisk . . . :** The virtual disk drive that holds the VM image

>> **dlsvr01350:** The server's network interface

>> **DLSVR01-ip:** A public IP address that has been allocated to the VM

>> **DLSVR01-nsg:** A network security group that was automatically created to manage the server's security

You can manage any of these resources to manage the resource from the portal. For example, Figure 3-8 shows the resource page for the DLSVR01 server.

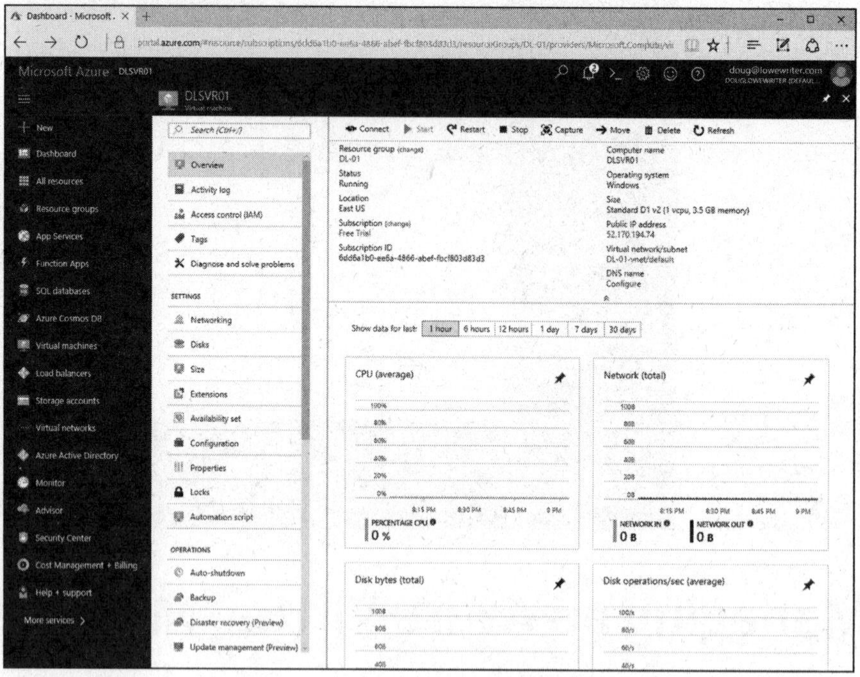

FIGURE 3-8: Managing a server from the Azure portal.

Across the top of the VM's resource page, you'll find a strip of icons useful for managing the machine:

🔌 Connect

 >> **Connect:** Lets you connect to the VM (see "Connecting to an Azure Virtual Machine," later in this chapter).

▶ Start

 >> **Start:** Starts the VM, if it isn't already running.

↻ Restart

 >> **Restart:** Restarts the VM.

■ Stop

 >> **Stop:** Stops the VM.

🔲 Capture

 >> **Capture:** Creates an image of the VM. You can later use this image to create a new VM.

→ Move

 >> **Move:** Lets you move the VM to another resource group or to another Azure subscription.

🗑 Delete

 >> **Delete:** Deletes the VM.

↻ Refresh

 >> **Refresh:** Updates the display with current information.

Notice also that along the left side of the resource page for a VM is a menu of other activities you can use to manage the machine. For example, you can adjust the machine's size configuration by clicking the Size option (found under Settings). This displays a list of the VM size options, as shown in Figure 3-9.

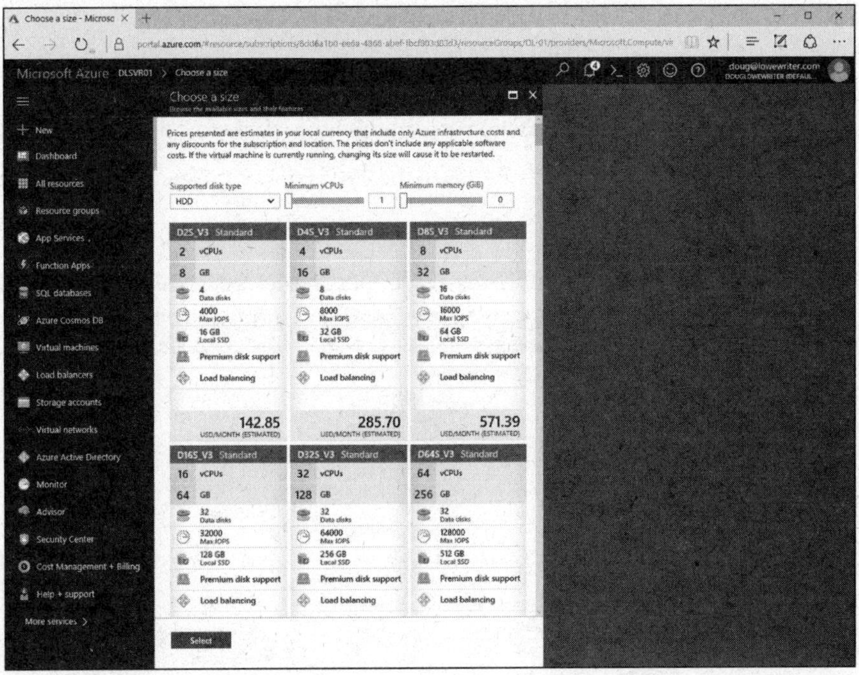

FIGURE 3-9: Resizing an Azure virtual machine.

Connecting to an Azure Virtual Machine

When an Azure VM is up and running, you can connect to it remotely using Remote Desktop Connection, just as you can connect to any other VM. The easiest way to do so is to follow these steps:

1. **Open the VM in the Dashboard (refer to Figure 3-8).**

2. **Click Connect in the toolbar.**

   This downloads a remote desktop connection file (.rdp).

3. **When prompted, click Save As.**

   The Save As dialog box appears.

4. **Select a location to save the** `.rdp` **file and then click Save.**

   The `.rdp` file is saved to the location you specify. You're given the option to open the file.

5. **Click Open to open the connection.**

   Remote Desktop Connection fires up, connects to the Azure VM, and then asks for credentials.

6. **Enter the username and password for the administrator account you specified when you created the machine, and then click OK.**

   You are connected to the VM, as shown in Figure 3-10.

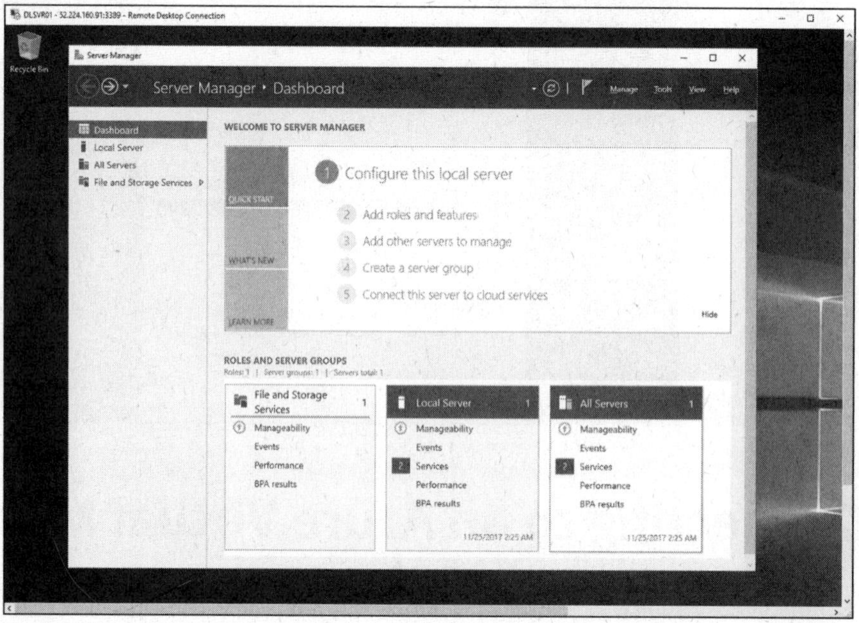

FIGURE 3-10: Connecting to an Azure virtual machine.

> **Signing up for an AWS account**

> **Creating a virtual machine in AWS**

> **Managing an AWS virtual machine instance**

> **Connecting to an AWS virtual machine instance**

Chapter **4**

Amazon Web Services

ike Microsoft Azure, Amazon Web Services (AWS) is a cloud computing service that includes numerous ways to virtualize your IT infrastructure in the cloud. AWS is the grandfather of cloud-based infrastructure providers — it got its start way back in 2002. Since then, AWS has developed into the largest cloud provider in the world. Amazon's online retail space itself is hosted on AWS, as are many other familiar services, including Netflix, Hulu, and Ancestry.com.

AWS provides services that span the full range of cloud-based services, including Infrastructure as a Service (IaaS), Platform as a Service (PaaS), and Software as a Service (SaaS). In this chapter, I give you a brief look at the range of cloud services that AWS provides. Then you'll learn how to create and manage a virtual machine (VM) on AWS.

Looking at What Amazon Web Services Can Do

AWS has well over 2,000 distinct services available on its platform. They're organized into several categories:

>> **Compute:** Provides cloud-base virtual computing resources. The main service in this category is Amazon's cloud-based virtualization platform, known as *Amazon Elastic Compute Cloud* (EC2). With EC2, you can create and manage VMs that run at Amazon's data centers. You can select from several different pricing models, depending on your needs. Multiple operating system choices are available, including Windows Server 2016 and several variations of Linux. And you can configure VMs with a single processor and as little as 1GB of RAM to as many as 64 processors and 488GB of RAM.

Naturally, the larger the machine configuration and the more it is used, the more it will cost. The smallest server can be run for just a few dollars per month (in fact, free for 12 months) — perfect for experimenting with AWS to familiarize yourself with its features.

>> **Networking:** Lets you set up virtual networks that enable your AWS cloud components to communicate with one another and also with your physical network. Amazon Virtual Private Cloud (VPC) lets you set up a private network at Amazon's data centers so that you can extend your own private network into Amazon's cloud, allowing EC2 machines to seamlessly integrate into your own network.

>> **Storage and Content Delivery:** Amazon Elastic File System (EFS) is a cloud-based storage system designed to work with EC2 VMs to provide cloud-based data storage. In addition to EFS, AWS provides several other specialized types of cloud storage for various types of content.

>> **Database:** Relational Database Service (RDS) provides basic relational database capabilities similar to Microsoft SQL Server, and several other database offerings provide non-relational database services.

>> **Application Services:** Provide features such as email, messaging, media encoding, workflow management, and many others.

>> **Administration and Security:** Provides basic directory and security services for AWS.

>> **Developer and Management:** Provides features for developers creating and managing custom applications on AWS.

>> **Analytics:** Features for managing and analyzing large data sets.

>> **Enterprise Applications:** Provides several enterprise-class applications, including a desktop virtualization solution called Workspaces, a document-management solution called WorkDocs, and an email and calendaring system called WorkMail.

But wait, there's more! AWS also includes Internet of Things (IoT) solutions for managing your coffee pots and toasters, features for game development features, and who knows what else!

Creating an Amazon Web Services Account

Before you can use AWS, you must first set up an AWS account. The good news is that Amazon offers a free account you can use to experiment with AWS. Basic AWS services are free for 12 months, which gives you plenty of time to familiarize yourself with the many capabilities and features of AWS.

Setting up the free account is easy, but you'll have to fork over a credit card number. So you'll want to keep a good eye on your account, just in case you step over the line of what's free and begin incurring monthly charges.

To set up your account, just browse to `http://aws.amazon.com` and follow the links to set up a free account.

Here's what you get your first year with the free account:

>> 750 hours per month of compute usage on a small virtual machine called a *micro instance*, which has just one processor core and 1GB of RAM)

>> 5GB of EFS storage

>> 750 hours per month of Amazon RDS relational database

>> An assortment of other free services, too detailed to list here

Note that all these services are free for a period of one year. After the first year, normal charges are incurred.

TIP

The full list of what is free for 12 months is detailed and definitely subject to change. I suggest you examine the details to be sure you understand exactly what's free and what will be charged. And check your billing summary frequently to avoid surprises.

Examining the Amazon Web Services Console

When you've created your free AWS account, you can access the AWS Console by following these steps:

1. **Go to** http://aws.amazon.com.

The AWS home page appears, as shown in Figure 4-1.

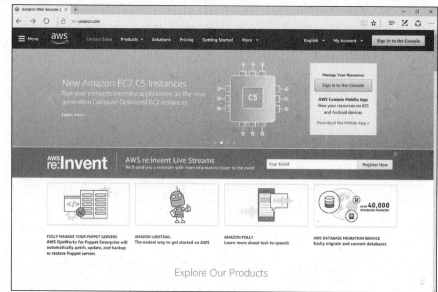

FIGURE 4-1:
The AWS home page.

2. **Click the Sign In to the Console button.**

You're taken to a sign-in screen.

3. **Enter your username and click Next.**

You're prompted for your password.

4. **Enter your password and click Sign In.**

The AWS Console appears, as shown in Figure 4-2.

Explore the console! Start by clicking Services in the menu bar at the top of the page. This reveals a menu of services you can access via the console, as shown in Figure 4-3.

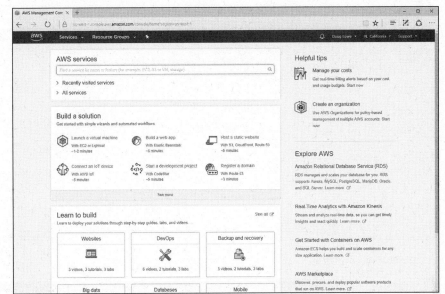

FIGURE 4-2:
The AWS Console.

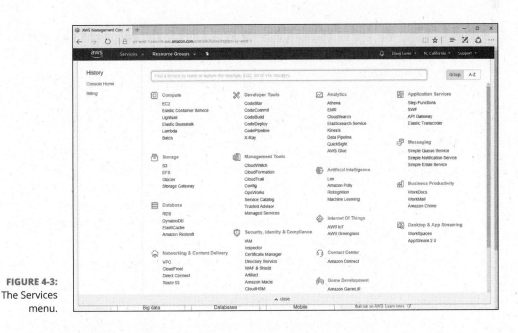

FIGURE 4-3:
The Services menu.

You can click any of the services listed in this menu to view the dashboards for the various services. For example, Figure 4-4 shows the EC2 Dashboard, which shows information about EC2 VMs.

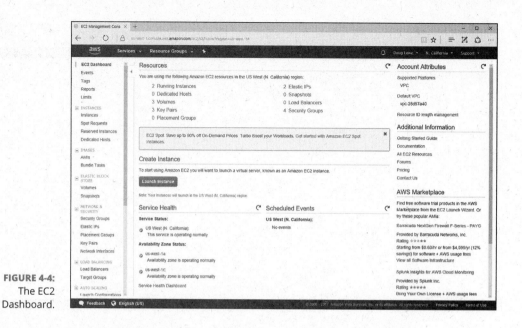

FIGURE 4-4:
The EC2
Dashboard.

Creating a Windows Virtual Machine

To create a VM, navigate to the EC2 Dashboard as described in the previous section (refer to Figure 4-4). Then follow these steps:

1. **Click the Launch Instance button.**

Step 1 of the Launch Instance Wizard is displayed, as shown in Figure 4-5. This page displays a list of machine images you can choose for your virtual machine.

Scroll through the list to see the variety of images that are available for your virtual machines. You'll find a wide array of both Linux- and Windows-based images.

2. **Click the Microsoft Windows Server 2016 Base image.**

This image provides a basic Windows Server 2016 VM.

You're taken to Step 2 of the Launch Instance Wizard, which invites you to choose an instance type, as shown in Figure 4-6. The instance type determines the performance characteristics of the VM. Here, you'll find various combinations of virtual CPUs, memory, storage, and network performance options.

For this example, we select the t2.micro type, which provides one CPU and 1GB of memory. This instance type is eligible for the AWS free-usage tier, which gives you 750 hours of usage per month for the first 12 months of your account.

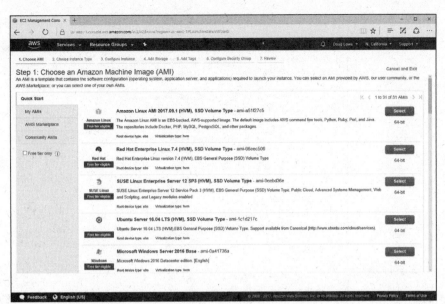

FIGURE 4-5:
Choosing a machine image.

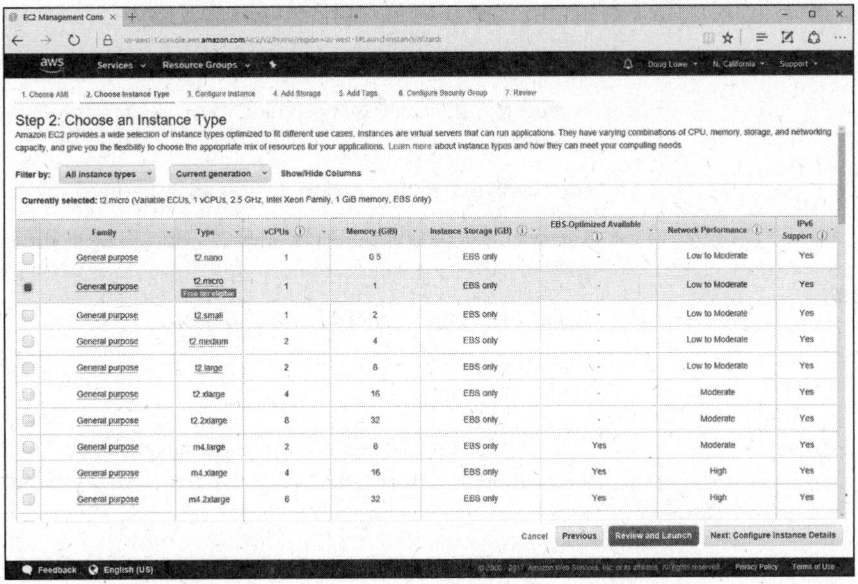

FIGURE 4-6:
Choosing an instance type.

3. **Select the t2.micro instance type and click Next: Configure Instance Details.**

This summons Step 3 of the wizard, which allows you to set a variety of options for the VM, as shown in Figure 4-7.

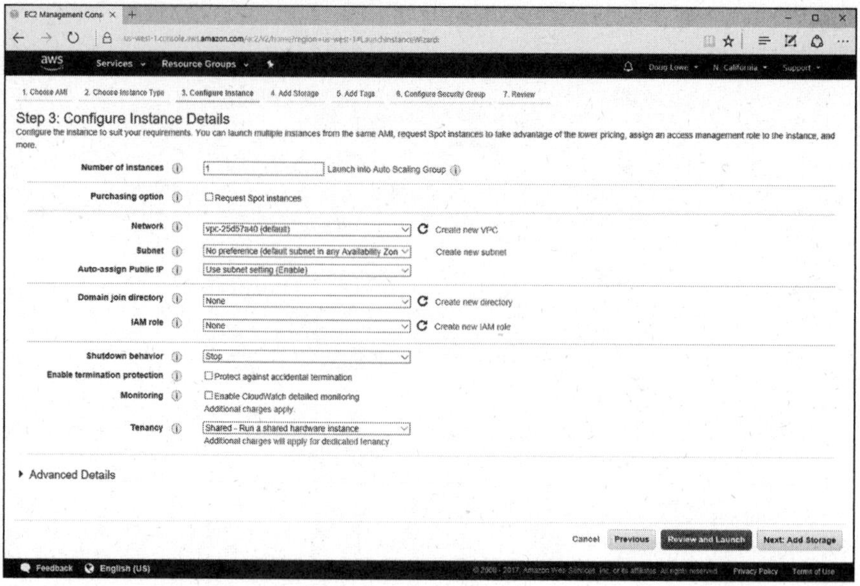

FIGURE 4-7:
Configuring
instance details.

4. **Select the configuration options you want.**

The following options are available on this page:

- *Number of Instances:* Use this option if you want to create more than one VM instance.

- *Purchasing Option:* This option doesn't apply to the t2.micro instance type.

- *Network:* Select the virtual network you want to use. If you haven't yet created a virtual network, you can click Create New VPC to create one.

- *Subnet:* Select the subnet you want to use.

- *Auto-Assign Public IP:* Use this option to enable automatic assignment of an IP for the instance.

- *Domain Join Directory:* Use this option to join an Active Directory domain. (Click Create New Directory to create a new directory if one doesn't already exist.)

- *IAM Role:* To join a directory, you must select an IAM role to authenticate your identity. To create one, click Create New IAM Role.

- *Shutdown Behavior:* Use this option to select what happens when the host operating system is shut down. The options are Stop or Terminate; in most cases, you should leave this setting set to Stop.

- *Enable Termination Protection:* Enable this feature to prevent the instance from being stopped. If you enable this feature, you'll have to disable it before you can shut down the machine.

- *Monitoring:* Enables monitoring, which gathers statistics about the machine's performance. Amazon charges for monitoring, so enable this option only if you're sure you need it.

- *Tenancy:* Use this option to select whether you want this instance to run in shared hardware or on dedicated hardware. Amazon charges more for dedicated tenancy, so select shared tenancy unless you specifically need dedicated hardware.

5. Click Next: Add Storage.

This brings up Step 4 of the wizard, which lets you configure the storage for the VM (see Figure 4-8).

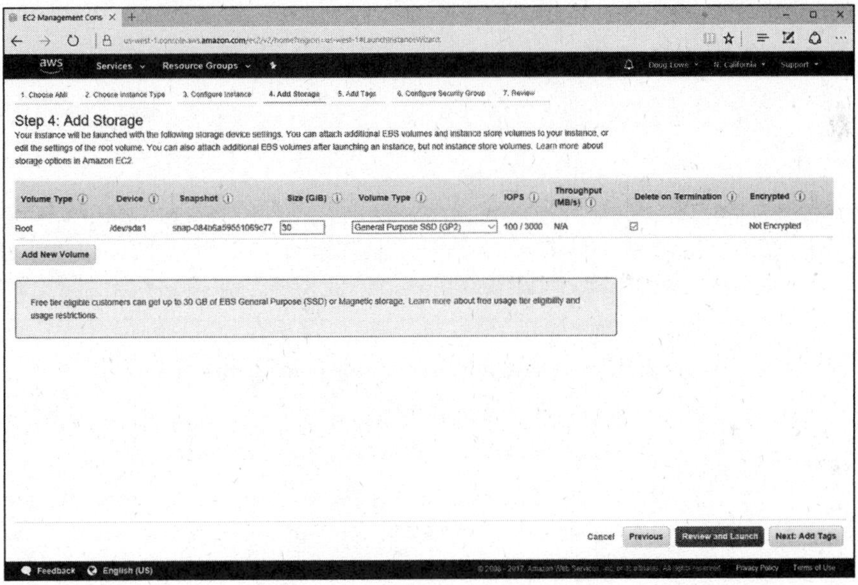

FIGURE 4-8: Adding storage.

6. Configure the storage for the VM.

By default, a single disk volume is created for the instance. You can change the amount of space allocated for this volume (in Figure 4-8, 30GB has been allocated by default), and you can change the disk type. The default is General Purpose SSD, but you can change it to less expensive Magnetic Disk if you want.

You can add additional disk volumes by clicking the Add New Volume button. When you click this button, an additional disk volume is added; you can then specify the size and volume type for the new volume.

7. **Click Next: Add Tags.**

The page shown in Figure 4-9 is displays.

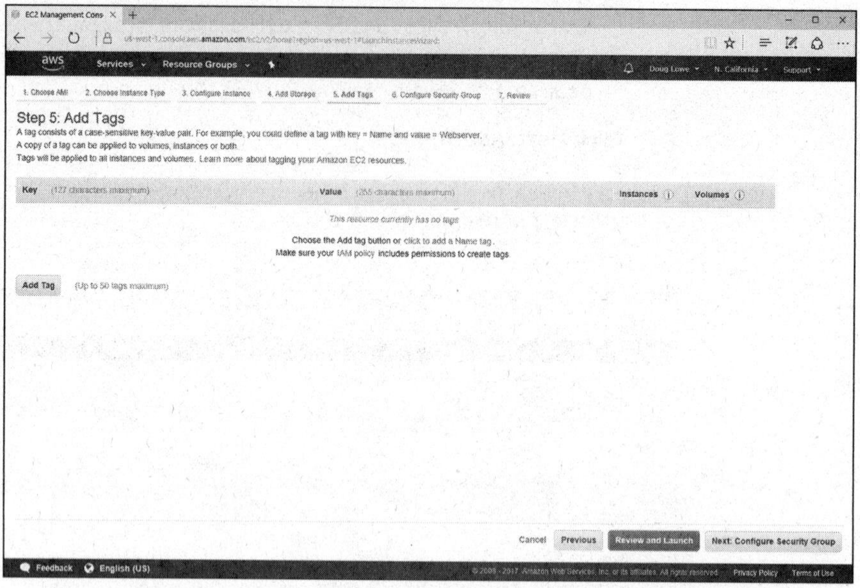

FIGURE 4-9:
Adding tags.

8. **If you want, add one or more tags to the instance.**

AWS tags let you add keywords and associated values to your instances, as well as to other types of resources, such as volumes.

For your first experimental VM instance, you don't need to add tags. But if you end up using more than a few VMs in AWS, you may want to apply tags to help keep them organized. For example, you might create a keyword named Stack to indicate whether a machine is part of your production stack or your test stack. For production machines, you would specify Production for the Stack keyword; for test machines, you'd specify Test.

To add a tag, simply click the Add Tag button. Then enter the tag and value.

9. **Click Next: Configure Security Group.**

This brings up the Configure Security Group page, shown in Figure 4-10. This page lets you configure one or more firewall rules that limit access to the VM.

10. **Configure the firewall rules.**

The default security group provides a single firewall rule that allows Remote Desktop Protocol (RDP) access from any IP address. If you want, you can limit RDP access to a specific address by entering the address in the Source column.

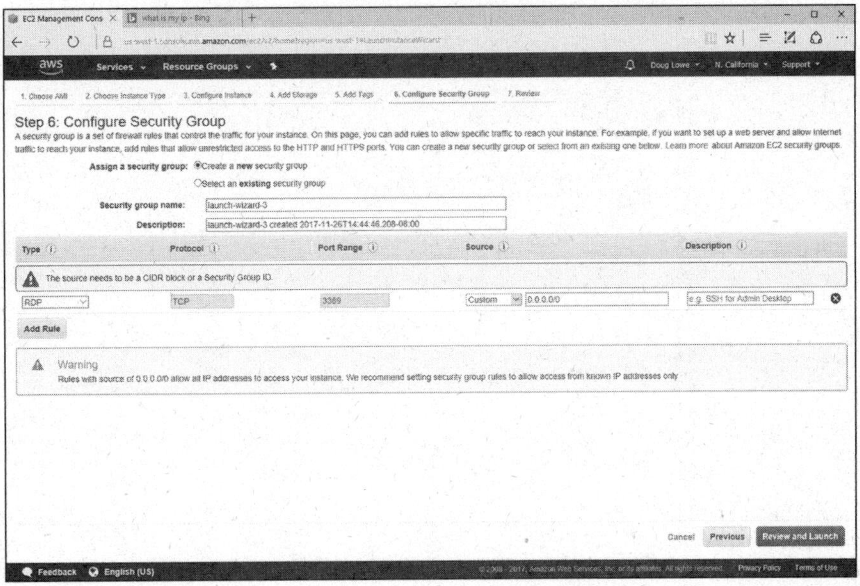

FIGURE 4-10:
Configuring the
security group.

TIP

Change the source drop-down from Custom to My IP; AWS will figure out the IP address of your computer and set the rule to allow access only from that IP address.

If you want to allow other types of traffic to the machine, you'll need to add additional rules. For example, to enable HTTP or HTTPS traffic, you'll need to add rules to allow HTTP and HTTPS.

11. **Click Review and Launch.**

This takes you to the final page of the wizard, which displays a summary of the instance settings that you can review before you create the instance (see Figure 4-11).

12. **Review the settings.**

You can click the Edit links to the right of each group of settings if you need to make any changes.

13. **Click Launch.**

AWS prompts you to select a key pair to provide security for your instance. A *key pair* is a combination of a public key that AWS keeps and a private key stored in a file that you're responsible for storing. You *must* keep the private key file in a safe place; without it, you won't be able to access your instance!

As Figure 4-12 shows, AWS asks you to enter a name for the key pair. You can then download the key pair file and save it on your computer.

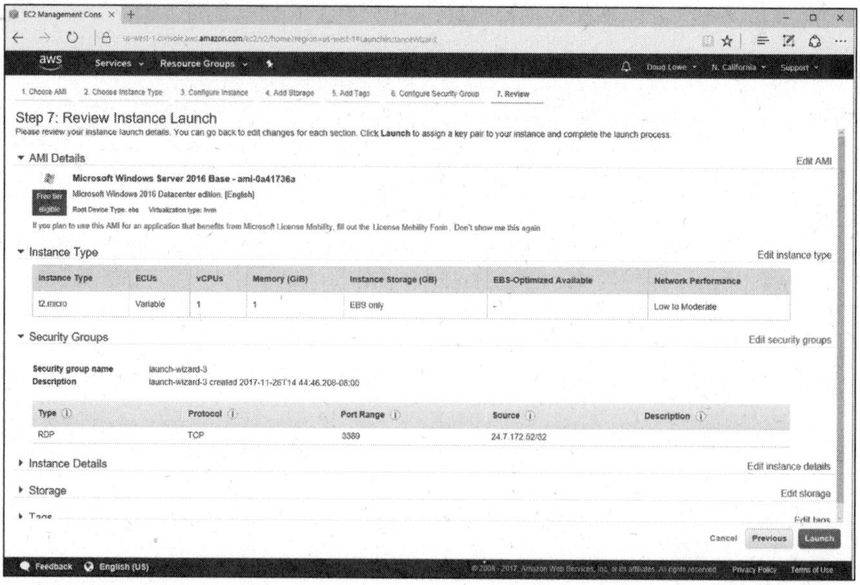

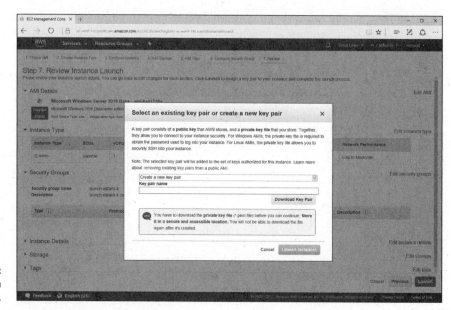

FIGURE 4-11:
Reviewing the
instance settings.

FIGURE 4-12:
Creating a
key pair.

14. Enter a name for the key pair.

Use whatever name you want, but make sure it's memorable.

15. Click Download Key Pair.

Windows asks what you want to do with the downloaded file.

16. Click Save As, navigate to a safe location, and click Save.

17. Click Launch Instances.

AWS displays a Launch Status page that indicates the status of your request, as shown in Figure 4-13.

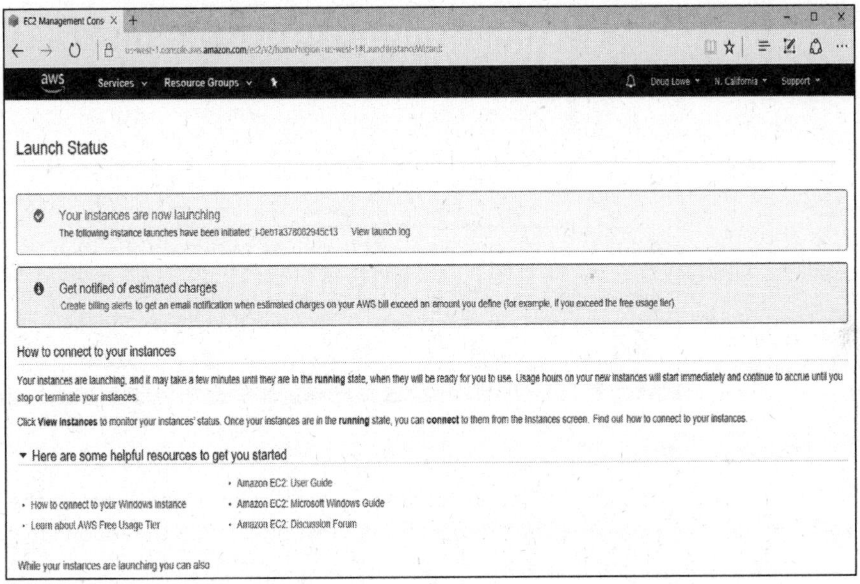

FIGURE 4-13:
Your instances are being created!

Managing an Amazon Web Services Virtual Machine

You can manage your VM instances by opening the EC2 Dashboard and then clicking Instances in the menu that appears at the left side of the Dashboard page. This brings up a list of all EC2 VM instances, as shown in Figure 4-14.

TIP

To add or change the name of an instance, hover the mouse over the Name column for the instance you want to rename and click the pencil icon that appears. You can then type a name for the instance.

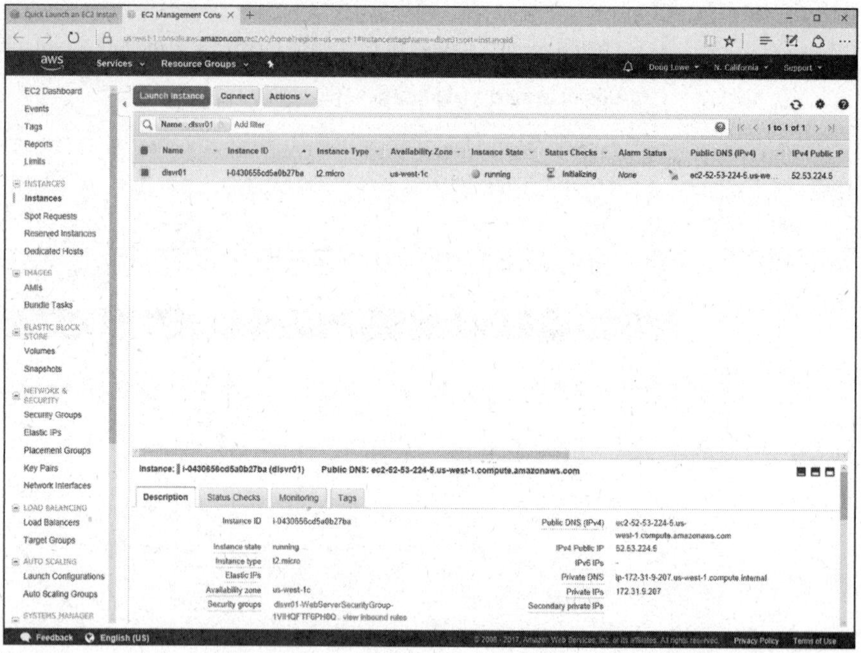

FIGURE 4-14:
Managing EC2
instances.

To manage an instance, right-click anywhere in the row for the instance you want to manage. This brings up a context menu with the following commands:

>> **Connect:** Connects to the instance using Remote Desktop Connection.

>> **Get Windows Password:** Lets you retrieve the Windows administrator password; you'll have to supply the key pair file that was downloaded when you created the instance.

>> **Launch More Like This:** Lets you create one or more clones of the instance.

>> **Instance State:** Lets you start, stop, reboot, or terminate the instance.

>> **Instance Settings:** Lets you change settings for the instance. Note that if the instance is stopped, you can change the instance type to increase the amount of RAM or the processor resources available to the instance.

>> **Image:** Create an image of the instance that you can later use to create new instances.

>> **Networking:** Changes network settings for the instance.

>> **CloudWatch Monitoring:** Enables monitoring services for the instance.

Connecting to an Amazon Web Services Virtual Machine

When an AWS VM is up and running, you can connect to it remotely using Remote Desktop Connection, just as you can connect to any other VM. The easiest way to do so is to follow these steps:

1. **In the EC2 Instance Dashboard, right-click the instance you want to connect to and choose Connect.**

   The Connect to Your Instance dialog box, shown in Figure 4-15, appears.

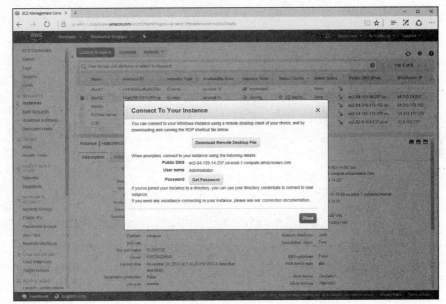

FIGURE 4-15:
Connecting to an instance.

2. **Click Download Remote Desktop File.**

This downloads a remote desktop connection file (`.rdp`).

3. **When prompted, click Save As.**

The Save As dialog box appears.

4. **Select a location to save the** `.rdp` **file and click Save.**

The `.rdp` file is saved to the location you specify. You're given the option to open the file.

5. **Back in the Connect to Your Instance dialog box, click Get Password.**

AWS asks you to specify the key pair file you downloaded when you created the instance, as shown in Figure 4-16.

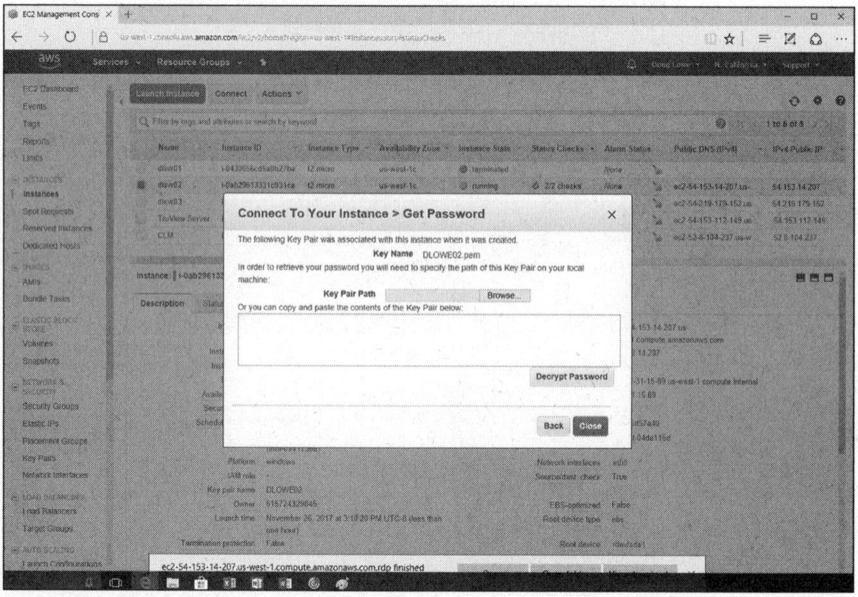

FIGURE 4-16: Entering the path to the key pair file.

6. **Click the Browse button, navigate to your key path file, select it, and click Open.**

AWS shows the contents of the key path file in the text box.

7. Click Decrypt Password.

AWS decrypts the password and displays it, as shown in Figure 4-17. (Well, sort of — I airbrushed out the actual password. Don't get all excited, though. I've already terminated this machine, so don't waste your time trying to hack into it!)

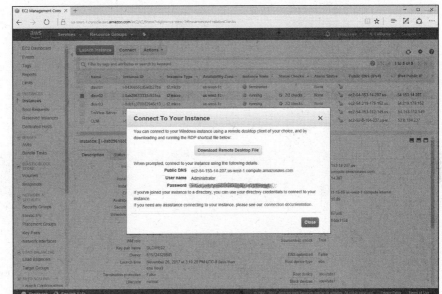

FIGURE 4-17:
AWS shows you
the Administrator
password.

TIP

Notice that the password generated by AWS consists of 32 random characters. You'll never in a lifetime commit that to memory, and you should under no circumstances copy and paste this password into a document on your computer. My recommendation is that when you log in to the server, you change its Administrator password to something you can remember without writing down.

8. Navigate to the .rdp file you saved in Step 4 and double-click to open it.

Remote Desktop Connection fires up, connects to the instance, and prompts you for credentials to log in.

9. Enter the username (Administrator) and password (see Step 7) and click OK.

Congratulations! You've successfully logged in to your first AWS EC2 instance, as shown in Figure 4-18!

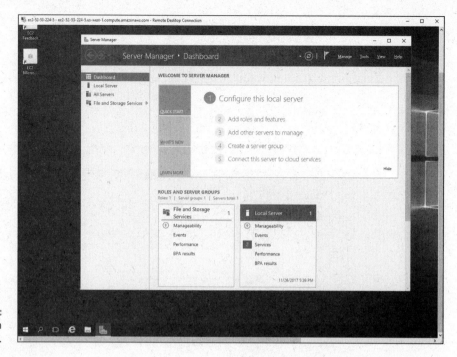

FIGURE 4-18:
The console of an EC2 instance.

Chapter 5

Desktop Virtualization

Virtualization is most often applied to server computers. However, more and more organizations are also applying virtualization to desktops, replacing traditional Windows desktop computers with virtual desktops that are accessed from a nontraditional type of device.

In this chapter, I present a basic overview of desktop virtualization and its benefits and introduce you to some of the technologies that can be used to implement virtual desktop infrastructure (VDI).

Introducing Desktop Virtualization

The term *desktop virtualization* refers to any software that separates an end-user's Windows desktop environment from the hardware that the environment runs on. Desktop virtualization is meant to address some of the fundamental weaknesses of the traditional practice of giving each user his or her own Windows workstation.

Here are just a few of the problems that desktop virtualization addresses:

» Windows workstations must be configured individually for each user. If your organization has 100 workstations and you decide to update your accounting software, you have to figure out how to deploy the update to 100 computers.

>> Windows software frequently needs to be updated. Updates are normally delivered via Windows Update. However, deploying Windows updates separately to all your desktop computers is fraught with peril. A particular Windows update might work well on 99 percent of all computers, which means that if your organization has 100 computers, that update is likely to not work on at least one of them. That means a trip to that computer to diagnose the problem caused by the update and get the user back up and running.

>> If a user's computer fails, that computer must be replaced. To replace the computer, you'll need to rebuild the user's profile, reinstall the user's applications, and perform other configuration work to restore the user's desktop environment.

>> Windows computers have a dreaded thing called the C: drive. Any data stored on the C: drive belongs to that computer alone and is not easily backed up to the network. Thus, if the user's C: drive dies, its data is likely to die with it.

>> If a user moves to another desk or office, the user must take her computer with her.

>> If a user wants to work from home, the user can't easily access her desktop environment from her home computer. There are solutions for this problem, such as remote access software like GoToMyPC (www.gotomypc.com), but those solutions introduce problems of their own.

>> If a user has a laptop computer in addition to a desktop computer, the user must make a special effort to ensure that the data on the desktop computer is synchronized with the data on the laptop.

>> The user may have devices with different platforms than his or her desktop computer. For example, a user might have a Windows computer at work, a MacBook Pro at home, and an Apple iPad for the road. These platforms aren't compatible with one another, so the user can't run the same software on all three.

Desktop virtualization addresses all these problems (and more) by moving the user's desktop environment from a desktop computer to a central host computer. Then the user can access the desktop environment from any device that is compatible with the VDI technology chosen to virtualize the desktop. The advantages of this arrangement are many:

>> If the user's computer dies, the user's desktop does not die with it. You can replace the failed computer with any other computer and simply reconnect to the virtual desktop.

>> Operating systems and application software can be centrally managed. There is no need to visit a user's desk to install or update software.

>> The user's desktop can be accessed from different types of devices. So, a user can access his or her desktop from a Windows computer, a MacBook, an iPad, an Android table, or even from an iPhone or Android phone.

>> You can use thin clients at users' desks rather than full-blown Windows computers. A *thin client* is a small computer that has just enough processing power (CPU, RAM, and disk) to run the client piece of the desktop virtualization platform. Typically, the thin client runs an embedded version of Linux that is specially configured to run the client software that accesses the virtual desktop. In most cases, the end-user is not even aware that this is happening — to the user, the experience is identical to having a standard Windows computer at his or her desk.

>> In some desktop virtualization environments, multiple users share a common Windows environment, which means that an application needs to be installed only once for it to be available for multiple users, and operating system patches need to be applied just once rather than to multiple computers.

>> All data is kept on the host computers, which means the data can be centrally managed and backed up.

Considering Two Approaches to Desktop Virtualization

There are at least two distinct approaches to implementing desktop virtualization. The first approach is to simply create a separate virtual machine for each user and provide a way for the users to efficiently connect to their virtual machines. This approach is usually referred to as *virtual desktop infrastructure* (VDI). VDI solutions are usually built using traditional virtualization products such as Microsoft's Hyper-V or VMware's ESXi hypervisor.

The second approach is to use a single server that is designed to support multiple users and provide a way for each user to connect to his or her session on the server. This approach is often called *terminal services*, because it's based on the terminal services role that is a standard part of all versions of Windows Server.

TECHNICAL STUFF

Technically, with Windows Server 2008, Microsoft changed the name of Terminal Services to *Remote Desktop Services* to emphasize the role of Terminal Services for virtualizing desktops. The IT industry is pretty reluctant to change its phraseology, however, so most IT professionals still call it *terminal services* even though that term has been obsolete for almost a decade.

The remaining sections of this chapter describe two popular desktop virtualization products that use these two approaches. The first is VMware's Horizon View, which builds on VMware's virtualization platform. The second is Citrix XenApp, which builds on Windows Terminal Services.

Looking at VMware's Horizon View

With VMware's virtualization infrastructure, you could easily implement desktop virtualization by simply creating virtual machines for each of your users' desktops and having your users connect to their virtual machines using Remote Desktop Connection (RDC). However, you'll quickly start to realize some of the limitations of this approach.

First, you'll probably discover that the RDC client is not very efficient when it comes to intensive graphics applications. Watching YouTube videos over RDC can be frustrating, as can working with graphically oriented programs such as Adobe Photoshop.

You'll also discover that managing users' access to virtual desktop machines is difficult with vSphere. vSphere is designed to create and manage virtual servers that are typically accessed only by IT personnel. Access to those servers is controlled through Active Directory credentials; in other words, if you don't know the password, you can't log in. But vSphere isn't really designed to create hundreds of desktop VMs and make them available to hundreds of users.

To address these and other issues, VMware offers a product called VMware Horizon View that builds on the core functions of vSphere and adds features specifically designed for desktop virtualization. Here's a short list of some of the more important features of Horizon:

- » **vSphere Desktop:** A version of vSphere specifically designed for running up to tens of thousands of desktop virtual machines

- » **vCenter Desktop:** A version of vCenter designed specifically for managing virtual resources such as hosts, RAM, processors, and disk storage in a virtual desktop environment

- » **Horizon View:** A management tool designed to provision and deploy virtual desktops

- » **Horizon View Client:** Client software for accessing virtual desktops on a variety of platforms, including Windows, Mac, iOS, and Amazon devices

>> **Horizon View Composer:** A tool for cloning desktop VMs and for managing software and operating system updates on pools of similar desktop VMs

Looking at Citrix XenApp

Citrix XenApp is a desktop virtualization environment that uses Windows Terminal Services to enable multiple users to access remote desktops from a variety of client devices, including Windows, Mac, iOS, and Amazon devices. Unlike VMware's Horizon View, XenApp does not create a separate virtual machine for each user. Instead, when users connect to XenApp, they log in to separate terminal services sessions on a common Windows Server. The users then have access to all the resources and applications that are available to the Windows Server.

Users connect with XenApp by using a client application called the Citrix Receiver, which can be run on Windows, Mac, iOS, or Android devices. Figure 5-1 shows Citrix Receiver running on a Windows 10 system.

FIGURE 5-1:
Citrix Receiver.

When you configure a XenApp server, you create and publish *desktops* and *applications* that users can remotely connect to. Then, when the user connects to the XenApp server, the user is shown the applications that he or she is authorized to use. For example, Figure 5-1 shows a typical Citrix Receiver screen connected to a XenApp server. In this case, the user is authorized to open a desktop and two applications.

Desktop Virtualization

If the user connects to a desktop, the user sees an entire Windows desktop environment, complete with a Start menu that grants access to applications, as well as Explorer to browse disk resources. Figure 5-2 shows the Citrix Receiver connected to a desktop.

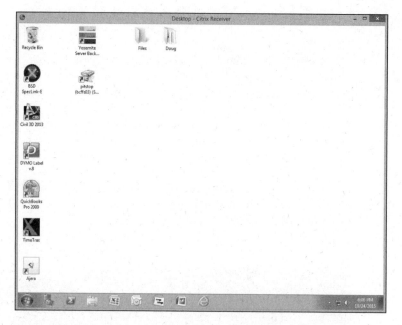

FIGURE 5-2:
Connecting to a desktop.

On the other hand, a user can connect to an individual application rather than to a desktop. This feature is called *application virtualization.* When you connect to an application, that application runs on the server but only that one application's window is shown on the user's device. In other words, the user sees the individual application rather than a complete desktop. The user can then use the application as if the application were natively running on his or her device, even if the user's device is a non-Windows device.

Figure 5-3 shows an example of Microsoft Excel running on an iPhone 6 Plus via Citrix Receiver. As you can see, Citrix Receiver makes the desktop Microsoft Excel application available on my iPhone exactly as it's available on my Windows desktop. In fact, I could choose File ⇨ Open to summon an Open dialog box which would allow me to browse the network to open any file that would be available to me from my Windows desktop. This feature effectively extends my desktop applications to my iPhone.

FIGURE 5-3:
Viewing Excel on
an iPhone.

6

Implementing Windows Server 2016

Contents at a Glance

Chapter **1**

Installing Windows Server 2016

This chapter presents the procedures that you need to follow to install Windows Server — specifically, Windows Server 2016. Note that although the specific details provided are for Windows Server 2016, installing a previous version is very similar, as is installing the older Windows Server 2008. So you won't have any trouble adapting these procedures if you're installing an older version.

Planning a Windows Server Installation

Before you begin the Setup program to actually install a Windows Server operating system, you need to make several preliminary decisions, as the following sections describe.

Checking system requirements

Before you install a Windows Server operating system, you should make sure that the computer meets the minimum requirements. Table 1-1 lists the official minimum requirements for Windows Server 2016. (The minimums for Windows

Server 2012 are the same.) Table 1-1 also lists what I consider to be more realistic minimums if you expect satisfactory performance from the server as a moderately used file server.

TABLE 1-1

Minimum Hardware Requirements for Windows Server 2016 (Standard Edition)

Item	Official Minimum	A More Realistic Minimum
CPU	1.4 GHz	3 GHz
RAM	512MB	4GB
Free disk space	32GB	100GB

Note that there is no 32-bit version of Windows Server 2016. A 64-bit processor is required, but that shouldn't be a problem, as nearly all computers manufactured since around 2007 have 64-bit processors.

Note also that if you're installing Windows Server 2016 on a virtual machine, you'll need at least 800MB of RAM to complete the installation. After Windows Server 2016 is installed, you can back the RAM down to 512MB if you wish.

Reading the release notes

Like all versions of Windows Server, Windows Server 2016 provides a set of release notes that you should read before you start Setup, just to check whether any of the specific procedures or warnings it contains applies to your situation.

At the time I wrote this, those notes weren't available yet. But you can find them online by searching for *Windows Server 2016 Release Notes* to find the link.

Deciding whether to upgrade or install

Windows offers two installation modes: full installation or upgrade installation.

A *full installation* deletes any existing operating system(s) it finds on the computer and configures the new operating system from scratch. If you do a full installation onto a disk that already has an operating system installed, the full installation offers to keep any existing data files that it finds on the disk.

An *upgrade installation* assumes that you already have a previous Windows Server 2012 (either Windows Server 2012 or Windows Server 2012 R2) installation in place.

The operating system is upgraded to Windows Server 2016, preserving as many settings from the previous installation as possible. You cannot upgrade Windows Server 2008 or earlier to Windows Server 2016.

Here are some points to ponder before you perform an upgrade installation:

>> You can't upgrade a client version of Windows to a server version.

>> With an upgrade installation, you don't have to reinstall any applications that were previously installed on the disk.

>> Always perform a full backup before doing an upgrade installation!

Considering your licensing options

Two types of licenses are required to run a Windows Server operating system: a *server license*, which grants you permission to run a single instance of the server, and *Client Access Licenses* (CALs), which grant users or devices permission to connect to the server. When you purchase Windows Server, you ordinarily purchase a server license plus some number of CALs.

To complicate matters, there are two distinct types of CALs: per-user and per-device. *Per-user* CALs limit the number of users who can access a server simultaneously, regardless of the number of devices (such as client computers) in your organization. By contrast, *per-device* CALs limit the number of unique devices that can access the server, regardless of the number of users in your organization.

Thinking about multiboot

Windows includes a *multiboot* feature that lets you set up the computer so that it has more than one operating system. When you boot up the computer, you can select the operating system you want to boot up from a menu.

TIP

Although you may be tempted to use the multiboot features to maintain previous operating system installations, I recommend against it. A much better alternative is to install Windows Server into a virtual machine using virtualization technology such as Microsoft's Hyper-V or VMware. Virtualization allows you to install a complete operating system such as Windows Server 2016 within an already-installed operating system. (Note that the Windows Server 2016 installation illustrated in this chapter and throughout this book is installed on a Hyper-V virtual machine running within Windows 10.)

Planning your partitions

Partitioning enables you to divide a physical disk into one or more separate units called *partitions.* Each disk can have up to four partitions. All four of the partitions can be primary partitions. A *primary partition* contains one — and only one — file system. Alternatively, you can create up to three primary partitions and one extended partition, which can be subdivided into one or more logical drives. Then each logical drive can be formatted with a file system.

Windows Server 2016 offers you two file systems: NTFS and ReFS. NTFS is the tried-and-true file system that has been the standard file system for going on 20 years. The partition that Windows Server 2016 boots from must be NTFS. However, other partitions can be either NTFS or ReFS.

Although you can set up partitions for a Windows Server in many ways, the following two approaches are the most common:

>> **Allocate the entire disk as a single partition that will be formatted with NTFS.** The operating system is installed into this partition, and disk space that isn't needed by the operating system or other network applications can be shared.

>> **Divide the disk into two partitions.** Install the operating system and any other related software (such as Exchange Server or a backup utility) on the first partition. If the first partition will contain just the operating system, 100GB is a reasonable size, although you can get by with as little as 32GB if space is at a premium. Then use the second partition for application data or network file shares.

TIP

Note that the disk partitioning scheme is independent of any hardware-based RAID configuration your server may employ. Your server may actually include five physical hard drives that are combined by the hardware disk controller to form a single logical drive, for example. Within this logical drive, you can create one or more operating-system partitions.

Deciding your TCP/IP configuration

Before you install the operating system, you should have a plan for implementing TCP/IP on the network. Here are some of the things you need to decide or find out:

>> What are the IP subnet address and mask for your network?

>> What is the domain name for the network?

>> What is the host name for the server?

- » Will the server obtain its address from DHCP?

- » Will the server have a static IP address? If so, what?

- » Will the server be a DHCP server?

- » What is the Default Gateway for the server (that is, what is the IP address of the network's Internet router)?

- » Will the server be a DNS server?

In almost all cases, you should assign the server a static IP address.

TIP

For more information about planning your TCP/IP configuration, see Book 3.

Choosing workgroups or domains

A *domain* is a method of placing user accounts and various network resources under the control of a single directory database. Domains ensure that security policies are applied consistently throughout a network and greatly simplify the task of managing user accounts on large networks.

A *workgroup* is a simple association of computers on a network that makes it easy to locate shared files and printers. Workgroups don't have sophisticated directory databases, so they can't enforce strict security.

Workgroups should be used only for very small networks with just a few users. Truthfully, any network that is large enough to have a dedicated server running Windows Server 2016 is too large to use workgroups. So, if you're installing a Windows Server, you should always opt for domains.

After you decide to use domains, you have to make two basic decisions:

- » **What will the domain name be?** If you have a registered Internet domain name, such as mydomain.com, you may want to use it for your network's domain name. Otherwise, you can make up any name you want.

- » **What computer or computers will be the domain controllers for the domain?** If this server is the first server in a domain, you must designate it as a domain controller. If you already have a server acting as a domain controller, you can either add this computer as an additional domain controller or designate it a member server.

You can always change the role of a server from a domain controller to a member server, and vice versa, if the needs of your network change. If your network has more than one server, it's always a good idea to create at least two domain controllers. That way, if one fails, the other one can take over.

TIP

Before You Install . . .

After you've made the key planning decisions for your Windows Server installation, but before you actually start the Setup program, you should take a few precautionary steps. The following sections describe what you should do before you perform an upgrade installation.

Note: The first two steps apply only to upgrades. If you're installing a Windows Server on a new system, you can skip those steps.

Backing up

Do a complete backup of the server before you begin. Although Windows Setup is reliable, sometimes, something serious goes wrong, and data is lost.

TIP

You don't have to back up the drive to external media, such as tape. If you can find a network disk share with enough free space, back up to it.

Checking the event logs

Look at the event logs of the existing server computer to check for recurring errors. You may discover that you have a problem with a SCSI device or your current TCP/IP configuration. It's better to find out now rather than in the middle of setup.

Disconnecting UPS devices

If you've installed an uninterruptible power supply (UPS) device on the server and connected it to your computer via a USB cable, you should temporarily disconnect the serial cable before you run Setup. When Setup is complete, you can reconnect the UPS device.

Running Setup

Now that you've planned your installation and prepared the computer, you're ready to run the Setup program. The following procedure describes the steps that you must follow to install Windows Server 2016 on a virtual machine using an ISO image of the installation DVD. Before you begin this procedure, you'll need to download the ISO file from Microsoft's website. Search for *Windows Server 2016 Download* to find the download site.

1. **Configure the new virtual machine with the specifications you want to use, mount the installation ISO file on the virtual DVD drive, and start the VM.**

   After a few moments, the Windows Setup Wizard fires up and asks for your language, time and currency format, and keyboard layout.

2. **Click Next.**

   The Welcome screen appears, as shown in Figure 1-1.

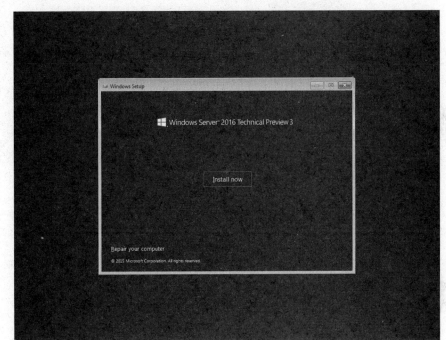

FIGURE 1-1:
Welcome to
Windows Setup!

3. **Click Install Now.**

   Windows asks which edition of the operating system you want to install, as shown in Figure 1-2.

   Two editions are available:

   - Windows Server 2016 (also known as Server Core), a streamlined version of the operating system that does not have a graphical user interface (GUI). You must manage this edition of the server remotely using PowerShell or Windows Management Console.

   - Windows Server 2016 with Desktop Experience, a more user-friendly version of the server with a GUI modeled after Windows 10.

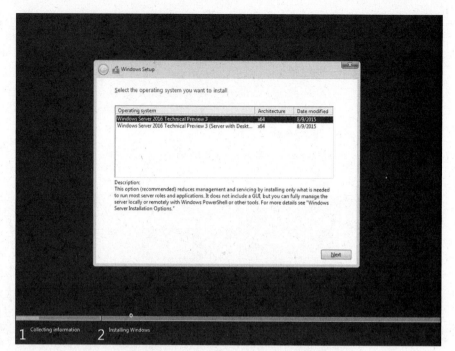

FIGURE 1-2:
Selecting the OS
edition to install.

For this book, I use the Desktop Experience version to demonstrate how to
manage various aspects of Windows Server 2016.

4. **Select the edition you want to install and then click Next.**

   The Setup Wizard displays the License Agreement information. Read it if you
   enjoy legalese.

5. **Click I Accept the License Terms and then click Next.**

   The Setup Wizard asks whether you want to perform an upgrade installation or
   a full installation.

6. **Click the installation option you want to use.**

   Setup continues by displaying the computer's current partition information.
   You can select the partition that you want to use for the installation. If necessary, you can reconfigure your partitions from this screen by deleting existing
   partitions or creating new ones. I assume here that you want to create a single
   partition that uses all available space on the drive.

7. **Select the partition on which you want to install Windows and then click
   Next.**

   Setup formats the drive and then copies files to the newly formatted drive. This
   step usually takes a while. I suggest you bring along your favorite book. Start
   reading at Chapter 1.

After all the files have been copied, Setup reboots your computer. Then Setup examines all the devices on the computer and installs any necessary device drivers. You can read Chapter 2 of your book during this time.

When Setup finishes installing drivers, it asks for the password you want to use for the computer's Administrator account, as shown in Figure 1-3.

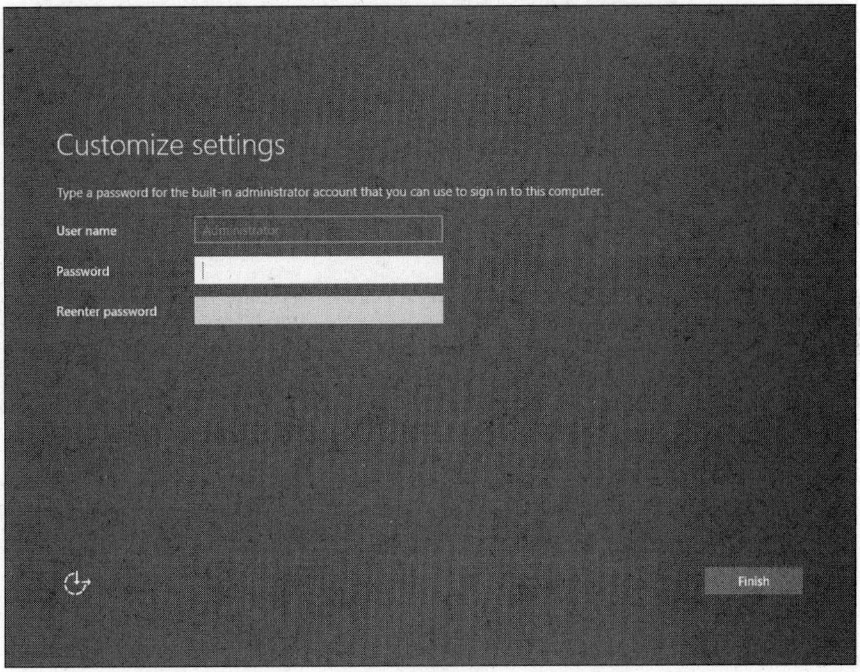

Customize settings

Type a password for the built-in administrator account that you can use to sign in to this computer.

User name	Administrator
Password		
Reenter password		

Finish

FIGURE 1-3:
Setting the
Administrator
password.

8. **Enter the Administrator password twice and then click Finish.**

REMEMBER

Be sure to write this password down somewhere and keep it in a secure place. If you lose this password, you won't be able to access your server.

After you've set the Administrator password, Windows displays the login screen shown in Figure 1-4.

9. **Press Ctrl+Alt+Del, and log in using the Administrator account.**

You have to enter the password you created in Step 7 to gain access.

When you're logged in, Windows displays the Server Manager Dashboard, as shown in Figure 1-5.

FIGURE 1-4:
Press Ctrl+Alt+Del
to log in.

Press Ctrl+Alt+Delete to unlock.

8:28

Thursday, September 10

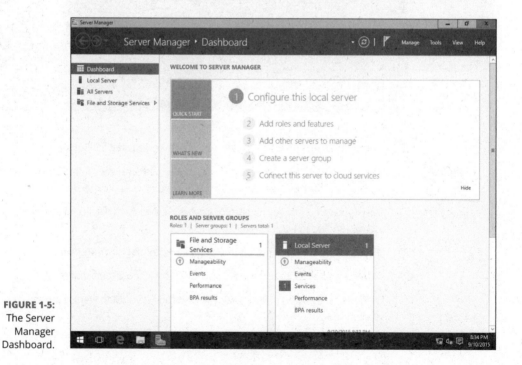

FIGURE 1-5:
The Server
Manager
Dashboard.

The Server Manager Dashboard provides links that let you complete the configuration of your server. Specifically, you can

- Click Configure This Local Server to configure server settings such as the computer's name and the domain it belongs to, network settings such as the static IP address, and so on.

- Click Add Roles and Features to add server roles and features. (For more information, see "Adding Server Roles and Features," later in this chapter.)

- Click Add Other Servers to Manage to manage other servers in your network.

- Click Create a Server Group to create a customized group of servers.

- Click Connect This Server to Cloud Services if you integrate cloud services with your server.

Adding Server Roles and Features

Server roles are the roles that your server can play on your network — roles such as file server, web server, or DHCP or DNS server. *Features* are additional capabilities of the Windows operating system itself, such as the .NET Framework or Windows Backup. Truthfully, the distinctions between roles and features are a bit arbitrary. The web server is considered to be a role, for example, but the Telnet server is a feature. Go figure.

The following procedure describes how to install server roles. The procedure for installing server features is similar.

1. **Click Add Roles and Features on the Server Manager Dashboard.**

   The Add Roles and Features Wizard appears, as shown in Figure 1-6.

2. **Click Next.**

   The wizard asks which of two installation types you want to perform. In most cases, you want to leave the default choice (Role-Based or Feature-Based Installation) selected. Select the alternative (Remote Desktop Services Installation) only if you're configuring a remote virtual server.

3. **Click Next.**

   The wizard lets you select the server you want to install roles or features for, as shown in Figure 1-7. In this example, only one server is listed. If you'd chosen Add Other Servers to Manage in the Server Manager Dashboard to add other servers, those servers would appear on this page as well.

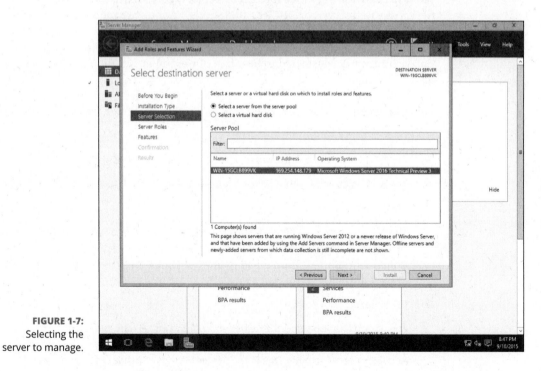

FIGURE 1-6:
The Add Roles
and Features
Wizard.

FIGURE 1-7:
Selecting the
server to manage.

4. **Select the server you want to manage and then click Next.**

   The Select Server Roles page, shown in Figure 1-8, appears. This page lets you select one or more roles to add to your server.

5. **Select one or more roles to install.**

   You can click each role to display a brief description of it. If you click DHCP Server, for example, the following text is displayed:

   ```
   Dynamic Host Configuration Protocol (DHCP) Server enables you to centrally
       configure, manage, and provide temporary IP addresses and related
       information for client computers.
   ```

6. **Click Next.**

   The Select Features page appears, as shown in Figure 1-9. This page lists additional server features that you can install.

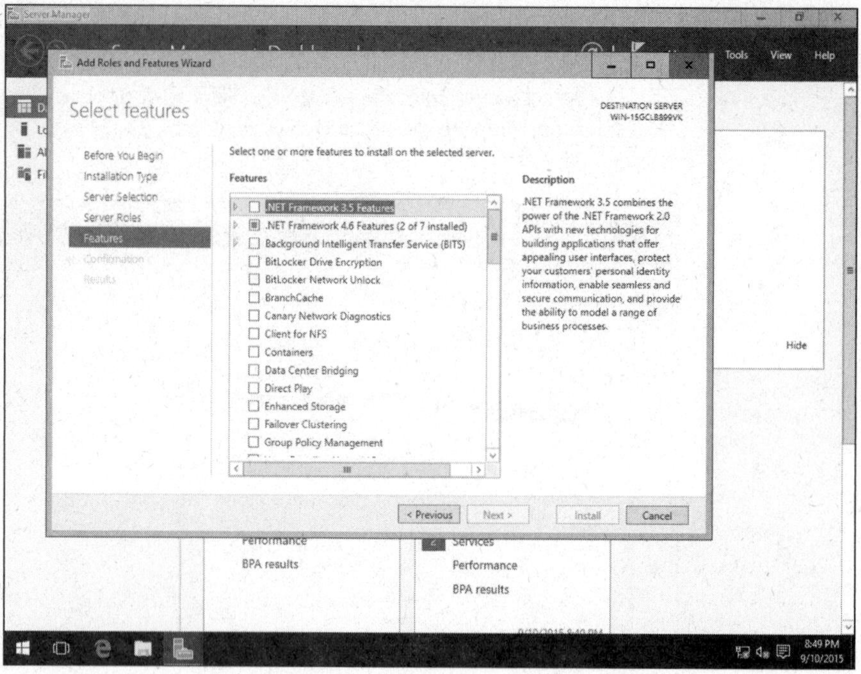

FIGURE 1-9:
The Select
Features page.

7. **Select the features you want to install.**

   Again, you can select each feature to see a brief text description of the service.

8. **Click Next.**

   A confirmation page appears, listing the roles and features you've selected.

9. **Click Install.**

   Windows installs the server role and its features. A progress screen is displayed during the installation so that you can gauge the installation's progress. When the installation finishes, a final results page is displayed.

10. **Click OK.**

    You're done!

> » **Using Remote Desktop Connection to administer a server from the comfort of your desktop**
>
> » **Perusing the list of Microsoft Management Consoles**
>
> » **Customizing your own management console**

Chapter **2**

Configuring Windows Server 2016

This chapter provides an introduction to the most important tools that you'll use to administer Windows Server 2016.

Using the Administrator Account

Windows comes with a built-in account named *Administrator* that has complete access to all the features of the server. As a network administrator, you frequently log on using the Administrator account to perform maintenance chores.

Because the Administrator account is so powerful, you should always enforce good password practices for it. In other words, don't use your dog's name as the Administrator account password. Instead, pick a random combination of letters and numbers. Then change the password periodically.

REMEMBER

Write down the Administrator account password, and keep it in a secure location. Note that by *secure location*, I don't mean taped to the front of the monitor. Keep it in a safe place where you can retrieve it if you forget it, but where it won't easily fall into the hands of someone who's looking to break into your network.

Note that you cannot delete or disable the Administrator account. If Windows allowed you to do that, you could potentially find yourself locked out of your own system.

TIP

As much as possible, you should avoid using the Administrator account. Instead, you should create accounts for each of your system administrators and grant them administrator privileges by assigning their accounts to the Administrators group.

Although you can't delete or disable the Administrator account, you can rename it. Some network managers use this ability to hide the true Administrator account. To do this, just follow these steps:

1. **Rename the Administrator account.**

Write down the new name you use for the Administrator account, along with the password, and store it in a top-secret secure location.

2. **Create a new account named Administrator, and assign it a strong password, but don't give this account any significant privileges.**

This new account will become a "decoy" Administrator account. The idea is to get hackers to waste time trying to crack this account's password. Even if a hacker does manage to compromise this account, he won't be able to do anything when he gets in.

Using Remote Desktop Connection

One of the most useful tools available to system administrators is a program called *Remote Desktop Connection*, or *RDC* for short. RDC lets you connect to a server computer from your own computer and use it as though you were actually sitting at the server. In short, RDC lets you administer your server computers from your own office.

Enabling remote access

Before you can use Remote Desktop Connection to access a server, you must enable remote access on the server. To do that, follow these steps (on the server computer, not your desktop computer):

1. **Open the Control Panel and then click System.**

   This step brings up the System settings page.

2. **Click the Remote Settings link.**

   This step brings up the remote access options, as shown in Figure 2-1.

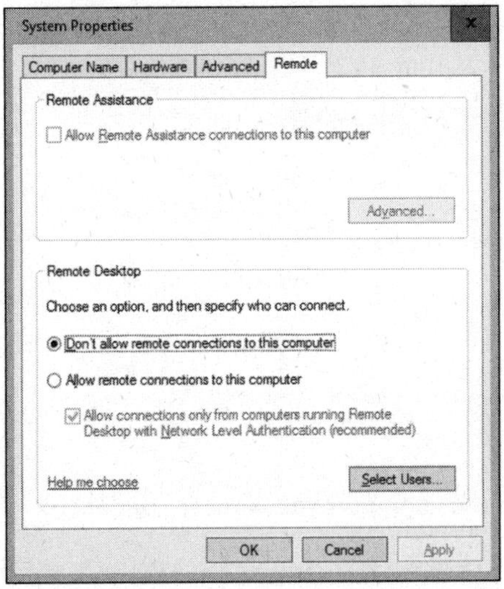

FIGURE 2-1:
Configuring
remote access.

System Properties dialog box showing the Remote tab with Remote Assistance and Remote Desktop settings.

3. **Select the Allow Remote Connections to This Computer radio button.**

4. **Click OK.**

You're done! Repeat this procedure for each server computer you want to allow access to.

Here are a few other points to ponder concerning remote access:

>> You can click the Select Users button to create a list of users who are authorized to access the computer remotely. Note that all members of the Administrators group are automatically granted access, so you don't have to add administrators to this list.

WARNING

>> There's no question that RDC is convenient and useful. It's also inherently dangerous, however. Don't enable it unless you've taken precautions to secure your Administrator accounts by using strong passwords; also, you should already have a firewall installed to keep unwanted visitors out of your network. For more information on account security, see Book 9, Chapter 1.

Connecting remotely

After you've enabled remote access on a server, you can connect to the server by using the Remote Desktop Client that's automatically installed with Windows. Here's the procedure:

1. **Choose Start⇨All Programs⇨Accessories⇨Remote Desktop Connection.**

   The Remote Desktop Connection client comes to life, as shown in Figure 2-2.

FIGURE 2-2:
Connecting with
Remote Desktop
Connection.

2. **Enter the name of the computer you want to connect to.**

   Alternatively, you can use the drop-down list to select the computer from the list of available computers.

3. **Click the Connect button.**

   You're connected to the computer you selected, and the computer's logon screen is displayed.

4. **Log on, and use the computer.**

   After you log on, you can use the computer as though you were sitting right in front of it.

Here are a few other tips for working with the Remote Desktop Connection client:

>> When you're using the Remote Desktop Connection client, you can't just Alt+Tab to another program running on the client computer. Instead, you must first minimize the RDC client's window by clicking its minimize button. Then you can access other programs running on your computer.

>> If you minimize the RDC client window, you have to provide your logon credentials again when you return. This security feature is there in case you forget that you have an RDC session open.

>> If you use RDC a lot on a particular computer (such as your own desktop computer), I suggest that you create a shortcut to RDC and place it on the desktop, at the top of the Start menu, or in the Quick Launch portion of the taskbar.

>> RDC has several useful configuration options that you can access by clicking the Options button.

Using Microsoft Management Console

Microsoft Management Console, also known as *MMC*, is a general-purpose management tool that's used to administer many different types of objects on a Windows system. Throughout this minibook, you see many examples of MMC for working with objects such as user accounts, disk drives, event logs, and so on. This section provides a general overview of how to use MMC.

By itself, MMC doesn't actually manage anything. Instead, it's a framework that accepts management snap-ins, which do the actual managing. The main point of MMC is that it provides a consistent framework for building management snap-ins so that all the snap-ins behave in similar ways. As a result, you don't have to struggle to learn completely different tools to manage various aspects of Windows Server 2016.

Another advantage of MMC is that you can create your own custom management consoles with just the right combination of snap-ins. Suppose that you spend most of your time managing user accounts, disk devices, and IIS (Internet Information Services, the web server that comes with Windows Server 2016), and studying event logs. You can easily craft a management console with just these four snap-ins. For more information, see the section "Customizing MMC," later in this chapter.

Working with MMC

There are several ways to open a Microsoft Management Console window. The easiest is to open one of the predefined consoles that come with Windows Server 2016. To access these consoles, press the Windows key and then select Administrative Tools.

You can also start MMC from a command prompt. To start MMC without opening a snap-in, just type **mmc** at a command prompt. To open a specific console, type the path to the console file after mmc. The following command, for example, opens the Computer Management console:

```
mmc \Windows\System32\compmgmt.msc
```

Figure 2-3 shows a typical Microsoft Management Console window, displaying the Active Directory Users and Computers snap-in. As you can see, the MMC window consists of two panes. The pane on the left is a tree pane that displays a hierarchical tree of the objects that you can manage. The pane on the right is a Details pane that shows detailed information about the object that's selected in the tree pane.

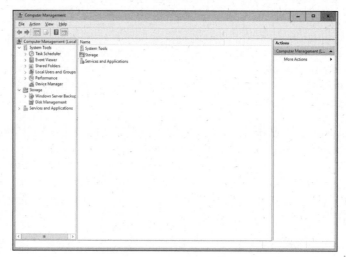

FIGURE 2-3:
A typical MMC window.

The procedures for working with the information in the Details pane vary depending on the console you're viewing. Most of the consoles, however, display lists of some kind, such as settings or user accounts. Double-clicking an item usually brings up a Properties dialog box that lets you view or set properties for the object. In most cases, you can click the column headings at the top of the list to change the order in which the list items are displayed.

MMC also includes a menu and toolbar with commands and buttons that vary depending on the item selected in the tree. In particular, the Action menu contains commands that apply to the current item. The Action menu includes a New User command when you're working with the Active Directory Users and Computers console, for example, and a Defragment command when you view the Disk Defragmenter item in the Computer Management Console. As you work with different items within the different consoles, be sure to check the Action menu frequently to find out what commands are available.

Taking an overview of the MMC consoles

The Tools menu in Server Manager Dashboard gives you direct access to many useful management consoles. You find detailed descriptions of several of these tools later in this minibook. The following paragraphs give you a brief overview of the most important of these consoles:

>> **Active Directory Domains and Trusts:** Manages the domain and trust relationships for the server.

>> **Active Directory Sites and Services:** Manages Active Directory services.

>> **Active Directory Users and Computers:** Lets you create and modify user accounts.

>> **Component Services:** Lets you manage how COM+ (Component Object Model) services work on the server. You mess with this console only if you're involved in developing applications that use COM+ services.

>> **Computer Management:** Provides access to several useful tools for managing a server. In particular, the Computer Management console provides the following management tools:

- *Event Viewer:* Lets you view event logs.

- *Shared Folders*: Lets you manage shared folders for a file server. In addition to finding out what shares are available, you can use this tool to find out which users are connected to the server and which files are open.

- *Local Users and Groups* (available only on servers that aren't domain controllers): Lets you manage local user and group accounts. For a domain controller, you use the Active Directory Users and Computers console to manage user accounts.

- *Performance*: Lets you monitor system performance counters.

- *Device Manager*: Lets you manage the hardware devices connected to a server. You'll probably use it only if you're having a problem with the server that you suspect may be hardware-related.

- *Disk Management*: Lets you view the physical disks and volumes that are available to the system. You can also use this tool to create and delete partitions, set up RAID volumes, format disks, and so on.

- *Services:* Lets you manage system services. You can use this tool to start or stop services such as Exchange email services, TCP/IP services such as DNS and DHCP, and so on.

- *WMI Control:* Lets you configure *Windows Management Instrumentation services,* which track management data about computers, users, applications, and other objects in large Enterprise networks.

- >> **DHCP:** Manages the DHCP server.

- >> **DNS:** Manages the DNS server.

- >> **Domain Controller Security Policy:** Lets you set security policy for a domain controller.

- >> **Event Viewer:** Lets you view event logs.

- >> **Group Policy Management:** Lets you set system policies that can be applied to objects such as users and groups.

- >> **Internet Information Services (IIS) Manager:** Lets you manage the services provided by IIS (Microsoft's web server) if IIS is installed on the server.

- >> **ODBC Data Sources:** Manages database connections that use ODBC. You'll probably use this console only if you're a developer or database administrator.

- >> **Performance Monitor:** Lets you monitor a server's performance and twiddle with various settings that can have positive or negative effects on performance.

- >> **Services:** Lets you start and stop Windows services. (It's also available via the Computer Management console.)

Customizing MMC

One of the best things about Microsoft Management Console is that you can customize it so that the tools you use most often are grouped together in whatever combination you choose. To create a custom console, first start Microsoft Management Console without loading a console by pressing the Windows key, typing **cmd** and pressing Enter to open a command prompt, and then entering the command **mmc**. This action creates an empty console, as shown in Figure 2-4.

Adding snap-ins

After you've created an empty console, you can customize it by adding whatever snap-ins you want to make use of in the console. To add a snap-in, follow these steps:

1. **Choose File⇨Add/Remove Snap-In.**

This command brings up the Add or Remove Snap-Ins dialog box, shown in Figure 2-5.

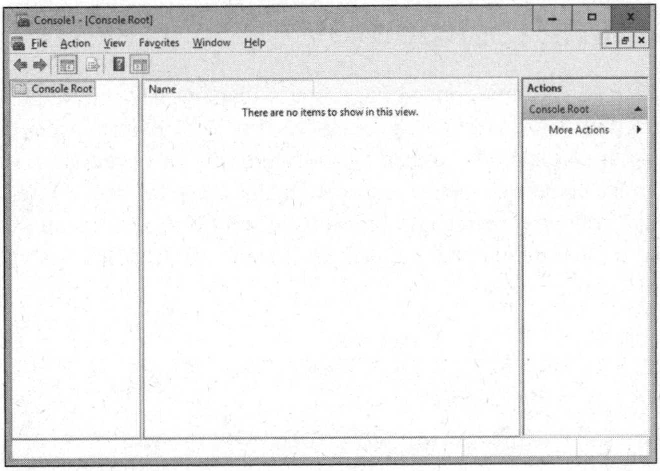

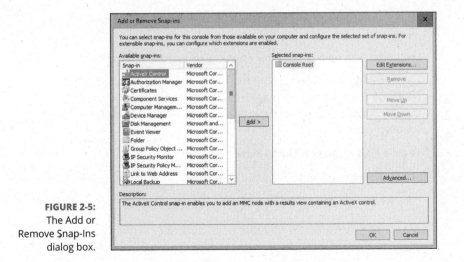

FIGURE 2-4:
An empty MMC
console.

2. **Select the snap-in you want to add and then click the Add button.**

Depending on which snap-in you select, a dialog box appears, asking whether you want to use the add-in to manage settings on your own computer or on a local computer.

3. **Repeat Step 2 if you want to add other snap-ins to the console.**

4. **Click OK.**

The console is equipped with the snap-ins you've selected.

FIGURE 2-5:
The Add or
Remove Snap-Ins
dialog box.

Adding taskpads

A *taskpad* is a customized page that's displayed within a console. Taskpads are designed to provide quick access to the most common chores for a particular snap-in. A taskpad can display shortcuts that run programs, execute menu commands, open web pages, or open folders. Figure 2-6 shows a simple taskpad that I created for managing local user accounts. As you can see, it includes icons that let you quickly add an account, delete an account, and change an account's password.

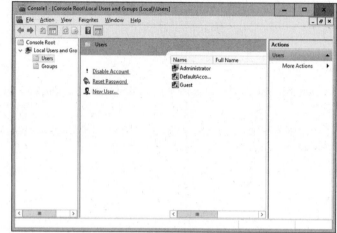

FIGURE 2-6:
A taskpad for managing user accounts.

To add a taskpad, follow these steps:

1. **Select the tree node where you want the taskpad to appear.**

    Each taskpad you create is specific to a tree node. The taskpad shown in Figure 2-6, for example, is displayed only when you select a user account. To create this taskpad, I opened the Local Users and Groups node and selected the Users node.

2. **Choose Action⇨New Taskpad View.**

    This step brings up the New Taskpad View Wizard, as shown in Figure 2-7.

3. **Click Next.**

    The Taskpad Style page appears, as shown in Figure 2-8.

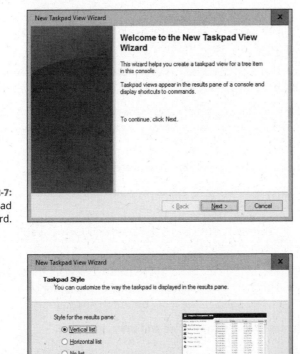

FIGURE 2-7:
The New Taskpad
View Wizard.

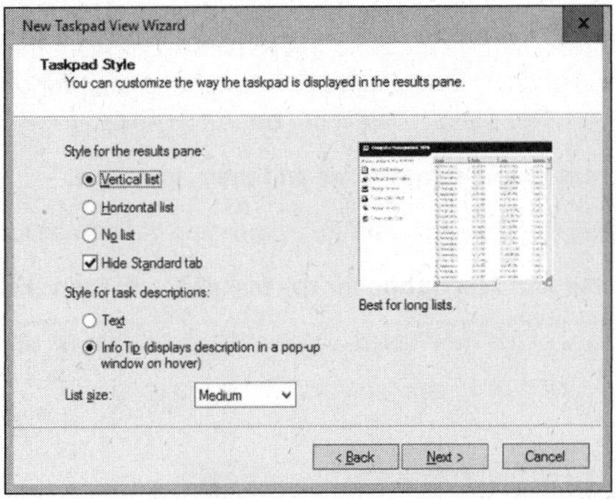

FIGURE 2-8:
Setting the style
options for a new
taskpad page.

This page provides the following options for formatting the taskpad display:

- *Vertical List*: If you want to include the list from the details page, you can select this option to place taskpad icons to the left of the list. I selected this option for the taskpad shown in Figure 2-6.

- *Horizontal List*: This option places the taskpad icons below the details-page list.

- *No List*: This option creates a taskpad with no list, just taskpad icons.

- *Hide Standard Tab*: Each taskpad can have a standard view, which simply lists all the items in the taskpad without showing custom tasks. The Hide Standard Tab check box, which is selected by default, hides this tab. Most of the time, you'll want to leave this check box selected.

- *Text*: This option displays descriptive information below each taskpad icon.

- *InfoTip*: This option displays descriptive information as a pop-up tip that appears when you hover the mouse over the icon.
- *List Size*: This drop-down list lets you select how much of the taskpad area should be devoted to the list. The options are Small, Medium, and Large.

TIP

It's a good thing that this wizard wasn't designed by a fast-food company. If it had been, the options for List Size would be Large, Extra Large, and MegaSuperKing.

4. **Select the taskpad options you want and then click Next.**

   The next page of the wizard presents two options that let you control when the taskpad should be displayed:

   - *Selected Tree Item*: The taskpad is displayed only for the specific tree item that you selected in Step 1.
   - *All Tree Items That Are the Same Type As the Selected Item*: The taskpad is displayed not only for the selected tree item, but also for other items of the same type. This option is the more common choice.

5. **Select the taskpad display option and then click Next.**

   The next page of the wizard asks for a name and description for the taskpad.

6. **Type a name and description for the taskpad, and then click Next.**

   The final page of the New Taskpad View Wizard is displayed, as shown in Figure 2-9.

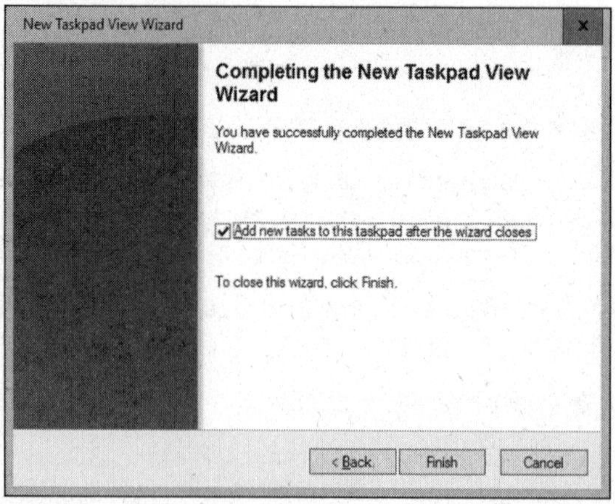
New Taskpad View Wizard
Completing the New Taskpad View Wizard
You have successfully completed the New Taskpad View Wizard.
Add new tasks to this taskpad after the wizard closes
To close this wizard, click Finish.
< Back
Finish
Cancel

FIGURE 2-9: The final page of the New Taskpad View Wizard.

7. **Select the Add New Tasks to This Taskpad After the Wizard Closes check box and then click Finish.**

This step completes the New Taskpad View Wizard but automatically launches the New Task Wizard so that you can begin adding tasks to the taskpad. The New Task Wizard begins by displaying a typical greeting page.

8. **Click Next.**

The page shown in Figure 2-10 is displayed. This page lets you select one of three types of shortcuts to create on the taskpad:

- *Menu Command*: Lets you choose one of the console's menu commands. All three of the shortcuts shown in the taskpad in Figure 2-6 are menu commands.

- *Shell Command:* Lets you run another program, start a batch file, or open a web page.

- *Navigation*: Lets you go to one of the views you've added to the Favorites menu. (If you want to add shortcuts that navigate to different taskpads in a console, first add each taskpad view to your Favorites menu by navigating to the taskpad and choosing Favorites⇨Add to Favorites.)

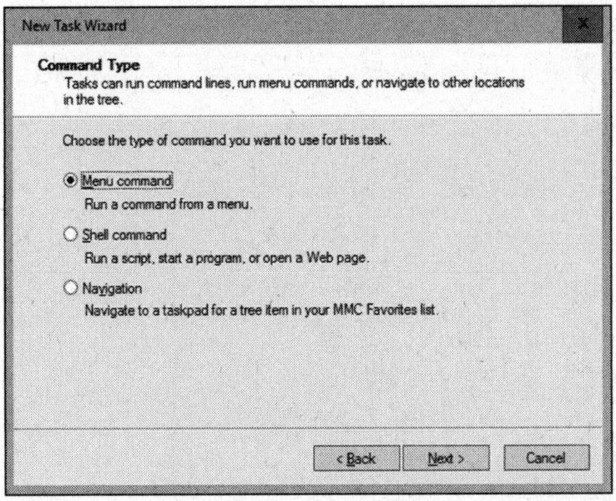

FIGURE 2-10:
The New Task Wizard gives you several choices for adding new tasks to a taskpad.

9. **Choose the type of shortcut command you want to create and then click Next.**

The page that's displayed next depends on which option you selected in Step 8. The rest of this procedure assumes that you selected the Menu Command option, which displays the page shown in Figure 2-11.

10. **Choose the command you want to use and then click Next.**

    The available commands are listed in the Available Commands list box. Note
    that you can bring up several different lists of available commands by choosing
    an option from the Command Source drop-down list.

    When you click Next, the wizard asks for a name and description for the
    command you've selected.

11. **Enter a name and description for the command and then click Next.**

    This step brings up the page shown in Figure 2-12.

12. **Choose the icon you want to use and then click Next.**

Note that in many cases, the New Task Wizard suggests an appropriate icon. If you select a Delete command, for example, the standard Delete icon will be selected.

When you click Next, the final page of the wizard is displayed, as shown in Figure 2-13.

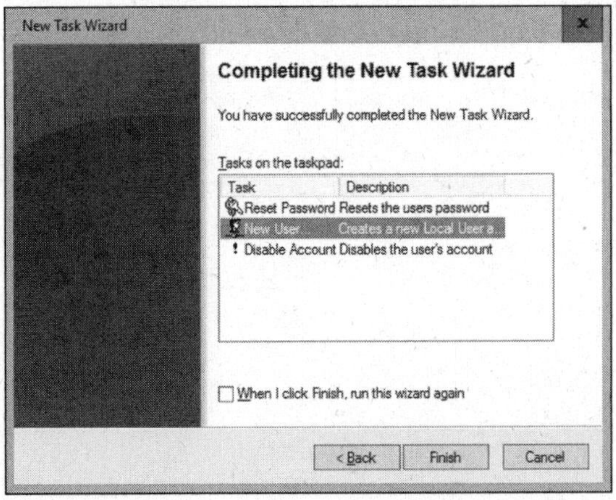

FIGURE 2-13:
The final page
of the New Task
Wizard.

[Figure: New Task Wizard dialog box titled "Completing the New Task Wizard" showing "You have successfully completed the New Task Wizard." with a list of Tasks on the taskpad: Reset Password — Resets the users password; New User — Creates a new Local User a...; Disable Account — Disables the user's account. A check box "When I click Finish, run this wizard again" and Back, Finish, Cancel buttons.]

13. **If you want to create additional tasks, select the When I Click Finish, Run This Wizard Again check box; click Finish; and repeat Steps 8–13.**

You can run the wizard as many times as necessary to add tasks to your taskpad.

14. **When you're finished adding tasks, deselect the When I Click Finish, Run This Wizard Again check box, and click Finish.**

You're done!

Here are a few other pointers for working with taskpads:

» You can edit an existing taskpad by selecting the tree node that displays the taskpad and choosing Action⇨Edit Taskpad View. This command brings up a Properties dialog box that lets you change the taskpad layout options and add or remove tasks.

» To delete a taskpad, select the tree node that displays the taskpad, and choose Action⇨Delete Taskpad View.

TIP

Don't forget to save (File⇨Save) often while you're creating custom taskpads.

Chapter **3**

Configuring Active Directory

Active Directory is among the most important features of Windows Server, and much of your time as a network administrator will be spent keeping Active Directory neat and tidy. This chapter lays some foundation by explaining what Active Directory is and how it works.

What Directories Do

Everyone uses directory services of one type or another every day. When you look up someone's name in a phone book, you're using a directory service. But you're also using a directory service when you make a call: When you enter someone's phone number into your touch-tone phone, the phone system looks up that number in its directory to locate that person's phone.

Almost from the very beginning, computers have had directory services. When I got started in the computer business back in the 1970s, I used IBM mainframe computers and a transaction-processing system called CICS that's still in widespread use today. CICS relied on many different directories to track such things as files available to the system, users that were authorized to access the system, and application programs that could be run.

But the problem with this directory system, and with most other directory systems that were popular in those days, is that it was made up of many small directory systems that didn't know how to talk to one another. I have the very same problem at home. I have my own little personal address book that has phone numbers and addresses for my friends and family members. I have a Day-Timer book with a bunch of other phone numbers and addresses. Then I have a church directory that lists everyone who goes to my church. Oh, and there's the list of players on the softball team I coach, and of course, my cellphone has a directory.

All counted, I probably have a dozen sources for phone numbers that I routinely call. So when I need to look up someone's phone number, I first have to decide which directory to look in. Some of my friends are listed in two or three of these sources, which raises the possibility that their listings are out of sync.

That's exactly the type of problem that Active Directory is designed to address. Before I get into the specifics of Active Directory, however, I show you the directory system that Microsoft used on Windows networks before Active Directory became available.

Remembering the Good Ol' Days of NT Domains

Active Directory was introduced with Windows 2000 Server. Before then, the directory management system in a Windows network was managed by Windows NT domains, which stored directory information in a database called the Security Account Manager (SAM) database.

PDCs and BDCs

The most important thing to know about NT domains is that they are *servercentric* — that is, every Windows NT domain is under the control of a Windows NT server computer that hosts the primary copy of the SAM database. This server is called the *Primary Domain Controller (PDC)*.

Large networks couldn't work efficiently if all directory access had to be channeled through a single computer, of course. To solve that bottleneck problem, Windows NT domains can also be serviced by one or more *Backup Domain Controllers (BDCs)*. Each BDC stores a read-only copy of the SAM database, and any changes made to the SAM database on the PDC must be propagated down to the BDC copies of the database.

Note that although any of the BDC servers can service access requests such as user logons, all changes to the SAM database must be made via the PDC. Then those changes are copied to the BDC servers. Naturally, this arrangement raises the possibility that the PDC and BDC database are out of sync.

If the PDC should fail for some reason, one of the BDCs can be promoted so that it becomes the PDC for the domain. This promotion allows the domain to continue to function while the original PDC is repaired. Because the BDC is an important backup for the PDC, it's important that all NT networks have at least one BDC.

Trusts

Many organizations have directory needs that are too complicated to store on just one NT domain PDC. In that case, the organization can create two or more separate domains for its network, each with its own PDC and BDCs. Then the organization can set up trusts among its domains.

Simply put, a *trust* is a relationship in which one domain trusts the directory information stored in another domain. The domain that does the trusting is called — you guessed it — the *trusting domain,* and the domain that contains the information being trusted is called the *trusted domain.*

Trust relationships work in one direction. Suppose that you have two domains, named DomainA and DomainB, and a trust relationship is set up so that DomainA trusts DomainB. That means that users whose accounts are defined in DomainB can log on to DomainA and access resources. The trust relationship doesn't work in the other direction, however: Users in DomainA can't log on and access resources defined in DomainB.

Also, trust relationships aren't *transitive.* (There's a word that takes you back to high-school algebra.) That means that even if DomainA trusts DomainB and DomainB trusts DomainC, DomainA doesn't automatically trust DomainC. For DomainA to trust DomainC, you'd have to create a separate trust relationship between DomainA and DomainC.

NetBIOS names

One other important characteristic of Windows NT domains is that they use NetBIOS names. Thus, NT names such as computer names and domain names are limited to 15 characters.

TECHNICAL STUFF

Actually, NetBIOS names are 16 characters long. But NT uses the last character of the 16-character NetBIOS name for its own purposes, so that character isn't available for use. As a result, NT names can be only 15 characters long.

Active Directory to the Rescue

Active Directory solves many of the inherent limitations of Windows NT domains by creating a distributed directory database that keeps track of every conceivable type of network object.

Active Directory is a comprehensive directory management system that tracks just about everything worth tracking in a Windows network, including users, computers, files, folders, applications, and much more. Much of your job as a network administrator involves working with Active Directory, so it's vital that you have a basic understanding of how it works.

One of the most important differences between Active Directory and NT domains is that Active Directory isn't servercentric. In other words, Active Directory isn't tied to a specific server computer, the way a Windows NT domain is. Although Active Directory still uses domains and domain controllers, these concepts are much more flexible in Active Directory than they are in Windows NT.

Another important difference between Active Directory and NT domains is that Active Directory uses the same naming scheme that's used on the Internet: Domain Name System (DNS). Thus, an Active Directory domain might have a name like `sales.mycompany.com`.

Understanding How Active Directory Is Structured

Like all directories, Active Directory is essentially a database management system. The Active Directory database is where the individual objects tracked by the directory are stored. Active Directory uses a *hierarchical* database model, which groups items in a treelike structure.

The terms *object, organizational unit, domain, tree,* and *forest* are used to describe the way Active Directory organizes its data. The following sections explain the meaning of these important Active Directory terms.

Objects

The basic unit of data in Active Directory is called an *object.* Active Directory can store information about many kinds of objects. The objects you work with most are users, groups, computers, and printers.

Figure 3-1 shows the Active Directory Manager displaying a list of built-in objects that come preconfigured with Windows Server 2016. To get to this management tool, choose Start➪Administrative Tools➪Active Directory Users and Computers. Then click the Builtin node to show the built-in objects.

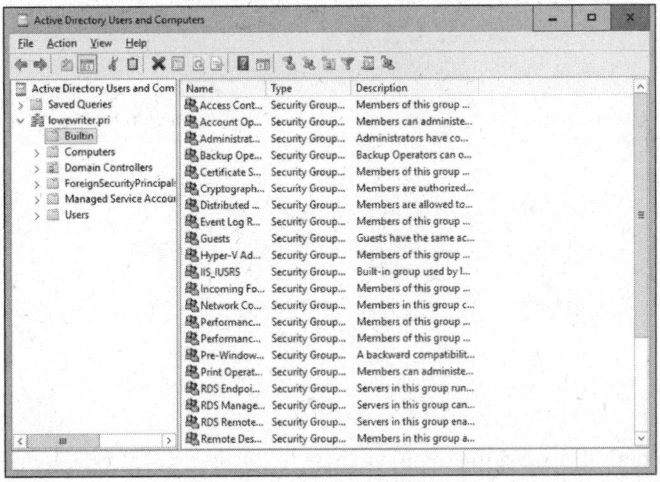

FIGURE 3-1:
Objects displayed by the Active Directory Manager console.

Objects have descriptive characteristics called *properties* or *attributes.* You can call up the properties of an object by double-clicking the object in the management console.

Domains

A *domain* is the basic unit for grouping related objects in Active Directory. Typically, domains correspond to departments in a company. A company with separate Accounting, Manufacturing, and Sales departments might have domains named (you guessed it) Accounting, Manufacturing, and Sales. Or the domains may correspond to geographical locations. A company with offices in Detroit, Dallas, and Denver might have domains named det, dal, and den.

Note that because Active Directory domains use DNS naming conventions, you can create subdomains that are considered to be child domains. You should always create the top-level domain for your entire network before you create any other domain. If your company is named Nimbus Brooms, and you've registered NimbusBroom.com as your domain name, you should create a top-level domain named NimbusBroom.com before you create any other domains. Then you can create subdomains such as Accounting.NimbusBroom.com, Manufacturing.NimbusBroom.com, and Sales.NimbusBroom.com.

TIP

If you have Microsoft Visio, you can use it to draw diagrams for your Active Directory domain structure. Visio includes several templates that provide cool icons for various types of Active Directory objects. Figure 3-2 shows a diagram that shows an Active Directory with four domains created with Visio.

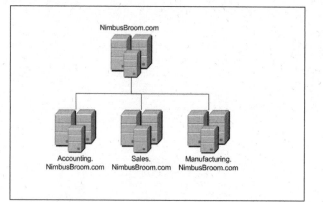

FIGURE 3-2:
Domains for a company with three departments.

Note that these domains have little to do with the physical structure of your network. In Windows NT, domains usually are related to the network's physical structure.

Every domain must have at least one *domain controller,* which is a server that's responsible for the domain. Unlike a Windows NT PDC, however, an Active Directory domain controller doesn't have unique authority over its domain. In fact, a domain can have two or more domain controllers that share administrative duties. A feature called *replication* works hard at keeping all the domain controllers in sync.

Organizational units

Many domains have too many objects to manage together in a single group. Fortunately, Active Directory lets you create one or more *organizational units,* also known as OUs. OUs let you organize objects within a domain, without the extra work and inefficiency of creating additional domains.

One reason to create OUs within a domain is to assign administrative rights to each OU of different users. Then these users can perform routine administrative tasks such as creating new user accounts or resetting passwords.

Suppose that the domain for the Denver office, named den, houses the Accounting and Legal departments. Rather than create separate domains for these departments, you could create organizational units for the departments.

Trees

A *tree* is a set of Active Directory names that share a namespace. The domains NimbusBroom.com, Accounting.NimbusBroom.com, Manufacturing.NimbusBroom.com, and Sales.NimbusBroom.com make up a tree that's derived from a common root domain, NimbusBroom.com.

The domains that make up a tree are related to one another through *transitive trusts*. In a transitive trust, if DomainA trusts DomainB and DomainB trusts DomainC, DomainA automatically trusts DomainC.

TIP

Note that a single domain all by itself is still considered to be a tree.

Forests

As its name suggests, a *forest* is a collection of trees. In other words, a forest is a collection of one or more domain trees that do *not* share a common parent domain.

Suppose that Nimbus Brooms acquires Tracorum Technical Enterprises, which already has its own root domain named TracorumTech.com, with several subdomains of its own. You can create a forest from these two domain trees so that the domains can trust each other. Figure 3-3 shows this forest.

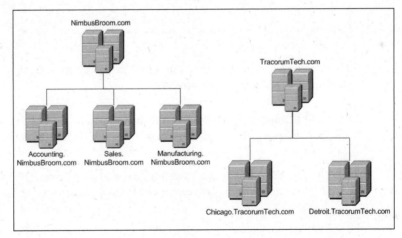

FIGURE 3-3:
A forest with
two trees.

The key to Active Directory forests is a database called the global catalog. The *global catalog* is sort of a superdirectory that contains information about all the objects in a forest, regardless of the domain. If a user account can't be found in the current domain, the global catalog is searched for the account. The global catalog provides a reference to the domain in which the account is defined.

Creating a New Domain

To create a domain, you start by designating a Windows Server 2016 system to be the new domain's controller. You can do that by using the Server Manager to install Active Directory services. After you've installed Active Directory services, click the Notifications icon near the top-right corner of the Server Manager, and choose Promote This Server to a Domain Controller. This command launches the wizard shown in Figure 3-4.

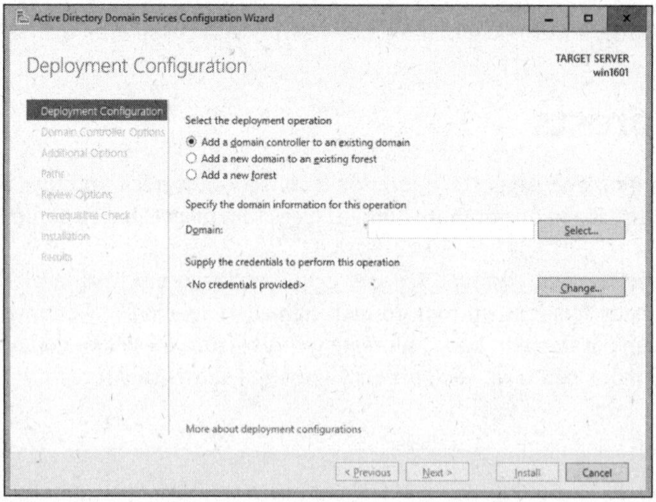

FIGURE 3-4:
Creating
a domain
controller.

This wizard lets you designate the server as a domain controller. As you can see, the wizard gives you three options:

» **Add a Domain Controller to an Existing Domain:** Choose this option if you've already created the domain and want to add this server as a domain controller.

» **Add a New Domain to an Existing Forest:** If you've already created a forest but want to create a new domain within the existing forest, choose this option.

» **Add a New Forest:** This option is the one to choose if you're setting up a new domain in a brand-new forest.

When you create a new domain, the configuration wizard asks you for a name for the new domain. If you're creating the first domain for your network, use your company's domain name, such as NimbusBroom.com. If you're creating a subdomain, use a name such as Sales.NimbusBroom.com.

Creating an Organizational Unit

Organizational units can simplify the task of managing large domains by dividing users, groups, and other objects into manageable collections. By default, Active Directory domains include several useful OUs. The Domain Controllers OU, for example, contains all the domain controllers for the domain.

If you want to create additional organizational units to help manage a domain, follow these steps:

1. **In Server Manager, choose Tools⇨Active Directory Users and Computers.**

   The Active Directory Users and Computers console appears, as shown in Figure 3-5.

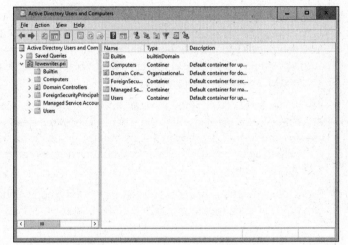

FIGURE 3-5:
The Active Directory Users and Computers console.

2. **Right-click the domain you want to add the OU to, and choose New⇨Organizational Unit.**

   The New Object – Organizational Unit dialog box appears, as shown in Figure 3-6.

3. **Type a name for the new organization unit.**

4. **Click OK.**

   You're done!

Configuring Active Directory

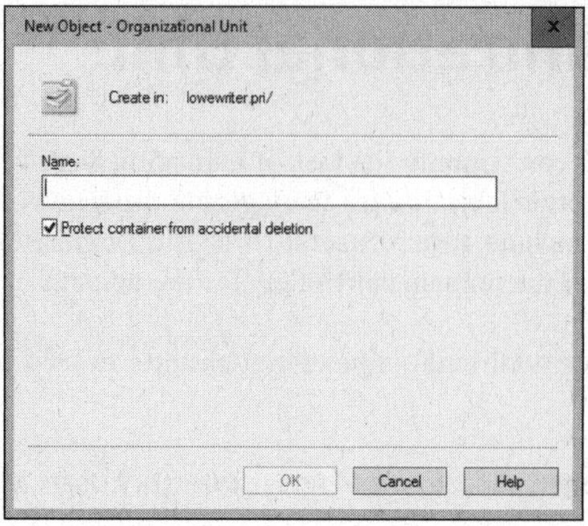

FIGURE 3-6:
Creating a new organizational unit.

Here are just a few more thoughts about OUs to ponder as you drift off to sleep:

» You can delegate administrative authority for an OU to another user by right-clicking the OU and choosing Select Delegate Control from the contextual menu. Then you can select the user or group that will have administrative authority over the OU. You can also choose which administrative tasks will be assigned to the selected user or group.

» Remember that OUs aren't the same as groups. *Groups* are security principals, which means that you can assign them rights. Thereafter, when you assign a user to a group, the user is given the rights of the group. By contrast, an OU is merely an administrative tool that lets you control how user and group accounts are managed.

» For more information about how to create user and group accounts as well as other Active Directory objects, turn to Book 6, Chapter 4.

Chapter **4**

Configuring User Accounts

E very user who accesses a network must have a *user account*. User accounts let you control who can access the network and who can't. In addition, user accounts let you specify what network resources each user can use. Without user accounts, all your resources would be open to anyone who casually dropped by your network.

Understanding Windows User Accounts

User accounts are among the basic tools for managing a Windows server. As a network administrator, you'll spend a large percentage of your time dealing with user accounts — creating new ones, deleting expired ones, resetting passwords for forgetful users, granting new access rights, and so on. Before I get into the specific procedures of creating and managing user accounts, this section presents an overview of user accounts and how they work.

Local accounts versus domain accounts

A *local account* is a user account that's stored on a particular computer and applies only to that computer. Typically, each computer on your network will have a local account for each person who uses that computer.

By contrast, a *domain account* is a user account that's stored by Active Directory and can be accessed from any computer that's a part of the domain. Domain accounts are centrally managed. This chapter deals primarily with setting up and maintaining domain accounts.

User account properties

Every user account has several important account properties that specify the characteristics of the account. The three most important account properties are

>> **Username:** A unique name that identifies the account. The user must enter the username when logging on to the network. The username is public information. In other words, other network users can (and often should) find out your username.

>> **Password:** A secret word that must be entered to gain access to the account. You can set up Windows so that it enforces password policies, such as the minimum length of the password, whether the password must contain a mixture of letters and numerals, and how long the password remains current before the user must change it.

>> **Group membership:** The group or groups to which the user account belongs. Group memberships are the key to granting access rights to users so that they can access various network resources, such as file shares or printers, or perform certain network tasks, such as creating new user accounts or backing up the server.

Many other account properties record information about the user, such as the user's contact information, whether the user is allowed to access the system only at certain times or from certain computers, and so on. I describe some of these features in later sections of this chapter, and some are described in more detail in Book 6, Chapter 6.

Creating a New User

To create a new domain user account in Windows Server 2016, follow these steps:

1. **Choose Start ⇨ Administrative Tools ⇨ Active Directory Users and Computers.**

   This command fires up the Active Directory Users and Computers management console, as shown in Figure 4-1.

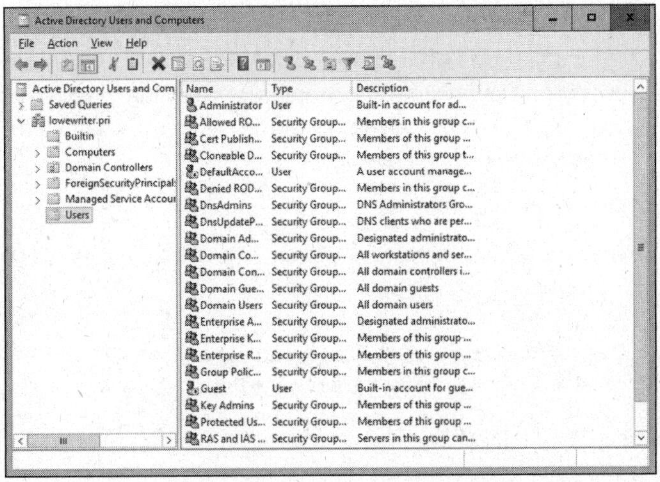

FIGURE 4-1: The Active Directory Users and Computers management console.

2. **Right-click the organizational unit that you want to add the user to and then choose New ⇨ User.**

   This command summons the New Object – User Wizard, as shown in Figure 4-2.

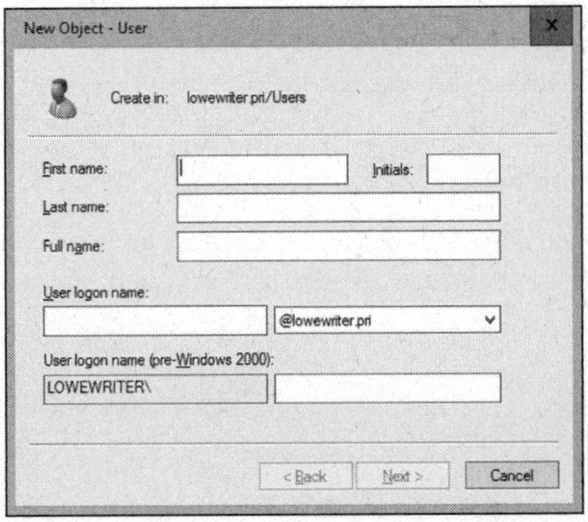

FIGURE 4-2: Creating a new user.

Configuring User Accounts

3. Type the user's first name, middle initial, and last name.

As you type the name, the New Object Wizard automatically fills in the Full Name field.

4. Change the Full Name field if you want it to appear different from what the wizard proposes.

You may want to reverse the first and last names so the last name appears first, for example.

5. Type the user logon name.

This name must be unique within the domain.

TIP

Pick a naming scheme to follow when creating user logon names. You can use the first letter of the first name followed by the complete last name, the complete first name followed by the first letter of the last name, or any other scheme that suits your fancy.

6. Click Next.

The second page of the New Object – User Wizard appears, as shown in Figure 4-3.

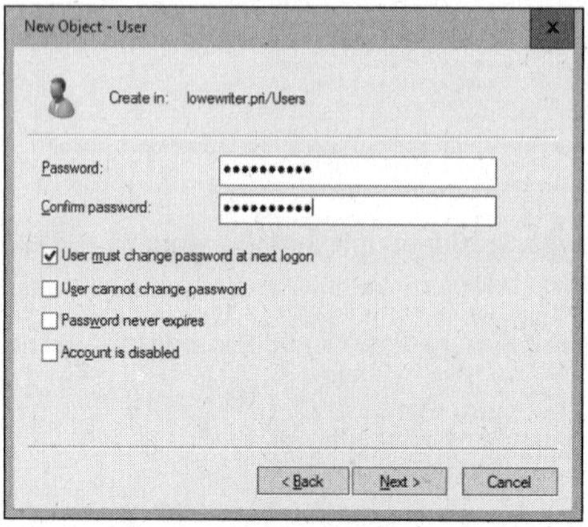

New Object - User

Create in: lowewriter.pri/Users

Password: ●●●●●●●●●●
Confirm password: ●●●●●●●●●●

☑ User must change password at next logon
☐ User cannot change password
☐ Password never expires
☐ Account is disabled

< Back   Next >   Cancel

FIGURE 4-3:
Setting the user's password.

7. Type the password twice.

You're asked to type the password twice, so type it correctly. If you don't type it identically in both boxes, you're asked to correct your mistake.

8. **Specify the password options that you want to apply.**

The following password options are available:

- User Must Change Password at Next Logon.

- User Cannot Change Password.

- Password Never Expires.

- Account Is Disabled.

For more information about these options, see the section "Setting account options," later in this chapter.

9. **Click Next.**

You're taken to the final page of the New Object – User Wizard, as shown in Figure 4-4.

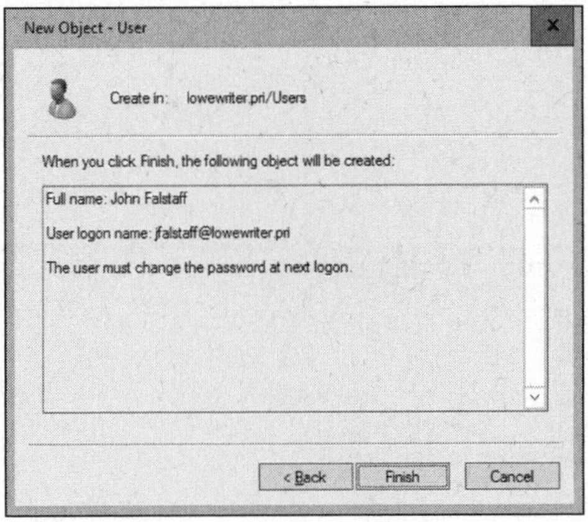

FIGURE 4-4: Verifying the user account information.

10. **Verify that the information is correct and then click Finish to create the account.**

If the account information isn't correct, click the Back button, and correct the error.

You're done! Now you can customize the user's account settings. At minimum, you'll probably want to add the user to one or more groups. You may also want to add contact information for the user or set up other account options.

TIP

An alternate way to create a new user is to simply copy an existing user. When you copy an existing user, you provide a new username and password and Windows copies all the other property settings from the existing user to the new user.

Setting User Properties

After you've created a user account, you can set additional properties for the user by right-clicking the new user and choosing Properties from the contextual menu. This command brings up the User Properties dialog box, which has about a million tabs that you can use to set various properties for the user. Figure 4-5 shows the General tab, which lists basic information about the user, such as the user's name, office location, and phone number.

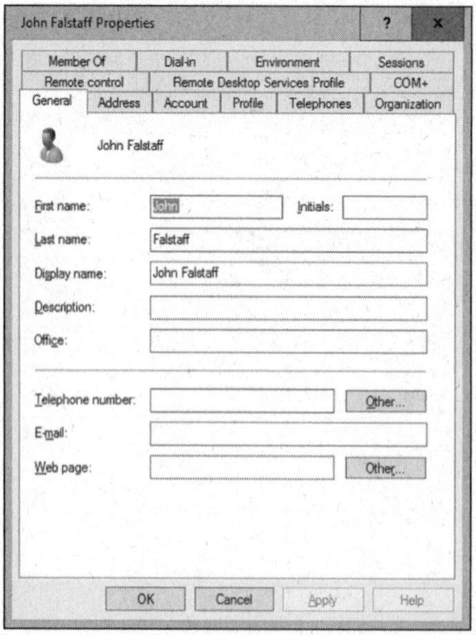

FIGURE 4-5:
The General tab.

The following sections describe some of the administrative tasks that you can perform via the various tabs of the User Properties dialog box.

Changing the user's contact information

Several tabs of the User Properties dialog box contain contact information for the user:

>> **Address:** Lets you change the user's street address, post office box, city, state, zip code, and so on

>> **Telephones:** Lets you specify the user's phone numbers

>> **Organization:** Lets you record the user's job title and the name of his or her boss

Setting account options

The Account tab of the User Properties dialog box, shown in Figure 4-6, features a variety of interesting options that you can set for the user. From this dialog box, you can change the user's logon name. In addition, you can change the password options that you set when you created the account, and you can set an expiration date for the account.

The following account options are available in the Account Options list box:

>> **User Must Change Password at Next Logon:** This option, which is selected by default, allows you to create a one-time-only password that can get the user started with the network. The first time the user logs on to the network, he or she is asked to change the password.

>> **User Cannot Change Password:** Use this option if you don't want to allow users to change their passwords. (Obviously, you can't use this option and the preceding one at the same time.)

>> **Password Never Expires:** Use this option if you want to bypass the password-expiration policy for this user so that the user will never have to change his or her password.

>> **Store Password Using Reversible Encryption:** This option stores passwords by using an encryption scheme that hackers can easily break, so you should avoid it like the plague.

>> **Account Is Disabled:** This option allows you to create an account that you don't yet need. As long as the account remains disabled, the user won't be able to log on. See the section "Disabling and Enabling User Accounts," later in this chapter, to find out how to enable a disabled account.

>> **Smart Card Is Required for Interactive Logon:** If the user's computer has a smart card reader to read security cards automatically, check this option to require the user to use it.

>> **Account Is Trusted for Delegation:** This option indicates that the account is trustworthy and can set up delegations. This advanced feature usually is reserved for Administrator accounts.

>> **Account Is Sensitive and Cannot Be Delegated:** This option prevents other users from impersonating this account.

>> **Use DES Encryption Types for This Account:** This option beefs up the encryption for applications that require extra security.

>> **Do Not Require Kerberos Preauthentication:** Select this option if you use a different implementation of the Kerberos protocol.

Specifying logon hours

You can restrict the hours during which the user is allowed to log on to the system by clicking the Logon Hours button on the Account tab of the User Properties dialog box. This button brings up the Logon Hours for [User] dialog box, shown in Figure 4-7.

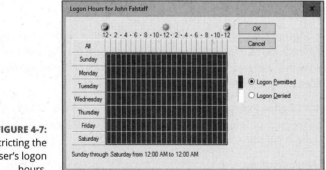

FIGURE 4-7: Restricting the user's logon hours.

Initially, the Logon Hours dialog box is set to allow the user to log on at any time of day or night. To change the hours that you want the user to have access, click a day and time or a range of days and times; choose either Logon Permitted or Logon Denied; and click OK.

Restricting access to certain computers

Normally, a user can use his or her user account to log on to any computer that's part of the user's domain. You can restrict a user to certain computers, however, by clicking the Log On To button on the Account tab of the User Properties dialog box. This button brings up the Logon Workstations dialog box, as shown in Figure 4-8.

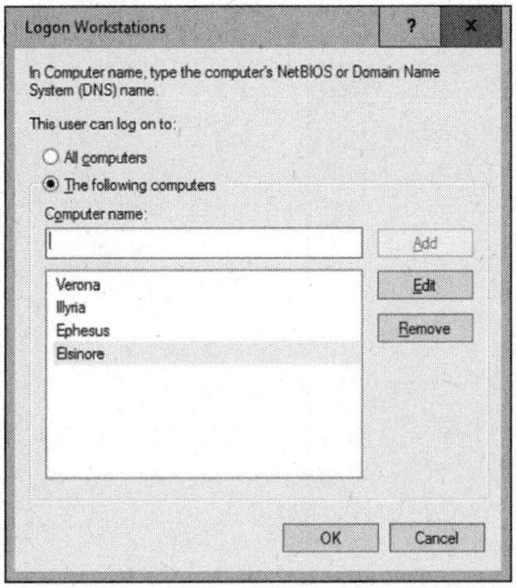

FIGURE 4-8:
Restricting the user to certain computers.

To restrict the user to certain computers, select the radio button labeled The Following Computers. Then, for each computer you want to allow the user to log on from, type the computer's name in the text box, and click Add.

TIP

If you make a mistake, you can select the incorrect computer name and then click Edit to change the name or Remove to delete the name.

Setting the user's profile information

The Profile tab, shown in Figure 4-9, lets you configure the user's profile information. This dialog box lets you configure three bits of information related to the user's profile:

>> **Profile Path:** This field specifies the location of the user's roaming profile. For more information, see the section "Working with User Profiles," later in this chapter.

>> **Logon Script:** This field is the name of the user's logon script. A *logon script* is a batch file that's run whenever the user logs on. The main purpose of the logon script is to map the network shares that the user requires access to.

Logon scripts are carryovers from early versions of Windows NT Server. In Windows Server 2016, profiles are the preferred way to configure the user's computer when the user logs on, including setting up network shares. Many administrators still like the simplicity of logon scripts, however. For more information, see the section "Creating a Logon Script," later in this chapter.

>> **Home Folder:** This section is where you specify the default storage location for the user.

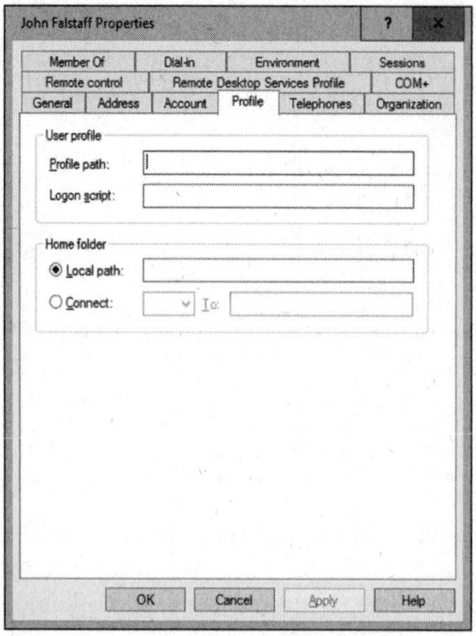

FIGURE 4-9:
The Profile tab.

TIP

The Profile tab lets you specify the location of an existing profile for the user, but it doesn't actually let you set up the profile. For more information about setting up a profile, see the section "Working with User Profiles," later in this chapter.

Resetting User Passwords

By some estimates, the single most time-consuming task of most network administrators is resetting user passwords. It's easy to think that users are forgetful idiots, but put yourself in their shoes. Administrators insist that they set their passwords to something incomprehensible, such as 94kD82leL384K; that they change it a week later to something more unmemorable, such as dJUQ63DWd8331; and that they don't write it down. Then administrators get mad when they forget their passwords.

So when a user calls and says that he or she forgot his or her password, the least the administrator can do is be cheerful when resetting it. After all, the user probably spent 15 minutes trying to remember it before finally giving up and admitting failure.

Here's the procedure to reset the password for a user domain account:

1. Log on as an administrator.

You must have administrator privileges to perform this procedure.

2. In Server Manager, choose Tools⇨Active Directory Users and Computers.

The Active Directory Users and Computers management console appears.

3. Click Users in the console tree.

4. In the Details pane, right-click the user who forgot his or her password, and choose Reset Password from the contextual menu.

5. Type the new password in both password boxes.

You have to type the password twice to ensure that you type it correctly.

6. If desired, select the User Must Change Password at Next Logon option.

If you select this option, the password that you assign will work for only one logon. As soon as the user logs on, he or she will be required to change the password.

7. Click OK.

That's all there is to it! The user's password is reset.

Disabling and Enabling User Accounts

If you want to temporarily prevent a user from accessing the network, you can disable his or her account. Then you can enable the account later, when you're ready to restore the user to full access. Here's the procedure:

1. Log on as an administrator.

You must have administrator privileges to perform this procedure.

2. From Server Manager, choose Tools⇨Active Directory Users and Computers.

The Active Directory Users and Computers management console appears.

3. **Click Users in the console tree.**

4. **In the Details pane, right-click the user that you want to enable or disable; then choose either Enable Account or Disable Account from the contextual menu to enable or disable the user.**

Deleting a User

Deleting a user account is surprisingly easy. Just follow these steps:

1. **Log on as an administrator.**

   You must have administrator privileges to perform this procedure.

2. **Choose Start ⇨ Administrative Tools ⇨ Active Directory Users and Computers.**

   The Active Directory Users and Computers management console appears.

3. **Click Users in the console tree.**

4. **In the Details pane, right-click the user that you want to delete and then choose Delete from the contextual menu.**

   Windows asks whether you really want to delete the user, just in case you're kidding.

5. **Click Yes.**

   Poof! The user account is deleted.

WARNING

Deleting a user account is a permanent, nonreversible action. Do it only if you're absolutely sure that you'll never want to restore the user's account. If there's any possibility of restoring the account later, you should disable the account rather than delete it.

Working with Groups

A *group* is a special type of account that represents a set of users who have common network access needs. Groups can dramatically simplify the task of assigning network access rights to users. Rather than assign access rights to each user individually, you can assign rights to the group itself. Then those rights automatically extend to any user you add to the group.

The following sections describe some of the key concepts that you need to under-stand to use groups, along with some of the most common procedures you'll employ when setting up groups for your server.

Group types

Two distinct types of groups exist:

>> **Security groups:** Most groups are security groups, which extend access rights to members of the group. If you want to allow a group of users to access your high-speed color laser printer, for example, you can create a group called ColorPrintUsers. Then you can grant permission to use the printer to the ColorPrintUsers group. Finally, you can add individual users to the ColorPrintUsers group.

>> **Distribution groups:** Distribution groups aren't used as much as security groups are. They're designed as a way to send email to a group of users by specifying the group as the recipient.

Group scope

A group can have any of three distinct *scopes*, which determine what domains the group's members can belong to:

>> **Domain local:** A group with *domain local scope* can have members from any domain. The group can be granted permissions only from the domain in which the group is defined, however.

>> **Global:** A group with *global scope* can have members only from the domain in which the group is defined. The group can be granted permissions in any domain in the forest, however. (For more information about forests, refer to Book 6, Chapter 3.)

>> **Universal scope:** Groups with *universal scope* are available in all domains that belong to the same forest.

As you can probably guess, universal scope groups are usually used only on very large networks.

One common way you can use domain local and global groups is as follows:

1. **Use domain local groups to assign access rights for network resources.**

To control access to a high-speed color printer, for example, create a domain local group for the printer. Grant the group access to the printer, but don't add any users to the group.

2. **Use global groups to associate users with common network access needs.**

Create a global group for users who need to access color printers, for example. Then add each user who needs access to a color printer membership to the group.

3. **Finally, add the global group to the domain local group.**

That way, access to the printer is extended to all members of the global group.

This technique gives you the most flexibility when your network grows.

Default groups

Windows Server 2016 comes with several predefined groups that you can use. Although you shouldn't be afraid to create your own groups when you need them, there's no reason to create your own group if you find a default group that meets your needs.

Some of these groups are listed in the Builtin container in the Active Directory Users and Computers management console. Others are listed in the Users container. Table 4-1 lists the most useful default groups in Builtin, and Table 4-2 lists the default groups in the Users container.

TABLE 4-1 **Default Groups Located in the Builtin Container**

Group	Description
Account Operators	This group is for users who should be allowed to create, edit, or delete user accounts but shouldn't be granted full administrator status.
Administrators	This group is for the system administrators who have full control of the domain. The Administrator account is a default member of this group. You should create only a limited number of accounts that belong to this group.
Backup Operators	This group is for users who need to perform backup operations. Because this group must have access to the files that are backed up, it presents a security risk, so you should limit the number of users that you add to this group.

Group	Description
Guests	This group allows members to log on but little else. The default Guest account is a member of this group.
Network Configuration	This group is allowed to twiddle with network configuration settings, including releasing and renewing DHCP leases.
Print Operators	This group grants users access to printers, including the ability to create and share new printers and to manage print queues.
Remote Desktop Users	This group can remotely log on to domain controllers in the domain.
Replicator	This group is required to support directory replication. Don't add users to this group.
Server Operators	These users can log on locally to a domain controller.
Users	These users can perform common tasks, such as running applications and using local and network printers.

TABLE 4-2   **Default Groups Located in the Users Container**

Group	Description
Cert Publishers	These users can publish security certificates for users and computers.
DnsAdmins	This group is installed if you install DNS. It grants administrative access to the DNS Server service.
DnsUpdateProxy	This group is installed if you install DNS. It allows DNS clients to perform dynamic updates on behalf of other clients, such as DHCP servers.
Domain Admins	These users have complete control of the domain. By default, this group is a member of the Administrators group on all domain controllers, and the Administrator account is a member of this group.
Domain Computers	This group contains all computers that belong to the domain. Any computer account created becomes a member of this group automatically.
Domain Controllers	This group contains all domain controllers in the domain.
Domain Guests	This group contains all domain guests.
Domain Users	This group contains all domain users. Any user account created in the domain is added to this group automatically.
Group Policy	These users can modify group policy for the domain.
IIS_WPG	This group is created if you install IIS. It's required for IIS to operate properly.
RAS and IAS Servers	This group is required for RAS and IAS servers to work properly.

Creating a group

If none of the built-in groups meets your needs, you can create your own group by following these steps:

1. **Log on as an administrator.**

   You must have administrator privileges to perform this procedure.

2. **From Server Manager, choose Tools ⇨ Active Directory Users and Computers.**

   The Active Directory Users and Computers management console appears.

3. **Right-click the domain to which you want to add the group and then choose New ⇨ Group from the contextual menu.**

   The New Object – Group dialog box appears, as shown in Figure 4-10.

4. **Type the name for the new group.**

   Enter the name in both text boxes.

5. **Choose the group scope.**

   The choices are Domain Local, Global, and Universal. For groups that will be granted access rights to network resources, choose Domain Local. Use Global for groups to which you'll add users and Domain Local groups. Use Universal groups only if you have a large network with multiple domains.

6. **Choose the group type.**

   The choices are Security and Distribution. In most cases, choose Security.

7. **Click OK.**

   The group is created.

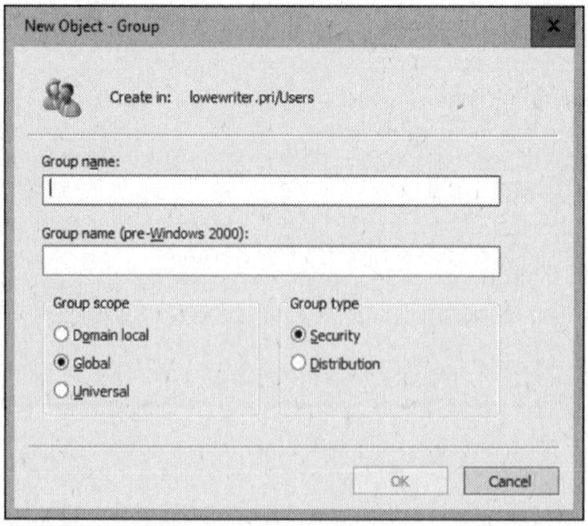

FIGURE 4-10: Creating a new group.

Adding a member to a group

Groups are collections of objects, called *members.* The members of a group can be user accounts or other groups. When you create a group, it has no members. As a result, the group isn't useful until you add at least one member.

Follow these steps to add a member to a group:

1. Log on as an administrator.

You must have administrator privileges to perform this procedure.

2. Choose Start⇨Administrative Tools⇨Active Directory Users and Computers.

The Active Directory Users and Computers management console appears.

3. Open the folder that contains the group to which you want to add members and then double-click the group.

The Group Properties dialog box appears.

4. Click the Members tab.

The members of the group are displayed, as shown in Figure 4-11.

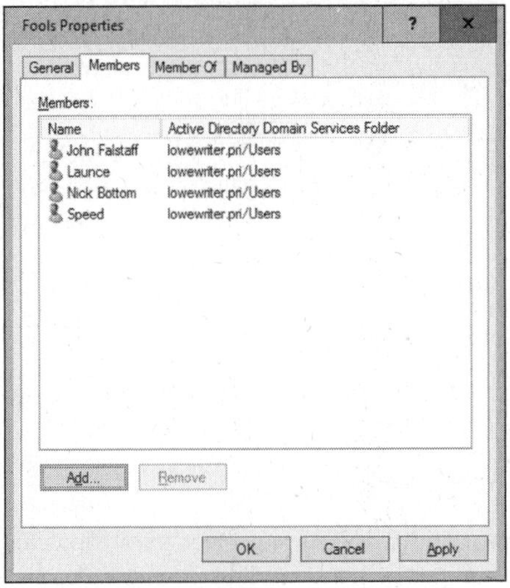

FIGURE 4-11:
Adding members
to a group.

5. Click Add, type the name of a user or another group that you want to add to this group, and click OK.

The member is added to the list.

6. **Repeat Step 5 for each user or group that you want to add.**

   Keep going until you've added everyone!

7. **Click OK.**

That's all there is to it.

TIP

The Group Properties dialog box also has a Member Of tab that lists each group that the current group is a member of.

Adding members to a group is only half the process of making a group useful. The other half is adding access rights to the group so that the members of the group can actually *do* something. The procedures for doing that are covered in Book 6, Chapter 5.

Working with User Profiles

User profiles automatically maintain desktop settings for Windows users. By default, a user profile is stored on the user's local computer. The following items are just some of the settings that are stored as part of the user profile:

>> **Desktop settings** in the Display Properties dialog box, including wallpaper, screen savers, and color schemes

>> **Start-menu programs** and Windows toolbar options

>> **Favorites,** which provide easy access to the files and folders that the user accesses frequently

>> **Application Data,** such as option settings, custom dictionaries, and so on

>> **Cookies,** used for Internet browsing

>> **Recent Documents,** which keeps shortcuts to the documents most recently accessed by the user

>> **Templates,** which stores user templates

>> **Network,** which keeps shortcuts to the user's network locations

>> **Send To,** which keeps shortcuts to document-handling utilities

>> **Local Settings,** such as history and temporary files

>> **Printers,** which keeps shortcuts to the user's printers

>> **Documents,** which stores the user's local documents

Types of user profiles

Four types of user profiles exist:

>> **Local user profile:** A local user profile is stored on the user's local computer and is applied only when the user logs on to that computer. A local user profile is created automatically when a new user logs on.

>> **Roaming user profile:** A roaming user profile is created on a network share. That way, the user can access the roaming profile when he or she logs on to any computer on the network.

>> **Mandatory user profile:** A mandatory user profile is a roaming user profile that the user is not allowed to change. One benefit of mandatory user profiles is that users can't mess up their desktop settings. Another benefit is that you can create a single mandatory profile that can be used by multiple users.

>> **Temporary user profile:** If a roaming or mandatory profile isn't available for some reason, a temporary user profile is automatically created for the user. The temporary profile is deleted when the user logs off, so any changes that the user makes while using a temporary profile are lost at the end of the session.

Roaming profiles

A *roaming user profile* is simply a user profile that has been copied to a network share so that it can be accessed from any computer on the network.

Before you can create roaming user profiles, you should create a shared folder on the server to hold the profiles. You can name the shared folder anything you like, but most administrators call it Users. For information on the procedure to create a shared folder, see Book 6, Chapter 5.

After you've created the shared Users folder, you can copy the profile to the server by following these steps at the user's local computer:

1. **Log on to the computer by using an account other than the one you want to make a user account.**

   Windows won't let you copy the profile that you're logged on with.

2. **Click the Start button, type the word Profile, and choose the Configure Advanced User Profile Properties option from the menu that appears.**

   This step brings up the User Profiles dialog box, shown in Figure 4-12.

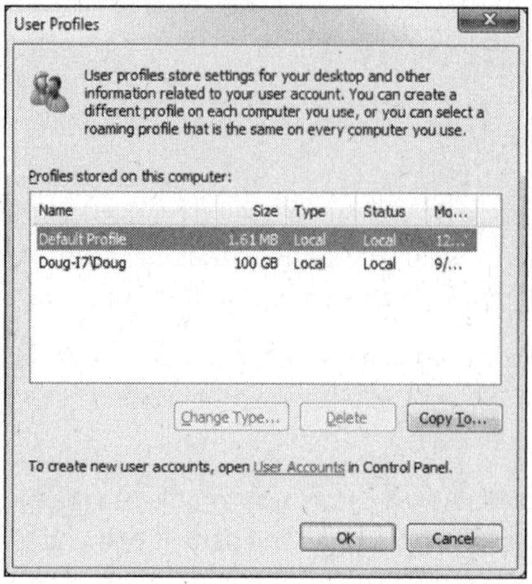

FIGURE 4-12:
The User Profiles
dialog box.

3. **Select the profile that you want to copy and then click Copy To.**

   A Copy To dialog box appears.

4. **Type the path and name for the roaming profile in the Copy Profile To box.**

   To copy a profile named Doug to the Users share on a server named Server01, for example, type **\\Server01\Users\Doug**.

5. **Click OK.**

   The profile is copied.

Now you can go back to the server, log on as an administrator, and follow these steps to designate a roaming profile for the user's domain account:

1. **From the Server Manager, choose Tools⇔Active Directory Users and Computers.**

   The Active Directory Users and Computers management console appears.

2. **Right-click the user account, and choose Properties from the contextual menu.**

   The User Properties dialog box appears.

3. **Click the Profile tab.**

   The Profile tab appears. (This tab is shown in Figure 4-9, earlier in this chapter, so I won't repeat it here.)

4. **Type the path and name of the profile in the Profile Path text box.**

The path and name that you type here should be the same path and name that you used to copy the profile to the server.

5. **Click OK.**

Creating a Logon Script

A *logon script* is a batch file that's run automatically whenever a user logs on. The most common reason for using a logon script is to map the network shares that the user needs access to. Here's a simple logon script that maps three network shares:

```
echo off
net use m: \\server1\shares\admin
net use n: \\server1\shares\mktg
net use o: \\server2\archives
```

Here, two shares on server1 are mapped to drives M and N, and a share on server2 is mapped as drive O.

If you want, you can use the special variable %username% to get the user's username. This variable is useful if you've created a folder for each user, and you want to map a drive to each user's folder, as follows:

```
net use u: \\server1\users\%username%
```

If a user logs on with the username dlowe, for example, drive U is mapped to \\server1\users\dlowe.

TIP

Scripts should be saved in the Scripts folder, which is buried deep in the bowels of the SYSVOL folder — typically, c:\Windows\SYSVOL\Sysvol*domainname*\Scripts, where *domainname* is your domain name. Because you need to access this folder frequently, I suggest creating a shortcut to it on your desktop.

After you've created a logon script, you can assign it to a user by using the Profile tab of the User Properties dialog box. For more information, see the section "Setting the user's profile information," earlier in this chapter.

Configuring User Accounts

Chapter **5**

Configuring a File Server

n this chapter, you discover how to set up and manage file and print servers for Windows Server 2016. Because the features for file and print servers are essentially the same for previous versions of Windows Server, the techniques presented in this chapter should work for older versions as well.

Understanding Permissions

Before I get into the details of setting up a file server, you need to have a solid understanding of the concept of permissions. *Permissions* allow users to access shared resources on a network. Simply sharing a resource such as a disk folder or a printer doesn't guarantee that a given user is able to access that resource. Windows makes this decision based on the permissions that have been assigned to various groups for the resource and group memberships of the user. If the user belongs to a group that has been granted permission to access the resource, the access is allowed. If not, access is denied.

In theory, permissions sound pretty simple. In practice, however, they can get pretty complicated. The following paragraphs explain some of the nuances of how access control and permissions work:

> » Every object — that is, every file and folder — on an NTFS volume has a set of permissions called the *Access Control List (ACL)* associated with it.

>> The ACL identifies the users and groups who can access the object and specifies what level of access each user or group has. A folder's ACL may specify that one group of users can read files in the folder, whereas another group can read and write files in the folder, and a third group is denied access to the folder.

>> Container objects — files and volumes — allow their ACLs to be inherited by the objects that they contain. As a result, if you specify permissions for a folder, those permissions extend to the files and child folders that appear within it.

Table 5-1 describes the six permissions that can be applied to files and folders on an NTFS volume.

TIP

>> Actually, the six file and folder permissions comprise various combinations of *special permissions* that grant more detailed access to files or folders. Table 5-2 lists the special permissions that apply to each of the six file and folder permissions.

>> It's best to assign permissions to groups rather than to individual users. Then if a particular user needs access to a particular resource, add that user to a group that has permission to use the resource.

TABLE 5-1   **File and Folder Permissions**

Permission	Description
Full Control	The user has unrestricted access to the file or folder.
Modify	The user can change the file or folder's contents, delete the file or folder, read the file or folder, or change the attributes of the file or folder. For a folder, this permission allows you to create new files or subfolders within the folder.
Read & Execute	For a file, this permission grants the right to read or execute the file. For a folder, this permission grants the right to list the contents of the folder or to read or execute any of the files in the folder.
List Folder Contents	This permission applies only to folders; it grants the right to list the contents of the folder.
Read	This permission grants the right to read the contents of a file or folder.
Write	This permission grants the right to change the contents of a file or its attributes. For a folder, this permission grants the right to create new files and subfolders within the folder.

TABLE 5-2 **Special Permissions**

Special Permission	Full Control	Modify	Read & Execute	List Folder Contents	Read	Write
Traverse Folder/Execute File	*	*	*	*		
List Folder/Read Data	*	*	*	*	*	
Read Extended Attributes	*	*	*	*	*	
Create Files/Write Data	*	*				*
Create Folders/Append Data	*	*				*
Write Attributes	*	*				*
Write Extended Attributes	*	*				*
Delete Subfolders and Files	*					
Delete	*	*				
Read Permissions	*	*	*	*	*	*
Change Permissions	*					
Take Ownership	*					
Synchronize	*	*	*	*	*	*

Understanding Shares

A *share* is simply a folder that is made available to other users via the network. Each share has the following elements:

>> **Share name:** The name by which the share is known over the network. To make the share name compatible with older computers, you should stick to eight-character share names whenever possible.

>> **Path:** The path to the folder on the local computer that's being shared, such as `C:\Accounting`.

>> **Description:** An optional one-line description of the share.

>> **Permissions:** A list of users or groups who have been granted access to the share.

When you install Windows and configure various server roles, special shared resources are created to support those roles. You shouldn't disturb these special shares unless you know what you're doing. Table 5-3 describes some of the most common special shares.

TABLE 5-3

Special Shares

Share Name	Description
drive$	The root directory of a drive; for example, C$ is the root share for the C: drive.
ADMIN$	Used for remote administration of a computer. This share points to the operating system folder (usually, C: \Windows).
IPC$	Used by named pipes, a programming feature that lets processes communicate with one another.
NETLOGON	Required for domain controllers to function.
SYSVOL	Another required domain controller share.
PRINT$	Used for remote administration of printers.
FAX$	Used by fax clients.

Notice that some of the special shares end with a dollar sign ($). These shares are *hidden shares* that aren't visible to users. You can still access them, however, by typing the complete share name (including the dollar sign) when the share is needed. The special share C$, for example, is created to allow you to connect to the root directory of the C: drive from a network client. You wouldn't want your users to see this share, would you? (Shares such as C$ are also protected by privileges, of course, so if an ordinary user finds out that C$ is the root directory of the server's C: drive, he or she still can't access it.)

Managing Your File Server

To manage shares on a Windows Server 2016 system, open the Server Manager, and select File and Storage Services in the task pane on the left side of the window. Then click Shares to reveal the management console shown in Figure 5-1.

The following sections describe some of the most common procedures that you'll use when managing your file server.

Using the New Share Wizard

To be useful, a file server should offer one or more *shares* — folders that have been designated as publicly accessible via the network. To create a new share, use the New Share Wizard, as described in the following procedure:

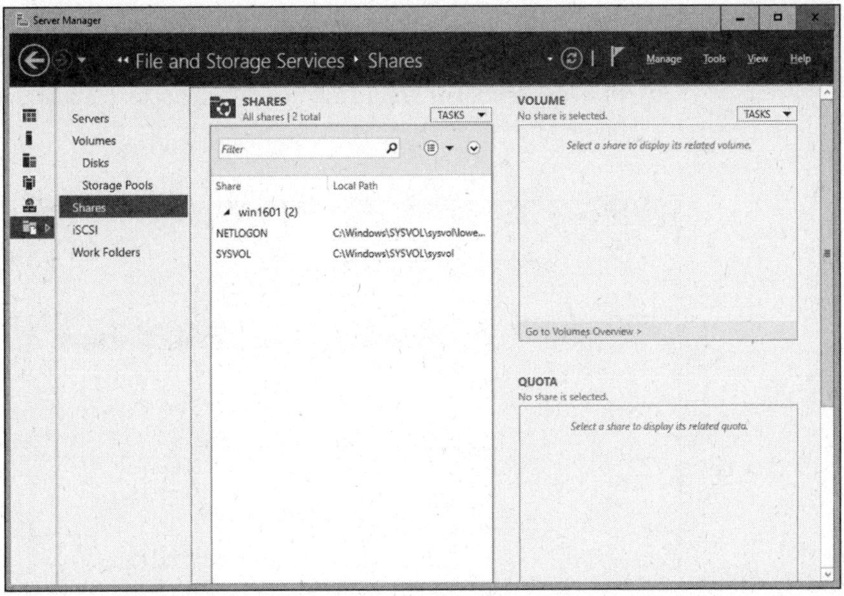

FIGURE 5-1:
Managing shares
in Windows
Server 2016.

1. **In Server Manager, click File and Storage Services, click Shares, and then choose New Share from the Tasks drop-down menu.**

   The opening screen of the New Share Wizard appears, as shown in Figure 5-2. Here, the wizard asks you what folder you want to share.

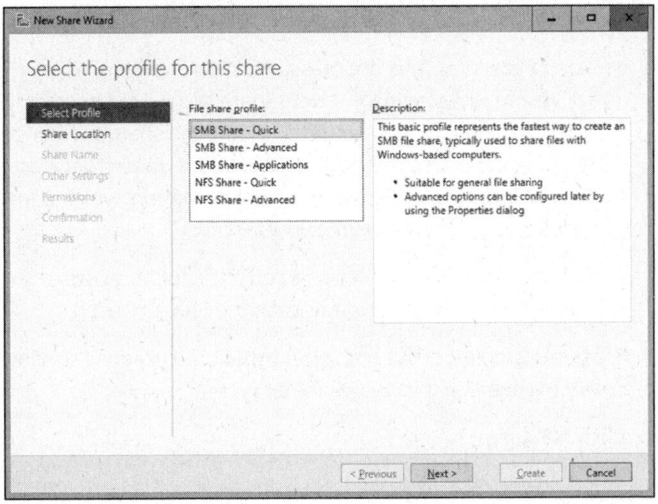

FIGURE 5-2:
The New Share
Wizard comes
to life.

2. **Select SMB Share – Quick in the list of profiles and then click Next.**

Next, the New Share Wizard asks for the location of the share, as shown in Figure 5-3.

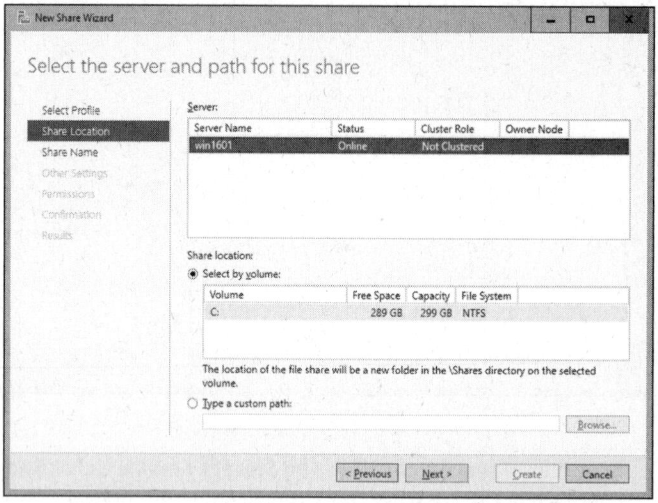

FIGURE 5-3:
The wizard asks where you'd like to locate the share.

3. **Select the server you want the share to reside on.**

For this example, I chose the server named win1601.

4. **Select the location of the share by choosing one of these two options:**

- *Select by Volume:* This option selects the volume on which the shared folder will reside while letting the New Share Wizard create a folder for you. If you select this option, the wizard will create the shared folder on the designated volume. Use this option if the folder doesn't yet exist and you don't mind Windows placing it in the default location, which is inside a folder called Shares on the volume you specify.

- *Type a Custom Path:* Use this option if the folder exists or if you want to create one in a location other than the Shares folder.

For this example, I chose the Select by Volume example to allow the wizard to create the share in the Shares folder on the C: drive.

5. **Click Next.**

The dialog box shown in Figure 5-4 appears.

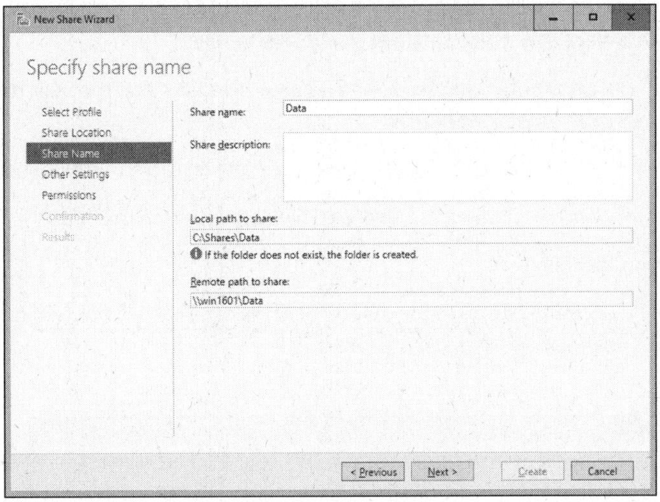

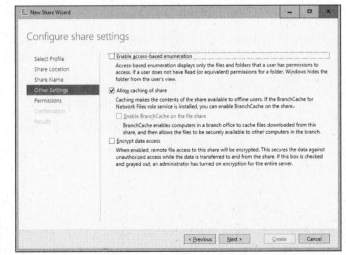

FIGURE 5-4:
The wizard asks
for the share
name and
description.

6. **Type the name that you want to use for the share in the Share Name box.**

The default name is the name of the folder being shared. If the folder name is long, you can use a more succinct name here.

For this example, I entered the share name Data.

7. **Enter a description for the share.**

For this example, I left the description blank.

8. **Click Next.**

The dialog box shown in Figure 5-5 appears.

FIGURE 5-5:
Specifying the
share settings.

9. **Select the share settings you'd like to use:**

   - *Enable Access-Based Enumeration*: Hides files that the user does not have permission to access

   - *Allow Caching of Share*: Makes the files available to offline users

   - *Encrypt Data Access:* Encrypts files accessed via the share

10. **Click Next.**

    The wizard displays the default permissions that will be used for the new share, as shown in Figure 5-6.

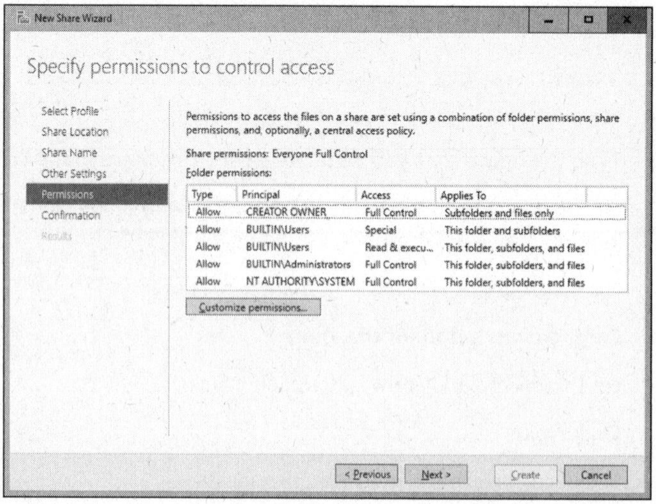

FIGURE 5-6:
Setting the share permissions.

11. **If you want to customize the permissions, click Customize Permissions.**

    This button summons the Advanced Security Settings for Data dialog box, which lets you customize both the NTFS and the share permissions.

12. **Click Next.**

    The confirmation page appears, as shown in Figure 5-7.

13. **Verify that all the settings are correct and then click Create.**

    The share is created, and a results dialog box is displayed, as shown in Figure 5-8.

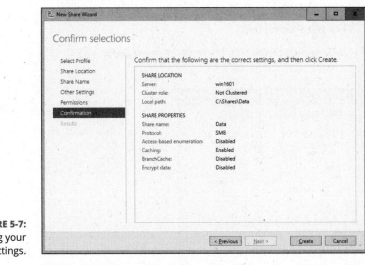

FIGURE 5-7:
Confirming your
share settings.

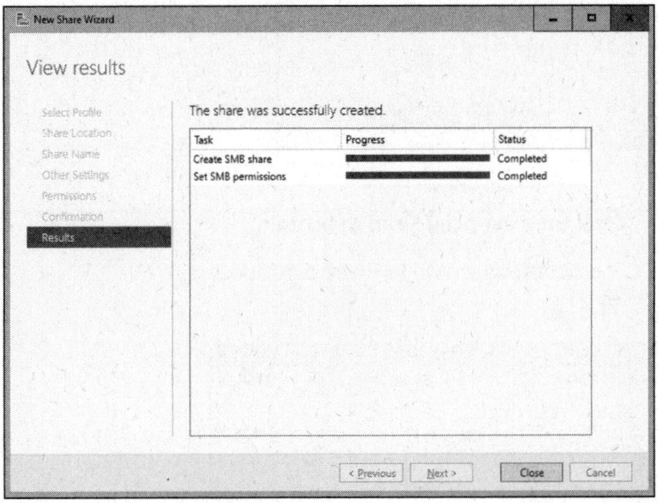

FIGURE 5-8:
You're done!

Sharing a folder without the wizard

If you think wizards should be confined to *Harry Potter* movies, you can set up a share without bothering with the wizard. Just follow these steps:

1. **Press the Windows key, click Computer, and navigate to the folder that you want to share.**

2. **Right-click the folder, and choose Properties from the contextual menu.**

   This action brings up the Properties dialog box for the folder.

3. Click the Sharing tab.

The Sharing tab comes to the front, as shown in Figure 5-9.

4. Click the Advanced Sharing button.

The dialog box shown in Figure 5-10 appears.

5. **Select the Share This Folder check box to designate the folder as shared.**

The rest of the controls in this dialog box will be unavailable until you select this check box.

6. **Type the name that you want to use for the share in the Share Name box, and type a description of the share in the Comments box.**

The default name is the name of the folder being shared. If the folder name is long, you can use a more succinct name here.

The description is strictly optional but sometimes helps users determine the intended contents of the folder.

7. **If you want to specify permissions now, click Permissions.**

This button brings up a dialog box that lets you create permissions for the share. For more information, see the next section, "Granting permissions."

8. **Click OK.**

The folder is now shared.

Granting permissions

When you first create a file share, all users are granted read–only access to the share. If you want to allow users to modify files in the share or allow them to create new files, you need to add permissions. Here's how to do this via Windows Explorer:

1. **Open Windows Explorer by pressing the Windows key and clicking Computer; then browse to the folder whose permissions you want to manage.**

2. **Right-click the folder you want to manage, and choose Properties from the contextual menu.**

The Properties dialog box for the folder appears.

3. **Click the Sharing tab; then click Advanced Sharing.**

The Advanced Sharing dialog box appears.

4. **Click Permissions.**

The dialog box shown in Figure 5-11 appears. This dialog box lists all the users and groups to whom you've granted permission for the folder. When you select a user or group from the list, the check boxes at the bottom of the list change to indicate which specific permissions you've assigned to each user or group.

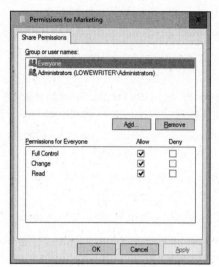

FIGURE 5-11:
Setting the share
permissions.

FIGURE 5-11:
Setting the share
permissions.

5. **Click Add.**

The dialog box shown in Figure 5-12 appears.

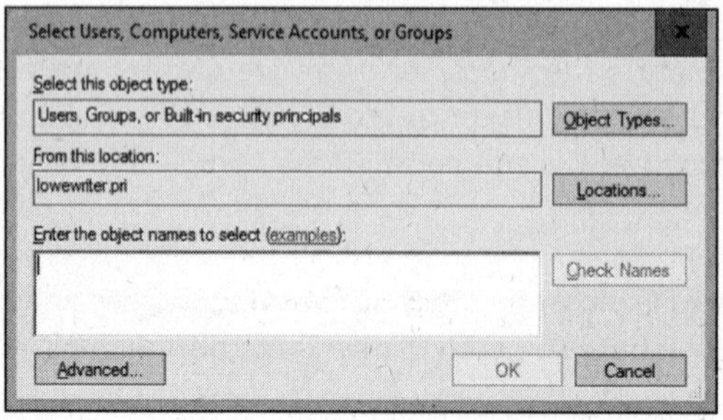

FIGURE 5-12:
The Select Users,
Computers,
Service Accounts,
or Groups
dialog box.

6. **Type the name of the user or group to whom you want to grant permission and then click OK.**

If you're not sure of the name, click Advanced. This action brings up a dialog box that lets you search for existing users. You can click the Find Now button to display a list of all users and groups in the domain. Alternatively, you can enter the first part of the name that you're looking for before you click Find Now to search more specifically.

When you click OK, you return to the Share Permissions tab, with the new user or group added.

TIP

7. **Select the appropriate Allow and Deny check boxes to specify which permissions to allow for the user or group.**

8. **Repeat Steps 5 through 7 for any other permissions that you want to add.**

9. **When you're done, click OK.**

Here are a few other thoughts to ponder concerning adding permissions:

TIP

>> If you want to grant full access to everyone for this folder, don't bother adding another permission. Instead, select the Everyone group and then select the Allow check box for each permission type.

>> You can remove a permission by selecting the permission and then clicking Remove.

REMEMBER

>> The permissions assigned in this procedure apply only to the share itself. The underlying folder can also have permissions assigned to it. If that's the case, whichever of the restrictions is most restrictive always applies. If the share permissions grant a user Full Control permission but the folder permission grants the user only Read permission, for example, the user has only Read permission for the folder.

Chapter **6**

Using Group Policy

Group policy refers to a feature of Windows operating systems that lets you control how certain aspects of Windows and other Microsoft software work throughout your network. Many features that you might expect to find in a management console, such as Active Directory Users and Computers, are controlled by group policy instead. You must use group policy to control how often users must change their passwords, for example, and how complicated their passwords must be. As a result, group policy is an important tool for any Windows network administrator.

Unfortunately, group policy can be a confusing beast. In fact, it's one of the most confusing aspects of Windows network administration. So don't be put off if you find this chapter more confusing than other chapters in this minibook. Group policy becomes clear after you spend some time actually working with it.

Understanding Group Policy

Here it is in a nutshell: Group policy consists of a collection of *group policy objects* (also called *GPOs)* that define individual policies. These policy objects are selectively applied to both users and computers. Each policy object specifies how some aspect of Windows or some other Microsoft software should be configured. A group policy object might specify the home page that's initially displayed when any user launches Internet Explorer, for example. When a user logs on to the domain, that policy object is retrieved and applied to the user's Internet Explorer configuration.

Group policy objects can apply to either computers or users. A policy that applies to a computer will be enforced for any user of the computer, and a policy that applies to a user will be enforced for that user no matter what computer he or she logs on to. As a network administrator, you'll be concerned mostly with policies that apply to users. But computer policies are useful from time to time as well.

To use group policy, you have to know how to do two things: (1) create individual group policy objects, and (2) apply — or *link* — those objects to user and computer objects. Both tasks can be a little tricky.

The trick to creating group policy objects is finding the particular setting you want to employ. Trying to find a specific group policy among the thousands of available policies can be frustrating. Suppose that you want to force all network users to change their passwords every 30 days. You know that a group policy controls the password-expiration date. But where is it? You'll find help with this aspect of working with group policy in the section titled "Creating Group Policy Objects," later in this chapter.

After you've created a group policy object, you then are faced with the task of linking it to the users or computers you want it to apply to. Creating a policy that applies to all users or computers is simple enough. But things get more complicated if you want to be more selective — for example, if you want the policy to apply only to users in a particular organizational unit (OU) or to users that belong to a particular group. You'll find help for this aspect of working with group policy in the section "Filtering Group Policy Objects," later in this chapter.

Enabling Group Policy Management on Windows Server 2016

Before you can work with group policy on a Windows Server 2016, you must enable group policy on the server. The procedure is simple enough and needs to be done only once for each server. Here are the steps:

1. **In the Server Manager, click Add Roles and Features.**

2. **Follow the wizard until you get to the Select Features page, which is shown in Figure 6-1.**

3. **If the Group Policy Management check box is not already checked, select it.**

4. **Click Next.**

5. **When the confirmation page appears, click Install.**

Be patient; installation may take a few minutes.

6. **Click Close.**

You're done!

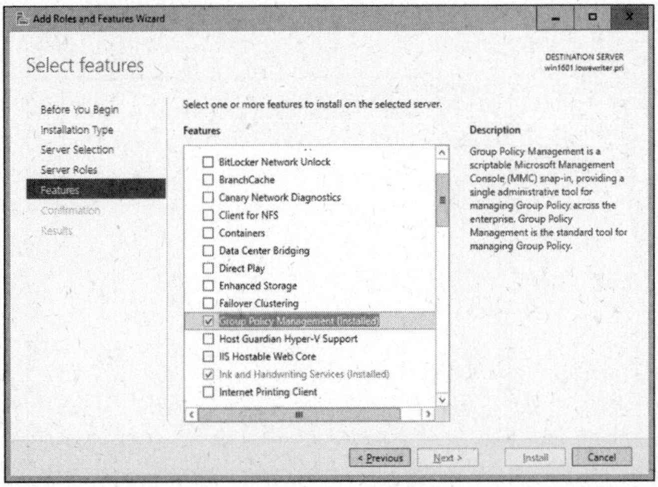

FIGURE 6-1:
Enabling
group policy
management
on Windows
Server 2016.

After you've completed this procedure, a new command titled Group Policy Management appears on the Tools menu in the Server Manager.

Creating Group Policy Objects

The easiest way to create group policy objects is to use the Group Policy Management console, which you can run from the Server Manager by choosing Tools⇨Group Policy Management.

A single group policy object can consist of one setting or many individual group policy settings. The Group Policy Management console presents the thousands of group policy settings that are available for your use in several categories. The more you work with group policy, the more these categories will begin to make sense. When you get started, you can expect to spend a lot of time hunting through the lists of policies to find the specific one you're looking for.

The easiest way to learn how to use the Group Policy Management console is to use it to create a simple group policy object. In the following procedure, I show you how to create a GPO that defines a group policy enabling Windows Update for all computers in a domain so that users can't disable Windows Update.

1. **In the Server Manager, choose Tools ⇨ Group Policy Management.**

   The Group Policy Management console appears, as shown in Figure 6-2.

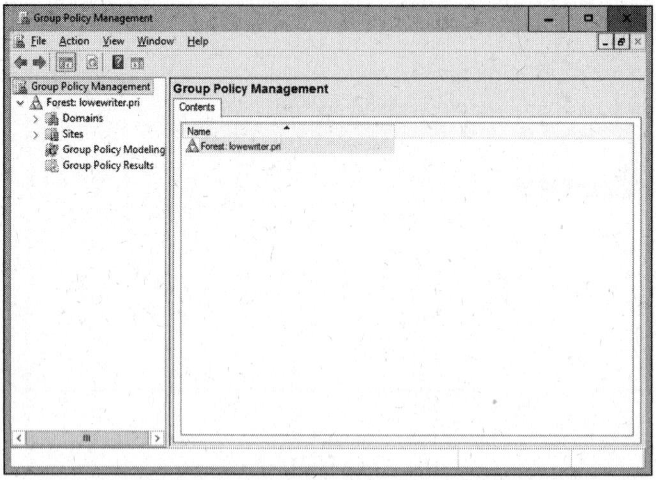

FIGURE 6-2:
The Group Policy Management console.

2. **In the Navigation pane, drill down through the Domains node to the node for your domain, then select the Group Policy Objects node for your domain.**

3. **Right-click the Group Policy Objects node and then choose New from the contextual menu that appears.**

   This command brings up the dialog box shown in Figure 6-3.

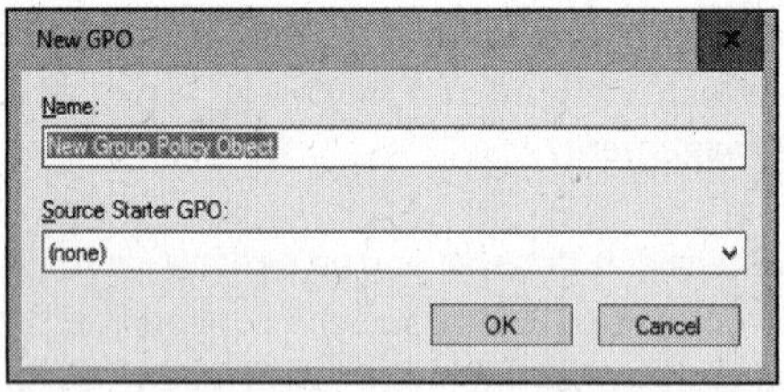

FIGURE 6-3:
Creating a new group policy object.

4. **Type a name for the group policy object and then click OK.**

   For this example, type something like Windows Update for a policy that will manage the Windows Update feature.

   When you click OK, the group policy object is created and appears in the Group Policy Objects section of the Group Policy Management window.

5. Double-click the new group policy.

The group policy opens, as shown in Figure 6-4. Note that at this stage, the Location section of the group policy doesn't list any objects. As a result, this policy is not yet linked to any Active Directory domains or groups. I get to that topic in a moment. First, I create the policy settings.

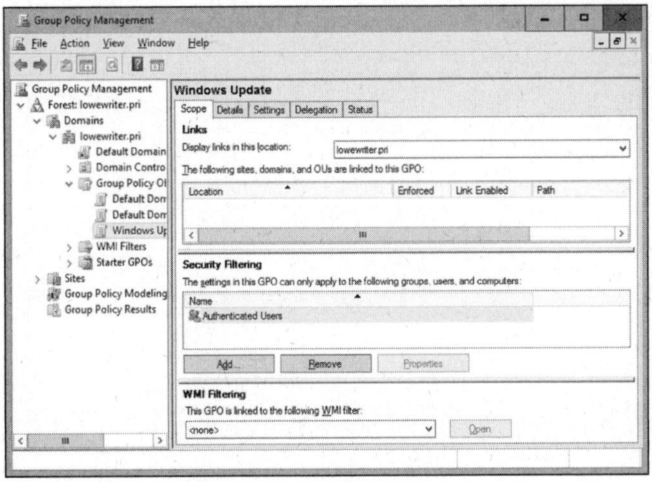

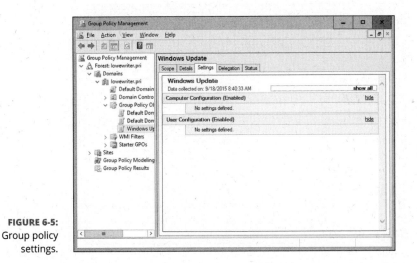

FIGURE 6-4:
A new group policy object.

6. Click the Settings tab.

The message "Generating Report" appears for a moment, and then the group policy settings are displayed, as shown in Figure 6-5.

FIGURE 6-5:
Group policy settings.

7. **Right-click Computer Configuration and then choose Edit from the contextual menu.**

This command opens the Group Policy Management Editor, as shown in Figure 6-6, where you can edit the Computer Configuration policies.

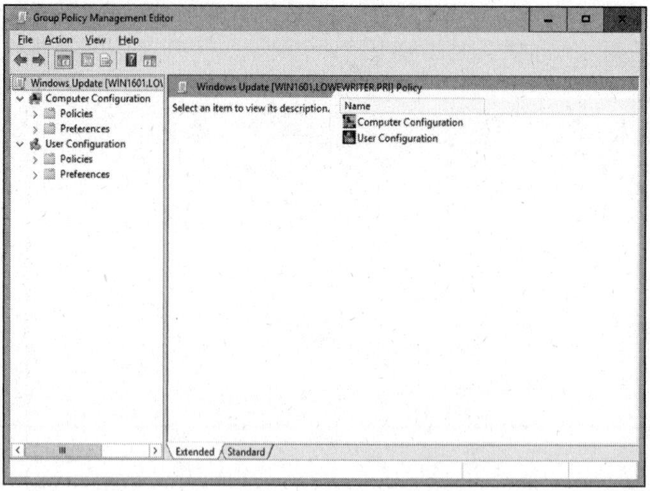

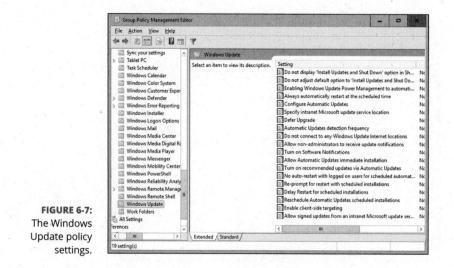

FIGURE 6-6:
Editing group
policy.

8. **In the Navigation pane, navigate to Computer Configuration ⇨ Administrative Templates ⇨ Windows Components ⇨ Windows Update.**

This step brings up the Windows Update policy settings, as shown in Figure 6-7.

FIGURE 6-7:
The Windows
Update policy
settings.

9. **Double-click Configure Automatic Updates.**

This step brings up the Configure Automatic Updates dialog box, as shown in Figure 6-8.

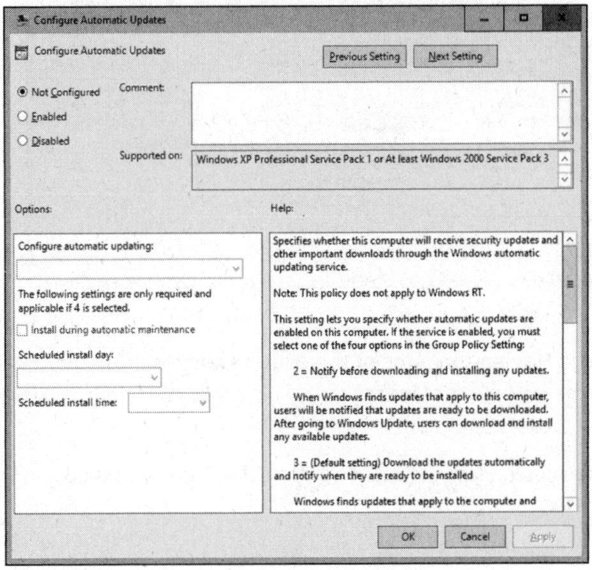

FIGURE 6-8:
The Configure
Automatic
Updates
dialog box.

10. **Select Enabled to enable the policy.**

11. **Configure the Windows Update settings however you want.**

For this example, I configure Windows Update so that updates are automatically downloaded every day at 3 a.m.

12. **Click OK.**

You return to the Group Policy Management Editor.

13. **Close the Group Policy Management Editor window.**

This step returns you to the Group Policy Management settings window.

14. **Right-click Computer Configuration, and choose Refresh from the contextual menu.**

The Windows Update policy is visible, as shown in Figure 6-9. (To show the full details of the policy, I expanded the Administrative Templates and Windows Components/Windows Update sections of the policy report.)

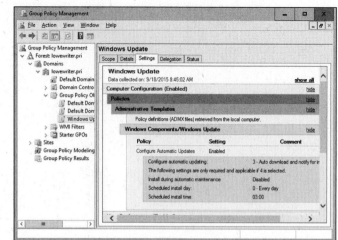

FIGURE 6-9:
The Windows
Update policy.

15. In the Navigation pane of the Group Policy Management window, drag the new Windows Update policy object to the top-level domain (in this case, `lowewriter.pri`).

When you release the mouse button, the dialog box shown in Figure 6-10 appears.

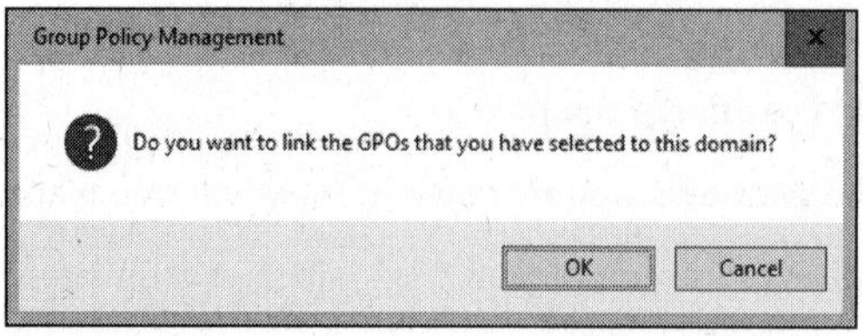

FIGURE 6-10:
Confirming
the scope.

16. Click OK.

The domain is added to the scope, as shown in Figure 6-11.

17. Close the Group Policy Management window.

The new group policy is now active.

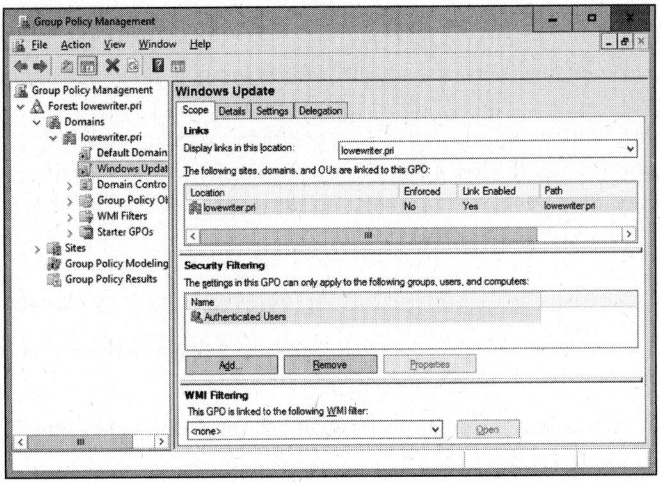

FIGURE 6-11:
The policy is finished.

Filtering Group Policy Objects

One of the most confusing aspects of group policy is that even though it applies to users and computers, you don't associate group policy objects with users or computers. Instead, you link GPOs to sites, domains, or organizational units (OUs). At first glance, this aspect may seem to limit the usefulness of group policy. For most simple networks, you'll work with group policy mostly at the domain level and occasionally at the OU level. Site-level group policy objects are used only for very large or complex networks.

Group policy wouldn't be very useful if you had to assign exactly the same policy to every user or computer within a domain. And although OUs can help break down group policy assignments, even that capability is limiting, because a particular user or computer can be a member of only one OU. Fortunately, group policy objects can have *filters* that further refine which users or computers the policy applies to. Although you can filter policy objects so that they apply only to individual users or computers, you're more likely to use groups to apply your group policy objects.

Suppose that you want to use group policy to assign two different default home pages for Internet Explorer. For the Marketing department, you want the default home page to be www.dummies.com, but for the Accounting department, you'd like the default home page to be www.beancounters.com. You can easily accomplish this task by creating two groups named Marketing and Accounting in Active Directory Users and Computers, and assigning the marketing and accounting users to the appropriate groups. Next, you can create two group policy objects: one for the Marketing department's home page and the other to assign the Accounting department's home page. Then you can link both of these policy objects to the domain and use filters to specify which group each policy applies to.

For the following procedure, I've created two group policies, named IE Home Page Dummies and IE Home Page Beancounter, as well as two Active Directory groups, named Marketing and Accounting. Here are the steps for filtering these policies to link correctly to the groups:

1. **Choose Start ⇨ Administrative Tools ⇨ Group Policy Management.**

   The Group Policy Management console appears. (Refer to Figure 6-2 for a refresher on what it looks like.)

2. **In the Navigation pane, navigate to the group policy object you want to apply the filter to.**

   For this example, I navigated to the IE Home Page Dummies policy, as shown in Figure 6-12.

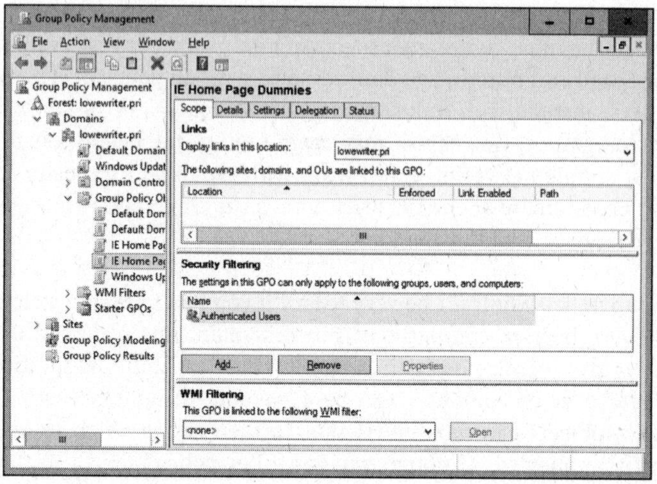

FIGURE 6-12: The IE Home Page Dummies policy.

3. **In the Security Filtering section, click Authenticated Users and then click Remove.**

   This step removes Authenticated Users so that the policy won't be applied to all users.

4. **Click Add.**

   This step brings up the Select User, Computer, or Group dialog box, as shown in Figure 6-13.

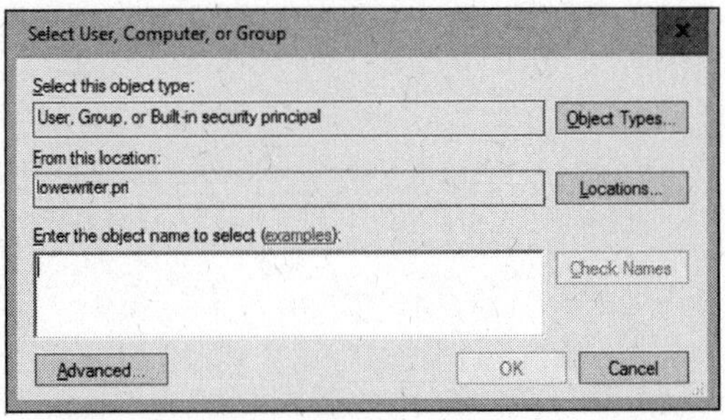

FIGURE 6-13:
The Select User,
Computer, or
Group dialog box.

5. **Type Marketing in the text box and then click OK.**

   The policy is updated to indicate that it applies to members of the Marketing group, as shown in Figure 6-14.

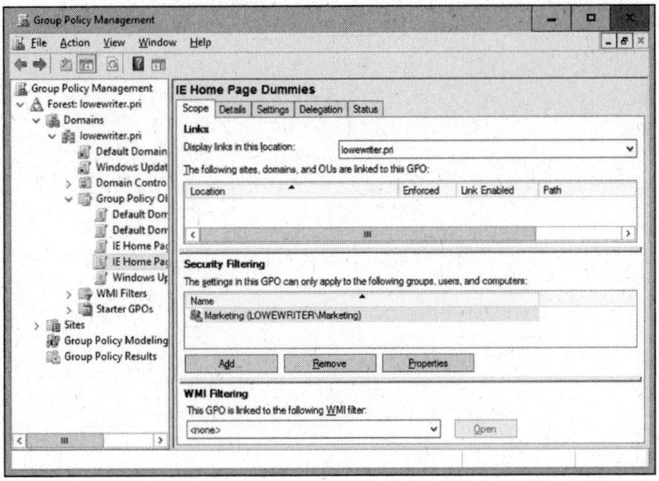

FIGURE 6-14:
A policy that
uses a filter.

6. **Repeat Steps 2 through 5 for the IE Home Page Beancounter policy, applying it to the Accounting group.**

   You're done!

Chapter **7**

Configuring Internet Information Services

Internet Information Services (IIS) is the web server that comes with Windows Server. It's an essential piece of software for hosting public websites, and it's also a must for any network that includes an intranet with web pages designed to be used by your network users.

In this chapter, you find out how to set up IIS and perform the most common types of maintenance chores, such as creating new websites.

Installing IIS

IIS is a free component of Windows Server, but it's not installed by default. After you've completed the installation of Windows Server, you must add the Web Server Role to enable IIS. The following procedure is for Windows Server 2016, but the procedure for Windows Server 2012 (or 2008, for that matter) is similar:

1. **Open the Server Manager; then choose Add Roles and Features.**

   The Add Roles and Features Wizard comes to life.

2. **Follow the steps of the Add Roles and Features Wizard up to the Select Server Roles step.**

   The Select Server Roles page is shown in Figure 7-1.

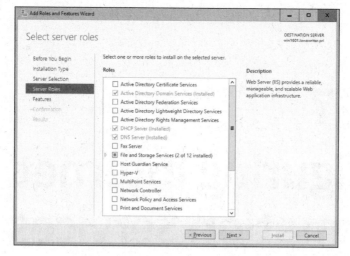

3. **Select the Web Server (IIS) check box and then click Next.**

   The Add Roles and Features Wizard asks whether you want to install the related IIS Management Console, as shown in Figure 7-2.

4. **Click Add Features; then click Next.**

   The Select Features page appears.

5. **Click Next.**

The Features page appears.

6. **Click Next.**

The Web Server Role (IIS) page appears, as shown in Figure 7-3.

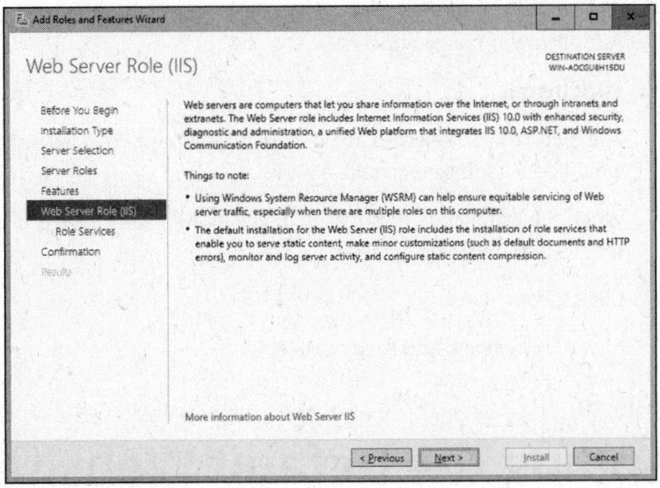

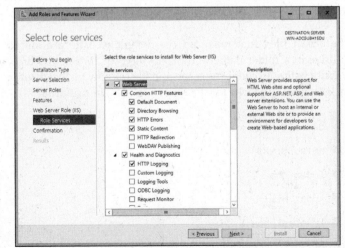

FIGURE 7-3:
The Web Server
Role (IIS) page
of the Add Roles
and Features
Wizard.

7. **Click Next.**

The Select Role Services page appears, as shown in Figure 7-4. This page lists a variety of optional services that can be configured for IIS.

FIGURE 7-4:
The Select Role
Services page of
the Add Roles
and Features
Wizard.

8. **Select the services you want to configure for IIS.**

If you want, you can study this list and try to anticipate which features you think you'll need. Or you can just leave the default options selected.

TIP

You can always return to the Add Roles and Features Wizard to add features you leave out here.

9. **Click Next.**

A confirmation page appears.

10. **Click Install.**

The features you selected are installed. This may take a few minutes, so now would be a good time to take a walk.

When the installation finishes, an Installation Results page is displayed to verify that IIS was properly installed.

11. **Click Close.**

IIS is now installed and ready to use!

Understanding the Default Website

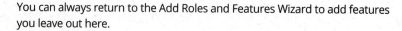

Initially, IIS is configured with a single website, called the *default website.* You can test that IIS is up and running by logging in as a standard user (not an administrator), opening a browser window on the server and typing **http://localhost** in the address bar. You can also reach this page by entering your local domain name in the address bar, such as **lowewriter.pri.** Figure 7-5 shows the standard welcome page that appears when you browse to the default site.

The actual files that make up the default website are stored on the server's C: drive in a folder named \inetpub\wwwroot. When you browse to the default website without requesting a specific file (simply by **localhost** in the address bar, for example), IIS looks for the following files, in this order:

- » default.htm
- » default.asp
- » index.htm
- » index.html
- » iisstart.htm
- » default.aspx

FIGURE 7-5:
The default
website.

Initially, `c:\inetpub\wwwroot` contains just two files: `iisstart.htm` and `welcome.png`. The `iisstart.htm` file is the file that's displayed when you browse to the website; it contains the HTML necessary to display the image contained in the `welcome.png` file, which is the image you actually see on the page.

You can preempt the standard page for the default website by providing your own file using one of the preceding names. You can follow these steps, for example, to create a simple `default.htm` file that displays the words *Hello World!* as the start page for the default website:

1. **Log in as an administrator, open an Explorer window, and browse to**
    `c:\inetpub\wwwroot`.

2. **Choose File⇨New⇨Text Document, type** default.htm **for the filename,
    and press Enter.**

3. **Right-click the** `default.htm` **file you just created, and choose Open
    With⇨Notepad from the contextual menu.**

4. **Enter the following text in the Notepad window:**

    ```
    <HTML>
    <BODY>
    <H1>Hello World!</H1>
    </BODY>
    </HTML>
    ```

5. **Choose File⇨Save to save the file and then choose File⇨Exit to quit
    Notepad.**

6. **Log out, log in as a standard user, and open a browser window.**

7. **Type** http://localhost **in the address bar, and press Enter.**

   The page shown in Figure 7-6 appears.

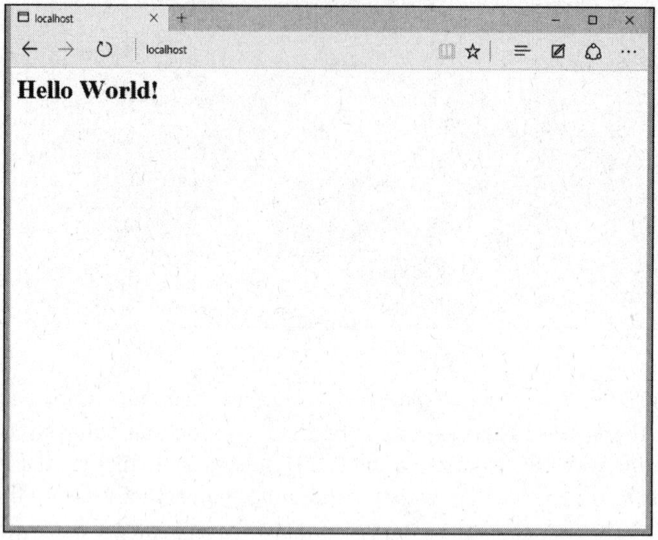

FIGURE 7-6:
Hello World!

Creating Websites

IIS has the ability to host multiple websites. This is an extremely useful feature not only for web servers that host public sites, but also for web servers that host internal (intranet) sites. You might create a separate intranet website for Human Resources and assign it the website name hr. Then, assuming that the domain name is lowewriter.pri, users can browse to the website by using the address hr.lowewriter.pri.

Here are the steps:

1. **Using Windows Explorer, create a folder in which you will save the files for the new website.**

   For this example, I created a folder named c:\HR-Web-Site.

2. **In Server Manager, choose Tools⇨Internet Information Services (IIS) Manager.**

   The IIS Manager springs to life, as shown in Figure 7-7.

FIGURE 7-7:
The IIS Manager.

3. **In the navigation pane, open the primary domain and Sites node. Then right-click Sites and choose Add Website from the contextual menu.**

The Add Website dialog box appears, as shown in Figure 7-8.

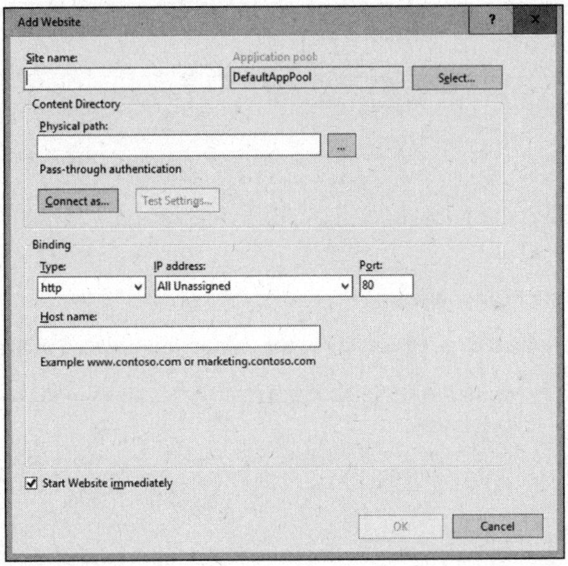

FIGURE 7-8:
The Add Website dialog box.

4. **Enter a name for the website in the Site Name text box.**

For this example, I used HR.

Configuring Internet Information Services

5. **Click the Browse button (the one with the ellipsis), browse to the folder you created in Step 1, and then click OK.**

For this example, I browsed to C:\HR-Web-Site.

6. **In the Host Name text box, enter the exact DNS name you want to use for the site.**

For this example, I entered hr.lowewriter.pri.

7. **Click OK.**

The newly created website appears below the Sites node in the IIS Manager, as shown in Figure 7-9.

FIGURE 7-9: The HR website appears in the IIS Manager.

8. **Close the IIS Manager.**

9. **Create a web page to display in the folder you created in Step 1.**

For this example, I used Notepad to create a text file named default.htm, with the following text:

```
<HTML>
<BODY>
<H1>Welcome to the HR Website!</H1>
</BODY>
</HTML>
```

10. **In Server Manager, choose Tools ⇨ DNS.**

This brings up the DNS Manager console, as shown in Figure 7-10.

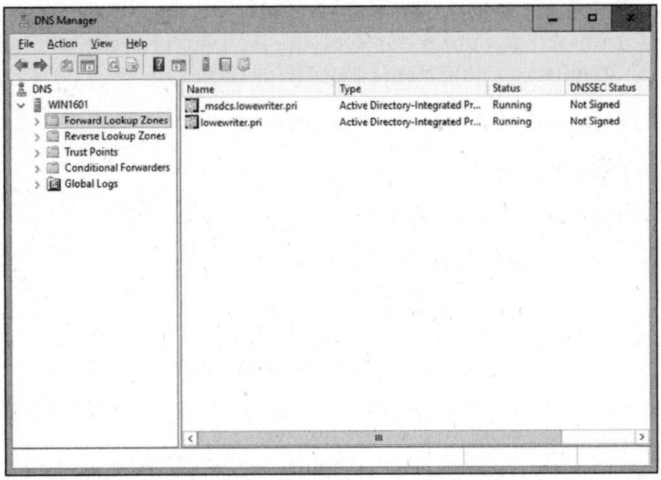

FIGURE 7-10:
The DNS Manager console.

11. **In the navigation pane, navigate to the node for your domain.**

   In this example, I navigated to `lowewriter.pri`.

12. **Choose Action⇨New Alias (CNAME)**

   The New Resource Record dialog box appears, as shown in Figure 7-11.

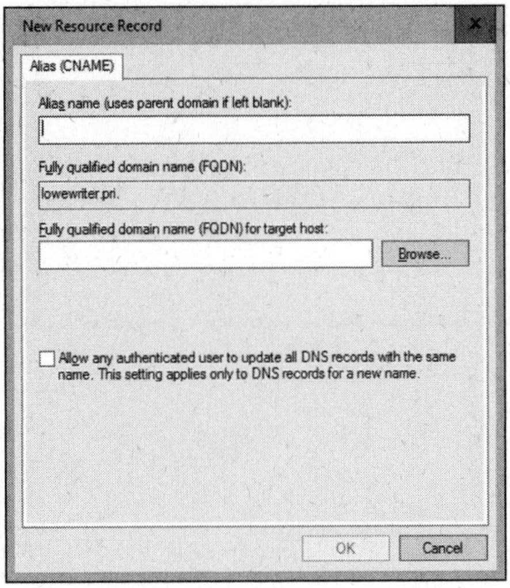

FIGURE 7-11:
Creating a CNAME record.

13. **Enter the alias name you want to use in the Alias Name text box.**

   For this example, I entered simply `hr`.

14. Enter the computer name of your web server in the text box labeled Fully Qualified Domain Name (FQDN) for Target Host.

For this example, I entered `1server01`.

15. Click OK.

The DNS alias is created.

16. Close the DNS Manager console.

17. Open a browser window.

18. Browse to the alias address you just created.

For this example, I browsed to `hr.lowewriter.pri`. Figure 7-12 shows the resulting page.

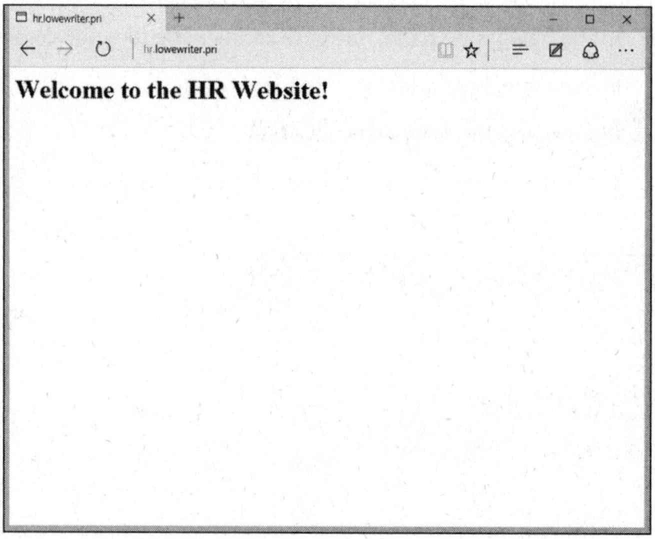

FIGURE 7-12:
Viewing a
website.

Chapter **8**

Configuring Exchange Server 2016

Although not strictly a part of Windows Server, Exchange Server is the mail server software that's used on most Windows networks. Yes, I know Microsoft doesn't call Exchange Server a *mail server*. It's a *messaging and collaboration server*. But the basic reason for Exchange Server's existence is email. The other messaging and collaboration features are just icing on the cake.

In this chapter, you discover how to perform the most commonly requested maintenance chores for Exchange Server, such as how to create a new mailbox, grant a user access to an additional mailbox, and deal with mailbox size limits. The examples shown in this chapter are for Exchange Server 2016, but the procedures are similar for previous versions.

Creating a Mailbox

In previous versions of Exchange, you managed mailboxes using the Exchange Management Console. In the 2013 and 2016 versions of Exchange, you use the web-based Exchange Administrative Center (EAC) instead. To start EAC, choose Start ➪ All Apps ➪ Microsoft Exchange 2016 ➪ Exchange Administrative Center.

When you create a new mailbox, you can either specify either an existing Active Directory user or use EAC to create a new Active Directory user and mailbox at the same time. The following procedure describes the steps you should follow to create a new Active Directory user with a mailbox:

1. **Open the Exchange Administrative Center by choosing Start ⇨ All Apps ⇨ Microsoft Exchange Server 2016 ⇨ Exchange Administrative Center.**

2. **When prompted, enter your username and password.**

   The EAC comes to life, as shown in Figure 8-1.

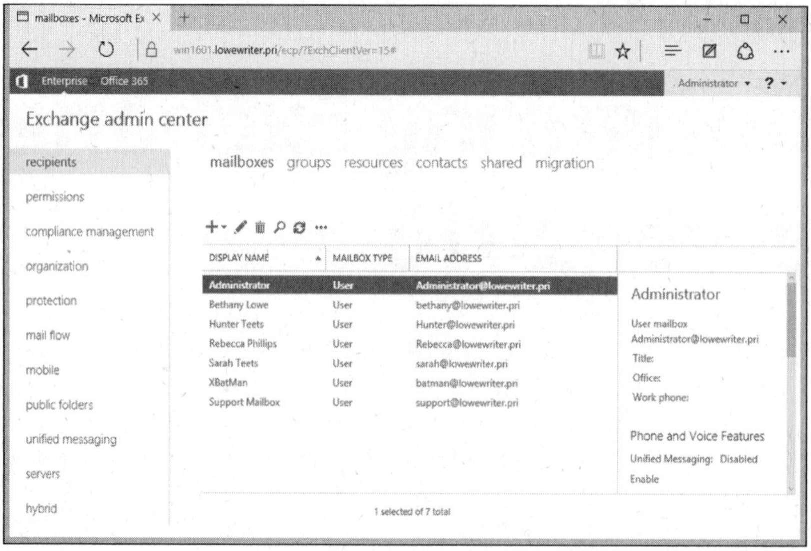

FIGURE 8-1: The Exchange Administrative Center.

3. **Click the plus sign (+) icon above the list of mailboxes, and then choose User Mailbox.**

   The User Mailbox page appears, as shown in Figure 8-2.

4. **Enter the alias for the new mailbox.**

   The alias is the portion of the email address that appears before the at (@) sign. For example, in the email address `mitchell@lowewriter.com`, the alias is `mitchell`.

5. **Choose New User.**

6. **Type the user's first name, middle initial, and last name.**

   As you type the name, the Display Name field is automatically filled in.

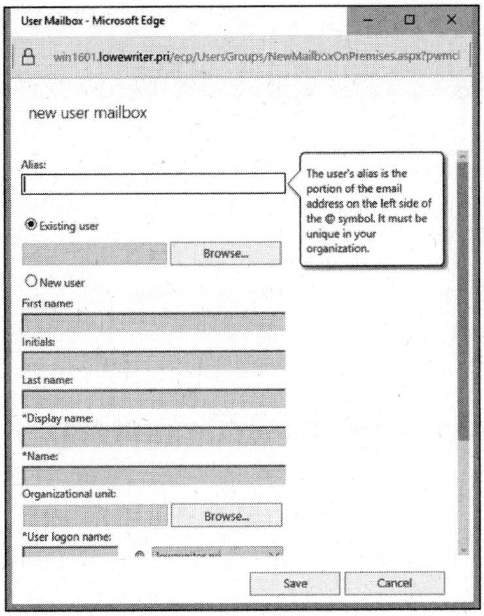

FIGURE 8-2:
Creating a user
mailbox.

7. **Change the Display Name field if you want it to appear different from what was proposed.**

   You may want to reverse the first and last names so the last name appears first, for example.

8. **Enter the user logon name.**

   This name must be unique within the domain and will be used to form the user's email address.

9. **Enter the password twice.**

   You're asked to type the password twice, so type it correctly. If you don't type it identically in both boxes, you're asked to correct your mistake.

10. **If the password is temporary, select the User Must Change Password at Next Logon check box.**

    This setting requires the user to change the temporary password the first time he or she logs on.

11. **Click Save.**

    The user's mailbox is created and appears in the EAC Recipients page, as shown in Figure 8-3.

12. **Pat yourself on the back; then click Finish.**

    You're done!

Configuring Exchange
Server 2016

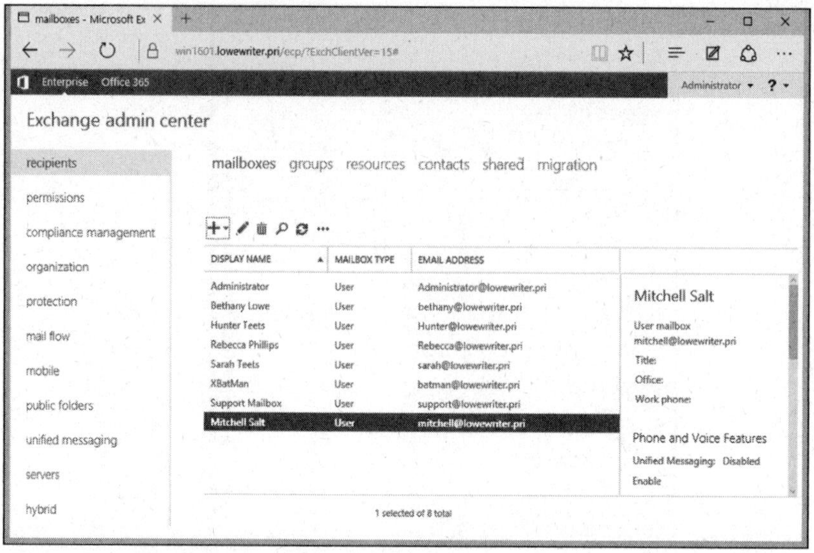

FIGURE 8-3:
The new
user's mailbox
appears in the
Recipients page.

Managing Mailboxes

After you've set up a mailbox, you can use the Exchange Administrative Center to
manage the settings of the mailbox. To do that, just select the mailbox you want
to manage, and click the Edit icon. This action brings up the User Mailbox page,
which is the portal to many of the most frequently used features of Exchange.

The following sections describe several commonly used features you can enable
when you edit a mailbox.

Enabling mailbox features

Exchange Mailbox Features refers to several features of Exchange mailboxes that
are controlled via the Mailbox Features tab of the User Mailbox page. This tab is
shown in Figure 8-4.

The following paragraphs describe some of the features that are controlled from
this tab:

>> **Outlook on the Web:** Lets the user access his or her Exchange mailbox from
a web browser rather than from an Outlook client. With this feature enabled,
the user can read email from any computer that has an Internet connection.

>> **Exchange ActiveSync:** Activates the ActiveSync feature, which allows
Exchange data to synchronize with mobile devices such as iPhones or
Windows Mobile phones.

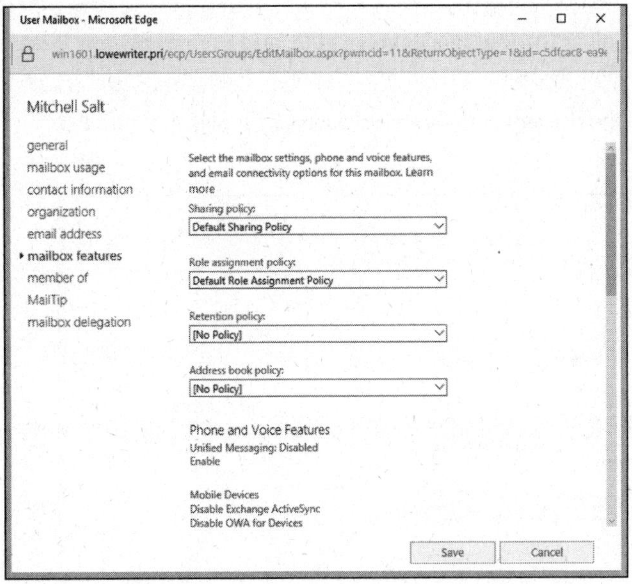

FIGURE 8-4:
The Mailbox
Features tab.

>> **MAPI:** Enables email using the MAPI protocol.

>> **POP3:** Enables email using the POP3 protocol.

>> **IMAP4:** Enables email using the IMAP4 protocol.

>> **Archiving:** Enables the Exchange Archive feature, which is available only with the Enterprise edition of Exchange.

>> **Mail Flow:** Lets you set delivery options such as creating an automatic forwarder, as described in the next section.

>> **Message Size Restrictions:** Lets you set the maximum size of incoming or outgoing messages.

Creating a forwarder

A *forwarder* is a feature that automatically forwards any incoming email to another email address. This feature is most often used when an employee is on vacation or leave and the employee's manager has requested that someone else temporarily handle the absent employee's email.

To configure a forwarder, follow these steps:

1. In Exchange Administrative Center, open the User Mailbox page for the user.

2. **Select the Mailbox Features tab, and then click View Details in the Mail Flow section.**

The delivery options are displayed, as shown in Figure 8-5.

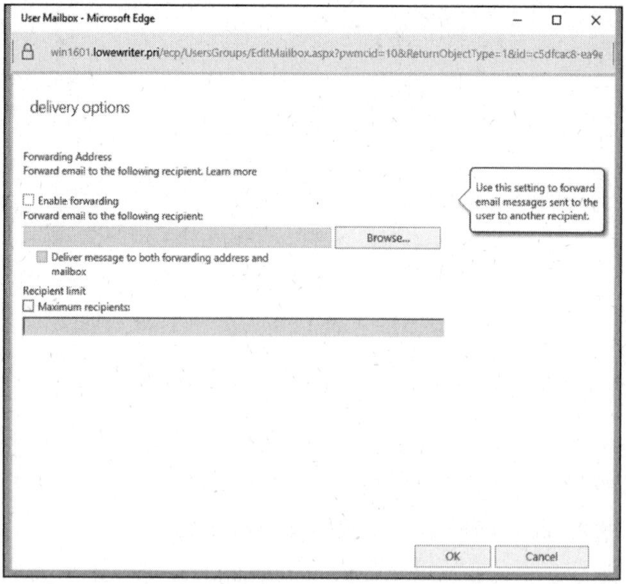

FIGURE 8-5:
Setting the delivery options.

3. **Select the Enable Forwarding check box.**

4. **Click the Browse button.**

The Select Recipient window appears, as shown in Figure 8-6.

5. **Select the recipient you want to forward the email to and then click OK.**

The name you selected is displayed in the text box next to the Browse button in the Delivery Options page (refer to Figure 8-5).

6. **If you want the email to be delivered to this user's mailbox in addition to the forwarding address, select the Deliver Message to Both Forwarding Address and Mailbox check box.**

If you leave this option deselected, only the forwarding address will receive the email; the mail won't be delivered to this user's mailbox.

7. **Click OK to close the Delivery Options page.**

You return to the User Mailbox page.

8. **Click Save to save your changes.**

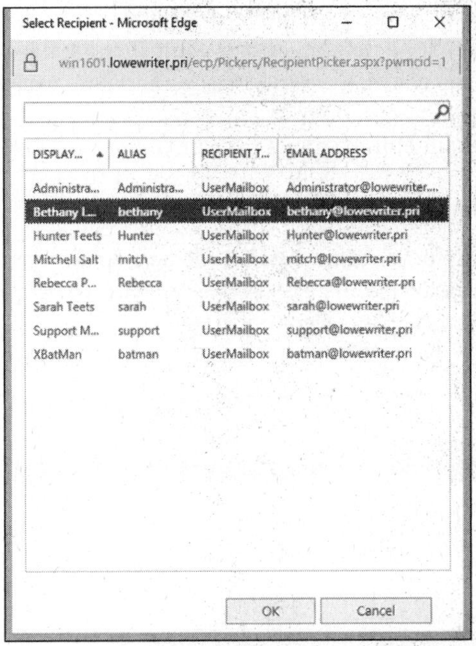

FIGURE 8-6:
Select the
recipient for
the forwarder.

Setting mailbox storage limits

Exchange lets you set a limit on the size of each user's mailbox. In a very small organization, you can probably get away without imposing strict mailbox size limits. But if your organization has 20 or more users, you need to limit the size of each user's mailbox to prevent the Exchange private mail store from getting out of hand.

Exchange provides five kinds of storage limits for user mailboxes:

» **Issue Warning At:** When this limit is exceeded, an email warning is sent to the user to let him know that his mailbox is getting large.

» **Prohibit Send At:** When this limit is reached, the user can't send email, but the mailbox continues to receive email. The user won't be able to send emails again until she deletes enough emails to reduce the mailbox size below the limit.

» **Prohibit Send and Receive At:** When this limit is reached, the mailbox shuts down and can neither send nor receive emails.

» **Keep Deleted Items for (Days):** Most users don't realize it, but when they permanently delete an item from their mailbox, the item isn't really permanently deleted. Instead, Exchange retains the item for the period specified by this limit. The default is 14 days.

» **Keep Deleted Mailboxes for (Days):** This limit specifies how long Exchange should retain mailboxes that you delete.

You can (and should) set a default storage limit that applies to all mailboxes in your organization. You can also override these limits for specific users.

To configure the default storage limits for all mailboxes, follow these steps:

1. In Exchange Administrative Center, select Databases.

A list of databases for your Exchange environment appears, as shown in Figure 8-7. In this example, there is just one database. For larger Exchange environments, you may see several databases.

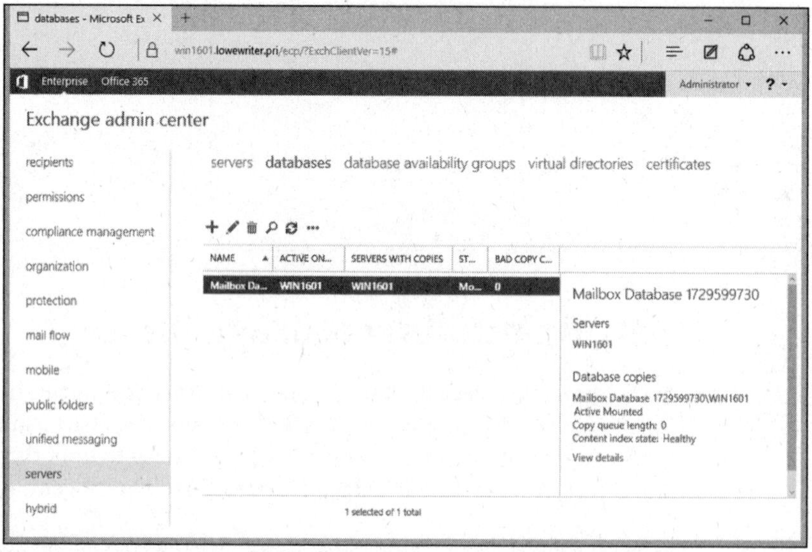

FIGURE 8-7:
The Exchange
Admin Center
Databases page.

2. Double-click the database whose limits you want to change.

The Mailbox Database page appears, as shown in Figure 8-8.

3. Select Limits.

The Mailbox Database Limits page is displayed, as shown in Figure 8-9.

4. Change the Storage Limits settings to meet your needs.

By default, the storage limits are set quite high: Warnings are issued at about 1.9GB, send permission is revoked at 2GB, and both send and receive permissions are revoked at 2.3GB. These limits are generous, but bear in mind that if you have 100 users, your mailbox database may grow to 200GB. You may want to set lower limits.

5. Click Save.

The limits you set take effect immediately.

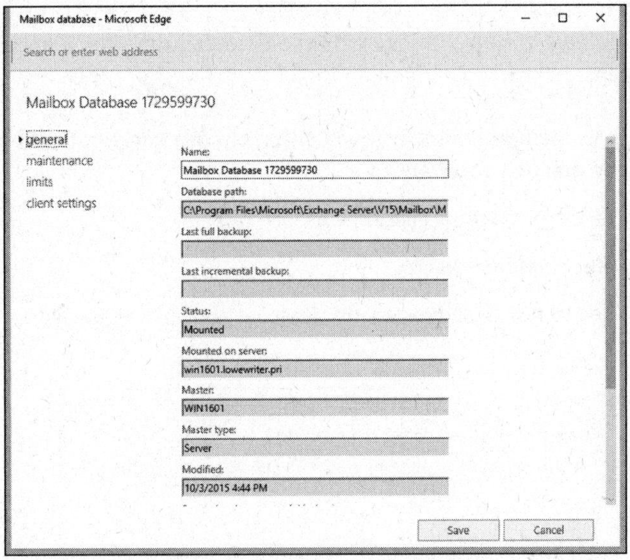

FIGURE 8-8:
The Mailbox
Database page.

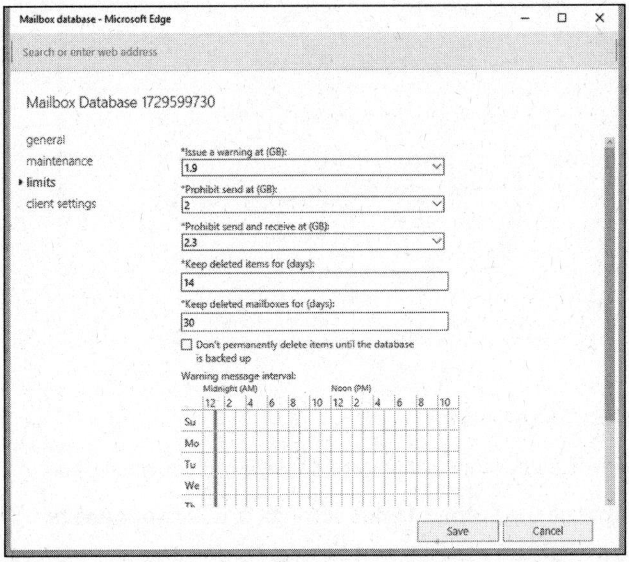

FIGURE 8-9:
The Mailbox
Database
Limits page.

If you impose restrictive default storage limits for your users, you may want to relax the limits on a case-by-case basis. Some users may require a larger mailbox because of the type of work they do, and you probably don't want to impose a tight limit on your boss.

Fortunately, it's easy to override the default limits for a specific user. Here are the steps:

1. **In Exchange Administrative Center, choose Recipients, then double-click the mailbox you want to edit.**

The user's mailbox page appears.

2. **Select Mailbox Usage.**

The Mailbox Usage page is displayed, as shown in Figure 8-10.

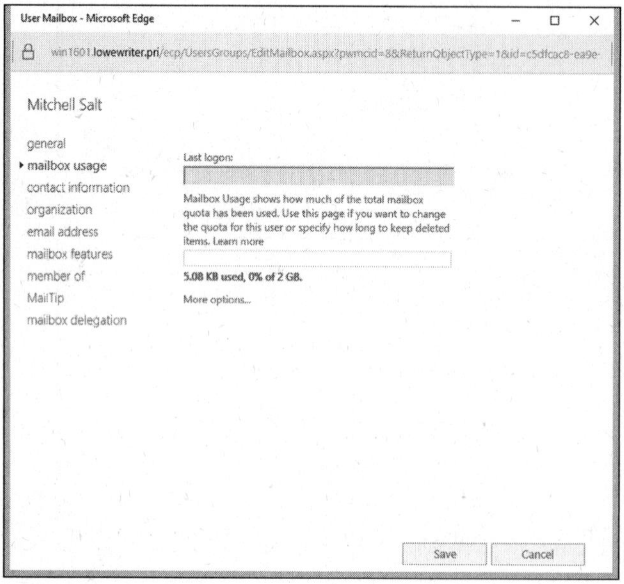

FIGURE 8-10:
The Mailbox
Usage page.

3. **Click More Options.**

The mailbox limits options are displayed, as shown in Figure 8-11.

4. **Change the Storage Limits settings to meet your needs.**

You can adjust any of the mailbox limits up or down to create limits for the user that are either more or less restrictive than the defaults for the database.

5. **Click Save.**

The limits you set take effect immediately.

You can configure many other features of Exchange via the Exchange Management Console. You should take some time to explore all the nodes in the navigation pane and to examine the Properties dialog boxes for the various types of Exchange objects that appear when you select each node.

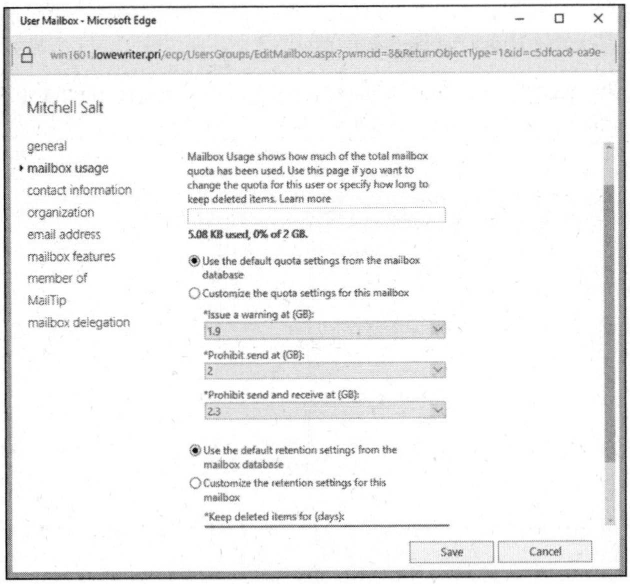

FIGURE 8-11:
Setting the
default storage
limits.

Configuring Outlook for Exchange

After you've created an Exchange mailbox for a user, you can configure that user's Outlook client software to connect to the user's account. Although you can do this configuration directly within Outlook, it's better to do it outside Outlook, using the Control Main Mail applet. Here are the steps:

1. **Open Control Panel, and open the Mail applet.**

    The dialog box shown in Figure 8-12 appears.

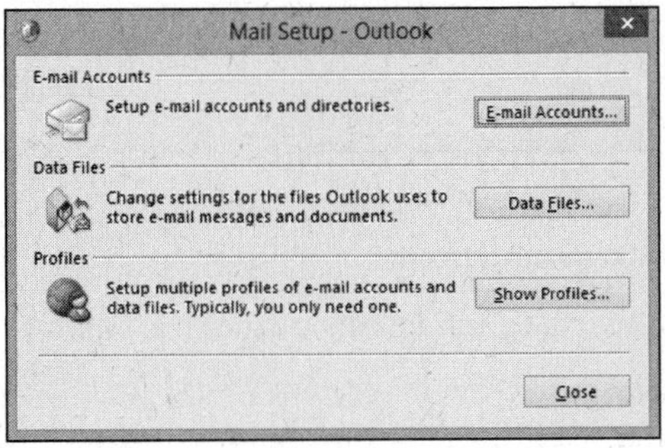

FIGURE 8-12:
The Mail Setup
dialog box.

2. Click the Show Profiles button.

The dialog box shown in Figure 8-13 appears, listing the mail profiles that already exist on the computer.

3. Double-click the user's profile.

The Mail Setup dialog box shown in Figure 8-14 appears.

4. Click the E-mail Accounts button.

The Account Settings dialog box appears, as shown in Figure 8-15.

5. Click the New icon.

An Add E-mail Account dialog box appears. Don't enter your email address as prompted in this dialog box; instead, proceed to Step 6.

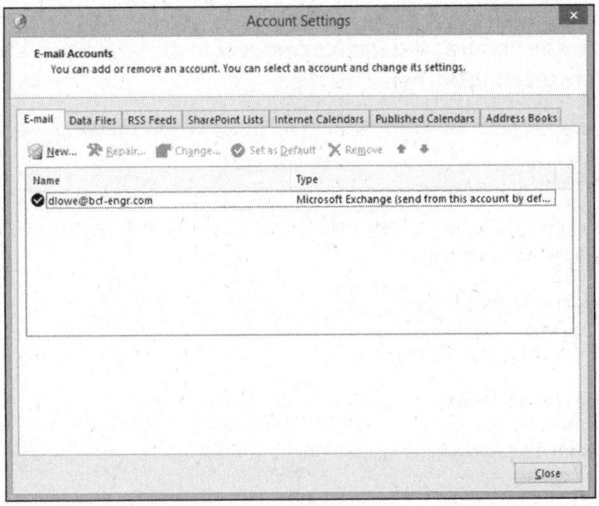

FIGURE 8-15:
The Account
Settings
dialog box.

6. **Click the Manually Configure Server Settings or Additional Server Types option and then click Next.**

A dialog box asks you what type of email account you want to create. The choices are (a) Outlook.com or Exchange ActiveSync Compatible Service or (b) POP 3 or IMAP.

7. **Select the Outlook.com or Exchange ActiveSync Compatible Service option and then click Next.**

The Server Settings dialog box shown in Figure 8-16 appears.

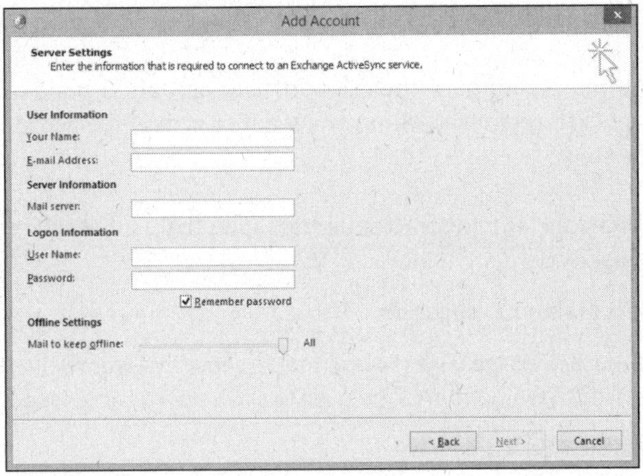

FIGURE 8-16:
You must
identify the
Exchange server
and provide a
username.

8. **Enter the name of the Exchange server and the username in the appropriate text boxes; then click Next.**

   After your account information is verified, a confirmation message is displayed.

9. **Click OK.**

   The confirmation message disappears, and the last page of the E-Mail Accounts Wizard appears.

10. **Click the Finish button.**

    The wizard is dismissed.

11. **Choose File ⇨ Exit.**

12. **Restart Outlook.**

    The mailbox should be configured.

Viewing Another Mailbox

Sometimes, you want to set up Outlook so that in addition to the user's main mailbox, he or she has access to another user's mailbox. Suppose that you create a user named Support so that your customers can send email to Support@YourCompany.com to ask technical support questions. If you don't set up at least one of your users so that he or she can read the Support mailbox, any mail sent to Support@YourCompany.com will languish unanswered. Assuming that this situation isn't what you want, you can set up one or more of your users to access the Support mailbox so that those users can read and respond to the mail.

First, you must configure the Support user account's mailbox so that it grants access rights to each user whom you want to access the account. To do that, follow these steps:

1. **In Exchange Administrative Center, open the User Mailbox page for the user.**

2. **Select Mailbox Delegation.**

   The Mailbox Usage page is displayed, as shown in Figure 8-17. (For this figure, I scrolled to the bottom of the page to show the Full Access settings.)

3. **Click the Add icon.**

   The Select Full Access page opens, as shown in Figure 8-18.

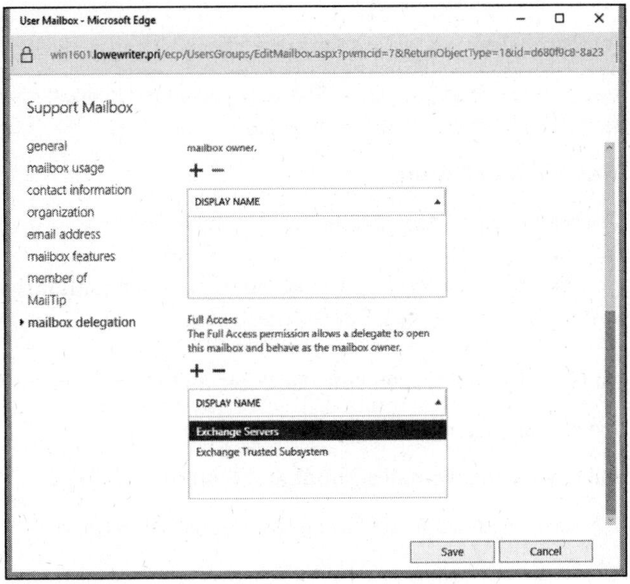

FIGURE 8-17:
The Mailbox
Delegation page.

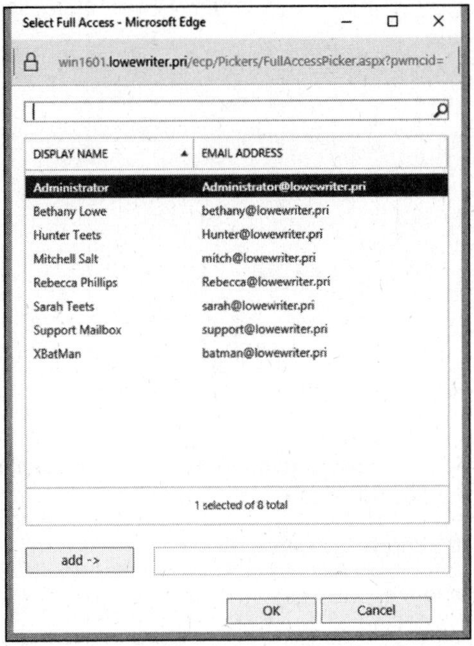

FIGURE 8-18:
The Select Full
Access page.

4. **Select the user you want to grant access to; then click OK.**

   You're returned to the wizard. The user you added is selected in the list of users who have access to the mailbox.

5. **Click the Save button.**

   The mailbox rights are updated.

After you've granted access to the account, you can configure the user's Outlook to read the Support account. Follow these steps:

1. **On the user's computer, start Outlook, and choose Tools➪Account.**

   The Account Settings dialog box is displayed.

2. **Select your main email account and then click Change.**

   The Server Settings dialog box appears, as shown in Figure 8-19.

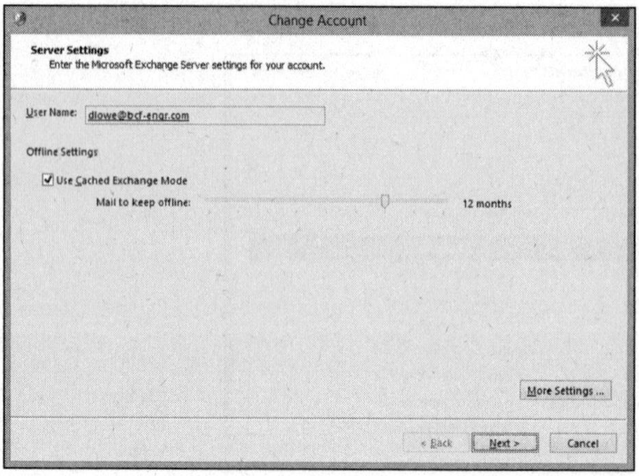

FIGURE 8-19:
The Server
Settings
dialog box.

3. **Click the More Settings button to open the Microsoft Exchange dialog box and then click the Advanced tab.**

   The Advanced tab is shown in Figure 8-20.

4. **Click the Add button.**

   A dialog box appears, prompting you for the name of the mailbox you want to add.

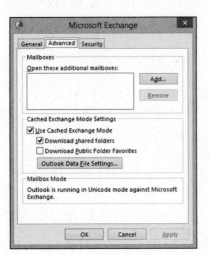

FIGURE 8-20:
The Advanced tab.

5. **Type the name of the mailbox you want to add and then click OK.**

   The mailbox is added to the list box in the Microsoft Exchange dialog box (refer to Figure 8-20).

6. **Click OK.**

   You're returned to the Server Settings dialog box.

7. **Click Next and then click Finish.**

   You're done! Now you can view the Support mailbox.

TIP

To view the mailbox, you need to open the Folder List window in Outlook (by choosing View⇨Folder List). Then you can double-click the Support mailbox in the list to open it.

Chapter **9**

Configuring SQL Server 2014

S QL Server 2014 is the latest and greatest version of the most common database server used on Microsoft networks.

This chapter introduces you to the basics of installing and running SQL Server 2014. It begins with a basic introduction to relational databases and SQL. Then it shows you how to manage a SQL Server database by using SQL Server 2014 Management Studio.

Note: The information in this chapter applies to previous versions of SQL Server as well.

What Is a Database?

A *database* is simply an organized collection of information. Here are some examples of databases from everyday life:

>> Your personal address book

>> The shoebox that contains your tax records for the year

- » Your baseball card collection

- » All those parking tickets conveniently stuffed into your car's glove compartment

- » The phone book (well, from everyday life in the good ol' days anyway)

- » That pile of score cards that has been accumulating in the bottom of your golf bag for 15 years

You can think of each of these databases as a collection of records. In database lingo, a *record* consists of all the useful information that you can gather about a particular thing. In your address book, each record represents one of your friends (or enemies). For your tax records database, each receipt in the shoebox is a record.

Each snippet of information that makes up a record is called a *field*. Using the address book as an example once again, each person's record (that is, each entry in your address book) consists of several fields: name; street address; city; state; zip code; phone number; email address; and other information that may be optional, such as the person's birthday, whether you sent a Christmas card to the person last year, or how much money the person owes you.

SQL Server is designed to create and manage computerized databases that are similar to these noncomputerized databases. Like your address book or shoebox full of tax records, a SQL Server database is a collection of records, and each record is a collection of fields. The biggest difference is that in a SQL Server database, the information is stored on a server computer's hard drive rather than in a shoebox.

What Is a Relational Database?

SQL Server is a database management server that creates and maintains relational databases. Unfortunately, the term *relational database* is one of the most used and abused buzzwords in the computer business. The term has at least three meanings. A *relational database* can be

- » **A database in which data is stored in tables:** In a relational database, groups of similar records are called *tables*. A database usually consists of more than one table; in fact, it isn't uncommon for a single database to have dozens of tables. You can establish relationships between and among these tables based on common information. A sales database, for example, might contain a table of customer information and a table of invoices, with both tables containing a customer-number column that establishes a relationship between the tables.

>> **A database model based on a Coneheads branch of mathematics called Set Theory:** This is actually the most technically precise definition of a relational database, but only computer geeks know or care. Contrary to popular belief, the term *relational database* is derived not from the ability to create relationships among tables, but from the term *relation,* a mathematical term that refers to the way data is arranged into tables of rows and columns.

(It's a little-known fact that relational-database theory was developed at around the same time that the Coneheads from the planet Remulak first visited Earth, back in the 1970s. I've always suspected that these two developments are — dare I say it? — related.)

>> **A database that's accessed via SQL:** *SQL,* which stands for *Structured Query Language,* provides a practical way to access data stored in relational tables. A database that's based on SQL is inherently relational because SQL stores its data in tables and is based on Set Theory. SQL Server, as its name implies, is based on SQL.

From a practical point of view, the third definition is the most important: A relational database is a database that you can access via SQL. Thus, SQL Server is used for relational databases. The next section dives a little more deeply into what SQL is.

What Is SQL?

SQL, which stands for *Structured Query Language,* is a language designed to extract, organize, and update information in relational databases. Originally, SQL was envisioned as an English-like query language that untrained end-users could use to access and update relational database data. In reality, SQL is nothing like English, and it's far too complicated and esoteric for untrained users, but it has become the overwhelming favorite among programmers who develop applications that access relational databases.

SQL dialects

Like most computer languages, SQL has several dialects. In fact, each major brand of SQL database server has its own dialect of SQL. These dialects are 95 percent the same, so a basic SQL statement is likely to work the same way regardless of the database server you use it with. But the ways that the more advanced features of SQL work have many variations.

The version of SQL used by Microsoft's SQL Server is known as *T-SQL.*

HOW DO YOU PRONOUNCE SQL?

Here's something you've probably wondered ever since you first saw the letters *SQL*: How do you pronounce it? Two schools of thought exist on the subject:

- Spell out the letters: *S-Q-L.*

- Pronounce it like the word *sequel.*

Either way is acceptable, but *sequel* is hipper.

You can always tell how a writer pronounces *SQL* by checking to see whether the author writes "a SQL query" or "an SQL query."

You can impress even the staunchest SQL expert by pointing out that originally, the language was called SEQUEL by the IBM engineers who created the first version way back in the 1970s. *SEQUEL* stood for *Structured English Query Language.* Someone must have correctly pointed out that aside from borrowing a few words from English, such as `select` and `create`, SEQUEL actually bore no resemblance whatsoever to English. So *English* was dropped from the name, and the acronym was shortened from SEQUEL to SQL.

SQL statements

Like other programming languages, SQL uses statements to get its work done. Table 9-1 lists the most commonly used statements.

TABLE 9-1 **Common SQL Statements**

SQL Statement	What It Does
Use	Identifies the name of the database that subsequent SQL statements apply to.
select	Retrieves data from one or more tables. This is the SQL statement that's used the most.
Insert	Inserts one or more rows into a table.
delete	Deletes one or more rows from a table.
update	Updates existing rows in a table.
create	Creates tables and other database objects.
alter	Alters the definition of a table or other database object.
drop	Deletes a table or other database object.

Using the select statement

As the name *Structured Query Language* suggests, queries are what SQL is all about. Thus, the select statement is the most important of the SQL statements. A select statement extracts data from one or more tables in a database and creates a *result set* containing the selected rows and columns.

In a select statement, you list the table or tables from which you want to retrieve the data; the specific columns you want to retrieve (you may not be interested in everything that's in the table); and other clauses that indicate which specific rows should be retrieved, what order the rows should be presented in, and so on.

Here's a simple select statement that retrieves data from a table named movie, which contains information about your favorite movies:

```
select title, year
from movie
order by year
```

Now take this statement apart piece by piece:

» select title, year names the columns you want included in the query result (title and year).

» from movie names the table you want the rows retrieved from (movie).

» order by year indicates that the result should be sorted in sequence by the year column so that the oldest movie appears first.

In other words, this select statement retrieves the title and date for all the rows in the movie table and sorts them into year sequence.

If you want the query to retrieve all the columns in each row, you can use an asterisk instead of naming the individual columns:

```
select * from movie order by year;
```

Both examples so far include an order by clause. In a SQL database, the rows stored in a table are not assumed to be in any particular sequence. As a result, if you want to display the results of a query in sequence, you must include an order by clause in the select statement.

Suppose that you want to find information about one particular video title. To select certain rows from a table, use the where clause in a select statement:

```
select title, year from movie
where year <= 1980
order by year
```

Here, the select statement selects all rows in which the year column is less than or equal to 1980. The results are ordered by the year column.

Perhaps you want to retrieve all rows except those that match certain criteria. Here's a query that ignores movies made in the 1970s (which is probably a good idea, with exceptions like *The Godfather* and *Young Frankenstein*):

```
select title, year from movie
where year < 1970 or year > 1979
order by year;
```

You can do much more with select statements, of course. But this chapter isn't about SQL itself; it's about installing and using SQL Server. So get ready to move on to the good stuff.

Using SQL Server 2014 Management Studio

SQL Server Management Studio is a component of SQL Server 2014 that runs on workstation computers and lets you manage any or all of the SQL Server instances on your network. You run it by choosing Start⇨ SQL Server Management Studio on any computer on which you have installed the Management Studio. SQL Server Management Studio begins by displaying a Connect to Server dialog box, as shown in Figure 9-1. You can use this dialog box to connect to any SQL Server instance on your network.

FIGURE 9-1:
Connecting to a SQL Server instance.

To connect to a SQL Server instance, specify the instance name and your logon credentials, and then click Connect. After you've connected, SQL Server Management Studio displays the screen shown in Figure 9-2.

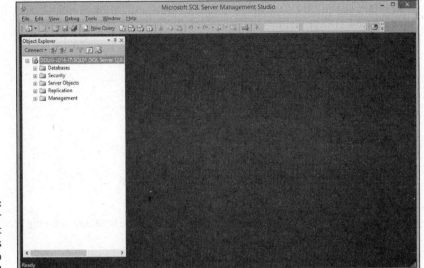

FIGURE 9-2:
SQL Server
Management
Studio has
connected to
an instance!

The following sections explain how to perform some of the most common SQL Server chores: creating databases and tables, viewing database data, and so on.

Creating a New Database

To create a new database, follow these steps:

1. **Right-click the Databases node in the Navigation pane (on the left side of SQL Server Management Studio window), and choose New Database from the contextual menu that appears.**

   This brings up the New Database dialog box, shown in Figure 9-3.

2. **Type a name for the new database in the Database Name field.**

3. **In the Owner field, enter the domain username of the user who is responsible for the database.**

   You can leave this field set to the default if you want to be listed as the owner.

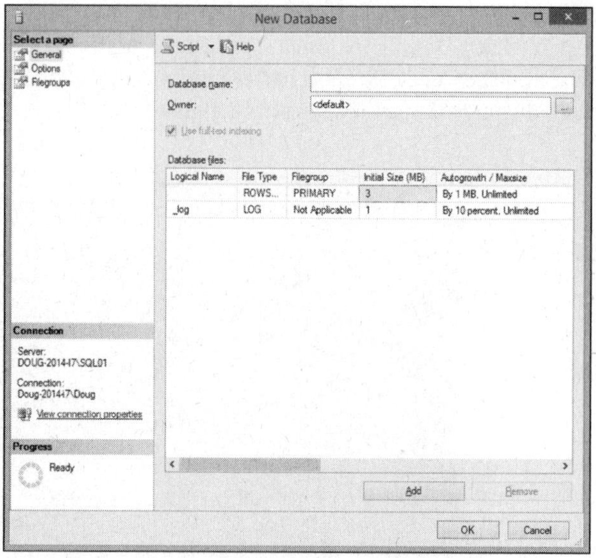

FIGURE 9-3:
Creating a new
database.

4. **If you want, change the settings for the database and log files.**

You can change the following settings:

- *Initial Size:* This setting refers to the amount of disk space initially allocated to the files. The defaults are a ridiculously small 3MB for the database and 1MB for the log files. Unless your databases are going to be extremely small, you probably should increase these defaults.

- *Autogrowth:* This setting sets the incremental amount by which the database grows when it exceeds the allocated capacity. Again, you'll probably want to change these amounts for any but the smallest databases.

- *Path:* This setting points the way to the folder where the files are stored. By default, the files are created under the Program Files folder on the server's C: drive. You may want to change this setting to a more appropriate location. (You'll have to scroll the database files section of the New Database dialog box to the right to see this setting.)

- *File Name:* You can change this setting if you want to use a filename that's different from the database name. (You'll have to scroll the database files section of the New Database dialog box to the right to see this setting.)

Note that you can change additional options by clicking Options or Filegroups in the top-left corner of the New Database dialog box. These pages link to additional pages of options you can set to tweak the behavior of the database.

5. **Click OK.**

SQL Server grinds and whirs for a few moments while it creates the new database. When it's finished, the database appears below the Databases node, as shown in Figure 9-4.

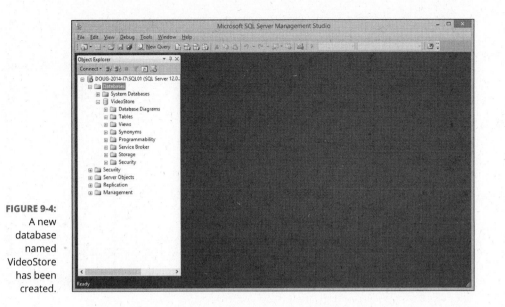

FIGURE 9-4:
A new
database
named
VideoStore
has been
created.

The new database is ready to use. It won't be very useful until you define some tables, of course, so read on.

Creating Tables

A database is nothing more than a container for various types of database objects. The most important of these objects are *tables*, which hold the actual data that makes up the database. A database isn't very useful without at least one table. Most real–world databases have more than one table; in fact, many databases have dozens of tables.

To create a table, follow these steps:

1. **Right-click the Tables node for the database, and choose Table from the contextual menu.**

   The window shown in Figure 9-5 appears.

2. **Type the name of the first column of the table and then press the Tab key.**

3. **Choose the data type for the column and then press the Tab key.**

   SQL Server has several data types to choose among for each column. Use the drop-down list to choose the appropriate type.

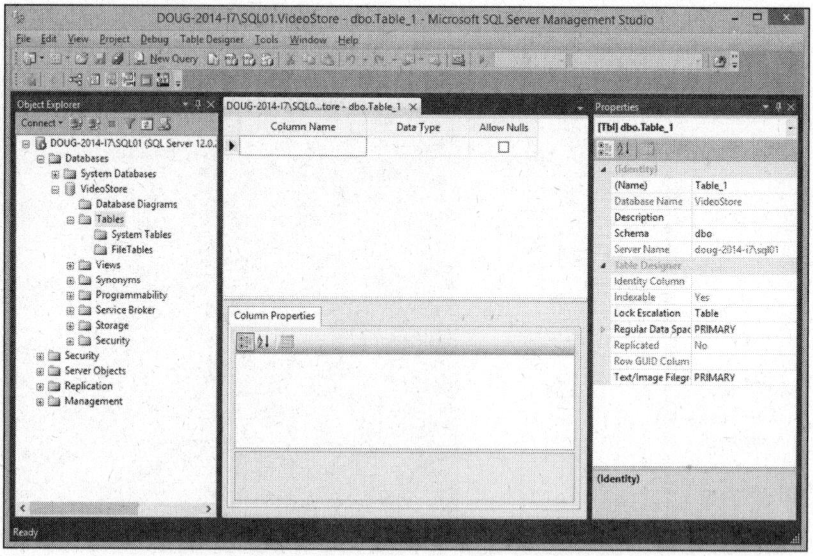

DOUG-2014-I7\SQL01.VideoStore - dbo.Table_1 - Microsoft SQL Server Management Studio

FIGURE 9-5:
Creating a
new table.

4. Use the Allow Nulls check box to indicate whether the column should allow null values; then press the Tab key.

Nulls are among the most confusing aspects of database design and programming. In a SQL database, *null* means that the item doesn't have a value. It's different from zero (for numbers) or an empty string (for text). Allowing a column to have null values introduces programming complexities, because when you retrieve the value of a column, the program has to anticipate that the value may be missing. But prohibiting nulls (by deselecting the check box) also introduces complexities, because you have to make sure that you provide an explicit value for every column.

TECHNICAL STUFF

The phrase *null value* is actually an oxymoron. Because *null* means the absence of a value, it doesn't make sense to say that a column can have a null value or that the value of a column is null.

5. Repeat Steps 2 through 4 to create additional columns.

Figure 9-6 shows how the table looks after several columns have been defined.

6. When all the columns have been created, select the column you want to use as a key field for the table, right-click the column, and choose Set Primary Key from the contextual menu.

A little key icon appears next to that column to indicate that it's the primary key.

(The *primary key* provides a unique value that can be used to identify each row in the table. Most tables use a single column, such as Customer Number or Invoice Number, as the primary key. But some tables create the primary key by combining two or more columns. This type of key is called a *composite key.*)

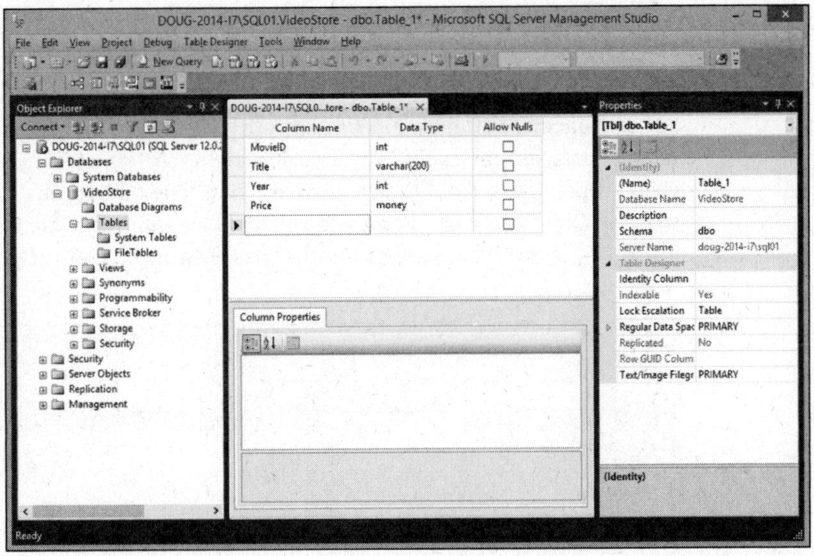

Configuring SQL
Server 2014

FIGURE 9-6:
A table with
several columns.

7. **Right-click the table-name tab that appears above the list of columns, and choose Save from the contextual menu.**

   A Save dialog box appears, prompting you to enter a name for the table.

8. **Type a name for the table and then click OK.**

   The table is created. You're done!

Note that each column has a properties page that appears when you select the column. You can set a variety of properties for each column, including the following:

>> **Default Value:** A value that's supplied for the column if no value is provided when a row is created. This property is especially useful for columns that don't allow null values.

>> **Description:** A text description that you can use to explain the purpose of the column.

>> **Identity Specification:** Used to create an *identity field,* which is a field whose value is generated automatically when rows are created. Often, an identity field is used as the primary key field for a table when it's desirable for the table to have a primary key, but no other column in the table provides a unique value for each row.

   When you create an identity field, you can specify two settings that affect how the values are generated: the seed and the increment. The *seed* is the value used for the first row in the table. The *increment* is a value that's added to the seed for each subsequent row. If you specify 1000 for the seed and 1 for the increment, the rows in the table will be numbered 1001, 1002, 1003, and so on.

Editing Tables

SQL Management Studio includes a spreadsheetlike feature that lets you edit the contents of database tables directly. To use it, right-click the table you want to edit, and choose Open Table from the contextual menu. The table opens in a spreadsheetlike window. Then you can add data to the table by entering table values for each row. Figure 9-7 shows a table after some data has been added via the Open Table command.

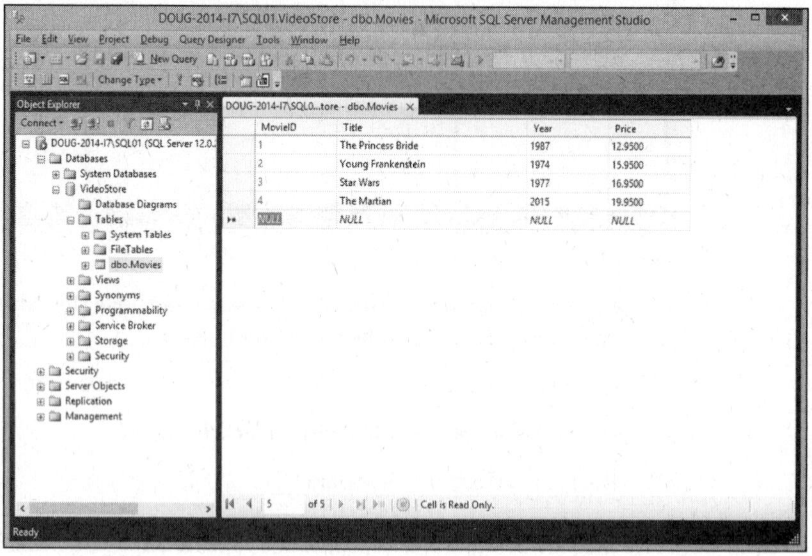

FIGURE 9-7:
A table with several rows added via the Open Table command.

Note that in addition to inserting new rows, you can edit existing rows. You can also delete one or more rows by selecting the rows you want to delete and pressing the Delete key.

Working with Queries

SQL Management Studio includes a query tool that lets you type SQL commands and execute them. You can type any SQL statement you want in a query window and then click the Execute button to execute the query.

There are two important rules to follow when you work with queries:

» Each SQL statement in the query should end with a semicolon.

» You must begin the query with a use statement that provides the name of the database.

Here's an example of a query that follows these two rules:

```
use VideoStore;
select * from movies;
```

The use statement indicates that the query applies to the VideoStore database, and the select statement retrieves all the data from the movies table.

To use the query tool, click the New Query button on the toolbar. Then enter the statements for your query in the window, and click the Execute button on the toolbar. The results of the query are displayed in the window, as shown in Figure 9-8.

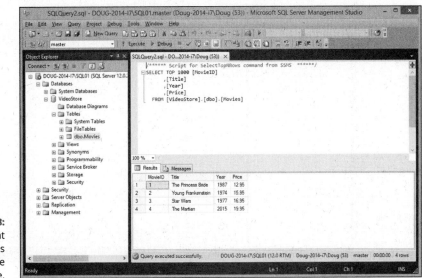

FIGURE 9-8:
A query that retrieves data from the Movies table.

Working with Scripts

One final feature of SQL Management Studio I want to cover in this chapter is the use of scripts. Although you can create databases by using the graphical features presented earlier in this chapter (in the sections "Creating a New Database" and "Creating Tables"), it's actually much better practice to write SQL scripts that contain the CREATE commands necessary to create the database, as well as its tables and other objects. That's because during the development and operation of any database application, you often need to delete the database and re-create it from scratch. By scripting these actions, you can delete the database and re-create it simply by running a script.

Fortunately, SQL Management Studio can generate scripts from existing databases and tables. Thus, you can use the visual design features of SQL Management Studio to create your databases initially; then you can generate scripts that let you delete and re-re-create the database easily.

To create a script for a database or table, just right-click the database or table and choose one of the Script As commands from the contextual menu. Figure 9-9 shows the script that results when I right-click the movies table and choose Script Table As⇨CREATE To⇨New Query Window. As you can see, this command generated a CREATE TABLE statement along with other advanced SQL statements to create the Movies table automatically.

FIGURE 9-9:
A script that creates the Movies table.

After you've created the script, you can save it to a text file by clicking the Save button. Then you can run the script at any time by following these steps:

1. **Choose File ⇨ Open ⇨ File.**

2. **Select the file you saved the script to.**

3. **Click Open.**

4. **Click the Execute button to run the script.**

The only limitation of this technique is that although you can generate scripts to define your databases and tables, you can't automatically generate scripts to insert data into your tables. If you want scripts that insert data, you have to manually create the INSERT statements to insert the data.

Chapter **10**

Windows Commands

Although Windows sports a fancy graphical interface that makes it possible to perform most network management tasks by pointing and clicking, you can also do almost any network management task from a command prompt. Whether you choose to do so is largely a matter of personal style. Some network administrators pride themselves on being able to type Windows commands blindfolded and with two fingers on each hand tied behind their backs. Others have fully embraced the graphical user interface and think the command line is for administrators with Unix envy.

So the choice is yours. Skip this chapter if the thought of typing commands causes you to lose sleep. If you're willing to venture forth, this chapter begins with an overview of working from the command prompt. Then it describes some of the more useful Windows commands. Finally, this chapter introduces the fine (and almost lost) art of writing batch files.

TIP

Windows Server 2016 also includes an alternative command environment known as PowerShell. *PowerShell* is an advanced command processor that has many sophisticated features that are designed especially for creating powerful scripts. For more information, see Chapter 11 of this minibook.

Using a Command Window

Command prompts are even older than video monitors. The first computer I worked on used a teletype machine as its terminal, so the command prompt was printed on paper rather than displayed onscreen. Surprisingly, though, the concept of the command prompt hasn't changed much since those days. The system displays a prompt to let you know it's waiting for a command. When you type the command and press the Enter key, the system reads your command, interprets it, executes it, displays the results, and then displays the prompt again so that you can enter another command.

Opening and closing a command window

To get to a command prompt on a Windows server, follow these steps:

1. **Press the Windows key on your keyboard, and then type** cmd.

2. **Press the Enter key.**

   The command prompt window appears, as shown in Figure 10-1.

FIGURE 10-1:
The command prompt.

You can type any commands you want in the window.

TIP

To exit the command prompt, type **Exit**, and press Enter. This action properly terminates cmd.exe and closes the command prompt window. If you try to close the command prompt window by clicking its Close button, Windows is forced to shut down cmd.exe. The process works, but you have to click your way through an intervening dialog box and wait a few seconds while Windows terminates cmd.exe. Entering the Exit command is a much faster method.

Editing commands

Most of the time, you just type commands by using the keyboard. If you make a mistake, you just retype the command, being careful not to repeat the mistake. cmd.exe, however, has several built-in editing features that can simplify the task of correcting a mistaken command or entering a sequence of similar commands:

>> Press the right-arrow key to recall the text of the last command that you entered, one letter at a time. When you get to the spot where the new command should differ from the previous command, start typing.

>> Press F3 to recall all the previous commands from the current cursor position to the end of the line.

>> If you want to repeat a command that you've used recently, press the up-arrow key. This action recalls up to 50 of the most recently executed commands. You can press Enter to execute a command as is, or you can edit the command before you execute it.

Using the Control menu

Although the command window has no menu bar, it does have a menu that you can access via the control box in the top-left corner of the window. Besides the commands found on this menu for all windows (such as Move, Size, and Minimize), this menu includes three additional commands:

>> **Edit:** The Edit command leads to a submenu with several choices. Several of these commands work together so that you can copy information from the command window to the Clipboard, and vice versa. If you choose Edit⇨Mark, you're placed in a special editing mode that lets you highlight text in the command window with the mouse. (Normally, the mouse doesn't do anything in the command window.) Then you can choose Edit⇨Copy or just press Enter to copy the text that you selected to the Clipboard.

You can also use the Edit menu to paste text from the Clipboard, to scroll the window, and to search the window for text.

>> **Default:** This command lets you set default properties for the command window.

>> **Properties:** This command displays a Properties dialog box that you can use to change the appearance of the window. You can change the font size, choose background colors, and make other adjustments to make the command window look good on your computer.

Special Command Tricks

Before I get into the details of using specific commands, I want to describe some techniques you should familiarize yourself with. In many cases, these techniques can let you accomplish in a single command what would otherwise take dozens of separate commands.

Wildcards

Wildcards are among the most compelling reasons to use the command prompt. With wildcards, you can process all the files that match a particular naming pattern with a single command. Suppose that you have a folder containing 500 files, and you want to delete all the files that contain the letters *Y2K* and end with the extension .doc, which happens to be 50 files. If you open a Documents window, you'll spend ten minutes picking these files out from the list. From a command window, you can delete them all with the single command del *Y2K*.doc.

You can use two wildcard characters. An asterisk stands for any number of characters, including zero, and an exclamation point stands for just one character. Thus, !Text.doc would match files with names like aText.doc, xText.doc, and 4Text.doc, but not abcText.doc or just Text.doc. *Text.doc, however, would match any of the names mentioned in the previous sentence.

Wildcards work differently in Windows than they did in MS-DOS. In MS-DOS, anything you typed after an asterisk was ignored. Thus, ab*cd.doc was the same as ab*.doc. In Windows, the asterisk wildcard can come before static text, so ab*cd.doc and ab*.doc are *not* the same.

Chaining commands

You can enter two or more commands on the same line by separating the commands with an ampersand (&), like this:

```
C:\>copy *.doc a: & del *.doc
```

Here, the copy command copies all the .doc files to the A: drive. Then, the del command deletes the .doc files.

Although that technique may be convenient, it's also dangerous. What if the A: drive fills up so that all the files can't be copied? In that case, the del command executes anyway, deleting the files that didn't get copied.

A safer alternative is to use two ampersands, telling Windows to execute the second command only if the first command finishes successfully:

```
C:\>copy *.doc a: && del *.doc
```

Now the del command will be executed only if the copy command succeeds.

You can also use two pipe characters (the *pipe* is the vertical bar character that's above the backslash on the keyboard) to execute the second command only if the first command fails. Thus,

```
C:\>copy *.doc a: || echo Oops!
```

displays the message Oops! if the copy command fails.

Finally, you can use parentheses to group commands. Then you can use the other symbols in combination:

```
C:\>(copy *.doc a: && del *.doc) || echo Oops!
```

Here, the files are copied and then deleted if the copy was successful. If either command fails, the message is displayed.

Redirection and piping

Redirection and piping are related techniques. *Redirection* lets you specify an alternative destination for output that will be displayed by a command or an alternative source for input that should be fed into a command. You can save the results of an ipconfig /all command to a file named myconfig.txt like this:

```
C:\>ipconfig /all > myconfig.txt
```

Here, the greater-than sign (>) is used to redirect the command's console output.

If a command accepts input from the keyboard, you can use input redirection to specify a file that contains the input you want to feed to the command. You can create a text file named lookup.txt with subcommands for a command such as nslookup. Then you can feed those scripted subcommands to the nslookup command, like this:

```
C:\>nslookup < lookup.txt
```

Piping is a similar technique. It takes the console output from one command and feeds it into the next command as input. Piping is often used with special commands called *filters*, which are designed to read input from the console, modify the data in some way, and then write it to the console.

Suppose that you want to display the contents of a file named `users.txt` sorted into alphabetical order. You can use the `Type` command, which displays a file on the console, and then pipe the output into the `Sort` command, a filter that sorts its input and displays the sorted output on the console. The resulting command looks like this:

```
C:\>type users.txt | sort
```

The vertical bar is often called the *pipe character* because it's the symbol used to indicate piping.

Environment variables

The command shell makes several *environment variables* available to commands. Environment variables all begin and end with percent signs. You can use an environment variable anywhere in a command. The command

```
C:\>echo %OS% running on a %PROCESSOR_IDENTIFIER%
```

displays a line such as this:

```
Windows_NT running on an x86 Family 15 Model 2 Stepping 8, GenuineIntel
```

Interestingly, later versions of Windows Server all display `Windows_NT` for the operating-system name.

If the environment variable represents a path, you may need to enclose it in quotation marks, like this:

```
C:\>dir "%HOMEPATH%"
```

This command displays the contents of the user's home directory. The quotation marks are required here because the environment variable expands to a pathname that may include spaces, and the command shell requires that long filenames that include spaces be enclosed in quotation marks.

Table 10-1 lists the environment variables that are available to you and your commands.

TABLE 10-1 **Environment Variables**

Variable	Description
%ALLUSERSPROFILE%	The location of the All Users profile
%APPDATA%	The path where applications store data by default
%CD%	The path to the current directory
%CMDCMDLINE%	The command line that was used to start the command shell
%CMDEXTVERSION%	The version number of the command shell
%COMPUTERNAME%	The computer's name
%COMSPEC%	The path to the command shell executable (cmd.exe)
%DATE%	The current date in the format generated by the date /t command
%ERRORLEVEL%	The error returned by the most recent command
%HOMEDRIVE%	The drive letter of the user's home directory
%HOMEPATH%	The path to the user's home directory
%HOMESHARE%	The network path to the user's shared home directory
%LOGONSERVER%	The name of the domain controller the user logged on to
%NUMBER_OF_PROCESSORS%	The number of processors on the computer
%OS%	The name of the operating system
%PATH%	The current search path
%PATHEXT%	A list of the extensions the operating system treats as executable files
%PROCESSOR_ARCHITECTURE%	The chip architecture of the processor
%PROCESSOR_IDENTIFIER%	A description of the processor
%PROCESSOR_REVISION%	The revision level of the processor
%PROMPT%	The current prompt string
%RANDOM%	A random number between 1 and 32,767
%SYSTEMDRIVE%	The drive containing the operating system
%SYSTEMROOT%	The path to the operating system
%TEMP%	The path to a temporary folder for temporary files
%TMP%	Same as %TEMP%

(continued)

TABLE 10-1 *(continued)*

Variable	Description
%TIME%	The time in the format produced by the `time /t` command
%USERDOMAIN%	The name of the user's domain
%USERNAME%	The user's account name
%USERPROFILE%	The path to the user's profile
%WINDIR%	The path to the operating-system directory

Batch files

A *batch file* is simply a text file that contains one or more commands. Batch files are given the extension .bat and can be run from a command prompt as though they were commands or programs. You can also run a batch file from the Start menu by choosing Start⇨Run, typing the name of the batch file, and clicking OK.

As a network administrator, you'll find plenty of uses for batch files. Most of them won't be very complicated. Here are some examples of very simple batch files I've used:

» I once used a one-line file to copy the entire contents of an important shared network drive to a user's computer every night at 10 p.m. The user wanted a quick-and-dirty backup solution that would complement the regular tape backups that ran every night.

» I've also used a pair of short batch files to stop and then restart an Exchange server before and after nightly backups.

» If I frequently need to work with several related folders at the same time, I create a short batch file that opens Explorer windows for each of the folders. (You can open an Explorer window from a batch file simply by typing the path to the folder that you want to open as a command.) Then I place the batch file on my desktop so that I can get to it quickly.

You can also use batch files to create logon scripts that are executed whenever a user logs on. Microsoft keeps trying to get users to use profiles instead of logon scripts, but many networks still use logon scripts.

The EventCreate Command

The `EventCreate` command lets you create an event that's added to one of the Windows event logs. This command can be useful if you want to make a note of something unusual that's happened. It's often used in batch files to mark the start or completion of a task such as a nightly backup.

Here's the basic syntax:

```
eventcreate [options]
eventcreate /T type /D "description" /ID eventide
[/L logname] [/SO sourcename]
[/S system [/U username [/P password]]]
```

Here's a description of the options:

- » **/T:** Specifies the type. The options are Information, Warning, and Error.
- » **/D:** Provides a descriptive message that's saved in the log. Use quotes if the message contains more than one word.
- » **/ID:** A number from 1 to 1,000.
- » **/L:** The name of the log to write the event to. The default is Application.
- » **/SO:** A string that represents the source of the event. The default is EventCreate. If you specify this option, you must also specify the /L option.
- » **/S:** The name of the system on which the event should be recorded.
- » **/U:** The user account to use when logging the event. You can specify this option only if you also specify /S.
- » **/P:** The password. You can specify this option only if you also specify /U.

Here's an example that writes an informational message to the Application log:

```
eventcreate /t information /id 100 /d "Nightly processing completed"
   /L Application /SO Nightly
```

Figure 10-2 shows an event created by the preceding command.

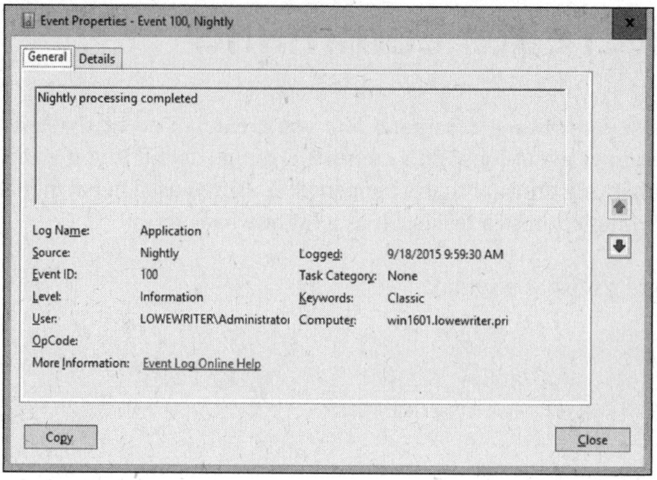

FIGURE 10-2:
An event generated by the EventCreate command.

Net Commands

Among the most useful commands for network administrators are the Net Services commands. All these commands are two-word commands beginning with Net — such as Net Use and Net Start. In the following sections, I present the Net commands in alphabetical order for handy reference. First, though, I want to point out a few details about the Net commands:

» You can get a quick list of the available Net commands by typing **net /?** at a command prompt.

» You can get brief help for any Net command by typing **net help *command***. To display help for the Net Use command, for example, type **net help use**. (Yes, we all could use some help.)

» Many of the Net commands prompt you for confirmation before completing an operation. For these commands, you can specify /Y or /N to bypass the confirmation prompt. You'll want to do that if you include these commands in a batch file that runs unattended. Note that you can use /Y or /N on any Net command, even if it doesn't prompt you for confirmation. So I suggest that you place /Y on every Net command in a batch file that you intend to run unattended.

The Net Accounts command

This command updates user account policies for password requirements. Here's the command syntax:

```
net accounts [/forcelogoff:{minutes | no}]
[/minpwlen:length] [/maxpwage:{days | unlimited}]
[/minpwage:days] [/uniquepw:number]
[/domain]
```

The following paragraphs describe the parameters for the Net Accounts command:

>> **forcelogoff:** Specifies how long to wait before forcing a user off the system when the user's logon time expires. The default value, no, prevents users from being forced to log off. If you specify a number, the user will be warned a few minutes before being forcibly logged off.

>> **minpwlen:** Specifies the minimum length for the user's password. *Length* can be 0 through 127. The default is 6.

>> **maxpwage:** Specifies the number of days a user's password is considered to be valid. Unlimited means that the password will never expire. *Days* can be from 1 through 49,710, which is about 135 years. The default is 90.

>> **minpwage:** Specifies the minimum number of days after a user changes a password before the user can change it again. The default value is 0. You usually should set this value to 1 day to prevent users from bypassing the Uniquepw policy.

>> **uniquepw:** Indicates how many different passwords the user must use before he or she is allowed to reuse the same password. The default setting is 5. The range is 0 through 24.

>> **domain:** Specifies that the operation should be performed on the primary domain controller rather than on the local computer.

If you enter Net Accounts without any parameters, the command simply displays the current policy settings.

Here's an example that sets the minimum and maximum password ages:

```
C:\>net accounts /minpwage:7 /maxpwage:30
```

The Net Computer command

This command creates or deletes a computer account. Here's the syntax:

```
net computer \\computername {/add | /del}
```

The following paragraphs describe the parameters for the Net Computer command:

>> **Computername:** Specifies the computer to add or delete

>> **add:** Creates a computer account for the specified computer

>> **del:** Deletes the specified computer account

Here's an example that adds a computer named Theodore:

```
C:\>net computer \\theodore /add
```

The Net Config command

This command lets you view or configure various network services. Here's the syntax:

```
net config [{server|workstation}] [options]
```

To configure server settings, use this syntax:

```
net config server [/autodisconnect:time] [/srvcomment:"text"] [/hidden:{yes
   | no}]
```

The following paragraphs describe the parameters for the Net Config command:

>> **server:** Lets you display and configure the Server service while it's running.

>> **workstation:** Lets you display and configure the workstation service while it's running.

>> **autodisconnect:** Specifies how long a user's session can be inactive before it's disconnected. Specify –1 to never disconnect. The range is –1 to 65,535 minutes, which is about 45 days. The default is 15 minutes.

>> **srvcomment:** Specifies a description of the server. The comment can be up to 48 characters long and should be enclosed in quotation marks.

>> **hidden:** Specifies whether the server appears in screens that display available servers. Hiding a server doesn't make the server unavailable; it just means that the user will have to know the name of the server to access it. The default is No.

Here's an example that sets a server's descriptive comment:

```
C:\>net config server /srvcomment:"DHCP Server"
```

The Net Continue command

This command continues a service you've suspended with the net pause command. Here's the syntax:

```
net continue service
```

Here are some typical services that you can pause and continue:

- **netlogon:** The Net Logon service.
- **schedule:** The Task Scheduler service.
- **server:** The Server service.
- **workstation:** The Workstation service.

Here's an example that continues the Workstation service:

```
C:\>net continue workstation
```

If the service name has embedded spaces, enclose the service name in quotation marks. This command continues the NT LM Security Support Provider service:

```
C:\>net continue "nt lm security support provider"
```

The Net File command

This command lists all open shared files and the number of file locks placed on each file. You can also use this command to close files and remove locks, which is a useful procedure when a user manages to accidentally leave a file open or locked. Here's the syntax:

```
C:\>net file [id [/close]]
```

The following paragraphs describe the Net File command's parameters:

- **id:** The file's identification number.
- **close:** Closes an open file and releases any locks that were placed on the file.

To close a file, you must issue the command from the server where the file is shared.

`net files` works, too.

To close an open file, first run `net file` without any parameters to list the open files. Here's a sample of the output that you can expect from `net file`:

```
File Path Username #locks
---------------------------------------------
0 C:\BUDGET.DOC WARD 0
1 C:\RECIPE.MDF JUNE 4
```

Next, run `net file` again, specifying the file number displayed for the file that you want to close. To close the `RECIPE.MDF` file, for example, use this command:

```
C:\>net file 1 /close
```

The Net Group command

This command lets you add, display, or change global groups. This command has several different syntaxes, depending on how you intend to use it.

To display information about a group or to change a group's comment, use this syntax:

```
net group groupname [/comment:"text"] [/domain]
```

To create a new group, use this syntax:

```
net group groupname /add [/comment:"text"] [/domain]
```

To delete a group, use this syntax:

```
net group groupname /delete [/domain]
```

Finally, to add or remove users from a group, use this syntax:

```
net group groupname username[ ...] {/add | /delete} [/domain]
```

The following paragraphs describe the parameters that you can use with the `net group` command:

» *groupname:* Specifies the name of the group to add, change, or delete. If you specify this parameter and no others, a list of users in the group appears.

» `comment:` Specifies a comment for the group. The comment can be up to 48 characters in length and should be enclosed in quotation marks.

» `domain:` Specifies that the operation should be performed on the primary domain controller rather than on the local computer.

» `add:` Creates a new group or adds users to an existing group. Before you add a user to a group, you must create a user account for the user.

» `delete:` Removes a group or removes users from the group.

» *username:* Specifies one or more usernames to be added to or removed from the group. If you list more than one name, separate the names with spaces.

TIP

Windows isn't picky: You can specify `net groups` rather than `net group` if you want.

This example lists all the groups on a server:

```
C:\>net group
```

This example adds a group named Admin:

```
C:\>net group Admin /add
```

This example adds three users to the Admin group:

```
C:\>net group Admin Ward Wally June /add
```

This example lists the users in the Admin group:

```
C:\>net group Admin
```

The Net Help command

This command displays help for the `net` command or for a specific `net` subcommand. Here's the basic syntax:

```
net help [command]
```

The *command* parameter can be any of the following commands:

accounts	helpmsg	stop
computer	localgroup	time
config	pause	use
continue	session	user
file	share	view
group	start	
help	statistics	

TIP

You can type **net help services** to display a list of services that you can start via the Net Start command.

The Net Helpmsg command

This command displays an explanation of network error codes. Here's the syntax:

```
net helpmsg message#
```

The *message#* parameter should be the four-digit number displayed when the error occurred. If you get an error with message 2180, for example, use this command to see an explanation of the error:

```
C:\>net helpmsg 2180
The service database is locked.
EXPLANATION
Another program is holding the service database lock.
ACTION
Wait for the lock to be released and try again later. If it is possible to
    determine which program is holding the lock, then end that program.
```

The Net Localgroup command

This command lets you add, display, or change local groups. This command has several different syntaxes, depending on how you intend to use it.

To display information about a local group or to change a local group's comment, use this syntax:

```
net localgroup groupname [/comment:"text"] [/domain]
```

To create a new group, use this syntax:

```
net localgroup groupname /add [/comment:"text"] [/domain]
```

To delete a group, use this syntax:

```
net localgroup groupname /delete [/domain]
```

Finally, to add users to or remove users from a group, use this syntax:

```
net localgroup groupname username[ ...] {/add | /delete} [/domain]
```

The following paragraphs describe the parameters that you can use with the net localgroup command:

>> *groupname:* Specifies the name of the group to add, change, or delete. If you specify this parameter and no others, a list of users in the group appears.

>> **comment:** Specifies a comment for the group. The comment can be up to 48 characters in length and should be enclosed in quotation marks.

>> **domain:** Specifies that the operation should be performed on the primary domain controller rather than on the local computer.

>> **add:** Creates a new group or adds users to an existing group. Before you add a user to a group, you must create a user account for the user.

>> **delete:** Removes a group or removes users from the group.

>> *username:* Specifies one or more usernames to be added to or removed from the group. If you list more than one name, separate the names with spaces.

This example lists all the local groups:

```
C:\>net localgroup
```

This example adds a local group named Admin:

```
C:\>net localgroup Admin /add
```

This example adds three users to the Admin local group:

```
C:\>net localgroup Admin Ward Wally June /add
```

This example lists the users in the Admin group:

```
C:\>net localgroup Admin
```

The Net Pause command

This command temporarily pauses a service. It's a good idea to pause a service for a while before you stop the service altogether. That gives users who are currently using the service a chance to finish any pending tasks, while at the same time preventing other users from beginning new sessions with the service. To reactivate the service later, use the net continue command.

The syntax to pause a service is

```
net pause service
```

Here are some typical services that you can pause:

>> **netlogon:** The Net Logon service

>> **schedule:** The Task Scheduler service

>> **server:** The Server service

>> **workstation:** The Workstation service

Here's an example that pauses the Workstation service:

```
CL>net pause workstation
```

If the service name has embedded spaces, enclose the service name in quotation marks. This command pauses the NT LM Security Support Provider service, for example:

```
C:\>net pause "nt lm security support provider"
```

The Net Session command

This command lets you view current server connections and kick users off, if you feel inclined. Here's the syntax:

```
net session [\\ComputerName] [/delete]
```

Here's what the parameters do:

» *computerName*: Indicates which computer's session you want to view or disconnect. If you omit this parameter, all sessions are listed.

» `delete`: Disconnects the computer's session. Any open files are immediately closed. If you use this parameter without specifying a computer name, all computers currently connected to the server are disconnected.

WARNING

This command is an obviously dangerous one. If you disconnect users while they're updating files or before they have a chance to save their work, they'll be hopping mad.

To find out who is connected to a computer, use this command:

```
C:\>net session
Computer User name Client type Opens Idle time
----------------------------------------------------------
\\DEN Ward Windows XP 1 00:00:4
\\BEDROOM Administrator Windows 2008 0 02:15:17
```

The Net Share command

This command lets you manage shared resources. To display information about all shares or a specific share, use this syntax:

```
net share [ShareName]
```

To create a new share, use this syntax:

```
net share ShareName=path [{/users:number|/unlimited}] [/remark:"text"] [/cache:
    {manual|automatic|no}]
```

To change the properties of an existing share, use this syntax:

```
net share ShareName [{/users:number|unlimited}] [/remark:"text"] [/cache:
    {manual|automatic|no}]
```

To delete an existing share, use this syntax:

```
net share {ShareName|drive:path} /delete
```

Here's what the parameters do:

>> **ShareName:** Specifies the share name. Use this parameter by itself to display information about the share.

>> **path:** Specifies the path to the folder to be shared. The path should include a drive letter. If the path includes spaces, enclose it in quotation marks.

>> **users:** Specifies how many users can access the share concurrently.

>> **unlimited:** Specifies that an unlimited number of users can access the share concurrently.

>> **remark:** Creates a descriptive comment for the share. The comment should be enclosed in quotation marks.

>> **cache:** Specifies the caching option for the share.

>> **delete:** Stops sharing the folder.

If you use net share without any parameters, all the current shares are listed, as shown in this example:

```
C:\>net share
Sharename Resource Remark

-------------------------------------------------------------
ADMIN$ C:\WINNT Remote Admin
C$ C:\ Default Share
print$ C:\WINNT\SYSTEM\SPOOL
IPC$ Remote IPC
         LASER LPT1 Spooled Laser printer
```

The following example creates a share named Docs:

```
C:\>net share Docs=C:\SharedDocs /remark:"Shared documents"
```

The Net Start command

This command lets you start a networking service or display a list of all the services that are currently running. The syntax is

```
net start [service]
```

In most cases, you'll use this command to start a service that you've previously stopped with the net stop command. In that case, you should first run the net start command without any parameters to find the name of the service that you want to stop. Make a note of the exact spelling of the service that you want to stop. Then use the net stop command to stop the service. When you want to restart the service, use the net start command again — this time specifying the service to start.

Suppose that you need to stop your DNS server. Using net start, you discover that the name of the service is DNS Server, so you use the following command to stop it:

```
C:\>net stop "DNS Server"
```

Later, you can use this command to restart the service:

```
C:\>net start "DNS Server"
```

The Net Statistics command

This command lists the statistics log for the local Workstation or Server service. The syntax is

```
net statistics [{workstation | server}]
```

You can specify workstation or server to indicate the service for which you'd like to view statistics.

If you use net statistics workstation, the following information appears:

>> The computer name

>> The date and time when the statistics were last updated

>> The number of bytes and server message blocks (SMB) received and transmitted

>> The number of read and write operations that succeeded or failed

>> The number of network errors

>> The number of sessions that failed, disconnected, or were reconnected

>> The number of connections to shared resources that succeeded or failed

If you use Net Statistics Server, the following information is listed:

>> The computer name

>> The date and time when the statistics were last updated

- **»** The number of sessions that have been started, disconnected automatically, and disconnected because of errors
- **»** The number of kilobytes sent and received, and the average response time
- **»** The number of password and permission errors and violations
- **»** The number of times the shared files, printers, and communication devices were used
- **»** The number of times the size of the memory buffer was exceeded

The Net Stop command

This command lets you stop a networking service. The syntax is

```
net stop service
```

To use this command, first run the `net start` command to determine the exact spelling of the service that you want to stop. If the service name includes spaces, enclose it in quotation marks.

You can restart the service later by using the `net start` command.

The following example stops the DNS service:

```
C:\>net stop "DNS Server"
```

The Net Time command

This command synchronizes the computer's clock with the clock on another computer. To access a clock on another computer in the same domain or workgroup, use this form:

```
net time \\ComputerName [/set]
```

To synchronize time with a domain, use this form:

```
net time /domain[:DomainName] [/set]
```

To use an RTS time server, use this syntax:

```
net time /rtsdomain[:DomainName] [/set]
```

To specify the computer to use for Network Time Protocol, use this syntax:

```
net time [\\ComputerName] [/querysntp] [/setsntp[:NTPServerList]]
```

To set the computer's clock to match the Server01 clock, use this command:

```
C:\>net time \\Server01 /set
```

The Net Use command

This command connects to or disconnects from a shared resource on another computer and maps the resource to a drive letter. Here's the complete syntax:

```
net use [{drive | *}]
[{\\computername\sharename]
[{password | *}]]
[/user:[domainname\]username]
[/savecred]
[/smartcard]
[{/delete | /persistent:{yes | no}}]
```

To set up a home directory, use this syntax:

```
net use [drive [/home[{password | *}]
[/delete:{yes | no}]]
```

And to control whether connections should be persistent, use this:

```
net use [/persistent:{yes | no}]
```

Here's what the parameters do:

>> **drive:** Specifies the drive letter. (Note that for a printer, you should specify a printer device such as LPT1: here instead of a drive letter.) If you specify an asterisk, Windows will determine what drive letter to use.

>> **\\computername\sharename:** Specifies the server and share name to connect to.

>> **password:** Provides the password needed to access the shared resource. If you use an asterisk, you're prompted for the password.

>> **user:** Specifies the username to use for the connection.

>> **savecred:** Saves the credentials for reuse later if the user is prompted for a password.

>> **smartcard:** Specifies that the connection should use a smart card for authorization.

>> **delete:** Deletes the specified connection. If you specify an asterisk (*), all network connections are canceled.

>> **persistent:** Specifies whether connections should be persistent.

>> **home:** Connects to the home directory.

To display all current connections, type **net use** with no parameters.

The following example shows how to create a persistent connection to a drive named Acct on a server named Server01, using drive K:

```
C:\>net use k: \\Server01\Acct /persistent: yes
```

The following example drops the connection:

```
C:\>net use k: /delete
```

The Net User command

This command creates or changes user accounts. To display a user's information, use this form:

```
net user username
```

To update user information, use this form:

```
net user [username [password | *] [options]] [/domain]
```

To add a new user, use this form:

```
net user username [password | *] /add [options] [/domain]
```

To delete a user, use this form:

```
net user username /delete [/domain]
```

Most of the parameters for this command are straightforward. The `options` parameters, however, can have a variety of settings. Table 10-2 lists the descriptions of these options as presented by the `Net Help Users` command.

TABLE 10-2 **The Options Parameters**

Options	Description
/ACTIVE:{YES | NO}	Activates or deactivates the account. If the account isn't active, the user can't access the server. The default is YES.
/COMMENT:"text"	Provides a descriptive comment about the user's account (maximum of 48 characters). Enclose the text in quotation marks.
/COUNTRYCODE:nnn	Uses the operating-system country code to implement the specified language files for a user's help and error messages. A value of 0 signifies the default country code.
/EXPIRES:{date | NEVER}	Causes the account to expire if date is set. NEVER sets no time limit on the account. An expiration date is in the form mm/dd/yy or dd/mm/yy, depending on the country code. The month can be a number, spelled out, or abbreviated with three letters. The year can be two or four numbers. Use slashes (/), not spaces, to separate parts of the date.
/FULLNAME:"name"	Is a user's full name (rather than a username). Enclose the name in quotation marks.
/HOMEDIR:pathname	Sets the path for the user's home directory. The path must exist.
/PASSWORDCHG:{YES | NO}	Specifies whether users can change their own passwords. The default is YES.
/PASSWORDREQ:{YES | NO}	Specifies whether a user account must have a password. The default is YES.
/PROFILEPATH[:path]	Sets a path for the user's logon profile.
/SCRIPTPATH:pathname	Is the location of the user's logon script.
/TIMES:{times | ALL}	Is the logon hours. TIMES is expressed as day[-day][,day[-day]],time[-time] [,time[-time]], limited to 1-hour increments. Days can be spelled out or abbreviated. Hours can be 12- or 24-hour notation. For 12-hour notation, use am or pm (without periods) or a.m. or p.m. ALL means that a user can always log on, and a blank value means that a user can never log on. Separate day and time entries with a comma, and separate multiple day and time entries with a semicolon.
/USERCOMMENT:"text"	Lets an administrator add or change the User Comment for the account.
/WORKSTATIONS:	Lists as many as eight computers from which a user {ComputerName[,...] | *} can log on to the network. If /WORKSTATIONS has no list or if the list is *, the user can log on from any computer.

To display information for a particular user, use the command like this:

```
C:\>net user Doug
```

To add a user account for Theodore Cleaver with the username Beaver, use this command:

```
C:\>net user Beaver /add /fullname:"Theodore Cleaver"
```

The Net View command

This command displays information about your network. If you use it without parameters, it displays a list of the computers in your domain. You can use parameters to display resources that are being shared by a particular computer. Here's the syntax:

```
net view [\\computername] [/domain[:domainname]]
net view /network:nw [\\computername]
```

Here's what the parameters do:

>> *computername:* Specifies the computer whose shared resources you want to view.

>> *domainname:* Specifies the domain you want to view, if it's other than the current domain.

Here's typical output from a net view command:

```
C:\>net view
Server Name Remark

---------------------------------------------------
\\Server01 Main file server
\\Print01 Main print server
```

The RunAs Command

The runas command lets you run a program from a command prompt by using the credentials of another user account. Here's the basic syntax:

```
runas /user:username [other parameters] program
```

To run the Microsoft Management Console with the dom1 domain's administrator account, for example, you can use this command:

```
runas /user:dom1\administrator mmc
```

Assuming that the username is valid, you'll be prompted for the user's password. Then the program will be run using the specified user's account.

Here are some of the parameters you can use with the RunAs command:

>> **/user:** Specifies the domain and username. You can use either of two forms to specify the domain and username: domain\username or user-name@domain.

>> **/profile:** Specifies that the user's profile should be loaded. (This option is on by default, so you don't have to specify it explicitly.)

>> **/noprofile:** Doesn't load the user's profile. Although this parameter can cause the application to load faster, it can also prevent some applications from functioning properly.

>> **/env:** Uses the current environment instead of the user's.

>> **/netonly:** Indicates that the user account isn't valid in the current domain. (If you use /netonly, the username must be specified in the form domain\username; the username@domain form won't work.)

>> **/savecred:** Saves the password so that it has to be entered only the first time the RunAs command is used.

WARNING

Using the /savecred parameter is an extremely bad idea, as it creates a gaping security hole. In short, after you've used /savecred, any user at the computer can use the RunAs command to run any program with administrator privileges.

>> **/smartcard:** Specifies that the user's credentials will be supplied by a smart card device.

Windows Commands

Chapter **11**

Using PowerShell

I n the preceding chapter, you learn how to use a variety of Windows commands from a standard command prompt to perform various Windows administrative chores. In this chapter, you learn how to use a significantly more advanced command-line interface called *PowerShell.* PowerShell is to the Windows command prompt what a Tesla is to a Model A. Both cars look good, but the Model A was popular 90 years ago and took forever to get to its top speed of 65 miles per hour. The Tesla will get you to 155 miles per hour in less than 30 seconds.

Truth be told, I'd rather drive the Model A. But that's because I like things that are old like me. For real command-line performance, however, I suggest you spend some time learning PowerShell. You won't regret it.

TIP

This short chapter can't possibly cover everything there is to know about Power-Shell. For more information, see Microsoft's PowerShell site at www.microsoft. com/powershell.

Using PowerShell

PowerShell runs in a command window that's very similar to the standard Windows command prompt. However, the procedure to open it is a bit different:

1. **Press the Windows key on your keyboard, and then type** PowerShell.

2. **Press the Enter key.**

The PowerShell window appears, as shown in Figure 11-1.

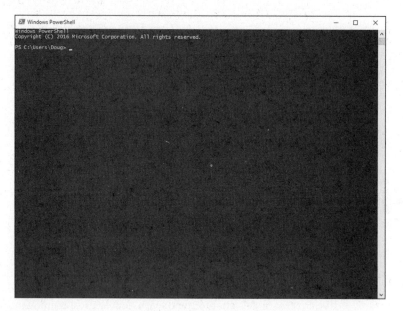

FIGURE 11-1:
The PowerShell
window.

TIP

If you want to perform administrative functions while in PowerShell, you'll need to open PowerShell as an administrator. To do that, right-click the Windows PowerShell icon and choose Run As Administrator.

WARNING

PowerShell is an incredibly powerful administrative tool, and opening a PowerShell window as an administrator can be risky if you aren't sure what you're doing. I suggest that while you're learning PowerShell, you do so on your desktop computer rather than on one of your servers. At least if you make serious mistakes on your own desktop computer, you won't bring down everyone else! (I'm half joking here. As a network administrator, you know how to be careful. But it's a good idea to experiment on your own computer or one you've designated as a sandbox rather than on a critical server!)

As with a standard command shell, you can type any commands you want in the window. However, you'll notice a few differences right off the bat:

>> Though it's not apparent in the figure, the background for a PowerShell window is blue rather than black.

>> The title bar indicates that you're in Windows PowerShell.

>> The welcome banner at the top of the window announces that you're using PowerShell.

>> Although the command prompt is similar to the prompt for a standard command shell, the current directory is prefixed with *PS* to remind you that you're in PowerShell.

TIP

You can formally exit PowerShell by typing **exit** and pressing Enter. Or, you can just close the window.

You can enter and edit commands within a PowerShell window pretty much the same as you do in a standard command shell. However, one difference you'll find useful is that the Tab key serves as an auto-complete feature: If you type a partial command and then press the Tab key, Windows will try to finish the command for you. Because most PowerShell commands are a bit long compared to their standard Windows command counterparts, this can be a real timesaver.

Give it a try: Open a PowerShell window and then type **get-r** and press the Tab key. PowerShell automatically expands this to the first standard PowerShell command that starts with get-r:

```
PS C:\Users\Doug> Get-Random
596196043
PS C:\Users\Doug>
```

As you can see, the shell expands your text to Get-Random, a PowerShell command that returns a random number. (Run this command several times; you'll see a different number each time.)

Understanding PowerShell Commands

PowerShell supports four distinctly different kinds of commands you can run directly from the PowerShell prompt:

>> **Native commands:** A *native command* is a standard Windows command that you would ordinarily run at a normal command prompt. Traditional commands such as xcopy, ipconfig, and ping can all be run from a PowerShell prompt.

>> **Cmdlets:** A *cmdlet* (which is short for *commandlet*) is the basic built-in PowerShell command. All cmdlet names follow a consistent *verb-noun* format. In the example in the preceding section, the verb is Get and the noun is Random.

(For more information about cmdlets, see the section "Using Cmdlets" later in this chapter.)

>> **Scripts**: A *script* is a collection of PowerShell commands saved to a text file with the extension .ps1. You can run a script at a PowerShell prompt simply by typing the name of the script, without the extension. In short, scripts are PowerShell's equivalent for batch files. (For more information about scripts, see the section "Using Scripts" later in this chapter.)

>> **Functions**: A *function* is a set of PowerShell commands that you give a name. Then you can run the named set of commands using the function's name as if it were a command. Here's a simple example that creates and then calls a function:

```
PS C:\Users\Doug> function rnd {Get-Random}
PS C:\Users\Doug> rnd
948203949
PS C:\Users\Doug>
```

The first command entered above creates a function named rnd. The list of commands to be executed for the function is enclosed within curly braces; in this example, just a single command is used (Get-Random). This line creates a function named rnd that runs the Get-Random cmdlet.

The second command calls the rnd function. As you can see, PowerShell responds to the rnd function by displaying another random number.

Note that functions are usually used within scripts. And because they're a somewhat advanced topic, I won't be covering them further in this chapter. (For more information, you can refer to Microsoft's PowerShell website at www.microsoft.com/powershell.)

Using Cmdlets

Cmdlets are the bread and butter of PowerShell. At first glance, cmdlets seem similar to native commands, but actually they're quite different. The most obvious difference is how they're named. All cmdlets are named using a simple *verb-name* convention, where the first word is one of several standardized verbs (such as *get*, *create*, or *show*) and the noun is a somewhat less standardized name of the object that the verb acts on. For example, in the Get-Random cmdlet, the verb is Get and the noun is Random.

Nouns in PowerShell are always singular. For example, the command that retrieves a list of all system services is called get-service, not get-services.

All cmdlets follow this naming convention, which makes it easy to remember cmdlet names, at least once you work with PowerShell long enough to learn the most common verb and noun names.

You can see a listing of all the verbs by running the get-verb cmdlet (again, singular: get-verb, not get-verbs). The get-verb command displays a list of 98 different verbs that can be used in cmdlets — too many to show here. Run the command at a PowerShell prompt to get a feel for the types of verbs that are used in cmdlets.

Incidentally, PowerShell names are not case-sensitive. Thus, you don't have to capitalize the verbs and nouns when you type PowerShell commands. Get-Random and get-random have exactly the same effect.

Using Parameters

Most cmdlets let you use *parameters* that allow you to customize the behavior of the cmdlet. Parameter names are preceded by a hyphen and followed by the parameter value. For example:

```
PS C:\Users\Doug> Get-Random -Minimum 1 -Maximum 10
2
PS C:\Users\Doug>
```

This cmdlets returns a random number between 1 and 10; in the above example, the number returned happens to be 2, but each time you run the cmdlet you'll get a different random value.

Many parameters have default values, so if you omit a parameter, the default value is used. For the Get-Random cmdlet, the default value for -Minimum is 1, so you can omit it, as in this example:

```
Get-Random -Maximum 10
```

Some parameters can accept two or more values. In that case, you simply separate the values by commas.

You don't always have to type the full name of a parameter; PowerShell will do its best to figure out which parameter you intend. For example, the following command works:

```
Get-Random 1 -Max 10
```

In fact, this command works, too, because Ma is enough to distinguish –Maximum from –Minimum:

```
Get-Random -Ma 10
```

However, the following command doesn't work:

```
Get-Random -M 10
```

Here, PowerShell can't tell whether you mean to use the –Minimum parameter or the –Maximum parameter.

Some parameters don't have values; in that case, you just list the parameter name without a subsequent value, as in this example:

```
PS C:\Users\Doug> Get-ChildItem -recurse
```

This cmdlet, Get-ChildItem, is PowerShell's equivalent to the dir command: It lists the contents of the current directory. The –recurse parameter tells Get-ChildItem to list not just the current directory, but all subdirectories as well.

PowerShell defines a set of *common parameters* that work in a consistent way across many different cmdlets. These common parameters are listed in Table 11-1. Note that not all cmdlets implement all the common parameters. But the point is that when a cmdlet provides the feature indicated by one of these common parameters, the name of the common parameter will be used. (Of special interest is the –whatif parameter, which lets you check out what a complicated cmdlet will do before you actually run it.)

Some cmdlet parameters are positional, which means that you can omit the parameter name and just list the parameter values. For the Get_Random cmdlet, –Maximum is the first positional parameter. So, if you simply specify a value without a parameter name, Get-Random uses the value as the –Maximum parameter:

```
Get-Random 10
```

TABLE 11-1   **PowerShell Common Parameters**

Parameter	What It Does
–WhatIf	Displays a message that indicates what the cmdlet will do without actually doing anything.
–Confirm	Prompts the user before proceeding.
–Verbose	Displays additional explanatory information.
–ErrorAction	Indicates what to do if an error occurs. Possible actions are Continue, Ignore, Inquire, SilentlyContinue, Stop, and Suspend.
–ErrorVariable	Provides the name of a variable used to hold error information.
–WarningAction	Indicates what to do if a warning message is generated. Actions are the same as for –ErrorAction.
–WarningVariable	Provides the name of a variable used to hold warning information.
–OutVariable	Provides the name of a variable used to hold the cmdlet's output.
–Debug	Displays messages that are sometimes helpful when debugging a cmdlet.

One final bit about parameters: If you omit a required parameter, PowerShell will prompt you to enter its value. You'll see an example of this in the section, "Using Aliases" later in this chapter.

Getting Help

PowerShell includes an extensive collection of help information that you can access via the Get-Help cmdlet. Simply provide the name of the cmdlet you need help with as a positional parameter. For example, here is the Get-Help output for the Get-Random cmdlet:

```
PS C:\Users\Doug> Get-Help Get-Random

NAME
    Get-Random

SYNOPSIS
    Gets a random number, or selects objects randomly from a collection.
```

```
SYNTAX
    Get-Random [-InputObject] <Object[]> [-Count <Int32>] [-SetSeed <Int32>]
    [<CommonParameters>]

    Get-Random [[-Maximum] <Object>] [-Minimum <Object>] [-SetSeed <Int32>]
    [<CommonParameters>]


DESCRIPTION
    The Get-Random cmdlet gets a randomly selected number. If you submit a
    collection of objects to Get-Random , it gets one or more randomly selected
    objects from the collection.

    Without parameters or input, a Get-Random command returns a randomly
    selected 32-bit unsigned integer between 0 (zero) and Int32.MaxValue
    (0x7FFFFFFF, 2,147,483,647).

    You can use the parameters of Get-Random to specify a seed number, minimum
    and maximum values, and the number of objects returned from a submitted
    collection.


RELATED LINKS
    Online Version: http://go.microsoft.com/fwlink/?LinkId=821799

REMARKS
    To see the examples, type: "get-help Get-Random -examples".
    For more information, type: "get-help Get-Random -detailed".
    For technical information, type: "get-help Get-Random -full".
    For online help, type: "get-help Get-Random -online"

PS C:\Users\Doug>
```

You can use several additional parameters to get even more help information:

» –Examples: Displays examples of the cmdlet, along with a detailed explanation of what each example does.

» –Detailed: Provides more detailed help.

» –Full: Displays all available help information.

» –Online: Opens a web browser homed on Microsoft's help page for the cmdlet. (This is actually the most useful form of help; see Figure 11-2 for an example of the help page for the Get_Random cmdlet.)

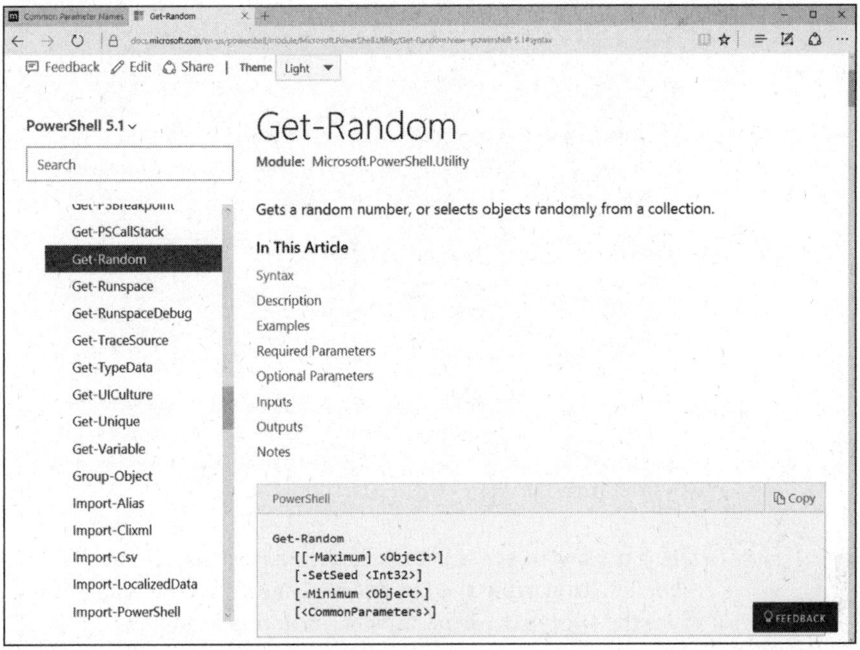

FIGURE 11-2:
Online help for
a PowerShell
cmdlet.

Using Aliases

By now, you may be grumbling that PowerShell is a bit verbose. Indeed, most cmdlet names are pretty long. And although PowerShell will attempt to figure out what parameter names you mean if you don't spell them out completely, Power-Shell doesn't give you the same grace with cmdlet names: If you don't spell out a cmdlet name in its entirety, PowerShell displays a rude error message.

Fortunately, PowerShell does provide relief in the form of aliases. An *alias* is an alternative name for a cmdlet. You can make up your own aliases, or you can use a somewhat large number of built-in aliases.

For example, earlier I show an example of the Get-ChildItem cmdlet used to list the contents of a folder. Get-ChildItem is the PowerShell equivalent of the dir command, and PowerShell provides dir as an alias for the Get-ChildItem com-mand. So although Get-ChildItem is the cmdlet to list the contents of a folder, you can call the Get-ChildItem cmdlet by entering dir at a PowerShell prompt.

Thus, you can display the contents of a folder like this:

```
PS C:\Users\Doug> dir


    Directory: C:\Users\Doug
```

```
Mode              LastWriteTime        Length Name
----              -------------        ------ ----
d-r---      1/4/2018   10:18 PM               Contacts
d-r---      1/4/2018   10:18 PM               Desktop
d-r---      1/4/2018   10:18 PM               Documents
d-r---      1/4/2018   10:18 PM               Downloads
d-r---      1/4/2018   10:18 PM               Favorites
d-r---      1/4/2018   10:18 PM               Links
d-r---      1/4/2018   10:18 PM               Music
d-r---      1/4/2018   10:19 PM               OneDrive
d-r---      1/4/2018   10:18 PM               Pictures
d-r---      1/4/2018   10:18 PM               Saved Games
d-r---      1/4/2018   10:18 PM               Searches
d-r---      1/4/2018   10:18 PM               Videos

PS C:\Users\Doug>
```

If you want to see a list of all the aliases that are available, use the Get-Alias cmdlet. To narrow the list down to show just the aliases for a particular cmdlet, use the –Definition parameter, as in this example:

```
PS C:\Users\Doug> Get-Alias -Definition Get-ChildItem

CommandType     Name                                               Version
    Source

-------------   ----                                               -------
    -------
Alias           dir -> Get-ChildItem
Alias           gci -> Get-ChildItem
Alias           ls -> Get-ChildItem

PS C:\Users\Doug>
```

Here, you can see that three aliases are defined for the Get-ChildItem cmdlet: dir, gci, and ls. Dir is the Windows equivalent to Get-ChildItem, gci is simply an abbreviation for Get-ChildItem, and ls is the Linux equivalent.

If you want to create your own aliases, you can use the Set-Alias command. This cmdlet requires two parameters: –name, which provides the name of the alias, and –value, which indicates the cmdlet that will be aliases. For example:

```
Set-Alias -Name ListFiles -Value Get-ChildItem
```

This creates a new alias for the Get-ChildItem cmdlet named ListFiles.

To remove an alias, you have to use the Remove-Item cmdlet, as in this example:

```
Remove-Item Alias:ListFiles
```

In this case, you indicate that you want to remove an Alias item, followed by a colon and the name of the alias you want to remove.

Using the Pipeline

The verb-noun naming convention isn't the most important difference between PowerShell and other command shells. The real difference is how PowerShell cmdlets deal with piped input and output. PowerShell takes the idea of piping to a new level.

In Chapter 10 of this minibook, I explain how to use piping to chain two standard Windows commands together so that the output from the first command is piped into the second command. For example:

```
C:\>type users.txt | sort
```

Here, the `type` command displays the contents of a text file named `users.txt`. But instead of being displayed on the screen, the output from the `type` command is fed into the `sort` command, which sorts the text and then displays it on the screen. The result is that the contents of the `users.txt` file are displayed on the screen in sorted order.

With a standard Windows command, the input and output for commands that can use piping is always simple text. Thus, the `type` command creates text output, and the `sort` command reads text input and creates more text output. When the shell gets to the end of a sequence of piped commands, the output from the last command is displayed on the screen.

With cmdlets, the information that is piped is not simple text but complete objects. An *object* is an amalgamation of data, as well as executable code. Objects have *properties,* which are named characteristics of the object, and *methods,* which are named functions that the object can perform. Methods are important in Power-Shell, but using them is an advanced topic that's beyond the scope of this chapter. So I'm focusing here on properties.

Consider the `Get-ChildItem` cmdlet, which lists the contents of a folder:

```
PS C:\Users\Doug> Get-ChildItem

    Directory: C:\Users\Doug
```

```
Mode              LastWriteTime        Length Name
----              -------------        ------ ----
d-r----      1/4/2018   10:18 PM              Contacts
d-r----      1/4/2018   10:18 PM              Desktop
d-r----      1/4/2018   10:18 PM              Documents
d-r----      1/4/2018   10:18 PM              Downloads
d-r----      1/4/2018   10:18 PM              Favorites
d-r----      1/4/2018   10:18 PM              Links
d-r----      1/4/2018   10:18 PM              Music
d-r----      1/4/2018   10:19 PM              OneDrive
d-r----      1/4/2018   10:18 PM              Pictures
d-r----      1/4/2018   10:18 PM              Saved Games
d-r----      1/4/2018   10:18 PM              Searches
d-r----      1/4/2018   10:18 PM              Videos

PS C:\Users\Doug>
```

This cmdlet doesn't actually produce the text that is displayed in the PowerShell window. Instead, it returns a collection of file system objects. These file system objects have a number of important properties, among them Name, Length, LastWriteTime, and Mode.

The Get-ChildItem cmdlet puts this collection in the *pipeline,* which is a repository for objects that passed from one cmdlet to another. In most cases, you only invoke one cmdlet at a time in PowerShell. In that case, the output from the cmdlet you invoke is passed to the end of the pipeline, which automatically renders the contents of the pipeline as text. Hence, the list of file system objects is converted to text form and displayed in the PowerShell window.

You can easily manipulate the output displayed for a cmdlet by piping the output to one of several commonly used cmdlets that sort, filter, or otherwise format the objects in the pipeline. For example, if you want to show the contents of a folder in reverse alphabetical order, you can pipe the Get-ChildItem cmdlet's output into the Sort-Object cmdlet and use the –Descending parameter to reverse the order:

```
PS C:\Users\Doug> Get-ChildItem | Sort-Object –Descending

    Directory: C:\Users\Doug


Mode              LastWriteTime        Length Name
----              -------------        ------ ----
d-r----      1/4/2018   10:18 PM              Videos
d-r----      1/4/2018   10:18 PM              Searches
d-r----      1/4/2018   10:18 PM              Saved Games
d-r----      1/4/2018   10:18 PM              Pictures
d-r----      1/4/2018   10:19 PM              OneDrive
d-r----      1/4/2018   10:18 PM              Music
```

```
d-r----         1/4/2018  10:18 PM            Links
d-r----         1/4/2018  10:18 PM            Favorites
d-r----         1/4/2018  10:18 PM            Downloads
d-r----         1/4/2018  10:18 PM            Documents
d-r----         1/4/2018  10:18 PM            Desktop
d-r----         1/4/2018  10:18 PM            Contacts


PS C:\Users\Doug>
```

As you can see, PowerShell uses the vertical-bar character (also known as the pipe character) to indicate piping.

If you want to pick and choose which properties to display when you use Get-ChildItem, you can use the Select-Object cmdlet. For example:

```
PS C:\Users\Doug> Get-ChildItem | Select-Object -Property Name


Name
----

Contacts
Desktop
Documents
Downloads
Favorites
Links
Music
OneDrive
Pictures
Saved Games
Searches
Videos


PS C:\Users\Doug>
```

In this example, the Select-Object cmdlet's Property method indicates that you want to include only the Name property. The result is a list of filenames.

You can select more than one property by separating the property names with commas, as in this example:

```
PS C:\Users\Doug> Get-ChildItem | Select-Object -Property Name, LastWriteTime

Name        LastWriteTime
----        -------------
Contacts    1/4/2018 10:18:49 PM
Desktop     1/4/2018 10:18:49 PM
Documents   1/4/2018 10:18:49 PM
```

```
Downloads      1/4/2018 10:18:49 PM
Favorites      1/4/2018 10:18:49 PM
Links          1/4/2018 10:18:49 PM
Music          1/4/2018 10:18:49 PM
OneDrive       1/4/2018 10:19:05 PM
Pictures       1/4/2018 10:18:49 PM
Saved Games    1/4/2018 10:18:49 PM
Searches       1/4/2018 10:18:49 PM
Videos         1/4/2018 10:18:49 PM

PS C:\Users\Doug>
```

Here's an example that invokes three cmdlets: the first gets the contents of the current folder, the second selects just the Name property, and the third sorts the list in descending order:

```
PS C:\Users\Doug> Get-ChildItem | Select-Object -Property Name | Sort-Object
    -Descending

Name
----
Pictures
OneDrive
Music
Videos
Searches
Saved Games
Documents
Desktop
Contacts
Links
Favorites
Downloads

PS C:\Users\Doug>
```

The more you learn about PowerShell, the more you'll come to rely on the pipeline to tailor PowerShell to meet your precise needs.

Using Providers

One of the most interesting things about PowerShell is the concept of providers. A *provider* is a source of data that is consumed by many of PowerShell's commands. For example, the Get-ChildItem command consumes information from a provider called FileSystem, which represents the host computer's file system.

PowerShell provides several providers besides FileSystem. To see them all, you can use the Get-PSProvider command:

```
PS C:\Users\Doug> Get-PSProvider

Name            Capabilities                          Drives

----            ------------                          ------

Registry        ShouldProcess, Transactions           {HKLM,
   HKCU}
Alias           ShouldProcess                         {Alias}
Environment     ShouldProcess                         {Env}
FileSystem      Filter, ShouldProcess, Credentials    {C}
Function        ShouldProcess                         {Function}
Variable        ShouldProcess                         {Variable}

PS C:\Users\Doug>
```

Depending on the environment in which you run the Get-PSProvider cmdlet, you may see additional providers as well.

All providers are modeled on the concept of a file system, meaning that providers present their data to PowerShell cmdlets through one or more drives which contain items organized into folders. This might seem confusing at first, but you'll get used to it once you start to work with it.

Looking at the output from the Get-PSProvider cmdlet, you can see that the FileSystem provider lists just one drive, identified as C. If more disk drives were available on the computer, additional drive letters would appear.

Other providers list their drives using short words or abbreviations rather than single letters. For example, the Alias provider has a single drive, named Alias. Similarly, the Registry provider has two drives, named HKLM and HKCU. (If you're familiar with the Windows Registry, you'll recognize these as the common abbreviations for HKEY_Local_Machine and HKEY_Current_User, respectively.)

By default, the Get-ChildItem cmdlet uses the FileSystem provider, starting at the current folder location. However, you can easily switch the provider for Get-Children by specifying an alternative path. For example, to see a list of all available aliases, you can use this command:

```
Get-Children Alias:\
```

Notice that the drive name Alias is followed by a colon and a single backslash in much the same way that the root folder of the FileSystem C drive would be written as C:\.

You can change the default location for cmdlets that work with providers by using the Set-Location cmdlet. For example:

```
Set-Location Alias:\
```

Having set the default location to the root of the Alias drive, subsequent cmdlets such as Get-ChildItem will automatically pull data from the Alias provider rather than from the FileSystem provider.

Using Scripts

A *script* is a collection of PowerShell commands saved to a text file with the extension .ps1. You can run a script at a PowerShell prompt simply by typing the name of the script, without the extension. Thus, scripts are PowerShell's equivalent for batch files.

Scripts are a great way to simplify routine Windows administration tasks. Any time you find yourself entering the same cmdlets over and over again, consider placing the cmdlets in a script. Then you can simply run the script, and let the script take care of the details of each command.

For example, suppose you routinely want to know what processes are consuming the most memory resources. You can do that using a combination of several cmdlets:

>> Use Get-Process to get a list of active processes.

>> Use Select-Object to select just the ProcessName and WS properties. (WS stands for *working set,* which is one of the key memory indicators in a Windows system.)

>> Use Sort-Object to sort the result in descending order on the WS property.

>> Use Select-Object again to select just the top ten results.

The resulting command would look like this:

```
PS C:\Users\Doug> Get-Process | Select-Object -Property ProcessName, WS |
    Sort-Object -descending WS | Select-Object -first 10

ProcessName          WS
-----------          --
MicrosoftEdgeCP 269713408
MicrosoftEdgeCP 243097600
```

```
WINWORD          169254912
SearchUI         158670848
MsMpEng          120512512
SelfService       98873344
EXCEL             89866240
explorer          87056384
MicrosoftEdge     78503936
powershell        70873088


PS C:\Users\Doug>
```

But that's a lot to type. To save all the wear and tear on your fingers and your keyboard, you can create a `.ps1` file with the command, as shown in Figure 11-3.

```
Get-Process | Select-Object -Property ProcessName, WS | Sort-Object -descending
    WS | Select-Object -first 10
```

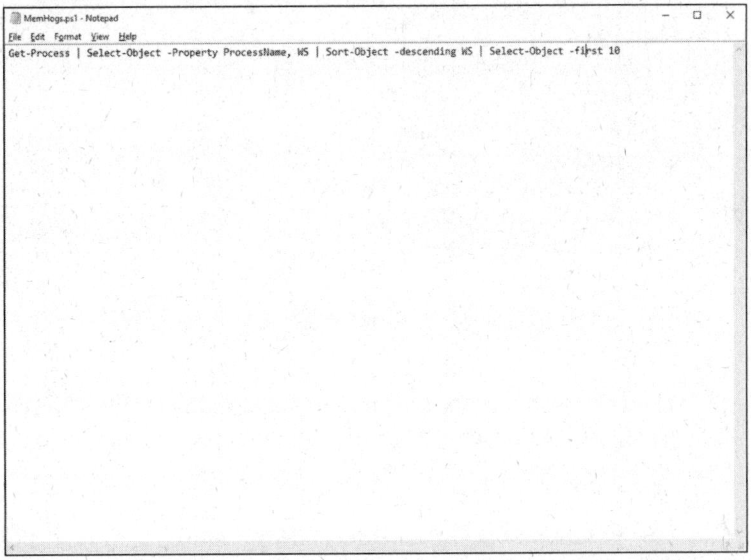

FIGURE 11-3:
A PowerShell
script.

Then you can invoke the whole thing just by running the `.ps1` file.

However, before you can run scripts in PowerShell, you have to make a few preparations:

>> **Run PowerShell with administrator permissions.** You can do that by right-clicking the PowerShell icon and choosing Run As Administrator.

» **Enable script execution by using the** Set-ExecutionPolicy **cmdlet.** For example:

```
Set-ExecutionPolicy unrestricted
```

When you run this command, the cmdlet will ask for your permission to enable unrestricted script execution.

» **Save your scripts to a location you can easily access.** For example, use C:\Scripts.

After you've enabled scripting, you can run a script by entering the script filename (including path) at the prompt:

```
PS C:\Windows\system32> c:\scripts\memhogs

ProcessName          WS
-----------          --
MicrosoftEdgeCP 269381632
MicrosoftEdgeCP 237064192
WINWORD         179699712
SearchUI        164970496
MsMpEng         117723136
SelfService      98873344
explorer         89452544
MicrosoftEdge    77590528
EXCEL            75345920
powershell       74674176


PS C:\Windows\system32>
```

There is much more to scripting than the limits of this short chapter allows me to go into. Here are some additional features you can explore on Microsoft's Power-Shell website:

» Variables, which let you store and later retrieve values and objects.

» Functions, which let you create a set of PowerShell commands that you give a name to. Then you can run the named set of commands using the function's name as if it were a command.

» Advanced Functions, which let you create functions with parameters.

» Logic statements, including While, Do...While, Do...Until, For, Foreach, If, and Switch.

7

Implementing Linux

Contents at a Glance

Chapter **1**

Installing a Linux Server

This chapter presents the procedures that you need to follow to install Linux on a server computer. The details provided are specifically for Fedora 26, a free Linux distribution sponsored by Red Hat. However, the procedures for installing other distributions of Linux are similar, so you won't have any trouble adapting these procedures if you're using a different distribution.

Planning a Linux Server Installation

Before you begin the installation program, you need to make a number of preliminary decisions. The following sections describe the decisions that you need to make before you install Linux.

Checking system requirements

Before you install Linux, make sure that the computer meets the minimum requirements. Although the minimum requirements for Linux are considerably less than those for the latest version of Windows Server, you can't run Linux on an abacus. The following paragraphs summarize the minimum capabilities you need:

>> **A 1GHz processor or faster:** You probably won't find a computer that doesn't meet this requirement.

>> **1GB of RAM or more:** Today most computers have at least 1GB of RAM.

>> **A hard drive with enough free space to hold the packages that you need to install:** A suitable minimum is 10GB.

>> **A CD or DVD-ROM drive from which to install the operating system**

>> **Just about any video card and monitor combination:** You don't need anything fancy for a server. In fact, fancy video cards often lead to hardware compatibility issues. Stick to a basic video card.

>> **An Ethernet network interface**

For the purposes of this chapter, I'll be installing Fedora into a Hyper-V virtual machine configured with 4GB of RAM, two processor cores, and 100GB of disk space. (For information about setting up a Hyper-V virtual machine, refer to Book 5, Chapter 1.)

Choosing a distribution

Because the *kernel* (that is, the core operating functions) of the Linux operating system is free, several companies have created their own *distributions* of Linux, which include the Linux OS along with a bundle of packages, such as administration tools, web servers, and other useful utilities, as well as printed documentation.

The following are some of the more popular Linux distributions:

>> **Fedora:** One of the popular Linux distributions. You can download Fedora free from http://fedoraproject.org. You can also obtain it by purchasing any of several books on Fedora that include the Fedora distribution on DVD or CD-ROM.

Fedora comes in two editions: a Workstation edition and a Server edition. The main difference between the two is that the Workstation edition includes a graphical user interface (GUI), whereas the Server edition relies on the command-line interface. Because the GUI is easier to work with when you're learning Linux, I recommend you use the Workstation edition.

All the examples in this book are based on Fedora Workstation 26.

>> **Ubuntu:** A Linux distribution that has gained popularity in recent years. It focuses on ease of use. For more information, go to www.ubuntu.com.

>> **SUSE:** Pronounced *SOO-zuh,* like the name of the famous composer of marches; a popular Linux distribution sponsored by Novell. You can find more information at www.suse.com.

>> **Slackware:** One of the oldest Linux distributions and still popular, especially among Linux old-timers. A full installation of Slackware gives you all the tools

that you need to set up a network or Internet server. See www.slackware.com for more information.

I CAN'T SEE MY C: DRIVE!

Linux and Windows have a completely different method of referring to your computer's hard drives and partitions. The differences can take some getting used to for experienced Windows users.

Windows uses a separate letter for each drive and partition on your system. For example, if you have a single drive formatted into three partitions, Windows identifies the partitions as drives C:, D:, and E:. Each of these drives has its own root directory, which can, in turn, contain additional directories used to organize your files. As far as Windows is concerned, drives C:, D:, and E: are completely separate drives even though the drives are actually just partitions on a single drive.

Linux doesn't use drive letters. Instead, Linux combines all the drives and partitions into a single directory hierarchy. In Linux, one of the partitions is designated as the *root* partition. The root partition is roughly analogous to the root directory of the C: drive on a Windows system. Then, the other partitions can be *mounted* on the root partition and treated as if they were directories on the root partition. For example, you may designate the first partition as the root partition and then mount the second partition as /user and the third partition as /var. Then, any files stored in the /user directory would actually be stored in the second partition, and files stored in the /var directory would be stored in the third partition.

The directory to which a drive mounts is called the drive's *mount point.*

Notice that Linux uses regular forward slash characters (/) to separate directory names rather than the backward slash characters (\) used by Windows. Typing backslashes instead of regular slashes is one of the most common mistakes made by new Linux users.

While I'm on the subject, Linux uses a different convention for naming files, too. In Windows, filenames end in a three- or four-letter extension that's separated from the rest of the filename by a period. The extension is used to indicate the file type. For example, files that end in .exe are program files, but files that end in .doc are word-processing documents.

Linux doesn't use file extensions, but periods are often used in Linux filenames to separate different parts of the name — and the last part often indicates the file type. For example, ldap.conf and pine.conf are both configuration files.

All distributions of Linux include the same core components: the Linux kernel, an X Server, popular windows managers such as GNOME and KDE, compilers, Internet programs such as Apache, Sendmail, and so on. However, not all Linux distributions are created equal. In particular, the manufacturer of each distribution creates its own installation and configuration programs to install and configure Linux.

The installation program is what makes or breaks a Linux distribution. All the distributions I list in this section have easy-to-use installation programs that automatically detect the hardware that's present on your computer and configure Linux to work with that hardware, thus eliminating most — if not all — manual configuration chores. The installation programs also let you select the Linux packages that you want to install and let you set up one or more user accounts besides the root account.

Going virtual

Another common way to install Linux is in a virtual machine running within the Windows operating system. In fact, all the examples in this minibook were tested using VMware Workstation Player, a free virtualization platform you can download from www.vmware.com. You can also use Microsoft's Hyper-V or any of several other virtualization products, many of which are free. For more information, see Book 5.

Deciding on your TCP/IP configuration

Before you install the OS, you should have a plan for how you will implement TCP/IP on the network. Here are some of the things you need to decide or find out:

>> The public IP subnet address and mask for your network

>> The domain name for the network

>> The host name for the server

>> Whether the server obtains its address from DHCP

>> Whether the server has a static IP address — and if so, what

>> Whether the server is a DHCP server

>> The default gateway for the server — that is, the IP address of the network's Internet router

>> Whether the server is a DNS server

TIP

If the server will host TCP/IP servers (such as DHCP or DNS), you'll probably want to assign the server a static IP address.

For more information about planning your TCP/IP configuration, see Book 2.

Installing Fedora 26

After you plan your installation and prepare the computer, you're ready to actually install Linux. The following procedure describes the steps you must follow to install Fedora 26 on a virtual machine using a downloaded .iso file containing the Fedora installation media.

Note that, for this example, I chose to install the workstation version of Fedora. You can also install the server version of Fedora, but the server version does not configure a graphical user interface (GUI) by default. The workstation version works well as a server and provides GUI tools to simplify basic configuration tasks.

1. **Download the Fedora 26 .iso file from the Fedora project's download page, connect it to the virtual machine's optical drive, and start the virtual machine.**

   The download is located at https://getfedora.org.

   When you start the VM, a bunch of text messages fly across the screen. Eventually, the first page of the setup program is displayed, as shown in Figure 1-1.

2. **Choose your language, and then click Continue.**

   The Installation Summary page is displayed, as shown in Figure 1-2.

3. **Click Installation Destination.**

   The installation program displays the Installation Destination screen, shown in Figure 1-3.

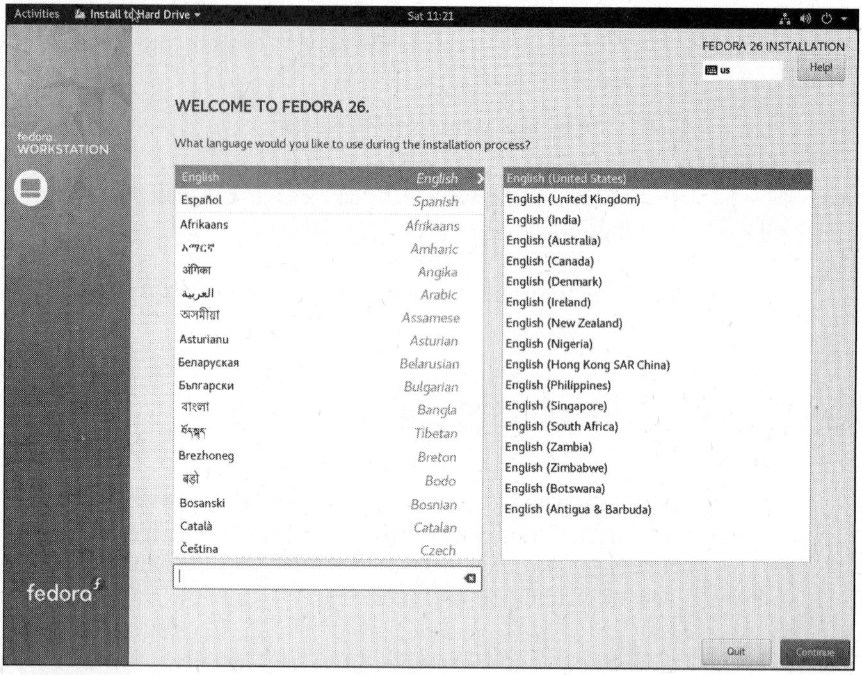

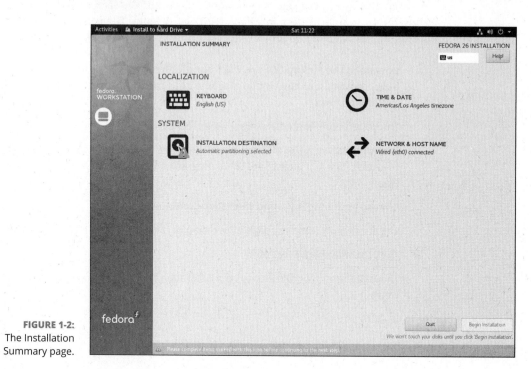

FIGURE 1-1:
Choose a language to begin the Fedora installation.

FIGURE 1-2:
The Installation Summary page.

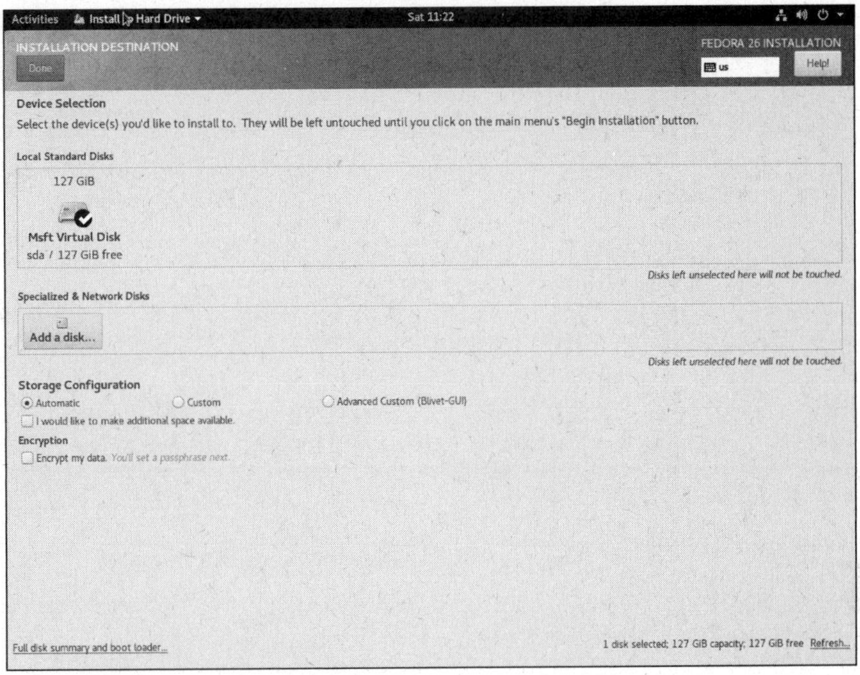

FIGURE 1-3:
The Installation
Destination
screen.

4. **If necessary, adjust the installation destination settings.**

The Installation Destination screen indicates the disk volume on which Fedora will be installed. The default setting is to automatically create a partition on the empty primary drive and then install Fedora into the new partition. You should adjust these settings only if you want to install Fedora into a different location.

5. **Click Done.**

You're returned to the Installation Summary screen.

6. **Click Time & Date.**

The Time & Date screen appears, as shown in Figure 1-4.

7. **Select the correct time zone and location, and then click Done.**

You're returned to the Installation Summary page.

8. **Click Network & Host Name.**

The Network & Host Name screen is displayed, as shown in Figure 1-5.

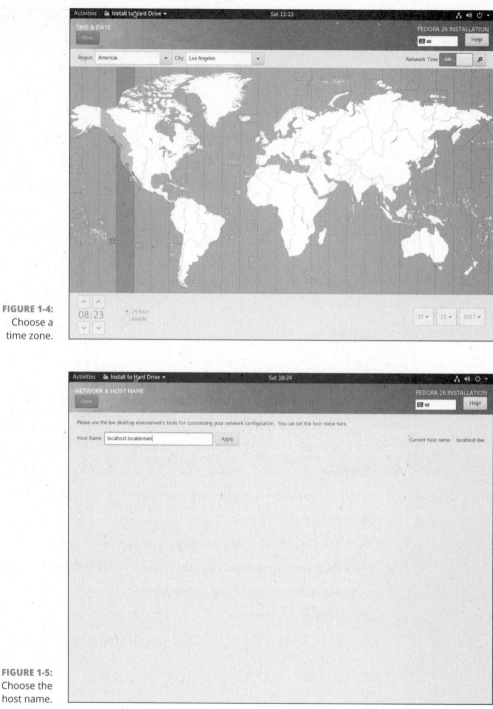

FIGURE 1-4:
Choose a
time zone.

FIGURE 1-5:
Choose the
host name.

9. **Enter the name you want to assign this computer and then click Done.**

You're returned to the Installation Summary screen.

10. **Click Begin Installation.**

The Configuration screen is displayed, as shown in Figure 1-6.

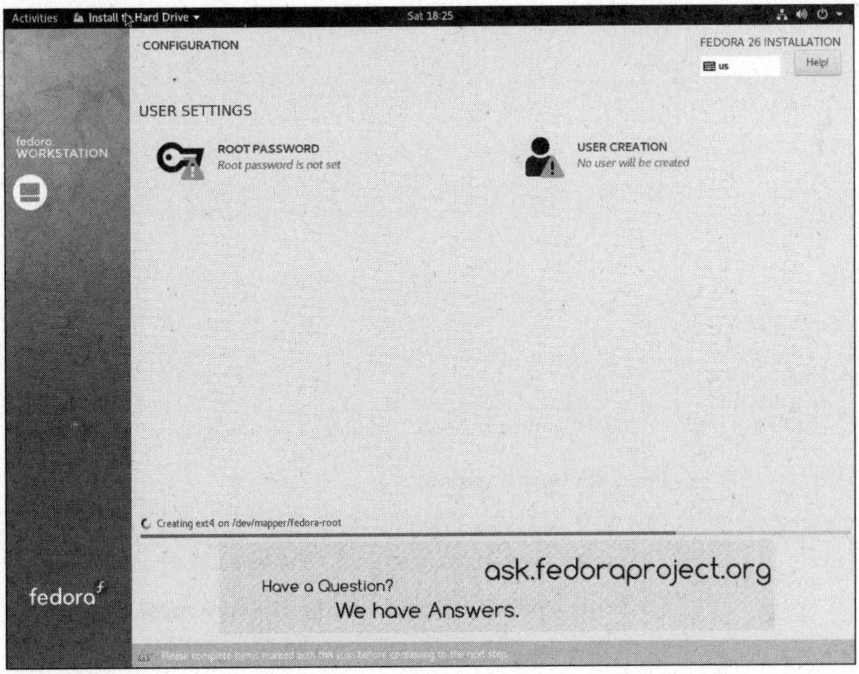

FIGURE 1-6:
The Configuration
screen.

11. **Click Root Password.**

The Root Password screen is displayed, as shown in Figure 1-7.

12. **Enter a password for the root account.**

It's vital that the root account is protected by a strong password, so choose a good one. Write down the password somewhere and store it in a secure location away from the computer.

13. **Click Done.**

You're returned to the Configuration screen.

Installing a Linux Server

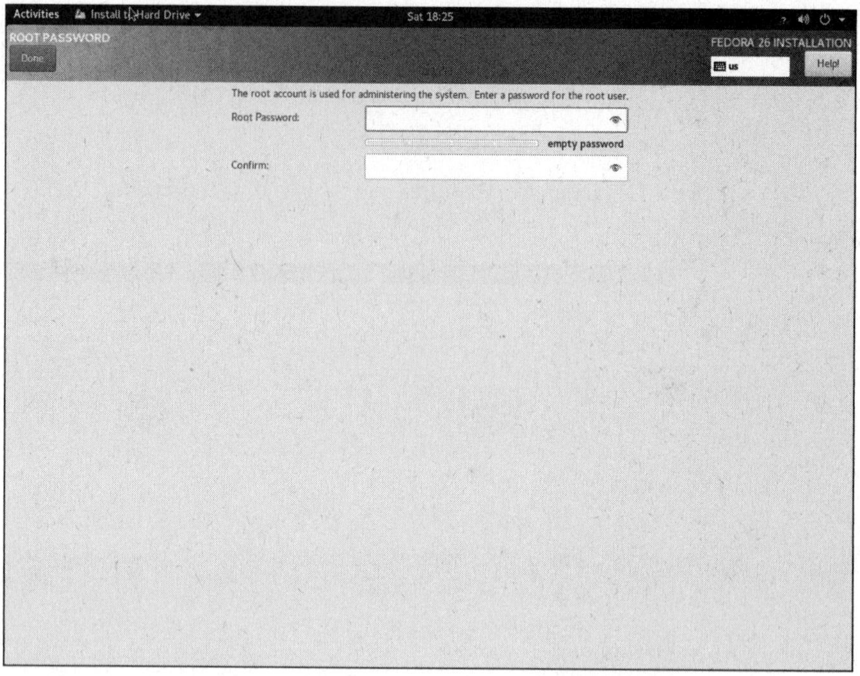

The root account is used for administering the system. Enter a password for the root user.

Root Password:

empty password

Confirm:

FIGURE 1-7:
Entering a
password for the
root account.

14. **Click User Creation.**

The Create User screen appears, as shown in Figure 1-8. This screen lets you create a user account so you'll have at least one user other than the root.

15. **Enter a name and password for the user account, and then click Done.**

You're returned to the Configuration screen.

16. **Wait a few minutes until the installation finishes.**

Fedora displays an installation progress bar while the software installs. When the installation completes, the screen shown in Figure 1-9 appears.

17. **Click Quit and then restart the computer.**

Installation is done!

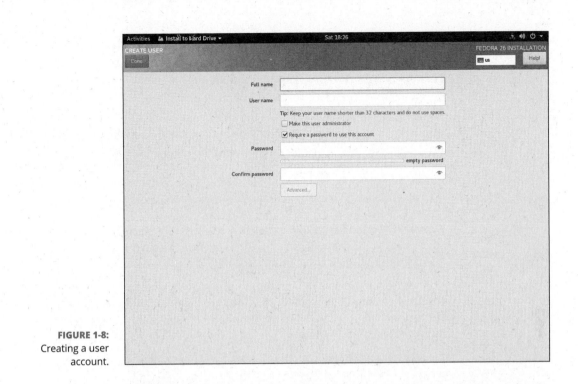

FIGURE 1-8:
Creating a user
account.

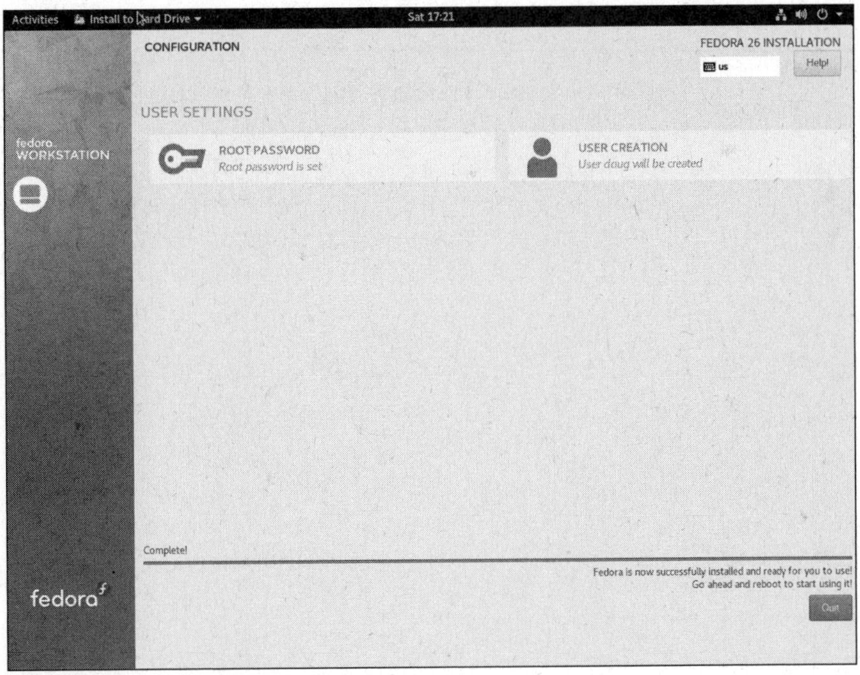

FIGURE 1-9:
Fedora
announces
that it is done!

VIRTUAL CONSOLES AND THE INSTALLATION PROGRAM

Linux is inherently a command-line–oriented OS. Graphical user interfaces — including the installation program's GUI — are provided by an optional component called *X Window System.* However, while you're working with the GUI of the installation program, Linux keeps several additional command-line consoles open. Normally, you don't need to use every one of these consoles during installation. However, if something goes wrong during installation, these consoles may be useful:

- **Console 1: The Installation dialog box.** This is the main installation console. You see it when Setup first starts. After the GUI takes over, it's hidden in the background. You can call it up by pressing Ctrl+Alt+F1.

- **Console 2: Shell prompt.** This console provides you with a shell prompt, from which you can enter Linux commands. If you need to do something manually during installation, you can do it from this console. The keyboard shortcut is Ctrl+Alt+F2.

- **Console 3: Install log.** This console lists messages generated by the installation program. You can get to it by pressing Ctrl+Alt+F3.

- **Console 4: System log.** This console displays system-related messages. You can get to it by pressing Ctrl+Alt+F4.

- **Console 5: Other messages.** Still more messages may appear in this console, which you can open by pressing Ctrl+Alt+F5.

- **Console 6: X graphical display.** This is the console where the GUI of the installation program is displayed. If you use a Ctrl+Alt keyboard combination to view any of the other logs, press Ctrl+Alt+F7 to return to the installation GUI.

Chapter **2**

Configuring Linux

Before you can set up Linux to do serious networking, you need to discover the basics of getting around Linux. In this chapter, you find out those basics. You see how to log on and off Linux, how the Linux file system works, and how to use commands. I also introduce you to GNOME, the graphical user interface (GUI) that's used most with Fedora and many other Linux distributions. Finally, I show you the basics of setting up a Linux user account.

In this chapter, I assume that you have plenty of experience with Windows, so I focus mostly on the differences between Linux and Windows — which, unfortunately, are myriad.

Linux: It Isn't Windows

Before I get into the details of actually using a Linux system, you need to understand some basic differences between Linux and Windows that will puzzle you at first. Linux looks a lot like Windows, but underneath, it's very different. You won't have any trouble finding out how to point and click your way through the GNOME user interface, but before long, you'll run into Linux file-naming conventions, terminal windows, configuration files, and a host of other significant differences.

The following sections describe some of the more important differences between Linux and Windows.

X Window

Linux doesn't have a built-in graphical user interface (GUI) as Windows does. Instead, the GUI in Linux is provided by an optional component called *X Window System.* You can run Linux without X Window, in which case you interact with Linux by typing commands. If you prefer to use a GUI, you must install and run X Window.

X Window is split into two parts:

>> A server component, called an *X Server,* handles the basic chores of managing multiple windows and providing graphics services for application programs.

>> A user interface (UI) component, called a *window manager,* provides UI features such as menus, buttons, toolbars, a taskbar, and so on. Several different window managers are available, each with a different look and feel. The most popular is GNOME. I describe it in more detail later in this chapter, in the section "Using GNOME."

Virtual consoles

Linux is a true multiuser OS. This means that you can log on to Linux by using one user account and then log on by using a different account, so that you're logged on twice at the same time. You switch back and forth between the different user sessions, and actions that you take in one session don't affect any of your other sessions.

In addition to an X Window client such as GNOME, Linux provides a traditional text-based environment — a *console* — through which you can enter Linux commands to perform any function available in Linux. The more you work with Linux, the more you'll discover the limitations of even a sophisticated GUI such as GNOME. When that happens, you'll turn to a console where you can enter brute-force commands.

Because Linux is a multiuser system, it lets you work with more than one console. In fact, you actually have six virtual consoles at your disposal. You can switch to a particular virtual console by pressing Ctrl+Alt+F1 through F6. For example, to switch to virtual console 3, press Ctrl+Alt+F3.

TIP

When a GUI such as GNOME is running, you can switch to it by pressing Ctrl+Alt+F7.

Understanding the file system

The Linux file system is a bit different from the Windows file system. Two of the most obvious differences are actually superficial:

>> Linux uses forward slashes rather than backward slashes to separate directories. Thus, /home/doug is a valid path in Linux; \Windows\System32 is a valid path in Windows.

>> Linux filenames don't use extensions. You can use periods within a filename, but unlike Windows, the final period doesn't identify a file extension.

The fundamental difference between the Linux and Windows file system is that Linux treats everything in the entire system as a file, and it organizes everything into one gigantic tree that begins at a single root. When I say, "Everything is treated as a file," I mean that hardware devices such as floppy drives, serial ports, and Ethernet adapters are treated as files.

The root of the Linux file system is the root partition from which the OS boots. Additional partitions, including other devices that support file systems such as CD-ROM drives, floppy drives, or drives accessed over the network, can be grafted into the tree as directories called *mount points.* Thus, a directory in the Linux file system may actually be a separate hard drive.

Another important aspect of the Linux file system is that the directories that compose a Linux system are governed by a standard called the Filesystem Hierarchy Standard (FHS). This standard spells out which directories a Linux file system should have. Because most Linux systems conform to this standard, you can trust that key files will always be found in the same place.

Table 2-1 lists the top-level directories that are described in the FHS.

TABLE 2-1 **Top-Level Directories in a Linux File System**

Directory	Description
/bin	Essential command binaries
/boot	Static files of the boot loader
/dev	Devices
/etc	Configuration files for the local computer
/home	Home directories for users

(continued)

TABLE 2-1 *(continued)*

Directory	Description
/lib	Shared libraries and kernel modules
/mnt	Mount point for file systems mounted temporarily
/opt	Add-on applications and packages
/root	Home directory for the root user
/sbin	Essential system binaries
/tmp	Temporary files
/usr	Read-only, shared files such as binaries for user commands and libraries
/var	Variable data files

On Again, Off Again

Any user who accesses a Linux system, whether locally or over a network, must be authenticated by a valid user account on the system. In the following sections, you find out how to log on and off of a Linux system and how to shut down the system.

Logging on

When Linux boots up, it displays a series of startup messages as it starts the various services that compose a working Linux system. Assuming that you selected X Window when you installed Linux, you're eventually greeted by the screen shown in Figure 2-1. To log on to Linux, click your username, then type your password and press Enter. (Note that this logon procedure is for Fedora. Other distributions have similar logon procedures.)

TIP

As a part of the installation process (described in Chapter 1 of this minibook), you created a user account other than the root account. You should use this user account rather than the root user account whenever possible. Use the root account only when you are making major changes to the system's configuration. When you're doing routine work, log on as an ordinary user in order to avoid accidentally corrupting your system.

When you log on, Linux grinds its gears for a moment and then displays the GNOME desktop, which I describe later in this chapter.

FIGURE 2-1:
Begin by
logging on.

Logging off

After you've logged on, you'll probably want to know how to log off. To do so, click the power icon in the upper-right corner of the screen, click your account name, and then choose Log Out. A dialog box asks whether you're sure that you want to log out. Click Log Out.

Shutting down

As with any OS, you should never turn off the power to a Linux server without first properly shutting down the system. You can shut down a Linux system by using one of these two techniques:

>> Press Ctrl+Alt+Delete.

>> Click the power icon in the upper-right corner of the screen, click the power icon in the menu that appears, and then choose Power Off.

Using GNOME

Figure 2-2 shows a typical GNOME desktop. Although the GNOME desktop looks a lot different from the Windows desktop, many of the basic skills used for working with Microsoft Windows — such as moving or resizing windows, minimizing or maximizing windows, and using drag-and-drop to move items between windows — are almost exactly the same in GNOME.

FIGURE 2-2:
The desktop.

The following paragraphs describe some of the key features of the GNOME desktop:

>> The Activities Overview provides a single access point for all GNOME applications. It provides fast access to common functions, such as Internet browsing, email, or file management, as well as desktop access to other applications. You can access Activities Overview by pressing the Windows key on the keyboard or clicking Activities in the top-left corner. (The screen in Figure 2-2 shows the Activities Overview open.)

>> The search box in the top-middle portion of the desktop is the easiest way to find things in GNOME. For example, if you want to run the gedit program to edit a text file, search for *gedit*. Or if you want to fiddle with network settings, search for *network*.

>> To log off, click the down-arrow at the upper right of the screen. Then click the arrow that appears next to your name and choose Log Out. (You can also click Account Settings to change your password. Or, you can click the power icon to shut down the computer.)

Getting to a Command Shell

You can get to a command shell in one of two basic ways when you need to run Linux commands directly. The first is to press Ctrl+Alt+Fx to switch to one of the virtual consoles, where Fx is one of the function keys, from F1 through F12. (If you aren't sure which function key to use to open a virtual console, refer to the "Virtual consoles" section in this chapter.) Then, you can log on and run commands to your heart's content. When you're done, press Ctrl+Alt+F7 to return to GNOME.

Alternatively, you can open a command shell directly in GNOME by opening the Activities Overview, clicking Applications, opening the Utilities collection, and then clicking the Terminal icon. This opens a command shell in a window right on the GNOME desktop, as shown in Figure 2-3. Because this shell runs within the user account that GNOME is logged on as, you don't have to log on. You can just start typing commands. When you're done, type **Exit** to close the window.

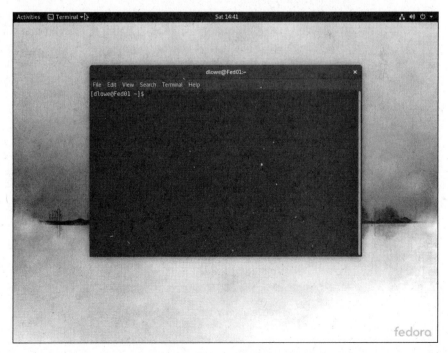

FIGURE 2-3:
A terminal window.

Enabling the SUDO Command

Throughout the remaining chapters of this minibook, you'll see many examples of commands entered in a terminal window that begin with the word sudo. This command is an essential part of Linux administration. It lets you execute Linux commands with permissions of the root user account.

The sudo command is required because many Linux administrative commands can only be run by the root user. You can simply log in as the root user to run such commands, but that's considered a risky practice because the root user can do virtually anything in a Linux environment. It's safer to log in with an ordinary user account and use sudo to enable access to administrative functions.

For example, you'll often use the dnf command to install new software on a Linux system. The dnf command is one of those commands that can only be run by the root user. So you'll need to use sudo to run the dnf command. To use sudo, you simply prefix the command you want to run with the word sudo, as in the following example:

```
sudo dnf install dhcp
```

Here, the command dnf install dhcp will be run as the root user. Note that for security purposes, the sudo command prompts you for your own password before it runs the dnf command.

To enable your user account for sudo, the root user must add your account name to a group called wheel, because by default the sudo program is configured to allow all users in this group to run commands as the root user. To add yourself to the wheel group, you must edit a configuration file called group, which is found in the etc/ folder. Here are the steps to edit this file:

1. **Log in as the root user.**

   The GNOME desktop appears.

2. **Click Activities at the top left of the GNOME desktop, and then choose Files.**

   The File Manager appears, as shown in Figure 2-4.

3. **Click Other Locations in the navigation pane on the left side of the File Manager window; then click Computer.**

   The folders at the computer's root level appear, as shown in Figure 2-5.

4. **Double-click the etc folder.**

   The files in the etc folder appear.

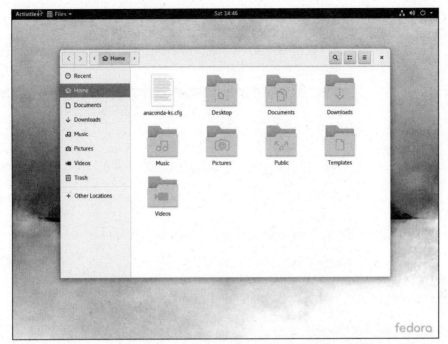

FIGURE 2-4:
The File Manager window.

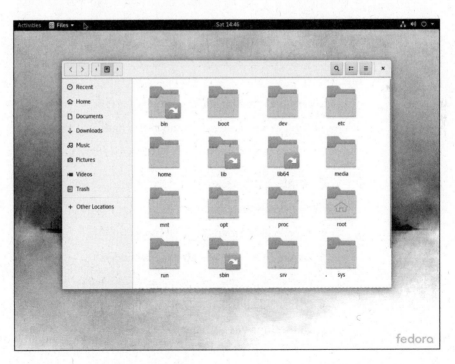

FIGURE 2-5:
The root-level folders.

5. **Locate and double-click the file named** group.

The group file is opened in the gedit text editor, as shown in Figure 2-6.

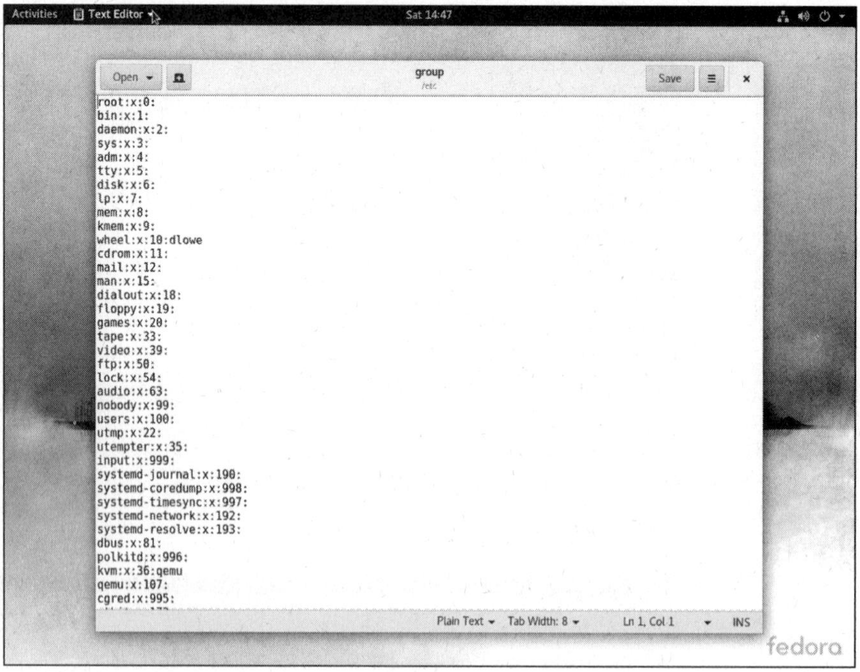

FIGURE 2-6:
Editing the
group file.

6. **Locate the line that starts with** wheel:x:10:

7. **Add your username to the end of this line.**

For example, since my username is dlowe, I edited the line to read as follows:

```
wheel:x:10:dlowe
```

8. **Click the Save button.**

The group file is saved with your changes.

9. **Close the** gedit **and File Manager windows.**

You're done! You can now use the sudo command.

Don't forget that you're still logged in as the root user. You should now log off and log in again using your personal user account.

Managing User Accounts

One of the most common network administration tasks is adding a user account. The Setup Agent prompts you to create a user account the first time you start Linux after installing it. However, you'll probably need to create additional accounts.

Each Linux user account has the following information associated with it:

>> **Username:** The name the user types to log on to the Linux system.

>> **Full name:** The user's full name.

>> **Home directory:** The directory that the user is placed in when he or she logs on. In Fedora, the default home directory is /home/username. For example, if the username is blowe, the home directory is /home/blowe.

>> **Shell:** The program used to process Linux commands. Several shell programs are available. In most distributions, the default shell is /bin/bash.

>> **Group:** You can create group accounts, which make it easy to apply identical access rights to groups of users.

>> **User ID:** The internal identifier for the user.

You can add a new user by using the useradd command. For example, to create a user account named kgearhart, using default values for the other account information, open a terminal window or switch to a virtual console and type this command:

```
sudo useradd kgearhart
```

The useradd command has many optional parameters that you can use to set account information, such as the user's home directory and shell.

Fortunately, most Linux distributions come with special programs that simplify routine system management tasks. Fedora is no exception. It comes with a program called User Manager, shown in Figure 2-7. To start this program, open a terminal window and type the following command:

```
sudo system-config-users
```

If you're prompted to install the User Manager program, type **y**.

To create a user with User Manager, click the Add User button. This brings up a dialog box that asks for the user's name, password, and other information. Fill out this dialog box and then click OK.

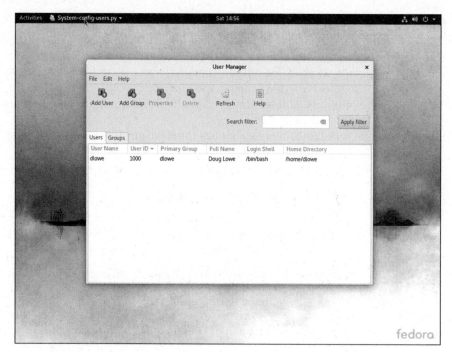

FIGURE 2-7:
Managing users
and groups.

The User Manager also lets you create groups. You can simplify the task of administering users by applying access rights to groups rather than individual users. Then, when a user needs access to a resource, you can add the user to the group that has the needed access.

To create a group, click the Add Group button. A dialog box appears, asking for the name of the new group. Type the name you want and then click OK.

To add a user to a group, click the Groups tab in the User Manager. Then, double-click the group to which you want to add users. This brings up the Group Properties dialog box. Click the Group Users tab and then select the users that you want to belong to the group.

Chapter **3**

Basic Linux Network Configuration

n many cases, configuring a Linux server for networking is a snap. When you install Linux, the installation program automatically detects your network adapters and installs the appropriate drivers. Then, you're prompted for basic network configuration information, such as the computer's IP address, host name, and so on.

However, you may need to manually change your network settings after installation. You may also need to configure advanced networking features that aren't configured during installation. In this chapter, you discover the basic procedures for configuring Linux networking services.

Using the Network Configuration Program

Before you can use a network interface to access a network, you have to configure the interface's basic TCP/IP options, such as its IP address, host name, Domain Name System (DNS) servers, and so on. This configuration is automatically set up when you install Linux, but you may need to change it later on. In this section, I show you how to do that by using Fedora's Network settings program. You can access this program by clicking your name in the top-right corner of the screen, choosing Settings, and then choosing Network.

TIP

If you prefer a more masochistic approach to configuring your network, see the section "Working with Network Configuration Files," later in this chapter.

The Network Configuration program lets you configure the basic TCP/IP settings for a network interface by pointing and clicking your way through tabbed windows. Here are the steps:

1. **Click Activities and type** Network. **Then click the Network icon (shown in the margin).**

The Network application appears, as shown in Figure 3-1.

FIGURE 3-1:
The Network application.

2. **Select the network interface that you want to configure and then click the Options button (shown in the margin).**

This summons the editing window, as shown in Figure 3-2.

3. **Click the IPv4 Settings tab.**

The screen shown in Figure 3-3 is displayed.

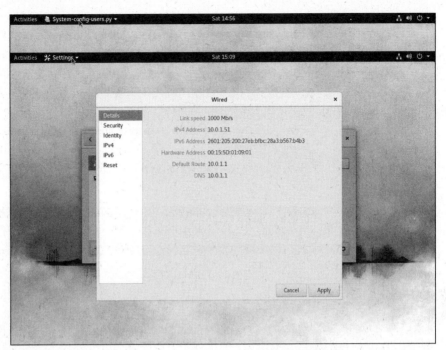

FIGURE 3-2:
Editing a network
connection.

FIGURE 3-3:
Configuring
IPv4 settings.

Basic Linux Network
Configuration

CHAPTER 3 **Basic Linux Network Configuration**   **611**

4. To configure the device to use DHCP, select Automatic (DHCP) in the Addresses drop-down.

If you plan on setting up this computer to be your network's DHCP or DNS server, you shouldn't select this check box. Instead, you should assign a static IP address as described in Step 5.

5. To configure the device with a static IP address, select Manual in the Method drop-down.

This enables the controls shown in Figure 3-4.

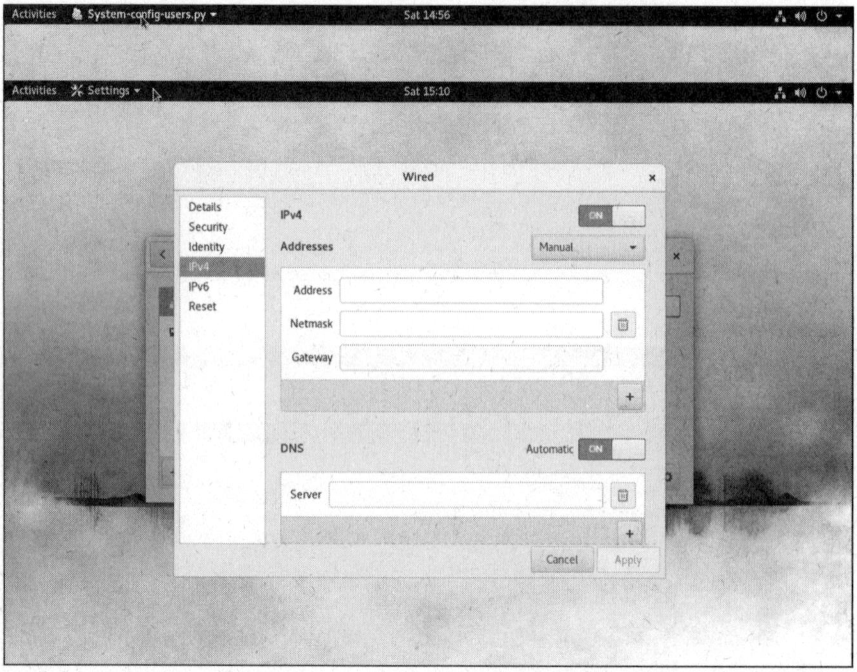

FIGURE 3-4:
Manual IP
configuration.

6. Enter the Address, Netmask, and Gateway addresses.

The IP address should be located on your network's private subnet. Typically, you'll use an address in the form 192.168.*x.x*.

TIP

If you're setting up this computer to be the gateway router that will manage traffic between your local network and the Internet, use a static address that's easy to remember, such as 192.168.1.1.

The subnet mask should be the mask that's appropriate for the IP address you choose. For a 192.168.*x.x* address, use 255.255.255.0.

The default gateway address should be the address of the gateway router that links your network to the Internet. If this computer *is* the gateway router, specify the gateway address provided to you by your Internet service provider (ISP).

7. **Enter the IP addresses for the DNS servers that you want to use in the DNS Server text box.**

If your network runs its own DNS server, you can specify its address here. Otherwise, you have to get the DNS server addresses from your ISP.

To enter more than one DNS server address, enter the first DNS address, then click the plus sign (+) button located beneath and to the right of the DNS server address to display a text box for the second DNS server address.

8. **Click Apply.**

Any changes you made to the network configuration are saved, and you return to the Network application.

9. **Restart the network services.**

For the gory details on how to do that, see the next section.

Restarting Your Network

Whenever you make a configuration change to your network, you must restart Linux networking services for the change to take effect. If you find that annoying, just be thankful that you don't have to restart the entire computer. Simply restarting the network services is sufficient.

Open a console by pressing Ctrl+Alt+*n*, where *n* is a number from 2–7. Log in using the root account and then enter the following command:

```
service network restart
```

To confirm that the service was properly restarted, you'll see a message similar to this:

```
Restarting network (via systemctl): [ OK ]
```

Working with Network Configuration Files

Like other OS services, the Linux network is configured by settings that are specified in configuration files that you can find in the /etc directory or in one of its subdirectories. Graphical configuration programs, such as Fedora Network Configuration, are actually little more than glorified text editors that enable you to select network configuration options from user-friendly screens and then save your configuration changes to the standard configuration files. If you prefer to do the grunt work yourself, you can open the configuration files in a text editor and make changes to them directly.

WARNING

Any time you open a configuration file in a text editor, you run the risk of messing up your system's configuration. So be careful!

Table 3-1 lists the main Linux network configuration files and describes what each file does. The details of these files are described in the sections that follow.

TABLE 3-1 **Linux Network Configuration Files**

File	Location	Description
network	/etc/sysconfig	Basic network configuration
hostname	/etc	Specifies the host name (obsolete, but should still be present)
ifcfg-xxxx	-/etc/sysconfig/ network-scripts	IP settings for the network adapter named xxxx
hosts	/etc	Lists host address mappings
resolv.conf	/etc	Lists DNS nameservers
nsswitch.conf	/etc	Specifies the name search order
xinetd.conf	/etc	Specifies which network services are started automatically

The Network file

The Network file, which lives in /etc/sysconfig, specifies basic configuration settings for your network. Here's a typical Network file:

```
NETWORKING=yes
HOSTNAME=LSERVER
GATEWAY=192.168.1.1
```

This file specifies that networking is enabled, the computer's host name is LSERVER, and the default gateway address is 192.168.1.1.

The following paragraphs describe all the settings that are valid for this file:

>> NETWORKING: Specifies YES or NO to enable or disable networking for the computer.

>> HOSTNAME: Specifies the host name for this computer. You should also specify this name in /etc/hostname, although that file is considered obsolete and is used only by some old programs. Note that this can be a simple host name (like LSERVER) or a fully qualified domain name (like Lserver.LoweWriter.com).

>> FORWARD_IPV4: Specifies YES or NO to enable or disable IP forwarding. Specify FORWARD_IPV4=YES to set up a router.

>> GATEWAY: Specifies the IP address of the computer's Default Gateway. If the network has a gateway router, specify its address here. If this computer is the network's gateway router, specify the gateway IP address provided by your ISP.

>> GATEWAYDEV: Specifies the interface (such as eth0) that should be used to reach the gateway.

The ifcfg files

Each network interface has an ifcfg configuration file located in /etc/sysconfig/network-scripts. The device name is added to the end of the filename. So, for example, the configuration file for an interface named p2p1 is called ifcfg-p2p1.

TIP

This file is created and updated by the Network Configuration program, so you don't have to edit it directly (if you don't want to).

Here's a typical ifcfg file for an interface that has a static IP address:

```
DEVICE=p2p1
BOOTPROTO=none
ONBOOT=yes
USERCTL=no
IPADDR=192.168.1.200
NETMASK=255.255.255.0
BROADCAST=192.168.1.255
NETWORK=192.168.1.0
```

Here's an example for an interface that uses DHCP:

```
DEVICE=p2p1
BOOTPROTO=dhcp
ONBOOT=yes
USERCTL=no
```

Here, the ifcfg file doesn't have to specify the IP address information because the interface gets that information from a DHCP server.

The following paragraphs describe the settings that you're most likely to see in this file:

>> DEVICE: The name of the device, such as eth0 or eth1.

>> USERCTL: Specifies YES or NO to indicate whether local users are allowed to start or stop the network.

>> ONBOOT: Specifies YES or NO to indicate whether the device should be enabled when Linux boots up.

>> BOOTPROTO: Specifies how the device gets its IP address. Possible values are NONE for static assignment, DHCP, or BOOTP.

>> BROADCAST: The broadcast address used to send packets to everyone on the subnet: for example, 192.168.1.255.

>> NETWORK: The network address: for example, 192.168.1.0.

>> NETMASK: The subnet mask: for example, 255.255.255.0.

>> IPADDR: The IP address for the adapter.

The Hosts file

The Hosts file is a simple list of IP addresses and the host names associated with each address. You can think of the Hosts file as a local DNS database of sorts. Whenever Linux needs to resolve a DNS name, it first looks for the name in the Hosts file. If Linux finds the name there, it doesn't have to do a DNS lookup; it simply uses the IP address found in the Hosts file.

For small networks, common practice is to list the host name for each computer on the network in the Hosts file on each computer. Then, whenever you add a new computer to the network, you just update each computer's Hosts file to include the new computer. That's not so bad if the network has just a few computers, but you wouldn't want to do it that way for a network with 1,000 hosts. That's why other name resolution systems are more popular for larger networks.

The default Linux Hosts file looks something like this:

```
# Do not remove the following line, or various programs that require
# network functionality will fail.
127.0.0.1 localhost.localdomain localhost
```

Here, the names localhost.localdomain and localhost both resolve to 127.0.0.1, which is the standard local loopback address.

Here's an example of a Hosts file that has some additional entries:

```
# Do not remove the following line, or various programs that require
# network functionality will fail.
127.0.0.1 LServer localhost.localdomain localhost
192.168.1.1 linksys
192.168.1.100 ward.cleaver.com ward
192.168.1.101 june.cleaver.com june
192.168.1.102 wally.cleaver.com wally
192.168.1.103 theodore.cleaver.com theodore beaver
```

Here, I defined host names for each of the Cleaver family's four computers and their Linksys router. Each computer can be accessed by using one of two names (for example, ward.cleaver.com or just ward), except the last one, which has three names.

The resolv.conf file

The resolv.conf file lists the DNS nameservers that can be consulted to perform DNS lookups. A typical resolv.conf file looks like this:

```
nameserver 192.168.1.110
nameserver 204.127.198.19
nameserver 63.249.76.19
```

If you have set up a nameserver on your own network, its IP address should be the first one listed.

The nsswitch.conf file

This configuration file controls how name resolution works when looking up various types of objects, such as host addresses and passwords. Listing 3-1 shows the sample nsswitch.conf file that comes with Fedora Linux. As you can see, this file is loaded with comments that explain what the various settings do.

You can use the files, db, and dns keywords to specify how objects should be retrieved. files specifies that the local file should be used, db specifies a database lookup, and dns specifies that a DNS server should be consulted.

The order in which you list these keywords determines the order in which the data sources are searched. Thus, if you want host names to be resolved first by the local Hosts file and then by DNS, you should include the following line in nsswitch:

```
hosts: files dns
```

LISTING 3-1: **A Sample** /etc/nsswitch.conf **File**

```
#
# /etc/nsswitch.conf
#
# An example Name Service Switch config file. This file should be
# sorted with the most-used services at the beginning.
#
# The entry '[NOTFOUND=return]' means that the search for an
# entry should stop if the search in the previous entry turned
# up nothing. Note that if the search failed due to some other reason
# (like no NIS server responding) then the search continues with the
# next entry.
#
# Legal entries are:
#
# nisplus or nis+ Use NIS+ (NIS version 3)
# nis or yp Use NIS (NIS version 2), also called YP
# dns Use DNS (Domain Name Service)
# files Use the local files
# db Use the local database (.db) files
# compat Use NIS on compat mode
# hesiod Use Hesiod for user lookups
# [NOTFOUND=return] Stop searching if not found so far
#
# To use db, put the "db" in front of "files" for entries you want to be
# looked up first in the databases
#
# Example:
#passwd: db files nisplus nis
#shadow: db files nisplus nis
#group: db files nisplus nis
passwd: files
shadow: files
group: files
initgroups: files
#hosts: db files nisplus nis dns
hosts: files dns
# Example - obey only what nisplus tells us...
#services: nisplus [NOTFOUND=return] files
```

```
#networks: nisplus [NOTFOUND=return] files
#protocols: nisplus [NOTFOUND=return] files
#rpc: nisplus [NOTFOUND=return] files
#ethers: nisplus [NOTFOUND=return] files
#netmasks: nisplus [NOTFOUND=return] files
bootparams: nisplus [NOTFOUND=return] files
ethers: files
netmasks: files
networks: files
protocols: files
rpc: files
services: files
netgroup: files
publickey: nisplus
automount: files
aliases: files nisplus
```

The xinetd.conf file

Xinetd is a service that oversees a variety of networking services, such as Telnet or Finger. Xinetd listens for requests on the ports on which these services talk and automatically starts the service when a connection is made. Xinetd is controlled by the configuration file xinetd.conf, which is found in the /etc directory, and each of the services controlled by Xinetd is in turn controlled by a configuration file found in the /etc/xinet.d directory.

You should leave most of the settings in these configuration files alone unless you've studied up on Xinetd. (You can find out more about it at www.github/xinetd-org.) However, you may want to modify the configuration files in order to enable or disable specific services.

Each service controlled by Xinetd has a configuration file in the /etc/xinet.d directory. Each configuration file ends with a line that enables or disables the service. For example, here's the configuration file for Telnet, /etc/xinet.d/telnet:

```
# default: on
# description: The telnet server serves telnet sessions; it uses \
# unencrypted username/password pairs for authentication.
service telnet
{
Flags = REUSE
socket_type = stream
wait = no
user = root
server = /usr/sbin/in.telnetd
log_on_failure += USERID
```

```
disable = yes
}
```

Here, the last line disables Telnet. You can enable the Telnet service by changing the last line to disable = no.

Displaying Your Network Configuration with the ifconfig Command

Linux doesn't have an ipconfig command like Windows. Instead, the command that you use to display information about your network configuration is ifconfig. You can also use this command to set network configuration options, but in most cases, using the Network Configuration program or directly editing the network configuration files is easier.

If you enter ifconfig without any parameters, you get output similar to the following:

```
lo: flags=73<UP,LOOPBACK,RUNNING> mtu 16436
inet addr:127.0.0.1 netmask:255.0.0.0
inet6 ::1 prefixlen 128 scopeid 0x10<host>
loop txqueuelen 0 (local loopback)
RX packets 12 bytes 720 (720.0 B)
RX errors 0 dropped 0 overruns 0 frame 0
TX packets 12 bytes 720 (720.0 B)
TX errors 0 dropped 0 overruns 0 frame 0
p2p1: flags=4163<UP,BROADCAST,RUNNING,MULTICAST> mtu 1500
inet addr:10.0.2.15 netmask:255.255.255.0 broadcast 10.0.2.255
inet6 fe00::a00:27ff:fe08::3f5a prefixlen 64 scopeid 0x20<link>
ether 08:00:27:08:3f:5a txqueuelen 1000 (Ethernet)
RX packets 273 bytes 208816 (203.9 KiB)
RX errors 0 dropped 0 overruns 0 frame 0
TX packets 278 bytes 27696 (27KiB)
TX errors 0 dropped 0 overruns 0 frame 0
```

From this output, you can tell that the IP address of the Ethernet adapter (p2p1) is 10.0.2.15, the broadcast address is 10.0.2.255, and the netmask is 255.255.255.0. You can also see transmit and receive statistics as well as information about the hardware configuration, such as the MAC address and the adapter's interrupt and memory base address assignments.

Linux offers many other commands that can help you configure and troubleshoot a network. Many of these commands are described in detail in Chapter 8 of this minibook.

Chapter **4**

Running DHCP and DNS

O ne of the main reasons why many network administrators add Linux servers to their networks is to run Internet services, such as DHCP and DNS. These services were originally developed for the Unix environment, so they tend to run better under Linux than they do under Windows.

Well, that's the theory, at least. The most recent versions of Windows are probably just as good at running these services as Linux. Still, if you prefer to set up these services on a Linux server, this chapter is for you.

Running a DHCP Server

DHCP is the TCP/IP protocol that automatically assigns IP addresses to hosts as they come on the network. (DHCP stands for Dynamic Host Configuration Protocol, but that won't be on the test.) For a very small network (say, fewer than ten hosts), you don't really need DHCP: You can just configure each computer to have a static IP address. For larger networks, however, DHCP is almost a must. Without DHCP, you have to manually plan your entire IP address scheme and manually configure every computer with its IP information. Then, if a critical address — such as your Internet gateway router or your DNS server address — changes, you have to manually update each computer on the network. As you can imagine, DHCP can save you a lot of time.

Even for small networks, however, DHCP can be a timesaver. For example, suppose that you have a notebook computer that you take back and forth between your home and office. If you don't set up a DHCP server at home, you have to change the computer's static IP address each time you move the computer. With DHCP, the computer can change IP addresses automatically.

For the complete lowdown on DHCP, please read Book 2, Chapter 5. In the following sections, I show you how to install and configure a DHCP server on the Fedora 12 Linux distribution.

Installing DHCP

You can quickly find out whether DHCP is installed on your system by entering the following command from a shell prompt:

```
sudo dnf install dhcp
```

If DHCP has already been installed, the dnf command will let you know that the package is already installed and that it has nothing to do. Otherwise, the dnf command will ask your permission to install the package:

```
Total download size: 801 k
Installed size: 1.5 M
Is this ok [y/N]:
```

Enter **y** to proceed with the installation. After a few moments, dnf will announce that the installation is complete.

Configuring DHCP

You configure DHCP settings through a file called dhcpd.conf that lives in the /etc directory. Fedora provides you with a sample configuration file located in the directory

```
/usr/share/doc/dhcp-version/dhcpd.conf.sample
```

Open this file in the text editor and then save it to the /etc directory, changing its name from dhcpd.conf.sample to just dhcpd.conf. Then, edit the file to reflect the settings that you want to use.

Listing 4-1 shows the sample configuration file that comes with Fedora. (The exact contents of this file vary from release to release and include additional comments that I've removed for the sake of brevity.)

LISTING 4-1:

A Sample dhcpd.conf **File**

```
ddns-update-style interim;
ignore client-updates;
subnet 192.168.0.0 netmask 255.255.255.0 {
# --- default gateway
option routers 192.168.0.1;
option subnet-mask 255.255.255.0;
option nis-domain "domain.org";
option domain-name "domain.org";
option domain-name-servers 192.168.0.1;
option time-offset -18000; # Eastern Standard Time
# option ntp-servers 192.168.0.1;
# option netbios-name-servers 192.168.0.1;
# --- Selects point-to-point node (default is hybrid). Don't change this
# -- unless you understand Netbios very well
# option netbios-node-type 2;
range dynamic-bootp 192.168.0.128 192.168.0.255;
default-lease-time 21600;
max-lease-time 43200;
# we want the nameserver to appear at a fixed address
host ns {
next-server marvin.redhat.com;
hardware ethernet 12:34:56:78:AB:CD;
fixed-address 207.175.42.254;
}
}
```

The following paragraphs describe some of the key points of this file:

>> ddns-update-style: The DHCP standards group is in the midst of deciding exactly how DHCP will handle changes to DNS data. This option specifies that the interim method should be used. This line is required — so don't mess with it.

>> subnet: This line specifies a subnet that's managed by this DHCP server. Following the subnet ID and netmask is an opening bracket; all the options that appear between this bracket and the closing bracket in the last line of the file belong to this subnet. In some cases, your DHCP server may dole out IP configuration information for two or more subnet groups. In that case, you need additional subnet groups in the configuration file.

>> option routers: This line provides the IP address of the Default Gateway.

>> option subnet-mask: This line provides the subnet mask for the subnet.

>> option nis-domain: This line provides the NIS domain name. This line is important only if you've set up one or more NIS servers.

- » `option domain-name`: This line provides the domain name for the network.

- » `option domain-name-servers`: This line provides the IP addresses of your DNS servers.

- » `range`: This line specifies the range of addresses that the DHCP server will assign for this subnet.

- » `default-lease-time`: This line determines the default lease time in seconds.

- » `max-lease-time`: This line determines the maximum life of a lease.

- » `host`: This line specifies a reservation. The host group specifies the MAC address for the host and the fixed IP address to be assigned.

Starting DHCP

After you set up the configuration file, you can start DHCP by opening a terminal window or virtual console and entering the following command:

```
dhcpd start
```

If an error exists in the configuration file, a message to that effect is displayed. You have to edit the file in order to correct the error and then start the DHCP service again.

You should also restart the service whenever you make a change to the configuration file. To restart DHCP, enter this command:

```
dhcpd restart
```

To automatically start DHCP whenever you start the computer, run this command:

```
chkconfig -level 35 dhcpd on
```

Running a DNS Server

Linux comes with BIND, the best DNS server that money can buy. BIND is an extremely powerful program. Some people make entire careers of setting up and configuring BIND. In these few short pages, I just touch on the very basics of setting up a DNS server on your network.

TIP

You can find plenty of details about DNS in Book 2, Chapter 6. Please review that chapter before playing with BIND on your Linux system.

Installing BIND

You can quickly find out whether BIND is installed on your system by entering the following command from a shell prompt:

```
sudo dnf install bind
```

If BIND has already been installed, the dnf command will let you know that the package is already installed and that it has nothing to do. Otherwise, the dnf command will ask your permission to install the package. Enter **y** to install the package.

Looking at BIND configuration files

Although Fedora Linux includes a handy BIND configuration tool, you still need to know the location and purpose of each of BIND's basic configuration files. These files are described in the following sections.

named.conf

This file, found in the /etc directory, is the basic BIND configuration file. This file contains global properties and links to the other configuration files.

WARNING

Because the Fedora BIND configuration tool edits this file, you shouldn't edit this file directly. If you need to set your own configuration options, use named.custom instead.

Here's a typical named.conf file:

```
## named.conf - configuration for bind
#
# Generated automatically by redhat-config-bind, alchemist et al.
# Any changes not supported by redhat-config-bind should be put
# in /etc/named.custom
#
controls {
inet 127.0.0.1 allow { localhost; } keys { rndckey; };
};
```

```
include "/etc/named.custom";
include "/etc/rndc.key";
zone "0.0.127.in-addr.arpa" {
type master;
file "0.0.127.in-addr.arpa.zone";
};
zone "localhost" {
type master;
file "localhost.zone";
};
zone "lowewriter.com" {
type master;
file "lowewriter.com.zone";
};
```

The line `include "/etc/named.custom";` is what causes the `named.custom` file to be read in. The `zone` lines name the zone files for each domain for which the server is responsible.

By default, this file always includes two zones:

» `0.0.127.in-addr.arpa`: The reverse-lookup zone for `localhost`

» `localhost`: The zone file for the local computer

Any other zones that you added through the Fedora BIND configuration tool appear in this file as well.

named.custom

This file, also found in /etc, lets you add information to the `named.conf` file. Here's a typical `named.custom` file:

```
## named.custom - custom configuration for bind
#
# Any changes not currently supported by redhat-config-bind should be put
# in this file.
#
zone "." {
type hint;
file "named.ca";
};
options {
directory "/var/named/";
};
```

One reason to use this file is if you want to include zone files that you create yourself without the aid of the Fedora BIND configuration program. If you want to include your own zone file, just add a zone statement that names the zone file. For example, suppose that you want to add a zone named cleaver.com, and you manually created the cleaver.com.zone. To include this zone, add these lines to the named.custom file:

```
zone "cleaver.com" {
type master;
file "cleaver.com.zone";
};
```

named.ca

This file, located in the /var/named directory, lists the names and addresses of the Internet's root servers. It's a fascinating file to look at because it helps to unveil the mystery of how the Internet really works. You shouldn't change it, however, unless, of course, you happen to be the administrator of one of the Internet's root servers — in which case, I hope you're not reading this book to learn how BIND works.

Listing 4-2 shows a typical named.ca file. The exact contents of this file varies from release to release.

| LISTING 4-2: | **A Sample** named.ca **File** |

```
; <<>> DiG 9.9.2-P1-RedHat-9.9.2-6.P1.fc18 <<>> +bufsize=1200
+norec @a.root-servers.net
; (2 servers found)
;; global options: +cmd
;; Got answer:
;; ->>HEADER<<- opcode: QUERY, status: NOERROR, id: 25828
;; flags: qr aa; QUERY: 1, ANSWER: 13, AUTHORITY: 0, ADDITIONAL: 23
;; OPT PSEUDOSECTION:
; EDNS: version: 0, flags:; udp: 512
;; QUESTION SECTION:
;. IN NS
;; ANSWER SECTION:
. 518400 IN NS a.root-servers.net.
. 518400 IN NS b.root-servers.net.
. 518400 IN NS c.root-servers.net.
. 518400 IN NS d.root-servers.net.
. 518400 IN NS e.root-servers.net.
```

(continued)

LISTING 4-2: **(continued)**

```
.   518400 IN NS f.root-servers.net.
.   518400 IN NS g.root-servers.net.
.   518400 IN NS h.root-servers.net.
.   518400 IN NS i.root-servers.net.
.   518400 IN NS j.root-servers.net.
.   518400 IN NS k.root-servers.net.
.   518400 IN NS l.root-servers.net.
.   518400 IN NS m.root-servers.net.
;; ADDITIONAL SECTION:
a.root-servers.net. 3600000 IN A    198.41.0.4
a.root-servers.net. 3600000 IN AAAA 2001:503:ba3e::2:30
b.root-servers.net. 3600000 IN A    192.228.79.201
c.root-servers.net. 3600000 IN A    192.33.4.12
d.root-servers.net. 3600000 IN A    199.7.91.13
d.root-servers.net. 3600000 IN AAAA 2001:500:2d::d
e.root-servers.net. 3600000 IN A    192.203.230.10
f.root-servers.net. 3600000 IN A    192.5.5.241
f.root-servers.net. 3600000 IN AAAA 2001:500:2f::f
g.root-servers.net. 3600000 IN A    192.112.36.4
h.root-servers.net. 3600000 IN A    128.63.2.53
h.root-servers.net. 3600000 IN AAAA 2001:500:1::803f:235
i.root-servers.net. 3600000 IN A    192.36.148.17
i.root-servers.net. 3600000 IN AAAA 2001:7fe::53
j.root-servers.net. 3600000 IN A    192.58.128.30
j.root-servers.net. 3600000 IN AAAA 2001:503:c27::2:30
k.root-servers.net. 3600000 IN A    193.0.14.129
k.root-servers.net. 3600000 IN AAAA 2001:7fd::1
l.root-servers.net. 3600000 IN A    199.7.83.42
l.root-servers.net. 3600000 IN AAAA 2001:500:3::42
m.root-servers.net. 3600000 IN A    202.12.27.33
m.root-servers.net. 3600000 IN AAAA 2001:dc3::35
;; Query time: 78 msec
;; SERVER: 198.41.0.4#53(198.41.0.4)
;; WHEN: Mon Jan 28 15:33:31 2013
;; MSG SIZE rcvd: 699
```

TIP

An organization named InterNIC keeps the named.ca file up to date. You can download the most current version of named.ca from the InterNIC FTP site at ftp.internic.net. Every once in awhile, InterNIC publishes a new version of this file, so you should check now and then to make sure that your file is current.

named.local

This file, located in `/var/named`, is a zone file for your local computer — that is, for the `localhost` domain. Rarely (if ever) do you need to modify it. It typically looks like this:

```
$TTL 86400
@ IN SOA localhost. root.localhost. (
1997022700 ; Serial
28800 ; Refresh
14400 ; Retry
3600000 ; Expire
86400 ) ; Minimum
IN NS localhost.
1 IN PTR localhost.
```

Zone files

Each zone for which your DNS server is authoritative should have a zone file, named *domain*.zone and located in the `/var/named` directory. If you like to edit DNS records directly, you can create this file yourself. Or you can use the point-and-click interface of the Fedora BIND configuration tool to automatically create the file.

Here's a typical zone file, named `lowewriter.com.zone`:

```
$TTL 86400
@ IN SOA ns207.pair.com. root.localhost (
2 ; serial
28800 ; refresh
7200 ; retry
604800 ; expire
86400 ; ttl
)
IN NS ns000.ns0.com.
IN NS ns207.pair.com.
@ IN MX 1 sasi.pair.com.
www IN A 209.68.34.15
```

Table 4-1 lists the most common types of records that appear in zone files. For a complete description of each of these record types, see Book 2, Chapter 6.

TABLE 4-1 **Common Resource Record Types**

Type	Name	Description
SOA	Start Of Authority	Identifies a zone
NS	Name Server	Identifies a name server that is authoritative for the zone
A	Address	Maps a fully qualified domain name to an IP address
CNAME	Canonical Name	Creates an alias for a fully qualified domain name
MX	Mail Exchange	Identifies the mail server for a domain
PTR	Pointer	Maps an IP address to a fully qualified domain name for reverse lookups

Restarting BIND

BIND runs as a service called `named`. As a result, when you make changes to your DNS configuration, you have to restart the `named` service to apply the changes. To do that, use this command:

```
service named restart
```

You can also restart the `named` service from the Service Configuration tool. Choose Main Menu⇨System Settings⇨Server Settings⇨Services. This brings up a dialog box that lists all the running services. Scroll down the list to find `named`, select it, and then click the Restart button.

Chapter **5**

Doing the Samba Dance

U ntil now, you probably thought of Samba as a Brazilian dance with intri-
cate steps and fun rhythms. In the Linux world, however, *Samba* refers to
a file- and printer-sharing program that allows Linux to mimic a Windows
file and print server so that Windows computers can use shared Linux directories
and printers. If you want to use Linux as a file or print server in a Windows network, you need to know how to dance the Samba.

Understanding Samba

Because Linux and Windows have such different file systems, you can't create a
Linux file server simply by granting Windows users access to Linux directories.
Windows client computers can't access files in the Linux directories. Too many
differences exist between the file systems. For example:

» Linux filenames are case sensitive, whereas Windows filenames are not. For
example, in Windows, `File1.txt` and `file1.txt` are the same file. In Linux,
they're different files.

» In Linux, periods aren't used to denote file extensions. Linux filenames don't
use extensions.

» Windows has file attributes like *read-only* and *archive*. Linux doesn't have
these.

More fundamentally, Windows networking uses the Server Message Block (SMB) protocol to manage the exchange of file data among file servers and clients. Linux doesn't have SMB support built in.

That's why Samba is required. Samba is a program that mimics the behavior of a Windows-based file server by implementing the SMB protocol. So when you run Samba on a Linux server, the Windows computers on your network see the Linux server as if it were a Windows server.

Like a Windows server, Samba works by designating certain directories as shares. A *share* is simply a directory that's made available to other users via the network. Each share has the following elements:

>> **Name:** The name by which the share is known over the network. Share names should be eight characters whenever possible.

>> **Path:** The path to the directory on the Linux computer that's being shared, such as \Users\Doug.

>> **Description:** A one-line description of the share.

>> **Access:** A list of users or groups who have been granted access to the share.

Samba also includes a client program that lets a Linux computer access Windows file servers.

Why did Samba's developers choose to call their program Samba? Simply because the protocol that Windows file and print servers use to communicate with each other is SMB. Add a couple of vowels to *SMB*, and you get *Samba*.

Installing Samba

To install Samba, open a console or terminal window and enter the following command:

```
sudo dnf install samba.x86_64
```

Assuming that Samba is not already installed, dnf will ask for your permission to install Samba. Enter **y** to proceed. Be patient while the package downloads and installs.

TIP

One sure way to render a Samba installation useless is to enable the default Linux firewall settings on the computer that runs Samba. The Linux firewall is designed to prevent users from accessing network services, such as Samba. It's designed to be used between the Internet and your local network — not between Samba and your local network. Although you can configure the firewall to allow access to Samba only to your internal network, a much better option is to run the firewall on a separate computer. That way, the firewall computer can concentrate on being a firewall, and the file server computer can concentrate on being a file server.

Starting and Stopping Samba

Before you can use Samba, you must start its two daemons, smbd and nmbd. (*Daemon* is the Linux term for *service* – a program that runs as a background task.) Both daemons can be started at once by starting the SMB service. From a command shell, use this command:

```
sudo service smb start
```

Whenever you make a configuration change, such as adding a new share or creating a new Samba user, you should stop and restart the service with this command:

```
sudo service smb restart
```

If you prefer, you can stop and start the service with separate commands:

```
sudo service smb stop
sudo service smb start
```

If you're not sure whether Samba is running, enter this command:

```
sudo service smb status
```

You get a message indicating whether the smbd and nmbd daemons are running.

To configure Samba to start automatically when you start Linux, use this command:

```
sudo chkconfig –level 35 smb on
```

See the upcoming Tip for an explanation of level 35.

To make sure that the chkconfig command worked right, enter this command:

```
chkconfig –list smb
```

You should see output similar to the following:

```
Smb 0:off 1:off 2:off 3:on 4:off 5:on 6:off
```

TIP

You can independently configure services to start automatically for each of the six *boot levels* of Linux. Boot level 3 is normal operation without an X Server; level 5 is normal operation with an X Server. So setting SMB to start for levels 3 and 5 makes SMB available — regardless of whether you're using a graphical user interface (GUI). (Read more about X Server in Chapter 2 of this minibook.)

Editing the smb.conf File

To configure Samba, you have to roll up your sleeves and edit the Samba configuration file, which is called smb.conf and is usually located in the /etc/samba directory.

Figure 5-1 shows you the smb.conf file being edited in the standard text editor program, which you can access by double-clicking the configuration file.

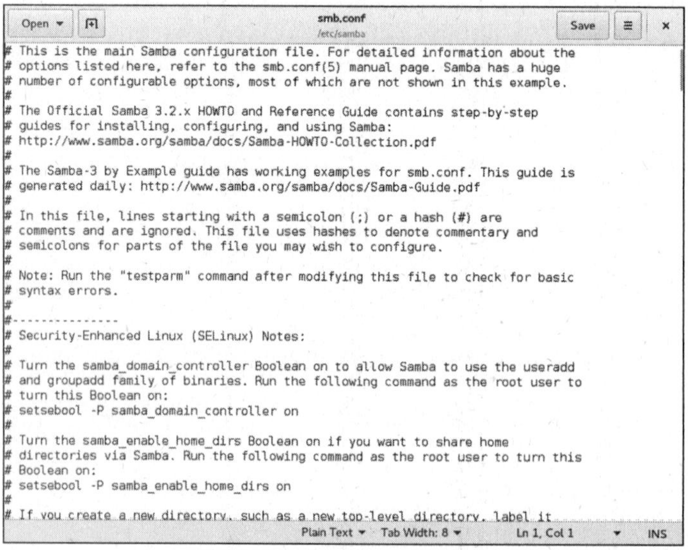

FIGURE 5-1:
Editing the
smb.conf file.

Any line in the smb.conf file that begins with a hash mark (#) or semicolon (;) is a comment. The default smb.conf file is loaded with comments that describe what each configuration line does. Plus, you can find many sample configuration entries that are commented out. The sample configuration lines are marked with a semicolon to distinguish them from explanatory text lines, which begin with a hash mark.

TIP

Before you edit the smb.conf file, make a backup copy of it. That way, if you mess up the file beyond recognition, you can revert to the backup copy.

The smb.conf file consists of several predefined sections that define several types of options, followed by one or more sections that define shares.

The overall structure of the smb.conf file is something like this:

```
[global]
    Global settings

[homes]
    Home folder settings

[printers]
    Printing settings

[sharename1]
    Settings for first share

[sharename2]
    Settings for second share
```

Configuring global settings

To make your Samba server visible on the network, you need to configure its server settings by editing the [Global] section of the smb.conf file. The following paragraphs describe the settings you're likely to change:

>> workgroup: The workgroup name must match the name of the workgroup or domain used by the computers that will access this Samba server.

>> server string: You can enter any descriptive text you want for this setting.

>> interfaces: Indicates which network interface the Samba server uses. You can omit this option if the computer has just one interface.

>> `security`: The security model used by the Samba server. The options are as follows:

- *ADS (Active Directory Security):* This mode configures the Samba server to use a Windows domain controller to verify the user. If you specify this option, the domain controller will be determined based on the computer's DNS settings.

- *Domain:* This mode configures the Samba server to use an old-style Windows NT domain. You should use this option only if your network hasn't been upgraded since Bill Clinton was president.

- *Server:* This mode configures Samba to use another Samba server to authenticate users. If you have more than one Samba server, this feature lets you set up user accounts on just one of the servers. Specify the name of the Samba server in which you want to perform the authentication in the Authentication Server text box.

- *Share:* This mode authorizes users separately for each share that they attempt to access.

- *User:* This is the default mode. It requires that users provide a valid username and password when they first connect to a Samba server. That authentication then grants them access to all shares on the server, subject to the restrictions of the account under which they are authorized.

Creating a share

To be useful, a file server should offer one or more *shares* — directories that have been designated as publicly accessible via the network.

Before you create a share, you should create the directory that will hold the share's data. You can create this folder anywhere you want. I usually create a directory named `shares` in the `var` directory, and then create individual shared directories in `\var\shares`. For example, you can use the following command to create a directory named `myshare`:

```
mkdir /var/shares/myshare
```

Then, to grant full access to all users on this folder, use this command:

```
chmod 777 /var/shares/myshare
```

After you've created a directory to share, you can create the Samba share by adding a share definition to the end of the `smb.conf` file. For example:

```
[myshare]
    path = /var/shares/myshare
    comment = Sample Share
    writable = yes
```

If you add these lines to the end of the smb.conf file and restart the SMB service, a share named myshare will be added to the Samba server. The files for this share will be stored in the /var/shares/myshare directory, and users who connect to the share will be able to read or write files to the share.

Using the Samba Client

Earlier in this chapter, I show you how to set up Samba's server program so that you can enable a Linux computer to operate as a file server in a Windows network, thus allowing Windows clients to access files in shared directories on the Linux computer. That's the most common reason for using Samba.

But Samba can also work the other way around: It includes a program called smbclient that lets you access Windows file servers from a Linux computer. The smbclient program works much like an FTP client, so if you've used FTP before, you'll have no trouble understanding how it works.

smbclient is a command line tool, so you need to log on to a virtual console or open a terminal window. Then, enter the smbclient command, followed by the server and share name, like this:

```
smbclient //server01/share01
```

When the client successfully accesses the share, you are greeted by the friendly SMB prompt:

```
smb:\>
```

Then, you can enter smbclient commands to access the data in the shared directory. Table 5-1 summarizes the more common commands that are available at the smb:\> prompt.

Doing the Samba Dance

TABLE 5-1   **Commonly Used smbclient Commands**

Command	Description
cd *directory*	Changes to the specified directory on the remote system
del *filename*	Deletes the specified file or files on the remote system
dir	Lists files in the current directory on the remote system
exit	Terminates the session
get remote-file local-file	Copies the specified remote file to the specified local file
lcd *directory*	Changes the local current directory to the specified directory
md *directory*	Creates a directory on the remote system
mget *wildcard-mask*	Copies all files that match the wildcard mask from the remote system to the local system
mput *wildcard-mask*	Copies all files that match the wildcard mask from the local system to the remote system
put *local-file remote-file*	Copies the specified file from the local system to the remote system
rd *directory*	Deletes the specified directory on the remote system

Chapter **6**

Running Apache

All the popular Linux distributions come with Apache, the most popular web server on the Internet today. In most cases, Apache is installed and configured automatically when you install Linux. Then setting up a web server for the Internet or an intranet is simply a matter of tweaking a few Apache configuration settings and copying your HTML document files to Apache's home directory.

Installing Apache

To install Apache, open a console or terminal window and enter the following command:

```
sudo dnf install httpd
```

Assuming that Apache is not already installed, dnf will ask for your permission to install Apache. Enter **y** to proceed. Be patient while the package downloads and installs.

You'll also want to install the graphical configuration program by running the following command:

```
sudo dnf install system-config-httpd
```

Starting and Stopping Apache

Before you can use Apache, you must start the httpd daemon. From a command shell, use this command:

```
sudo service httpd start
```

Whenever you make a configuration change, you should stop and restart the service with this command:

```
sudo service httpd restart
```

If you prefer, you can stop and start the service with separate commands:

```
sudo service httpd stop
sudo service httpd start
```

If you're not sure whether Apache is running, enter this command:

```
sudo service httpd status
```

You get a message indicating whether the httpd daemon is running.

To configure Apache to start automatically when you start Linux, use this command:

```
sudo chkconfig --level 35 httpd on
```

To make sure that the chkconfig command worked right, enter this command:

```
sudo chkconfig --list httpd
```

You should see output similar to the following:

```
sudo httpd 0:off 1:off 2:off 3:on 4:off 5:on 6:off
```

Confirming That Apache Is Running

You can test to see whether Apache is up and running by opening the Firefox browser (choose Applications➪ Internet➪ Firefox Web Browser) and typing **localhost** in the address bar. If Apache is running on the server, a page such as the one shown in Figure 6-1 appears.

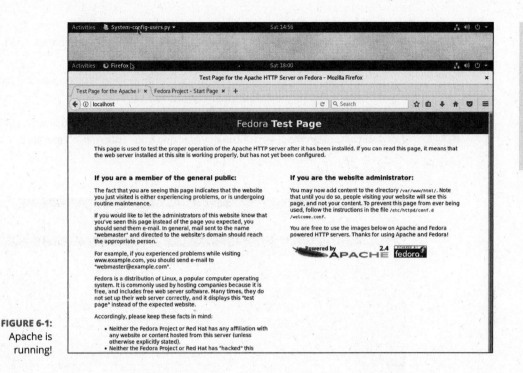

FIGURE 6-1:
Apache is running!

If this doesn't work, first make sure that you can ping your Linux server from the remote system. To do that, type **ping** followed by the IP address of the Linux server. If the ping command times out, you have a connectivity problem that you need to correct.

If you can ping the Linux server but still can't reach the Apache server home page, here are a few things to check:

» Make sure that the httpd service is running as described in the "Starting and Stopping Apache" section, earlier in this chapter.

» Make sure that the Linux firewall is turned off or configured to allow HTTP traffic. In Fedora, you can manage the firewall settings from the GNOME-based Security Level Configuration tool. To run it, click Activities, type **Firewall**, and then click the Firewall icon. Then select WWW (HTTP) in the list of trusted services. Figure 6-2 shows the System Settings Configuration tool with the firewall enabled and the HTTP service trusted.

TIP

If you don't have the Security Level Configuration tool, you can install it using the following command:

```
sudo dnf install system-config-securitylevel
```

WARNING

Do *not* disable the firewall altogether unless you have another firewall, such as a firewall router, between your Linux server and your Internet connection.

FIGURE 6-2:
Trusting the HTTP service.

Using the HTTP Configuration Tool

Apache should run fine using the default configuration settings made when you install it. You can change various configuration settings, however, either by editing the Apache configuration files or by using the HTTP configuration tool, as shown in Figure 6-3. To start this tool, choose Activities⇨Applications⇨Http.

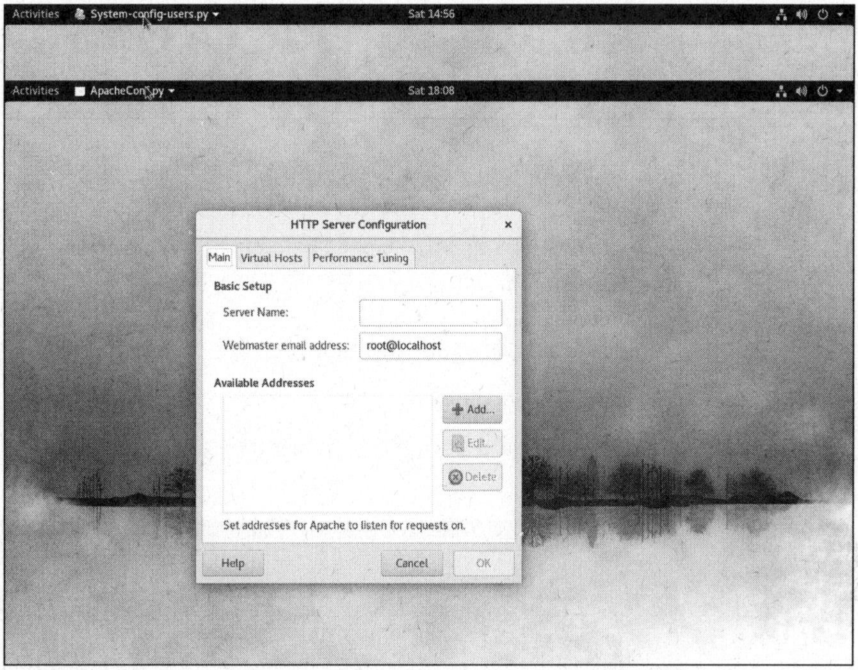

FIGURE 6-3:
Configuring
Apache's HTTP
settings.

The Main tab of the HTTP configuration tool provides the basic configuration settings for Apache. Here, you can set the following options:

>> **Server Name:** This option sets the name that the Apache server will return. If you leave this name blank, Apache will figure out the actual name of the Linux server and return it, so you need to set this option only if you want to use a different name for your Apache server.

>> **Webmaster Email Address:** This is the email address of the webmaster for this web server.

>> **Available Addresses:** This list box shows the addresses that Apache will service HTTP requests for. By default, Apache will reply to HTTP requests from any computer that makes the request on port 80, the standard HTTP port. You can change the port or restrict access, however, as described in the following section.

Whenever you use the HTTP configuration tool to change Apache's configuration, you need to restart Apache. You can do so by entering this command from a console prompt:

```
service httpd restart
```

Allowing or Restricting Access to an Apache Server

To allow or restrict access to your Apache server, you can alter the Available Addresses list in the Main tab of the HTTP configuration tool by using the Add, Edit, and Delete buttons. To allow access to the HTTP standard port 80 for your server, follow these steps:

1. **Open the HTTP Configuration Tool.**

2. **Click the Add button.**

   The Add Address dialog box, shown in Figure 6-4, appears.

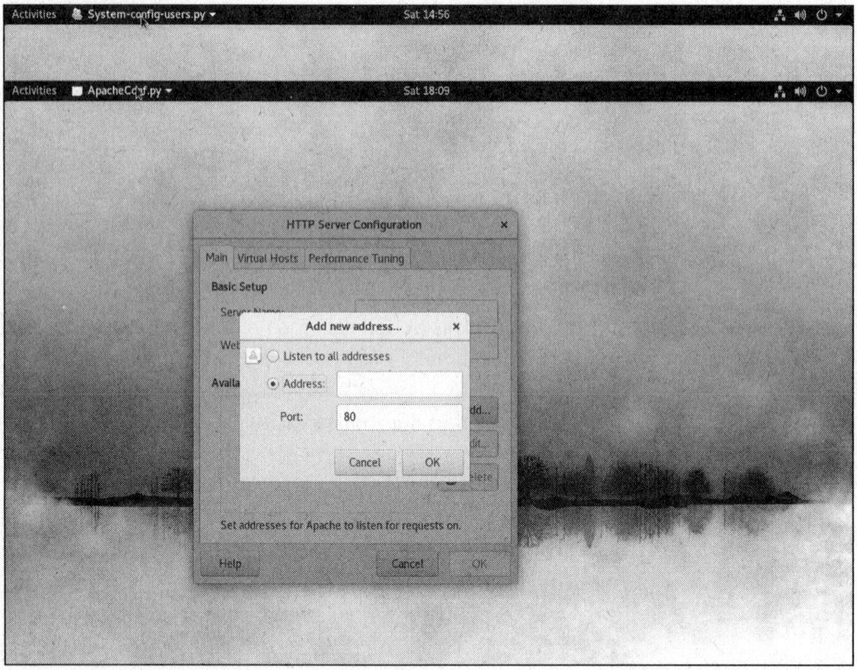

FIGURE 6-4: Adding an address.

3. **Select the Listen to All Addresses option.**

4. **Click OK.**

   You are returned to the HTTP Configuration tool; an entry entitled "All available addresses on port 80" now appears in the Available Addresses list.

To change the port that the Apache server uses, select All Available Addresses on Port 80 in the Available Addresses list and click Edit. This brings up the dialog box shown in Figure 6-4. Then specify the port you want to use, and click OK.

If you want to restrict access to certain IP addresses, select the All Available Addresses line, click the Edit button, select the Address radio button, and then enter the address you want to allow access to. You can enter a single IP address, but you're more likely to enter a partial IP address or an IP/netmask combination. For example, to allow access to all addresses from 212.66.5.0 to 212.66.5.255, you can enter either of the following:

```
212.66.5
212.66.5.0/255.255.255.0
```

If you want to allow access to a list of specific IP addresses, you can add lines to the Available Addresses list box. First, though, you should remove the All Available Addresses line or edit it to allow just a single address. Then click the Add button to add addresses you want to allow.

Configuring Virtual Hosts

A *virtual host* is simply a website with its own domain name hosted by an Apache server. By default, Apache is set up to serve just one virtual host, but you can add more virtual hosts. As a result, a single Apache server is able to host more than one website.

If I were so inclined, I might set up an Apache server to host my own personal website (www.lowewriter.com) that has information about my books and a second website (www.hauntedlowes.com) that has information about my favorite hobby: decorating my house for Halloween. Both of these websites could be implemented as virtual hosts on a single Apache server.

To configure a virtual host (including the default virtual host, if you have only one), you use the Virtual Hosts tab of the HTTP configuration tool, as shown in Figure 6-5.

Configuring the default host

Even if you don't plan on creating additional virtual hosts, you can still use the Virtual Hosts tab to configure the default virtual host for your website. To do so, select the virtual host in the Virtual Hosts list, and click the Edit button. This brings up the dialog box shown in Figure 6-6.

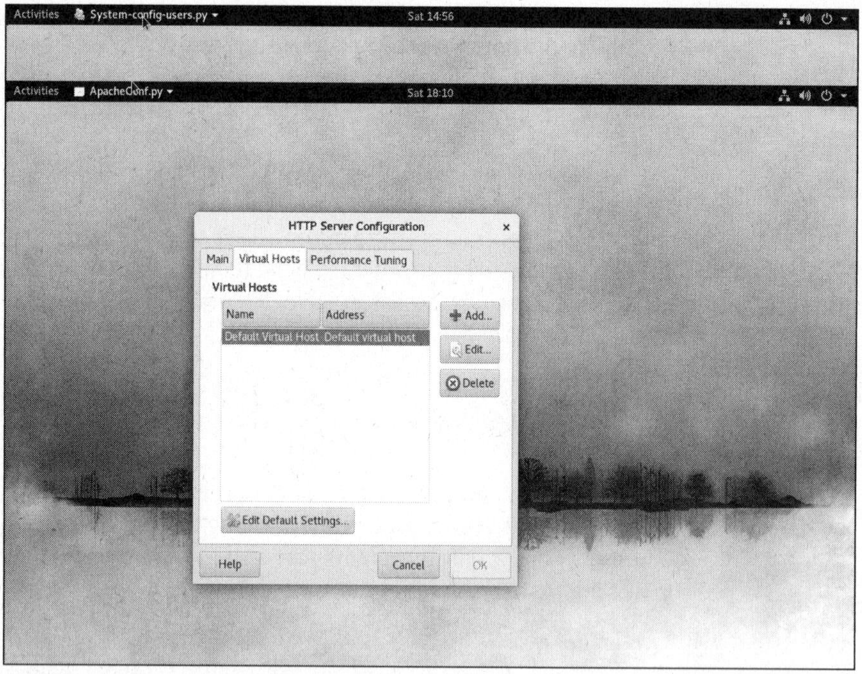

FIGURE 6-5:
The Virtual
Hosts tab.

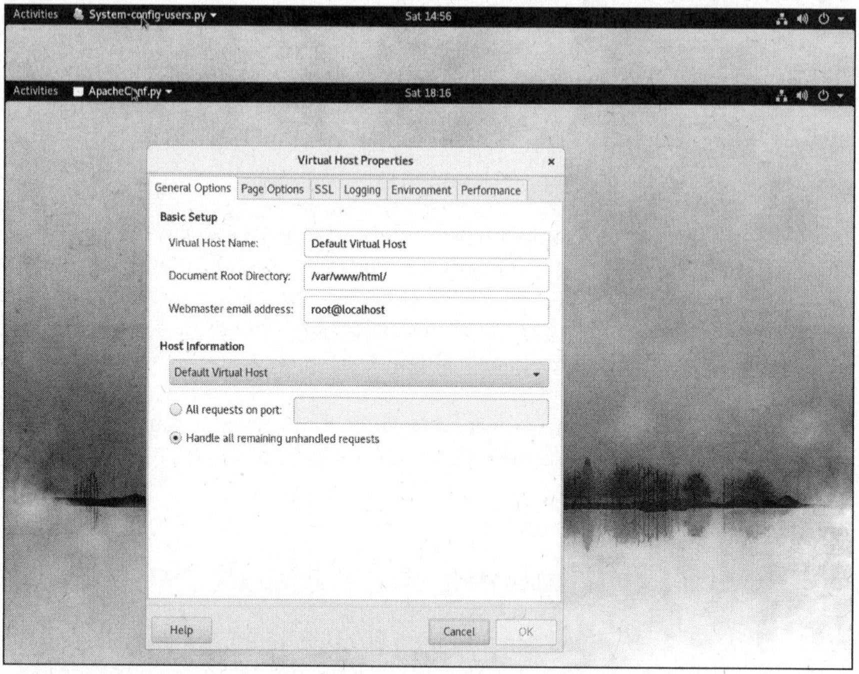

FIGURE 6-6:
Editing the virtual
host's properties.

From this dialog box, you can configure a variety of important settings for the virtual host:

>> **Virtual Host Name:** You use this name to refer to the virtual host.

>> **Document Root Directory:** This is the file system location that contains the HTML documents for the website. The default is /var/www/html, but you can specify a different location if you want to store your HTML files somewhere else.

>> **Webmaster Email Address:** Each virtual host can have its own webmaster email address. If you leave this option blank, the address specified for the main HTTP configuration (refer to Figure 6-3) is used.

>> **Host Information:** This section of the dialog box lets you specify what HTTP requests should be serviced by this virtual host.

You can use the other tabs of the Virtual Host Properties dialog box to configure additional options. Figure 6-7 shows the Page Options tab, where you can set the following options:

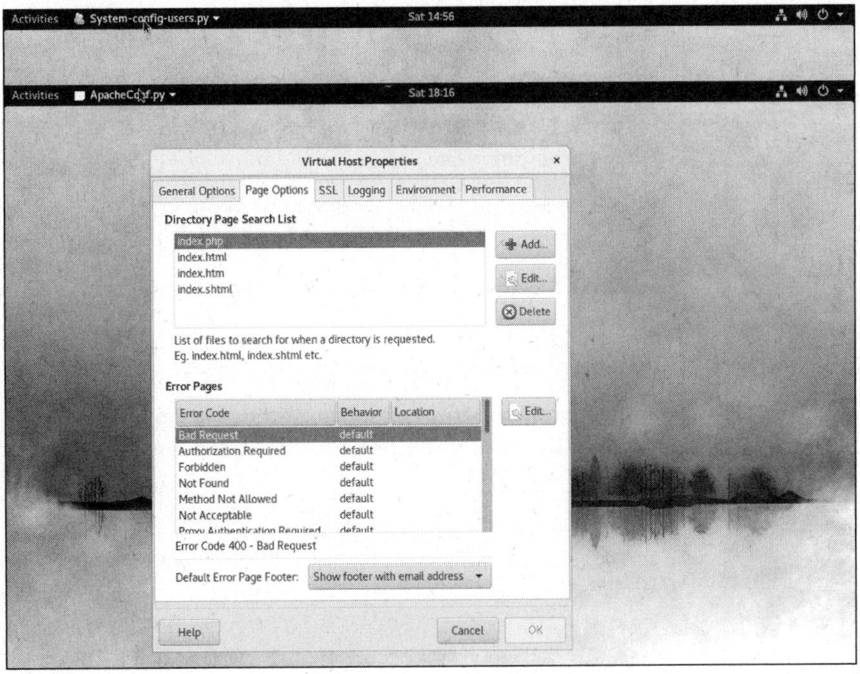

FIGURE 6-7: The Page Options tab lets you set the directory search list and custom error pages.

>> **Directory Page Search List:** This list specifies the default page for the website. The default page is displayed if the user doesn't indicate a specific page to retrieve. Then Apache looks for each of the pages listed in the Directory Page Search list and displays the first one it finds. You can use the Add, Edit, and Delete buttons to modify this list.

>> **Error Pages:** This list lets you change the default error pages that are displayed when an HTTP error occurs. The most common HTTP error, Not Found, happens when the user requests a page that doesn't exist. If you want to create a custom error page to let the user know that the page doesn't exist or that some other error has occurred, this list is the place to do it.

Creating a virtual host

If you want to host more than one website on an Apache server, you can create additional virtual hosts. Just follow these steps:

1. **Click the Add button on the Virtual Hosts tab of the HTTP configuration tool (refer to Figure 6-5).**

   This brings up the virtual host properties, which you've already seen in Figure 6-6.

2. **In the Host Information section, choose Name Based Virtual Host from the drop-down list.**

   The Virtual Host Properties dialog box morphs into the dialog box shown in Figure 6-8.

3. **Enter the IP address and the host name for the virtual host.**

   The IP address is usually the IP address assigned to the Apache server, and the host name is the DNS name used to access the virtual host.

4. **If you want to provide an alias for the virtual host, click the Add button, enter the alias name, and click OK.**

   An alias is often used for websites that are used on an intranet rather than on public websites. If you're setting up an intranet website for your company suggestion box, for example, the full DNS name for the virtual host might be suggestionbox.mycompany.com. But if you provide just suggestionbox as an alias, users can access the suggestion-box website by using suggestionbox rather than suggestionbox.mycompany.com as the website address.

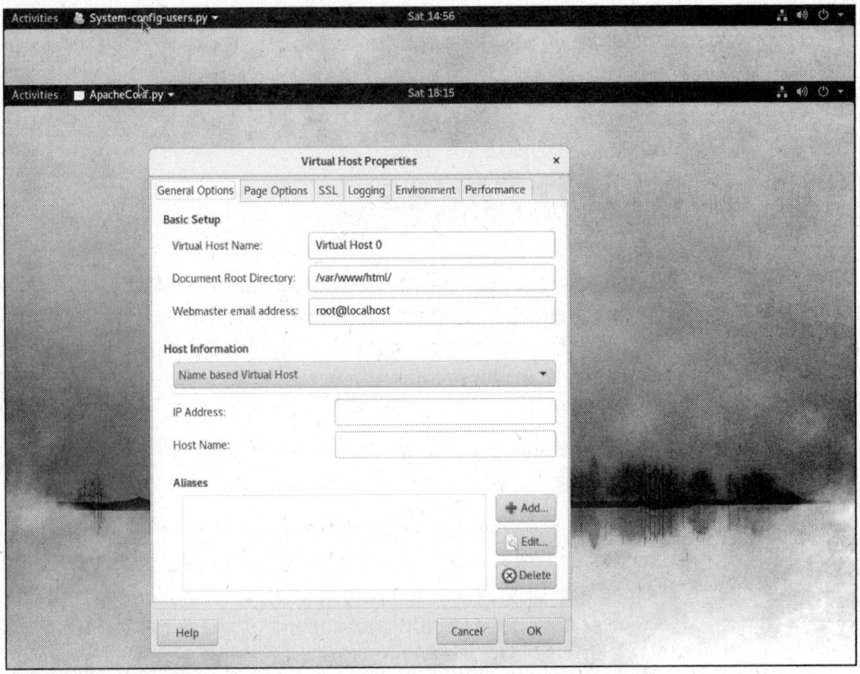

FIGURE 6-8:
Creating a new
virtual host.

5. **Use the other tabs of the Virtual Host Properties dialog box to configure additional options.**

You might want to use the Page Options tab (refer to Figure 6-7) to change the Directory Page Search List or designate custom error pages, for example.

6. **Click OK.**

The virtual host is created. You're returned to the HTTP configuration tool, where the new virtual host appears in the Virtual Hosts list.

Manually Editing Apache's Configuration Files

If you're allergic to GUI configuration tools, you can configure your Apache server by editing the configuration files directly. Apache's configuration settings are located in three separate configuration files, named `httpd.conf`, `srm.conf`, and `access.conf`. These files are located in `/etc/httpd/conf` in Fedora Core Linux, but they may be in a different location in other Linux distributions. Be sure to study the Apache documentation before you start messing with these files!

TIP

Whenever you make a configuration change to Apache, you should restart Apache by using the `service httpd restart` command.

Creating Web Pages

This section is about how to create and edit HTML content for your website. Plenty of good books on how to do that are available, including my own *Creating Web Pages For Dummies Quick Reference* (Wiley). Rather, I just want to point out a few key things that you need to know to set up a website with Apache:

» The default location for web documents is `/var/www/html`. When you create web pages for your site, save them in that directory.

» When a user visits your website by typing just the domain name without a filename (`www.mydomain.com` instead of `www.mydomain.com/file1.html`), Apache displays the file named `index.html` or `index.htm`. You should give the home page for your website one of these two names.

» If you're a programmer, you can build complicated web-based applications with PHP, which is installed along with Apache.

Chapter **7**

Running Sendmail

Sendmail, which is a standard part of most Linux distributions, is one of the most popular mail server programs on the Internet. You can use Sendmail as an alternative to expensive mail server programs, such as Microsoft Exchange Server, to provide email services for your LAN. This chapter shows you how to set up and use Sendmail on a Linux server.

WARNING

Spam artists — unscrupulous marketers who clutter the Internet with millions of unsolicited emails — are constantly on the prowl for unprotected Sendmail servers, which they can use to launch their spam campaigns. If you don't protect your server, sooner or later, a spammer will coax your computer into spending almost all its time sending out the spammer's email. To protect your server from becoming an indentured spam servant, you can configure it to refuse any mail that merely wants to use your computer to relay messages to other computers. See the sidebar "Don't be an open relay!" later in this chapter.

Understanding Email

Before I get into the details of installing and configuring Sendmail, I want to review some basics of how Internet email works. First, you need to understand that email consists of messages that are delivered according to an Internet protocol commonly referred to as SMTP. Simple Mail Transfer Protocol was first codified in 1983, long before Al Gore invented the Internet. Several enhancements have been made along the way, but most email on the Internet today is delivered using this nearly ancient protocol.

Interestingly, the software that delivers 70 percent of all the email on the Internet — Sendmail — also originated in the same year. In 1983, Eric Allman developed the first version of the Sendmail program as part of the Berkeley Software Distribution (BSD) of Unix, one of the earliest versions of Unix made publicly available.

The following paragraphs describe some of the key features of email that you should know about if you plan on setting up a Linux server running Sendmail:

» **Mailbox:** A *mailbox* is a simple text file that holds incoming email messages until they are processed by a mail user agent. In Fedora Linux, each user has a mailbox file in /var/mail.

» **Mail User Agent (MUA):** A program that end-users can use to send and receive mail. The most widely used MUA is Microsoft Outlook. Linux comes with several MUAs. The most basic is Mail, a text-based MUA that lets you read and compose email messages from a console prompt. Fedora also includes a sophisticated graphical MUA called *Evolution,* which is similar in many ways to Microsoft Outlook. Both are described later in this chapter.

» **Mail Transfer Agent (MTA):** A program that transfers email messages between computers. Sendmail, which most of this chapter is devoted to, is an MTA. When a user uses an MUA to send an email message, the MUA delivers the message to an MTA, which then transfers the message to the intended recipient.

» **Mail Delivery Agent (MDA):** A program that accepts incoming mail from an MTA and places it in the intended recipient's mailbox. A basic MDA simply copies each message to the mailbox, but more advanced MDAs can be used to filter the incoming mail to eliminate spam or check for viruses. The default MDA for Fedora Linux is Procmail. Fedora also includes SpamAssassin, which you can use to filter spam from your incoming mail.

Installing Sendmail

To install Sendmail, open a console or terminal window and enter the following commands:

```
sudo dnf install sendmail
sudo dnf install sendmail-cf
sudo dnf install m4
```

Assuming that the Sendmail packages are not already installed, dnf will ask for your permission to install the required packages. Enter **y** to proceed. Be patient while the package downloads and installs.

Modifying sendmail.mc

Sendmail is probably one of the most difficult programs to configure that you'll ever encounter. In fact, the basic configuration file, sendmail.cf, is well more than 1,000 lines long. You don't want to mess with this file if you can possibly avoid it.

Fortunately, you don't have to. The sendmail.cf configuration file is generated automatically from a much shorter file called sendmail.mc. This file contains special macros that are processed by a program called m4. The m4 program reads the macros in the sendmail.mc file and expands them to create the actual sendmail.cf file.

Even so, the sendmail.mc file is a few hundred lines long. Configuring Sendmail isn't for the faint of heart.

WARNING

You can find the sendmail.mc and sendmail.cf files in the /etc/mail directory. Before you edit these files, you should make backup copies of the current files. That way, if you mess up your mail configuration, you can quickly return to a working configuration by reinstating your backup copies.

After you make backup copies, you can safely edit sendmail.mc. When you're finished, you can regenerate the sendmail.cf file by entering these commands:

```
cd /etc/mail
m4 sendmail.mc > sendmail.cf
service sendmail restart
```

The first command changes the current working directory to /etc/mail. Then, the second command compiles the sendmail.mc command into the sendmail.cf command. Finally, the third command restarts the Sendmail service so that the changes will take effect.

You need to be aware of two strange conventions used in the sendmail.mc file:

>> **Comments:** Unlike most configuration files, comments don't begin with a hash mark (#). Instead, they begin with the letters dn1.

>> **Strings:** Strings are quoted in an unusual way. Instead of regular quotation marks or apostrophes, strings must begin with a backquote (`` ` ``), which is located to the left of the numeral 1 on the keyboard and ends with an apostrophe (`'`), located to the right of the semicolon. So a properly quoted string looks like this:

```
MASQUERADE_AS(`mydomain.com')
```

Pretty strange, eh?

The following sections describe the common configuration changes that you may need to make to sendmail.mc.

Enabling connections

The default configuration allows connections only from localhost. If you want Sendmail to work as a server for other computers on your network, look for the following line in the sendmail.mc file:

```
DAEMON_OPTIONS(`Port=smtp,Addr=127.0.0.1, Name=MTA')dnl
```

Add dnl to the beginning of this line to make it a comment.

DON'T BE AN OPEN RELAY!

An *open relay* is a mail server that's configured to allow anyone to use it as a relay for sending mail. In short, an open relay sends mail when neither the sender nor the recipient is a local user. Spammers love open relays because they can use them to obscure the true origin of their junk email. As a result, open relays are a major contributor to the Internet spam problem.

Fortunately, the default configuration for the current version of Sendmail (8.14) is to not allow open relaying. As a result, you have to go out of your way to become an open relay with Sendmail. In fact, you'll have to look up the lines you'd need to add to sendmail.mc to enable open relaying. I'm certainly not going to list them here.

If you do need to allow relaying for specific hosts, create a file named relay-domains in /etc/mail. Then, add a line for each domain you want to allow relaying for. This line should contain nothing but the domain name. Then restart Sendmail.

Enabling masquerading

Masquerading allows all the mail being sent from your domain to appear as if it came from the domain (for example, wally@cleaver.net) rather than from the individual hosts (like wally@wally.cleaver.net). To enable masquerading, add lines similar to these:

```
MASQUERADE_AS(`cleaver.net')dnl
FEATURE(masquerade_envelope)dnl
FEATURE(masquerade_entire_domain)dnl
MASQUERADE_DOMAIN(`cleaver.net')dnl
```

Setting up aliases

An *alias* — also known as a *virtual user* — is an incoming email address that is automatically routed to local users. For example, you may want to create a generic account such as sales@mydomain.com and have all mail sent to that account delivered to a user named *willie*. To do that, you edit the file /etc/mail/virtusers. This file starts out empty. To create a virtual user, just list the incoming email address followed by the actual recipient.

For example, here's a virtusers file that defines several aliases:

```
sales@mydomain.com willie
bob@mydomain.com robert
marketing@mydomain.com robert
```

After you make your changes, you should restart the Sendmail service.

Using SpamAssassin

SpamAssassin is a spam-blocking tool that uses a variety of techniques to weed the spam out of your users' mailboxes. SpamAssassin uses a combination of rule filters that scan for suspicious message content and other telltale signs of spam, as well as blacklists from known spammers. The following sections explain how to install and use it.

Installing SpamAssassin

To configure SpamAssassin for basic spam filtering, follow these steps:

1. Ensure that Procmail is installed as your MDA.

In Fedora, Procmail is installed by default. To make sure it's enabled, open the file `/etc/mail/sendmail.mc` and make sure it includes the following line:

```
FEATURE(local_procmail,`',`procmail -t -Y -a $h -d $u')dnl
```

If this line is missing, add it and then restart Sendmail.

2. Ensure that the `spamassassin` daemon is running.

You can do that by entering this command at a console prompt:

```
sudo service spamassassin status
```

If SpamAssassin isn't running, enter this command:

```
sudo chkconfig --level 35 spamassassin on
```

TIP

Whenever you make a configuration change, you should stop and restart the service with this command:

```
sudo service spamassassin restart
```

3. Create a file named `procmailrc` in the `/etc` directory.

Use `gedit` or your favorite text editor. The file should contain these two lines:

```
:0fw
| /usr/bin/spamc
```

These lines cause Procmail to run all incoming mail through the SpamAssassin client program.

4. Restart Sendmail and SpamAssassin.

You can do this from Applications➪Server Settings➪Services, or you can enter these commands at a console prompt:

```
sudo service sendmail restart
sudo service spamassassin restart
```

SpamAssassin should now be checking for spam. To make sure it's working, send some email to one of the mailboxes on your system and then open the mailbox file for that user in \var\mail and examine the message that was sent. If the message headers include several lines that begin with *X-Spam*, SpamAssassin is doing its job.

Customizing SpamAssassin

You can configure SpamAssassin by editing the configuration file /etc/mail/ spamassassin/local.cf. This file contains SpamAssassin rules that are applied system wide although you can override these rules for individual users by creating a user_prefs file in each user's $HOME/.spamassassin directory.

In Fedora, the default local.cf file contains the following lines:

```
required_hits 5
report_safe 0
rewrite_header Subject [SPAM]
```

These lines cause SpamAssassin to add the word [SPAM] to the start of the subject line for any message that scores 5 or higher on SpamAssassin's spam scoring algorithm.

TIP

Although you can configure SpamAssassin to automatically delete messages that score above a specified value, most antispam experts recommend against it. Instead, adding a word such as [SPAM] to the header lets each user decide how he wants to handle spam by using a message filter on his email client that either deletes the marked messages or moves them to a Spam folder.

No matter how you configure SpamAssassin, you will inevitably get some false positives. For example, a long-lost friend who moved to Nigeria will email you a joke about Viagra using a Hotmail account. Odds are good that SpamAssassin will mark this message as spam. That's why arbitrarily deleting messages marked as spam isn't such a great idea, especially on a system-wide basis. Better to simply mark the messages and then let your users decide how to deal with the spam.

Blacklisting and whitelisting email addresses

SpamAssassin lets you blacklist or whitelist a specific email address or an entire domain. When you *blacklist* an address, any mail from the address will automatically be blocked, regardless of the message contents. Conversely, when you *whitelist* an address, all mail from the address will be allowed through, even if the message would otherwise be blocked as spam.

TIP

Whitelisting is a powerful tool for making sure that the people you correspond with on a regular basis don't get their email accidentally blocked by SpamAssassin. As a result, it's a good idea to add your friends, relatives, and especially your customers to a whitelist.

Likewise, blacklisting lets you mark spammers who have managed to get their spam into your system in spite of SpamAssassin's best efforts to detect their true intent.

To whitelist an address, add a line such as the following to `/etc/mail/spamassassin/local.rc`:

```
whitelist_from wally@cleaver.com
```

This allows all mail from `wally@cleaver.com` to be delivered, even if the mail might otherwise look like spam.

To blacklist an address, add a line like this:

```
blacklist_from auntida@myrelatives.com
```

This blocks all mail from your Aunt Ida.

Using the Mail Console Client

The most basic client for creating and reading email is the `mail` command. Although it doesn't have many advanced features, it is fast, so some Linux users like to use it for sending simple messages. (It is also sometimes used in scripts.) To install the `mail` command, open a terminal window and enter the following command:

```
sudo dnf install mailx
```

To read mail, open a command console, log on using the account whose mail you want to read, and enter the command `mail`. A list of all messages in your mailbox will be displayed. You can then use any of the commands listed in Table 7-1 to work with the messages in the mailbox or compose new mail messages.

TABLE 7-1

Mail Commands

Command	Explanation
?	Display a list of available commands.
q	Quit.
h	List the headers for all messages in the mailbox.
n	Type the next message.
t *list*	Type the specified messages. For example, t 3 types message 3, and t 4 5 types messages 4 and 5.
d *list*	Deletes one or more messages. For example, d 4 deletes message 4.
R *list*	Reply to message sender.
r *list*	Reply to message sender and all recipients.
m user	Compose a new message addressed to the specified user.

To compose a new message from a command prompt, follow these steps:

1. **Type** mail **followed by the email address of the recipient.**

   For example:

   ```
   mail wally@cleaver.com
   ```

   Mail responds by prompting you for the subject.

2. **Type the subject line and press Enter.**

   Mail then waits for you to enter the text of the message.

3. **Type the message text. Use the Enter key to start new lines.**

   You can enter as many lines as you want for the message.

4. **To send the message, enter a line consisting of only a period.**

You're done! The message is on its way.

Using Evolution

Evolution is a graphical email client that's similar in many ways to Microsoft Outlook, as Figure 7-1 shows. It includes not only email features, but also a contact list, a calendar, a task manager, and other Outlook-like features.

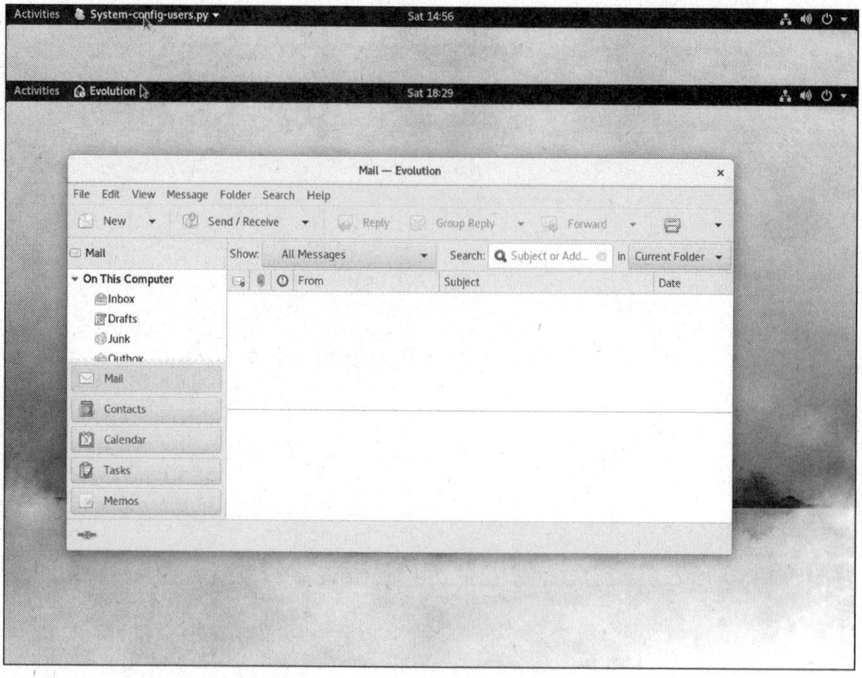

FIGURE 7-1:
Evolution looks a
lot like Outlook.

Evolution is installed automatically as part of a Fedora Workstation install. You can install it manually with the following command:

```
sudo dnf install evolution.x86_64
```

To start Evolution, click the E-mail icon that's located in the panel at the top of the GNOME screen. The first time you run Evolution, a configuration wizard will guide you through the necessary configuration. You need to supply basic information about your email account, such as your email address and the name of your mail server.

» **Identifying file and directory commands**

» **Discovering commands that help with packages and services**

» **Figuring out commands for managing users and groups**

» **Becoming familiar with networking commands**

Chapter **8**

Linux Commands

inux has several nice graphical user interfaces (GUI) to choose from, and many of the more common Linux networking functions have graphical configuration utilities. Still, many Linux configuration tasks can be done only from a command shell. In many cases, though, the configuration utility provides access only to the most basic configuration parameters, so if you want to configure advanced features, you have to use commands. In fact, some network features don't even have a graphical configuration utility, so you have no choice but to use commands.

Even when GNOME-based alternatives are available, you'll often resort to using commands because frankly, that's what Linux was built to do. Unlike Windows, Linux relies on commands as its primary means of getting things done. If you're going to work with Linux, knowing the basic commands presented in this chapter is a must.

Command Shell Basics

A *shell* is a program that accepts commands from a command prompt and executes them. The shell displays a prompt to let you know it's waiting for a command. When you type the command and press Enter, the system reads your command, interprets it, executes it, displays the results, and then displays the prompt again so that you can enter another command.

TIP

Linux commands are case-sensitive, so be careful about capitalization when you type Linux commands.

Getting to a shell

You can work with Linux commands directly from one of the six virtual consoles. If you like the responsiveness of text mode, virtual consoles are for you. To switch to a virtual console, press Ctrl+Alt+Fx. For example, press Ctrl+Alt+F1 to switch to virtual console 1. When you're in a virtual console, you have to answer the logon prompt with a valid username and password. To return to GNOME, press Ctrl+Alt+F7.

The alternative is to work in a terminal window within the GNOME environment. If you have an older computer, you may find that the terminal window is a little unresponsive. If your computer is relatively new, however, the terminal window will be just as responsive as the text-mode virtual console. Plus, you'll have the benefit of a scroll bar that lets you scroll to see text that otherwise would have flown off the screen.

To open a terminal window, click Activities, click Show Applications, click Utilities, then click the Terminal icon. This opens a command shell in a window right on the GNOME desktop, as shown in Figure 8-1. Because this shell runs within the user account GNOME is logged on as, you don't have to log on. You can just start typing commands. When you're done, type **Exit** to close the window.

TIP

Since you'll use Terminal often to enter commands, I suggest you make it a favorite so it always appears when you click Activities. To make Terminal a favorite, click Activities, then click Show Applications, then click Utilities. Finally, right-click Terminal and choose Add to Favorites.

WARNING

For normal Linux users, the command shell prompt character is a dollar sign ($). If you see a hash mark (#) as the prompt character, it means you're logged on as root. Whenever you see a hash prompt, you should be extra careful about what you do because you can easily get yourself into trouble by deleting important files or otherwise corrupting the system.

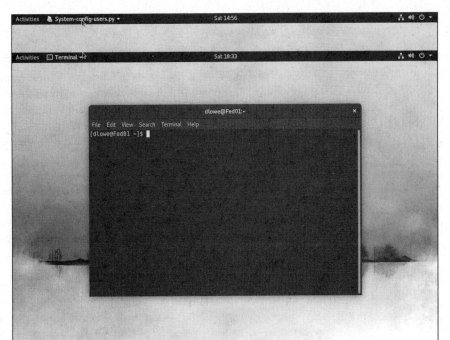

FIGURE 8-1:
A terminal
window.

Editing commands

Most of the time, you just type commands using the keyboard. If you make a mistake, you just type the command again, being careful not to repeat the mistake. However, Linux shells have several built-in editing features that can simplify the task of correcting a mistaken command or entering a sequence of similar commands:

>> **Repeat:** If you want to repeat a command that you've used recently, press the up-arrow key. This action recalls your most recently executed commands. You can press Enter to execute a command as is, or you can edit the command before you execute it.

>> **Autocomplete:** The shell has a handy autocomplete feature that can finish partially spelled directory, file, or command names. Just type part of the name and then press Tab. If you've typed enough for the shell to figure out what you mean, the shell finishes the name for you. Otherwise, it just beeps, in which case you can type a few more letters and try again. In some cases, the shell displays a list of items that match what you've typed so far to help you know what to type next.

Wildcards

Wildcards are one of the most powerful features of command shells. With wildcards, you can process all the files that match a particular naming pattern with a single command. For example, suppose that you have a folder with 500 files in it, and you want to delete all the files that contain the letters Y2K and end with .doc, which happens to be 50 files. If you try to do this in GNOME, you'll spend ten minutes picking these files out from the list. From a shell, you can delete them all with the single command rm *Y2K*.doc.

You can use two basic wildcard characters. An asterisk (*) stands for any number of characters, including zero, and an exclamation mark (!) stands for just one character. Thus, !Text.doc matches files with names like aText.doc, xText.doc, and 4Text.doc, but not abcText.doc or just Text.doc. However, *Text.doc matches any of those filenames.

You can also use brackets to indicate a range of characters to choose from. For example, report[123] matches the files report1, report2, or report3. You can also specify report[1–5] to match report1, report2, report3, report4, or report5. The wildcard r[aeiou]port matches files named raport, report, riport, roport, or ruport. As you can see, the possibilities are almost endless.

Redirection and piping

Redirection and piping are related techniques. *Redirection* lets you specify an alternative destination for output that will be displayed by a command or specify an alternative source for input that should be fed into a command. For example, you can save the results of an ifconfig command to /home/doug/myconfig like this:

```
$ ifconfig > /home/doug/myconfig
```

Here, the greater-than sign (>) is used to redirect the command's console output.

If a command accepts input from the keyboard, you can use input redirection to specify a file that contains the input that you want to feed to the command. For example, you can create a text file named lookup.commands with subcommands for a command such as nslookup. Then, you can feed those scripted subcommands to the nslookup command, like this:

```
$ nslookup < /home/doug/lookup.commands
```

Piping is a similar technique. It takes the console output from one command and feeds it into the next command as input. One of the most common uses of piping is to send the output of a command that displays a lot of information to the more program, which displays the output one page at a time. For example:

```
$ ifconfig | more
```

The vertical bar (|) is often called the *pipe character* because it's the symbol used to indicate piping.

Environment variables

The shell makes several environment variables available to commands. An *environment variable* is a predefined value you can use in your commands to provide commonly used information, such as the name of the current user or the operating system version. You can use an environment variable anywhere in a command by typing **$** (dollar sign) followed by the environment variable name. For example, this command

```
$ echo This is $HOSTNAME running on an $HOSTTYPE
```

displays a line such as

```
This is LSERVER running on an i386
```

Table 8-1 lists some of the more useful environment variables that are available to you and your commands.

TABLE 8-1

Environment Variables

Variable	Description
HOME	The current user's home directory
HOSTNAME	The computer's host name
HOSTTYPE	The host computer type
OSTYPE	The operating system
PATH	The search order for executable programs
PROMPT_COMMAND	The command used to generate the prompt
PWD	The present working directory
SHELL	The shell being used
USERNAME	The current username

Shell scripts

A *shell script* is simply a text file that contains one or more commands which you can execute in sequence by running the script. The simplest shell scripts are just lists of commands, but advanced shell scripts can include complicated scripting statements that border on a full-featured programming language.

TIP

You can create shell scripts by using any text editor. The easiest text editor to use is gedit, which you can access from the GNOME desktop by choosing Activities⇨Applications⇨gedit. If you want your friends to think you're a Linux guru, however, take a few moments to learn how to use vi, a powerful text-mode editor. To create or edit a file in vi, type the command **vi** followed by a filename. Then, type away. To use a vi command, press Esc(ape) and then type one of the commands listed in Table 8-2.

TABLE 8-2

Common vi Commands

Command	Explanation
i	Enters insert mode so that you can enter text at the cursor location. Move the cursor to the point where you want to enter the text first. When you're finished inserting text, press Esc to return to command mode.
:w	Saves the file. (w stands for write.)
:q	Quit.
:wq	Write and then quit.
:q!	Quit without saving.
/string	Search forward for string.
?string	Search backward for string.
n	Repeat the last search.
u	Undo the previous command.

After you create a shell script, you have to grant yourself execute permission to run the script. For example, to grant yourself permission to run a script named myscript, use this command:

```
$ chmod 755 myscript
```

To run a shell script, you use the sh command and provide the name of the script file. For example:

```
$ sh myscript
```

Running a command with root-level privileges

Many Linux commands perform actions that can only be done by the root user. To avoid the need to switch back and forth between your normal user account and the root user account, you can use the `sudo` command to perform any command using root-level permissions. To do so, just prefix the command you want to execute with the word `sudo`. For example:

```
sudo dnf install httpd
```

Here, the command `dnf install httpd` is executed using root-level permissions.

To use `sudo`, your Linux account must be configured by the root user to allow root-level access. For more information about how to do that, refer to Chapter 2 of this minibook.

Directory- and File-Handling Commands

Because much of Linux administration involves working with configuration files, you frequently need to use the basic directory- and file-handling commands presented in this section.

The pwd command

This command displays the current directory, which is called the *present working directory* — hence the command name `pwd`. Here's the syntax:

```
pwd
```

Enter this command, and you get output similar to the following:

```
$ pwd
/home/doug
```

The cd command

The `cd` command changes the current working directory. The syntax is as follows:

```
cd directory
```

You may want to follow the `cd` command with a `pwd` command to make sure that you changed to the right directory. For example:

```
$ cd /etc/mail
$ pwd
/etc/mail
```

To change to a subdirectory of the current directory, omit the leading slash from the directory name. For example:

```
$ pwd
/home
$ cd doug
$ pwd
/home/doug
```

You can also use the double-dot (`..`) to represent the parent of the current directory. Thus, to move up one level, use the command `cd ..`, as follows:

```
$ pwd
/home/doug
$ cd ..
$ pwd
/home
```

The mkdir command

To create a new directory, use the `mkdir` command. It has the following syntax:

```
mkdir directory
```

Here's an example that creates a subdirectory named `images` in the current directory:

```
$ mkdir images
```

This example creates a directory named /home/doug/images:

```
$ mkdir /home/doug/images
```

The rmdir command

The `rmdir` command removes a directory. It has the following syntax:

```
rmdir directory
```

Here's an example:

```
$ rmdir /home/doug/images
```

Here, the /home/doug/images directory is deleted. Note that the directory must be empty to be removed, so you have to first delete any files in the directory.

The ls command

The ls command lists the contents of the current directory. Here's the syntax:

```
ls [options] directory
```

The following paragraphs describe the more important options for the ls command:

>> -a: Lists all the files in the directory, including files that start with a period

>> -c: Sorts entries by the time the files were last modified

>> -d: Lists only directory names

>> -l: Displays in long format

>> -r: Displays files in reverse order

>> -R: Lists the contents of all subdirectories, and subdirectories of subdirectories, and subdirectories of subdirectories of subdirectories; in other words, lists subdirectories recursively

>> -s: Displays file sizes

>> -S: Sorts files by size

>> -t: Sorts files by timestamp.

>> -u: Sorts files by the time the files were last accessed.

>> -X: Sorts files by their extensions.

Without arguments, the ls command lists all the files in the current directory, like this:

```
$ pwd
/etc/mail
$ ls
```

```
access helpfile Makefile submit.cf virtusertable
access.db local-host-names sendmail.cf submit.cf.bak virtusertable.db
domaintable mailertable sendmail.mc submit.mc
domaintable.db mailertable.db statistics trusted-users
```

You can limit the display to certain files by typing a filename, which can include wildcards. For example:

```
$ ls a*
access access.db
```

You can also specify the directory that you want to display, like this:

```
$ ls /etc/httpd
conf conf.d logs modules run
```

To display detailed information about the files in the directory, use the –l switch, as in this example:

```
$ ls /etc/mail/s* -l
-rw-r--r-- 1 root root 57427 Jul 19 16:35 sendmail.cf
-rw-r--r-- 1 root root 5798 Feb 24 16:15 sendmail.mc
-rw------- 1 root root 628 Jul 24 17:21 statistics
-rw-r--r-- 1 root root 39028 Jul 19 17:28 submit.cf
-r--r--r-- 1 root root 39077 Feb 24 16:15 submit.cf.bak
-rw-r--r-- 1 root root 953 Feb 24 16:15 submit.mc
```

The cp command

The cp command copies files. Here's the basic syntax:

```
cp [options] source-file destination-file
```

The following list describes the more important options for the cp command:

>> –a: The same as –dpR.

>> –b: Makes backup copies of existing files before they're overwritten. Sounds like a good plan to me.

>> –d: Copies links rather than the files the links point to.

>> –f: Removes files that will be overwritten.

>> –i: Interactively prompts for each file to be overwritten.

>> –l: Creates links to files rather than actually copying file contents.

- **»** −p: Preserves ownership and permissions.

- **»** −R: Copies the contents of subdirectories recursively.

- **»** −s: Creates symbolic links to files rather than actually copying file contents.

- **»** −u: Replaces destination files only if the source file is newer.

To make a copy of a file within the same directory, use cp like this:

```
$ cp sendmail.cf sendmail.cf.backup
```

If you want to copy a file to another directory without changing the filename, use cp like this:

```
$ cp sendmail.cf /home/doug
```

You can use wildcards to copy multiple files:

```
$ cp send* /home/doug
```

To include files in subdirectories of the source file, use the −R switch, like this:

```
$ cp -R /etc/*.cf /home/doug
```

In this example, all files in the /etc directory or any of its subdirectories that end with .cf are copied to /home/doug.

The rm command

The rm command deletes files. The syntax is as follows:

```
rm [options] file
```

The options are described in the following paragraphs:

- **»** −f: Removes files that will be overwritten

- **»** −i: Interactively prompts for each file to be overwritten

- **»** −R: Copies the contents of subdirectories recursively

To delete a single file, use it like this:

```
$ rm any.old.file
```

To delete multiple files, use a wildcard:

```
$ rm any.*
```

To delete an entire directory, use the –r switch:

```
$ rm -r /doug/old.files
```

The mv command

The mv command moves files or renames them. In Linux, moving and renaming a file is essentially the same thing. Moving a file changes the file's directory location but leaves its name the same. Renaming a file leaves the file in the same directory but changes the file's name.

The syntax of the mv command is

```
mvp [options] source-file destination
```

The following paragraphs describe the options:

- ❯❯ –b: Makes backup copies of existing files before they're overwritten. Still sounds like a good plan to me.
- ❯❯ –f: Removes files that will be overwritten.
- ❯❯ –i: Interactively prompts for each file to be overwritten.
- ❯❯ –u: Replaces destination files only if the source file is newer.

To move a file to another directory, provide a filename for the first argument and a directory for the second, like this:

```
$ mv monthly.report /home/Debbie/
```

To rename a file, provide filenames for both arguments:

```
$ mv monthly.report august.monthly.report
```

The touch command

The touch command is one of the more interesting Linux file management commands. Here's the syntax:

```
touch [options] file
```

Here are some of the options that you can use:

>> –a: Changes the access time only

>> –c: Doesn't create files that don't exist

>> –m: Changes the modification time only

The basic form of the touch command looks like this:

```
$ touch monthly.report
```

If you use touch on an existing file, the touch command changes the modification date of the file. If you use it on a command that doesn't exist, the touch command creates a new, empty file.

The cat command

The cat command displays the contents of a file. It has the following syntax:

```
cat [options] [filename...]
```

The filename is optional. If you omit the filename, the cat command obtains its input from the console, which you can redirect if you want.

And, you can specify more than one filename. If you do, the files are combined to create a single output stream.

Here are some of the options you can use:

>> –A: Displays new line characters as $, tab characters as ^I, and control characters with a caret (^)

>> –b: Numbers all nonblank lines as they're displayed

>> –e: Displays new line characters as $ and control characters with a caret (^)

>> –E: Displays new line characters as $

>> –n: Numbers lines as they are displayed

>> –s: Squeezes multiple spaces down to a single space

>> –t: Displays tab characters as ^I and control characters with a caret (^)

>> –T: Displays tab characters as ^I

>> –v: Shows nonprinting control characters with a caret (^)

Here's a basic example:

```
$ cat /etc/hosts
# Do not remove the following line, or various programs
# that require network functionality will fail.
127.0.0.1 LSERVER localhost.localdomain localhost
$
```

If you don't provide any filename arguments, the cat command copies text from the keyboard and displays it on the console. You can use the cat command along with output redirection to quickly create a short text file, like this:

```
$ cat >mytext
This is line one.
This is line two.
This is line three.
<ctrl+D>
```

For the last line, press Ctrl+D. This signals the end of the input to the cat command.

Commands for Working with Packages and Services

As a Linux administrator, you frequently need to start and stop services and check the status of installed packages or install new packages. The following sections describe the Linux commands that help you to perform these tasks.

The service command

You use the service command to check the status of services and to start, stop, or restart services. You need to restart a service whenever you make a configuration change in order for your changes to take effect. Here's the basic syntax:

```
service [service] [ start | stop | restart ]
```

The following paragraphs describe some typical uses of the service command:

>> To check the status of the httpd service (Apache), use this command:

```
$ service httpd status
```

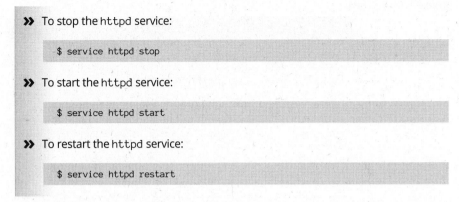

» To stop the httpd service:

```
$ service httpd stop
```

» To start the httpd service:

```
$ service httpd start
```

» To restart the httpd service:

```
$ service httpd restart
```

The only trick to using the service command is that you have to know the name of the service. If you're not sure of the name, you can run the service command to display the status of all services, like this:

```
$ service --status-all
```

It will take a few moments to list all the services, but after the command is done, you can scroll through the list to find the service that you're looking for.

Table 8-3 lists some of the more common services.

TABLE 8-3

Common Linux Services

Service	Description
atd	Runs commands scheduled by the at command
autof	Automatically mounts file systems
crond	Runs programs at specified times
dhcpd	The DHCP server
finger	The Internet finger service
httpd	The Apache web server
imap	The IMAP mail protocol
imaps	Secure IMAP service (SSL)
ipop3	The POP3 mail protocol
iptables	Automatic packet filtering for firewalls

(continued)

Linux Commands

TABLE 8-3 *(continued)*

Service	Description
isdn	ISDN services
named	The BIND DNS server
netf	The network file system
network	Activates and deactivates all network interfaces
nfs	Native Unix/Linux network file sharing
pop3s	Secure POP3 service (SSL)
sendmail	The Sendmail service
smb	The Samba file- and printer-sharing service
snmpd	SNMP
telnet	The Telnet server

The yum and dnf commands

yum, which stands for *Yellowdog Updater Modified,* is a tool for installing and updating packages on a Linux system. Until recently, yum was the preferred way to install packages on a Linux system. One of the chief advantages of yum over earlier package managers is that yum not only installs packages you tell it to install, but also automatically installs any packages that are prerequisites to the packages you ask yum to install.

yum has recently been superseded by a faster package manager called dnf. dnf and yum share pretty much the same command line options, so yum and dnf commands are mostly interchangeable.

Although dnf has many command line options, the most common way to use it is as follows:

```
dnf install package-name
```

For example, to install a package named sendmail, you would use this command:

```
dnf install sendmail
```

Note that installing a package is an action that requires root-level permissions to perform, so you'll usually use dnf or yum along with the sudo command, like this:

```
sudo dnf install sendmail
```

Commands for Administering Users

The following sections describe the Linux commands that you can use to create and manage user accounts from a command shell.

TIP

You should log on as root to perform these tasks.

The useradd command

The useradd command creates a user account. Here's the basic syntax for adding a new user:

```
useradd [options] username
```

You can also use this command to change the default options for new users. In that case, the syntax is more like this:

```
useradd -D [options]
```

If you use −D with no options, a list of the current default settings will be shown.

The options are as follows:

>> -c comment: Typically the user's full name

>> −d home-dir: The home directory of the new user

>> −e date: The expiration date for the user

>> −f time: The number of days between logons before the user is considered expired

>> −g group: The initial logon group for the user

>> −G groups: Additional groups the user should belong to

>> −m: Creates the new user's home directory if it doesn't exist already

>> -s shell-path: Specifies the user's logon shell

The following option is valid only with –D (which sets a default option):

>> –b *base-dir*: Provides the default base directory if a home directory is not specified

In its most basic form, the useradd command creates a user with default option settings:

```
$ useradd theodore
```

This command creates a user named theodore.

Here's a command that specifies the user's full name in the comment option:

```
$ useradd -c 'Theodore Cleaver' theodore
```

The following command creates a temporary account named ghost that expires on Halloween 2016:

```
$ useradd -e 2016-10-31 ghost
```

If you want to see what the default values are for account options, use the –D option without any other parameters:

```
$ useradd -D
GROUP=100
HOME=/home
INACTIVE=-1
EXPIRE=
SHELL=/bin/bash
SKEL=/etc/skel
```

The usermod command

The usermod command modifies an existing user. It has the following syntax:

```
usermod [options] username
```

The options are as follows:

>> c *comment*: Typically the user's full name

>> –d *home-dir*: The home directory of the new user

>> –e *date*: The expiration date for a logon

» −f *time*: The number of days between logons before the user is considered expired

» −g *group*: The initial logon group for the user

» −G *groups*: Additional groups the user should belong to

» −m: Creates the new user's home directory if it doesn't exist already

» −s *shell-path*: Specifies the user's logon shell

» −1: Locks an account

» −u: Unlocks an account

Here's an example that changes a user's full name:

```
$ usermod −c 'The Beave' theodore
```

The userdel command

The userdel command deletes a user. It has a simple syntax:

```
userdel [-r] username
```

If you specify −r, the user's home directory is deleted along with the account.

The chage command

The chage command modifies date policies for a user's passwords. It has the following syntax:

```
chage [options] username
```

The following paragraphs describe the options you can use:

» −m *days*: Specifies the minimum number of days allowed between password changes.

» −M *days*: Specifies the maximum number of days allowed between password changes.

» −d *date*: The date of the last password change.

» −E *date*: The date on which the account will expire.

>> –W *days*: The number of days prior to the password expiring that the user will be warned the password is about to expire.

>> –I *days*: The number of days of inactivity after the password has expired that the account is locked out. Specify 0 to disable this feature.

Here's an example that sets an account to expire on Halloween 2016:

```
$ chage -E 2016-10-31 ghost
```

If you specify a username but no other options, you're prompted to enter each option. This is a lot easier than trying to remember all the switches!

The passwd command

The passwd command changes the password for a user account. Its syntax is

```
passwd [user]
```

If you don't supply a user, the password for the current user is changed.

The passwd command prompts you to enter the new password twice to prevent the possibility of mistyping the password.

The newusers command

The newusers command provides an easy way to create a group of new user accounts. It reads a text file that contains one line for each new user, listing the user's name and password.

Here's the syntax of the newusers command:

```
newusers [filename]
```

If you omit the filename, newusers accepts input from the console.

Suppose that you have a file named /root/island.users that contains these lines:

```
gilligan ml9jiedr
skipper 1hiecr8u
professor dr0uxiaf
maryann choe7rlu
ginger jiuqled5
```

```
mrhowell j1emoaf1
lovie zo2priak
```

You can then create these seven stranded user accounts by issuing this command:

```
$ newusers /root/island.users
```

WARNING

Because the newusers file contains unencrypted passwords, you shouldn't leave it lying around. Require these new users to change their passwords immediately and delete the file you used to create the users.

The groupadd command

The groupadd command creates a new group. It has the following syntax:

```
groupadd [options] group
```

Although you have several possible options to use, the only one you're likely to need is -r, which creates a system group that has special privileges.

Here's an example that creates a group named castaways:

```
$ groupadd castaways
```

That's all you have to do to create a new group. To administer the group, you use the gpasswd command.

The groupdel command

The groupdel command deletes a group. It has the following syntax:

```
groupdel group
```

Here's an example that deletes a group named castaways:

```
$ groupdel castaways
```

Poof! The group is gone.

The gpasswd command

You use the gpasswd command to administer a group. This command has several different syntax options.

To change the group password:

```
gpasswd [ -r | -R ] group
```

To add a user:

```
gpasswd -a user group
```

To remove a user:

```
gpasswd -d user group
```

To create group administrators and/or members:

```
gpasswd [-A administrators...] [-M members... ] group
```

The options are as follows:

>> -r: Removes the password from the group.

>> -R: Disables access to the group via the newgrp command.

>> -a: Adds the specified user to the group.

>> -d: Deletes the specified user from the group.

>> -A: Specifies one or more group administrators. Use commas with no intervening spaces to separate the administrators from each other. Each administrator must be an existing user.

>> -M: Specifies one or more group members. Use commas with no intervening spaces to separate the members from each other. Each member must be an existing user.

The following example adds seven group members and one administrator to a group called castaways:

```
$ gpasswd -A skipper -M skipper,gilligan,professor,maryann,
ginger,mrhowell,lovie castaways
```

If the rest of the group finally decides to throw Gilligan off the island, they can remove him from the group with this command:

```
$ gpasswd -d gilligan castaways
```

Commands for Managing Ownership and Permissions

This section presents the details of the chown and chmod commands, which are the essential tools for assigning file system rights in the Linux environment.

The chown command

The chown command changes the owner of a file. Typically, the user who creates a file is the owner of the file. However, the owner can transfer the file to someone else via this command. The basic syntax of this command is

```
chown user file
```

For example, to change the owner of a file named rescue.plans to user professor, use this command:

```
$ chown professor rescue.plans
```

To change ownership of all the files in the directory named /home/island to professor, use this command:

```
$ chown professor /home/island
```

TIP

Issuing the following command would be a really bad idea:

```
$ chown gilligan rescue.plans
```

The chgrp command

Every file has not only an individual owner, but also a group owner. You can change the group ownership by using the chgrp command, which has the following basic syntax:

```
chgrp group file
```

For example, to grant the castaways group ownership of the file rescue.plans, use this command:

```
$ chgrp castaways rescue.plans
```

To change group ownership of all the files in the directory named /home/island to castaways, use this command:

```
$ chgrp castaways /home/island
```

The chmod command

The chmod command lets you change the permissions for a Linux file. Before explaining the syntax of the chmod command, you need to look at the cryptic way that Linux reports file permissions. Linux grants three different types of permissions — read, write, and execute — for three different scopes: owner, group, and everyone. That's a total of nine permissions.

When you use the ls command with the –l option, the permissions are shown as a ten-character string that begins with a hyphen if the entry is for a file or a d if the entry is for a directory. Then, the next nine letters are the nine permissions, in this order:

>> Read, write, execute for the owner

>> Read, write, execute for the group

>> Read, write, execute for everyone

The letters r, w, or x appear if the permission has been granted. If the permission is denied, a hyphen appears.

For example, suppose the ls –l command lists these permissions:

```
-rw-r--r--
```

You interpret this permission string like this:

>> The first hyphen indicates that this is a file, not a directory.

>> The next three positions are rw-. Therefore, the owner has read and write permission on this file, but not execute permission.

>> The next three positions are r--. That means the group owner has read permissions but not write or execute permission.

>> The last three positions are also r--. That means that everyone else has read permission but not write or execute permission.

The full syntax of the `chmod` command is pretty complex. However, you can do most of what you need to do with this form:

```
chmod specification file
```

Here, `specification` is in the form `u=rwx`, `g=rwx`, or `o=rwx` to set the permissions for the user (owner), group, and others (everyone). You don't have to specify `r`, `w`, and `x`; you just list the permissions that you want to grant. For example, to grant read and write permission for the user to a file named `rescue.plans`, use this command:

```
$ chmod u=rw rescue.plans
```

You can also combine specifications, like this:

```
$ chmod u=rw,g=rw,o=r rescue.plans
```

To revoke all rights for the user, group, or others, don't type anything after the equal sign. For example, this command revokes all rights for others:

```
$ chmod o= rescue.plans
```

Networking Commands

The following sections present Linux commands that are used to display information about the network or configure its settings.

The hostname command

The `hostname` command simply displays the computer's host name. It has the following syntax:

```
hostname [name]
```

If you use this command without any parameters, the computer's host name is displayed. If you specify a name, the computer's host name is changed to the name you specify.

The ifconfig command

`ifconfig` displays and sets configuration options for network interfaces. Although you can configure an Ethernet adapter using this command, you'll rarely have to.

Linux does a pretty good job of automatically configuring network adapters, and the GNOME-based Network Configuration tool supplied with the Red Hat distribution should be able to handle most network configuration chores. So you'll use ifconfig mostly to display network configuration settings.

The basic syntax for ifconfig is

```
ifconfig interface [address] [netmask mask]
[broadcast broadcast]
```

Here are the options that you can use on the ifconfig command:

» *interface*: The symbolic name for your network adapter. It's typically eth0 for the first Ethernet adapter or eth1 for the second adapter.

» *address*: The IP address you want to assign to the interface, such as 192.168.1.100.

» *netmask*: The subnet mask to use, such as 255.255.255.0.

» *broadcast*: The broadcast, which should be the highest address on the subnet. For example: 192.168.1.255.

If you enter ifconfig without any parameters, the ifconfig command displays the current status of your network adapters, like this:

```
eth0 Link encap:Ethernet HWaddr 00:20:78:16:E0:6A
UP BROADCAST RUNNING MULTICAST MTU:1500 Metric:1
RX packets:0 errors:0 dropped:0 overruns:0 frame:0
TX packets:11 errors:0 dropped:0 overruns:0 carrier:0
collisions:0 txqueuelen:100
RX bytes:0 (0.0 b) TX bytes:2916 (2.8 Kb)
Interrupt:11 Base address:0xd000
eth1 Link encap:Ethernet HWaddr 00:40:05:80:51:F3
inet addr:192.168.3.100 Bcast:192.168.3.255 Mask:255.255.255.0
UP BROADCAST RUNNING MULTICAST MTU:1500 Metric:1
RX packets:2358 errors:0 dropped:0 overruns:0 frame:0
TX packets:1921 errors:0 dropped:0 overruns:0 carrier:0
collisions:0 txqueuelen:100
RX bytes:265194 (258.9 Kb) TX bytes:424467 (414.5 Kb)
Interrupt:3 Base address:0xc000
lo Link encap:Local Loopback
inet addr:127.0.0.1 Mask:255.0.0.0
UP LOOPBACK RUNNING MTU:16436 Metric:1
RX packets:93707 errors:0 dropped:0 overruns:0 frame:0
TX packets:93707 errors:0 dropped:0 overruns:0 carrier:0
collisions:0 txqueuelen:0
RX bytes:6393713 (6.0 Mb) TX bytes:6393713 (6.0 Mb)
```

To change the IP address of an adapter, use ifconfig like this:

```
$ ifconfig eth0 192.168.1.200
```

The netstat command

The netstat command lets you monitor just about every aspect of a Linux server's network functions. This command can generate page after page of interesting information — if you know what it all means.

The two most common reasons to use netstat are to display the routing table and to display open TCP/IP connections. The syntax for displaying the routing table is

```
netstat -r
```

This results in a display similar to this:

```
Kernel IP routing table
Destination Gateway Genmask Flags MSS Window irtt Iface
192.168.1.0 * 255.255.255.0 U 0 0 0 eth1
192.168.1.0 * 255.255.255.0 U 0 0 0 eth0
127.0.0.0 * 255.0.0.0 U 0 0 0 lo
```

To display TCP/IP connections, use this syntax:

```
netstat -l
```

This results in a display similar to the following:

```
Active Internet connections (only servers)
Proto Recv-Q Send-Q Local Address Foreign Address State
tcp 0 0 *:1024 *:* LISTEN
tcp 0 0 LSERVER:1025 *:* LISTEN
tcp 0 0 *:netbios-ssn *:* LISTEN
tcp 0 0 *:sunrpc *:* LISTEN
tcp 0 0 *:http *:* LISTEN
tcp 0 0 *:x11 *:* LISTEN
tcp 0 0 *:ssh *:* LISTEN
tcp 0 0 LSERVER:ipp *:* LISTEN
tcp 0 0 LSERVER:smtp *:* LISTEN
tcp 0 0 *:https *:* LISTEN
udp 0 0 *:1024 *:*
udp 0 0 LSERVER:1026 *:*
udp 0 0 192.168.1.20:netbios-ns *:*
udp 0 0 192.168.1.20:netbios-ns *:*
udp 0 0 *:netbios-ns *:*
```

```
udp 0 0 192.168.1.2:netbios-dgm *:*
udp 0 0 192.168.1.2:netbios-dgm *:*
udp 0 0 *:netbios-dgm *:*
udp 0 0 *:940 *:*
udp 0 0 *:sunrpc *:*
udp 0 0 *:631 *:*
```

From this display, you can tell which Linux services are actively listening on TCP/IP ports.

The ping command

The `ping` command is the basic troubleshooting tool for TCP/IP. You use it to determine whether basic TCP/IP connectivity has been established between two computers. If you're having any kind of network trouble between two computers, the first troubleshooting step is almost always to see whether the computers can ping each other.

The basic syntax of `ping` is straightforward:

```
ping [options] address
```

The options can be

>> –c: The number of packets to send. If you omit this, `ping` continues to send packets until you interrupt it.

WARNING

>> –d: Floods the network with packets, as many as 100 per second. Use with care!

>> –i: Specifies how many seconds to wait between sending packets. The default is one second. If you're having intermittent connection problems, you may try letting `ping` run for a while with this option set to a higher value, such as 60, to send a packet every minute.

>> –R: Displays the route the packets take to get to the destination computer.

TIP

`ping` will continue to ping the destination computer until you interrupt it by pressing Ctrl+Z.

You can specify the host to ping by using an IP address, as in this example:

```
$ ping 192.168.1.100
PING 192.168.1.100 (192.168.1.100) 56(84) bytes of data.
```

```
64 bytes from 192.168.1.100: icmp_seq=1 ttl=128 time=0.382 ms
64 bytes from 192.168.1.100: icmp_seq=2 ttl=128 time=0.345 ms
64 bytes from 192.168.1.100: icmp_seq=3 ttl=128 time=0.320 ms
64 bytes from 192.168.1.100: icmp_seq=4 ttl=128 time=0.328 ms
```

You can also ping by using a DNS name, as in this example:

```
$ ping www.lowewriter.com
PING www.lowewriter.com (209.68.34.15) 56(84) bytes of data.
64 bytes from www.lowewriter.com (209.68.34.15): icmp_seq=1 ttl=47 time=88.9 ms
64 bytes from www.lowewriter.com (209.68.34.15): icmp_seq=2 ttl=47 time=87.9 ms
64 bytes from www.lowewriter.com (209.68.34.15): icmp_seq=3 ttl=47 time=88.3 ms
64 bytes from www.lowewriter.com (209.68.34.15): icmp_seq=4 ttl=47 time=87.2 ms
```

The route command

The route command displays or modifies the computer's routing table. To display the routing table, use route without any parameters. To add an entry to the routing table, use this syntax:

```
route add [ -net | -host ] address [options]
```

To delete an entry, use this syntax:

```
route del [ -net | -host ] address [options]
```

The available options are as follows:

>> netmask *mask*: Specifies the subnet mask for this entry

>> gw *address*: Specifies the gateway address for this entry

>> dev *if*: Specifies an interface (such as eth0 or eth1) for this entry

If you enter route by itself, with no parameters, you'll see the routing table, as in this example:

```
$ route
Kernel IP routing table
Destination Gateway Genmask Flags Metric Ref Use Iface
192.168.1.0 * 255.255.255.0 U 0 0 0 eth1
192.168.1.0 * 255.255.255.0 U 0 0 0 eth1
169.254.0.0 * 255.255.0.0 U 0 0 0 eth1
127.0.0.0 * 255.0.0.0 U 0 0 0 lo
default 192.168.1.1 0.0.0.0 UG 0 0 0 eth1
```

Suppose that your network has a second router that serves as a link to another private subnet, 192.168.2.0 (subnet mask 255.255.255.0). The interface on the local side of this router is at 192.168.1.200. To add a static route entry that sends packets intended for the 192.168.2.0 subnet to this router, use a command like this:

```
$ route add 192.168.2.0 netmask 255.255.255.0 gw 192.168.1.200
```

The traceroute command

The traceroute command displays a list of all the routers that a packet must go through to get from the local computer to a destination on the Internet. Each one of these routers is a *hop*. If you're unable to connect to another computer, you can use traceroute to find out exactly where the problem is occurring.

Here's the syntax:

```
traceroute [-i interface] host
```

Although several options are available for the traceroute command, the one you're most likely to use is -i, which lets you specify an interface. This is useful if your computer has more than one network adapter.

8
Managing a Network

Contents at a Glance

Chapter **1**

Welcome to Network Administration

Help wanted. Network administrator to help small business get control of a network run amok. Must have sound organizational and management skills. Only moderate computer experience required. Part-time only.

Does this ad sound like one that your company should run? Every network needs a network administrator, whether the network has 2 computers or 200. Of course, managing a 200-computer network is a full-time job, whereas managing a 2-computer network isn't. At least, it shouldn't be.

This chapter introduces you to the boring job of network administration. Oops . . . you're probably reading this chapter because you've been elected to be the network manager, so I'd better rephrase that: This chapter introduces you to the wonderful, exciting world of network management! Oh, boy! This is going to be fun!

Knowing What Network Administrators Do

Simply put, network administrators administer networks, which means that they take care of the tasks of installing, configuring, expanding, protecting, upgrading, tuning, and repairing the network. Network administrators take care of the network hardware, such as cables, hubs, switches, routers, servers, and clients, as well as network software, such as network operating systems, email servers, backup software, database servers, and application software. Most importantly, network administrators take care of network users by answering their questions, listening to their troubles, and solving their problems.

On a big network, these responsibilities constitute a full-time job. Large networks tend to be volatile: Users come and go, equipment fails, cables break, and life in general seems to be one crisis after another.

Smaller networks are much more stable. After you get your network up and running, you probably won't have to spend much time managing its hardware and software. An occasional problem may pop up, but with only a few computers on the network, problems should be few and far between.

Regardless of the network's size, all network administrators must attend to several common chores:

>> **Equipment upgrades:** The network administrator should be involved in every decision to purchase new computers, printers, or other equipment. In particular, the network administrator should be prepared to lobby for the most network-friendly equipment possible, such as network-ready printers, ample network disk storage, and an adequate backup system.

>> **Configuration:** The network administrator must put on the pocket protector whenever a new computer is added to the network. The network administrator's job includes considering what changes to make to the cabling configuration, what computer name to assign to the new computer, how to integrate the new user into the security system, what rights to grant the user, and so on.

>> **Software upgrades:** Every once in a while, your trusty OS vendor (likely, Microsoft) releases a new version of your network operating system (NOS). The network administrator must read about the new version and decide whether its new features are beneficial enough to warrant an upgrade. In most cases, the hardest part of upgrading to a new version of your network operating system is determining the *migration path* — that is, how to upgrade your entire network to the new version while disrupting the network or its users as little as possible. Upgrading to a new NOS version is a major chore, so you need to carefully consider the advantages that the new version can bring.

>> **Patches:** Between upgrades, Microsoft releases patches and service packs that fix minor problems with its server operating systems. For more information, see the section "Patching Up Your Operating System and Software" later in this chapter. (Other software vendors also regularly release patches and service packs, so it isn't only Microsoft software that must be kept up to date.)

>> **Performance maintenance:** One of the easiest traps that you can get sucked into is the quest for network speed. The network is never fast enough, and users always blame the hapless network manager. So the administrator spends hours and hours tuning and tweaking the network to squeeze out that last 2 percent of performance.

>> **Ho-hum chores:** Network administrators perform routine chores, such as backing up the servers, archiving old data, freeing up server hard drive space, and so on. Much of network administration is making sure that things keep working and finding and correcting problems before any users notice that something is wrong. In this sense, network administration can be a thankless job.

>> **Software inventory:** Network administrators are also responsible for gathering, organizing, and tracking the entire network's software inventory. You never know when something is going to go haywire on Joe in Marketing's ancient Windows XP computer and you're going to have to reinstall that old copy of WordPerfect. Do you have any idea where the installation discs are?

Choosing the Part-Time Administrator

The larger the network, the more technical support it needs. Most small networks — with just a dozen or so computers — can get by with a part-time network administrator. Ideally, this person should be a closet computer geek: someone who has a secret interest in computers but doesn't like to admit it. Someone who will take books home and read them over the weekend. Someone who enjoys solving computer problems just for the sake of solving them.

The job of managing a network requires some computer skills, but it isn't entirely a technical job. Much of the work that the network administrator does is routine housework. Basically, the network administrator dusts, vacuums, and mops the network periodically to keep it from becoming a mess.

Here are some additional ideas on picking a part-time network administrator:

>> The network administrator needs to be an organized person. Conduct a surprise office inspection and place the person with the neatest desk in charge of the network. (Don't warn anyone in advance, or everyone may mess up his or her desk intentionally the night before the inspection.)

>> Allow enough time for network administration. For a small network (say, no more than 20 or so computers), an hour or two each week is enough. More time is needed upfront as the network administrator settles into the job and

discovers the ins and outs of the network. After an initial settling-in period, though, network administration for a small office network doesn't take more than an hour or two per week. (Of course, larger networks take more time to manage.)

>> Make sure that everyone knows who the network administrator is and that the network administrator has the authority to make decisions about the network, such as what access rights each user has, what files can and can't be stored on the server, how often backups are done, and so on.

>> Pick someone who is assertive and willing to irritate people. A good network administrator should make sure that backups are working *before* a hard drive fails and make sure that antivirus protection is in place *before* a virus wipes out the entire network. This policing will irritate people, but it's for their own good.

>> In most cases, the person who installs the network is also the network administrator. This is appropriate because no one understands the network better than the person who designs and installs it.

>> The network administrator needs an understudy — someone who knows almost as much about the network, is eager to make a mark, and smiles when the worst network jobs are delegated.

>> The network administrator has some sort of official title, such as Network Boss, Network Czar, Vice President in Charge of Network Operations, or Dr. Network. A badge, a personalized pocket protector, or a set of Spock ears helps, too.

Establishing Routine Chores

Much of the network administrator's job is routine stuff — the equivalent of vacuuming, dusting, and mopping. Or if you prefer, changing the oil and rotating the tires every 3,000 miles. Yes, it's boring, but it has to be done.

>> **Backup:** The network administrator needs to make sure that the network is properly backed up. If something goes wrong and the network isn't backed up, guess who gets the blame? On the other hand, if disaster strikes, yet you're able to recover everything from yesterday's backup with only a small amount of work lost, guess who gets the pat on the back, the fat bonus, and the vacation in the Bahamas?

>> **Protection:** Another major task for network administrators is sheltering your network from the evils of the outside world. These evils come in many forms, including hackers trying to break into your network and virus programs arriving through email.

>> **Clean-up:** Users think that the network server is like the attic: They want to throw files up there and leave them forever. No matter how much storage your network has, your users will fill it up sooner than you think. So the network manager gets the fun job of cleaning up the attic once in a while. Oh, joy. The best advice I can offer is to constantly complain about how messy it is up there and warn your users that spring cleaning is coming up.

Managing Network Users

Managing network technology is the easiest part of network management. Computer technology can be confusing at first, but computers aren't nearly as confusing as people. The real challenge of managing a network is managing the network's users.

The difference between managing technology and managing users is obvious: You can figure out computers, but you can never really figure out people. The people who use the network are much less predictable than the network itself. Here are some tips for dealing with users:

>> **Training:** Training is a key part of the network manager's job. Make sure that everyone who uses the network understands it and knows how to use it. If the network users don't understand the network, they may unintentionally do all kinds of weird things to it.

>> **Respect:** Never treat your network users like they're idiots. If they don't understand the network, it isn't their fault. Explain it to them. Offer a class. Buy them each a copy of *Networking All-in-One For Dummies* and tell them to read it during their lunch hour. Hold their hands. But don't treat them like idiots.

>> **Aids:** Make up a network cheat sheet that contains everything that the users need to know about using the network on one page. Make sure that everyone gets a copy.

>> **Responsive:** Be as responsive as possible when a network user complains of a network problem. If you don't fix the problem soon, the user may try to fix it. You probably don't want that.

TIP

The better you understand the psychology of network users, the more prepared you'll be for the strangeness they often serve up. Toward that end, I recommend that you read the *Diagnostic and Statistical Manual of Mental Disorders* (also known as *DSM-IV*) cover to cover.

Patching Up Your Operating System and Software

One of the annoyances that every network manager faces is applying software patches to keep your OS and other software up to date. A software *patch* is a minor update that fixes small glitches that crop up from time to time, such as minor security or performance issues. These glitches aren't significant enough to merit a new version of the software, but they're important enough to require fixing. Most patches correct security flaws that computer hackers have uncovered in their relentless attempts to prove that they're smarter than security programmers.

Periodically, all the recently released patches are combined into a *service pack*. Although the most diligent network administrators apply all patches as they're released, many administrators just wait for the service packs.

For all versions of Windows, you can use Windows Update to apply patches to keep your operating system and other Microsoft software up to date. You can find Windows Update in the Start menu. Windows Update automatically scans your computer's software and creates a list of software patches and other components that you can download and install. You can also configure Windows Update to automatically notify you of updates so that you don't have to remember to check for new patches.

For larger networks, you can set up a server that runs Microsoft's Windows Software Update Services (WSUS) to automate software updates. WSUS, which is a built-in role on Windows Server 2012 and later, essentially lets you set up your own Windows Update site on your own network. Then, you have complete control over how software updates are delivered to the computers on your network.

Discovering Software Tools for Network Administrators

Network administrators need certain tools to get their jobs done. Administrators of big, complicated, and expensive networks need big, complicated, and expensive tools. Administrators of small networks need small tools.

Some of the tools that the administrator needs are hardware tools, such as screw-drivers, cable crimpers, and hammers. The tools that I'm talking about here, however, are software tools. Here's a sampling of the tools you'll need:

>> **A diagramming tool:** A diagramming tool lets you draw pictures of your network. Visio (from Microsoft) is great for drawing the types of diagrams you'll want to make as a network administrator.

>> **A network discovery program:** For larger networks, you may want to invest in a network discovery program such as Spiceworks (`www.spiceworks.com`) that can automatically document your network's structure for you. These programs scan the network carefully, looking for computers, printers, routers, and other devices. They then create a database of the network components, draw diagrams for you, and chug out helpful reports.

>> **The network's built-in tools:** Many software tools that you need to manage a network come with the network itself. As the network administrator, read through the manuals that come with your network software to see what management tools are available. For example, Windows includes a `net diag` command that you can use to make sure that all the computers on a network can communicate with each other. (You can run `net diag` from an MS-DOS prompt.) For TCP/IP networks, you can use the TCP/IP diagnostic commands summarized in Table 1-1.

>> **System Information:** This program that comes with Windows is a useful utility for network managers.

>> **A protocol analyzer:** A *protocol analyzer* monitors and logs the individual packets that travel along your network. (Protocol analyzers are also called *packet sniffers*.) You can configure the protocol analyzer to filter specific types of packets, watch for specific types of problems, and provide statistical analysis of the captured packets. Most network administrators agree that Wireshark (`www.wireshark.org`) is the best protocol analyzer available. And it's free!

>> **Network Monitor:** All current versions of Windows include Network Monitor, which provides basic protocol analysis and can often help solve pesky network problems.

TABLE 1-1 TCP/IP Diagnostic Commands

Command	What It Does
arp	Displays address resolution information used by the Address Resolution Protocol (ARP)
hostname	Displays your computer's host name
ipconfig	Displays current TCP/IP settings
nbtstat	Displays the status of NetBIOS over TCP/IP connections
netstat	Displays statistics for TCP/IP
nslookup	Displays Domain Name System (DNS) information
ping	Verifies that a specified computer can be reached
route	Displays the PC's routing tables
tracert	Displays the route from your computer to a specified host

Building a Library

One of Scotty's best lines in the original *Star Trek* series was when he refused to take shore leave so he could get caught up on his technical journals. "Don't you ever relax?" asked Kirk. "I am relaxing!" Scotty replied.

To be a good network administrator, you need to read computer books. Lots of them. And you need to enjoy doing it. If you're the type who takes computer books with you to the beach, you'll make a great network administrator.

You need books on a variety of topics. I'm not going to recommend specific titles, but I do recommend that you get a good, comprehensive book on each of the following topics:

>> Network security and hacking

>> Wireless networking

>> Network cabling and hardware

>> Ethernet

>> Windows Server 2008, 2012, and 2016

>> Windows 7, 8, 8.1, and 10

>> Linux

>> TCP/IP

>> DNS

>> Sendmail or Microsoft Exchange Server, depending on which email server you use

In addition to books, you may also want to subscribe to some magazines to keep up with what's happening in the networking industry. Here are a few you should probably consider, along with their web addresses:

>> *InformationWeek:* www.informationweek.com

>> *InfoWorld:* www.infoworld.com

>> *Network Computing:* www.networkcomputing.com

>> *Network World:* www.networkworld.com

>> *2600 The Hacker Quarterly* (a great magazine on computer hacking and security): www.2600.com

TIP

The Internet is one of the best sources of technical information for network administrators. You'll want to stock your browser's Favorites menu with plenty of websites that contain useful networking information. In addition, you may want to subscribe to one of the many online newsletters that deliver fresh information on a regular basis via email.

Getting Certified

Remember the scene near the end of *The Wizard of Oz* when the Wizard grants the Scarecrow a diploma, the Cowardly Lion a medal, and the Tin Man a testimonial?

Network certifications are kind of like that. I can picture the scene now:

> *The Wizard:* "And as for you, my network-burdened friend, any geek with thick glasses can administer a network. Back where I come from, there are people who do nothing but configure Cisco routers all day long. And they don't have any more brains than you do. But they do have one thing you don't have: certification. And so, by the authority vested in me by the Universita Committeeatum E Pluribus Unum, I hereby confer upon you the coveted certification of CND."
>
> *You:* "CND?"

The Wizard: "Yes, that's, uh, *Certified Network Dummy.*"

You: "The Seven Layers of the OSI Reference Model are equal to the Sum of the Layers on the Opposite Side. Oh, joy, rapture! I feel like a network administrator already!"

My point is that certification in and of itself doesn't guarantee that you really know how to administer a network. That ability comes from real-world experience — not exam crams.

Nevertheless, certification is becoming increasingly important in today's competitive job market. So you may want to pursue certification, not just to improve your skills, but also to improve your résumé. Certification is an expensive proposition. Each test can cost several hundred dollars, and depending on your technical skills, you may need to buy books to study or enroll in training courses before you take the tests.

You can pursue two basic types of certification: vendor-specific certification and vendor-neutral certification. The major software vendors such as Microsoft and Cisco provide certification programs for their own equipment and software. CompTIA, a nonprofit industry trade association, provides the best-known vendor-neutral certification.

The following sections describe some of the certifications offered by CompTIA, Microsoft, Novell, and Cisco.

CompTIA

```
http://certifications.comptia.org
```

- **A+** is a basic certification for an entry-level computer technician. To attain A+ certification, you have to pass two exams: one on computer hardware, the other on operating systems.

- **Linux+ Powered by LPI** covers basic Linux skills such as installation, operations, and troubleshooting. This certification is vendor neutral, so it doesn't depend on any particular version of Linux.

- **Network+** is a popular vendor-neutral networking certification. It covers four major topic areas: Media and Topologies, Protocols and Standards, Network Implementation, and Network Support.

- **Server+** covers network server hardware. It includes details such as installing and upgrading server hardware, installing and configuring an NOS, and so on.

>> **Cloud+** covers building cloud infrastructure.

>> **Security+** is for security specialists. The exam topics include general security concepts, communication security, infrastructure security, basics of cryptography, and operational/organizational security.

Microsoft

`www.microsoft.com/learning/mcp`

>> **MTA** (Microsoft Technology Associate) is a general certification in either IT Infrastructure, Database, or Developer technology.

>> **MCSE** (Microsoft Certified Solutions Expert) is a prestigious certification for networking professionals who design and implement networks. To gain this certification, you have to pass several rigorous exams. Microsoft offers separate Windows Server 2008 and Windows Server 2012 certification tracks.

>> **MCSA** (Microsoft Certified Solutions Associate) is for networking professionals who administer existing networks.

Cisco

`www.cisco.com/web/learning/certifications`

>> **CCENT** (Cisco Certified Entry Network Technician) is an entry-level certification. A CCENT should be able to install, configure, and operate Cisco equipment for branch-level networks.

>> **CCNA** (Cisco Certified Network Associate) is an entry-level apprentice certification. A CCNA should be able to install, configure, and operate Cisco equipment for small networks (under 100 nodes).

>> **CCNP** (Cisco Certified Network Professional) is a professional-level certification for Cisco equipment. A CCNP should be able to install, configure, and troubleshoot Cisco networks of virtually any size. Several variants are available for cloud, data center, routing, security, service provider, and routing.

>> **CCDP** (Cisco Certified Design Professional) is for network design professionals. The CCNA certification is a prerequisite for the CCDP.

>> **CCDE** (Cisco Certified Design Expert) is an expert-level design certification.

» **CCIE** (Cisco Certified Internetwork Expert) is an expert-level certification, which can be had in several varieties, including routing, security, wireless, and service provider.

» **CCAr:** (Cisco Certified Architect) is the top dog of Cisco certifications.

» **CCT** (Cisco Certified Technician) is a certification for those who can diagnose and repair Cisco equipment.

» **And much more!** There are many more Cisco certifications to choose from, including certification for security, voice technology, wireless networking, and more.

Gurus Need Gurus, Too

No matter how much you know about computers, plenty of people know more than you do. This rule seems to apply at every rung of the ladder of computer experience. I'm sure that a top rung exists somewhere, occupied by the world's best computer guru. However, I'm not sitting on that rung, and neither are you. (Not even Bill Gates is sitting on that rung. In fact, Bill Gates got to where he is today by hiring people on higher rungs.)

As the local computer guru, one of your most valuable assets can be a knowledgeable friend who's a notch or two above you on the geek scale. That way, when you run into a real stumper, you have a friend to call for advice. Here are some tips for handling your own guru:

» In dealing with your own guru, don't forget the Computer Geek's Golden Rule: "Do unto your guru as you would have your own users do unto you." Don't pester your guru with simple stuff that you just haven't spent the time to think through. If you have thought it through and can't come up with a solution, however, give your guru a call. Most computer experts welcome the opportunity to tackle an unusual computer problem. It's a genetic defect.

» If you don't already know someone who knows more about computers than you do, consider joining your local PC users' group. The group may even have a subgroup that specializes in your networking software or may be devoted entirely to local folks who use the same networking software that you use. Odds are good that you're sure to make a friend or two at a users' group meeting. Also, you can probably convince your boss to pay any fees required to join the group.

> » If you can't find a real-life guru, try to find an online guru. Check out the various computing newsgroups on the Internet. Subscribe to online newsletters that are automatically delivered to you via email.

Helpful Bluffs and Excuses

As network administrator, you just won't be able to solve a problem sometimes, at least not immediately. You can do two things in this situation. The first is to explain that the problem is particularly difficult and that you'll have a solution as soon as possible. The second solution is to look the user in the eyes and, with a straight face, try one of these phony explanations:

> » Blame it on the version of whatever software you're using. "Oh, they fixed that with version 39."

> » Blame it on cheap, imported memory chips.

> » Blame it on Democrats. Or Republicans. Doesn't matter.

> » Blame it on oil company executives.

> » Blame it on global warming.

> » Hope that the problem wasn't caused by stray static electricity. Those types of problems are very difficult to track down. Tell your users that not properly discharging themselves before using their computers can cause all kinds of problems.

> » You need more memory.

> » You need a bigger hard drive.

> » You need a faster processor.

> » Blame it on Jar-Jar Binks.

> » You can't do that in Windows 10.

> » You can only do that in Windows 10.

> » Could be a virus.

> » Or sunspots.

> » No beer and no TV make Homer something something something. . . .

Chapter **2**

Managing Remotely

One of the first things you'll realize when you become a network administrator is that you quickly tire of walking all over the building to get to your servers or to users' computers. As a result, you'll soon discover that one of your best secret weapons is the ability to manage computers remotely.

Windows provides two distinct built-in ways to do this:

» **Remote Desktop Connection (RDC)** is designed to let you log into a Windows computer from a remote location. This is useful for managing a server without having to actually go to the computer room and accessing the server's console, or for accessing a virtual server that has no physical console.

» **Remote Assistance** is used to connect to an existing session of another Windows computer so that you can provide technical support for the other user.

This chapter shows you how to use both of these features.

Enabling Remote Desktop Connection

Before you can use RDC to access a server, you must enable remote access on the server. To do that, follow these steps (on the server computer, not your desktop computer):

1. **Open the Control Panel and click System.**

   This step brings up the System settings page.

2. **Click the Remote Settings link.**

   The remote access options appear, as shown in Figure 2-1.

3. **Select the Allow Remote Connections to This Computer radio button.**

4. **Click OK.**

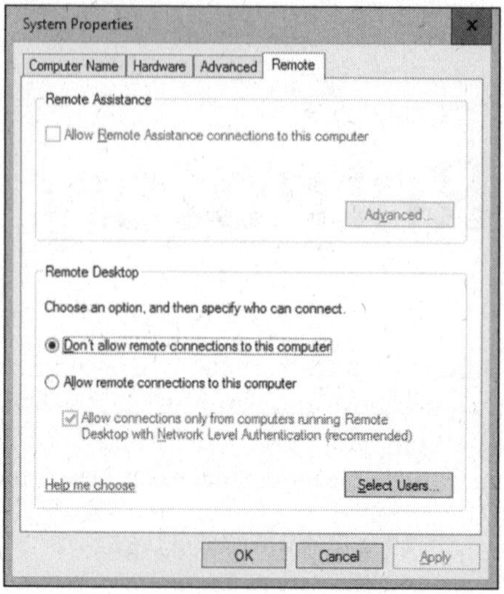

FIGURE 2-1:
Configuring
remote access.

You're done! Repeat this procedure for each server computer you want to allow access to.

You can click the Select Users button to create a list of users who are authorized to access the computer remotely. Note that all members of the Administrators group are automatically granted access, so you don't have to add administrators to this list.

WARNING

There's no question that RDC is convenient and useful. It's also inherently dangerous, however. Don't enable it unless you've taken precautions to secure your Administrator accounts by using strong passwords. Also, you should already have a firewall installed to keep unwanted visitors out of your network.

Connecting Remotely

After you've enabled remote access on a server, you can connect to the server by using the remote desktop client that's automatically installed with Windows. Here's the procedure:

1. **Click the Start button and type the word Remote. Then click the Remote Desktop Connection icon.**

The Remote Desktop Connection client comes to life, as shown in Figure 2-2.

FIGURE 2-2:
Connecting with
Remote Desktop
Connection.

2. **Enter the name of the computer you want to connect to.**

Alternatively, you can use the drop-down list to select the computer from the list of available computers.

You can also enter the IP address of the computer you want to connect to.

3. **Click the Connect button.**

You're connected to the computer you selected, and then prompted for login credentials, as shown in Figure 2-3.

4. **Enter your username and password, and then click OK.**

Assuming you enter valid credentials, the desktop of the remote computer is displayed, as shown in Figure 2-4.

5. **Use the remote computer!**

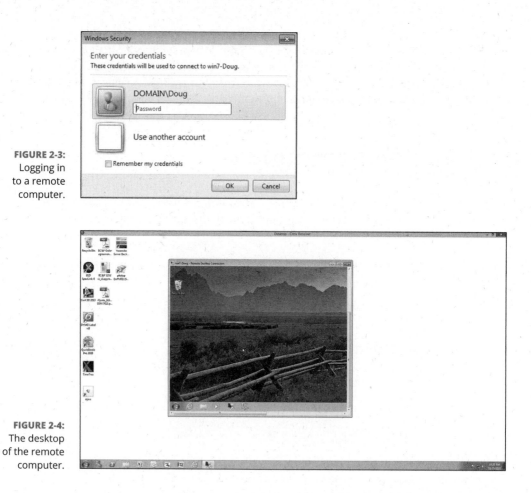

FIGURE 2-3:
Logging in
to a remote
computer.

FIGURE 2-4:
The desktop
of the remote
computer.

You may notice in Figure 2-4 that the Remote Desktop window is not large enough to display the entire desktop of the remote computer. As a result, scroll bars appear to allow you to scroll the desktop horizontally or vertically. You can always maximize the Remote Desktop window to see the entire desktop of the remote computer.

TIP

Here are a few other tips for working with Remote Desktop Connection:

>> **Remote Desktop allows only one user at a time to log in to the remote computer.** If another user is remotely logged in when you try to connect, you'll get a notice informing you that another user is already logged on. You

can either cancel or attempt to barge in on the other user's remote session. If you choose the latter option, the other user will see a message stating that you want to connect. If the other user accepts your request, the other user is logged off and you're logged in. If the other user denies your request, your attempt to log in is canceled. If the user does not respond, eventually Windows will kick the other user off and let you in.

» **When you're using the Remote Desktop Connection client, you can't just press Alt+Tab to get another program running on the client computer.** Instead, you must first minimize the RDC client's window by clicking its minimize button. Then you can access other programs running on your computer.

» **If you minimize the RDC client window, you have to provide your logon credentials again when you return.** This security feature is there in case you forget that you have an RDC session open.

TIP

If you use RDC a lot on a particular computer (such as your own desktop computer), I suggest that you create a shortcut to RDC and place it on the desktop, at the top of the Start menu, or in the Quick Launch portion of the taskbar.

» **RDC has several useful configuration options that you can access by clicking the Options button.**

For more information about these options, refer to the section "Configuring Remote Desktop Options" later in this chapter.

Using Keyboard Shortcuts for Remote Desktop

When you're working in a Remote Desktop session, some of the standard Windows keyboard shortcuts don't work exactly as you expect them to. Table 2-1 lists the special keyboard shortcuts you can use in a Remote Desktop session.

TABLE 2-1 **Keyboard Shortcuts for Remote Desktop**

Shortcut	What It Does
Ctrl+Alt+Break	Toggles between full-screen and windowed views.
Ctrl+Alt+Pause	Similar to Ctrl+Alt+Break, but instead of maximizing the remote window to full screen, it displays the remote window against a black background.
Alt+Insert	Cycles between applications running on the remote desktop, the same as Alt+Tab on your local machine.
Alt+PageUp	Same as Alt+Insert.
Alt+PageDown	Similar to Alt+Insert, but reverses the order in which applications are cycled. This is the same as Alt+Shift+Tab on your local machine.
Ctrl+Alt+End	Sends a Ctrl+Alt+Del to the remote desktop.
Alt+Home	Brings up the Start menu on the remote system.
Alt+Delete	Opens the Windows menu on a window in the remote desktop. (The Windows menu is the one at the top left of every window, with options to move, resize, minimize, maximize, and close the window.)
Ctrl+Alt+Plus Sign (+)	Captures a screen image of the entire remote desktop and saves it to the Clipboard. This is the same as pressing Print Screen on your local machine.
Ctrl+Alt+Minus Sign (–)	Captures an image of the current window and saves it to the Clipboard. This is the same as pressing Alt+Tab on your local machine.

Configuring Remote Desktop Options

Before you connect to a remote desktop session, you can set a variety of options that affect how the remote desktop session will behave. To summon these options, click the Start button, type the word **Remote**, and then click the Remote Desktop Connection icon. When the Remote Desktop Connection window appears (refer to Figure 2-2), click the Show Options button at the bottom left of the window. This brings up the Remote Desktop options, as shown in Figure 2-5.

Figure 2-5 shows the General tab of the Remote Desktop options. On this tab, you can enter the name or IP address of the computer you want to access remotely and the username you want to connect with. You can also save the settings you've created via the other tabs or open a settings file you've previously saved.

TIP

When you click the Save or Save As buttons, your settings are saved to an .rdp file. .rdp files are associated with the Remote Desktop Connection program, so you can double-click an .rdp file to open a saved connection. In other words, an .rdp file is a handy shortcut to a remote connection.

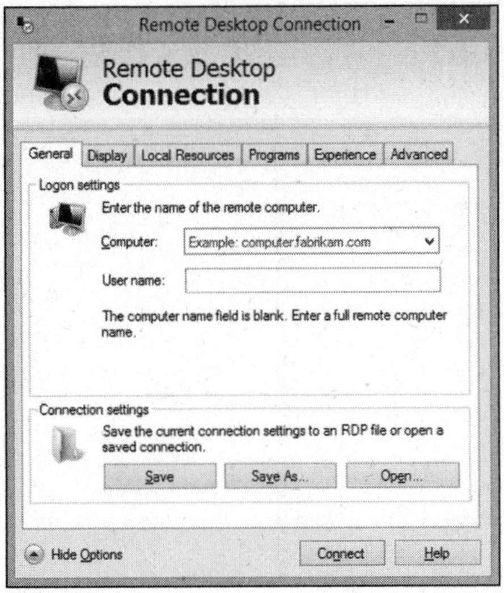

FIGURE 2-5:
Setting the
options for
Remote Desktop
Connection.

The following sections describe the additional options that are available on the other Remote Desktop Connection tabs.

Setting the Display options

Figure 2-6 shows the Display tab of the Remote Desktop Connection dialog box. The following paragraphs describe each of the options available from this tab:

>> **Display Configuration size slider:** Use this control to set the size of your remote desktop display. If you drag the slider all the way to the right, the remote desktop will be displayed in full-screen mode. As you move the slider to the left, various display resolutions will appear. Choose the display size you want the remote computer to open up in.

>> **Use All My Monitors for the Remote Session:** If your computer has more than one monitor, select this check box to use all your monitors for the remote session. If you want to open the remote desktop in full-screen mode on just one of your monitors, leave this box deselected.

>> **Choose the Color Depth of the Remote Session drop-down list:** Use this drop-down list to choose the color quality of the remote desktop. Over slower connections, reducing the color depth will help performance.

>> **Display the Connection Bar When I Use the Full Screen:** The connection bar is a thin bar at the top of the screen that enables you to switch back to normal windowed mode. If you deselected this box, you'll have to remember that you can press Ctrl+Alt+Break to switch between full-screen and windowed mode.

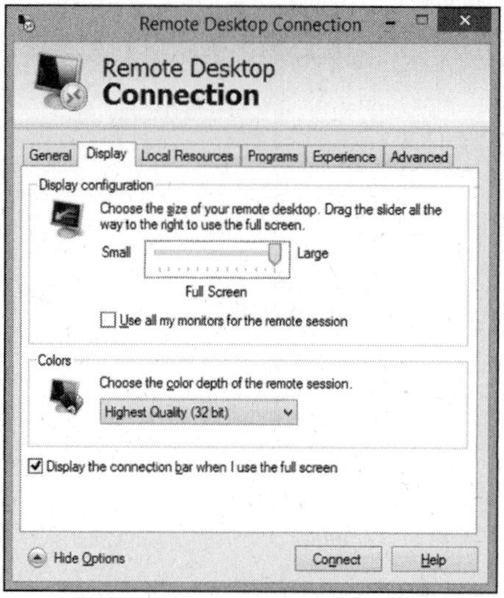

FIGURE 2-6:
Setting the Display options for Remote Desktop Connection.

Setting the Local Resources options

The Local Resources tab, shown in Figure 2-7, lets you set the following options:

FIGURE 2-7:
Setting the Local Resources options for Remote Desktop Connection.

>> **Remote Audio:** Click the Settings button to bring up a dialog box that lets you choose whether to play audio on the remote computer using the remote computer's sound card, the local computer's sound card, or not at all. This display box also lets you choose whether to allow audio recording during the remote session.

» **Apply Windows Key Combinations drop-down list:** This drop-down list lets you specify how Windows keyboard shortcuts are to be interpreted — on the remote computer, on the local computer, or on the remote computer only when it's running in full-screen mode.

» **Local Devices and Resources:** The Printers check box lets you access local printers from the remote session. The Clipboard check box synchronizes the local and remote clipboards, so that when you copy something to the Clipboard in the remote session, you can return to the local session and paste the Clipboard contents (or vice versa).

You can also share local drives with the remote session. To do so, click More, and then select the drives that you want to make available to the remote session, as shown in Figure 2-8.

FIGURE 2-8: Sharing drives with the remote computer.

Setting the Programs options

The Programs tab, shown in Figure 2-9, lets you specify a program that will automatically run when you connect to the remote computer. You can specify the path to the program's executable file, and you can also specify the working directory for the program.

For example, if you always want Active Directory Users and Computers to start when you log in to your domain controller, you can set up an .rdp file with the start program set to the path to Active Directory Users and Computers (%SystemRoot%System32\dsa.msc). Then, you don't have to manually start this program when you log in to your domain controller.

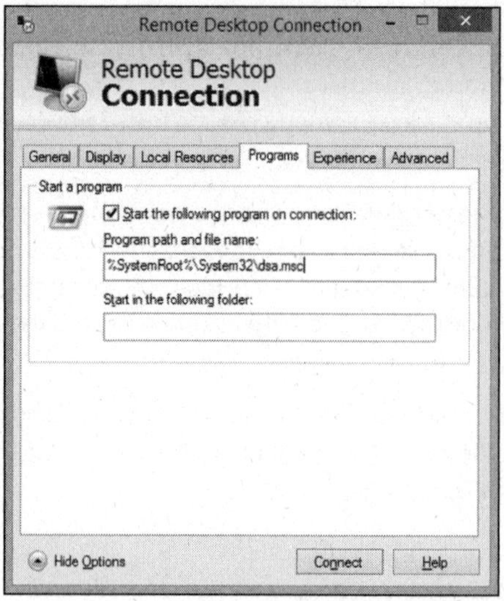

FIGURE 2-9:
Setting programs to automatically run in a remote session.

Setting the Experience options

The options on the Experience tab, shown in Figure 2-10, control various settings that affect the responsiveness of your remote connection. The options are as follows:

» **Choose Your Connection Speed to Optimize Performance drop-down list:** This allows you to optimize the amount of information sent back and forth over the network based on your expected connection speed. At slower speeds, features such as the desktop background, font smoothing, window animations, and so on, will be suppressed. The default setting is to let Windows choose which features to use based on the actual speed of the connection.

» **Persistent Bitmap Caching:** If you select this box, copies of bitmap images are stored on the local computer so they don't have to be transferred across the network every time they're needed.

» **Reconnect If the Connection Is Dropped:** If you select this box, the connection will be automatically reestablished if the connection is broken.

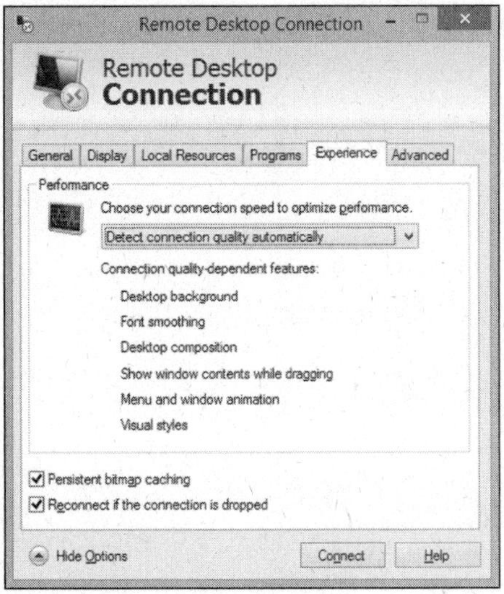

FIGURE 2-10:
Setting the
Experience
options for a
Remote Desktop
session.

Setting the Advanced options

The Advanced tab of the Remote Desktop Connections window, shown in Figure 2-11, lets you control two features:

>> **Server Authentication:** Determines what to do if an authentication problem such as an unknown security certificate is encountered when connecting to the server. The default action is to warn the user, but allow the user to continue if desired. You can change this setting to always connect in spite of the authentication problem, or to never connect when a problem is encountered.

>> **Connect from Anywhere:** These settings are used only when you use an advanced server role called Remote Desktop Gateway to manage remote access to computers on your network. For more information about this server role, search the Internet for *Remote Desktop Gateway*. (This subject is beyond the scope of this book.)

Using Remote Assistance

One of the most annoying aspects of providing technical support for network users is that you often have to go to the user's desk to see what's going on with his or her computer. That's annoying enough if the other user's desk is across the room or down the hall, but it's almost unworkable if the user you need to support is across town or in a different city or state altogether.

Fortunately, Windows includes a handy feature called Remote Assistance, which is designed to let you provide technical support to an end-user without going to the user's location. With Remote Assistance, you can see the user's screen in a window on your own screen, so you can watch what the user is doing. You can even take control when necessary to perform troubleshooting or corrective actions to help solve the user's problems.

Note that there are commercial alternatives to Windows Remote Assistance that do a much better job at this task. This chapter shows you how to use Remote Assistance because it's free and all Windows computers since Windows XP have it.

Enabling Remote Assistance

Before you can lend assistance to a remote computer, Remote Assistance must be enabled on that computer. It is best to enable Remote Assistance before you need it, so that when the time comes, you can easily access your users' computers. But the procedure is simple enough that you can probably walk a user through the steps over the phone so that you can then gain access.

Here are the steps for Windows 7 and later:

1. **Click the Start button, type** Remote Assistance, **and click Enable Remote Assistance Invitations to Be Sent from This Computer.**

This brings up the System Properties dialog box, shown in Figure 2-12.

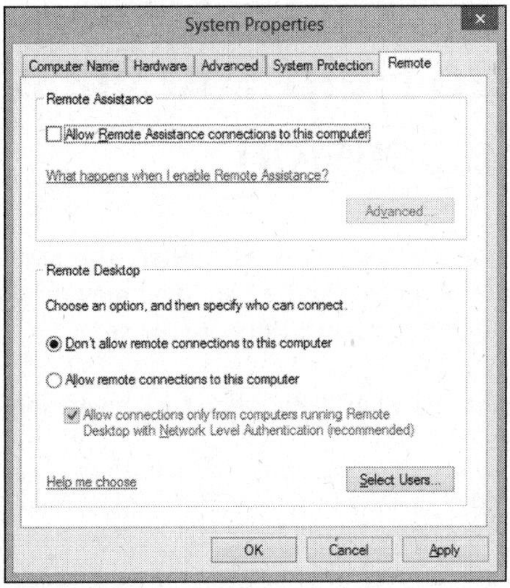

FIGURE 2-12:
Enabling Remote Assistance.

2. **Select the Allow Remote Connections to This Computer option.**

3. **Click the Advanced button.**

The Remote Assistance Settings dialog box appears, as shown in Figure 2-13.

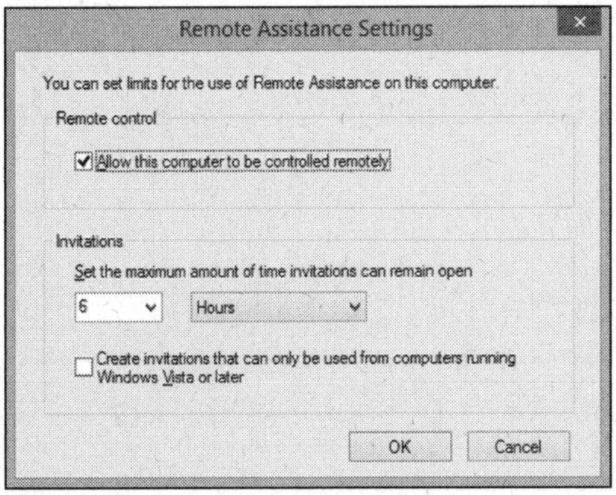

FIGURE 2-13:
Setting the advanced Remote Assistance options.

4. **Select the Allow This Computer to Be Controlled Remotely check box.**

   This option will allow you to later take control of this computer remotely.

5. **Click OK.**

   You're returned to the System Properties dialog box.

6. **Click OK.**

You're done. You can now initiate Remote Assistance sessions from this computer.

Inviting Someone to Help You via a Remote Assistance Session

The user requesting remote assistance must initiate the request before you can connect to the user's computer to provide help. You may need to guide your user through this procedure over the phone. Here are the steps:

1. **Click the Start button, type** Invite, **and then click Invite Someone to Connect to Your PC.**

   The Windows Remote Assistance window appears, as shown in Figure 2-14.

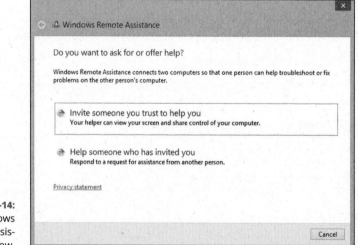

FIGURE 2-14:
The Windows
Remote Assis-
tance window.

2. **Click Invite Someone You Trust to Help You.**

The screen shown in Figure 2-15 appears.

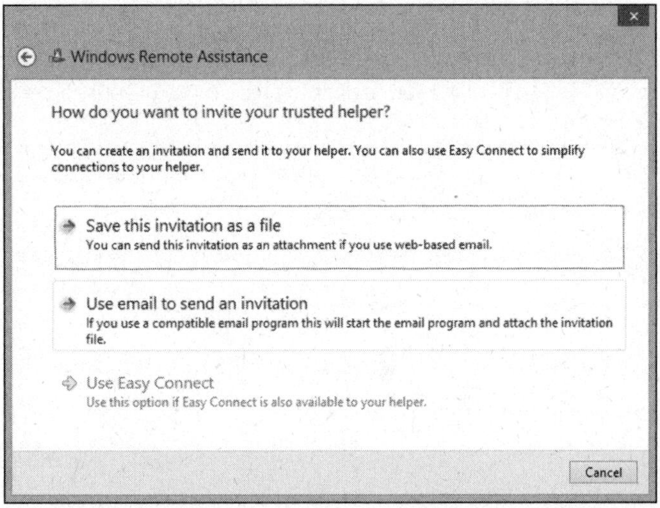

FIGURE 2-15:
Inviting someone
to help you.

3. **Click Save This Invitation as a File, and save the invitation file to a convenient disk location.**

This option creates a special file that you can save to disk. A Save As dialog box appears, allowing you to save the invitation file in any disk location you want. You can then email the invitation to your helper, who can use the invitation to connect to your PC.

4. **If you use Microsoft Outlook, you can alternatively choose Use Email to Send an Invitation. This option fires up Outlook and creates an email with the invitation file already attached.**

Either way, a password will be displayed, as shown in Figure 2-16. You'll need to provide this password to your helper when requested. (Typically, you'll do that over the phone.)

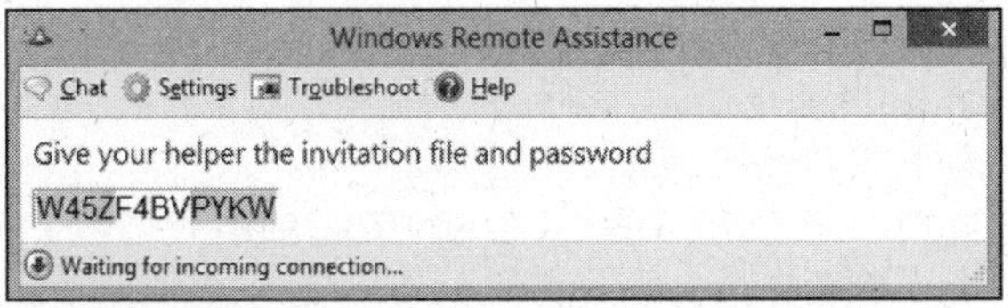

FIGURE 2-16:
You'll need to tell
your helper the
password.

5. **Email the invitation file to the person you want to help you.**

Use your preferred email program to send the invitation file as an attachment.

6. **Wait for your helper to request the password.**

When your helper enters the password into his or her Remote Assistance screen, the Remote Assistance session is established. You'll be prompted for permission to allow your helper to take control of your computer, as shown in Figure 2-17.

7. **Click Yes.**

Your helper now has access to your computer. To facilitate the Remote Assistance session, the toolbar shown in Figure 2-18 appears. You can use this toolbar to chat with your helper or to temporarily pause the Remote Assistance session.

Responding to a Remote Assistance Invitation

If you've received an invitation to a Remote Assistance session, you can establish the session by following these steps:

1. **Click the Start button, type** Invite, **and then click Invite Someone to Connect to Your PC.**

This brings up the Windows Remote Assistance window (refer to Figure 2-14).

2. **Click Help Someone Who Has Invited You.**

3. **Click Use an Invitation File.**

   An Open dialog box appears.

4. **Locate the invitation file you were sent, select it, and click Open.**

   You're prompted to enter the Remote Assistance password, as shown in Figure 2-19.

FIGURE 2-19:
Enter the Remote
Assistance
password.

> **Remote Assistance** ✕
>
> Enter the password to connect to the remote computer
>
> You can get this password from the person requesting assistance. A Remote Assistance session will start after you type the password and click OK.
>
> Enter password:
>
> [   ]
>
> OK   Cancel

TIP

As an alternative to Steps 1 through 3, you can simply double-click the invitation file you received. This will launch Windows Remote Assistance and prompt you for the password.

5. **Enter the password given to you by the user requesting help, and then click OK.**

   The remote user is prompted to grant you permission to start the Remote Assistance session (this is where the remote user sees the screen that was shown in Figure 2-17). When the user grants permission, the Remote Assistance session is established. You can now see the user's screen in the Remote Assistance window, as shown in Figure 2-20.

6. **To take control of the remote user's computer, click Request Control.**

   The remote user will be prompted to allow control. Assuming that permission is granted, you can now control the other computer.

7. **Do your thing.**

   Now that you're connected to the remote computer, you can perform whatever troubleshooting or corrective actions are necessary to solve the user's problems.

8. **If necessary, use the Chat window to communicate with the user.**

   You can summon the Chat window by clicking the Chat button in the toolbar. Figure 2-21 shows a chat in progress.

9. **To conclude the Remote Assistance session, simply close the Remote Assistance window.**

   The remote user is notified that the Remote Assistance session has ended.

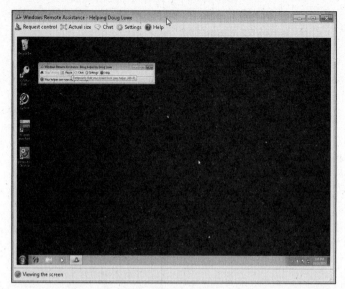

FIGURE 2-20:
A Remote
Assistance
session in
progress.

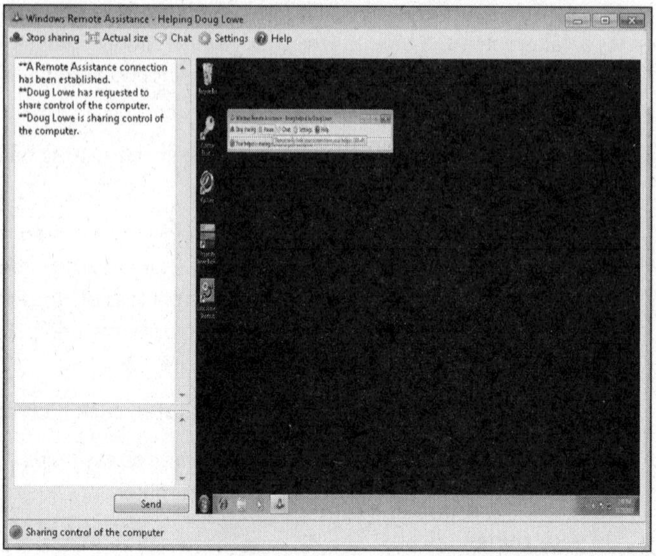

FIGURE 2-21:
Using the chat
window.

Chapter 3

Managing Network Assets

n a small network, keeping track of the computers that live on the network is easy. For example, in a small office with four or five employees, you can just walk around the room and make sure that everyone's computer is still there. If one of the computers is missing, you know you've lost one!

But in a larger network, keeping track of the assets on the network can become a major burden. With dozens, hundreds, or even thousands of devices to keep track of, you need some kind of organized system to keep track of everything. Other-wise, you'll soon find yourself asking questions like these, and struggling to come up with answers:

>> When Bob in Accounting left the company two years ago, did we get his laptop back? If so, where is it?

>> When we hired Paige last summer, did we set her up with a MacBook or a Dell laptop? Or did we give her Bob's laptop?

>> What kind of printer did we set up in the Redmond office?

>> When Richard became a remote worker, did we give him a mobile hotspot?

> » Analisa's car was broken into last night and her Surface Pro was stolen. Was it the 4GB i5 model or the 16GB i7 model?
>
> » Juan Carlos is going to be out of town for a conference next week. Do we have a laptop he can borrow?

This chapter gives you some suggestions on what to do when it becomes impossible to keep all this stuff in your head.

Introducing IT Asset Management

IT asset management (ITAM) is a program that assumes the responsibility for managing the life cycle of all IT assets within an organization. IT assets include *hardware assets* (such as computers, tablets, and mobile phones) and *software assets* (such as licenses of Office 365, Adobe Acrobat Standard, and Exchange Server 2016).

Ideally, an ITAM system should track all of an organization's IT assets through each asset's entire life cycle, from acquisition to retirement. For a hardware asset such as a computer, the life cycle includes the following:

> » **Acquisition:** Consideration of alternative proposals for the asset, planned usage of the asset, development of new or application of existing policies related to the asset, and the actual purchase of the asset
>
> » **Deployment:** Installation and configuration of the asset for use by a specific user
>
> » **Support:** Any necessary reconfiguration, repair, upgrades, or installation of new software that may be done during the asset's useful life
>
> » **Redeployment:** For example, when a desktop computer is redeployed to a different user or application
>
> » **Retirement:** When an asset is taken out of service due to obsolescence or changing business needs
>
> » **Disposition:** When the asset is physically disposed of (e-wasted or sold) and is no longer owned by the organization

Software assets have a similar but distinct characteristic life cycle. The main distinction is that software typically falls under one of several licensing models that permit deployment to a varying number of users and have a predictable maintenance cost that is set by the vendor. For example, a software asset such as Office 365 is a subscription that is charged per user, per month. Some software, such as AutoDesk's AutoCAD, can be obtained with multiuser licenses that are administered by AutoDesk's cloud-based licensing services and paid annually. Each software vendor provides its own licensing options. The ITAM program should be able to accommodate a variety of licensing models so that you can track your software assets.

Why Bother?

Whew, this sounds like a lot of work. It's true: Maintaining an accurate and detailed record of all your IT assets is a bit of an undertaking. Before you commit to it, you should understand some of the benefits of doing so. Here are some of the top reasons I suggest you take the time:

>> To prevent loss due to theft or neglect of equipment

>> To reduce cost by not purchasing unnecessary equipment and by repurposing existing equipment for new applications

>> To improve performance by retiring and replacing obsolete equipment

>> To comply with auditing or regulatory requirements

>> To control the cost of maintaining equipment

>> To ensure proper recovery of lost or damaged equipment, especially if an insurance claim is necessary

>> To prevent the serious security threat that occurs when assets are lost

One of the most important, and often overlooked, benefits is that your users will take much better care of their equipment if they know that *you* care about the equipment enough to keep a record of it.

Getting Organized

The first step for creating a system to track the assets on your network is to get organized. Start by making a list of the various types of IT assets that exist within your organization. This list might include

>> Desktop computers

>> Portable computers

>> Tablets

>> Smartphones

- » MiFi devices (hotspots)
- » Printers
- » Scanners
- » IP phones
- » Servers
- » Switches
- » Wireless access points
- » Routers

ISO/IEC 19770

To provide a standardized way of doing IT asset management, the International Organization for Standardization (ISO) along with the International Electrotechnical Commission (IEC) have adopted a standard known as ISO/IEC 19770. This standard provides guidelines for consistent processes and technology use to track primarily software assets.

There are five sections of the guidelines:

- ISO/IEC 19770-1 lays out a process for verifying that an organization is tracking IT assets properly.

- ISO/IEC 19770-2 provides a data format for recording software identification (SWID) tags.

- ISO/IEC 19770-3 spells out a data format for recording software licensing information in the form of entitlements (ENT).

- ISO/IEC 19770-4 documents a data format for tracking resource utilization measurement (RUM).

- ISO/IEC 19770-5 is a general overview and glossary.

Quite a few vendors have implemented various aspects of ISO/IEC 19770. In particular, most Windows installer programs create ISO/IEC 19770-2 SWID tags that register software installed on a computer. When looking for software to assist you with IT asset management, ISO/IEC 19770 compliance is a definite plus.

After you've compiled this list, you can start to focus on which types of assets will most benefit from tracking in an asset management system. For example, you may decide that parts of the infrastructure (such as servers, switches, and routers) don't need to be tracked. After all, there are probably a limited number of them, and they don't move around much. The other types of devices, on the other hand, move around as often as employees are hired or leave, change jobs, or have new requirements.

After you've identified what types of assets you need to track, you can home in on the specifics. For example, you can make a list of each of your desktop computers, including the make and model of the computer, basic specifications (such as CPU type, RAM, and disk capacity), when it was acquired, and who is using it.

What to Track

Managing Network Assets

When putting together a database for tracking IT assets, you should carefully consider the type of information you want to track. Strive to find the right balance between tracking so much information that the recordkeeping becomes a burden versus tracking so little information that the database is useless.

At the minimum, I recommend you track the following:

>> **Asset identifier:** See the section "Picking a Number" later in this chapter for tips on creating an identifier.

>> **Type of asset:** Develop a list of asset types and use a standard name for each type of asset (for example, "WK" for "workstation").

>> **Manufacturer, product name, model number, and serial number.**

>> **Asset's status:** For example, "Deployed," "In Inventory," "Retired," or "Disposed."

>> **Date the asset was acquired.**

>> **The user currently assigned to the asset.**

>> **The date the asset was assigned to the current user.**

You can easily track this information in a simple spreadsheet; just create a column for each data point and start entering your inventory.

But ideally, you may want to track more than just this basic information for each asset. In particular, you may want to track the entire history of the asset. To do that, you'll need detailed records to record each event during the asset's life cycle. These records should include the following:

>> Asset identifier

>> Event type (for example, "Deployed," "Serviced," "Returned to Inventory," "Retired," and so on)

>> Event date

>> Name of the user

>> Name of the technician

>> Description

A spreadsheet won't do for tracking this type of life-cycle information. Instead, you'll need a bona-fide database. If you're smart with Microsoft Access or SQL databases, you can easily design your own database. But you may find it easier in the long run (and ultimately less expensive) to use professionally designed IT asset management software to track this level of detail. For more information, refer to the section "Using Asset-Tracking Software" later in this chapter.

Taking Pictures

Besides all the useful data spelled out in the previous section, consider including a photograph of each asset in your asset database. As they say, a picture is worth a thousand words!

Including a picture can be especially useful if the asset is stolen or damaged and an insurance claim is made. A good photograph coupled with an accurate description can go a long ways toward establishing the legitimacy of a loss claim.

Picking a Number

To keep track of your computer inventory, you'll need to assign each device in your inventory a unique identifier. You can call this identifier an *asset identifier, asset number, tracking number,* or anything else that makes sense to you. The most important aspect of this identifier is that it is unique. To avoid confusion, every IT asset tracked by your asset management system must have a unique identifier.

If your initial goal is to keep track of Windows computers, you may be tempted to use each computer's Active Directory computer name to uniquely identify your assets. However, that's a shortsighted choice, for two reasons:

>> Even if you initially start with Windows computers, you'll eventually realize that you also need to track other types of devices, such as smartphones, tablets, and cellular hotspots. Not all these devices lend themselves to Active Directory naming conventions.

>> More important, it's easy to change the name of a Windows computer. If you rename a device, you'll have to remember to rename the device in your asset database.

Instead of using the Active Directory computer name, I suggest you create your own asset ID for every device in your inventory. In keeping with good database normalization rules, this ID should *not* indicate the type of device. In other words, I recommend against using something like "NB-002" for "Notebook #2" or "18-001 for "the first device purchased in 2018." Instead, use simple sequential identification numbers that have no meaning or purpose other than to uniquely identify each device.

TECHNICAL STUFF

In case you're interested, *database normalization* refers to the design of database structures that meet an idealized concept known as *normal form.* One of the basic normalization rules is that every column should signify one and only one thing; a single column should not be overloaded with two or more meanings. So, the asset ID should not represent both a sequence number *and* a type. Instead, the type should be indicated in a separate column. (To be fair, I should point out that many common unique identifiers *are* overloaded with additional information. For example, an automobile vehicle identification number [VIN] includes many attributes about the vehicle, including the country, manufacturer, plant, and model year in addition to a sequence number. And the venerable MAC address, which uniquely identifies network hardware, indicates the manufacturer as well as a unique serial number.)

Making Labels

One of the basic steps in keeping track of your computer equipment is to physically apply a label on every piece of equipment maintained in your asset inventory. That way, you'll always be able to correlate a specific piece of equipment with its record in the database.

DEVELOPING AN EQUIPMENT LOSS POLICY

At the same time you're developing an asset management system for your organization, you may also want to consider developing a policy on how lost or damaged equipment is handled. This is especially true if you intend to hold employees responsible for loss or damage of equipment issued to them.

The policy should spell out exactly what the expectations of the company are regarding the proper care of the equipment, as well as the consequences of losing or damaging the equipment. The policy should specifically address what happens in the following circumstances:

- Theft from a locked vehicle versus an unlocked vehicle

- Misplaced equipment

- Damage as a result of abuse versus accidental damage or ordinary wear and tear

If the policy is to require reimbursement by the employee or a payroll deduction to cover the loss, make sure that the employee is aware of the policy and signs a written agreement at the time the equipment is issued. You should also check with your attorney to make sure that payroll deductions are allowed in your state.

At the minimum, the label should include the unique asset identifier as well as identifying information for your organization such as the company name and perhaps a phone number, street address, and URL. Any other information is superfluous and will probably make your task more difficult.

Here are a few tips for making labels:

>> Don't use a handheld or desktop label maker unless you have only a few assets to track. You'll quickly grow tired of manually keying in the information for each label. Instead, use a computer-attached label printer. Several companies make excellent label printers; check out DYMO (www.dymo.com), Brother (www.brother-usa.com), and Zebra (www.zebra.com).

>> Consider printing the asset ID number in barcode format. Then you can use a barcode reader whenever you need to read the label. This can save considerable time when servicing the asset.

>> Use tamper-proof label tape when printing labels. It costs a bit more but is worth it.

>> Affix the labels in a consistent location for each device type.

>> Always affix the label to the device itself, not to a protective case.

>> If possible, incorporate your company's branding into the design of the label. Get help from the marketing or publicity department to make sure your labels are consistent with company branding.

Tracking Software

Managing Network Assets

So far, we've only talked about keeping track of hardware assets. Besides hardware, you'll also need to keep track of the software assets within your organization. Make a thorough list of all the software used by your organization, along with information about the software version, how the software is licensed, how many and what types of seats you own, and who in your organization uses the software. If you don't do this, you'll find yourself unnecessarily purchasing software you already own or installing more copies of a program than your license permits.

Many software products offer their own license management portals you can use to manage their licenses. Examples include the following:

>> If you use Microsoft Volume Licensing for your Microsoft software, you can use the Volume Licensing Center (available via www.microsoft.com/licensing)

>> You can manage Office 365 from the Office 365 admin center. Just log in at www.office.com, and then choose Admin from the app launcher. (You must have admin permissions, of course.)

>> For Adobe Creative Suite products (such as Acrobat, Photoshop, InDesign, and so on), log in to the team management portal at http://accounts.adobe.com. This portal allows you to view all your Adobe subscription licenses and purchase additional seats if needed.

Most other software companies that offer subscription-based software licensing offer their own portals.

Using Asset-Tracking Software

A simple spreadsheet may suffice for a very basic asset-tracking system, but eventually you'll outgrow the spreadsheet. When that happens, you'll need to move to a bona-fide database system. If you're a skilled database developer, you can create a system on your own. But why spend so much time inventing something that many software vendors have already developed? A simple web search will reveal that there are plenty of IT asset–tracking systems available. Some are low-cost or even free and provide just the basics. Others are capable of tracking inventory for the largest IT systems. The trick, as with any software, is to find the product that meets your current needs, can grow with you as your organization grows, and fits your budget.

When searching for asset management software, here are a few features I suggest you look for:

» **Simple installation and management:** Asset management is an ideal application for a cloud-based service rather than an on-premises install.

» **Secure access:** If you do go with a cloud-based option, it's imperative that the data be secure.

» **Web-based interface:** That way, a client install is not required. It will be very helpful to access your asset management software from any computer on your network so that you don't have to return to your office to look up or update an asset's record.

» **Mobile app support:** This allows you to easily scan a barcode label with your smartphone or tablet to call up an asset's record.

» **Customizable fields:** This allows you to set up the tracking records to meet your own unique needs.

» **Customizable reports:** These let you meet your organization's reporting standards.

» **Import capabilities:** This allows you to convert your current asset-tracking spreadsheets to the new system. Spreadsheet imports can also sometimes help with bulk entry of data; it's often easier to enter data in spreadsheet format than it is to work through a multitude of data-entry screens.

» **Pricing that scales with volume:** That way, you don't pay for capacity you don't need.

» **Responsive support and good training resources.**

Other Sources of Asset-Tracking Information

In addition to dedicated asset-tracking service, there are several other places you can go for information that can be helpful for tracking IT assets. Here are a few:

» **Cellphone vendor portals:** All major mobile phone providers have online portals for managing your accounts. These portals typically let you view and edit all the phone lines on your account, with details including who the phone is assigned to, how much usage the phone has incurred, the exact make and model of the phone, and when the phone is eligible for upgrade. If a phone is lost or stolen, you can disable or deactivate the device.

These vendor portals also track MiFi hotspot devices as well.

» **Copier vendor portals:** If your organization leases its copiers and has a support plan, your provider probably has a service and support portal you can use to manage your devices. This portal can give you up-to-date information about the make, model, and location of each of your copiers. And you can keep track of maintenance and supplies needed for the copiers.

» **Switch or router management pages:** Modern switches and routers include management pages that can be useful for managing network assets. For example, the management page for a switch can reveal information about the devices that are attached to each of the switch's ports. Some switches provide basic information such as IP address, but others provide detailed information including the computer name for Windows computers connected to the switch.

Chapter **4**

Managing the Help Desk

A few years ago, I helped purchase and configure a cloud-based gadget that displays company information on a large-screen TV located in the office's main lobby. It took a bit of fiddling to get it figured out, but when we did, it turned out to be a great solution for the problem at hand.

We recently needed to expand to a second large-screen TV that would display the exact same information on a second screen. So I purchased another one of the same gadgets and spent most of an entire morning trying to figure out how to get it integrated into our account. Finally, in exasperation, I called the vendor's help desk for support. They politely asked if I had read the instructions, which I hadn't, and then gently guided me through the super-simple two-step process. The second gadget was up and running within about five minutes.

The moral of the story is that sometimes even people who should know better (a.k.a., *me*) don't follow the instructions and end up needing help. I needed the help desk.

If you work at a small company where you're pretty much the entire IT department, you probably *are* the help desk. As your company grows, that situation will not be sustainable. In a small organization (say, less than 40 people), it may be possible for one person to manage the entire IT infrastructure, including setting up and maintaining server hardware and software, as well as network equipment and application software, and still manage to field occasional phone calls from users who need help. But as more employees are brought on, you'll eventually need to set up a formal help desk with staff dedicated to solving users' problems.

In this chapter, I give you a brief overview of what to consider when setting up and managing an effective help desk.

Establishing the Help Desk's Charter

Whether you're starting from scratch or evaluating the effectiveness of an existing help desk, the best place to start is to create a charter for the help desk. Without a clear charter, you'll never be able to measure your help desk's effectiveness.

The charter should spell out the core mission of the help desk, which certainly includes solving IT problems encountered by users of your organization's computer systems. The charter should also address considerations such as the following:

- » How does the mission of the help desk fit in with the company's core values?

- » Where does the help desk fit within the company's overall organization? Who does it report to?

- » Does the help desk seek to solve *all* IT problems, or does it have a more limited scope? In other words, if a user doesn't understand how to create and use a Microsoft Excel Pivot Table, is it within the scope of the help desk to provide that training? Or is the help desk's mission limited to helping users when Excel is broken, not when the user doesn't know how it works?

- » Should the help desk prioritize the needs of some users over others when deciding how to allocate resources? For example, is one department, such as factory production or payroll, a higher priority than other, less time-critical departments? Should executive management get higher priority response than other users?

- » Are there specific performance metrics you can identify to measure the effectiveness of the help desk? Is it the total number of calls handled, the percentage of problems solved on the first call? Or is it a positive score on user satisfaction surveys?

- » How responsive do you expect your help desk to be? Is it important that a live human being always answers the help-desk phone? Does that person need to be a technician who can actually solve problems, or is it acceptable to have a non-technical person field the calls and assign him or her to the appropriate technician?

The help-desk charter should be developed by a team representing all the stakeholders. This should include not just IT staff and executive management, but also representatives from the various departments that will be supported by the help desk.

The charter should also be reviewed periodically to assess whether the help desk is meeting the needs of its users. This assessment should also include representation from all the stakeholders.

Tracking Support Tickets

The most important tool that a help desk uses to manage support requests is the *support ticket*. A support ticket tracks the status of a support request, from inception to completion, and should record every pertinent detail related to the request, including the following:

>> **Basic identification information for the person requesting the ticket:** This may include name and contact information, a short title (which can be created by the user requesting the support or by help-desk staff), the date and time the ticket was created, a detailed description of the problem, and identification of the support technician initially assigned to the ticket.

>> **The ticket category:** You'll need to devise a list of categories that is appropriate for your company, but you'll likely include categories similar to the following:

- Login and password
- New user onboarding
- Employee separation
- Hardware
- Email
- Printing
- Intranet
- Microsoft Office
- Virus/malware
- Phones
- Other

>> **An indication of the ticket's status:** Here's an example of status options:

- Received
- Assigned

- In Progress

- Escalated

- Resolved

- Closed

>> **All correspondence including emails, messages, and detailed notes of all phone conversations:** These records should include the date and time of the correspondence.

>> **Screen shots, event logs, and any other pertinent files.**

>> **Detailed descriptions of everything that has been done to resolve the issue.**

>> **Details of how the issue was ultimately resolved.**

TIP

Ideally, the user who initiated a support request should have access to the ticket and the opportunity to contribute notes to it. Keeping users in the loop will help with overall satisfaction of the trouble resolution process and can help them appreciate that their problem has not been forgotten but is indeed being worked on.

The entire ticketing database should also be available to help-desk staff so that they can review previous issues. A support technician should be able to search the database for tickets created by the same user or other users who have reported similar problems. That way, the technician can avoid re-inventing the wheel.

You may be tempted to keep track of your help-desk tickets in a home-grown database, perhaps using a database program such as Microsoft Access or a more general program such as Microsoft OneNote. However, you'll soon outgrow the home-grown solution when you discover that it isn't as flexible as you need it to be, isn't very searchable, and doesn't have the features that can make your help desk shine, such as automatic reminders or built-in workflows for delegating or escalating issues.

Fortunately, there is plenty of good software available to help you manage your help desk's trouble tickets. Just do a web search for the keywords *help-desk software*, and you'll find dozens of options to choose from.

Deciding How to Communicate with Users

Users must have a reliable and responsive method of communicating with the help desk. Here are some of the best options to consider:

>> **Phone:** The most obvious way to communicate is via phone. If your help desk is small, with just a few support technicians, you might simply publish the phone numbers or extensions of each of the technicians. For a larger help desk, you'll want to provide a single number for incoming calls and *not* publish the numbers for individual support technicians.

The advantage of the phone is that the contact is immediate (assuming someone actually answers the phone) and human (assuming the phone is answered by an actual person). The disadvantage is that it's difficult to triage incoming calls. Ideally, a single person should be responsible for answering incoming calls and transferring them to the appropriate technician.

You may want to consider setting up a phone tree, with options such as "Press 1 for help logging on," "Press 2 for help with accounting software," and so on. This is fine, as long as the tree is simple and users are quickly able to get to a real person who can help. If users have to make a bunch of touch-tone selections that ultimately drop them into a voicemail, they'll be frustrated.

A disadvantage of the phone is that there is no detailed record of the conversation. After each phone call, the technician should record the details of the call in the ticket. However, it isn't easy to note every detail accurately, so errors or misunderstandings are bound to creep in.

>> **Email:** This is a common and useful means of communicating with the help desk. Just set up a support mailbox using an easy-to-remember name like "Support" or "Help," and connect your technician's Outlook profiles to the support mailbox. Then support technicians can monitor the support mailbox and respond when new help requests are received.

One of the major advantages of email is that it creates an accurate record of correspondence. Emails can be attached to tickets, so technicians can quickly review previous activity on a ticket.

>> **Online chat:** An increasingly popular way for users to communicate with support technicians is through online chat. Many users prefer chat to email because it's more responsive, and prefer chat to phone because chat is less intrusive. Support staff often prefer chat as well because the lag time between messages allows them to work on more than one issue simultaneously. Win-win!

As an added bonus, a transcript of the chat can be copied into the ticket, preserving a record of the entire conversation.

There are many chat services available that lend themselves to use by support staff. One I'm fond of is Slack. In addition to simple chats, it offers video chats, screen sharing, file transfer, and many other features that can be useful to support teams. For more information, go to www.slack.com.

Providing Remote Support

An important element of help-desk support is the ability of the help-desk staff to access the user's computer without having to travel to the user's location. To do this, use remote support software, which allows a support technician to take control of a user's computer so that the technician can see exactly what the user sees. This is vital because most users aren't able to adequately describe what they see on the screen. In addition, the remote support software will allow the technician to remotely fix the issue without having to tediously talk the user through a series of steps and hope that the user follows the steps correctly.

An important consideration is whether you want your users to authorize remote support before the technician takes control of the user's computer. Most remote support programs, including Windows Remote Assistance (built in to Windows), require the user to enter a code to initiate the remote support session. However, some software allows the technician to take control of the user's computer without any notification or confirmation. This can be especially useful when the support technician needs the flexibility to access the user's computer at any time, but it can create security concerns.

For more information about remote support software, refer to Chapter 2 of this minibook.

Creating a Knowledge Base

An important aspect of any help desk is creating and maintaining a comprehensive knowledge base of common issues along with their solutions. Whenever a recurring issue is discovered, a member of the help-desk team who has good writing skills should be assigned to create a new article in the knowledge base. The article should clearly list the symptoms typically encountered along with a detailed, step-by-step solution that solves the problem.

The knowledge base should be shared throughout your company, perhaps on your company intranet. That way, users can search it on their own. Sharing a well-stocked knowledge base on your intranet can cut down on the number of support calls your help desk receives as users search it to find solutions on their own.

Creating a Self-Service Help Portal

One of the best ways to improve the efficiency of your help desk is to create a self-serve help-desk portal where users can look for their solutions on their own, create and track support tickets, initiate chat sessions, and so on.

Here's what a good help-desk portal should provide:

>> **Contact information for the help desk outlining all the methods a user can use to communicate with the support team:** Instead of just providing an email address, the Contacts section should include a link that creates an email message automatically addressed to the support team.

>> **A link that lets the user create a new support ticket:** The simplest way to do this would be to create a link that opens an email addressed to the support team, with the subject line pre-filled to something like "New Support Request." But a better alternative is to provide a simple form that allows the user to fill in fields to describe the issue. When the user clicks OK, the form creates a new support ticket that can be assigned to a support technician.

>> **A summary of the user's current and previous support tickets, with links to pull up detailed information about a specific ticket:** For a current ticket, the user should have the ability to add a comment. For a closed ticket, the user should have the ability to re-open the ticket, in case the problem recurs.

>> **Links to open chat sessions or to initiate a remote assistance session.**

>> **A search field that enables the user to search the knowledge base.**

>> **Information about current or upcoming outages, recent upgrades, or other noteworthy stuff.**

If your company has a staff of web developers (or if you happen to be a web developer), you can develop the help-desk portal yourself. Otherwise, you can find plenty of commercial options that will meet this need. (For more information, see the section "Using Help-Desk Management Software" later in this chapter.)

Using Satisfaction Surveys

It's always a good idea to follow up every support request with a brief survey asking the user to rate his or her satisfaction with the help desk's support. The easiest way to do this is to follow up with an email that contains a link to a survey page. Note that the survey should be short — just a few questions that can be shown on a single page.

Here are some suggested questions for the survey:

>> How satisfied are you with the support you received from the help desk for this issue?

>> Was your problem resolved in a timely manner?

>> Was the issue resolved during the initial contact (phone call, chat, or email)?

>> How understanding of your situation was the support technician?

>> Did the technician ensure that your issue was resolved before closing the ticket?

>> After the issue was resolved, did the technician ask if there were any other issues he or she could assist you with?

>> Do you have any comments?

A simple Internet search for terms such as *help-desk satisfaction survey* will turn up tons of software that can help with satisfaction surveys. One of the best known is Survey Monkey (www.surveymonkey.com). Survey Monkey even has a help-desk satisfaction survey template to help you get started (see Figure 4-1).

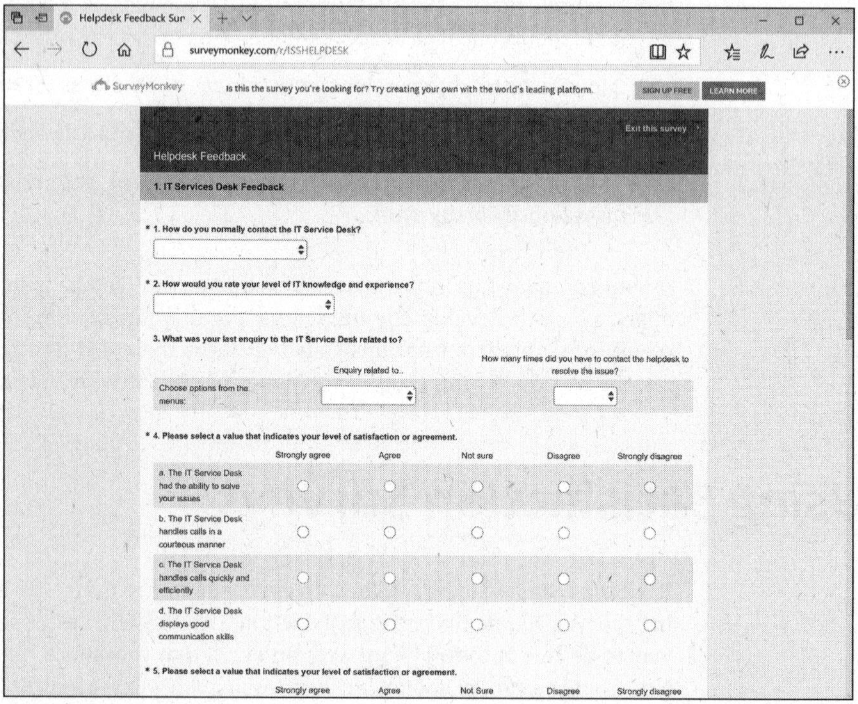

FIGURE 4-1:
Survey Monkey's help-desk satisfaction survey template.

Tracking Help-Desk Performance

If you want to know how efficient and effective your help–desk team is, you need to track a number of factors and periodically evaluate how you're doing. Here are some of the most important indicators to track on a monthly basis:

- **Total ticket count:** The most important baseline number you need to track is the total number of tickets your help desk receives. Unless you know how many tickets enter your help desk, you won't be able to make any sense of the other statistics. Keeping an eye on the growth of this number can help you justify the need for additional staff.

- **Tickets successfully resolved:** Hopefully, this number equals the number of tickets received. But it's important to note the differential, because sometimes you'll encounter issues that just can't be resolved. You want to pay close attention to these, to determine whether the problem is simply intractable, the user was unreasonable, or your staff just gave up.

- **Ticket categories:** Assuming you've created a good set of categories, tracking the overall percentage of tickets in each category will help you understand how to train and staff your help desk. (Can you say "pie chart"?)

- **Average/mean response time:** Track how long it takes to respond to incoming tickets. The faster the initial response, the less frustrated your users will be.

- **Average/mean resolution time:** Track how long it takes from the receipt of the ticket to its final resolution. Again, the faster the resolution, the more satisfied your users will be.

- **Average/mean hours spent per ticket:** The overall average is useful, but even more useful is the average hours per category. Some types of problems are simply more difficult to resolve than others.

- **User satisfaction:** This metric will come from your satisfaction surveys.

- **Staff performance:** Are the members of your help-desk team working effectively? If one team member tends to spend a substantially greater number of hours on certain categories of problems than other team members, the team member in question may be in need of more training. (On the other hand, it's entirely possible that the team member in question is the best one among the team to handle the most difficult problems, so the tough questions often get referred to him or her!)

Using Help-Desk Management Software

As you can tell from this chapter, running an efficient help desk is a big deal. And having an effective help desk is vital to your company's overall performance. The sooner the help desk can resolve your users' issues, the sooner your users can get back to productive work.

Instead of attempting to cobble together all the various pieces needed to run a help desk, consider acquiring a comprehensive package that includes all aspects of IT service management. Such software isn't cheap, but it can save your company money in the long run.

Good help-desk management software should include the following features:

>> **Ticket management:** Comprehensive management of trouble tickets from their inception to their resolution, with the ability to sort and filter by status, category, user, technician, and other factors. The ticketing system should allow for custom fields so that you can integrate your company's unique needs into the system.

>> **Self-service portal:** The software should make it easy for you to stand up a self-service portal that enables your users to find solutions without engaging the help desk.

>> **Knowledge base:** A good, customizable knowledge base is a must.

>> **Reporting:** The software should keep track of important performance metrics and should have reporting features that let you track how the help desk is doing.

>> **Asset management:** A definite plus. Some products offer this as an extra-charge feature. (For more information, please see Chapter 3 of this minibook.)

>> **Deployment flexibility:** Ideally, you should have the option to deploy the software on-site or use the software as a cloud-based service.

Search the Internet for *help-desk software* and you'll find many options to choose from. Here are just a few of the better known products — note that this list is by no means complete:

>> **ZenDesk** (www.zendesk.com): An excellent cloud-based solution that charges per-month subscription for each member of your help-desk team. Most organizations opt for the $19.99/month Professional plan or the $49/month Enterprise plan. (***Remember:*** This cost is per help-desk team member, not per end-user.) ZenDesk is consistently one of the top-ranked help-desk solution providers, so it should be one that you carefully consider.

>> **GoToAssist Service Desk** (www.gotoassist.com): A comprehensive help-desk solution that includes powerful remote assistance, from the makers of the popular GoToMeeting conferencing software.

>> **Salesforce** (www.salesforce.com): If your company is already a Salesforce customer, consider using its help-desk features to automate your help desk.

Chapter **5**

Solving Network Problems

F ace it: Networks are prone to breaking.

They have too many parts. Cables. Connectors. Cards. Switches. Routers. All these parts must be held together in a delicate balance, and the network equilibrium is all too easy to disturb. Even the best-designed computer networks sometimes act as if they're held together with baling wire, chewing gum, and duct tape.

To make matters worse, networks breed suspicion. After your computer is attached to a network, users begin to blame the network every time something goes wrong, regardless of whether the problem has anything to do with the network. You can't get columns to line up in a Word document? Must be the network. Your spreadsheet doesn't add up? The @#$% network's acting up again. The stock market's down? Arghhh!!!!!!

The worst thing about network failures is that sometimes they can shut down an entire company. It's not so bad if just one user can't access a particular shared folder on a file server. If a critical server goes down, however, your network users may be locked out of their files, applications, email, and everything else they need to conduct business as usual. When that happens, they'll be beating down your doors and won't stop until you get the network back up and running.

In this chapter, I review some of the most likely causes of network trouble and suggest some basic troubleshooting techniques that you can employ when your network goes on the fritz.

When Bad Things Happen to Good Computers

Here are some basic troubleshooting steps explaining what you should examine at the first sign of network trouble. In many (if not most) of the cases, one of the following steps can get your network back up and running:

1. **Make sure that your computer and everything attached to it is plugged in.**

TECHNICAL
STUFF

Computer geeks love it when a user calls for help, and they get to tell the user that the computer isn't plugged in or that its power strip is turned off. They write it down in their geek logs so that they can tell their geek friends about it later. They may even want to take your picture so that they can show it to their geek friends. (Most "accidents" involving computer geeks are a direct result of this kind of behavior. So try to be tactful when you ask a user whether he or she is sure the computer is actually turned on.)

2. **Make sure that your computer is properly connected to the network.**

3. **Note any error messages that appear on the screen.**

4. **Try restarting the computer.**

TIP

An amazing number of computer problems are cleared up by a simple restart of the computer. Of course, in many cases, the problem recurs, so you'll have to eventually isolate the cause and fix the problem. Some problems are only intermittent, and a simple reboot is all that's needed.

5. **Try the built-in Windows network troubleshooter.**

6. **Check the free disk space on your computer and on the server.**

When a computer runs out of disk space or comes close to it, strange things can happen. Sometimes you get a clear error message indicating such a situation, but not always. Sometimes the computer just grinds to a halt; operations that used to take a few seconds now take a few minutes.

7. **Do a little experimenting to find out whether the problem is indeed a network problem or just a problem with the computer itself.**

   See the section "Time to Experiment," later in this chapter, for some simple things that you can do to isolate a network problem.

8. **Try restarting the network server.**

   See the section "Restarting a Network Server," later in this chapter.

Fixing Dead Computers

If a computer seems totally dead, here are some things to check:

>> **Make sure that the computer is plugged in.**

>> **If the computer is plugged into a surge protector or a power strip, make sure that the surge protector or power strip is plugged in and turned on.** If the surge protector or power strip has a light, it should be glowing. Also, the surge protector may have a reset button that needs to be pressed.

>> **Make sure that the computer's On/Off switch is turned on.** This advice sounds too basic to even include here, but many computers have two power switches: an on/off switch on the back of the computer, and a push-button on the front that actually starts the computer. If you push the front button and nothing happens, check the switch on the back to make sure it's in the ON position.

REMEMBER

To complicate matters, newer computers have a Sleep feature, in which they appear to be turned off but really they're just sleeping. All you have to do to wake such a computer is jiggle the mouse a little. (I used to have an uncle like that.) It's easy to assume that the computer is turned off, press the power button, wonder why nothing happened, and then press the power button and hold it down, hoping it will take. If you hold down the power button long enough, the computer will actually turn itself off. Then, when you turn the computer back on, you get a message saying the computer wasn't shut down properly. Arghhh! The moral of the story is to jiggle the mouse if the computer seems to have nodded off.

>> **If you think the computer isn't plugged in but it looks like it is, listen for the fan.** If the fan is running, the computer is getting power, and the problem is more serious than an unplugged power cord. (If the fan isn't running but the computer is plugged in and the power is on, the fan may be out to lunch.)

>> **If the computer is plugged in and turned on but still not running, plug a lamp into the outlet to make sure that power is getting to the outlet.** You may need to reset a tripped circuit breaker or replace a bad surge protector. Or you may need to call the power company. (If you live in California, don't bother calling the power company. It probably won't do any good.)

>> **Check the surge protector.** Surge protectors have a limited life span. After a few years of use, many surge protectors continue to provide electrical power for your computer, but the components that protect your computer from power surges no longer work. If you're using a surge protector that is more than two or three years old, replace the old surge protector with a new one.

>> **Make sure that the monitor is plugged in and turned on.** The monitor has a separate power cord and switch. (The monitor actually has two cables that must be plugged in. One runs from the back of the monitor to the back of the computer; the other is a power cord that comes from the back of the monitor and must be plugged into an electrical outlet.)

>> **Make sure that all cables are plugged in securely.** Your keyboard, monitor, mouse, and printer are all connected to the back of your computer by cables.

Make sure that the other ends of the monitor and printer cables are plugged in properly, too.

REMEMBER

>> **If the computer is running but the display is dark, try adjusting the monitor's contrast and brightness.** Some monitors have knobs that you can use to adjust the contrast and brightness of the monitor's display. They may have been turned down all the way.

Ways to Check a Network Connection

The cables that connect client computers to the rest of the network are finicky beasts. They can break at a moment's notice, and by "break," I don't necessarily mean "to physically break in two." Although some broken cables look like someone got to the cable with pruning shears, most cable problems aren't visible to the naked eye.

>> **Twisted-pair cable:** If your network uses twisted-pair cable, you can quickly tell whether the cable connection to the network is good by looking at the back of your computer. Look for a small light located near where the cable plugs in; if this light is glowing steadily, the cable is good. If the light is dark or it's flashing intermittently, you have a cable problem (or a problem with the network card or the hub or switch that the other end of the cable is plugged in to).

TIP

If the light isn't glowing steadily, try removing the cable from your computer and reinserting it. This action may cure the weak connection.

>> **Patch cable:** Hopefully, your network is wired so that each computer is connected to the network with a short (six feet or so) patch cable. One end of the patch cable plugs into the computer, and the other end plugs into a cable connector mounted on the wall. Try quickly disconnecting and reconnecting the patch cable. If that doesn't do the trick, try to find a spare patch cable that you can use.

>> **Switches:** Switches are prone to having cable problems, too — especially switches that are wired in a "professional manner," involving a rat's nest of patch cables. Be careful whenever you enter the lair of the rat's nest. If you need to replace a patch cable, be very careful when you disconnect the suspected bad cable and reconnect the good cable in its place.

A Bunch of Error Messages Just Flew By!

Error messages that display when your computer boots can provide invaluable clues to determine the source of the problem.

If you see error messages when you start up the computer, keep the following points in mind:

>> **Don't panic if you see a lot of error messages.** Sometimes, a simple problem that's easy to correct can cause a plethora of error messages when you start your computer. The messages may look as if your computer is falling to pieces, but the fix may be very simple.

>> **If the messages fly by so fast that you can't see them, press your computer's Pause key.** Your computer comes to a screeching halt, giving you a chance to catch up on your error-message reading. After you've read enough, press the Pause key again to get things moving. (On keyboards that don't have a Pause key, pressing Ctrl+Num Lock or Ctrl+S does the same thing.)

TIP

>> **If you miss the error messages the first time, restart the computer and watch them again.**

>> **Better yet, press F8 when you see the Starting Windows message.** This displays a menu that allows you to select from several startup options. (Note that this won't work on Windows 8, 8.1, or 10.)

Double-Checking Your Network Settings

I swear that there are little green men who sneak into offices at night, turn on computers, and mess up TCP/IP configuration settings just for kicks. These little green men are affectionately known as *networchons*.

Remarkably, network configuration settings sometimes get inadvertently changed so that a computer, which enjoyed the network for months or even years, one day finds itself unable to access the network. So one of the first things you do, after making sure that the computers are actually on and that the cables aren't broken, is a basic review of the computer's network settings. Check the following:

>> At a command prompt, run `ipconfig` to make sure that TCP/IP is up and running on the computer and that the IP addresses, subnet masks, and default gateway settings look right.

>> Call up the network connection's Properties dialog box and make sure that the necessary protocols are installed correctly.

>> Open the System Properties dialog box (double-click System in Control Panel) and check the Computer Name tab.

>> Make sure that the computer name is unique and also that the domain or workgroup name is spelled properly.

>> Double-check the user account to make sure that the user really has permission to access the resources he needs.

TIP

For more information about network configuration settings, see Book 2, Chapters 3 and 6.

Time to Experiment

If you can't find some obvious explanation for your troubles — like the computer is unplugged — you need to do some experimenting to narrow down the possibilities. Design your experiments to answer one basic question: Is it a network problem or a local computer problem?

Here are some ways you can narrow down the cause of the problem:

>> **Try performing the same operation on someone else's computer.** If no one on the network can access a network drive or printer, something is probably wrong with the network. On the other hand, if the error occurs on

only one computer, the problem is likely with that computer. The wayward computer may not be reliably communicating with the network or configured properly for the network, or the problem may have nothing to do with the network at all.

»» If you're able to perform the operation on another computer without problems, try logging on to the network with another computer using your own username. Then see whether you can perform the operation without error. If you can, the problem is probably on your computer. If you can't, the problem may be with the way your user account is configured.

»» If you can't log on at another computer, try waiting for a bit. Your account may be temporarily locked out. This can happen for a variety of reasons — the most common of which is trying to log on with the wrong password several times in a row. If you're still locked out an hour later, call the network administrator and offer a doughnut.

Who's on First?

When troubleshooting a networking problem, it's often useful to find out who is actually logged on to a network server. For example, if a user can't access a file on the server, you can check whether the user is logged on. If so, you know that the user's account is valid, but the user may not have permission to access the particular file or folder that he's attempting to access. On the other hand, if the user isn't logged on, the problem may lie with the account itself or how the user is attempting to connect to the server.

It's also useful to find out who's logged on in the event that you need to restart the server. For more information about restarting a server, see the section, "Restarting a Network Server," later in this chapter.

To find out who is currently logged on to a Windows server, right-click the Computer icon on the desktop and choose Manage from the menu that appears. This brings up the Computer Management window. Open System Tools in the tree list and then open Shared Folders and select Sessions. A list of users who are logged on appears.

TIP

You can immediately disconnect all users by right-clicking Sessions in the Computer Management window and choosing All Tasks ⇨ Disconnect All. Be warned, however, that this can cause users to lose data.

Restarting a Client Computer

Sometimes, trouble gets a computer so tied up in knots that the only thing you can do is reboot. In some cases, the computer just starts acting weird. Strange characters appear on the screen, or Windows goes haywire and doesn't let you exit a program. Sometimes, the computer gets so confused that it can't even move. It just sits there, like a deer staring at oncoming headlights. It won't move, no matter how hard you press Esc or Enter. You can move the mouse all over your desktop, or you can even throw it across the room, but the mouse pointer on the screen stays perfectly still.

When a computer starts acting strange, you need to reboot. If you must reboot, you should do so as cleanly as possible. I know this procedure may seem elementary, but the technique for safely restarting a client computer is worth repeating, even if it is basic:

1. **Save your work if you can.**

   Choose File➪Save to save any documents or files that you were editing when things started to go haywire. If you can't use the menus, try clicking the Save button on the toolbar. If that doesn't work, try pressing Ctrl+S (the standard keyboard shortcut for the Save command).

2. **Close any running programs if you can.**

   Choose File➪Exit or click the Close button in the upper-right corner of the program window. Or press Alt+F4.

3. **Restart the computer.**

   - *Windows XP:* Choose Start➪Turn Off Computer to summon the Shut Down Windows dialog box. Select the Restart option, and then click OK.

   - *Windows 7 and Vista:* Click the Start button, click the right arrow that appears at the bottom-right corner of the Start menu, and then click Restart.

   - *Windows 8:* Oddly enough, shutting down Windows 8 is a bit challenging. You can stare at the Windows 8 desktop all day and not find an intuitive way to shut down your computer. The secret lies in the Charms Bar, which you can find by hovering the mouse over the lower-right corner of the screen. Next, click the Settings icon, and then click the Shut Down icon.

   - *Windows 8.1 and 10:* Click the Start button, click the Power Options button, and then choose Restart.

If restarting your computer doesn't seem to fix the problem, you may need to turn your computer off and then turn it on again. To do so, follow the previous procedure but choose Shut Down instead of Restart.

Here are a few things to try if you have trouble restarting your computer:

>> **If your computer refuses to respond to the Start⇨Shut Down command, try pressing Ctrl+Alt+Delete.**

This is called the "three-finger salute." It's appropriate to say, "Queueue" while you do it.

When you press Ctrl+Alt+Delete, Windows displays a dialog box that enables you to close any running programs or shut down your computer entirely.

>> **If pressing Ctrl+Alt+Delete doesn't do anything, you've reached the last resort. The only thing left to do is turn off the computer by pressing the power On/Off button and holding it down for a few seconds.**

WARNING

Turning off your computer by pressing the power button is a drastic action that you should take only after your computer becomes completely unresponsive. Any work you haven't yet saved to disk is lost. (Sniff.) (If your computer doesn't have a Reset button, turn off the computer, wait a few moments, and then turn the computer back on again.)

REMEMBER

If at all possible, save your work before restarting your computer. Any work you haven't saved is lost. Unfortunately, if your computer is totally tied up in knots, you probably can't save your work. In that case, you have no choice but to push your computer off the digital cliff.

Booting in Safe Mode

Windows provides a special startup mode called *Safe Mode* that's designed to help fix misbehaving computers. When you start your computer in Safe Mode, Windows loads only the most essential parts of itself into memory — the bare minimum required for Windows to work. Safe Mode is especially useful when your computer has developed a problem that prevents you from using the computer at all.

To boot in Safe Mode on a Windows 7 or earlier computer, first restart the computer. Then, as soon as the computer begins to restart, start pressing the F8 key — just tap away at it until a menu titled Advanced Boot Options appears. One of the options on this menu is Safe Mode; use the up- or down-arrow keys to select that option and then press Enter to boot in Safe Mode.

On a Windows 8, 8.1, or 10 computer, you can reboot into Safe Mode by holding down the Shift key when you choose the Restart command.

Using System Restore

System Restore is a Windows feature that periodically saves important Windows configuration information and allows you to later return your system to a previously saved configuration. This can often fix problems by reverting your computer to a time when it was working.

By default, Windows saves restore points whenever you install new software on your computer or apply a system update. Restore points are also saved automatically every seven days.

Although System Restore is turned on by default, you should verify that System Restore is active and running to make sure that System Restore points are being created. To do that, right-click Computer in the Start menu, choose Properties, and then click the System Protection tab. The dialog box shown in Figure 5-1 is displayed. Verify that the Protection status for your computer's C: drive is On. If it isn't, select the C: drive and click the Configure button to configure System Restore for the drive.

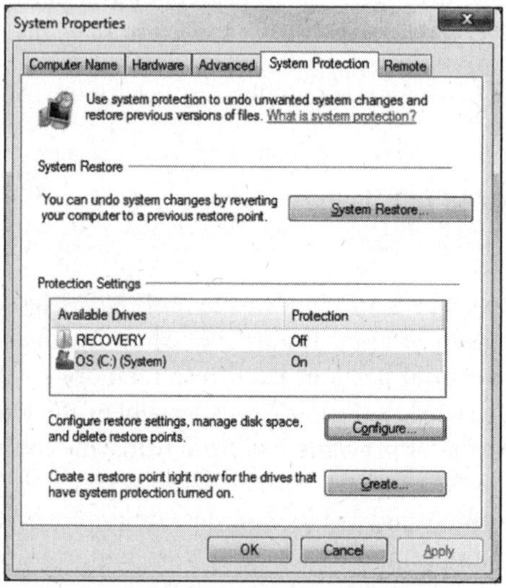

FIGURE 5-1:
The System Protection tab of the System Properties dialog box.

If your computer develops a problem, you can restore it to a previously saved restore point by clicking System Restore on the System Protection tab. This brings up the System Restore Wizard, as shown in Figure 5-2. This wizard allows you to select the restore point you want to use.

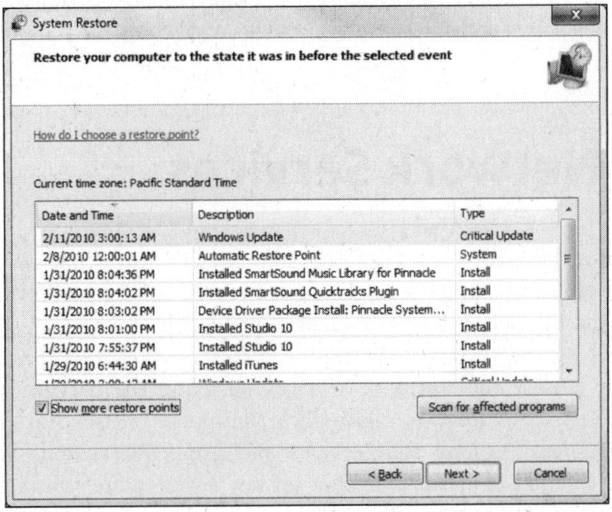

FIGURE 5-2:
Use System Restore to restore your system to an earlier configuration.

Here are a few additional thoughts to remember about System Restore:

>> System Restore *does not* delete data files from your system. Thus, files in your Documents folder won't be lost.

>> System Restore *does* remove any applications or system updates you've installed since the time the restore point was made. Thus, you need to reinstall those applications or system updates — unless, of course, you determine that an application or system update was the cause of your problem in the first place.

>> System Restore automatically restarts your computer. The restart may be slow because some of the changes made by System Restore happen after the restart.

>> Do *not* turn off or cut power to your computer during System Restore. Doing so may leave your computer in an unrecoverable state.

>> After completing a System Restore, you may discover that the user can't log on to the computer because the computer complains about the "domain trust relationship" being lost. This happens because the internal password that Active Directory uses to verify the identity of the computer has been reset by the System Restore to a previous version. The only solution is to log in to a local account on the computer, leave the domain, reboot the computer, log in again using a local account, rejoin the domain, and reboot the computer again. Sigh.

Restarting Network Services

Once in awhile, the OS service that supports the task that's causing you trouble inexplicably stops or gets stuck. If users can't access a server, it may be because one of the key network services has stopped or is stuck.

You can review the status of services by using the Services tool, as shown in Figure 5-3. To display it, right-click Computer on the Start menu and choose Manage; then, expand the Services and Applications node and click Services. Review this list to make sure that all key services are running. If an important service is paused or stopped, restart it.

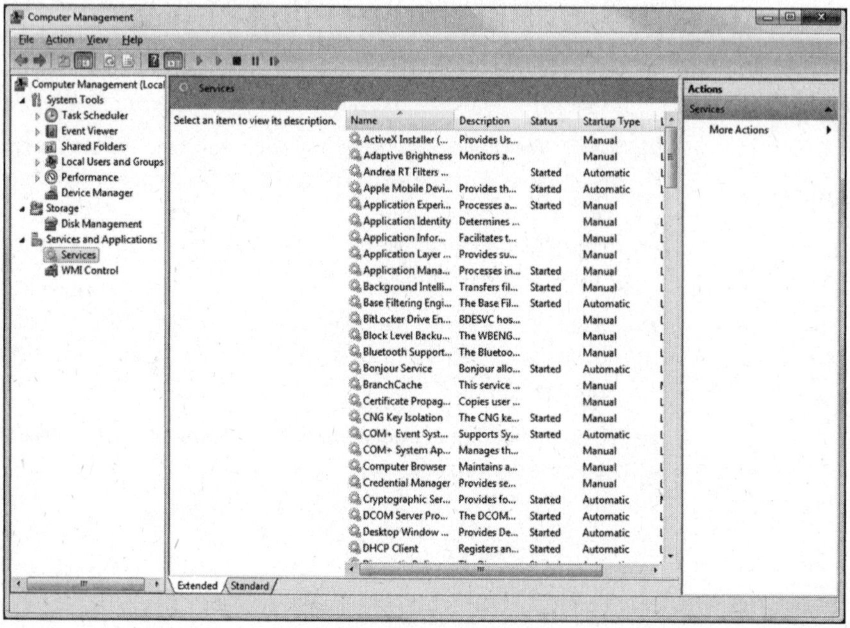

FIGURE 5-3: Looking at services.

Which services qualify as "important" depends on what roles you define for the server. Table 5-1 lists a few important services that are common to most versions of Windows. However, many servers require additional services besides these. In fact, a typical server will have many dozens of services running simultaneously.

TABLE 5-1   **Key Windows Services**

Service	Description
Computer Browser	Maintains a list of computers on the network that can be accessed. If this service is disabled, the computer won't be able to use browsing services, such as My Network Places.
DHCP Client	Enables the computer to obtain its IP address from a Dynamic Host Configuration Protocol (DHCP) server. If this service is disabled, the computer's Internet Protocol (IP) address won't be configured properly.
DNS Client	Enables the computer to access a Domain Name Server (DNS) server to resolve DNS names. If this service is disabled, the computer won't be able to handle DNS names, including Internet addresses and Active Directory names.
Server	Provides basic file- and printer-sharing services for the server. If this service is stopped, clients won't be able to connect to the server to access files or printers.
Workstation	Enables the computer to establish client connections with other servers. If this service is disabled, the computer won't be able to connect to other servers.

WARNING

Key services usually stop for a reason, so simply restarting a stopped service probably won't solve your network's problem — at least, not for long. You should review the System log to look for any error messages that may explain why the service stopped in the first place.

Restarting a Network Server

Sometimes, the only way to flush out a network problem is to restart the network server that's experiencing trouble.

WARNING

Restarting a network server is something you should do only as a last resort. Windows Server is designed to run for months or even years at a time without rebooting. Restarting a server invariably results in a temporary shutdown of the network. If you must restart a server, try to do it during off hours if possible.

TIP

Before you restart a server, check whether a specific service that's required has been paused or stopped. You may be able to just restart the individual service rather than the entire server. For more information, see the section "Restarting Network Services," earlier in this chapter.

Here's the basic procedure for restarting a network server:

1. **Make sure that everyone is logged off the server.**

The easiest way to do that is to restart the server after normal business hours, when everyone has gone home for the day. Then, you can just shut down the server and let the shutdown process forcibly log off any remaining users.

To find out who's logged on, refer to the earlier section, "Who's on First?"

2. **After you're sure the users have logged off, shut down the network server.**

You want to do this step behaving like a good citizen if possible — decently, and in order. Choose Start⇨Shut Down to shut down the server. This brings up a dialog box that requires you to indicate the reason for the shutdown. The information you supply here is entered into the server's System log, which you can review by using the Event Viewer.

3. **Reboot the server computer or turn it off and then on again.**

Watch the server start up to make sure that no error messages appear.

4. **Tell everyone to log back on and make sure that everyone can now access the network.**

Remember the following when you consider restarting the network server:

WARNING

- Restarting the network server is more drastic than restarting a client computer. Make sure that everyone saves his or her work and logs off the network before you do it! You can cause major problems if you blindly turn off the server computer while users are logged on.

- Obviously, restarting a network server is a major inconvenience to every network user. Better offer treats.

Looking at Event Logs

One of the most useful troubleshooting techniques for diagnosing network problems is to review the network operating system's built-in event logs. These logs contain information about interesting and potentially troublesome events that occur during the daily operation of your network. Ordinarily, these logs run in the background, quietly gathering information about network events. When something goes wrong, you can check the logs to see whether the problem generated a noteworthy event. In many cases, the event logs contain an entry that pinpoints the exact cause of the problem and suggests a solution.

To display the event logs in a Windows server, use Event Viewer, which is available from the Administrative Tools menu. For example, Figure 5-4 shows a typical Event Viewer. The tree listing on the left side of Event Viewer lists five categories of events that are tracked: Application, Security, System, Directory Service, and File Replication Service. Select one of these options to see the log that you want to view. For details about a particular event, double-click the event to display a dialog box with detailed information about the event.

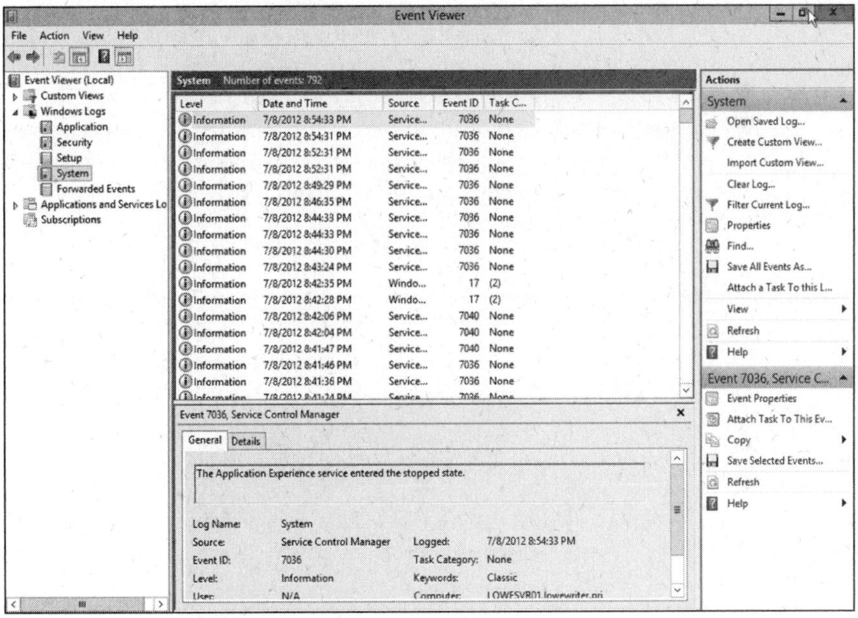

FIGURE 5-4:
Event Viewer.

Documenting Your Trials and Tribulations

For a large network, you probably want to invest in problem-management software that tracks each problem through the entire process of troubleshooting, from initial report to final resolution. For small- and medium-sized networks, it's probably sufficient to put together a three-ring binder with pre-printed forms. Or record your log in a Word document or an Excel spreadsheet.

Regardless of how you track your network problems, the tracking log should include the following information:

>> The real name and the network username of the person reporting the problem

>> The date the problem was first reported

>> An indication of the severity of the problem

>> Is it merely an inconvenience, or is a user unable to complete his or her work because of the problem? Does a work-around exist?

>> The name of the person assigned to resolve the problem

>> A description of the problem

>> A list of the software involved, including versions

>> A description of the steps taken to solve the problem

>> A description of any intermediate steps that were taken to try to solve the problem, along with an indication of whether those steps were "undone" when they didn't help solve the problem

>> The date the problem was finally resolved

Chapter **6**

Managing Software Deployment

An important task of any network administrator is managing the various bits and pieces of software that are used by your users throughout the network. Most, if not all, of your network users will have a version of Microsoft Office installed on their computers. Depending on the type of business, other software may be widely used. For example, accounting firms require accounting software; engineering firms require engineering software; and the list goes on.

Long gone are the days when you could purchase one copy of a computer program and freely install it on every computer on your network. Most software has built-in features — commonly called "copy protection" — designed to prevent such abuse. But even in the absence of copy protection, nearly all software is sold with a license agreement that dictates how many computers you can install and use the software on. As a result, managing software licenses is an important part of network management.

Some software programs have a license feature that uses a server computer to regulate the number of users who can run the software at the same time. As the network administrator, your job is to set up the license server and keep it running.

Another important aspect of managing software on the network is figuring out the most expedient way to install the software on multiple computers. The last thing you want to do is manually run the software's Setup program individually on each computer in your network. Instead, you'll want to use the network itself to aid in the deployment of the software.

Finally, you'll want to ensure that all the software programs installed throughout your network are kept up to date with the latest patches and updates from the software vendors.

This chapter elaborates on these aspects of network software management.

Understanding Software Licenses

Contrary to popular belief, you don't really buy software. Instead, you buy the right to use the software. When you purchase a computer program at a store, all you really own after you complete the purchase is the box the software comes in, the disks/discs the software is recorded on, and a license that grants you the right to use the software according to the terms offered by the software vendor. The software itself is still owned by the vendor.

That means that you're obligated to follow the terms of the license agreement that accompanies the software. Very few people actually read the complete text of a software agreement before they purchase and use software. If you do, you'll find that a typical agreement contains restrictions, such as the following:

>> **You're allowed to install the software on one and only one computer.** Some license agreements have specific exceptions to this, allowing you to install the software on a single computer at work and a single computer at home, or on a single desktop computer and a single notebook computer, provided that both computers are used by the same person. However, most software licenses stick to the one-computer rule.

>> **The license agreement probably allows you to make a backup copy of the disks/discs.** The number of backup copies you can make, though, is probably limited to one or two.

>> **You aren't allowed to reverse-engineer the software.** In other words, you can't use programming tools to dissect the software in an effort to learn the secrets of how it works.

>> **Some software restricts the kinds of applications it can be used for.** For example, you might purchase a student or home version of a program that prohibits commercial use. And some software — for example, Oracle's Java — prohibits its use for nuclear facilities.

>> **Some software has export restrictions that prevent you from taking it out of the country.**

>> **Nearly all software licenses limit the liability of the software vendor to replacing defective installation disks/discs.** In other words, the software vendor isn't responsible for any damage that might be caused by bugs in the software. In a few cases, these license restrictions have been set aside in court, and companies have been held liable for damage caused by defective software. For the most part, though, you use software at your own risk.

In many cases, software vendors give you a choice of several different types of licenses to choose from. When you purchase software for use on a network, you need to be aware of the differences between these license types so you can decide which type of license to get. The most common types are

>> **Retail:** The software you buy directly from the software vendor, a local store, or an online store. A retail software license usually grants you the right for a single user to install and use the software. Depending on the agreement, the license may allow that user to install the software on two computers — one at work and one at home. The key point is that only one user may use the software. (However, it is usually acceptable to install the software on a computer that's shared by several users. In that case, more than one user can use the software, provided they use it one at a time.)

The main benefit of a retail license is that it stays with the user when the user upgrades his or her computer. In other words, if you get a new computer, you can remove the software from your old computer and install it on your new computer.

>> **OEM:** For software that's installed by a computer manufacturer on a new computer. (OEM stands for *original equipment manufacturer*.) For example, if you purchase a computer from Dell and order Microsoft Office Professional along with the computer, you're getting an OEM license. The most important thing to know about an OEM license is that it applies only to the specific computer for which you purchased the software. You are never allowed to install the software on any computer other than the one for which you purchased the software.

Thus, if one day in a fit of rage you throw your computer out the fifth-floor window of your office and the computer smashes into little pieces in the parking lot below, your OEM version of Office is essentially lost forever. When you buy a replacement computer, you'll have to buy a new OEM license of Office for the new computer. You can't install the old software on the new computer.

If this sounds like a severe limitation, it is. However, OEM licenses are usually substantially less expensive than retail licenses. For example, a retail license of Microsoft Office 2016 Professional sells for about $500. The OEM version is less than $400.

>> **Volume:** Allows you to install and use the software on more than one computer. The simplest type of volume license simply specifies how many computers on which you can install the software. For example, you might purchase a 20-user version of a program that allows you to install the software on 20 computers. Usually, you're on the honor system to make sure that you don't exceed the quantity. You want to set up some type of system to keep track of this type of software license. For example, you can create an Excel spreadsheet in which you record the name of each person for whom you install the software.

Volume licenses can become considerably more complicated. For example, Microsoft offers several different types of volume license programs, each with different pricing and different features and benefits. Table 6-1 summarizes the features of the more popular license programs. For more information, refer to www.microsoft.com/licensing.

>> **Subscription:** A *subscription* isn't really a separate type of license but rather an optional add-on to a volume license. The added subscription fee entitles you to technical support and free product upgrades during the term of the subscription, which is usually annual. For some types of products, the subscription also includes periodic downloads of new data. For example, antivirus software usually includes a subscription that regularly updates your virus signature data. Without the subscription, the antivirus software would quickly become ineffective.

Note that many types of software that were traditionally offered under retail, OEM, or volume licensing–type plans are evolving toward subscription plans. Vendors such as Microsoft (for its Office 365), Adobe (for its Creative Design Suite) and AutoDesk (for its AutoCAD family of products) are moving in that direction, as are many others.

TABLE 6-1   Microsoft Volume License Plans

Plan	Features
Open License	Purchase as few as five end-user licenses.
Open Value	Purchase as few as five end-user licenses and receive free upgrades during the subscription term (three years).
Select License	This is a licensing program designed for companies with 250 or more employees.
Enterprise	This is an alternative to the Select License program that's designed to cost-effectively provide Windows Vista, Office, and certain other programs throughout an organization of at least 250 employees.

Using a License Server

Some programs let you purchase network licenses that enable you to install the software on as many computers as you want, but regulate the number of people who can use the software at any given time. To control how many people use the software, a special license server is set up. Whenever a user starts the program, the program checks with the license server to see whether a license is available. If so, the program is allowed to start, and the number of available licenses on the license server is reduced by one. Later, when the user quits the program, the license is returned to the server.

One of the most commonly used license server software is FlexNet Publisher, by Flexera Software. (This program used to be named FlexLM, and many programs that depend on it still distribute it as FlexLM.) It's used by AutoCAD as well as by many other network software applications. FlexNet Publisher uses special license files issued by a software vendor to indicate how many licenses of a given product you purchased. Although the license file is a simple text file, its contents are cryptic and generated by a program that only the software vendor has access to. Here's an example of a typical license file for AutoCAD:

```
SERVER server1 000ecd0fe359
USE_SERVER
VENDOR adskflex port=2080
INCREMENT 57000ARDES_2010_0F adskflex 1.000 permanent 6 \
VENDOR_STRING=commercial:permanent BORROW=4320
SUPERSEDE \
DUP_GROUP=UH ISSUED=07-May-2007 SN=339-71570316 SIGN="102D \
85EC 1DFE D083 B85A 46BB AFB1 33AE 00BD 975C 8F5C 5ABC 4C2F \
F88C 9120 0FB1 E122 BA97 BCAE CC90 899F 99BB 23C9 CAB5 613F \
E7BB CA28 7DBF 8F51 3B21" SIGN2="033A 6451 5EEB 3CA4 98B8 F92C \
184A D2BC BA97 BCAE CC90 899F 2EF6 0B45 A707 B897 11E3 096E 0288 \
787C 997B 0E2E F88C 9120 0FB1 782C 00BD 975C 8F5C 74B9 8BC1"
```

(Don't get any wild ideas here. I changed the numbers in this license file so that it won't actually work. I'm not crazy enough to publish an actual valid AutoCAD license file!)

One drawback to opting for software that uses a license server is that you have to take special steps to run the software when the server isn't available. For example, what if you have AutoCAD installed on a notebook computer, but you want to use it while you're away from the office? In that case, you have two options:

>> **Use virtual private network (VPN) software to connect to the network.**
After you're connected with the VPN, the license server will be available so you can use the software. (Read about VPNs in Book 4, Chapter 6.)

>> **Borrow a license.** When you borrow a license, you can use the software for a limited period of time while you're disconnected from the network. Of course, the borrowed license is subtracted from the number of available licenses on the server.

TIP

In most cases, the license server is a mission-critical application — as important as any other function on your network. If the license server goes down, all users who depend on it will be unable to work. Don't worry; they'll let you know. They'll be lining up outside your door demanding to know when you can get the license server up and running so they can get back to work.

Because the license server provides such an important function, treat it with special care. Make sure that the license server software runs on a stable, well-maintained server computer. Don't load up the license server computer with a bunch of other server functions.

And make sure that it's backed up. If possible, install the license server software on a second server computer as a backup. That way, if the main license server computer goes down and you can't get it back up and running, you can quickly switch over to the backup license server.

Options for Deploying Network Software

After you acquire the correct license for your software, the next task of the network administrator is to deploy the software: that is, installing the software on your users' computers and configuring the software so that it runs efficiently on your network. The following sections describe several approaches to deploying software to your network.

Deploying software manually

Most software is shipped on CD or DVD media along with a Setup program that you run to install the software. The Setup program usually asks you a series of questions, such as where you want the program installed, whether you want to install all the program's features or just the most commonly used features, and so on. You may also be required to enter a serial number, registration number, license key, or other code that proves you purchased the software. When all these questions are answered, the Setup program then installs the program.

If only a few of your network users will be using a particular program, the Setup program may be the most convenient way to deploy the program. Just take the installation media with you to the computer you want to install the program on, insert the disc into the CD/DVD drive, and run the Setup program.

WARNING

When you finish manually installing software from a CD or DVD, don't forget to remove the disc from the drive! It's easy to leave the disc in the drive, and if the user rarely or never uses the drive, it might be weeks or months before anyone discovers that the disc is missing. By that time, you'll be hard-pressed to remember where it is.

Running Setup from a network share

If you plan on installing a program on more than two or three computers on your network, you'll find it much easier to run the Setup program from a network share rather than from the original CDs or DVDs. To do so, follow these steps:

1. **Create a network share and a folder within the share where you can store the Setup program and other files required to install the program.**

I usually set up a share named Software and then create a separate folder in this share for each program I want to make available from the network. You should enable Read access for all network users, but allow full access only for yourself and your fellow administrators. (Read more about setting permissions in Book 6, Chapter 4.)

Read more about creating shares and setting permissions in Chapter 5 of Book 6.

2. **Copy the entire contents of the program's CD or DVD to the folder you create in Step 1.**

To do so, insert the CD or DVD in your computer's CD/DVD drive. Then, use Windows Explorer to select the entire contents of the disc and drag it to the folder you create in Step 1.

Alternatively, you can choose Start ⇨ Run to open a command prompt. Then, enter a command, such as this:

```
xcopy d:\*.* \\server1\software\someprogram\*.* /s
```

In this example, d: is the drive letter of your CD/DVD drive, *server1* is the name of your file server, and *software* and *someprogram* are the names of the share and folder you created in Step 1.

3. **To install the program on a client computer, open a Windows Explorer window, navigate to the share and folder you create in Step 1, and double-click the** Setup.exe **file.**

   This launches the Setup program.

4. **Follow the instructions displayed by the Setup program.**

   When the Setup program is finished, the software is ready to use.

WARNING

Copying the Setup program to a network share spares you the annoyance of carrying the installation discs to each computer you want to install the software on. It doesn't spare you the annoyance of purchasing a valid license for each computer, though! It's illegal to install the software on more computers than the license you acquired from the vendor allows.

Installing silently

Copying the contents of a program's installation media to a network share does spare you the annoyance of carrying the installation discs from computer to computer, but you still have to run the Setup program and answer all its annoying questions on every computer. Wouldn't it be great if there were a way to automate the Setup program so that after you run it, it runs without any further interaction from you? With many programs, you can.

In some cases, the Setup program itself has a command line switch that causes it to run silently. You can usually find out what command line switches are available by entering the following at a command prompt:

```
setup /?
```

With luck, you'll find that the Setup program itself has a switch, such as /quiet or /silent, that installs the program with no interaction, using the program's default settings.

TECHNICAL STUFF

If the Setup program doesn't offer any command line switches, don't despair. The following procedure describes a technique that often lets you silently install the software:

1. **Open an Explorer window and navigate to**

   - *Windows 10 (as well as 8.1, 8, 7, and Vista):* C:\Users\name\AppData\Local\Temp

   - *Windows XP:* C:\Documents and Settings*name*\Local Settings\Temp

   Then, delete the entire contents of this folder.

This is the Temporary folder where various programs deposit temporary files. Windows may not allow you to delete every file in this folder, but it's a good idea to begin this procedure by emptying the Temp folder as much as possible.

2. Run the Setup program and follow the installation steps right up to the final step.

When you get to the confirmation screen that says the program is about ready to install the software, stop! *Do not* click the OK or Finish button.

WARNING

3. Return to the Temp folder you open in Step 1, and then poke around until you find the `.msi` file created by the Setup program you run in Step 2.

The `.msi` file is the actual Windows Installer program that Setup runs to install the program. It may have a cryptic name, such as `84993882.msi`.

4. Copy the `.msi` file to the network share from which you want to install the program on your client computers.

For example, `\\server1\software\someprogram`.

5. (Optional) Rename the `.msi` file to `setup.msi`.

This step is optional, but I prefer to run `setup.msi` rather than `84993882.msi`.

6. Use Notepad to create a batch file to run the `.msi` file with the `/quiet` switch.

To create the batch file

1. Right-click in the folder where the `.msi` file is stored.

2. Choose New ⇨ Text Document.

3. Change the name of the text document to `Setup.bat`.

4. Right-click the `Setup.bat` file and choose Edit.

5. Add the following line to the file:

```
setup.msi /quiet
```

6. Save the file.

You can now install the software by navigating to the folder you created the `setup.bat` file in and double-clicking the `setup.bat` file.

Creating an administrative installation image

Some software, such as Microsoft Office and AutoCAD, comes with tools that let you create a fully configured silent setup program that you can then use to silently install the software. For Microsoft software, this silent setup program is called an "administrative installation image." (Note that the OEM versions of Microsoft Office don't include this feature. You need to purchase a volume license to create an administrative installation.)

To create an administrative image, you simply run the configuration tool supplied by the vendor. The configuration tool lets you choose the installation options you want to have applied when the software is installed. Then, it creates a network setup program on a network share that you specify. You can then install the software on a client computer by opening an Explorer window, navigating to the network share where you saved the network setup program, and running the network setup program.

Pushing out software with group policy

One final option you should consider for network software deployment is using Windows Group Policy to automatically install software to network users. Group Policy is a feature of recent versions of Windows Server (2003 and later) that lets you create policies that are assigned to users. You use the Windows Group Policy feature to specify that certain users should have certain software programs available to them.

Note that group policies aren't actually assigned to individual users, but to organizational units (OUs), which are used to categorize users in Active Directory. Thus, you might create a group policy to specify that everyone in the Accounting Department OU should have Microsoft Excel.

Then, whenever anyone in the Accounting department logs on to Windows, Windows checks to make sure that Excel is installed on the user's computer. If Excel is *not* installed, Windows advertises Excel on the computer. *Advertising* software on a computer means that a small portion of the software is downloaded to the computer — just enough to display an icon for the program on the Start menu and to associate Excel with the Excel file extensions (`.xls`, `.xlsx`).

If the user clicks the Start menu icon for the advertised application or attempts to open a document that's associated with the advertised application, the application is automatically installed on the user's computer. The user will have to wait a few minutes while the application is installed, but the installation is automatic.

For more information about setting up group policy software installation, search Google or any other search engine for *Group Policy Software.*

Keeping Software Up to Date

One of the annoyances that every network manager faces is applying software patches to keep the operating system and other software up to date. A software *patch* is a minor update that fixes the small glitches that crop up from time to time, such as minor security or performance issues. These glitches aren't significant enough to merit a new version of the software, but they're important enough to require fixing. Most patches correct security flaws that computer hackers have uncovered in their relentless attempts to wreak havoc on the computer world.

Periodically, all the recently released patches are combined into a service pack. Although the most diligent network administrators apply all patches when they're released, many administrators just wait for the service packs.

Windows includes the Windows Update feature that automatically installs patches and service packs when they become available. These patches apply not just to Windows but to other Microsoft software as well. To use Windows Update, open the Control Panel, click System and Security, and then click Windows Update. A window appears, such as the one shown in Figure 6-1.

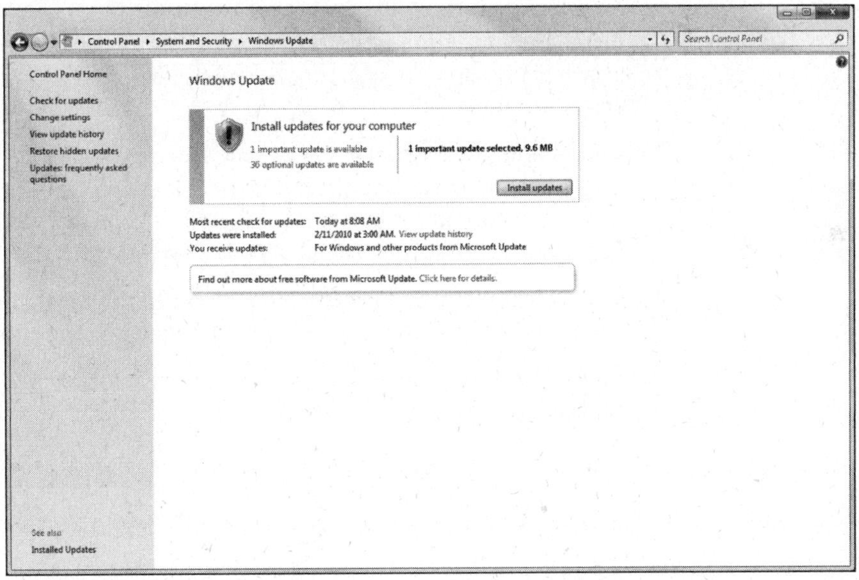

FIGURE 6-1:
Windows Update.

From the Windows Update window, you can click the Install Updates button to download any updates that apply to your computer. You can also configure Windows Update so that it automatically checks for updates and installs them without asking. To set this option, click the Change Settings link. This displays the Windows Update Change Settings page, as shown in Figure 6-2.

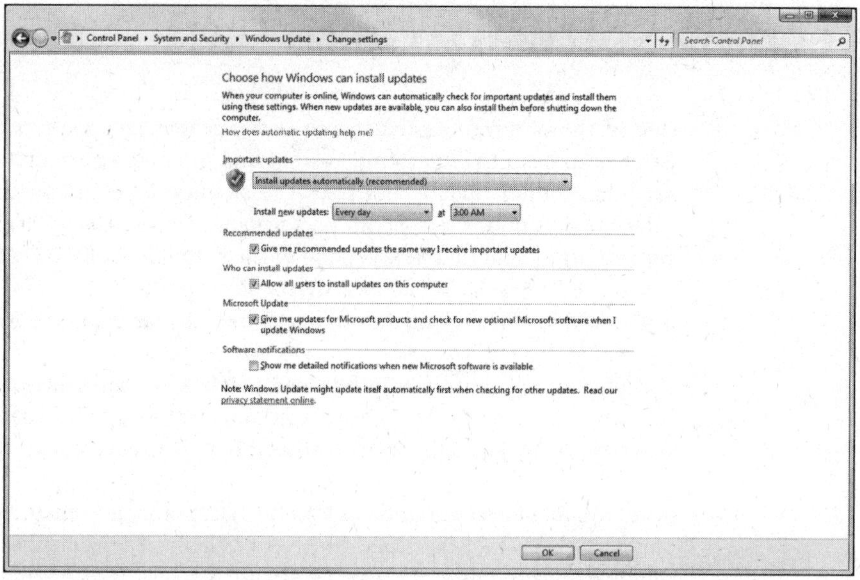

FIGURE 6-2:
Changing the
Windows Update
settings.

The Important Updates drop-down list gives you several options for automatic operation:

» **Install Updates Automatically:** Checks for updates on a regular basis and installs them without asking. You can specify how often to check for updates and at what time.

» **Download Updates But Let Me Choose Whether to Install Them:** If you're a picky computer user, you should choose this option. It automatically downloads the updates but then gives you the option of whether or not to install them. This lets you opt out of updates you may not want.

» **Check for Updates But Let Me Choose Whether to Download and Install Them:** This option lets you determine which updates should be downloaded.

» **Never Check for Updates:** This option disables automatic updates altogether.

Chapter **7**

Managing Email Retention

I f you've paid even the slightest attention to the news in recent years, you know that email scandals frequently dominate the headlines. The private Clinton email server, the Democratic National Committee email breach, and the 2016 election/Russia connection are just a few examples of major scandals that involve missing or undisclosed emails. But the vast majority of email discovery issues never make the rounds of CNN, MSNBC, and Fox News. Most email scandals are played out on a much smaller and more private scale: An employee complains of a harassing or inappropriate email from the boss; a contractor claims that inappropriate business practices on the part of your company led to a missed deadline or cost overrun; a malpractice or liability suit comes down to an email trail that indicates that top executives knew about the error and tried to sweep it under the rug.

When such matters come up, you (the IT administrator) will likely be called upon to search through your company's email repositories to find any and all email related to the matter. You need to be prepared for this inevitability. It'll happen sooner or later — I guarantee it.

The best way to prepare for an email search is to establish a clear and specific policy that spells out exactly what your company's practices are regarding the retention of emails. Are all emails retained indefinitely? Are all emails deleted after a relatively short period of time, such as two years? Do employees have the option to determine for themselves whether particular emails should be retained or discarded? If emails are to be retained, exactly where and how should they be saved? And if emails are to be discarded, what processes will be put in place to ensure that they're actually wiped from the system, so that no copies (or even fragments of copies) exist in unexpected places?

This chapter guides you through the factors you should consider when you prepare and implement a policy for retaining email. Having such a policy is a must: If a legal issue arises and no retention policy is in place, every bit of data storage in your entire organization may become subject to search.

Why Email Ends Up Everywhere

One of the basic problems with devising a good email retention policy is that copies of emails usually end up scattered about your network, often in multiple places, some of which may be unexpected, such as the following:

- **User Inbox or Sent Items folder:** Initially, incoming email arrives in a user's Inbox, and outgoing emails are stored in the user's Sent Items folder. Many users are good about cleaning out their Inboxes, but most rarely think to clean out their Sent Items folders.

- **Other user mailbox folders:** Many users create additional folders to store and organize incoming email. Some users have dozens of folders.

- **Deleted Items folder:** When a user deletes an email, the email isn't actually deleted; it's just moved to the Deleted Items folder. Unless the "deleted" email is later removed, it will remain in the Deleted Items folder indefinitely.

- **Other user mailboxes:** Users may forward incoming email, or an email may be CC'd to multiple users. So, a single email may exist in more than one user mailbox.

- **Auto-archive files:** If a user has set up auto-archiving, emails are automatically copied to .pst files when they're archived. Users can set up automatic archiving to save .pst files to a local disk or to a network share. And a single user can have multiple .pst files, possibly not all saved in the same location.

TIP

When you retire a computer, be sure to search the computer's local disks to see if it contains any .pst files. If so, you should preserve them before disposing of the computer.

- **Journal mailboxes:** If Exchange journaling is enabled, the journal mailbox contains a copy of all ingoing and outgoing email. When journaling is used, multiple mailboxes may be used (it's common to switch to a new mailbox when journal mailboxes become large).

>> **Exchange backups:** If your normal backup routine backs up your Exchange database (which it should), everything that was in your Exchange database at the time you made the backup is also in the backup copies. If you maintain more than one backup copy, each backup copy contains a copy of the Exchange database at the time the backup was made. Each one of these copies will have a different collection of emails, because the Exchange database is in a different state each time it's backed up. In other words, new emails will have been received between backups, and users may have deleted emails between backups. Thus, an email that is missing from the current Exchange database may be present in a backup copy of the Exchange database.

>> **Virtual machine (VM) backups:** If you use a backup tool that copies entire VM images, the backup copies of your Exchange server contain older versions of your Exchange database as well.

>> **Tape backups:** In some organizations, weekly or monthly tape backups are retained indefinitely. If your Exchange database or any archive .pst files are on those backups, each one contains a different set of email data that may or may not contain the particular emails that are of interest. If you have four years of monthly tape backups that contain your Exchange database, you may find yourself required to restore 48 incarnations of the database to search for relevant emails. Such a task would be a nightmare!

Creating a Retention Policy

An important part of any IT operation is to establish a clear written policy that addresses the questions of how email data will be retained. At a minimum, such a policy should address the issues described in the following sections.

Email classification

Not all emails are created equal; some are more worthy of retention than others. Unless your retention policy will treat all emails alike, you should spell out how emails will be classified and who will be responsible for determining which category an email belongs to. Generally, you'll want to leave it up to end-users to classify their own email. The policy should make it clear that users accept this responsibility and take it seriously, instead of just letting every incoming email accumulate in their Inboxes.

As a general rule, there are two broad categories of email: email that should be kept and email that shouldn't. More specifically:

» **Retained email:** Email that has lasting value and, therefore, should be retained. This may include the following types of email:

- Correspondence related to specific projects, sales, products, or whatever other type of business you're engaged in.

- Correspondence related to financial, administrative, personnel, or other internal business matters.

- Correspondence related to clients, vendors, contractors, suppliers, government agencies, providers, or whoever else you come in contact with as part of doing business.

» **Non-retained email:** Email that has no lasting value and, therefore, should be deleted as soon as possible. Examples might include the following:

- Personal correspondence not related to any business activity.

- Internal notices concerning things like holiday schedules, operating hours, or other routine business matters.

- Notices concerning computer, network, printer, phone, or other equipment status or availability. For example, if the copier breaks and someone sends an email indicating that the copier is down to the entire staff, that email doesn't need to be retained.

- Newsletters, updates, advertisements, and other routine correspondence from suppliers, trade organizations, subscription services, and the like.

- Spam messages or other unsolicited email.

Of course, there's a degree of individual discretion involved when determining whether a particular email should be considered retainable. No absolute rule can apply to every email, and reasonable people may disagree about whether an email should be considered worthy of retention. Employees should be encouraged to err on the side of preservation but should also be empowered to make their own decisions.

Retention duration

Many factors may influence how long your policy should direct that email should be retained. If your industry is subject to regulatory rules, you'll need to consult those rules to make sure your policy is in compliance. For example, in the United

States, the Federal Deposit Insurance Corporation (FDIC) requires that banks retain email for at least five years; the Internal Revenue Service (IRS) requires that tax-related correspondence be retained for seven years; and defense contractors must keep email for three years.

For your own purposes, you may decide that some emails should be retained permanently. For example, a consulting firm may want to keep all emails related to specific projects indefinitely, because you never know when an old project may be reactivated.

Mailbox size limits

In the old days of Exchange Server 2003 Standard Edition, Exchange databases were limited to a paltry 16GB. This limitation meant that you had to apply significant size limits to user mailboxes. Limits of 50MB or 100MB were common. With Exchange 2003 SP2, Microsoft raised the limit to 75GB, which helped but was still small enough that mailbox size limits were a must.

In Exchange Server 2010, the limit was increased dramatically to 1TB. Many administrators removed or increased their mailbox size limits, which was nice for the users but not necessarily a good idea. With large mailbox size limits, users tend to keep everything in their mailboxes, which can make it difficult to enforce any type of retention policy.

TIP

I recommend that you continue to impose a relatively small mailbox size limit on your users, unless you have a compelling reason not to. For example, you may want to set a default mailbox size limit of 100MB, but remove it for certain users such as the company CEO and your own mailbox, of course!

Auto-archive policies

The retention policy should spell out exactly how automatic archiving of user mailboxes should be performed, so that each user is not left to configure auto-archiving individually. You can then use Group Policy to globally configure the auto-archive settings.

One option (which I personally like) is to simply ban individual archiving, and then configure Outlook Group Policy to block the auto-archive features. This way, you can be certain that none of your users is creating .pst files and saving them in random locations on his computer or on your network. You'll probably get some pushback from your users over this, because many users depend on auto-archiving to keep their mailboxes clean while keeping all their old email. But if your policy is to ban auto-archiving, stick to your guns!

The other alternative is to allow auto-archiving but force the archive .pst files to a consistent location on the network. That way, you'll know where all the .pst files are, and you can easily back them up and keep track of the backup locations.

Impact of backup procedures

The email retention policy should explicitly spell out what impact (if any) the company's backup procedures have on email retention. In particular, make sure you document where any copies of Exchange databases and .pst files are kept.

TIP

Try to coordinate your backup procedures with your email retention policy to minimize the proliferation of backed-up email repositories. In other words, avoid keeping dozens of backup copies of Exchange databases or .pst files; instead, work to create a backup procedure that limits the number of email backups to just a few copies.

Configuring Exchange Retention Policies

Exchange Server has a powerful tool called Message Records Management (MRM), which lets you create and apply retention policies for your users' mailboxes. Using MRM effectively requires three distinct configurations, as described in the following sections.

Creating message retention tags

A *message retention tag* provides specific retention behavior for emails that have reached a certain age. To view or create retention tags, open the Exchange System Manager, go to the Mailbox node under Organization Configuration, and click the Retention Policy Tags tab. This displays the retention tags that already exist, as shown in Figure 7-1.

You can view or edit a retention tag by double-clicking it. You can create a new tag by right-clicking and choosing New Message Retention Tag. Figure 7-2 shows a retention tag.

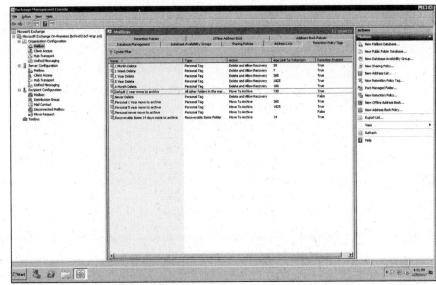

FIGURE 7-1:
Viewing message
retention tags.

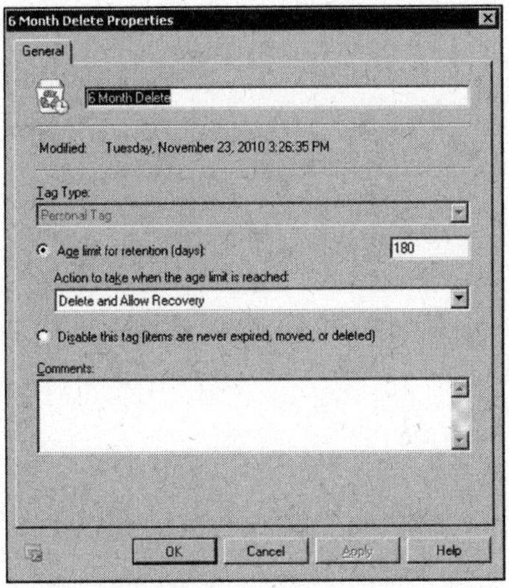

FIGURE 7-2:
A message
retention tag.

As you can see in Figure 7-2, each retention tag has five elements:

>> **Name:** Identifies the tag.

>> **Type:** Indicates the scope of the tag (that is, which emails the tag applies to). There are a total of 15 different tag types. Here are the most commonly used types:

- *Inbox:* Creates a default retention policy for the Inbox.

- *Sent:* Creates a default retention policy for the Sent Items folder.

Managing Email
Retention

- *Deleted Items:* Creates a default retention policy for the Deleted Items folder.

- *Drafts:* Creates a default retention policy for the Drafts folder.

- *All Other Items in This Mailbox:* Creates a default retention policy for folders that do not have a specify tag applied. Note that this includes custom folders created by users.

- *Personal:* Allows the user to tag individual messages to determine the disposition of his or her email messages, thus overriding the default retention tag for the folder. Users can also apply a Personal tag to a custom folder, overriding the retention policy established by the All Other Items in This Mailbox tag.

>> **Age:** Indicates how old an email must be for the tag to apply. The age is specified in days.

>> **Action:** An action that is triggered when an email associated with this tag reaches its expiration age. Here are the options:

- *Delete and Allow Recovery:* Deletes expired emails, but allows the user to recover them.

- *Permanently Delete:* Permanently deletes expired emails.

- *Mark as Past Retention Limit:* Marks the email so the user knows the email is past the limit.

- *Move to Archive:* Moves the email to an archive file.

As you can see in Figure 7-2, the Personal tag named "6 Month Delete" automatically moves emails marked with the tag to the Deleted Items folder when the email becomes six months old.

Creating message retention policies

A *message retention policy* is a combination of message retention tags that can be applied to individual mailboxes. Before you create a message retention policy, you need to first create all the tags you'll want to incorporate into the policy, including any Personal tags that allow users to determine the retention status of individual emails.

To create a message retention policy, follow these steps:

1. **Open the Exchange System Manager.**

2. **Select the Mailbox node under Organization Configuration.**

3. **Click the Retention Policies tab.**

The retention policies that already exist appear, as shown in Figure 7-3.

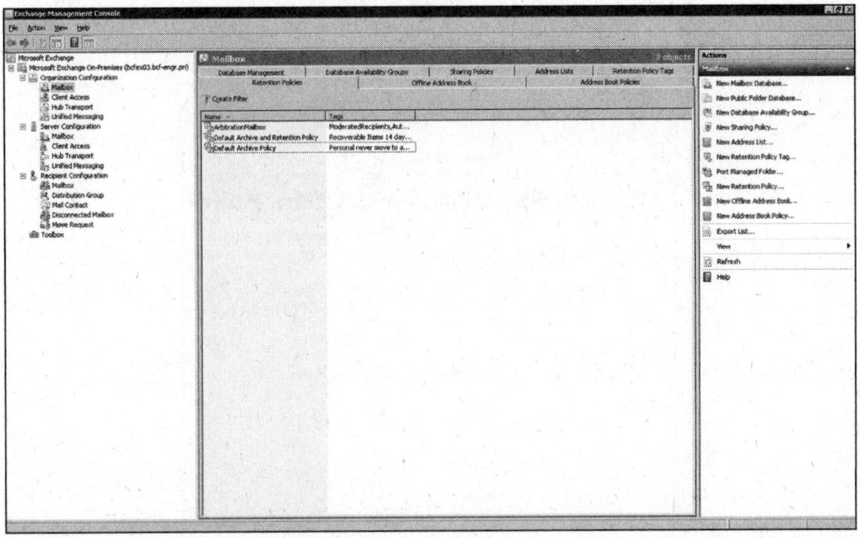

Managing Email
Retention

FIGURE 7-3:
Viewing retention
policies.

4. **Right-click in an empty area and choose New Retention Policy.**

The New Retention Policy Wizard appears, as shown in Figure 7-4.

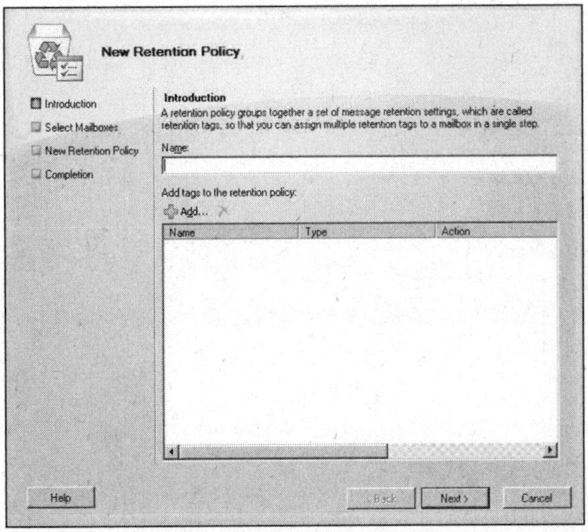

FIGURE 7-4:
The New
Retention Policy
Wizard.

5. Enter a name for your new policy.

For this example, I'll use the name "Test Policy."

6. Click the Add icon (the plus sign).

The dialog box shown in Figure 7-5 appears.

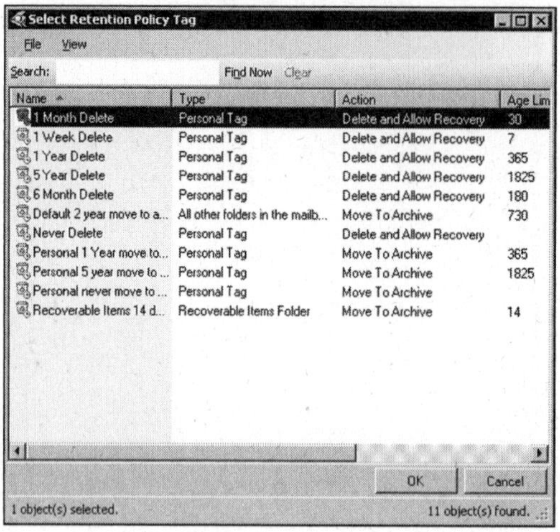

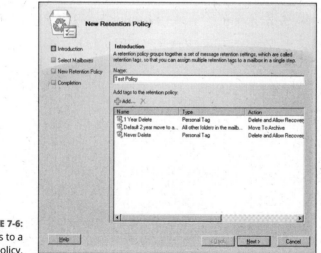

FIGURE 7-5:
Adding tags to a
new policy.

7. Select the tags you want to include in the policy and click OK.

You can use the Shift or Ctrl keys to select multiple tags.

Figure 7-6 shows the policy with some tags applied.

FIGURE 7-6:
Adding tags to a
new policy.

8. **Click Next.**

The next page of the wizard appears, as shown in Figure 7-7. Here, the wizard allows you to apply the new policy to one or more mailboxes. If you want to apply the policy to mailboxes, click the plus sign icon and select the mailboxes you want to use. However, I recommend that you first create the policy without assigning it to mailboxes; you can then assign the policy to mailboxes a few at a time to test the new policy.

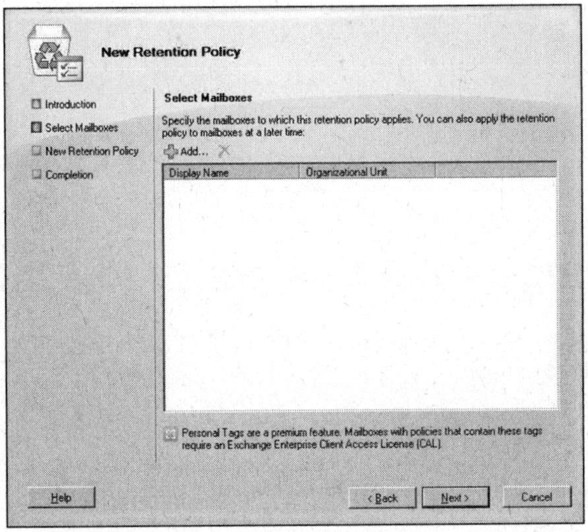

FIGURE 7-7:
The wizard asks
what mailboxes
to apply the
policy to.

9. **Click Next.**

The wizard displays a confirmation page, as shown in Figure 7-8.

10. **Review the policy details shown on the confirmation page and click New.**

Voilà! You have successfully created a new email retention policy. The wizard displays a congratulatory page, just to make you feel good.

11. **Click Finish.**

You're done.

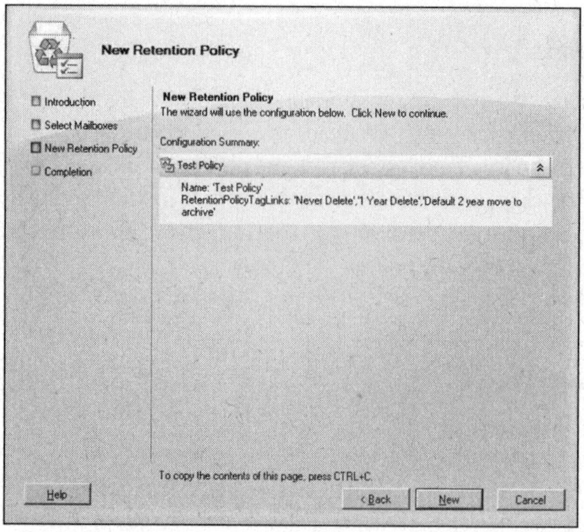

FIGURE 7-8:
The wizard
displays a
confirmation
page.

Applying a retention policy to a mailbox

After you've created a message retention policy, you can apply it to a mailbox by following these steps:

1. **Open the Exchange System Manager.**

2. **Select the Mailbox node under Recipient Configuration.**

3. **Right-click the mailbox you want to apply the policy to and choose Properties.**

   The mailbox properties page appears.

4. **Click the Mailbox Settings tab.**

   The Mailbox Settings page appears, as shown in Figure 7-9.

5. **Double-click Messaging Records Management.**

   The Messaging Records Management page appears, as depicted in Figure 7-10.

6. **Check the Apply Retention Policy check box, and then click the Browse button.**

   A list of your message retention policies appears, as shown in Figure 7-11.

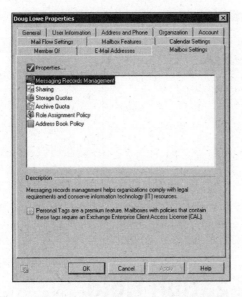

FIGURE 7-9:
Viewing the
Mailbox
Settings page.

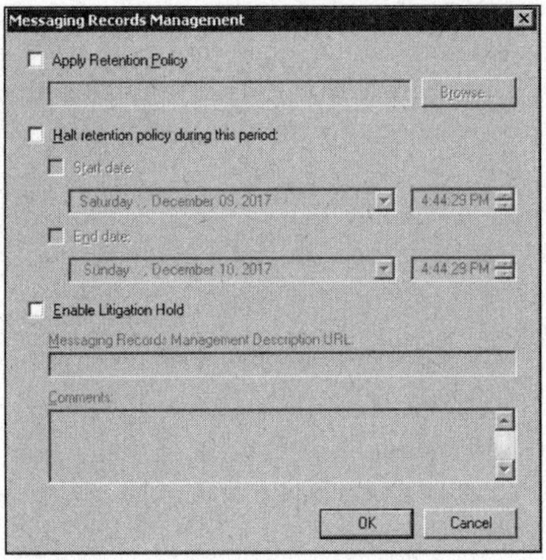

FIGURE 7-10:
The Messaging
Records
Management
page.

7. **Select the policy you want to apply.**

8. **Click OK to apply the policy.**

9. **Click OK to close the dialog box.**

After you've thoroughly tested the policy to ensure that it works as expected, you can roll it out to other mailboxes.

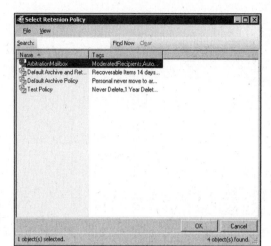

FIGURE 7-11:
The Messaging
Records Manage-
ment page.

Planning for a Litigation Hold

A *litigation hold* happens when a company determines that a legal claim has been made in which there is a possibility that emails may be demanded. Typically, a litigation hold has the following requirements:

» Users must be immediately notified that they are not allowed to delete *any* emails in their mailboxes. This applies to not only emails that they think are relevant to the legal matter, but to *all* emails.

» Any processes that automatically delete emails, including backup copies of emails, must be suspended.

» All mailboxes must be placed in a special Litigation Hold mode, which causes Exchange to keep a record of all mailbox changes including deletions. (For more information, see the procedure later in this section.)

» Conduct a compliance review of the email retention policy and make every effort to preserve all unforeseen email retention sources, including rogue .pst files residing in unexpected places such as on user computers.

» Be prepared to conduct a discover effort to recover emails requested, or to provide access to a third-party discovery team if directed.

If you need to place a mailbox in a Litigation Hold state, follow these steps:

1. **Open Exchange Server and navigate to the mailbox in question.**

2. **Open the Properties page for the mailbox in question and then click the Mailbox Settings tab (refer to Figure 7-9).**

3. **Double-click Message Records Management.**

   This brings up the Messaging Records Management dialog box, which was shown in Figure 7-10.

4. **Check the Enable Litigation Hold box.**

5. **If your email retention policy is posted to your company intranet, enter the URL in the Messaging Records Management Description URL field.**

6. **If you want, enter a comment in the Comments field.**

7. **Click OK.**

   You're returned to the Mailbox Settings configuration page.

8. **Click OK again.**

   The Litigation Hold is enabled.

To disable the Litigation Hold, repeat this procedure but uncheck the Enable Litigation Hold check box in Step 4.

Using the Exchange Journaling Feature

Microsoft Exchange provides a feature called *journaling* that can help you implement an email retention policy. Journaling is actually quite simple in concept: When you enable journaling, a copy of all incoming and outgoing email is automatically saved in a designated mailbox called the *journal mailbox*. There's nothing special about the journal mailbox; it's a normal Exchange mailbox just like any other, except that emails are automatically dumped into it by the Exchange journaling feature.

Here are a few points to ponder concerning journaling:

» The journal mailbox can get very large very fast. After all, any email sent by or received by any user will be copied to the journal mailbox. So you should consider periodically setting up new journal mailboxes. How often depends on the size of your organization and the number of emails the journal mailbox receives. You may want to set up a new journal mailbox every year, every three months, or every month.

» You can open the journal mailbox just like any other mailbox: Just create an Outlook profile (or use Outlook Web Access [OWA]) to log in to the mailbox using the mailbox username and password that you set up when you created the journal mailbox.

>> Access to the journal mailbox should be *very* limited. This mailbox almost certainly contains sensitive correspondence, because emails from every user are copied to it. Make sure you limit access to the mailbox and carefully protect the mailbox credentials.

>> If appropriate, you can implement journaling rules that control whose emails are copied to the journal. You may want to do this if only certain users generate email worthy of retention.

Using Exchange Online Archiving

You can use Microsoft's Exchange Online Archiving service to automatically archive your emails to Microsoft's cloud storage. Exchange Online Archiving includes advanced-use eDiscovery features that dramatically simplify the task of recovering retained emails when needed.

Exchange Online Archiving includes a web-based management console that lets you configure retention policies, enable litigation holds, and access archived emails. Users can access their own archived emails from within Outlook or OWA.

By storing your email archives on Microsoft's cloud storage, you don't have to worry about providing your own on-premises storage for email archiving. That means you also don't have to worry about backing it up; Microsoft provides its own secure and reliable backup service to safeguard your archive. And as with any cloud-based service, you don't have to worry about installing or maintaining the archive software; Microsoft takes care of that for you.

Exchange Online Archiving is included with the E3-level subscription of Office 365. If you're using an on-premises Exchange Server, you can subscribe to Exchange Online Archiving for $3 per user per month. Each user can archive up to 50GB of email, but additional storage is available at additional cost.

Chapter **8**

Managing Mobile Devices

A computer consultant once purchased a used BlackBerry device on eBay for $15.50. When he put in a new battery and turned on the device, he discovered that it contained confidential emails and personal contact information for executives of a well-known financial institution.

Oops!

It turns out that a former executive with the company sold his old BlackBerry on eBay a few months after he left the firm. He'd assumed that because he'd removed the battery, everything on the BlackBerry had been erased.

The point of this true story is that mobile devices such as smartphones and tablet computers pose a special set of challenges for network administrators. These challenges are now being faced even by administrators of small networks. Just a few years ago, only large companies had BlackBerry or other mobile devices that integrated with Exchange email, for example. Now it isn't uncommon for companies with just a few employees to have mobile devices connected to the company network.

This chapter is a brief introduction to mobile devices and the operating systems they run, with an emphasis on iPhone and Android devices. You'll find out how these devices can interact with Exchange email and the steps you can take to ensure their security.

The Many Types of Mobile Devices

Once upon a time, there were mobile phones and PDAs. A mobile phone was just that: a handheld telephone you could take with you. The good ones had nice features such as a call log, an address book, and perhaps a crude game but not much else. PDAs — *Personal Digital Assistants* — were little handheld computers designed to replace the old-fashioned Day-Timer books people used to carry around with them to keep track of their appointment calendars and address books.

All that changed when cellular providers began adding data capabilities to their networks. Now, cellphones can have complete mobile Internet access. This fact has resulted in the addition of sophisticated PDA features to mobile phones and phone features to PDAs so that the distinctions are blurred.

The term *mobile device* is used to describe a wide assortment of devices that you can hold in one hand and that are connected through a wireless network. The term *handheld* is a similar generic name for such devices. The following list describes some of the most common specifics of mobile devices:

» **Mobile phone:** A *mobile phone* (or *cellphone)* is a mobile device whose primary purpose is to enable phone service. Most mobile phones include features such as text messaging, address books, appointment calendars, and games, and they may provide Internet access.

» **Smartphone:** A *smartphone* is a mobile phone with advanced features that aren't typically found on mobile phones. There's no clearly drawn line between mobile phones and smartphones. One distinction is whether the phone can provide integrated access to corporate email. The screen on a smartphone is typically bigger than the screen on a traditional cellphone, and the most popular models (such as the iPhone and most Android devices) do not have a keyboard at all.

» **Android:** Android is an open-source operating system for smartphones developed by Google. Android is far and away the most popular platform for smartphones, being used on more than 80 percent of the smartphones sold in 2015.

>> **iOS:** iOS is the operating system used on Apple's popular iPhone and iPad mobile devices. Although outnumbered by Android devices, many people consider iOS devices to be more innovative than Android devices. The main thing that holds iOS back in market share is its cost: Apple devices are considerably more expensive than their Android equivalents.

>> **BlackBerry:** Once upon a time, BlackBerry was the king of the smartphone game. BlackBerry had a virtual monopoly on mobile devices that synchronized well with Microsoft Exchange. Now that Android and Apple devices do that just as well as (if not better) than BlackBerry, BlackBerry has fallen out of vogue. However, BlackBerry is still around, and there are still plenty of BlackBerry users out there. (Note that newer BlackBerry phones run Android rather than the old proprietary BlackBerry operating system.)

Considering Security for Mobile Devices

As a network administrator, one of your main responsibilities regarding mobile devices is to keep them secure. Unfortunately, that's a significant challenge. Here are some of the reasons why:

>> **Mobile devices connect to your network via other networks that are out of your control.** You can go to great lengths to set up firewalls, encryption, and a host of other security features, but mobile devices connect via public networks whose administrators may not be as conscientious as you.

>> **Mobile devices are easy to lose.** A user might leave her smartphone at a restaurant or hotel, or it might fall out of her pocket on the subway.

>> **Mobile devices run operating systems that aren't as security-conscious as Windows.**

>> **Users who wouldn't dare install renegade software on their desktop computers think nothing of downloading free games or other applications to their handheld devices.** Who knows what kinds of viruses or Trojans these downloads carry?

>> **Inevitably, someone will buy his own handheld device and connect it to your network without your knowledge or permission.**

Here are some recommendations for beefing up security for your mobile devices:

>> **Establish clear, consistent policies for mobile devices, and enforce them.**

>> **Make sure employees understand that they aren't allowed to bring their own devices into your network unless you have made special provisions to allow it**. In particular, I recommend you establish a separate subnet for employee-owned devices so that your employee devices don't contend for IP addresses with your main network. For more information about subnetting, refer to Book 3, Chapter 1.

>> **Train your users in the security risks associated with using mobile devices.**

>> **Implement antivirus protection for your mobile devices.**

Managing iOS Devices

In 2007, the Apple iPhone, one of the most innovative little gadgets in many, many years, hit the technology market. As a result, in just a few short years, the iPhone captured a huge slice of a market dominated almost exclusively by Research in Motion and its BlackBerry devices. Since then, the iPhone's share of the mobile–phone market has grown beyond that of the former king, BlackBerry.

The success of the iPhone was due in large part to the genius of its operating system, iOS. In 2010, Apple released the iPad, a tablet computer that runs the same operating system as the iPhone. And in 2012, Apple introduced a smaller version of the iPad: the iPad mini. Together, these devices are commonly known as "iOS devices."

Understanding the iPhone

The iPhone is essentially a combination of four devices:

>> A cellphone

>> An iPod

>> A digital camera

>> An Internet device with its own web browser (Safari) and applications, such as email, calendar, and contact management

The most immediately noticeable feature of the iPhone is its lack of a keyboard. Instead, nearly the entire front surface of the iPhone is a high-resolution, touch-sensitive LCD. The display is not only the main output device of the iPhone, but also its main input device. The display can become a keypad input for dialing a telephone number or a keyboard for entering text. You can also use various finger gestures, such as tapping icons to start programs or pinching to zoom in the display.

The iPhone has several other innovative features:

» An accelerometer tracks the motion of the iPhone in three directions. The main use of the accelerometer is to adjust the orientation of the display from landscape to portrait based on how the user is holding the phone. Some other applications — mostly games — use the accelerometer as well.

» A Wi-Fi interface lets the iPhone connect to local Wi-Fi networks for faster Internet access.

» GPS capability provides location awareness for many applications, including Google Maps.

» The virtual private network (VPN) client lets you connect to your internal network.

Of all the unique features of the iPhone, probably the most important is its huge collection of third-party applications that can be downloaded from a special web portal, the App Store. Many of these applications are free or cost just a few dollars. (Many are just 99 cents or $1.99.) As of this writing, more than 2.2 million apps — everything from business productivity to games — were available from the App Store.

Understanding the iPad

The iPad is essentially an iPhone without the phone but with a larger screen. Apart from these basic differences, an iPad is nearly identical to an iPhone. Any application that can run on an iPhone can also run on an iPad, and many applications are designed to take special advantage of the iPad's larger screen.

All the iOS information that follows in this chapter applies equally to iPhones and iPads.

Integrating iOS devices with Exchange

An iOS device can integrate with Microsoft Exchange email via the Exchange Active-Sync feature, which is enabled by default on Exchange 2010 and later versions.

To verify the Exchange ActiveSync feature for an individual mailbox, follow these steps:

1. **Choose Start ➪ Administrative Tools ➪ Active Directory Users and Computers.**

   The Active Directory Users and Computers console opens.

2. **Expand the domain and then locate the user you want to enable mobile access for.**

   Right-click the user and then choose Properties from the contextual menu.

3. **Click the Exchange Features tab.**

   The Exchange Features options are displayed, as shown in Figure 8-1.

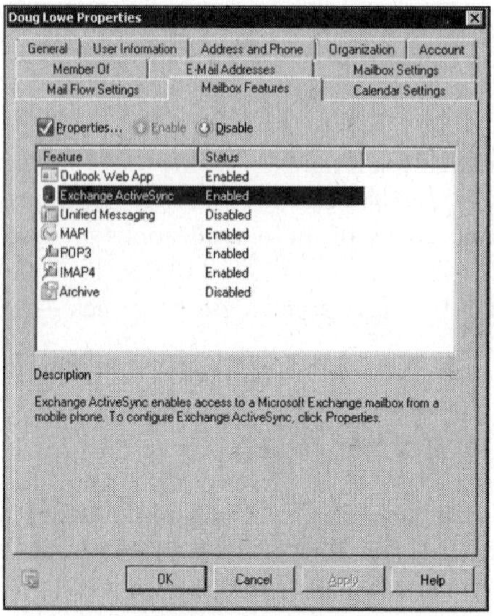

FIGURE 8-1: Enabling Exchange ActiveSync for a user.

4. **Ensure that the Exchange ActiveSync option is enabled.**

   If the options aren't already enabled, right-click each option and choose Enable from the contextual menu.

5. **Click OK.**

Repeat Steps 5 and 6 for any other users you want to enable mobile access for.

6. **Close Active Directory Users and Computers.**

That's all there is to it. After you enable these features, any users running Windows Mobile can synchronize their handheld devices with their Exchange mailboxes.

After ActiveSync is enabled for the mailbox, you can configure an iPhone or iPad to tap into the Exchange account by following these steps:

1. **On the iPhone or iPad, tap Settings and then tap Mail, Contacts, Calendars.**

The screen shown in Figure 8-2 appears. This screen lists any existing email accounts that may already be configured on the phone and also lets you add a new account.

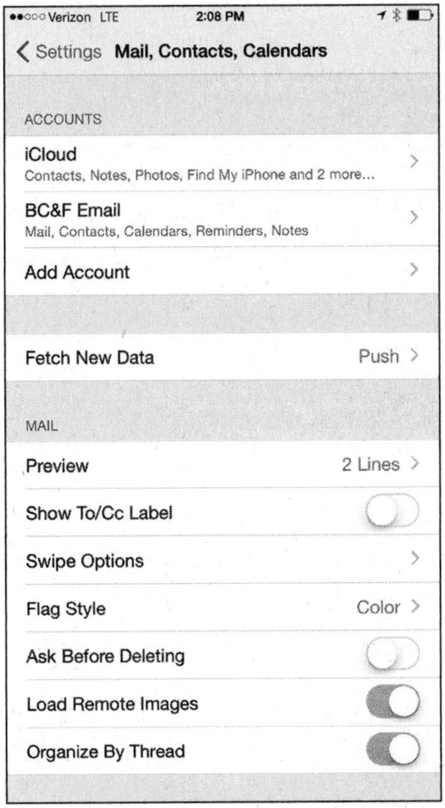

FIGURE 8-2:
Adding an email account.

(Managing Mobile Devices — side tab)

2. **Tap Add Account.**

The screen shown in Figure 8-3 appears, allowing you to choose the type of email account you want to add.

FIGURE 8-3:
The iPhone can support many types of email accounts.

3. **Tap Exchange.**

The screen shown in Figure 8-4 appears, where you can enter basic information for your Exchange account.

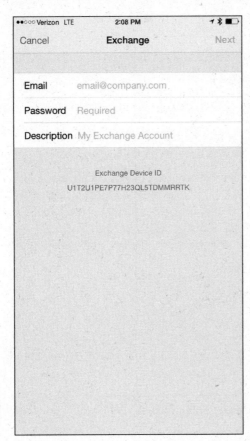

●●○○○ Verizon LTE   2:08 PM   ⚹ ✳ ◾

Cancel   **Exchange**   Next

Email   email@company.com

Password   Required

Description   My Exchange Account

Exchange Device ID

U1T2U1PE7P77H23QL5TDMMRRTK

FIGURE 8-4:
Enter your email
address and
password.

4. **Enter your email address, password, and a description of the account.**

5. **Tap Next.**

    The screen shown in Figure 8-5 appears.

6. **Enter either the DNS name or the IP address of your Exchange server in the Server field.**

    I entered smtp.lowewriter.com for my Exchange server, for example.

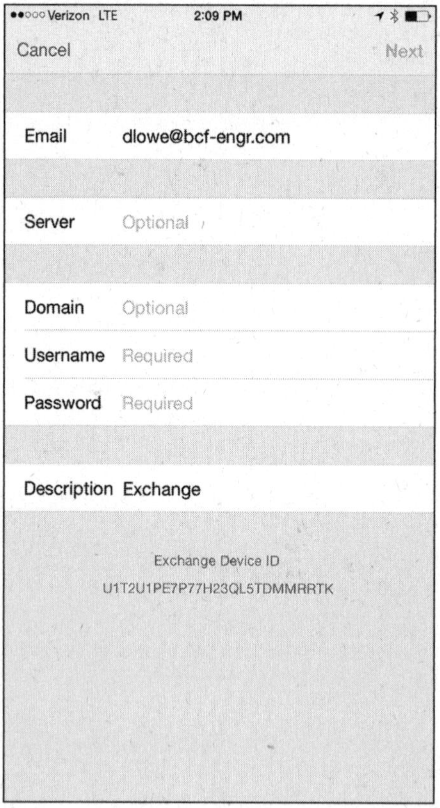

FIGURE 8-5:
Enter your
Exchange server
information.

7. **Enter your domain name, your Windows username, and your Windows password in the appropriate fields.**

8. **Tap Next.**

   The screen shown in Figure 8-6 appears. Here, you select which mailbox features you want to synchronize: Mail, Contacts, Calendars, Reminders, and/or Notes.

9. **Select the features you want to synchronize and then tap Done.**

   The email account is created.

After the email account has been configured, the user can access it via the Mail icon on the iPhone's home screen.

FIGURE 8-6:
Select features to synchronize.

Managing Android Devices

This section is a brief introduction to the Android platform. You find out a bit about what Android actually is, and you discover the procedures for setting up Exchange email access on an Android phone.

Crucial differences exist between Android phones and iPhones, however. The most important difference — in many ways, the *only* important difference — is that Android phones are based on an open-source OS derived from Linux, which can be extended and adapted to work on a wide variety of hardware devices from different vendors. With the iPhone, you're locked into Apple hardware. With an Android phone, you can buy hardware from a variety of manufacturers.

Looking at the Android OS

Most people associate the Android OS with Google, and it's true that Google is the driving force behind Android. The Android OS is an open-source OS managed by the Open Handset Alliance (OHA). Google still plays a major role in the development of Android, but more than 80 companies are involved in the OHA, including hardware manufacturers (such as HTC, Intel, and Motorola), software companies (such as Google and eBay), and mobile phone operators (such as T-Mobile and Sprint-Nextel).

TECHNICAL STUFF

Technically speaking, Android is more than just an OS. It's also a complete *software stack*, which comprises several key components that work together to create the complete Android platform:

>> **The OS core,** which is based on the popular Linux OS

>> **A middleware layer,** which provides drivers and other support code to enable the OS core to work with the hardware devices that make up a complete phone, such as a touch-sensitive display, the cellphone radio, the speaker and microphone, Bluetooth or Wi-Fi networking components, and so on

>> **A set of core applications** that the user interacts with to make phone calls, read email, send text messages, take pictures, and so on

>> **A software development kit (SDK)** that lets third-party software developers create their own applications to run on an Android phone, as well as a marketplace where the applications can be marketed and sold, much as the App Store lets iPhone developers market and sell applications for the iPhone

Besides the basic features provided by all OSs, here are a few bonus features of the Android software stack:

>> An optimized graphical display engine that can produce sophisticated 2-D and 3-D graphics

>> GPS capabilities that provide location awareness that can be integrated with applications such as Google Maps

>> Compass and accelerometer capabilities that can determine whether the phone is in motion and in which direction it's pointed

>> A built-in SQL database server for data storage

>> Support for several network technologies, including Bluetooth and Wi-Fi

>> Built-in media support, including common formats for still images, audio, and video files

Perusing Android's core applications

The Android OS comes preconfigured with several standard applications, which provide the functionality that most people demand from a modern smartphone. These applications include

>> **Dialer:** Provides the basic cellphone function that lets users make calls.

>> **Browser:** A built-in web browser that's similar to Google's Chrome browser.

>> **Messaging:** Provides text (SMS) and multimedia (MMS) messaging.

>> **Email:** A basic email client that works best with Google's Gmail but that can be configured to work with other email servers, including Exchange.

>> **Contacts:** Provides a contacts list that integrates with the Dialer and Email applications.

>> **Camera:** Lets you use the phone's camera hardware (if any) to take pictures.

>> **Calculator:** A simple calculator application.

>> **Alarm Clock:** A basic alarm clock. You can set up to three different alarms.

>> **Maps:** An integrated version of Google Maps.

>> **YouTube:** An integrated version of YouTube.

>> **Music:** An MP3 player similar to the iPod. You can purchase and download music files from Amazon.

>> **Market:** Lets you purchase and download third-party applications for the Android phone.

>> **Settings:** Lets you control various settings for the phone.

Integrating Android with Exchange

The Android's core Email application can integrate with Microsoft Exchange email. If you're using Exchange, you must enable Exchange Mobile Services and then enable ActiveSync for the user's mailbox.

After you enable Exchange Mobile Services and ActiveSync on your Exchange server, you can easily configure the Android phone for email access. Just run the Email application on the Android phone, and follow the configuration steps, which ask you for basic information such as your email address, username, password, and Exchange mail server.

9

Managing Cybersecurity

Contents at a Glance

Chapter **1**

Welcome to Cybersecurity

As an IT professional, cybersecurity is the thing most likely to keep you awake at night. Consider the following scenarios:

» Your phone starts ringing like crazy at 3 o'clock one afternoon because no one anywhere on the network can access any of their files. You soon discover that your network has been infiltrated by *ransomware*, nefarious software that has encrypted every byte of data on your network, rendering it useless to your users until you pay a ransom to recover the data.

» Your company becomes a headline on CNN because a security breach has resulted in the theft of your customers' credit card information.

» On his last day of work, a disgruntled employee copies your company contact list and other vital intellectual property to a flash drive and walks away with it along with his Swingline stapler. A few months later, your company loses its biggest contract to the company where this jerk now works.

There is no way you can absolutely prevent such scenarios from ever happening, but with proper security, you can greatly reduce their likelihood. This chapter presents a brief overview of some of the basic principles of securing your network. The remaining chapters in this minibook dive deeper into specific cybersecurity techniques.

But We're a Small Business . . . Do We Need Security?

It's tempting to think that cybersecurity is important only to large enterprises. In a small business, everyone knows and trusts everyone else. Folks don't lock up their desks when they take a coffee break, and although everyone knows where the petty cash box is, money never disappears.

Cybersecurity isn't necessary in an idyllic setting like this one — or is it? You bet it is. Here's why any network should be set up with built-in concern for security:

>> **Mitts off:** Even in the friendliest office environment, some information is and should be confidential. If this information is stored on the network, you want to store it in a directory that's available only to authorized users.

>> **Hmm:** Not all security breaches are malicious. A network user may be routinely scanning files and come across a filename that isn't familiar. The user may then call up the file, only to discover that it contains confidential personnel information, juicy office gossip, or your résumé. Curiosity, rather than malice, is often the source of security breaches.

>> **Trust:** Sure, everyone at the office is trustworthy now. However, what if someone becomes disgruntled, a screw pops loose, and he decides to trash the network files before jumping out the window? Or what if someone decides to print a few $1,000 checks before packing off to Tahiti?

>> **Temptation:** Sometimes the mere opportunity for fraud or theft can be too much for some people to resist. Give people free access to the payroll files, and they may decide to vote themselves a raise when no one is looking.

If you think that your network contains no data worth stealing, think again. For example, your personnel records probably contain more than enough information for an identity thief: names, addresses, phone numbers, Social Security numbers, and so on. Also, your customer files may contain your customers' credit card numbers.

>> **Malice:** Hackers who break into your network may not be interested in stealing your data. Instead, they may be looking to plant a *Trojan horse* program on your server, which enables them to use your server for their own purposes. For example, someone may use your server to send thousands of unsolicited spam email messages. The spam won't be traced back to the hackers; it will be traced back to you.

>> **Whoops:** Finally, bear in mind that not everyone on the network knows enough about how your operating system and the network work to be trusted with full access to your network's data and systems. One careless mouse click can wipe out an entire directory of network files. One of the best reasons for activating your network's security features is to protect the network from mistakes made by users who don't know what they're doing.

The Two Pillars of Cybersecurity

There are two basic elements that you must consider as part of your cybersecurity plan:

>> **Prevention:** The first pillar of cybersecurity is technology that you can deploy to prevent bad actors from penetrating your network and stealing or damaging your data. This technology includes firewalls that block unwelcome access, antivirus programs that detect malicious software, patch management tools that keep your software up to date, and antispam programs that keep suspicious email from reaching your users' inboxes.

Chapters 2 of this minibook addresses firewalls and antivirus software, while Chapter 3 shows you how to employ antispam software. For more information about patch management, refer to Book 8, Chapter 6.

TIP

The most important part of the prevention pillar is what I call the *human firewall.* Technology can only go so far in preventing successful cyber attacks. Most successful attacks are the result of users opening email attachments or clicking web links that they should have known were dangerous. Thus, in addition to providing technology to prevent attacks, you also need to make sure your users know how to spot and avoid suspicious email attachments and web links. (For more information, see the section "Securing the Human Firewall" later in this chapter.)

>> **Recovery:** The second pillar of cybersecurity is necessary because the first pillar isn't always successful. Successful cyber attacks are inevitable, so you need to have technology and plans in place to quickly recover from them when you do. You'll learn more about recovery technology in Chapters 4 and 5 of this minibook.

Considering Two Basic Approaches to Security

When you're planning how to implement security on your network, you should first consider which of two basic approaches to security you will take:

>> **Open-door:** You grant everyone access to everything by default and then place restrictions just on those resources to which you want to limit access.

>> **Closed-door:** You begin by denying access to everything and then grant specific users access to the specific resources that they need.

In most cases, an open-door policy is easier to implement. Typically, only a small portion of the data on a network really needs security, such as confidential employee records or secrets such as the Coke recipe. The rest of the information on a network can be safely made available to everyone who can access the network.

A closed-door approach results in tighter security, but can lead to the Cone of Silence Syndrome: Like Max and the Chief who can't hear each other talk while they're under the Cone of Silence, your network users will constantly complain that they can't access the information that they need. As a result, you'll find yourself frequently adjusting users' access rights. Choose the closed-door approach only if your network contains a lot of very sensitive information — and only if you're willing to invest time administrating your network's security policy.

TIP

Think of an open-door approach as an *entitlement model,* in which the basic assumption is that users are entitled to network access. In contrast, a closed-door policy is a *permissions model,* in which the basic assumption is that users aren't entitled to anything but must get permission for every network resource that they access.

Physical Security: Locking Your Doors

The first level of security in any computer network is physical security. I'm amazed when I walk into the reception area of an accounting firm and see an unattended computer sitting on the receptionist's desk. As often as not, the receptionist has logged on to the system and then walked away from the desk, leaving the computer unattended.

Physical security is important for workstations but vital for servers. Any hacker worth his salt can quickly defeat all but the most paranoid security measures if he or she can gain physical access to a server. To protect the server, follow these guidelines:

>> Lock the computer room.

>> Give the keys only to people you trust.

>> Keep track of who has the keys.

>> Mount the servers on cases or racks with locks.

>> Keep a trained guard dog in the computer room and feed it only enough to keep it hungry and mad. (Just kidding.)

REMEMBER

There's a big difference between a locked door and a door with a lock. Locks are worthless if you don't use them.

Client computers should be physically secure as well. Instruct users to not leave their computers unattended while they're logged on. In high-traffic areas (such as the receptionist's desk), users should secure their computers with the keylock. Additionally, users should lock their office doors when they leave.

Here are some other potential threats to physical security that you may not have considered:

>> **Off-hours personnel:** The nightly cleaning crew probably has complete access to your facility. How do you know that the person who vacuums your office every night doesn't really work for your chief competitor or doesn't consider computer hacking to be a sideline hobby? You don't, so you'd better consider the cleaning crew a threat.

>> **Dumpster diving:** What about your trash? Paper shredders aren't just for Enron accountants. Your trash can contain all sorts of useful information: sales reports, security logs, printed copies of the company's security policy, even handwritten passwords. For the best security, every piece of paper that leaves your building via the trash bin should first go through a shredder.

>> **Backups:** Where do you store your backup tapes? Don't just stack them up next to the server. Not only does that make them easy to steal, it also defeats one of the main purposes of backing up your data in the first place: securing your server from physical threats, such as fires. If a fire burns down your computer room and the backup tapes are sitting unprotected next to the server, your company may go out of business — and you'll certainly be out of a job. Store the backup tapes securely in a fire-resistant safe and keep a copy off-site, too.

> **» Switches:** I've seen some networks in which the servers are in a locked computer room, but the switches are in an unsecured closet. Remember that every unused port on a switch represents an open door to your network. The switches should be secured just like the servers.

Securing User Accounts

Next to physical security, the careful use of user accounts is the most important type of security for your network. Properly configured user accounts can prevent unauthorized users from accessing the network, even if they gain physical access to the network. The following sections describe some of the steps that you can take to strengthen your network's use of user accounts.

Obfuscating your usernames

Huh? When it comes to security, *obfuscation* simply means picking obscure usernames. For example, most network administrators assign usernames based on some combination of the user's first and last names, such as BarnyM or baMiller. However, a hacker can easily guess such a user ID if she knows the name of at least one employee. After the hacker knows a username, she can focus on breaking the password.

You can slow down a hacker by using more obscure names — and here's how:

> **»** Add a random three-digit number to the end of the name. For example: BarnyM320 or baMiller977.
>
> **»** Throw a number or two into the middle of the name. For example: Bar6nyM or ba9Miller2.
>
> **»** Make sure that usernames are different from email addresses. For example, if a user's email address is baMiller@Mydomain.com, do *not* use baMiller as the user's account name. Use a more obscure name.

WARNING

Do *not* rely on obfuscation to keep people out of your network! Security by obfuscation doesn't work. A resourceful hacker can discover even the most obscure names. The purpose of obfuscation is to slow down intruders — not to stop them. If you slow down an intruder, you're more likely to discover that she is trying to crack your network before she successfully gets in.

Using passwords wisely

One of the most important aspects of network security is using passwords. Usernames aren't usually considered secret. And even if you use obscure names, casual hackers will eventually figure them out.

Passwords, on the other hand, are indeed top secret. Your network password is the one thing that keeps an impostor from logging on to the network by using your username and therefore receiving the same access rights that you ordinarily have. *Guard your password with your life.*

Here are some tips for creating good passwords:

» Don't use obvious passwords, such as your last name, your kid's name, or your dog's name.

» Don't pick passwords based on your hobbies, either. A friend of mine is into boating, and his password is the name of his boat. Anyone who knows him can guess his password after a few tries. Five lashes for naming your password after your boat.

» Store your password in your head, not on paper. Especially bad: Writing down your password on a sticky note and sticking it on your computer's monitor. Ten lashes for that. (If you must write down your password, write it on digestible paper that you can swallow after you memorize the password.)

» Set expiration times for passwords. For example, you can specify that passwords expire after 30 days. When a user's password expires, the user must change it. Your users may consider this process a hassle, but it helps to limit the risk of someone swiping a password and then trying to break into your computer system later.

» You can also configure user accounts so that when they change passwords, they can't specify a password that they've used recently. For example, you can specify that the new password can't be identical to any of the user's past three passwords.

» You can also configure security policies so that passwords must include a mixture of uppercase letters, lowercase letters, numerals, and special symbols. Thus, passwords like DIMWIT or DUFUS are out. Passwords like 87dIM@wit or duF39&US are in.

» Use a biometric ID device, like a fingerprint reader, as a way to keep passwords. These devices store your passwords in a secret encoded file, then supply them automatically to whatever programs or websites require them — but only after the device has read your fingerprint. Fingerprint readers, which used to be exotic and expensive, are available for as little as $50.

A password-generator For Dummies

How do you come up with passwords that no one can guess but that you can remember? Most security experts say that the best passwords don't correspond to any words in the English language, but consist of a random sequence of letters, numbers, and special characters. Yet, how in the heck are you supposed to memorize a password like Dks4%DJ2, especially when you have to change it three weeks later to something like 3pQ&X(d8?

Here's a compromise solution that enables you to create passwords that consist of two four-letter words back to back. Take your favorite book (if it's this one, you need to get a life) and turn to any page at random. Find the first four- or five-letter word on the page. Suppose that word is When. Then repeat the process to find another four- or five-letter word; say you pick the word Most the second time. Now combine the words to make your password: WhenMost. I think you agree that WhenMost is easier to remember than 3PQ&X(D8 and is probably just about as hard to guess. I probably wouldn't want the folks at the Los Alamos Nuclear Laboratory using this scheme, but it's good enough for most of us.

Here are some additional thoughts on concocting passwords from your favorite book:

>> If the words end up being the same, pick another word. And pick different words if the combination seems too commonplace, such as WestWind or FootBall.

>> For an interesting variation, insert the page numbers on which you found both words either before or after the words. For example: 135Into376Cat or 87Tree288Wing. The resulting password will be a little harder to remember, but you'll have a password worthy of a Dan Brown novel.

>> To further confuse your friends and enemies, use archaic language: for example, medieval words from Chaucer's *Canterbury Tales.* Chaucer is a great source for passwords because he lived before the days of word processors with spell-checkers. He wrote *seyd* instead of *said, gret* instead of *great,* and *litel* instead of *little.* And he used lots of seven-letter and eight-letter words suitable for passwords, such as *glotenye* (gluttony), *benygne* (benign), and *opynyoun* (opinion). And he got an A in English.

TIP

>> If you do decide to go with passwords such as KdI22UR3xdkL, you can find random password generators on the Internet. Just go to a search engine, such as Google (www.google.com), and search for *password generator.* You can find web pages that generate random passwords based on criteria that you specify, such as how long the password should be, whether it should include letters, numbers, punctuation, uppercase and lowercase letters, and so on.

If you use any of these password schemes and someone breaks into your network, don't blame me. You're the one who's too lazy to memorize D#Sc$h4@bb3xaz5.

TIP

Recent research is suggesting that much of what we've believed about password security for the last 30 or so years may actually be counterproductive. Why? Two reasons:

>> The requirement to change passwords frequently and making them too complicated to memorize simply encourages users to write their passwords down, which makes them easy to steal.

>> A common way that passwords are compromised is by theft of the encrypted form of the password database, which can then be attacked using simple dictionary methods. Even the most complex passwords can be cracked using a dictionary attack if the password is relatively short; the most important factor in making passwords difficult to crack is not complexity but length.

As a result, the National Institute for Standards and Technology (NIST) recommends new guidelines for creating secure passwords:

>> Encourage longer passwords.

>> Drop the complexity requirement. Instead, encourage users to create passwords that they can easily remember. A simple sentence or phrase consisting of ordinary words will suffice, as long as the sentence or phrase is long. For example, "My password is a simple sentence" would make a good password.

>> Drop the requirement to change passwords periodically; it only encourages users to write down their passwords.

Old ways are difficult to change, and it will take a while for these new guidelines to catch on. Personally, I wouldn't drop the requirement to change passwords periodically without also increasing the minimum length to at least 15 characters.

Securing the administrator account

At least one network user must have the authority to use the network without any of the restrictions imposed on other users. This user — the *administrator* — is responsible for setting up the network's security system. To do that, the administrator must be exempt from all security restrictions.

Many networks automatically create an administrator user account when you install the network software. The username and password for this initial administrator are published in the network's documentation and are the same for all networks that use the same NOS. One of the first things that you must do after getting your network up and running is to change the password for this standard administrator account. Otherwise, your elaborate security precautions will be a complete waste of time. Anyone who knows the default administrator username and password can access your system with full administrator rights and privileges, thus bypassing the security restrictions that you so carefully set up.

Don't forget the password for the administrator account! If a network user forgets his password, you can log on as the supervisor and change that user's password. If you forget the administrator's password, though, you're stuck.

Securing the Human Firewall

Security techniques and technology — physical security, user account security, server security, and locking down your servers — are child's play compared with the most difficult job of network security: securing your network's users. All the best-laid security plans are for naught if your users write down their passwords on sticky notes and post them on their computers and click every link that shows up in their email.

The key to securing your network users is to empower your users to realize that they're an important part of your company's cybersecurity plan, and then show them what they can do to become an effective human firewall.

This necessarily involves training, and of course IT training is usually the most dreaded type of training there is. So, do your best to make the training fun and engaging rather than dull and boring.

If training isn't your thing, search the web. You'll find plenty of inexpensive options for online cybersecurity training, ranging from simple and short videos to full-length online courses.

You'll also need to establish a written cybersecurity policy and stick to it. Have a meeting with everyone to go over the security policy to make sure that everyone understands the rules. Also, make sure to have consequences when violations occur.

Here are some suggestions for some basic security rules you can incorporate into your security policy:

>> Never write down your password or give it to someone else.

>> Accounts should not be shared. Never use someone else's account to access a resource that you can't access under your own account. If you need access to some network resource that isn't available to you, you should formally request access under your own account.

>> Likewise, never give your account information to a co-worker so that he or she can access a needed resource. Your co-worker should instead formally request access under his or her own account.

>> Don't install any software or hardware on your computer — especially wireless access devices or modems — without first obtaining permission.

>> Don't enable file and printer sharing on workstations without first getting permission.

>> Never attempt to disable or bypass the network's security features.

Welcome to Cybersecurity

Chapter **2**

Managing Firewalls and Virus Protection

I f your network is connected to the Internet, a whole host of security issues bubble to the surface. You probably connected your network to the Internet so that your network's users could access the Internet. Unfortunately, however, your Internet connection is a two-way street. Not only does it enable your network's users to step outside the bounds of your network to access the Internet, but it also enables others to step in and access your network.

And step in they will. The world is filled with hackers looking for networks like yours to break into. They may do it just for fun, or they may do it to steal your customer's credit card numbers or to coerce your mail server into sending thousands of spam messages on their behalf. Whatever their motive, rest assured that your network will be broken into if you leave it unprotected.

This chapter presents an overview of two basic techniques for securing your network's Internet connection: firewalls and virus protection.

Firewalls

A *firewall* is a security-conscious router that sits between the Internet and your network with a single-minded task: preventing *them* from getting to *us*. The firewall acts as a security guard between the Internet and your local area network (LAN). All network traffic into and out of the LAN must pass through the firewall, which prevents unauthorized access to the network.

WARNING

Some type of firewall is a must-have if your network has a connection to the Internet, whether that connection is broadband (cable modem or digital subscriber line; DSL), T1, or some other high-speed connection. Without it, sooner or later a hacker will discover your unprotected network and tell his friends about it. Within a few hours, your network will be toast.

You can set up a firewall two basic ways. The easiest way is to purchase a *firewall appliance,* which is basically a self-contained router with built-in firewall features. Most firewall appliances include a web-based interface that enables you to connect to the firewall from any computer on your network using a browser. You can then customize the firewall settings to suit your needs.

Alternatively, you can set up a server computer to function as a firewall computer. The server can run just about any network operating system (NOS), but most dedicated firewall systems run Linux.

Whether you use a firewall appliance or a firewall computer, the firewall must be located between your network and the Internet, as shown in Figure 2-1. Here, one end of the firewall is connected to a network hub, which is in turn connected to the other computers on the network. The other end of the firewall is connected to the Internet. As a result, all traffic from the LAN to the Internet and vice versa must travel through the firewall.

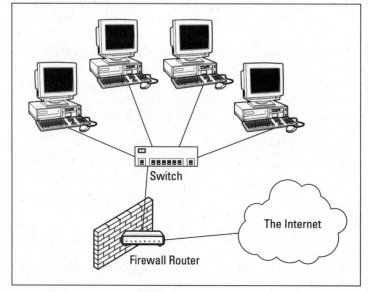

FIGURE 2-1:
Using a firewall appliance.

TECHNICAL STUFF

The term *perimeter* is sometimes used to describe the location of a firewall on your network. In short, a firewall is like a perimeter fence that completely surrounds your property and forces all visitors to enter through the front gate.

The Many Types of Firewalls

Firewalls employ four basic techniques to keep unwelcome visitors out of your network. The following sections describe these basic firewall techniques.

Packet filtering

A *packet-filtering* firewall examines each packet that crosses the firewall and tests the packet according to a set of rules that you set up. If the packet passes the test, it's allowed to pass. If the packet doesn't pass, it's rejected.

Packet filters are the least expensive type of firewall. As a result, packet-filtering firewalls are very common. However, packet filtering has a number of flaws that knowledgeable hackers can exploit. As a result, packet filtering by itself doesn't make for a fully effective firewall.

Packet filters work by inspecting the source and destination IP and port addresses contained in each Transmission Control Protocol/Internet Protocol (TCP/IP) packet. TCP/IP *ports* are numbers assigned to specific services that help to identify for which service each packet is intended. For example, the port number for the HTTP protocol is 80. As a result, any incoming packets headed for an HTTP server will specify port 80 as the destination port.

Port numbers are often specified with a colon following an IP address. For example, the HTTP service on a server whose IP address is 192.168.10.133 would be 192.168.10.133:80.

Literally thousands of established ports are in use. Table 2-1 lists a few of the most popular ports.

The rules that you set up for the packet filter either permit or deny packets that specify certain IP addresses or ports. For example, you may permit packets that are intended for your mail server or your web server and deny all other packets. Or, you may set up a rule that specifically denies packets that are heading for the ports used by NetBIOS. This rule keeps Internet hackers from trying to access NetBIOS server resources, such as files or printers.

TABLE 2-1 **Some Well-Known TCP/IP Ports**

Port	Description
20	File Transfer Protocol (FTP)
21	File Transfer Protocol (FTP)
22	Secure Shell Protocol (SSH)
23	Telnet
25	Simple Mail Transfer Protocol (SMTP)
53	Domain Name Server (DNS)
80	World Wide Web (HyperText Transport Protocol; HTTP)
110	Post Office Protocol (POP3)
119	Network News Transfer Protocol (NNTP)
137	NetBIOS Name Service
138	NetBIOS Datagram Service
139	NetBIOS Session Service
143	Internet Message Access Protocol (IMAP)
161	Simple Network Management Protocol (SNMP)
194	Internet Relay Chat (IRC)
389	Lightweight Directory Access Protocol (LDAP)
396	NetWare over IP
443	HTTP over TLS/SSL (HTTPS)

One of the biggest weaknesses of packet filtering is that it pretty much trusts that the packets themselves are telling the truth when they say who they're from and who they're going to. Hackers exploit this weakness by using a hacking technique called *IP spoofing*, in which they insert fake IP addresses in packets that they send to your network.

Another weakness of packet filtering is that it examines each packet in isolation without considering what packets have gone through the firewall before and what packets may follow. In other words, packet filtering is *stateless*. Rest assured that hackers have figured out how to exploit the stateless nature of packet filtering to get through firewalls.

In spite of these weaknesses, packet filter firewalls have several advantages that explain why they are commonly used:

>> **Efficient:** They hold up each inbound and outbound packet for only a few milliseconds while they look inside the packet to determine the destination and source ports and addresses. After these addresses and ports are determined, the packet filter quickly applies its rules and either sends the packet along or rejects it. In contrast, other firewall techniques have a more noticeable performance overhead.

>> **Almost completely transparent to users:** The only time a user will be aware that a packet-filter firewall is being used is when the firewall rejects packets. Other firewall techniques require that clients and/or servers be specially configured to work with the firewall.

>> **Inexpensive:** Even consumer-grade routers include built-in packet filtering.

Stateful packet inspection (SPI)

Stateful packet inspection (SPI) is a step up in intelligence from simple packet filtering. A firewall with stateful packet inspection looks at packets in groups rather than individually. It keeps track of which packets have passed through the firewall and can detect patterns that indicate unauthorized access. In some cases, the firewall may hold on to packets as they arrive until the firewall gathers enough information to make a decision about whether the packets should be authorized or rejected.

Stateful packet inspection was once found only on expensive, enterprise-level routers. Now, however, SPI firewalls are affordable enough for small- or medium-sized networks to use.

Circuit-level gateway

A *circuit-level gateway* manages connections between clients and servers based on TCP/IP addresses and port numbers. After the connection is established, the gateway doesn't interfere with packets flowing between the systems.

For example, you can use a Telnet circuit-level gateway to allow Telnet connections (port 23) to a particular server and prohibit other types of connections to that server. After the connection is established, the circuit-level gateway allows packets to flow freely over the connection. As a result, the circuit-level gateway can't prevent a Telnet user from running specific programs or using specific commands.

Application gateway

An *application gateway* is a firewall system that is more intelligent than a packet-filtering firewall, stateful packet inspection, or circuit-level gateway firewall. Packet filters treat all TCP/IP packets the same. In contrast, application gateways know the details about the applications that generate the packets that pass through the firewall. For example, a web application gateway is aware of the details of HTTP packets. As a result, it can examine more than just the source and destination addresses and ports to determine whether the packets should be allowed to pass through the firewall.

In addition, application gateways work as proxy servers. Simply put, a *proxy server* is a server that sits between a client computer and a real server. The proxy server intercepts packets that are intended for the real server and processes them. The proxy server can examine the packet and decide to pass it on to the real server, or it can reject the packet. Or, the proxy server may be able to respond to the packet itself without involving the real server at all.

For example, web proxies often store copies of commonly used web pages in a local cache. When a user requests a web page from a remote web server, the proxy server intercepts the request and checks whether it already has a copy of the page in its cache. If so, the web proxy returns the page directly to the user. If not, the proxy passes the request on to the real server.

Application gateways are aware of the details of how various types of TCP/IP servers handle sequences of TCP/IP packets to make more intelligent decisions about whether an incoming packet is legitimate or is part of an attack. As a result, application gateways are more secure than simple packet-filtering firewalls, which can deal with only one packet at a time.

The improved security of application gateways, however, comes at a price. Application gateways are more expensive than packet filters, both in terms of their purchase price and in the cost of configuring and maintaining them. In addition, application gateways slow network performance because they do more detailed checking of packets before allowing them to pass.

The Built-In Windows Firewall

Windows comes with a built-in packet-filtering firewall. If you don't have a separate firewall router, you can use this built-in firewall to provide a basic level of protection. Note, however, that you should rely on the Windows Firewall only as a last resort. If at all possible, use a separate firewall rather than the Windows Firewall to protect your network.

Here are the steps to activate the firewall in Windows:

1. **Choose Start⇨Control Panel.**

   In the Control Panel, click System and Security.

2. **On the System and Security page, click Windows Firewall.**

3. **On the Windows Firewall page, click Turn Windows Firewall On or Off.**

   The page shown in Figure 2-2 appears.

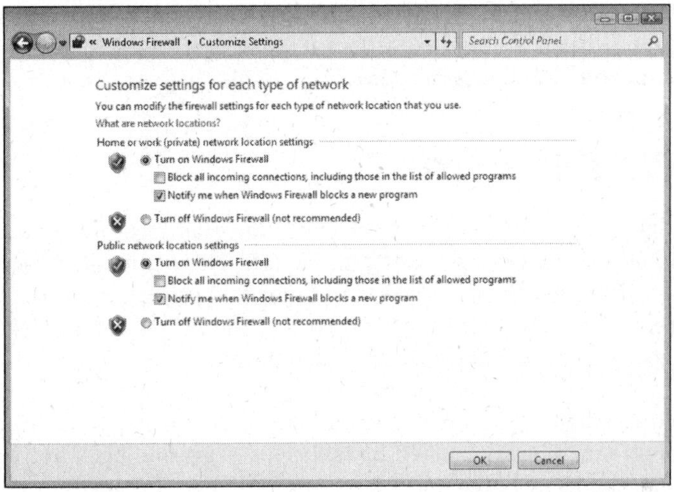

FIGURE 2-2:
Activating the
firewall.

4. **Select the Turn On Windows Firewall radio button.**

   Note that there are two such buttons: one for home and work (private)
   networks and one for public networks. If you have a separate router for your
   work or home network, you can leave the home and work (private) network
   firewall turned off. But always turn on the firewall for public networks.

5. **Click OK.**

   The firewall is enabled.

WARNING

Do *not* enable Windows Firewall if you're using a separate firewall router to protect your network. Because the other computers on the network are connected
directly to the router and not to your computer, Windows Firewall won't protect
the rest of the network. Additionally, as an unwanted side effect, the rest of the
network will lose the ability to access your computer.

Windows Firewall is turned on by default. If your computer is already behind a firewall, you should disable Windows Firewall. (In some cases, the network's group policy settings may prevent you from disabling Windows Firewall. In that case, you must change the group policy so that Windows Firewall can be disabled. For more information about group policy, see Book 8, Chapter 6.)

Virus Protection

Viruses are one of the most misunderstood computer phenomena around these days. What is a virus? How does it work? How does it spread from computer to computer? I'm glad you asked.

What is a virus?

Make no mistake — viruses are real. Now that most people are connected to the Internet, viruses have really taken off. Every computer user is susceptible to attacks by computer viruses, and using a network increases your vulnerability because it exposes all network users to the risk of being infected by a virus that lands on any one network user's computer.

Viruses don't just spontaneously appear out of nowhere. Viruses are computer programs that are created by malicious programmers who've lost a few screws and should be locked up.

What makes a virus a virus is its capability to make copies of itself that can be spread to other computers. These copies, in turn, make still more copies that spread to still more computers, and so on, ad nauseam.

Then, the virus patiently waits until something triggers it — perhaps when you type a particular command or press a certain key, when a certain date arrives, or when the virus creator sends the virus a message. What the virus does when it strikes also depends on what the virus creator wants the virus to do. Some viruses harmlessly display a "gotcha" message. Some send an email to everyone it finds in your address book. Some wipe out all the data on your hard drive. Ouch.

Many years ago, in the prehistoric days of computers, viruses were passed from one computer to another by latching themselves onto floppy disks. Whenever you borrowed a floppy disk from a buddy, you ran the risk of infecting your own computer with a virus that may have stowed away on the disk.

Virus programmers have discovered that email is a very efficient method to spread their viruses. Typically, a virus masquerades as a useful or interesting email attachment, such as instructions on how to make $1,000,000 in your spare time, pictures of naked celebrities, or a Valentine's Day greeting from your long-lost sweetheart. When a curious but unsuspecting user opens the attachment, the virus springs to life, copying itself onto the user's computer — sometimes sending copies of itself to all the names in the user's address book.

After the virus works its way onto a networked computer, the virus can then figure out how to spread itself to other computers on the network. It can also spread itself by burrowing into a flash drive so that when the flash drive is inserted into another computer, that computer may become infected as well.

Here are some more tidbits about protecting your network from virus attacks:

>> The term *virus* is often used to refer not only to true virus programs (which are able to replicate themselves) but also to any other type of program that's designed to harm your computer. These programs include so-called *Trojan horse* programs that usually look like games but are, in reality, ransomware.

>> A *worm* is similar to a virus, but it doesn't actually infect other files. Instead, it just copies itself onto other computers on a network. After a worm has copied itself onto your computer, there's no telling what it may do there. For example, a worm may scan your hard drive for interesting information, such as passwords or credit card numbers, and then email them to the worm's author.

>> Computer virus experts have identified several thousand "strains" of viruses. Many of them have colorful names, such as the I Love You virus, the Stoned virus, and the Michelangelo virus.

>> Antivirus programs can recognize known viruses and remove them from your system, and they can spot the telltale signs of unknown viruses. Unfortunately, the idiots who write viruses aren't idiots (in the intellectual sense), so they're constantly developing new techniques to evade detection by antivirus programs. New viruses are frequently discovered, and antivirus programs are periodically updated to detect and remove them.

Antivirus programs

The best way to protect your network from virus infection is to use an antivirus program. These programs have a catalog of several thousand known viruses that they can detect and remove. In addition, they can spot the types of changes that viruses typically make to your computer's files, thus decreasing the likelihood that some previously unknown virus will go undetected.

Windows comes with a built-in antivirus program called Windows Defender. Although it is serviceable, better alternatives are available. Popular options include Avast (www.avast.com), which is free and provides significantly better protection than Windows, Symantec Security by Symantec, and VirusScan Enterprise by McAfee.

REMEMBER

The people who make antivirus programs have their fingers on the pulse of the virus world and frequently release updates to their software to combat the latest viruses. Because virus writers are constantly developing new viruses, your antivirus software is next to worthless unless you keep it up to date by downloading the latest updates.

Here are several approaches to deploying antivirus protection on your network:

» **Install antivirus software on each network user's computer.** This technique would be the most effective if you could count on all your users to keep their antivirus software up to date. Because that's an unlikely proposition, you may want to adopt a more reliable approach to virus protection.

» **Managed antivirus services place antivirus client software on each client computer in your network.** Then, an antivirus server automatically updates the clients on a regular basis to make sure that they're kept up to date.

» **Server-based antivirus software protects your network servers from viruses.** For example, you can install antivirus software on your mail server to scan all incoming mail for viruses and remove them before your network users ever see them.

» **Some firewall appliances include antivirus enforcement checks that don't allow your users to access the Internet unless their antivirus software is up to date.** This type of firewall provides the best antivirus protection available.

Safe computing

Besides using an antivirus program, you can take a few additional precautions to ensure virus-free computing. If you haven't talked to your kids about these safe-computing practices, you had better do so soon.

» **Regularly back up your data.** If a virus hits you, and your antivirus software can't repair the damage, you may need the backup to recover your data. Make sure that you restore from a backup that was created before you were infected by the virus!

» **If you buy software from a store and discover that the seal has been broken on the disc package, take the software back.** Don't try to install it on your computer. You don't hear about tainted software as often as you hear about tainted beef, but if you buy software that's been opened, it may well be laced with a virus infection.

» **Use your antivirus software to scan your disk for virus infection after your computer has been to a repair shop or worked on by a consultant.** These guys don't intend harm, but they occasionally spread viruses accidentally, simply because they work on so many strange computers.

» **Don't open email attachments from people you don't know or attachments you weren't expecting.**

» **Use your antivirus software to scan any floppy disk or CD that doesn't belong to you before you access any of its files.**

Using Windows Action Center

Windows Action Center, which comes with Windows, monitors the status of security-related issues on your computer. You can summon the Windows Action Center by opening the Control Panel, clicking System and Security, and then clicking Action Center; see Figure 2-3.

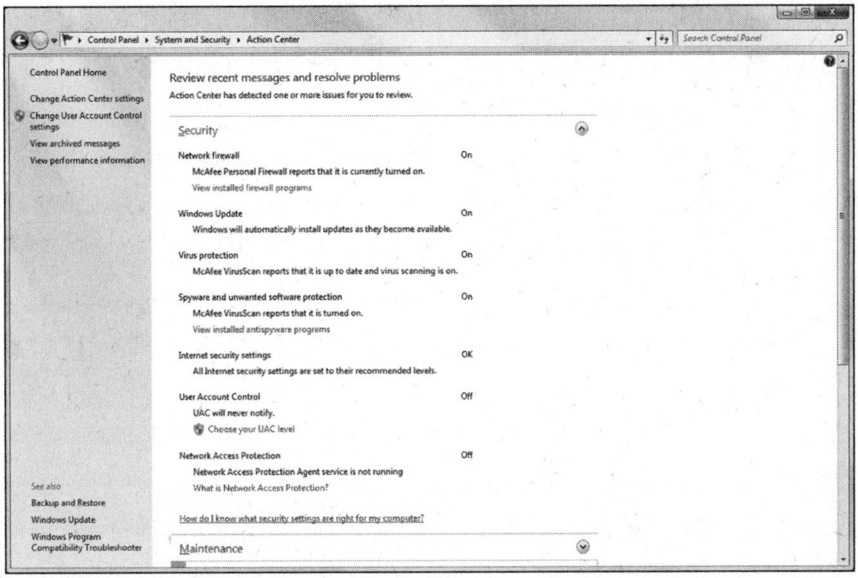

FIGURE 2-3:
The Windows
Action Center.

The Windows Action Center alerts you to issues with your computer's security status as well as reminds you of maintenance that should be done, such as installing operating system updates.

Here are additional points to ponder concerning the Windows Action Center:

» A flag icon appears in the notification area on the right end of the Windows taskbar to alert you to items you should attend to in the Windows Action Center.

» Earlier versions of Windows included a similar feature called the Windows Security Center, which you can access from the Control Panel.

Chapter **3**

Managing Spam

Spam, spam, spam, spam, spam, spam, and spam.

So goes the famous Monty Python sketch, in which a woman at a restaurant just wants to order something that doesn't have spam in it.

That pretty much sums up the situations with most people's inboxes these days. The legitimate email gets lost among the spam emails. Wouldn't you like to look at an inbox that wasn't filled with spam?

Nobody likes spam. You don't like it, and your users don't like it either. And believe me, they'll let you know if they're getting too much spam in their inboxes. They'll hold you personally responsible for every email with an offensive subject line, every email that tries to sell them stuff they aren't interested in, and every email that attempts to get them to provide their bank account password or credit card number.

As a network administrator, part of your job is protecting your users from spam. The holy grail of antispam is a solution that never allows a single piece of spam into anyone's inbox, but at the same time never mistakenly identifies a single legitimate piece of email as spam.

Good luck. This level of perfection doesn't exist. The best thing you can hope for is to find the right balance: a happy medium that lets only a small amount of actual spam through to users' inboxes and only occasionally misidentifies legitimate email as spam.

In this chapter, I explain what you need to know to find and deploy such a solution. I fill you in on the various kinds of spam, where spam comes from, how spammers get people's email addresses, and — most important — the many effective techniques you can employ to keep spam out of your users' inboxes.

Defining Spam

The most basic definition of *spam* is any email that arrives in your inbox that you didn't ask for. Spam is unsolicited email. It's email that isn't welcome, email that you aren't expecting. It's email from people you don't know or haven't heard of, usually trying to sell you something you aren't interested in or can't possibly need, and often trying to trick you into parting with either your money or your valuable personal information, or both.

One of the defining characteristics of spam is that it's sent out in bulk, often to thousands or even millions of recipients all at once. Most spam is not particularly well targeted. Instead of taking the time to figure out who might be interested in a particular product, spammers find it easier and cheaper to pitch their products to every email address they can get their hands on.

Spam is often compared to junk mail of the physical kind — the brochures, catalogs, and other solicitations that show up in your mailbox every day. In fact, spam is often called "junk email."

However, there is a crucial difference between physical junk mail and junk email. With physical junk mail, the sender must pay the cost of postage. As a result, even though junk mail can be annoying, most junk mail is carefully targeted. Junk mailers don't want to waste their money on postage to send mail to people who aren't interested in what they have to sell. They carefully measure response rates to ensure that their mailings are profitable.

In contrast, it costs very little money to send huge numbers of emails. To be sure, spam is expensive. But the bulk of the cost of spam is borne by the recipients, who must spend time and money to receive, store, and manage the unwelcome email, and by the network providers, who must build out their networks with ever greater capacity and speed to accommodate the huge volumes of spam emails that their networks must carry.

Estimates vary, but most studies indicate that as much as three-quarters of all the email sent via the Internet is spam. At the time that I wrote this, there were indications that spam was actually becoming less common, accounting for closer to half of all the emails sent. But some organizations report that 80 percent or 90 percent of the email that they receive is actually spam.

WARNING

One thing is sure: Spam is not just annoying; it's dangerous. Besides filling up your users' inboxes with unwanted email, spam emails often carry attachments that harbor viruses or other malware, or entice your users into clicking links that take them to websites that can infect your network. If your network is ever taken down by a virus, there's a very good chance that the virus entered your network by way of spam.

So, understanding spam and taking precautions to block it are an important part of any network administrator's job.

Sampling the Many Flavors of Spam

Spam is unsolicited and/or unwanted email. That's a pretty broad definition, but there are several distinct categories of spam:

>> **Advertisements:** Most spam is advertising from companies you've never heard of, trying to sell you products you aren't interested in. The most common type of product pitched by spam emails are pharmaceuticals, but spam also commonly promotes food supplements, knock-offs of expensive products such as watches or purses, weight-loss products, and so on.

>> **Phishing emails:** Among the most annoying and dangerous types of spam are phishing emails, which try to get you to divulge private information such as credit card account numbers or passwords. Phishing email masquerades as legitimate email from a bank or other well-known institution and often includes a link to a phony website that resembles the institution's actual website. For example, you might get an email informing you that there was a suspicious charge on your credit card, with a link you can click to log in to verify that the charge is legitimate. When you click the link, you're taken to a page that looks exactly like your credit card company's actual page. However, the phony page exists solely to harvest your username and password.

Another type of phishing email includes an attachment that claims to be an unpaid invoice or a failed parcel delivery notice. The attachment contains a Trojan that attempts to infect your computer with malware.

>> **Scams:** The most common type of email scam is called an *advance-fee scam,* in which you're promised a large reward or prize in the future for advancing a relatively small amount of money now in the form of a wire transfer or money order. You may have heard of or actually received the classic scam known as

the Nigerian prince scam, in which a person claiming to be a Nigerian prince needs your help to transfer a huge amount of money (for example, $40 million) but can't use an African bank account. The prince needs to use your personal bank account, and will pay you a percentage — perhaps $1 million — for your help. But you must first open a Nigerian account with a minimum balance — of perhaps $1,000 or $10,000 — to facilitate the transfer. All you have to do is wire the money, and they'll take care of the rest.

There are many variations of this story, but they all have one thing in common: They're too good to be true. They offer you a huge amount of money later, in exchange for a relatively small amount of money now.

>> **Ads for pornographic websites:** Such websites are notorious for being top sources of viruses and other malware.

>> **Get-rich-quick schemes:** Pyramid schemes, multilevel marketing schemes, phony real-estate schemes, you name it — they're all in a category of spam that promises to make you rich.

>> **Backscatter:** Backscatter is a particularly annoying phenomenon in which your inbox becomes flooded with dozens or perhaps hundreds of nondelivery reports (NDRs), indicating that an email that you allegedly sent didn't arrive. When you examine the NDRs, you can easily determine that you never sent an email to the intended recipient. What's actually going on here is that your email address has been used as the From address in a spam campaign, and you're receiving the NDRs from the mail servers of those spam emails that were not deliverable.

TIP

Though technically not spam, many users consider advertisements and newsletters from companies they *have* dealt with in the past to be a form of spam. An important element of the definition of spam is the word *unsolicited.* When you register at a company's website, you're effectively inviting that company to send you email.

Using Antispam Software

The most effective way to eliminate spam from your users' inboxes is to use antispam software. *Antispam software* examines all incoming email with the intent of distinguishing between spam and legitimate email. Depending on how the software is configured, email identified as spam is deleted, moved to a separate location, or simply marked as possible spam by adding a tag to the email's subject line.

Antispam software works by analyzing every piece of incoming email using sophisticated techniques that determine the likelihood that the email is, indeed, spam. When a certain threshold of probability is reached, the email is deemed to be spam and deleted, moved, or tagged. If the threshold is not reached, the email is passed on to the user as usual.

TIP

Microsoft Exchange mailboxes include a Junk folder that is often the ultimate destination of email identified as spam. You should always check your Junk folder whenever you can't find an email you're expecting.

Not all antispam programs use the Junk folder. Some programs store spam email outside of the user's mailbox, in a separate location on the network or perhaps on the cloud. These programs usually deliver a daily email (often called a *digest*) that lists the emails that were identified as spam. You should review this email whenever you can't find an email you're expecting.

Determining whether an email is spam is not an exact science. As a result, *false positives* (in which a legitimate piece of email is mistakenly identified as spam) and *false negatives* (in which a spam email is not detected as spam and makes it into the user's inbox) are not uncommon. False positives can result in your users not receiving emails they're expecting. False negatives can leave users scratching their heads wondering how in the world the spam filter didn't catch the spam. Sometimes email that to a human is obviously spam slips right by the antispam software.

The challenge of any antispam tool is finding the right balance of not too many false positives and not too many false negatives. Most antispam tools let you tune the filters to some degree, setting them to be more or less permissive — that is, erring on the side of more false negatives or more false positives. The stricter the filters are set, the more false positives you'll have. Loosening the filters will result in more false negatives.

TIP

The possibility of false negatives is one of the main reasons that it's rarely a good idea to configure an antispam program to simply delete spam. Most programs can be configured to delete only the most obvious spam emails — the ones that can be identified as spam with 100 percent certainty. Email that is probably spam but with less than 100 percent certainty should be marked as spam but not deleted.

Understanding Spam Filters

Antispam programs use a variety of different techniques to determine the probability of a given piece of email being spam. These techniques are employed by *filters*, which examine each piece of email; each filter uses a specific technique.

Here are some of the most commonly used filter types:

>> **Keyword checking:** The most obvious way to identify spam is to look for certain words that appear either in the email's subject line or in the email body. For example, a keyword checking filter might look for profanity, sexual terms, and other words or phrases such as "Get rich quick!"

Although this is the most obvious way to identify spam, it's also the least reliable. Spammers learned long ago to leave common words out of their spams to avoid these types of filters. Often they intentionally misspell words or substitute numbers or symbols for letters, such as the numeral 0 for the letter *o*, or the symbol ! for the letter *l*.

The biggest problem with keyword checking is that it often leads to false positives. Friends and relatives might intentionally or inadvertently use any of the banned words in their emails. Sometimes, the banned words appear in the middle of otherwise completely innocent words. For example, if you list *Cialis* as a keyword that you want blocked, you'll also block the words spe*cialis*t or so*cialis*t.

For these reasons, keyword filters are typically used only for the most obvious and offensive words and phrases, if they're used at all.

» **Bayesian analysis:** One of the most trusted forms of spam filtering is *Bayesian analysis,* which works by assuming that certain words occur more often in spam email than in other email. This sounds a lot like keyword checking, but Bayesian analysis is much more sophisticated than simple keyword checking. The Bayesian filter maintains an index of words that are likely to be encountered in spam emails. Each word in this index has a probability associated with it, and each word in the email being analyzed is looked up in this index to determine the overall probability of the email being spam. If the probability calculated from this index exceeds a certain threshold, the email is marked as spam.

Here's where the magic of Bayesian analysis comes in: The index is self-learning, based on the user's actual email. Whenever the filter misidentifies an email, the user trains the filter by telling the filter that it was incorrect. The user typically does this by clicking a button labeled "This is spam" or "This is not spam." When the user clicks either of these buttons, the filter adjusts the probability associated with the words that led it to make the wrong conclusion. So, when the filter encounters a similar email in the future, it's more likely to make the correct determination.

» **Sender Policy Framework (SPF):** Surprisingly, SMTP (the Internet email protocol) has very poor built-in security. In particular, any email server can easily send email that claims to be from any domain. This makes it easy to forge the From address in an email. SPF lets you designate via DNS which specific email servers are allowed to send email from your domain. An antispam SPF filter works by looking up the sending email server against the SPF records in the DNS of the domain specified by the email's From address.

» **Blacklisting:** Another trusted form of spam filtering is a *blacklist* (also known as *blocklist*), which uses a list of known spammers to block email from sources that aren't trustworthy. There are two types of blacklists: private and public. A private blacklist is a list that you set up yourself to designate sources you don't want to accept email from. A public blacklist is a list that is maintained by a company or organization and is available for others to use.

Note that simply blacklisting a sender email address isn't much help. That's because the sender email address is easy to forge. Instead, blacklists track individual email servers that are known to be sources of spam.

WARNING

Unfortunately, spammers don't usually set up their own servers to send out their spam. Instead, they hijack other servers to do their dirty work. Legitimate email servers can be hijacked by spammers and, thus, become spam sources, often without the knowledge of their owners. This raises the unfortunate possibility that your own email server might be taken over by a spammer, and you might find your email server listed on a public blacklist. If that happens, you won't be able to send email to anyone who uses that blacklist until you have corrected the problem that allowed your server to be hijacked and petitioned the blacklist owners to have your server removed.

» **Whitelisting:** One of the most important elements of any antispam solution is a *whitelist,* which ensures that email from known senders will never be blocked. Typically, the whitelist consists of a list of email addresses that you trust. When the antispam tool has confirmed that the From address in the email has not been forged (perhaps by use of an SPF filter), the whitelist filters looks up the address in the whitelist database. If the address is found, the email is immediately marked as legitimate email, and no other filters are applied. So, if the email is marked as legitimate by the whitelist filter, the other filters are not used.

TIP

Most whitelist filters will let you whitelist entire domains, as well as individual email addresses. You most certainly do *not* want to whitelist domains of large email providers such as gmail.com or comcast.net. But you should whitelist the domains of all your business partners and clients to ensure that emails from new employees at these key companies are never marked as spam.

Some antispam programs automatically add the recipient addresses of all outgoing emails to the whitelist. In other words, anyone that you send an email to is automatically added to the whitelist. Over time, this feature can drastically reduce the occurrence of false positives.

TIP

Use the whitelist to preemptively allow important email that you're expecting from new customers, vendors, or service providers. For example, if you switch payroll providers, find out in advance what email addresses the new provider will be using so that your payroll staff doesn't miss important emails.

» **Graylisting:** Graylisting is an effective antispam technique that exploits the fact that if a legitimate email server can't successfully deliver an email on its first attempt, the server will try again later, typically in 30 minutes. A graylist filter automatically rejects the first attempt to deliver a message but keeps track of the details of the message it rejected. Then, when the same message is received a second time, the graylist filter accepts the message and makes note of the sender so that future messages from the sender are accepted on the first attempt.

Graylisting works because spammers usually configure their servers to not bother with the second attempt. Thus, the graylist filter knows that if a second copy of the email arrives after the initial rejection, the mail is probably legitimate.

The drawback of graylisting is that the first time you receive an email from a new sender, the email will be delayed. Many users find that the benefit of graylisting is not worth the cost of the delayed emails, so they simply disable the graylist filter.

Looking at Three Types of Antispam Software

The many different antispam programs that are available fall into three broad categories: on-premises, appliance, and cloud based (hosted). The following sections describe the relative merits of each of these approaches to providing antispam for your organization.

On-premises antispam

An on-premises antispam program runs on a server on your network and interacts directly with your email server. Email that arrives at your server is passed over to the antispam program, which evaluates the email to determine whether it's spam or legitimate mail. The antispam software uses a variety of techniques to identify spam and can usually be configured for optimal performance. Email that is identified as legitimate is handed back to the email server for normal processing. Depending on how you configure the software, email that is identified as spam may be sent to your users' Junk folders or stored in some other location.

In smaller organizations, the antispam software can run on the same server as the email server (for example, Microsoft Exchange). In larger organizations, the antispam software can be configured to run on its own dedicated server, separate from the mail server(s).

Here are some of the advantages of using an on-premises antispam product:

» **You have complete control over the configuration and operation of the software.** Most on-premises antispam software is highly configurable, often providing a dozen or more distinct filtering methods, which you can customize in many different ways. (For more information, see the section "Understanding Spam Filters," earlier in this chapter.)

» **On-premises antispam software is usually tightly integrated not only with Microsoft Exchange but also with Microsoft Outlook.** Spam email typically appears in the users' Junk folders, and the software often provides an Outlook add-in that makes it easy for users to mark incorrectly identified email.

» **On-premises software is relatively inexpensive.** Typically, you pay an upfront fee to purchase the license, as well as an annual maintenance fee to receive regular updates not only to the software but also to the spam filters.

Here are the main disadvantages of on-premises antispam software:

» **You're responsible for installing, patching, configuring, updating, and otherwise maintaining the software.**

» **Because the relationship between the email server and the antispam software is complicated, on-premises antispam software periodically malfunctions.** Such a malfunction usually halts mail flow throughout your organization. It then becomes your responsibility to correct the problem so that mail begins flowing again. (This usually happens just at the moment when your boss is expecting an important email, and you find yourself diagnosing and fixing the problem while your boss watches over your shoulder.)

» **On-premises antispam software increases the workload on your servers, requiring additional resources in the form of processor time, RAM, disk storage, and network bandwidth.**

Antispam appliances

An *antispam appliance* is essentially an on-premises server in a dedicated box that you install at your location. The appliance is usually a self-contained Linux-based computer running antispam software that is pre-installed on the appliance. This makes the appliance essentially plug-and-play; you just set it up, connect it to your network, turn it on, and configure it using a simple web-based interface. When the appliance is up and running, it can provide many, if not all, of the features of on-premises antispam software.

Here are some of the main advantages of using an antispam appliance:

» **Because the appliance includes its own hardware and pre-installed operating system, you don't have to worry about purchasing hardware separately, installing an operating system, installing software, or any of the other tasks associated with setting up a server.**

» **After it's set up, an appliance will pretty much take care of itself.** You'll need to check on it once in a while, but appliances are designed to be self-sufficient.

>> **The appliance may provide other security features, such as antivirus and firewall protection.** Thus, a single appliance can handle many of your network's security and protection needs.

Using an antispam appliance is not without its disadvantages:

>> **Eventually, you'll outgrow the appliance.** For example, if the number of users on your network doubles, you may run out of disk space.

>> **If the appliance fails, you may have trouble getting it back up and running.** When a normal Windows server fails, you can usually troubleshoot the problem and get the server back up and running. Because of the self-contained nature of an appliance, troubleshooting it can be difficult when it's nonresponsive.

Cloud-based antispam services

A cloud-based antispam service (also called *hosted antispam*) is an Internet-based service that filters your email before it ever arrives at your mail server. When you use hosted antispam, you reconfigure your public DNS so that your mail server (the MX record) points to the cloud-based antispam server rather than to your mail server. That way, all email sent to your organization is first processed by the servers at the antispam service before it ever arrives at your mail server. Only those emails that are deemed to be legitimate are forwarded to your mail server; spam emails are stored in the cloud, where they can be reviewed and retrieved by your users if necessary.

Typically, you pay for hosted antispam based on how many users you have. For example, you might pay a monthly fee of $2 per user. As your organization grows, you simply purchase additional subscriptions.

Here are some of the main advantages of using cloud-based antispam:

>> **You get to skip the hassle of installing and configuring software, integrating the software with Exchange, maintaining and patching the software, and all the other chores associated with hosting your own server on your own premises.** Your monthly subscription charges cover the cost of someone else doing all that work.

>> **Because you don't have to buy software or hardware, there is no initial investment. You simply subscribe to the service and pay the monthly service charges.** (As an added bonus, if you're dissatisfied with the service, you can easily move to a different one. Switching to a different antispam appliance or on-premises solution is a much more complicated and expensive affair.)

>> **A cloud-based antispam solution scales easily with your organization. If you double the number of users, you simply pay twice as much per month.** You don't have to worry about running out of disk space, RAM, clock cycles, or network bandwidth.

>> **Cloud-based antispam takes a huge load off your network and your mail server.** Because someone else filters your spam for you, spam never enters your network. In most organizations, email is one of the most taxing applications running on the network. Using cloud-based antispam can easily cut incoming network traffic in half; in some cases, it might cut traffic by as much as 90 percent.

As you would expect, there are drawbacks to using cloud-based antispam:

>> **You give up some control.** Cloud-based services usually have fewer configuration options than on-premises software. For example, you'll probably have fewer options for customizing the spam filters.

>> **If the service goes down, so does your incoming email.** You won't be able to do anything about it except call technical support. And you can count on getting a busy signal, because when the service goes down, it isn't just you that's affected; it's all its customers. (Of course, this gives such services plenty of motivation to ensure that they fix the problem right away.)

Minimizing Spam

TIP

No antispam program is perfect, so you need to understand and expect that a certain amount of spam will get through to your inbox. Here are some tips that you (and your users) should keep in mind to minimize the amount of spam that gets through undetected:

>> **Never trust email that requests your password or credit card.** A bank will *never* send you an email notifying you of a potential problem and containing a link to its online portal's login page. Nor will a credit card company ever send you an email alerting you to potential fraud and containing a link to a page that requests your credit card number to verify the transaction. Such emails may look very convincing, but you can rest assured they're fraudulent.

If you're in doubt, do *not* click the link. Instead, open a browser window and navigate to the address you know for a fact to be the legitimate login page for your bank or credit card company's web portal.

>> **Never open attachments in spam.** Attachments in a spam email almost certainly contain malware. Often, the malware in a spam email harvests all the contacts from your computer and sends them to the spammer, or hijacks your computer so the spammer can use it to send spam email.

>> **Do not reply to spam.** If you reply to spam email, you merely confirm to the spammers that they've found a legitimate email address. You'll get even more spam.

>> **Use your antispam program's "This is spam" feature.** If your antispam program has a "This is spam" or similar button, be sure to use it. Doing so alerts the antispam program that it has missed a spam message, which helps improve the filters the antispam program uses to detect spam.

>> **Unsubscribe from legitimate emails.** Much of what many users consider to be spam is actually mail from legitimate organizations. If the spam is from a reputable organization, it probably isn't really spam; you probably at one time signed up to receive emails from the organization. Click the unsubscribe link on these types of emails to remove yourself from the mailing list.

WARNING

Spammers often include an unsubscribe link on their spam emails. If the email is actually spam, clicking the unsubscribe link is akin to replying to the spam — it simply confirms to the spammers that they've found a legitimate email address, and you'll just get more spam. Worse yet, the link may take you to a malicious website that will attempt to install malware on your computer. So, before you click the unsubscribe link, make sure that the email is indeed from a legitimate sender.

>> **Protect your email address.** Be careful who you give your email address to, especially when you fill out forms online. Make sure you give your email address only to trusted websites. And read the fine print when you sign up for an account — you'll often find check boxes that allow you to opt out of mailings such as newsletters or announcements about product updates and so on.

>> **Use an alternate email address.** One useful technique to manage the amount of spam you get is to set up a free email account with a provider such as Gmail. Then use this email account for websites that require an email address for registration when you don't want to use your real email address. You can delete or change the alternate email address if it becomes the target of spam.

>> **Don't publish your email address.** If you have a personal website or are on social media, don't publish your email address there. Spammers use scanning software that trolls the Internet looking for email addresses.

Chapter **4**

Managing Backups

I f you're the hapless IT manager, the safety of the data on your network is your responsibility. In fact, it's your primary responsibility. You get paid to lie awake at night worrying about your data. Will it be there tomorrow? If it's not, can you get it back? And — most important — if you can't get it back, will you have a job tomorrow?

This chapter covers the ins and outs of being a good, responsible, trustworthy network manager. No one gives out merit badges for this stuff, but someone should.

Backing Up Your Data

Having data backed up is the cornerstone of any disaster recovery plan. Without backups, a simple hard drive failure can set your company back days or even weeks while it tries to reconstruct lost data. In fact, without backups, your company's very existence is in jeopardy.

REMEMBER

The main goal of a backup is simple: Keep a spare copy of your network's critical data so that no matter what happens, you never lose more than one day's work. The stock market may crash, hanging chads may factor into another presidential election, and George Lucas may decide to make a pre-prequel. When you stay on top of your backups, though, you'll never lose more than one day's work.

The way to do this, naturally, is to make sure that data is backed up on a daily basis. For many networks, you can back up all the network hard drives every night. And even if full nightly backups aren't possible, you can still use techniques that can ensure that every file on the network has a backup copy that's no more than one day old.

Where to Back Up Your Data

If you plan on backing up the data on your network server's hard drives, you obviously need some type of media on which to back up the data. You could copy the data onto CDs, but a 500GB hard drive would need more than 750 CDs for a full backup. That's a few more discs than most people want to keep in the closet. You could use DVDs, but you'll still need about a dozen of them, as well as an hour or so to fill each one. Sigh. That means devoting a Saturday to creating your backup.

TIP

Because of the limitations of CDs and DVDs, most network administrators back up network data to another type of storage device. The three most common options are described in this list:

>> **Tape:** Magnetic tape is the oldest storage medium for backups and is still one of the most widely used. One big advantage of tape backups is that tape cartridges are small and can thus be easily transported to an off-site location.

>> **Network Attached Storage (NAS):** A *Network Attached Storage* device connects directly to your network. NAS devices are often used as backup devices because they're inexpensive. In addition, because they're relatively small and easy to remove, like tape, they can be transported off-site.

>> **Cloud backup:** An increasingly popular option is to use a third-party service to back up data to a remote location via the Internet. Cloud backup has the advantage of already being off-site.

Backing Up to Tape

One of the benefits of tape backup is that you can run it unattended. In fact, you can schedule a tape backup to run automatically during off-hours when no one is using the network. For unattended backups to work, though, you must ensure that you have enough tape capacity to back up your entire network server's hard drive without having to manually switch tapes. If your network server has only 100GB of data, you can easily back it up onto a single tape. If you have 1,000GB of data, however, invest in a tape drive that features a magazine changer that can hold several tapes and automatically cycle them in and out of the drive. That way, you can run your backups unattended.

You can choose from several distinct types of tape backup systems:

>> **Travan drives:** A popular style of tape backup for small servers is a Travan drive, which comes in a variety of models with tape capacities ranging from 20GB to 40GB. You can purchase a 20GB drive for less than $200.

>> **DAT, DLT, and LTO units:** For larger networks, you can get tape backup units that offer higher capacity and faster backup speed than Travan drives — for more money, of course. Digital Audio Tape (DAT) units can back up as much as 160GB on a single tape, and DLT (Digital Linear Tape) drives can store up to 800GB on one tape. The current generation of Linear Tape Open (LTO) drives can store 6TB on a single tape. DAT, DLT, and LTO drives can cost $1,000 or more, depending on the capacity.

>> **Robotic units:** If you're really up the backup creek, with dozens of terabytes to back up, you can get robotic tape backup units that automatically fetch and load tape cartridges from a library. That way, you can do complete backups without having to load tapes manually. As you can likely guess, these units aren't inexpensive: Small ones, which have a library of about eight tapes and a total backup capacity of more than 48TB, start at about $4,000.

Backup Software

All versions of Windows come with a built-in backup program. In addition, most tape drives come with backup programs that are often faster or more flexible than the standard Windows backup.

You can also purchase sophisticated backup programs that are specially designed for networks that have multiple servers with data that must be backed up. For a basic Windows file server, you can use the backup program that comes with Windows Server. Server versions of Windows come with a decent backup program that can run scheduled, unattended tape backups.

Backup programs do more than just copy data from your hard drive to tape. Backup programs use special compression techniques to squeeze your data so that you can cram more data onto fewer tapes. Compression factors of 2:1 are common, so you can usually squeeze 100GB of data onto a tape that would hold only 50GB of data without compression. (Tape drive manufacturers tend to state the capacity of their drives by using compressed data, assuming a 2:1 compression ratio. Thus, a 200GB tape has an uncompressed capacity of 100GB.)

WARNING

Whether you achieve a compression factor of 2:1 depends on the nature of the data you're backing up:

>> **Documents:** If your network is used primarily for Microsoft Office applications and is filled with Word and Excel documents, you'll probably get better than 2:1 compression.

>> **Graphics:** If your network data consists primarily of graphic image files, you probably won't get much compression. Most graphic image file formats are already compressed, so they can't be compressed much more by the backup software's compression methods.

Backup programs also help you keep track of which data has been backed up and which hasn't. They also offer options, such as incremental or differential backups, that can streamline the backup process, as I describe in the next section.

REMEMBER

If your network has more than one server, invest in good backup software. One popular choice is Baracuda Backup, made by BarracudaWare (www.barracudaware. com). Besides being able to handle multiple servers, one of the main advantages of backup software (such as Yosemite Backup) is that it can properly back up Microsoft Exchange server data.

Types of Backups

You can perform five different types of backups. Many backup schemes rely on full daily backups, but for some networks, using a scheme that relies on two or more of these backup types is more practical.

The differences among the five types of backups involve a little technical detail known as the archive bit. The *archive bit* indicates whether a file has been modified since it was backed up. The archive bit is a little flag that's stored along with the filename, creation date, and other directory information. Any time a program modifies a file, the archive bit is set to the On position. That way, backup programs know that the file has been modified and needs to be backed up.

The differences among the various types of backups center on whether they use the archive bit to determine which files to back up, as well as whether they flip the archive bit to the Off position after they back up a file. Table 4-1 summarizes these differences, which I explain in the following sections.

TABLE 4-1

How Backup Types Use the Archive Bit

Backup Type	Selects Files Based on Archive Bit?	Resets Archive Bits After Backing Up?
Normal	No	Yes
Copy	No	No
Daily	No*	No
Incremental	Yes	Yes
Differential	Yes	No

* Selects files based on the Last Modified date.

TIP

Backup programs allow you to select any combination of drives and folders to back up. As a result, you can customize the file selection for a backup operation to suit your needs. For example, you can set up one backup plan that backs up all a server's shared folders and drives, plus its mail server stores, but then leaves out folders that rarely change, such as the operating system folders or installed program folders. You can then back up those folders on a less-regular basis. The drives and folders that you select for a backup operation are collectively called the *backup selection.*

The archive bit would have made a good Abbott and Costello routine. ("All right, I wanna know who modified the archive bit." "What." "Who?" "No, What." "Wait a minute . . . just tell me what's the name of the guy who modified the archive bit!" "Right.")

Normal backups

A *normal backup* — also called a *full backup* — is the basic type of backup. In a normal backup, all files in the backup selection are backed up regardless of whether the archive bit has been set. In other words, the files are backed up even if they haven't been modified since the last time they were backed up. When each file is backed up, its archive bit is reset, so backups that select files based on the archive bit setting won't back up the files.

When a normal backup finishes, none of the files in the backup selection has its archive bit set. As a result, if you immediately follow a normal backup with an incremental backup or a differential backup, files won't be selected for backup by the incremental or differential backup because no file will have its archive bit set.

The easiest backup scheme is to simply schedule a normal backup every night. That way, all your data is backed up on a daily basis. Then, if the need arises, you can restore files from a single tape or set of tapes. Restoring files is more complicated when other types of backups are involved.

REMEMBER

Do normal backups nightly if you have the tape capacity to do them unattended — that is, without having to swap tapes. If you can't do an unattended normal backup because the amount of data to be backed up is greater than the capacity of your tape drive(s), you have to use other types of backups in combination with normal backups.

TIP

If you can't get a normal backup on a single tape, and you can't afford a second tape drive or a tape changer, take a hard look at the data that's being included in the backup selection. I recently worked on a network that was difficult to back up onto a single tape. When I examined the data that was being backed up, I discovered a large amount of static data that was essentially an online archive of old projects. This data was necessary because network users needed it for research purposes, but the data was read-only. Even though the data never changed, it was being backed up to tape every night, and the backups required two tapes. After I removed this data from the cycle of nightly backups, the backups were able to squeeze onto a single tape again.

If you remove static data from the nightly backup, make sure that you have a secure backup of the static data on tape, CD-RW, or some other media.

Copy backups

A *copy backup* is similar to a normal backup except that the archive bit isn't reset when each file is copied. As a result, copy backups don't disrupt the cycle of normal and incremental or differential backups.

Copy backups usually aren't incorporated into regular, scheduled backups. Instead, you use a copy backup when you want to do an occasional one-shot backup. If you're about to perform an operating system upgrade, for example, you should back up the server before proceeding. If you do a full backup, the archive bits are reset, and your regular backups are disrupted. If you do a copy backup, however, the archive bits of any modified files remain unchanged. As a result, your regular normal and incremental or differential backups are unaffected.

If you don't incorporate incremental or differential backups into your backup routine, the difference between a copy backup and a normal backup is moot.

Daily backups

A *daily backup* backs up just those files that changed the same day that the backup was performed. A daily backup examines the modification date stored with each file's directory entry to determine whether a file should be backed up. Daily backups don't reset the archive bit.

WARNING

I'm not a big fan of this option because of the small possibility that some files may slip through the cracks. Someone may be working late one night and modify a file after the evening's backups have completed — but before midnight — meaning that those files won't be included in the following night's backups. Incremental or differential backups, which rely on the archive bit rather than the modification date, are more reliable.

Incremental backups

An *incremental backup* backs up only those files that were modified since the last time you did a backup. Incremental backups are a lot faster than full backups because your network users probably modify only a small portion of the files on the server on any given day. As a result, if a full backup takes three tapes, you can probably fit an entire week's worth of incremental backups on a single tape.

When an incremental backup copies each file, it resets the file's archive bit. That way, the file will be backed up again before your next normal backup only when a user modifies the file again.

Here are some thoughts about using incremental backups:

TIP

>> **The easiest way to use incremental backups is the following:**

- A *normal* backup every Monday

  If your full backup takes more than 12 hours, you may want to do it on Friday so that it can run over the weekend.

- An incremental backup on each remaining normal business day (for example, Tuesday, Wednesday, Thursday, and Friday)

>> **When you use incremental backups, the complete backup consists of the full backup tapes and all the incremental backup tapes that you've made since you did the full backup.**

If the hard drive crashes, and you have to restore the data onto a new drive, you first restore Monday's normal backup and then restore each of the subsequent incremental backups.

>> **Incremental backups complicate restoring individual files because the most recent copy of the file may be on the full backup tape or on any of the incremental backups.**

TECHNICAL STUFF

Backup programs keep track of the location of the most recent version of each file to simplify the process.

>> **When you use incremental backups, you can choose whether you want to**

- Store each incremental backup on its own tape.

- Append each backup to the end of an existing tape.

TIP

Often, you can use a single tape for a week of incremental backups.

Differential backups

A *differential backup* is similar to an incremental backup except that it doesn't reset the archive bit when files are backed up. As a result, each differential backup represents the difference between the last normal backup and the current state of the hard drive.

To do a full restore from a differential backup, you first restore the last normal backup and then restore the most recent differential backup.

Suppose that you do a normal backup on Monday and differential backups on Tuesday, Wednesday, and Thursday, and your hard drive crashes Friday morning. On Friday afternoon, you install a new hard drive. To restore the data, you first restore the normal backup from Monday. Then you restore the differential backup from Thursday. The Tuesday and Wednesday differential backups aren't needed.

The main difference between incremental and differential backups is that

>> *Incremental* backups result in smaller and faster backups.

>> *Differential* backups are easier to restore.

If your users often ask you to restore individual files, consider using differential backups.

TIP

Local versus Network Backups

When you back up network data, you have two basic approaches to running the backup software:

>> You can perform a *local backup*, in which the backup software runs on the file server itself and backs up data to a tape drive that's installed in the server.

>> Or you can perform a *network backup*, in which you use one network computer to back up data from another network computer. In a network backup, the data has to travel over the network to get to the computer that's running the backup.

If you run the backups from the file server, you'll tie up the server while the backup is running, and users will complain that their server access has slowed to a snail's pace. On the other hand, if you run the backup over the network from a client computer or a dedicated backup server, you'll flood the network with gigabytes of data being backed up. Then your users will complain that the entire network has slowed to a snail's pace.

Network performance is one of the main reasons why you should try to run your backups during off-hours, when other users aren't accessing the network. Another reason to run backups during off-hours is so that you can perform a more thorough backup. If you run your backup while other users are accessing files, the backup program is likely to skip any files that are being accessed by users at the time the backup runs. As a result, your backup won't include those files. Ironically, the files most likely to get left out of the backup are often the files that need backing up the most, because they're the files that are being used and modified.

Here are some extra thoughts on client and server backups:

>> **Backing up directly from the server isn't necessarily more efficient than backing up from a client because data doesn't have to travel over the network.** The network may well be faster than the tape drive. The network probably won't slow down backups unless you back up during the busiest time of the day, when hordes of network users are storming the network gates.

>> **Any files that are open while the backups are running won't get backed up.** That's usually not a problem, because backups are run at off-hours when people have gone home. If someone leaves his computer on with a Word document open, however, that Word document won't be backed up. One way to solve this problem is to set up the server so that it automatically logs everyone off the network before the backups begin.

>> **Some backup programs have special features that enable them to back up open files.** These backup programs create a snapshot of the volume when it begins, thus making temporary copies of any files that are modified during the backup. The backup backs up the temporary copies rather than the versions being modified. When the backup finishes, the temporary copies are deleted.

How Many Sets of Backups Should You Keep?

Don't try to cut costs by purchasing one backup tape and reusing it every day. What happens if you accidentally delete an important file on Tuesday and don't discover your mistake until Thursday? Because the file didn't exist on Wednesday, it won't be on Wednesday's backup tape. If you have only one tape that's reused every day, you're outta luck.

The safest scheme is to use a new backup tape every day and keep all your old tapes in a vault. Pretty soon, though, your tape vault can start looking like the warehouse where they stored the Ark of the Covenant at the end of *Raiders of the Lost Ark.*

TIP

As a compromise between these two extremes, most users purchase several tapes and rotate them. That way, you always have several backup tapes to fall back on, just in case the file you need isn't on the most recent backup tape. This technique is *tape rotation*, and several variations are commonly used:

>> **The simplest approach is to purchase three tapes and label them A, B, and C.** You use the tapes on a daily basis in sequence: A the first day, B the second day, and C the third day; then A the fourth day, B the fifth day, C the sixth day, and so on. On any given day, you have three generations of backups: today's, yesterday's, and the day-before-yesterday's. Computer geeks like to call these the *grandfather, father,* and *son* tapes.

>> **Purchase five tapes and use one each day of the workweek.** This is another simple approach.

>> **A variation of the A, B, and C approach is to buy eight tapes.** Take four of them, and write *Tuesday* on one label, *Wednesday* on the second, *Thursday* on the third, and *Friday* on the fourth label. On the other four tapes, write *Monday 1, Monday 2, Monday 3,* and *Monday 4.* Now tack up a calendar on the wall near the computer, and number all the Mondays in the year: 1, 2, 3, 4, 1, 2, 3, 4, and so on.

On Tuesday through Friday, you use the appropriate daily backup tape. When you run a full backup on Monday, consult the calendar to decide which Monday tape to use. With this scheme, you always have four weeks' worth of Monday backup tapes, plus individual backup tapes for the rest of the week.

>> **If bookkeeping data lives on the network, make a backup copy of all your files (or at least all your accounting files) immediately before closing the books each month; then retain those backups for each month of the year**. This doesn't necessarily mean that you should purchase 12 additional tapes. If you back up just your accounting files, you can probably fit all 12 months on a single tape. Just make sure that you back up with the "append to tape" option rather than the "erase tape" option so that the previous contents of the tape aren't destroyed. Also, treat this accounting backup as completely separate from your normal daily backup routine.

WARNING

Keep at least one recent full backup at another location. That way, if your office should fall victim to an errant Scud missile or a rogue asteroid, you can re-create your data from the backup copy that you stored off-site. Make sure that the person entrusted with the task of taking the backups to this off-site location is trustworthy.

A Word about Tape Reliability

From experience, I've found that although tape drives are very reliable, they do run amok once in a while. The problem is that they don't always tell you when they're not working. A tape drive (especially one of the less-expensive Travan drives; refer to "All about Tapes and Tape Drives," earlier in this chapter) can spin along for hours, pretending to back up your data — but in reality, your data isn't being written reliably to the tape. In other words, a tape drive can trick you into thinking that your backups are working just fine. Then, when disaster strikes and you need your backup tapes, you may just discover that the tapes are worthless.

TIP

Don't panic! Here's a simple way to assure yourself that your tape drive is working. Just activate the "compare-after-backup" feature of your backup software. As soon as your backup program finishes backing up your data, it rewinds the tape, reads each backed-up file, and compares it with the original version on the hard drive. If all files compare, you know that your backups are trustworthy.

Here are some additional thoughts about the reliability of tapes:

>> The compare-after-backup feature doubles the time required to do a backup, but that doesn't matter if your entire backup fits on one tape. You can just run the backup after hours. Whether the backup and repair operation takes one

hour or ten doesn't matter, as long as it's finished by the time the network users arrive at work the next morning.

>> If your backups require more than one tape, you may not want to run the compare-after-backup feature every day. Be sure to run it periodically, however, to check that your tape drive is working.

>> If your backup program reports errors, throw away the tape, and use a new tape.

>> Actually, you should ignore that last comment about waiting for your backup program to report errors. You should discard tapes *before* your backup program reports errors. Most experts recommend that you should use a tape only about 20 times before discarding it. If you use the same tape every day, replace it monthly. If you have tapes for each day of the week, replace them twice yearly. If you have more tapes than that, figure out a cycle that replaces tapes after about 20 uses.

About Cleaning the Heads

An important aspect of backup reliability is proper maintenance of your tape drives. Every time you back up to tape, little bits and specks of the tape rub off onto the read and write heads inside the tape drive. Eventually, the heads become too dirty to read or write data reliably.

To counteract this problem, clean the tape heads regularly. The easiest way to clean them is to use a cleaning cartridge for the tape drive. The drive automatically recognizes when you insert a cleaning cartridge and then performs a routine that wipes the cleaning tape back and forth over the heads to clean them. When the cleaning routine is done, the tape is ejected. The whole process takes only about 30 seconds.

Because the maintenance requirements of drives differ, check each drive's user's manual to find out how and how often to clean the drive. As a general rule, clean drives once weekly.

The most annoying aspect of tape drive cleaning is that the cleaning cartridges have a limited life span, and unfortunately, if you insert a used-up cleaning cartridge, the drive accepts it and pretends to clean the drive. For this reason, keep track of how many times you use a cleaning cartridge and replace it as recommended by the manufacturer.

Backup and Virtualization

If your servers are virtualized using either VMware or Hyper-V, you may want to consider adopting an altogether different approach to backups. Instead of creating complicated schemes of weekly full backups and daily incremental backups that are based on backing up the hundreds of thousands (or even millions) of individual files on all your servers, a virtual backup solution can focus instead on backing up the files that represent entire virtual machines.

Virtualization presents an entirely different set of challenges and opportunities for backup and recovery. In a virtualized environment, each server is represented not by hundreds of thousands (or even millions) of files on a physical disk drive, but by just a few files that represent the contents of the entire server. These files are very large, but software exists that allows you to easily and quickly replicate these files onto other media.

Virtualization platforms such as VMware and Hyper-V have built-in capabilities to manage this replication, but you can also purchase third-party solutions that can turn this replication capability into a full-fledged backup solution. For example, the Swiss-based company Veeam (www.veeam.com) has a powerful backup solution that is specifically designed for virtual environments. With Veeam, you can do full and incremental backups of virtual machines in a way that lets you recover either individual files or entire machines. One of the best features of Veeam is that you can run a virtual server directly from a backup image, without the need to first do a time-consuming restore. This can cut your recovery time from hours to minutes. And, while continuing to run the machine from the backup image, you can simultaneously restore the machine to its primary media. After the restore is completed, Veeam will automatically switch over to the restored copy of the machine.

If your environment is virtualized, I definitely recommend you investigate options such as Veeam for your backup solution instead of using traditional backup methods.

Backup Security

Backups create an often-overlooked security exposure for your network: No matter how carefully you set up user accounts and enforce password policies, if any user (including a guest) can perform a backup of the system, that user may make an unauthorized backup. In addition, your backup tapes themselves are vulnerable to theft. As a result, make sure that your backup policies and procedures are secure by taking the following measures:

» **Set up a user account for the user who does backups.** Because this user account has backup permission for the entire server, guard its password carefully. Anyone who knows the username and password of the backup account can log on and bypass any security restrictions that you place on that user's normal user ID.

» **Counter potential security problems by restricting the backup user ID to a certain client and a certain time of the day.** If you're really clever (and paranoid), you can probably set up the backup user's account so that the only program it can run is the backup program.

» **Use encryption to protect the contents of your backups.**

» **Secure the backup tapes in a safe location, such as, um, a safe.**

Chapter **5**

Managing Disaster Recovery and Business Continuity Planning

On April Fools' Day about 30 years ago, my colleagues and I discovered that some loser had broken into the office the night before and pounded our computer equipment to death with a crowbar. (I'm not making this up.)

Sitting on a shelf right next to the mangled piles of what used to be a Wang minicomputer system was an undisturbed disk pack that contained the only complete backup of all the information that was on the destroyed computer. The vandal didn't realize that one more swing of the crowbar would have escalated this major inconvenience into a complete catastrophe. Sure, we were up a creek until we could get the computer replaced. And in those days, you couldn't just walk into your local Computers R Us and buy a new computer off the shelf — this was a Wang minicomputer system that had to be specially ordered. After we had the new computer, though, a simple restore from the backup disk brought us right back to where we were on March 31. Without that backup, getting back on track would have taken months.

I've been paranoid about disaster planning ever since. Before then, I thought that disaster planning meant doing good backups. That's a part of it, but I can never forget the day we came within one swing of the crowbar of losing everything.

Vandals are probably much smarter now: They know to smash the backup tapes as well as the computers themselves. Being prepared for disasters entails much more than just doing regular backups.

Nowadays, the trendy term for disaster planning is a business continuity plan (BCP). I suppose the term "disaster planning" sounded too negative, like we were planning for disasters to happen. The new term refocuses attention on the more positive aspect of preparing a plan that will enable a business to carry on with as little interruption as possible in the event of a disaster.

For more in-depth information about this topic, please refer to *IT Disaster Recovery Planning For Dummies*, by Peter Gregory (Wiley).

Assessing Different Types of Disasters

Disasters come in many shapes and sizes. Some types of disasters are more likely than others. For example, your building is more likely to be struck by lightning than to be hit by a comet. In some cases, the likelihood of a particular type of disaster depends on where you're located. For example, crippling snowstorms are more likely in New York than in Florida.

In addition, the impact of each type of disaster varies from company to company. What may be a disaster for one company may only be a mere inconvenience for another. For example, a law firm may tolerate a disruption in telephone service for a day or two. Loss of communication via phone would be a major inconvenience but not a disaster. To a telemarketing firm, however, a day or two with the phones down is a more severe problem because the company's revenue depends on the phones.

One of the first steps in developing a business continuity plan is to assess the risk of the various types of disasters that may affect your organization. Weigh the likelihood of a disaster happening with the severity of the impact that the disaster would have. For example, a meteor crashing into your building would probably be pretty severe, but the odds of that happening are miniscule. On the other hand, the odds of your building being destroyed by fire are much higher, and the consequences of a devastating fire would be about the same as those from a meteor impact.

The following sections describe the most common types of risks that most companies face. Notice throughout this discussion that although many of these risks are related to computers and network technology, some are not. The scope of business continuity planning is much larger than just computer technology.

Environmental disasters

Environmental disasters are what most people think of first when they think of disaster recovery. Some types of environmental disasters are regional. Others can happen pretty much anywhere.

>> **Fire:** Fire is probably the first disaster that most people think of when they consider disaster planning. Fires can be caused by unsafe conditions; carelessness, such as electrical wiring that isn't up to code; natural causes, such as lightning strikes; or arson.

>> **Earthquakes:** Not only can earthquakes cause structural damage to your building, but they can also disrupt the delivery of key services and utilities, such as water and power. Serious earthquakes are rare and unpredictable, but some areas experience them with more regularity than others. If your business is located in an area known for earthquakes, your BCP should consider how your company would deal with a devastating earthquake.

>> **Weather:** Weather disasters can cause major disruption to your business. Moderate weather may close transportation systems so that your employees can't get to work. Severe weather may damage your building or interrupt delivery of services, such as electricity and water.

>> **Water:** Flooding can wreak havoc with electrical equipment, such as computers. If floodwaters get into your computer room, chances are good that the computer equipment will be totally destroyed. Flooding can be caused not only by bad weather but also by burst pipes or malfunctioning sprinklers.

>> **Lightning:** Lightning storms can cause electrical damage to your computers and other electronic equipment from lightning strikes as well as surges in the local power supply.

Deliberate disasters

Some disasters are the result of deliberate actions by others. For example:

>> **Intentional damage:** Vandalism or arson may damage or destroy your facilities or your computer systems. The vandalism or arson may be targeted at you specifically, by a disgruntled employee or customer, or it may be random. Either way, the effect is the same.

REMEMBER

Don't neglect the possibility of sabotage. A disgruntled employee who gets hold of an administrator's account and password can do all sorts of nasty things to your network.

>> **Theft:** Theft is always a possibility. You may come to work someday to find that your servers or other computer equipment have been stolen.

>> **Terrorism:** Terrorism used to be something that most Americans weren't concerned about, but September 11, 2001, changed all that. No matter where you live in the world, the possibility of a terrorist attack is real.

Disruption of services

You may not realize just how much your business depends on the delivery of services and utilities. A BCP should take into consideration how you will deal with the loss of certain services:

>> **No juice:** Electrical power is crucial for computers and other types of equipment. During a power failure once (I live in California, so I'm used to it), I discovered that I can't even work with pencil and paper because all my pencil sharpeners are electric. Electrical outages are not uncommon, but the technology to deal with them is readily available. Uninterruptible power supply (UPS) equipment is reliable and inexpensive.

>> **No communications:** Communication connections can be disrupted by many causes. A few years ago, a railroad overpass was constructed across the street from my office. One day, a backhoe cut through the phone lines, completely cutting off our phone service — including our Internet connection — for a day and a half.

>> **No water:** An interruption in the water supply may not shut down your computers, but it can disrupt your business by forcing you to close your facility until the water supply is reestablished.

Equipment failure

Modern companies depend on many different types of equipment for their daily operations. The failure of any of these key systems can disrupt business until the systems are repaired:

>> **Computer equipment failure can obviously affect business operations.**

>> **Air-conditioning systems are crucial to regulate temperatures, especially in computer rooms.** Computer equipment can be damaged if the temperature climbs too high.

>> **Elevators, automatic doors, and other equipment may also be necessary for your business.**

Other disasters

You should assess many other potential disasters. Here are just a few:

>> Labor disputes

>> Loss of key staff because of resignation, injury, sickness, or death

>> Workplace violence

>> Public health issues, such as epidemics, mold infestations, and so on

>> Loss of a key supplier

>> Nearby disaster, such as a fire or police action across the street that results in your business being temporarily blocked off

Analyzing the Impact of a Disaster

With a good understanding of the types of disasters that can affect your business, you can turn your attention to the impact that these disasters can have on your business. The first step is to identify the key business processes that can be impacted by different types of disasters. These business processes are different for each company. For example, here are a few of the key business processes for a publishing company:

>> **Editorial,** such as managing projects through the process of technical editing, copyediting, and production

>> **Acquisition,** such as determining product development strategies, recruiting authors, and signing projects

>> **Human resource,** such as payroll, hiring, employee review, and recruiting

>> **Marketing,** including sales tracking, developing marketing materials, sponsoring sales conferences, and exhibiting at trade events

>> **Sales and billing,** such as filling customer orders, maintaining the company website, managing inventory, and handling payments

>> **Executive and financial,** such as managing cash flow, securing credit, raising capital, deciding when to go public, and deciding when to buy a smaller publisher or sell out to a bigger publisher

The impact of a disruption to each of these processes will vary. One common way to assess the impact of business process loss is to rate the impact of various degrees of loss for each process. For example, you may rate the loss of each process for the following time frames:

>> 0 to 2 hours

>> 2 to 24 hours

>> 1 to 2 days

>> 2 days to 1 week

>> More than 1 week

For some business processes, an interruption of two hours or even one day may be minor. For other processes, even the loss of a few hours may be very costly.

Developing a Business Continuity Plan

A BCP is simply a plan for how you will continue operation of your key business processes should the normal operation of the process fail. For example, if your primary office location is shut down for a week because of a major fire across the street, you won't have to suspend operations if you have a business continuity plan in place.

The key to a BCP is redundancy of each component that is essential to your business processes. These components include:

>> **Facilities:** If your company already has multiple office locations, you may be able to temporarily squeeze into one of the other locations for the duration of the disaster. If not, you should secure arrangements in advance with a real estate broker so that you can quickly arrange an alternate location. By having an arrangement made in advance, you can move into an emergency location on a moment's notice.

>> **Computer equipment:** It doesn't hurt to have a set of spare computers in storage somewhere so that you can dig them out to use in an emergency. Preferably, these computers would already have your critical software installed. The next best thing would be to have detailed plans available so that your IT staff can quickly install key software on new equipment to get your business up and running.

WARNING

Always keep a current set of backup media at an alternate location.

>> **Phones:** Discuss emergency phone services in advance with your phone company. If you're forced to move to another location on 24-hour notice, how

quickly can you get your phones up and running? And can you arrange to have your incoming toll-free calls forwarded to the new location?

» **Staff:** Unless you work for a government agency, you probably don't have redundant employees. However, you can make arrangements in advance with a temp agency to provide clerical and administrative help on short notice.

» **Stationery:** This sounds like a small detail, but you should store a supply of all your key stationery products (letterhead, envelopes, invoices, statements, and so on) in a safe location. That way, if your main location is suddenly unavailable, you don't have to wait a week to get new letterhead or invoices printed.

» **Hard copy files:** Keep a backup copy of important printed material (customer billing files, sales records, and so on) at an alternate location.

Holding a Fire Drill

Remember in grade school when the fire alarm would go off and your teacher would tell you and the other kids to calmly put down your work and walk out to the designated safe zone in an orderly fashion? Drills are important so that if a real fire occurs, you don't run and scream and climb all over each other in order to be the first one to get out.

Any disaster recovery plan is incomplete unless you test it to see whether it works. Testing doesn't mean that you should burn your building down one day to see how long it takes you to get back up and running. You should, though, periodically simulate a disaster in order to prove to yourself and your staff that you can recover.

The most basic type of disaster recovery drill is a simple test of your network backup procedures. You should periodically attempt to restore key files from your backup tapes just to make sure that you can. You achieve several benefits by restoring files on a regular basis:

» **Tapes are unreliable.** The only way to be sure that your tapes are working is to periodically restore files from them.

» **Backup programs are confusing to configure.** I've seen people run backup jobs for years that don't include all the data they think they're backing up. Only when disaster strikes and they need to recover a key file do they discover that the file isn't included in the backup.

>> **Restoring files can be a little confusing, especially when you use a combination of normal and incremental or differential backups.** Add to that the pressure of having the head of the company watching over your shoulder while you try to recover a lost file. If you regularly conduct file restore drills, you'll familiarize yourself with the restore features of your backup software in a low-pressure situation. Then, you can easily restore files for real when the pressure's on.

You can also conduct walk-throughs of more serious disaster scenarios. For example, you can set aside a day to walk through moving your entire staff to an alternate location. You can double-check that all the backup equipment, documents, and data are available as planned. If something is missing, it's better to find out now rather than while the fire department is still putting water on the last remaining hot spots in what used to be your office.

Appendix A: Directory of Useful Websites

Throughout this book, I mention many websites that you can visit to glean more information about various networking topics. This appendix gathers those sites into one convenient location and adds a bunch more that are also worth visiting from time to time. Happy surfing!

Certification

Here are the sites to check out for official certification information:

>> `www.microsoft.com/learning/mcp`: Microsoft's certification headquarters

>> `www.comptia.org`: Independent certification, including A+, Network+, and Security+

>> `www.ibm.com/certify`: IBM's certification home page

>> `www.cisco.com/certifications`: Cisco's certification home page

>> `www.vmware.com/certification`: The place to go for information about certification in VMware tools

>> `www.redhat.com/training/certification`: Red Hat's Linux certification home page

Hardware

The following websites are general resources for researching computer hardware:

>> `http://reviews.cnet.com`: CNET's reviews section offers reviews on all types of computer hardware, with a special section devoted to networking.

>> `www.hardwarecentral.com`: HardwareCentral is another good source for general computer hardware information, reviews, and advice.

>> `www.tomshardware.com`: Tom's Hardware Guide is the place to go if you want detailed information about the latest in computer components.

The following manufacturers offer high-end networking products, including servers, routers, switches, and so on:

>> `www.hpe.com`: This page is the home page for HPE's products.

>> `www.dell.com/servers`: This page is the home page for Dell server products.

>> `www.oracle.com/servers`: This page is the home page for Oracle (formerly Sun) servers.

Home and Small-Business Networking

The following websites have general information about home and small-business networking:

>> `www.home-network-help.com`: This excellent website is devoted to helping people get their home networks up and running. The site is loaded with step-by-step procedures and flowcharts.

>> `www.practicallynetworked.com`: This site is a great source of information for home networking, with general networking information, technology backgrounders, product reviews, troubleshooting advice, and more.

>> `www.hometoys.com`: This site provides information on all sorts of gadgets for the home, including networks.

>> `www.linksys.com`: This page is the home page of Linksys, one of the most popular manufacturers of networking devices for homes and small offices, including 10/100BaseT, wireless, and even phone and Powerline devices.

>> `www.netgear.com`: This page is the home page of NETGEAR, which makes home and small-office networking devices, including 10/100BaseT adapters and switches, wireless devices, and phone-line systems.

Linux

One of the best overall websites for everything Linux is `www.linux.org`. It's a central source of Linux information and news, and includes many links to Linux distributions and downloadable applications.

Here are the home pages for some of the most popular distributions:

» `www.redhat.com`: The website of the most popular Linux distribution

» `www.getfedora.org`: The home page of the Fedora project

» `www.ubuntu.com`: The website of the popular Ubuntu Linux distribution

» `www.caldera.com`: The Caldera distribution from SCO

» `www.slackware.com`: Slackware, one of the oldest Linux distributions

Here are the home pages for some popular Linux networking software:

» `www.isc.org/software/BIND`: The official page for BIND, the most popular DNS name server on the Internet

» `www.proofpoint.com/us/open-source-email-solution`: Official site for Sendmail, the SMTP mail exchange server

» `www.apache.org`: Official site for the Apache HTTP server

» `www.samba.org`: Official site for the Samba file and print server

Magazines

Here are some various magazines on networking topics:

» *2600 Magazine:* `www.2600.com`

» *InformationWeek:* `www.informationweek.com`

» *InfoWorld:* `www.infoworld.com`

» *IT Pro Magazine:* `www.itprotoday.com`

» *Linux Journal:* `www.linuxjournal.com`

» *Linux Magazine:* `www.linux-mag.com`

» *Network Computing:* `www.networkcomputing.com`

Microsoft

Microsoft's website is vast. Here are some links to a few useful areas within this huge website:

» `www.microsoft.com`: The entry point for Microsoft's website

» `www.microsoft.com/windows`: The home page for the Windows family of products

» `http://azure.microsoft.com`: The home page for Microsoft Azure

» `www.microsoft.com/exchange`: The home page for Exchange

» `www.microsoft.com/sqlserver`: The home page for SQL Server

» `www.microsoft.com/sharepoint`: The home page for SharePoint

» `http://technet.microsoft.com`: TechNet, a great source for technical information on Microsoft technologies

» `http://support.microsoft.com`: Microsoft's general support site

» `http://products.office.com`: The home page for Microsoft Office

Network Standards Organizations

The following websites are useful when you're researching network standards:

» `www.ansi.org`: The American National Standards Institute (ANSI), the official standards organization in the United States

» `www.ieee.org`: The Institute of Electrical and Electronics Engineers (IEEE), an international organization that publishes several key networking standards, including the official Ethernet standards (known as *IEEE 802.3*)

» `www.iso.org`: The International Organization for Standardization (ISO), a federation of more than 100 standards organizations throughout the world

» `www.internetsociety.org`: The Internet Society, an international organization for global coordination and cooperation on the Internet

» `www.ietf.org`: The Internet Engineering Task Force (IETF), responsible for the protocols that drive the Internet

» `www.iana.org`: The Internet Assigned Numbers Authority, which has responsibility for the IP address space

- » `www.w3c.org`: The World Wide Web Consortium (W3C), an international organization that handles the development of standards for the World Wide Web

- » `www.rfc-editor.org`: The official repository of RFCs (requests to create new standards), which includes a search facility that lets you look up RFCs by name or keyword

Reference

Several general-purpose and computer-specific reference sites provide encyclopedia-style articles or simple definitions of computer and networking terms. If you aren't sure what some new technology is, start at one of these sites:

- » `www.webopedia.com`: Webopedia is a great online dictionary of computer and Internet terms. Not sure what *direct sequence spread spectrum* means? Look it up at Webopedia!

- » `www.whatis.com`: Whatis.com is another great dictionary of computer and networking terms.

- » `www.howstuffworks.com`: This site has general information about many types of technology: computers, automobiles, electronics, science, and more. The computer section provides good low-level introductions to various computer topics, including computer hardware, the Internet, and security.

TCP/IP and the Internet

The following sites have interesting information about the Internet:

- » `www.internic.net`: The InterNIC website is a central point of information for domain registration. Check here for a list of accredited domain registrars.

- » `www.isc.org`: Members of the Internet Systems Consortium are the folks who do the twice-a-year domain survey to try to estimate how big the Internet really is.

For DNS information, try `www.dnsstuff.com`, which lets you perform a variety of DNS lookups to make sure that your DNS zones are set up correctly.

Check these sites to find information about web browsers:

>> `www.microsoft.com/ie`: The official home page for Internet Explorer.

>> `www.microsoft.com/edge`: The official home page for Edge, Microsoft's replacement for Internet Explorer.

>> `www.mozilla.org`: The home of Firefox, a popular alternative web browser. Many users consider Firefox to be the best web browser around.

>> `www.opera.com`: The home of Opera, another alternative to Internet Explorer.

>> `http://chrome.google.com`: The home of Google Chrome, Google's popular web browser.

Here are some sites that can do speed tests to let you know how fast your Internet connection is:

>> `www.speakeasy.net`: An independently operated speed test site

>> `www.speedtest.net`: Another independently operated speed test site

>> `http://fast.com`: Yet another speed test site.

>> `http://speedtest.att.com`: A speed test site run by AT&T

Wireless Networking

Wi-Fi Planet (`www.wi-fiplanet.com`) is a large site devoted to news, information, and product reviews for wireless networking.

Here are the websites for the most popular brands of wireless networking products:

>> **Cisco** (`www.cisco.com`): Cisco is the place to go for high-end wireless networking.

>> **D-Link** (`www.dlink.com`): D-Link is yet another manufacturer of inexpensive wireless products.

>> **Linksys** (`www.linksys.com`): Linksys is a manufacturer of wireless network cards and access points.

>> **Meraki** (`www.meraki.com`): Meraki, owned by Cisco, makes excellent cloud-managed wireless devices.

>> **NETGEAR** (www.netgear.com)**:** NETGEAR is another manufacturer of wireless components.

>> **SMC** (www.smc.com)**:** The home page for SMC, another manufacturer of wireless network products.

>> **Ubiquity** (www.ubnt.com)**:** Another excellent maker of wireless devices.

Smartphones

The following websites contain useful information about various smartphone platforms:

>> www.blackberry.com: The main website for BlackBerry

>> www.android.com: The home page for Google's Android platform

>> www.apple.com/iphone: The home page for Apple's iPhone

Appendix B: Glossary

10Base2: A now obsolete type of coax cable that was once the most often used cable for Ethernet networks; also known as *thinnet* or *cheapernet*. The maximum length of a single segment is 185 meters (600 feet). 10base2 is now all but obsolete.

10Base5: The original Ethernet coax cable, now pretty much obsolete; also known as *yellow cable* or *thick cable*. The maximum length of a single segment is 500 meters (1,640 feet).

10BaseT: Twisted-pair cable, commonly used for Ethernet networks; also known as *UTP*, *twisted pair*, or *twisted sister* (just kidding!). The maximum length of a single segment is 100 meters (330 feet). Of the three Ethernet cable types, this one is the easiest to work with.

100BaseFX: The Ethernet standard for high-speed fiber-optic connections.

100BaseT4: An alternative standard for 100 Mbps Ethernet using four-pair Category-3 cable.

100BaseTX: The leading standard for 100 Mbps Ethernet, which uses two-pair, Category-5 twisted-pair cable.

100VG AnyLAN: A standard for 100 Mbps Ethernet that isn't as popular as 100BaseT. Like 100BaseT, 100VG AnyLAN uses twisted-pair cable.

1000BaseT: A standard for 1,000 Mbps Ethernet using four-pair, Category-5, unshielded twisted-pair cable. 1000BaseT is also known as *Gigabit Ethernet*.

1 Trillion BaseT: Well, not really. But if current trends continue, we'll get there soon.

802.2: The forgotten IEEE standard. The more glamorous 802.3 standard relies on 802.2 for moral support.

802.3: The IEEE standard known in the vernacular as *Ethernet*.

802.11: The IEEE standard for wireless networking. Popular variants include 802.11a, 802.11b, 802.11g, 802.11n, and 802.11ac.

8088 processor: The microprocessor chip around which IBM designed its original PC, marking the transition from the Bronze Age to the Iron Age.

80286 processor: *Computo-habilis,* an ancient ancestor of today's modern computers.

80386 processor: *Computo-thirtwo-us,* the first 32-bit microprocessor chip used in personal computers, long since replaced by newer, faster, 64-bit designs.

80486 processor: The last of Intel's CPU chips to have a number instead of a name. It was replaced years ago by the Pentium processor, which was eventually replaced by the *i* series (i3, i5, i7, and i9), marking the return of numbers to Intel's CPUs.

access rights: A list of rights that tells you what you can and can't do with network files or directories.

account: The way by which the network knows who you are and what rights you have on the network. You can't get into the network without one.

acronym: An abbreviation made up of the first letters of a series of words. *See also* TLA.

Active Directory: The directory service in Windows networks.

Active Server Pages: An Internet feature from Microsoft that enables you to create web pages with scripts that run on the server rather than on the client; also known as *ASP.* The newest version is called *ASP.NET.*

ActiveSync: A Windows component used to synchronize data between computers.

adapter card: An electronic card that you can plug into one of your computer's adapter slots to give it some new and fabulous capability, such as displaying 16 billion colors.

address book: In an email system, a list of users with whom you regularly correspond.

administrator: The big network cheese who's responsible for setting things up and keeping them running. Pray that it's not you. The administrator is also known as the *network manager.*

allocation unit: Windows allocates space to files one allocation unit at a time; the allocation unit typically is 2,048 or 4,096 bytes, depending on the size of the disk. An allocation unit is also known as a *cluster.* Windows Server uses allocation schemes that are more efficient than those in standard Windows.

Android: A popular open-source mobile phone and tablet platform developed by Google.

antispam program: A program that prevents spam email from reaching your inbox.

antivirus program: A program that sniffs out viruses on your network and sends them into exile.

Apache: The most popular web server on the Internet. It comes free with most versions of Linux and is available free for Windows.

appliance: A self-contained computer system that comes preloaded with software to provide a commonly required function on a network. For example, security appliances are often used to provide firewall, antivirus, and antispam protection.

application layer: The highest layer of the OSI Reference Model, which governs how software communicates with the network.

archive bit: A flag that's kept for each file to indicate whether the file has been modified since it was last backed up.

ARCnet: An ancient network topology developed by Datapoint and now found only in history books. When my grandchildren are old enough, I'm going to tell them about the first computer network that I was responsible for, which actually used ARCnet and Datapoint minicomputers.

attributes: Characteristics that are assigned to files. DOS alone provides four attributes: system, hidden, read-only, and archive. Network operating systems generally expand the list of file attributes.

auto attendant: A feature of PBX systems that eliminates or reduces the need for human operators.

backbone: A trunk cable used to tie sections of a network together.

backup: A copy of your important files made for safekeeping in case something happens to the original files — something you should make every day, or even more often if you can.

banner: A fancy page that's printed between print jobs so that you can easily separate jobs from one another.

batch file: A file that contains one or more commands that are executed together as a set. You create the batch file by using a text editor and run the file by typing its name at the command prompt.

Bayesian filter: A type of spam filter that can be trained to identify spam emails.

benchmark: A repeatable test you use to judge the performance of your network. The best benchmarks are the ones that closely duplicate the type of work you routinely do on your network.

BES: See BlackBerry Enterprise Server (BES).

BlackBerry: A once-popular smartphone made by BlackBerry. These days, most IT administrators who still have to support BlackBerry are grumpy.

BlackBerry Enterprise Server (BES): Software that runs on a Windows server to enable BlackBerry devices to synchronize with Microsoft Exchange.

Bluetooth: (1) A Viking king who united Denmark and Norway in the tenth century. (2) A wireless networking protocol for short-range networks, used mostly for devices such as wireless keyboards, mice, and cellphones.

bot: A program that runs automated tasks over the Internet. Many bots are malicious in nature, prowling the web looking for information they can steal.

bottleneck: The slowest link in your network, which causes work to get jammed up. The first step in improving network performance is identifying the bottlenecks.

bridge: Not the popular card game, but a device that enables you to link two networks together. Bridges are smart enough to know which computers are on which side of the bridge, so they allow only those messages that need to get to the other side to cross the bridge. This device improves performance on both sides of the bridge.

broadband: A high-speed connection used for wide-area networking.

broadcast domain: In a network, a collection of nodes that can broadcast packets to one another via the data link layer. In TCP/IP, a subnet is a broadcast domain. One of the reasons for creating multiple subnets is to contain broadcast domains.

buffer: An area of memory that holds data en route to somewhere else. A hard drive buffer, for example, holds data as it travels between your computer and the hard drive.

bus: A type of network topology in which network nodes are strung out along a single run of cable called a *segment*. 10Base2 networks used a bus topology. *Bus* also refers to the row of expansion slots within your computer.

cable tie: Little strips of plastic that are especially handy for securing cables or bundling them together.

cache: A sophisticated form of buffering in which a large amount of memory is set aside to hold data so that it can be accessed quickly.

Carrier Sense Multiple Access with Collision Detection (CSMA/CD): The traffic-management technique used by Ethernet.

Category 3: An inexpensive form of unshielded twisted-pair (UTP) cable that is suitable only for 10 Mbps networks (10BaseT). Avoid using Category-3 cable for new networks.

Category 5: The higher grade of UTP cable that is suitable for 100 Mbps networks (100BaseTX) and Gigabit Ethernet (1000BaseT).

Category 5e: An enhanced version of Cat 5e that is suitable for Power over Ethernet (PoE). Cat 5e is the lowest grade Ethernet cable you should install.

Category 6: An even higher grade of UTP cable that's more reliable than Category-5 cable for Gigabit Ethernet.

CD-ROM: A high-capacity disc that uses optical technology to store data in a form that can be read but not written over.

central processing unit (CPU): The brains of the computer. *See* processor.

Centrex: A type of phone system similar to a PBX, except that the system is located on the phone company's premises, not on a customer's premises.

Certified Network Dummy (CND): Someone who knows nothing about networks but nevertheless gets the honor of installing one.

chat: What you do on the network when you talk live with another network user.

Chaucer: A dead English dude.

CHKDSK: A DOS command that checks the recordkeeping structures of a DOS hard drive for errors.

circuit: An end-to-end connection between transmitters and receivers, typically in phone systems.

click: What you do in Windows to get things done.

client: A computer that has access to the network but doesn't share any of its own resources with the network. *See also* server.

client/server: A vague term meaning roughly that the workload is split between a client computer and a server computer.

cloud: A popular term for the Internet, with the added connotation of being able to solve all your problems, prevent world hunger, and cure cancer.

cloud computing: An approach to networking in which certain elements of a network that were traditionally implemented within a LAN (such as file storage, backup, or email services) are instead implemented remotely via the Internet.

Clouseau: The most dangerous man in all of France. Some people say he only plays the fool.

cluster: *See* allocation unit.

CND: *See* Certified Network Dummy.

coaxial cable: A type of cable that contains two conductors. The center conductor is surrounded by a layer of insulation, which is then wrapped by a braided-metal conductor and an outer layer of insulation.

computer name: A unique name assigned to each computer on a network.

Cone of Silence: A running gag on the old TV series *Get Smart* in which a security device would be lowered over two people who needed to have a secure conversation. Unfortunately, the Cone of Silence worked so well that the people in it couldn't hear each other. (Anyone outside the Cone of Silence, however, could easily hear what the people in the cone were saying.)

console: In Windows, Linux, and many other operating systems, a text-mode command prompt.

Control Panel: In Windows, an application that enables you to configure various aspects of the Windows operating system.

core: A part of a processor that can independently process instructions. A single processor can contain multiple cores. Also, a single core can process two *threads* using a feature called *hyperthreading*.

CPU: *See* central processing unit (CPU).

crimp tool: A special tool used to attach connectors to cables. No network manager should be without one. Try not to get your fingers caught in it.

crossover cable: A cable used to connect two Ethernet devices directly to each other without the use of a switch.

CSMA/CD: *See* Carrier Sense Multiple Access with Collision Detection (CSMA/CD).

daisy-chain: A way of connecting computer components in which the first component is connected to the second, which is connected to the third, and so on. In Ethernet, you can daisy-chain hubs together.

DAT: *See* digital audiotape.

data link layer: The second layer of the OSI model, responsible for transmitting bits of data over the network cable.

dedicated server: A computer used exclusively as a network server.

delayed write: A hard-drive-caching technique in which data written to the hard drive is placed in cache memory and actually written to the hard drive later.

dial tone: The distinctive tone produced on a phone system to indicate that the system is ready to accept a call.

DID: *See* Direct Inward Dialing (DID).

differential backup: A type of backup in which only the files that have changed since the last full backup are backed up.

digital audiotape (DAT): A type of tape often used for network backups.

DIP switch: A bank of switches used to configure an old-fashioned adapter card. Modern cards configure themselves automatically, so DIP switches aren't required. *See also* jumper block.

Direct Inward Dialing (DID): A feature of PBX systems that lets you associate an external phone number with an extension on the PBX system.

directory hash: A popular breakfast food enjoyed by Linux administrators.

disk: A device (also known as a *hard drive*) that stores information magnetically. A hard drive is permanently sealed in an enclosure and has a capacity usually measured in thousands of megabytes, also known as *gigabytes*.

Disk Operating System (DOS): The original operating system for IBM and IBM-compatible computers.

distribution: A publicly available version of the Linux operating system. There are many distributions. One of the most popular is Fedora.

DNS: *See* Domain Name System (DNS).

domain: (1) In a Windows network, one or more network servers that are managed by a single network directory. (2) In the Internet, a name assigned to a network.

Domain Name System (DNS): The naming system used on the Internet, in which a network is given a domain name and individual computers are given host names.

DOS: *See* Disk Operating System (DOS).

dot-matrix printer: A prehistoric type of printer that works by applying various-colored pigments to the walls of caves. Once the mainstay printer for PCs, dot-matrix printers have given way to laser printers and inkjet printers. High-speed matrix printers still have their place on the network, though, and matrix printers have the advantage of being able to print multipart forms.

dumb terminal: Back in the heyday of mainframe computers, a monitor and keyboard attached to the central mainframe. All the computing work occurred at the mainframe; the terminal only displayed the results and sent input typed at the keyboard back to the mainframe.

DVD drive: A type of optical drive similar to a CD-ROM drive but with much higher storage capacity.

Eddie Haskell: The kid who's always sneaking around, poking his nose into other people's business, and generally causing trouble. Every network has one.

Edge: A Microsoft web browser designed to replace Internet Explorer in Windows 10.

editor: (1) A program for creating and changing text files. (2) A person who translates poorly written technical prose into understandable English.

email: Messages that are exchanged with other network users.

emoticon: A shorthand way of expressing emotions in email and chats by combining symbols to create smiles, frowns, and so on.

encryption: A security technique in which data is stored in an encoded (encrypted) form that can be decoded (or decrypted) only if the key used to encrypt the data is known.

enterprise computing: A trendy term that refers to a view of an organization's complete computing needs rather than just a single department's or group's needs.

Ethernet: The World's Most Popular Network Standard.

ETLA: *See* extended three-letter acronym (ETLA).

Exchange Server: The software that handles email services on a Windows server.

extended three-letter acronym (ETLA): An acronym with four letters. *See also* three-letter acronym (TLA).

false negative: With regards to spam, email that is mistakenly identified as legitimate when it's actually spam.

false positive: With regards to spam, email that is mistakenly identified as spam when it's actually legitimate.

Fast Ethernet: 100 Mbps Ethernet; also known as *100BaseT* or *100BaseTX*. This used to be considered fast; today, Fast Ethernet is actually incredibly slow.

FAT: *See* File Allocation Table (FAT).

FAT32: An improved way of keeping track of hard drive files that can be used with Windows 98 and later.

FDDI: *See* Fiber Distributed Data Interface (FDDI).

Fedora: A popular distribution of Linux.

Fiber Distributed Data Interface (FDDI): A 100 Mbps network standard used with fiber-optic backbone. When FDDI is used, FDDI/Ethernet bridges connect Ethernet segments to the backbone.

fiber-optic cable: A blazingly fast network cable that transmits data using light rather than electricity. Fiber-optic cable is often used as the backbone in large networks, especially where great distances are involved.

File Allocation Table (FAT): A recordkeeping structure once used on DOS and Windows computers to keep track of the location of every file on a hard drive.

file rights: The capability of a particular network user to access specific files on a network server.

file server: A network computer containing hard drives that are available to network users.

File Transfer Protocol (FTP): A method for retrieving files from the Internet.

filter: A software component that analyzes email to determine if the email is spam.

firewall: A special type of router that connects a LAN to the Internet while preventing unauthorized Internet users from accessing the LAN.

fish tape: A gadget that helps you pull cable through walls.

forest: A group of Active Directory domains.

FTP: *See* File Transfer Protocol (FTP).

full backup: A backup of all the files on a hard drive, whether or not the files have been modified since the last backup. *See also* differential backup.

gateway: A device that connects dissimilar networks. Gateways often connect Ethernet networks to mainframe computers or to the Internet.

GB: *See* gigabyte (GB).

generation backup: A backup strategy in which several sets of backup disks or tapes are retained; sometimes called *grandfather-father-son.*

generation gap: What happens when you skip one of your backups.

gigabyte (GB): *Roughly* a billion bytes of hard drive storage (1,024MB, to be precise). *See also* kilobyte (K), megabyte (MB), and terabyte (TB).

glass house: The room where the mainframe computer is kept. It's symbolic of the mainframe mentality, which stresses bureaucracy, inflexibility, and heavy iron.

GNOME: A graphical user interface that's popular on Linux systems.

grandfather-father-son: *See* generation backup.

group account: A type of security account that lets you group user accounts that have similar access rights.

guest: A user account that has no privileges. The guest account is designed to provide minimal network access to users who don't have a regular network account.

guru: Anyone who knows more about computers than you do.

HAL: (1) The evil computer in the classic science-fiction movie *2001: A Space Odyssey*. (2) *See* hardware abstraction layer (HAL).

hardware abstraction layer (HAL): A layer of software that isolates physical devices from software that uses those devices.

help desk: The team that handles technical support issues in an organization. Seldom thanked, almost always neglected — until, of course, they're needed.

hotspot: An area that has access to a public wireless network. Hotspots are commonly found in airports, hotels, and trendy coffee shops.

HTML: *See* HyperText Markup Language (HTML).

HTTP: *See* HyperText Transfer Protocol (HTTP).

HTTPS: A secure form of HyperText Transfer Protocol (HTTP) used to transmit sensitive data such as credit-card numbers.

hub: A passive and lazy layer-1 networking device that simply repeats everything it hears to anyone who will listen. Hubs are now considered obsolete, having been replaced by switches. *See also* switch.

HyperText Markup Language (HTML): The language used to compose pages that can be displayed via the World Wide Web.

HyperText Transfer Protocol (HTTP): The protocol used by the World Wide Web for sending HTML pages from a server computer to a client computer.

hyperthreading: An advanced technique that allows a single processor core to simultaneously process two distinct instruction threads, which creates the appearance of a single core acting as if it were actually two distinct cores.

hypervisor: Software that manages the execution of virtual machines in a virtualization environment.

I/O port address: Every I/O device in a computer — including network interface cards — must be assigned a unique address. In the old days, you had to configure the port address by using DIP switches or jumpers. Newer network cards automatically configure their own port addresses so that you don't have to mess with switches or jumper blocks.

i7 processor: A popular multicore processor made by Intel. (Variants include i3 and i5, which are not as powerful as the i7 but less expensive, and the i9, which is more powerful and, not surprisingly, more expensive.)

IEEE: *See* Institute of Electrical and Electronics Engineers (IEEE).

IIS: *See* Internet Information Services (IIS).

incremental backup: A type of backup in which only the files that have changed since the last backup are backed up. Unlike a differential backup, an incremental backup resets each file's archive bit as it backs it up. *See also* archive bit, differential backup, *and* full backup.

Industry Standard Architecture (ISA) bus: A once-popular type of expansion bus for accommodating adapter cards, now replaced by PCI.

inkjet printer: A type of printer that creates full-color pages by spraying tiny jets of ink onto paper.

Institute of Electrical and Electronics Engineers (IEEE): Where they send computer geeks who've had a few too many parity errors.

International Organization for Standardization (ISO): An international organization that maintains standards for many fields, including networking technology. Don't ask why the abbreviation is *ISO* instead of *IOS*.

Internet: A humongous network of networks that spans the globe and gives you access to just about anything you could ever hope for, provided that you can figure out how to work it. Spread across the Internet, you can find virtually the entire collective knowledge of the human race. In actuality, however, the Internet is used primarily to watch videos of cute kittens.

Internet Explorer: Microsoft's popular web browser.

Internet Information Services (IIS): Microsoft's web server. IIS is included with all versions of Windows Server.

Internet service provider (ISP): A company that provides access to the Internet for a fee.

interoperability: Providing a level playing field for incompatible networks to work together, kind of like NAFTA.

intranet: A network that resembles the Internet but is accessible only within a company or organization. Most intranets use the familiar World Wide Web interface to distribute information to company employees.

IP address: A string of numbers used to address computers on the Internet. If you enable TCP/IP on your network, you must provide an IP address for each computer on the network.

iPhone: A popular smartphone developed by Apple, best known for popularizing the trendy business of capitalizing the sEcond letter of words instead of the first.

ISA bus: *See* Industry Standard Architecture (ISA) bus.

ISDN: A digital telephone connection that lets you connect to the Internet at about twice the speed of a regular phone connection. It was once popular, but now, more cost-effective forms of high-speed Internet connections are available.

ISO: *See* International Organization for Standardization (ISO).

ISP: *See* Internet service provider (ISP).

Java: A programming language popular on the Internet.

JavaScript: A popular scripting language that can be used on web pages.

jumper block: A device used to configure an old-fashioned adapter card. To change the setting of a jumper block, you remove the jumper from one set of pins and place it on another.

K: *See* kilobyte (K).

Kerberos: (1) The mythical three-headed dog that guards the gates of Hades. (2) A network security protocol that authenticates users when they log on and grants the user a ticket that allows him or her to access resources throughout the network.

kilobyte (K): Roughly one thousand bytes (1,024, to be precise). *See also* gigabyte (GB), megabyte (MB), *and* terabyte (TB).

LAN: *See* local area network (LAN).

LAN Manager: An obsolete network operating system that Microsoft used to sell. Microsoft long ago put all its networking eggs in the Windows basket, so LAN Manager exists only on isolated islands along with soldiers who are still fighting World War II.

laser printer: A high-quality printer that uses lasers and photon torpedoes to produce beautiful output.

lemon-pudding layer: A layer near the middle of the OSI Reference Model that provides flavor and moistness.

Linux: An open-source version of the Unix operating system that's popular as a network server.

LLC sublayer: *See* logical link control (LLC) sublayer.

logical link control (LLC) sublayer: A sublayer of layer 2 of the OSI model whose main role is enabling different protocols to co-exist on the same network. The LLC is addressed by the IEEE 802.2 standard.

local area network (LAN): A network that is contained within a limited area, such as a single building.

local resources: Disk drives, printers, and other devices that are attached directly to a workstation rather than accessed via the network.

log in: *See* log on.

log on: The process of identifying oneself to the network (or a specific network server) and gaining access to network resources.

log out: The process of leaving the network. When you log out, any network drives or printers you were connected to become unavailable to you.

logon name: In a Windows network, the name that identifies a user uniquely to the network; same as *username* or *user ID*.

logon script: A batch file that is executed when a user logs on to a Windows domain.

Mac: A popular alternative to Windows, made by Apple.

MAC address: A unique network address given to every device ever manufactured.

MAC sublayer: *See* media access control (MAC) sublayer.

mail server: The server computer on which email messages are stored. This same computer also may be used as a file and print server, or it may be dedicated as a mail server.

mainframe: A huge computer kept in a glass house on raised floors and cooled with liquid nitrogen. In the olden days, the cable that connected the hard drives to the CPU was almost as big around as Arnold Schwarzenegger's forearms.

mapping: Assigning unused drive letters to network drives or unused printer ports to network printers. *See also* redirection.

MB: *See* megabyte (MB).

megabyte (MB): Roughly one million bytes (1,024K, to be precise). *See also* kilobyte (K), gigabyte (GB), *and* terabyte (TB).

media access control (MAC) sublayer: A sublayer of layer 2 of the OSI model whose main responsibility is interfacing with the hardware media. The MAC sublayer is best known for its device addresses, known as MAC addresses. The MAC is addressed by the IEEE 802.3 standard.

memory: The electronic storage where your computer stores data that's being manipulated and programs that are running. *See also* random access memory (RAM).

metaphor: A literary construction suitable for Shakespeare and Steinbeck but a bit overused by writers of computer books.

Metro: The original name for Windows 8 UI, a new graphical user interface introduced with Windows 8, optimized for use on touchscreen devices.

Microsoft Management Console (MMC): The primary management tool used to configure Windows features.

MMC: *See* Microsoft Management Console (MMC).

modem: A device that converts signals the computer understands to signals that can be accurately transmitted over the phone to another modem, which converts the signals back to their original form. Computers use modems to talk to each other. *Modem* is an abbreviation of *modulator–demodulator.*

mouse: The device used to move a pointer around on a screen. *Hint:* Don't pick it up and talk into it like Scotty did in *Star Trek IV.* That's very embarrassing, especially if you've traveled millions of miles to get here.

Mr. McFeeley: The nerdy-looking mailman on *Mister Rogers' Neighborhood.* He'd make a great computer geek. Speedy delivery!

multiboot: A technique that lets you install two or more operating systems on a single computer. When you power up a computer that uses multiboot, you must select which of the installed operating systems you want to boot.

multithreading: *See* hyperthreading.

MySQL: An open-source SQL database server for Linux systems.

NAS: *See* network accessible storage (NAS).

.NET: A Windows application environment that promises to simplify the task of creating and using applications for Windows and for the web.

NetBIOS: *See* Network Basic Input/Output System (NetBIOS).

NetWare: A once-popular network operating system, the proud child of Novell, Inc.

NetWare Directory Services: A feature of NetWare first introduced with Version 4, in which the resources of the servers are pooled together to form a single entity.

network: (1) A means of connecting computers (and other devices such as printers and smartphones) together so that they can share resources. (2) What this book is all about.

network accessible storage (NAS): A popular form of data storage in which a single storage appliance operates as an independent file server attached to a network.

Network Basic Input/Output System (NetBIOS): A high-level networking standard developed by IBM and used by most peer-to-peer networks. It can be used with NetWare as well.

network drive: A drive that resides somewhere out in the network rather than on your own computer.

network interface card (NIC): An adapter card that lets the computer attach to a network cable.

network layer: One of the layers somewhere near the middle of the OSI Reference Model. It addresses the interconnection of networks.

network manager: Hope that it's someone other than you.

Network Neighborhood: An icon used in older versions of Windows that enables you to access network servers and resources. In newer Windows versions, this icon is known as *My Network Places, Network Places,* or just *Network.*

network operating system (NOS): An operating system for networks, such as Linux or Windows Server 2003.

Network Places: An icon on the Windows Vista desktop that enables you to access network servers and resources. (In older versions of Windows, this icon is known as *Network Neighborhood* or *My Network Places.*)

network resource: A disk drive, printer, or other device that's located in a server computer and shared with other users. By contrast, a *local resource* is located in a user's computer.

NIC: *See* network interface card (NIC).

node: A device on the network, typically a computer or printer. A router is also a node.

NOS: *See* network operating system (NOS).

NTFS: A special type of disk format that you can use on Windows Server and Windows XP hard drives for improved performance and security.

obfuscation: A security technique that relies on using obscure names for security objects or particular user accounts. Avoiding obvious user account names can slow would-be intruders.

octet: A group of eight bits. In an IP address, each octet of the address is represented by a decimal number from 0 to 255.

offline: Not available on the network.

online: Available on the network.

Open System Interconnection (OSI) Reference Model: A seven-layer fruitcake framework upon which networking standards are hung.

operator: A user who has control of operational aspects of the network but doesn't necessarily have the power to grant or revoke access rights, create user accounts, and so on.

organizational unit: A grouping of objects in an Active Directory domain.

OSI: (1) The agency Lee Majors worked for in *The Six Million Dollar Man.* (2) *See* Open System Interconnection (OSI) Reference Model.

Outlook: A mail client from Microsoft, part of the Microsoft Office suite.

package: In Linux, a software component that can be separately installed and configured.

packet: A manageable chunk of data sent over the network. The size and makeup of a packet (also known as a *frame*) are determined by the protocol being used.

packet filter: A security technique used by firewalls. The firewall examines each packet that passes through it and blocks certain types of packets while allowing others to pass.

packet sniffer: *See* protocol analyzer.

parallel port: An all but obsolete type of data port that was used to connect printers. Parallel ports send data over eight "parallel" wires, one byte at a time. *See also* serial port *and* USB.

partition: (1) In disk management, a division of a single hard drive into several smaller units that are treated by the operating system as though they were separate drives. (2) In Hyper-V, the isolated space in which a virtual machine runs.

password: The only thing protecting your files from an impostor masquerading as you. Keep your password secret, and you'll have a long and happy life.

patch cable: A short cable used to connect a computer to a wall outlet, or one running from a patch panel to a switch, router, server, or other device.

patch panel: A metal plate, often attached to a rack, at which cables that run to user locations are terminated.

PBX: *See* Private Branch Exchange (PBX).

PCI: *See* Peripheral Component Interconnect (PCI).

peer-to-peer network: A network in which any computer can be a server if it wants to be, kind of like the network version of the Great American Dream. You can easily construct peer-to-peer networks by using Windows.

Peripheral Component Interconnect (PCI): The high-speed bus design found in modern Pentium computers.

permissions: Rights that have been granted to a particular user or group of users enabling them to access specific files.

physical layer: The lowest layer of the OSI Reference Model (whatever that is). It refers to the parts of the network you can touch: cables, connectors, and so on.

ping: A program that determines whether another computer is reachable. The ping program sends a message to the other computer and waits for a reply. If the reply is received, the other computer is reachable.

plenum cable: Fire-retardant cable that has a special Teflon coating. Usually required when cable is run through the ceilings in commercial buildings.

pocket protector: A status symbol among computer geeks.

Point-to-Point Protocol (PPP): The most common way of connecting to the Internet for World Wide Web access.

port: A connector on the back of your computer that you can use to connect a device such as a printer, modem, mouse, and so on.

PowerShell: A powerful command-line environment for managing Windows computers.

PPP: *See* Point-to-Point Protocol (PPP).

presentation layer: The sixth layer of the OSI Reference Model, which handles data conversions, compression, decompression, and other menial tasks.

print job: A report, letter, memo, or other document that has been sent to a network printer but hasn't printed yet. Print jobs wait patiently in the queue until a printer agrees to print them.

Print Manager: In old-style Windows (Windows 3.1 and Windows for Workgroups), the program that handles print spooling.

print queue: The line that print jobs wait in until a printer becomes available.

print server: A computer that handles network printing or a device such as a JetDirect, which enables the printer to attach directly to the network.

Private Branch Exchange (PBX): A phone system that manages shared access to one or more phones (called *extensions* or *stations)* to a limited number of external phone lines.

processor: A single chip that is responsible for executing the instructions of a computer. Also known as the *CPU.*

protocol: (1) The droid C-3PO's specialty. (2) The rules of the network game. Protocols define standardized formats for data packets, techniques for detecting and correcting errors, and so on.

protocol analyzer: A program that monitors packets on a network; also called a *packet sniffer.*

punch-down block: A gadget for quickly connecting a bunch of wires, used in telephone and network wiring closets.

queue: A list of items waiting to be processed. The term usually refers to the list of print jobs waiting to be printed, but networks have lots of other types of queues as well.

RAID: *See* Redundant Array of Independent Disks (RAID).

rack: A metal framework that computer and networking equipment can be bolted to in an effort to keep a computer room neat and orderly.

rackmountable: An adjective used to describe computer and network equipment that can be mounted to a rack.

RAM: *See* random access memory (RAM).

random access memory (RAM): A computer's memory chips.

RDC: *See* Remote Desktop Connection (RDC).

RDP: *See* Remote Desktop Protocol (RDP).

redirection: One of the basic concepts of networking, in which a device, such as a disk drive or printer, appears to be a local device but actually resides on the network. The networking software on your computer intercepts I/O requests for the device and redirects them to the network.

Redundant Array of Independent Disks (RAID): A bunch of hard drives strung together and treated as though they were one drive. The data is spread out over several drives, and one of the drives keeps checking information so that if any one of the other drives fails, the data can be reconstructed.

ReFS: *See* Resilient File System (ReFS).

Registry: The file where Windows keeps its configuration information.

Remote Desktop Assistance: A Windows feature that lets you take control of someone else's computer (with their consent) for the purpose of lending assistance (usually to troubleshoot a problem).

Remote Desktop Connection (RDC): A Windows feature that lets you log on to a Windows server from a remote computer so that you can manage it without physically going to the server.

Remote Desktop Protocol (RDP): The protocol used to enable Remote Desktop Connection.

Remote Installation Service (RIS): A feature of Windows Server operating systems that lets you install from a remote location without actually being present at the server.

repeater: A device that strengthens a signal so that it can travel on. Repeaters are used to lengthen the cable distance between two nodes. A *multiport repeater* is the same as a *hub*. Note that repeaters and hubs have been replaced by switches.

Resilient File System (ReFS): A file system introduced in Windows Server 2012 that improves on the older NTFS file system.

resource: A hard drive, hard drive directory, printer, modem, CD-ROM, or other device that can be shared on the network.

ring: A type of network topology in which computers are connected to one another in a way that forms a complete circle. Imagine the Waltons standing around the Thanksgiving table holding hands, and you have the idea of a ring topology.

RIS: *See* Remote Installation Service (RIS).

RJ-11: The kind of plug used by phone-system cabling.

RJ-45: The kind of plug used by 10BaseT and 100BaseT networks. It looks kind of like a modular phone plug, but it's bigger.

root: (1) The highest-level directory in a file system. (2) The administrator account in Linux.

root server: One of 13 powerful DNS servers located throughout the world that provide the core of the Internet's DNS service.

router: A device that interfaces two networks and controls how packets are exchanged between them. Routers are typically used to link a local Ethernet network to a broadband Internet connection.

Samba: A program that runs on a Linux server, allowing the Linux computer to work as a file and print server in a Windows network.

SAN: *See* Storage Area Network (SAN).

SATA: *See* Serial AT Attachment (SATA).

ScanDisk: A Windows command that examines your hard drive for physical defects.

scheduling software: Software that schedules meetings of network users, which works only if all network users keep their calendars up to date.

scope: In DHCP, a range of IP addresses that a DCHP server manages.

SCSI: See *Small Computer System Interface (SCSI)*.

segment: A single-run cable, which may connect more than two computers, with a terminator on each end.

Sendmail: An email server used on Unix and Linux systems. By some estimates, 70 percent or more of all mail on the Internet is handled by a version of Sendmail.

Serial AT Attachment (SATA): The most common type of hard drive interface in use today, popular because of its low cost and flexibility. For server computers, SCSI is the preferred drive interface. *See also* Small Computer System Interface (SCSI).

serial port: A port normally used to connect a modem or mouse to a DOS-based computer, sometimes called a *communications port. See also* parallel port.

server: A computer that's on the network and shares resources with other network users. The server may be *dedicated,* which means that its sole purpose in life is to provide service for network users, or it may be used as a client as well. *See also* client.

Server Message Block (SMB): The protocol that enables file sharing on Windows networks.

Service Pack: A collection of patches that are bundled together to bring an operating system up to a particular service level.

session layer: A layer somewhere near the middle of the beloved OSI Reference Model that deals with sessions between network nodes.

SFT: *See* System Fault Tolerance (SFT).

share name: A name that you assign to a network resource when you share it. Other network users use the share name to access the shared resource.

shared folder: A network server hard drive or a folder on a server hard drive that has been shared so that other computers on the network can access it.

shared resource: A resource, such as a hard drive or printer, that is made available to other network users.

SharePoint: A Microsoft software system that allows users to collaborate via the web.

shielded twisted pair (STP): Twisted-pair cable with shielding, used mostly for Token Ring networks. *See also* twisted pair.

Simple Network Management Protocol (SNMP): A standard for exchanging network management information between network devices that is anything but simple.

Small Computer System Interface (SCSI): A connection used mostly for hard drives but also suitable for CD-ROM drives, tape drives, and just about anything else. SCSI is also the winner of the Acronym Computer Geeks Love to Pronounce Most Award.

SMB: *See* Server Message Block.

smiley: A face made from various keyboard characters; often used in email messages to convey emotion. : –)

SNA: *See* Systems Network Architecture (SNA).

sneakernet: The cheapest form of network, in which users exchange files by copying them to discs and walking them between computers.

SNMP: *See* Simple Network Management Protocol (SNMP).

spam: Unsolicited and unwanted email.

spooling: A printing trick in which data that is intended for a printer is actually written to a temporary hard drive file and later sent to the printer.

SQL: *See* Structured Query Language (SQL).

SQL Server: Microsoft's database manager, which implements SQL databases.

SSID: A name that identifies a wireless network.

star: A type of network topology in which each node is connected to a central wiring hub. This topology gives the network a starlike appearance.

stateful packet inspection: An intelligent type of packet filtering that examines packets in groups rather than individually.

station: In a PBX system, a telephone that can be used for internal or external calls; also known as an *extension*.

storage area network (SAN): A type of data storage in which storage devices are networked together, usually with high-speed fiber connections.

STP: *See* shielded twisted pair (STP).

Structured Query Language (SQL): A popular method of organizing and accessing information in a database.

subnet mask: A bit pattern used to determine which bits of an IP address represent the subnet.

subnetting: An IP addressing technique that designates the first *n* bits of an IP address as the subnet address and the remaining bits as the host address.

switch: An efficient type of hub that sends packets only to the port that's connected to the packet's recipient rather than sending packets to all the ports, as a simple hub does.

System Fault Tolerance (SFT): A set of networking features designed to protect the network from faults, such as stepping on the line (known as a *foot fault*).

Systems Network Architecture (SNA): A networking standard developed by IBM that dates from the mid-Mainframerasic Period, approximately 65 million years ago. SNA is used by fine IBM mainframe and AS/400 minicomputers everywhere.

tape drive: The best way to back up a network server. Tape drives have become so inexpensive that even small networks should have one.

task: For a technically accurate description, enroll in a computer science graduate course. For a layperson's understanding of what a task is, picture the guy who used to spin plates on *The Ed Sullivan Show*. Each plate is a task. The poor guy had to move frantically from plate to plate to keep them all spinning. Computers work the same way. Each program task is like one of those spinning plates; the computer must service each one periodically to keep it going.

TB: *See* terabyte (TB).

TCP/IP: Transmission Control Protocol/Internet Protocol, the protocol used by the Internet.

terabyte (TB): Approximately one trillion bytes (1,024GB, to be precise). *See also* gigabyte (GB), kilobyte (K), *and* megabyte (MB).

terminator: (1) The little plug you have to use at each end of a segment of thin coax cable (10BaseT). (2) The former governor of California.

thinnet: *See also* 10Base2.

three-letter acronym (TLA): An acronym such as such as FAT (File Allocation Table), DUM (Dirty Upper Memory), or HPY (Heuristic Private Yodel).

time sharing: A technique used on mainframe computers to enable several users to access the computer at the same time.

time-out: How long a device waits while receiving data before it gives up.

TLA: *See* three-letter acronym (TLA).

token: The thing that gets passed around the network in a Token Ring topology. *See also* Token Ring.

Token Ring: A network that's cabled in a ring topology in which a special packet called a *token* is passed from computer to computer. A computer must wait until it receives the token before sending data over the network. (**Note:** Do not confuse it with the Tolkien ring, which could mean the ruin of Middle Earth.)

top-level domain: In DNS, a domain that appears immediately beneath the root domain. The common top-level domains include com, net, org, edu, gov, mil, and int.

topology: The shape of the network; how its computers and cables are arranged. *See also* bus, star, *and* ring.

touchscreen: A monitor that responds to a user's touch.

transport layer: One of those layers somewhere near the middle of the OSI Reference Model that addresses the way data is escorted around the network.

Trojan horse: A program that looks interesting but turns out to be something nasty, like a hard-drive reformatter.

trust: A relationship between domains in which one domain (the *trusting domain*) honors the information in the other domain (the *trusted domain*).

trustee rights: In NetWare, rights that have been granted to a particular user or group of users enabling them to access specific files.

twisted pair: A type of cable consisting of one or more pairs of wires that are twisted in a certain way to improve the cable's electrical characteristics. *See also* unshielded twisted pair *and* shielded twisted pair.

Uniform Resource Locator (URL): A fancy term for an Internet address.

uninterruptible power supply (UPS): A gizmo that switches to battery power whenever the power cuts out. The *Enterprise* didn't have one of these, which is why the lights always went out until Spock could switch to auxiliary power.

unshielded twisted pair (UTP): Twisted-pair cable that doesn't have a heavy metal shield around it. This type of cable is used for 10BaseT networks. *See also* twisted pair.

UPS: See uninterruptible power supply (UPS).

URL: *See* Uniform Resource Locator (URL).

USB: A high-speed serial interface that is found on most new computers. USB can be used to connect printers, scanners, mice, keyboards, network adapters, and other devices.

user ID: *See* logon name.

user profile: The way Windows keeps track of each user's desktop settings, such as window colors, wallpaper, screen savers, Start-menu options, favorites, and so on.

user rights: Network actions that a particular network user is allowed to perform after he or she has logged on to the network. *See also* file rights.

username: *See* logon name.

users' group: A local association of computer users, sometimes with a particular interest, such as networking.

UTP: *See* unshielded twisted pair (UTP). *See also* 10BaseT.

VBScript: A scripting language that can be used to add fancy features to web pages or create macros for Microsoft Office programs.

VGA: *See* Video Graphics Array (VGA).

Video Graphics Array (VGA): An obsolete standard in video monitors.

virtual disk: A virtualized disk resource that can be allocated to a virtual machine.

Virtual Local Area Network (VLAN): Enables you to create two or more broadcast domains on a single physical network.

virtual machine: A simulated computer system running on a host computer, which may support multiple virtual machines.

virtual memory: An operating-system technique in which the system simulates more memory than is physically present in the computer by swapping portions of memory out to disk.

virtual network: A simulated network created so that virtual machines can communicate with one another.

virtual private network (VPN): A secure connection between a computer and a remote network or between two remote networks.

virus: An evil computer program that slips into your computer undetected, tries to spread itself to other computers, and may eventually do something bad like trash your hard drive.

Visio: A program from Microsoft that draws diagrams. It's especially good at drawing network diagrams.

VLAN: *See* Virtual Local Area Network (VLAN).

VMware: The most popular software for implementing virtual machines.

Voice over IP (VoIP): A technique for routing telephone calls over the Internet instead of over traditional phone carriers.

voicemail: A feature of PBX and other types of phone systems in which a caller can record a message for the intended recipient of his or her call.

VoIP: *See* Voice over IP (VoIP).

VPN: *See* virtual private network (VPN).

web browser: A program that enables you to display information retrieved from the Internet's World Wide Web.

WEP: *See* Wired Equivalent Privacy (WEP).

Wi-Fi: The common name for wireless networking using the 802.11 protocols.

Wi-Fi Protected Access (WPA): A new and improved security standard for wireless networks.

Windows: The world's most popular operating system.

Windows 7: A popular and successful version of Windows that replaced Windows Vista in 2009.

Windows 8: The version of Windows that replaced Windows 7 in late 2012.

Windows 8.1: An updated version of Windows 8.

Windows 10: The replacement for Windows 8.1.

Windows 95: A version of Windows that became available in — you guessed it — 1995. Windows 95 was the first version of Windows that didn't require DOS.

Windows 98: The successor to Windows 95, introduced in 1998. Windows 98 included a new user interface that made the Windows desktop resemble the World Wide Web.

Windows CE: A version of Windows for very small computers, such as those found in phones and other handheld devices. Windows Mobile is based on Windows CE.

Windows for Workgroups: Microsoft's first network-aware version of Windows, now obsolete.

Windows Millennium Edition: The successor to Windows 98, designed especially for home users and featuring a Home Networking Wizard that simplifies the task of setting up a home network.

Windows Mobile: A version of the Windows operating system based on Windows CE and designed for handheld mobile devices, pocket computers, and smartphones.

Windows NT: The predecessor to Windows 2000. Windows NT is available in two versions: Windows NT Client for desktop computers and Windows NT Server for server computers.

Windows Server: The server version of Windows.

Windows Vista: The Windows version that replaced Windows XP in early 2007.

Windows XP: A popular and successful version of Windows, designed for home or professional users. It was replaced by Windows Vista in 2007.

Wired Equivalent Privacy (WEP): A security standard for wireless networks that makes wireless networking almost (but not quite) as secure as cabled networks.

wireless: A method of networking that uses radio signals instead of cables to transmit data.

wireless access point: A device that connects wireless devices to a cabled network.

wiring closet: Large networks need a place where cables can congregate. A closet is ideal.

workstation: *See* client.

World Wide Web (WWW): A graphical method of accessing information on the Internet.

WPA: *See* Wi-Fi Protected Access (WPA).

WWW: *See* World Wide Web (WWW).

X10: A low-bandwidth protocol for home automation that runs over your home's power lines.

yellow cable: See 10Base5.

zone: A portion of the DNS namespace that a particular DNS server is responsible for.

Index

appliance, 876

application gateway, 826

Application layer, 27, 81, 89, 106, 876

application servers, 240

application services, AWS for, 380

application virtualization, 402

applications (apps), cloud computing and, 69–70

APs (access points). *See* wireless access point (WAP)

archive bit, 849, 877

ARCnet, 877

ARCNET, 22

ARP (Address Resolution Protocol), 47, 105

arp command, 179–180, 700

ARPANET, 97, 101–102

ASA 5500-X models, 229–230

assigning IP addresses, 141

asterisk (*), 540, 664

asymmetrical technologies, 225

AT attachment (ATA), 260–261

atd service, 675

AT&T 258A, 277

attaching RJ-45 connectors, 28, 278–279

attachments, 844

attributes, 877

auto attendant, 877

auto-archiving files, 778, 781–782

autocompleting commands, 663

autodisconnect parameter, 548

autof service, 675

Automatic Private IP Addressing (APIPA), 148

autonomy, of Internet, 101

availability, as server consideration, 58

Avast (website), 830

AWS (Amazon Web Services), 72, 379

Azure (Microsoft)

  about, 365–366

  connecting to Azure VMs, 377–378

  creating an account, 367–368

  creating Windows Virtual Machines, 369–375

  managing Azure VMs, 375–377

  portal, 368–369

  services, 366–367

B

backbone, 877

backing up

  about, 782

  data

    about, 845–846

    cleaning heads, 856

    local *versus* network, 853–854

    locations for, 846

    number of, 854–855

    reliability of tape, 855–856

    security of backups, 857–858

    software for, 847–848

    to tape, 847

    types of backup, 848–852

  defined, 877

  before installing Windows Server 2016, 412

  network plans, 221

  as potential threat to physical security, 813

  as routine chore for network administrators, 696

  selecting, 849

  virtualization, 857

backquote, 654

backscatter, 836

backslash, 154

Backup Domain Controllers (BDCs), 438–439

Backup Operators group, 460

backup servers, 240–241

banner, 877

bare metal, 246

BarracudaWare (website), 848

basic IP configuration, displaying, 181

batch files, 544, 877

Bayesian analysis, 838

Bayesian filter, 877

BCP (Best Current Practice), 103

BCP (business continuity planning). *See also* disaster recovery

  about, 859–860

  developing, 864–865

BDCs (Backup Domain Controllers), 438–439

benchmark, 877

comment parameter, 551, 553

comments, in sendmail.mc file, 653

/COMMENT:"text" parameter, 561

common parameters, 570

communications

  disruption of, 862

  with users, 740–741

Component Services console, 427

composite key, 532

compression, 848

CompTIA, 702–703

Comptia (website), 867

Computer Browser, 761

Computer Management console, 427

computer name, 879

computername parameter, 548, 555, 562

%COMPUTERNAME% variable, 543

computernamesharename parameter, 559

computers

  accessing remotely, 330

  AWS for, 380

  client, restarting, 756–757

  equipment, as component of BCP, 864

  restricting access to, 455

%COMSPEC% variable, 543

Cone of Silence, 879

configuring

  DHCP, 622–624

  displaying options for, 685–687

  Exchange policies, 782–790

  files

    BIND, 625–630

    editing manually in Apache, 649–650

  iOS devices for Exchange email, 799–803

  network connections, 303–309

  network printers, 323–327

  Outlook for Exchange Server 2016, 515–518

  Remote Desktop options

    about, 712–713

    setting Advanced options, 717–718

    setting Display options, 713–714

    setting Experience options, 716–717

    setting Local Resources options, 714–715

    setting Programs options, 715–716

  as responsibility of network administrators, 694

  scopes, 143–147

  virtual hosts

    about, 645

    creating virtual hosts, 648–649

    default host, 645–648

  Windows clients

    about, 303

    configuring network connections, 303–309

    joining domains, 309–311

  Windows DHCP client, 147–149

  Windows DNS client, 177

  wireless access points, 284–286

–Confirm parameter, 571

Connect to Server dialog box, 320–321

connecting

  enabling, 654

  remotely, 709–711

  remotely with Remote Desktop Connection, 424–425

  servers, 242–243

  shares, 319–321

  to wireless networks, 286–288

consoles

  about, 598

  defined, 879

  Microsoft Management Console, 427–428

contact information, changing for users, 452

Contacts app, 805

container objects, 470

content delivery, AWS for, 380

Control menu, 539

Control Panel, 879

conversations, 88

copier vendor portals, 735

copy backups, 850–851

copy command, 540–541

"copy protection," 765

copying files in directories, 670–671

core, 879

enabling *(continued)*

Remote Desktop Connection (RDC), 708–709

sudo command, 604–606

user accounts, 457–458

WEP, 294–295

encryption keys

changing, 295

defined, 881

energy cost, as benefit of virtualization, 253

Enter key, 539

enterprise computing, 381, 881

enterprise routers, 229–230

entitlement model, 812

entrenched applications, as drawback of cloud computing, 68

/env: parameter, 563

environment variables, 542–544, 665

environmental disasters, 861

equipment failure, 862

equipment upgrades, as responsibility of network administrators, 694

error messages, 753

–ErrorAction parameter, 571

%ERRORLEVEL% variable, 543

–ErrorVariable parameter, 571

Essentials Edition (Windows Server 2016), 255–256

establishing

charters, 738–739

routine chores, 696–697

ESXi, 355–356

/etc directory, 599, 622–624, 625–626

Ethernet

about, 79, 90–92

defined, 881

Fast, 91, 92

Gigabit, 91, 93

Standard, 91, 92

Ethernet handoff, 127

Ethernet packet, 33–34

ETLA (three-letter acronym), 9

event logs

about, 762–763

checking, 412

Event Viewer

about, 763

console, 428

EventCreate command, 545–546

Evolution, 659–660

Exchange

integrating Android with, 805

integrating iOS devices with, 798–803

Exchange ActiveSync feature, 797–799

Exchange Administrative Center (EAC), 505–506

Exchange database, 779

Exchange journaling feature, 791–792

Exchange Mailbox Features, 508–509

Exchange Online Archiving, 792

Exchange Server 2016, managing

about, 505, 881

configuring Outlook for, 515–518

creating mailboxes, 505–508

managing mailboxes, 508–515

viewing other mailboxes, 518–521

exclamation point (!), 540, 664

exclusions, 139

exit command, 189, 190, 638

exiting command prompt, 538

Experience options, setting, 716–717

experimental specifications, 103

experimenting, 54–755

EXPIRE field, 171

/EXPIRES: parameter, 561

Extended Binary Coded Decimal Interchange Code (EBCDIC), 88

Extended Three-Letter Acronym (ETLA), 881. *See also* Three-letter acronym (TLA)

external interface, 127

F

F3, 539

facilities, as component of BCP, 864

flash memory, 260

flooding switches, 43–44

flushing local DNS cache, 183

folders. *See also* files

  permissions for, 470–471

  sharing without a wizard, 477–479

`forcelogoff` parameter, 547

forests

  about, 443

  adding, 444

  adding domains to existing, 444

  defined, 882

form factors, 61–63, 260

forward lookup, 174

forwarders, creating, 509–511

forwarding switches, 42–43, 44

`FORWARD_IPV4` setting, 615

FQDN (fully qualified domain names), 154

freeloaders, 289–290

FTP (File Transfer Protocol), 89, 106, 824, 882

full backups, 849–850, 882. *See also* differential
  backups

Full Control permission, 470

Full-Duplex transmission mode, 88

`/FULLNAME : "name"` parameter, 561

fully qualified domain names (FQDN), 154

functions, PowerShell, 568

G

G Suite, 69, 71, 72–73

G Suite for Business, 73

gateway, 126, 882

gateway router, 127

`GATEWAY` setting, 615

`GATEWAYDEV` setting, 615

GB (Gigabyte), 883

General tab (Remote Desktop), 712

generation backup, 882

generation gap, 883

generic domains, 155

geographic domains, 155–157

get command, 638

get-rich-quick schemes, 836

Gigabit Ethernet, 91, 93

Gigabyte (GB), 883

glass house, 883

global accessibility, as benefit of cloud
  computing, 68

global catalog, 443

global scope, 459–460

GNOME, 602–603, 883

Golden, Bernard (author)

  Virtualization For Dummies, 246

Google, 72–73, 816

Google App Engine, 73

Google Apps, 69

Google Chrome (website), 872

Google Cloud Print, 73

Google Drive, 73

Google Maps, 73

GoToAssist Service Desk (website), 747

GoToMyPC (website), 398

gpasswd command, 681–682

GPOs. *See* group policy objects (GPOs)

granting permissions, 479–481

graphics, backing up, 848

graylisting, 839–840

greater-than sign (>), 541, 664

Gregory, Peter (author)

  IT Disaster Recovery Planning For Dummies, 860

group account, 883

group membership, 448

group policy

  about, 483–484

  creating group policy objects (GPOs), 485–491

  enabling Group Policy Management on Windows
    Server 2016, 484–485

  filtering group policy objects (GPOs), 491–493

  pushing out software with, 774

Group Policy, 461

Group Policy Management

  console, 428

  enabling on Windows Server 2016, 484–485

IPC$ share, 472

ipconfig command
about, 83, 85, 141, 148–149, 180, 700
displaying
basic IP configuration, 181
detailed configuration information, 181–182
network configuration with, 620
flushing local DNS cache, 183
releasing IP leases, 183
renewing IP leases, 182–183

iPhone, 796–797, 885

ipop3 service, 675

IPSec (Internet Protocol Security), 332

iptables service, 675

IPv6, 115

IPX/SPX (Internetwork Packet Exchange/Sequenced Packet Exchange), 79, 98

IRC (Internet Relay Chat), 824

ISA (Industry Standard Architecture) bus, 884

ISC (Internet Systems Consortium), 100

ISDN, 885

isdn service, 676

ISO (International Organization for Standardization), 80, 870, 884

.iso file, 351–353

ISO/IEC 19770, 728

ISP (Internet service provider), 884

IT asset management, 726–727

IT Disaster Recovery Planning For Dummies (Gregory), 860

IT Pro Magazine (website), 869

iterative queries, 167

J

Java, 885

JavaScript, 885

Join a Domain dialog box, 310–311

joining domains, 309–311, 317–319

journal mailbox, 778

jumper block, 885. *See also* DIP switch

K

K (Kilobytes), 885

Kaufman, Marcia (author)
Hybrid Cloud For Dummies, 74

Kerberos, 885

keyboard, video, and mouse (KVM) switching, 62

keyboard shortcuts, for Remote Desktop, 711–712

keyword checking, 837–838

Kilobytes (K), 885

Kirsch, Daniel (author)
Hybrid Cloud For Dummies, 74

knowledge bases, creating, 742

KVM switch, 63

KVM (keyboard, video, and mouse) switching, 62

L

L2TP (Layer 2 Tunneling Protocol), 332

LAN. *See* local area network (LAN)

LAN Manager, 885

laser printer, 885

launching
Apache, 640
DHCP, 624
Evolution, 659–660
firewall in Windows 7/8, 826–828
Samba, 633–634
Windows Calculator, 111

Layer 2 Tunneling Protocol (L2TP), 332

layers. *See also* protocols
following packets through, 89–90
of the OSI model, 27, 81

lcd *directory* command, 638

LDAP (Lightweight Directory Access Protocol), 824

learning switches, 40–42, 44

leases
about, 136
duration of, 141
releasing, 148–149
renewing, 148–149

md *directory* command, 638

MDA (Mail Delivery Agent), 652

Media Access Control (MAC) address, 83, 141, 886

Megabytes (MB), 886

members, adding to groups, 463–464

memory. *See also* random access memory (RAM)
  amount of, 210
  defined, 886
  for server computers, 60

Meraki (website), 872

mesh topology, 22–23

message retention policy, 784–788

message retention tags, 782–784

Messaging app, 805

metaphor, 886

Metcalfe, Robert (graduate student), 93

metric, 200

Metro, 886

metropolitan area network (MAN), 17

mget subcommand, 638

Microsoft
  about, 73, 703
  certifications, 867
  licensing, 768
  website, 870

Microsoft Azure
  about, 365–366
  connecting to Azure VMs, 377–378
  creating an account, 367–368
  creating Windows Virtual Machines, 369–375
  managing Azure VMs, 375–377
  portal, 368–369
  services, 366–367

Microsoft Certified Solutions Associate (MCSA), 703

Microsoft Certified Solutions Expert (MCSE), 703

Microsoft Exchange Server, 237–238, 837

Microsoft Hyper-V
  about, 337
  creating virtual disks, 344–347
  creating virtual machines, 347–351
  creating virtual switches, 341–343

enabling, 339–340
installing operating systems, 351–353
panes, 340–341
virtual disks, 338–339

Microsoft Management Console (MMC)
  customizing
    about, 428
    adding snap-ins, 428–429
    adding taskpads, 430–435
  defined, 887
  managing Windows Server 2016 with
    about, 425
    consoles, 427–428
    working with, 425–426

Microsoft Office 365, 73

Microsoft PowerShell, 537

Microsoft SQL Server 2017, 240

Microsoft System Information, 211

Microsoft Technology Associate (MTA), 703

Microsoft Visio, 219

Microsoft Volume Licensing Center (website), 733

middleware layer, 804

minimizing spam, 843–844

MINIMUM field, 171

minpwage parameter, 547

minpwlen parameter, 547

mkdir command, 668

MMC (Microsoft Management Console)
  customizing
    about, 428
    adding snap-ins, 428–429
    adding taskpads, 430–435
  defined, 887
  managing Windows Server 2016 with
    about, 425
    consoles, 427–428
    working with, 425–426

mmc command, 425–426

MNAME field, 171

/mnt directory, 600

mobile applications, Azure and, 366

network interface card (NIC), 14, 30–31, 887
Network Interface layer, 104–105
network interfaces
  about, 8, 14
  for server computers, 60
Network layer, 27, 81, 84–86, 105, 888
network manager, 888
Network Monitor, 699
Network Neighborhood, 888
Network News Transfer Protocol (NNTP), 824
network operating systems (NOSes), 53–57, 888
Network Places, 888
network port. *See* network interface card (NIC)
network prefix notation, 121
network printers, configuring, 323–327
Network Properties dialog box, 177
network resource, 888
network servers, restarting, 761–762
network services, 54, 676, 760–761
NETWORK setting, 616
network settings, checking, 754
network software
  about, 16
  managing
    about, 765–766
    deploying, 770–774
    license server, 769–770
    licenses, 766–768
    updating, 775–776
Network Standards Organization, websites for, 870–871
network users, managing, 697–698
network virtualization, 252
Network World (website), 701
networking. *See also specific topics*
  about, 7–10
  AWS for, 380
  Azure and, 366
  benefits of, 10–12
  Linux commands for
    hostname, 685
    ifconfig, 685–687

    netstat, 687–688
    ping, 688–689
    route, 689–690
    traceroute, 690
NETWORKING setting, 615
networks
  about, 101
  clients compared with servers, 12–13
  components of, 14–16
  dedicated servers, 13–14
  defined, 887
  infrastructure, 25–36
  IP addresses and, 112–113
  peers, 13–14
  planning
    about, 207–208
    being purposeful, 208–209
    cable, 212–213
    considerations, 219–221
    diagrams, 219–220
    switches, 38–47, 213–215
    taking stock, 209–212
    TCP/IP implementation, 217–218
    topology, 19–23, 216–217
  printers, 323–327
  restarting in Linux, 613
  servers, 53–63
  size of, 17
  splitting, 129–130
New Host dialog box, 175–176
New Share Wizard, 472–481
newusers command, 680–681
NFS (Network File System), 89
nfs service, 676
NIC (network interface card), 14, 30–31, 887
NNTP (Network News Transfer Protocol), 824
node, 19, 888
nondelivery reports (NDRs), 836
/noprofile: parameter, 563
normal backups, 849–850
normal form, 731
NOSes (network operating systems), 53–57, 888

W

: w command, 666

W3C (World Wide Web Consortium), 80

wall jacks, 279–280

WAN (wide area network)

about, 17, 223

firewall, 230–232

Internet connection

about, 223–224

cable, 224–225

cellular network, 227

DSL, 224–225

fiber, 226–227

redundancy for, 232–233

remote locations/users, 233–234

T1 lines, 225–226

router

about, 227–228

cellular, 230

enterprise, 229–230

office, 228

WAP (wireless access point)

adding, 301

configuring, 284–286

defined, 898

installing, 283–284

multifunction, 284

placing outside firewall, 296–298

Warning! icon, 4

–WarningAction parameter, 571

–WarningVariable parameter, 571

water, 861, 862

weather, 861

web applications, Azure and, 366

web browser, 897

web interfaces, accessing network printers using, 326–327

web pages, creating, 650

web servers, 239–240

Web Services, Amazon (AWS)

about, 72, 379

connecting to AWS VMs, 393–396

Console, 382–384

creating an account, 381

creating Windows virtual machines, 384–391

managing AWV VMs, 391–393

uses for, 380–381

Webopedia (website), 871

websites

Amazon Web Services (AWS), 381

American National Standards Institute (ANSI), 870

Android, 873

Apache HTTP server, 869

Apple, 873

ASA 5500-X models, 229–230

Avast, 830

Azure portal, 368

BarracudaWare, 848

BIND, 869

BlackBerry, 873

Caldera, 869

certifications, 867

Cheat Sheet, 4

Cisco, 703, 867, 872

Class A address assignments, 116

CNET reviews, 867

Comptia, 867

CompTIA, 702

creating, 500–504

default, 498–500

Dell, 868

D-Link, 872

DNS lookups, 871

Edge, 872

Fedora, 586, 589, 869

Firefox, 872

G Suite, 71

Google, 816

Google Chrome, 872

GoToAssist Service Desk, 747

GoToMyPC, 398

hardware, 867–868

HardwareCentral, 867

home networking, 868

home-network-help, 868

World Wide Web (HyperText Transport Protocol; HTTP), 824

World Wide Web (WWW), 898

World Wide Web Consortium (W3C), 80, 871

worm, 829

WPA (Wi-Fi Protected Access)
  defined, 897
  using, 295–296

:wq command, 666

Write Attributes permission, 471

Write Extended Attributes permission, 471

Write permission, 470

WSUS (Windows Software Update Services), 698

WWW (World Wide Web), 898

X

X Window System, 596, 598

X10, 898

XenApp (Citrix), 401–403

Xeon, 59

xinetd.conf file, 614, 619–620

XOR operator, 110

Y

YouTube app, 805

yum command, 676–677

Z

ZenDesk (website), 747

zone files
  about, 169–170, 629–630
  CNAME records, 170, 173, 630
  defined, 898
  MX records, 170, 173–174, 630
  NS records, 170, 172, 630
  PTR records, 170, 173, 630
  A records, 170, 172–173, 630
  SOA records, 170–171, 630

zone transfer, 162

zones, 161–162

About the Author

Doug Lowe has written a whole bunch of computer books, including more than 50 *For Dummies* books, among them *Networking For Dummies*, 10th Edition; *Electronics All-in-One For Dummies*, 2nd Edition; *Java All-in-One For Dummies*, 6th Edition; and *PowerPoint 2016 For Dummies*. He lives in sunny Fresno, California, where the motto is "Fres-YES." He is the Information Technology Director at Blair, Church & Flynn Consulting Engineers in nearby Clovis, California.

Dedication

For Kristen. And for Dorothy, Kurt, and Hazel. We really miss you.

Author's Acknowledgments

I'd like to thank everyone who was involved with the seventh edition of this book, especially the most excellent project editor Elizabeth Kuball, who championed this book through all the editorial details needed to put a book of this scope together on time. Thanks also to Dan DiNicolo, who once again gave the manuscript a thorough review to ensure the technical accuracy of every sentence and in the process offered many excellent suggestions for improvements. And as always, thanks to all the behind-the-scenes people who chipped in with help I'm not even aware of.

Publisher's Acknowledgments

Acquisitions Editor: Amy Fandrei

Project Editor: Elizabeth Kuball

Copy Editor: Elizabeth Kuball

Technical Editor: Dan DiNicolo

Production Editor: Tamilmani Varadharaj

Cover Image: © asharkyu/Shutterstock

Take dummies with you everywhere you go!

Whether you are excited about e-books, want more from the web, must have your mobile apps, or are swept up in social media, dummies makes everything easier.

Find us online!

Leverage the power

Dummies is the global leader in the reference category and one of the most trusted and highly regarded brands in the world. No longer just focused on books, customers now have access to the dummies content they need in the format they want. Together we'll craft a solution that engages your customers, stands out from the competition, and helps you meet your goals.

Advertising & Sponsorships

Connect with an engaged audience on a powerful multimedia site, and position your message alongside expert how-to content. Dummies.com is a one-stop shop for free, online information and know-how curated by a team of experts.

- Targeted ads
- Video
- Email Marketing
- Microsites
- Sweepstakes sponsorship

20 MILLION PAGE VIEWS EVERY SINGLE MONTH

15 MILLION UNIQUE VISITORS PER MONTH

43% OF ALL VISITORS ACCESS THE SITE VIA THEIR MOBILE DEVICES

700,000 NEWSLETTER SUBSCRIPTION TO THE INBOXES OF *300,000* UNIQUE INDIVIDUALS EVERY WEEK

# of dummies

Custom Publishing

Reach a global audience in any language by creating a solution that will differentiate you from competitors, amplify your message, and encourage customers to make a buying decision.

- Apps
- Books
- eBooks
- Video
- Audio
- Webinars

Brand Licensing & Content

Leverage the strength of the world's most popular reference brand to reach new audiences and channels of distribution.

For more information, visit **dummies.com/biz**

Learning Made Easy

ACADEMIC

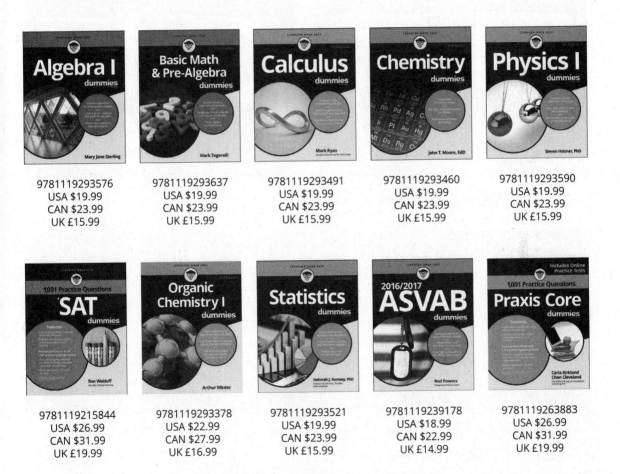

Algebra I *dummies*
Mary Jane Sterling
9781119293576
USA $19.99
CAN $23.99
UK £15.99

Basic Math & Pre-Algebra *dummies*
Mark Zegarelli
9781119293637
USA $19.99
CAN $23.99
UK £15.99

Calculus *dummies*
Mark Ryan
9781119293491
USA $19.99
CAN $23.99
UK £15.99

Chemistry *dummies*
John T. Moore, EdD
9781119293460
USA $19.99
CAN $23.99
UK £15.99

Physics I *dummies*
Steven Holzner, PhD
9781119293590
USA $19.99
CAN $23.99
UK £15.99

1001 Practice Questions SAT *dummies*
Ron Woldoff
9781119215844
USA $26.99
CAN $31.99
UK £19.99

Organic Chemistry I *dummies*
Arthur Winter
9781119293378
USA $22.99
CAN $27.99
UK £16.99

Statistics *dummies*
Deborah J. Rumsey, PhD
9781119293521
USA $19.99
CAN $23.99
UK £15.99

2016/2017 ASVAB *dummies*
Rod Powers
9781119239178
USA $18.99
CAN $22.99
UK £14.99

1001 Practice Questions Praxis Core *dummies*
Includes Online Practice Tests
Carla Kirkland
Chan Cleveland
9781119263883
USA $26.99
CAN $31.99
UK £19.99

Available Everywhere Books Are Sold

dummies.com

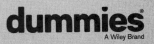

dummies®
A Wiley Brand

Small books for big imaginations

GETTING STARTED WITH **Coding**
Get Creative with Code!
Camille McCue, PhD

9781119177173
USA $9.99
CAN $9.99
UK £8.99

MODDING **Minecraft**
Build Your Own Minecraft Mods!
Sarah Guthals, PhD
Stephen Foster, PhD
Lindsey Handley, PhD

9781119177272
USA $9.99
CAN $9.99
UK £8.99

MAKING **YouTube** VIDEOS
Star in Your Own Video!
Nick Willoughby

9781119177241
USA $9.99
CAN $9.99
UK £8.99

DESIGNING **Digital Games**
Create Games with Scratch!
Derek Breen

9781119177210
USA $9.99
CAN $9.99
UK £8.99

GETTING STARTED WITH **Raspberry Pi**
Program Your Raspberry Pi!
Richard Wentk

9781119262657
USA $9.99
CAN $9.99
UK £6.99

EXPERIMENTING WITH **Science**
Think, Test, and Learn!
Jade J. Bullard, PhD

9781119291336
USA $9.99
CAN $9.99
UK £6.99

CREATING **Digital Animations**
Animate Stories with Scratch!
Derek Breen

9781119233527
USA $9.99
CAN $9.99
UK £6.99

GETTING STARTED WITH **Engineering**
Think Like an Engineer!
Camille McCue, PhD

9781119291220
USA $9.99
CAN $9.99
UK £6.99

WRITING **Computer Code**
Learn the Language of Computers!
Chris Minnick and Eva Holland

9781119177302
USA $9.99
CAN $9.99
UK £8.99

Unleash Their Creativity

dummies.com

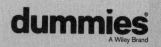

dummies®
A Wiley Brand